LEGAL RESEARCH, ANALYSIS, AND WRITING

THIRD EDITION

LEGAL RESEARCH, ANALYSIS, AND WRITING

Joanne Banker Hames

Yvonne Ekern

Pearson
Prentice Hall
Legal Series

PEARSON
Prentice
Hall

Upper Saddle River, New Jersey
Columbus, Ohio

Library of Congress Cataloging in Publication Data

Hames, Joanne Banker.
  Legal research, analysis, and writing/Joanne Banker Hames, Yvonne Ekern. — 3rd ed.
    p. cm.
  Rev. ed. of: Legal research, analysis, and writing/Joanne Banker Hames, Yvonne Ekern, 2006.
  Includes index.
  ISBN-13: 978-0-13-159480-7
  1. Legal research—United States. 2. Legal composition.   I. Ekern, Yvonne. II. Hames, Joanne Banker.
Legal research, analysis, and writing. III. Title.
  KF240.H36 2009
  340.072′073—dc22   2007052560

Editor in Chief: Vernon Anthony
Acquisitions Editor: Gary Bauer
Development Editor: Linda Cupp
Project Manager: Jessica Sykes
Production Coordination: Roxanne Klaas, S4Carlisle Publishing Services
Senior Operations Supervisor: Pat Tonneman
Art Director: Diane Y. Ernsberger
Cover Designer: Kristina Holmes
Cover art: SuperStock
Director of Marketing: David Gesell
Marketing Manager: Leigh Ann Sims
Marketing Coordinator: Alicia Dysert

This book was set in New Baskerville by S4Carlisle Publishing Services. It was printed and bound by Edwards Brothers. The cover was printed by Phoenix Color Corp./Hagerstown.

Pearson Prentice Hall™ is a trademark of Pearson Education, Inc.
Pearson® is a registered trademark of Pearson plc
Prentice Hall® is a registered trademark of Pearson Education, Inc.

Pearson Education Ltd., London
Pearson Education Singapore Pte. Ltd.
Pearson Education Canada, Ltd.
Pearson Education—Japan

Pearson Education Australia Pty. Limited
Pearson Education North Asia Ltd., Hong Kong
Pearson Educación de Mexico, S.A. de C.V.
Pearson Education Malaysia Pte. Ltd.

10 9 8 7 6 5 4 3
ISBN-13: 978-0-13-159480-7
ISBN-10:   0-13-159480-X

BRIEF CONTENTS

ABOUT THE AUTHORS

Yvonne Ekern is a full-time member of the Legal Analysis, Research, and Writing faculty at Santa Clara University's School of Law. For seven years she was the chairperson of the West Valley College Paralegal Program (ABA approved). Prior to attending law school, she taught high school English and math in California and Missouri. She graduated from the University of Idaho School of Law in 1985. While working in criminal and family law offices, she taught part-time in several Silicon Valley paralegal programs. Among the classes she teaches are Legal Research and Writing, Advanced Legal Research and Writing, Appellate Advocacy, Advanced Legal Research and Writing Using LEXIS, and Legal Analysis. She has over twenty-five years teaching experience. She was the principal and cofounder of Continuing Education for the Legal Assistant, a company dedicated to providing quality educational opportunities for working legal assistants. She has been a guest speaker at AAfPE conferences, chaired the AAfPE committee that developed the model curriculum for legal research, and was a member of the committee that developed the model curriculum for Introduction to Law. She is the co-author of the texts *Introduction to Law* and Constitutional Law: Principles and Practice.

Joanne Banker Hames is an attorney and paralegal educator who has been actively involved in paralegal education since 1977. She is an instructor in and the former coordinator for the ABA-approved paralegal program at DeAnza Community College in Cupertino, California. She earned her J. D. degree from Santa Clara University Law School and has been an active member of the California Bar since 1972. As an attorney, she has been involved in research and writing for legal memoranda and appellate briefs. Among the classes she teaches are Legal Research and Writing, Advanced Legal Research and Writing, and Advanced Legal Research Using LEXIS. She is the co-author of *Civil Litigation, Introduction to Law* and *Constitutional Law: Principles and Practice.*

CONTENTS

CHAPTER 4
HOW TO BRIEF A CASE   76

CHAPTER 5
CONSTITUTIONS, STATUTES, AND
ADMINISTRATIVE REGULATIONS   98

CHAPTER 6
STATUTORY AND CONSTITUTIONAL ANALYSIS   139

CHAPTER 7
SECONDARY SOURCES   165

CHAPTER 10
COMPUTER-ASSISTED LEGAL RESEARCH (CALR)   250

CHAPTER 11
BASIC LEGAL WRITING TOOLS   283

CHAPTER 12
PREDICTIVE LEGAL WRITING:
THE MEMORANDUM OF LAW   304

CHAPTER 13
PERSUASIVE WRITING: WRITING TO THE COURT   333

CHAPTER 14
LEGAL CORRESPONDENCE   370

PREFACE

GOALS

Beginning legal researchers generally ask four questions:

- How do I find the law?
- How do I know that I found the right law?
- How do I know when to stop?
- What do I do with the law now that I have it?

Experienced legal researchers know that successful research requires the ability to answer each of these questions.

They also know that researching the law requires more than knowledge of law books. It requires the ability to analyze factual and legal disputes; the ability to understand the written law, whether found in cases or statut`ory materials; the ability to apply the law to the factual disputes; and the ability to communicate one's findings. Our purpose in writing this book is to give students the basic knowledge and tools they need in order to research and analyze a problem and to communicate the results of that research and analysis to the appropriate person.

Our experience in teaching legal research classes in law school and paralegal programs confirms that all programs cover the same topics and assign similar projects. A review of the model curriculum for legal research and writing recommended by the American Association for Paralegal Education further illustrates the similarity. However, even within law schools or paralegal programs, the way in which legal research and writing is taught often differs. Some programs teach separate courses in legal research, legal writing, and legal analysis. Some programs recommend research before writing, while others require writing and analysis courses before research. This text is appropriate for a variety of instructional approaches to legal research, analysis, and writing. Realizing that there are legitimate reasons for different organizations we, offer suggestions for using the text with different approaches to teaching the subject.

ORGANIZATION

- Chapter 1 presents an introduction to legal research and writing as well as an overview of the legal system, with an emphasis on the way that laws originate. The distinction between federal and state laws is explained. This material provides even beginning students with the basic information and concepts needed to successfully undertake legal research.
- Chapter 2 introduces students to the beginning steps of legal research— analyzing the facts and issues to be researched.
- Chapter 3 explains how to find and analyze case law.
- Chapter 4 explains how to brief a case using the IRAC method of analysis.

- Chapters 5 and 6 explore statutes and constitutions. These chapters explain the publication and organization of these materials as well as how the laws should be read and analyzed.
- Chapters 7 and 8 explore numerous secondary sources and digests.
- Chapter 9 explains *Shepard's,* KeyCite, and other citators.
- Chapter 10 introduces computer-assisted legal research, although the use of the Internet as a research tool is included in all chapters.
- Chapter 11 explains the basic legal writing tools.
- Chapter 12 introduces predictive legal writing using the memorandum of law. This chapter also reviews the basic analysis methods (e.g., IRAC) introduced in earlier chapters and shows how these methods are incorporated into more formal legal writing.
- Chapter 13 introduces persuasive legal writing, with an emphasis on writing to a court.
- Chapter 14 introduces basic legal correspondence.

For courses covering only legal writing, the following chapters are appropriate:

- Chapters 1 and 2: Introductory Material (These chapters may be quickly reviewed depending on the students' educational background.)
- Chapter 4: How to Brief a Case
- Chapter 6: Statutory and Constitutional Analysis
- Chapter 11: Basic Legal Writing Tools
- Chapter 12: Predictive Legal Writing: The Memorandum of Law
- Chapter 13: Persuasive Writing: Writing to the Court
- Chapter 14: Legal Correspondence
- Appendix Materials

For courses covering only legal research, the following chapters are appropriate:

- Chapters 1 and 2: Introductory Material (These chapters may be quickly reviewed depending on the students' educational background.)
- Chapter 3: Finding and Analyzing Case Law
- Chapter 5: Constitutions, Statutes, and Administrative Regulations
- Chapter 7: Secondary Sources
- Chapter 8: Digests
- Chapter 9: Validating Your Research: Using *Shepard's,* KeyCite, and Other Citators
- Chapter 10: Computer-Assisted Legal Research (CALR)
- Appendix Materials

CHANGES TO THE THIRD EDITION

Legal research materials and the methods of doing legal research have changed considerably over the past few years. The availability of legal resources through the Internet has tremendous influence on the way research is conducted. No longer are researchers confined to a law library. The widespread use of all forms of computer-assisted legal research requires that legal researchers develop new skills. However, the law has not abandoned the written word and, as any experienced researcher knows, books are often preferred. The new skills that researchers must develop, therefore, cannot supplant traditional research skills, but must complement them. Chapter 10, Computer-Assisted Legal Research, was substantially revised to reflect current trends in legal research. Most chapters were revised in less substantial ways for the same reason. Chapters include online research activities and assignments near the end of the chapter.

In the third edition we added several features to help students develop basic research, writing, and analysis skills. We significantly expanded the chapters on legal writing. Chapters 11 through 14 address various types of legal writing. These chapters separate predictive writing from persuasive writing. Chapter 14, a new addition, introduces legal correspondence.

Recognizing that students are often frustrated and overwhelmed by the complexities of legal citation, we maintained a feature in each chapter called Citation Matters, introducing the student to one new facet of legal citation in each chapter. This allows students to gradually develop important citation skills. We also include a statement of Skill Objectives in each chapter so that students are better able to focus on the reading material. In order to provide students with more opportunities for legal analysis and writing, several shorter hypothetical research problems are included in the appendix material. This third edition includes expanded material in Appendix A. These research fact patterns now include case documents, such as transcripts and declarations. Appendix F is new; it contains partially written case briefs. Students will fill in the blank sections. Appendix G is also new. It contains supplemental case law for some of the chapter assignments and completion of the case briefs in Appendix F.

PRACTICAL APPROACH

Regardless of which instructional approach is followed, this text assists the instructor in presenting material in a practical and relevant way.

Each chapter opens with a short memorandum *From the Desk of W. J. Bryan, Esq.,* that contains a hypothetical factual situation to be researched and analyzed by a fictional research associate. The memorandum approach helps to introduce the topic of the chapter and to engage the student's imagination. Furthermore, because learning to do legal research requires hands-on experience, at the end of each chapter additional features appear. **Building Your Research Skills, Building Your Writing and/or Analysis Skills, and Building Your Online Skills—Assignments and Exercises** are included at the end of each chapter. These skill-building assignments and exercises contain research, analysis, and writing problems where students must often use a law library to complete. **Can You Figure It Out?** makes use of the numerous sample law book pages found in the chapters. In this section, students are asked practical research questions that can be answered by referring to the appropriate sample page in the text. Students should begin a practical approach to learning legal research even before entering the law library. A new feature encourages students to practice their **Online Legal Research** skills. All chapters continue to include a **Chapter Summary**, **Terms to Remember**, **Citation Matters,** and **Questions for Review**.

The **Case Project** allows students and instructors to select one hypothetical case (many of which are found in Appendix A) and to perform some research, analysis, or writing project in chapters. In this way, students see how the material covered in the different chapters is integrated.

FEATURES

A variety of features helps students and instructors.

- **Legal vocabulary** is identified in boldface type. The key terms are defined in the margins of the text where the terms appear. A comprehensive **Glossary** is also included at the end of the book.

- **Skill Objectives** are listed at the beginning of each chapter, helping students recognize the main points of the chapter.

- **Online Legal Research,** a new feature, offers students the opportunity to explore online legal research resources.

- **Citation Matters,** a feature that appears in each chapter, is a brief overview of major citation rules affecting legal writing.

- As previously stated, an interoffice memorandum called *From the Desk of W. J. Bryan, Esq.* opens the text of each chapter. This memorandum serves as an introduction to the subject matter, encouraging the student to think about the subject matter in a practical setting.

- **Research checklists** are found in several chapters, providing a quick, easy-to-read summary of the material found in the text.

- **Sample pages** from an assortment of law books are included in the research chapters. Practical exercises at the end of the chapter, found in the section **Can You Figure It Out?**, give students the opportunity to practice research skills *before* going to the library.

- Examples of actual **research memoranda** appear in appropriate chapters.

- A **Chapter Summary** is included in every chapter; it provides a short overview of the major concepts covered in the chapter.

- Basic **Questions for Review** follow the chapter summary. These questions are designed to focus the student on the most important concepts presented in the chapter.

- **Assignments, Activities, and Exercises** are included at the end of each chapter. These features includes library research problems, analysis exercises, and writing assignments.

- Most chapters include a feature we call **A Point to Remember.** This practical information is fashioned to help students focus on the skills and concepts that will help them in doing legal research, writing, and analysis.

- **Appendix A** includes several research problems that may be used as a basis for assignments for all chapters, giving students the opportunity to see the entire research process as it relates to one factual problem. Newly added to this appendix are case documents including transcripts and declarations. Other appendixes include a **short citation guide,** a **research strategies outline,** a **memorandum of points and authorities,** an **appellate brief, supplemental case law,** and **partially completed case briefs.**

- An **Instructor's Manual** is available, including answers to library research projects, answers to questions found in the feature **Can You Figure It Out?,** a test bank, transparency masters, and additional research problems.

- Icons in the table of contents and on the individual chapter outlines identify the chapter as primarily a research chapter (a book icon), a writing and analysis chapter (a pen icon), or a chapter emphasizing computer-assisted legal research (a computer icon).

To access supplementary materials online, instructors need to request an instructor access code. Go to **www .pearsonhighered.com/irc,** where you can register for an instructor access code. Within 48 hours after registering, you will receive a confirming e-mail, including an instructor access code. Once you have received your code, go to the site and log on for full instructions on downloading the materials you wish to use.

ACKNOWLEDGMENTS

Special thanks are extended to several individuals whose assistance and encouragement were invaluable: to Professor Gerald Uelman, who graciously shared with us his considerable research experiences, insight, and documents; Kenneth Rosenblatt, Deputy District Attorney and author of *High-Technology Crime;* and Mark Hames, Deputy District Attorney (retired), who also shared with us the fruits of their legal research and writing. We also thank our husbands, Bill Ekern and Mark Hames. Each contributed special talents and expertise to improving this text and each continues to be a source of encouragement and support. Finally, we thank the hundreds of paralegal and law students and paralegals who helped us formulate the tools and techniques to guide our future classes in their understanding of this complex and sometimes frustrating material.

Special thanks to the reviewers of this text: Lora Clark, Pitt Community College, Winterville, NC; Robert Loomis, Spokane Community College, Spokane, WA; Peggy Mathieson, West Valley College Paralegal Program; Christie Highlander, Southwestern Illinois College; Rick Barrett, Simpson College; and Pat Smith Nickell, Webber International University.

INTRODUCTION TO LEGAL RESEARCH, WRITING, AND ANALYSIS

CHAPTER OUTLINE

SKILL OBJECTIVES FOR CHAPTER 1

When you complete this chapter you should be able to

- Describe the role of a research associate.
- Explain the difference between a primary and a secondary source of law.

- List the types of materials often found in law libraries.
- List the common features of law books.
- Explain the effect of federalism on legal publications.
- Describe the sources of U.S. law.

FROM THE DESK OF W. J. BRYAN, ESQ.

TO: Research Assistant

I'm sorry I won't be here to greet you personally on your first day of work. Unfortunately, I need to be in court today. I am leaving a file on your desk for you to review. The case relates to a new client, Justin Meyers, who has been charged with murder. There may be a problem with the legality of a search and seizure and we need to do more research into this matter. After you read the documents in the file, including statements from several individuals, please write a brief memorandum of law outlining our client's legal rights.

You will need to familiarize yourself with our office library. The firm has a legal library containing all state and federal cases and codes, as well as selected secondary source materials. Hopefully all the books you need are available. You may be able to access information on various free Internet sites, but these sites are sometimes unreliable. The firm has subscriptions to both Westlaw and LEXIS and you can use these if necessary. However, these sources are not free and using them can be costly.

Just leave your memo on my desk and I will review it tomorrow morning.

1-1 INTRODUCTION

One of the most important skills for lawyers and paralegals is the ability to find and analyze the law and to communicate their findings, usually in writing. Many other professions also find legal research skills useful. Police officers, for example, often refer to code sections and case law in their jobs. Individuals in the business or corporate world also encounter legal questions. Questions of contract law, corporate law, and environmental regulations constantly arise in this setting.

Although this textbook is intended primarily for students pursuing a career in a legal environment, it provides a basic framework for legal research that any student should be able to follow. The subject matter of each chapter is introduced in a hypothetical factual scenario, found in a note from the desk of W. J. Bryan, Esq. As you go through the text you will learn where and how laws are published, how to find the law, how to analyze a factual situation and apply the relevant legal principles, and how to communicate your findings to clients, other attorneys, and the court. You will also learn how to access legal information through the Internet and how to evaluate the information you retrieve. At the end of each chapter are several practical research, analysis, and writing exercises. Some exercises can be completed with material found in the text. Others require that you visit a law library or access the Internet. In addition to the exercises found at the end of the

TABLE 1-1   Legal Terminology

Affirm	Precedent
Appeal	Real party in interest
Appellant	Remand
Appellee	Respondent
Civil	Reverse
Criminal	*Stare decisis*
Defendant	Writ of certiorari
Motion for summary judgment	Writ of habeas corpus
Plaintiff	Writ of mandate

chapters, Appendix A contains several hypothetical cases for research and writing assignments.

As you develop your research skills, you will also develop your legal vocabulary. The use of legal terminology may present problems for you. When you read cases, statutes, or other legal source material, you are reading material written by lawyers (or judges) for other lawyers. Many terms used in the law are not common in everyday language. Some legal concepts or ideas are expressed by using Latin terminology. Many words that you *think* you understand have special meanings when used in a legal context. It is essential, therefore, to have and use a **legal dictionary.** This is a tool that defines and explains legal terms. Another tool is a **legal thesaurus.** This provides synonyms for legal terms. This is particularly helpful when you use an **index.** Common legal terms used in case law are found in Table 1-1. Review this list and see how many you understand.

In addition to understanding the unique vocabulary of the law, a legal researcher also must be familiar with special abbreviations, known as **legal citations,** used to describe resource material. If you have ever written a term paper and used footnotes or a bibliography, you know that there are standard abbreviations for research sources such as books, magazines, and encyclopedias. The same is true for legal resource materials. An abbreviated or shorthand way of referring to a particular legal source is called a *legal citation.* The leading authority for legal citation form is *A Uniform System of Citation,* and commonly referred to as *The Bluebook.* This publication provides citation format and accepted abbreviations for almost all legal materials, both federal and state. While it is the most commonly used authority for citations, it is not the only one. The *ALWD Citation Manual,* created by the Association of Legal Writing Directors, is another popular citation guide. Additionally, your state may publish its own style manual or have rules regarding legal citation. Because of the importance of legal citations, each chapter in this text contains a feature, Citation Matters, dedicated to specific citation issues.

legal dictionary.   A dictionary defining and explaining legal terms.

legal thesaurus.   A book providing synonyms for legal words.

index.   A list of words and phrases that reflect the topics covered in the book.

legal citations.   Special abbreviations used to describe resource material.

1-2 LEGAL RESEARCH AND LAW PRACTICE

Although legal professionals and paraprofessionals spend considerable time studying the law before working in the field, they do not know the answer to every legal question. Even the most experienced lawyers must research the law. Laws change constantly. Legislatures routinely enact, amend, or repeal statutes. Courts decide new cases every day. Even constitutions are amended. When lawyers make legal arguments in court or give legal advice to clients, they must be certain about the current state of the law. Because laws are not the same throughout the various states, lawyers must be certain about the law in their jurisdiction. This often requires legal research.

The researcher's job rarely stops with just finding the law. In most cases, the law must be analyzed in relation to the facts of the particular case and the results of the research and analysis explained, usually in written form, to the appropriate person. This may be a client, another attorney, or a judge. Thus, the legal research process usually involves three steps—finding the law, analyzing the law, and then preparing a written explanation or argument based on the law.

Recall the hypothetical research problem mentioned at the beginning of the chapter. The research assistant here is asked to use a law library to find law related to a problem related to a police search. But the task does not end with finding the law. The research assistant must evaluate or analyze the law and determine how it affects the client's legal position. Finally, the research assistant must prepare a written memorandum summarizing the research and analysis conclusions.

BOX 1-1   THE LEGAL RESEARCH PROCESS

✓ Identify factual question raised by the client's problem.

✓ Find law that applies to factual question.

✓ Analyze law in relationship to factual question.

✓ Communicate findings.

1-3 THE ROLE OF THE RESEARCH ASSOCIATE

Only attorneys can give legal advice to clients. Therefore, if you are a paralegal or a law clerk, your legal research should be performed under the general supervision of an attorney. An attorney must review the research before a client is advised of the findings.

As a research assistant you may find yourself engaged in various responsibilities, including:

- Gathering or verifying the facts that raise a legal question
- Summarizing the facts
- Conducting legal research
- Summarizing relevant law
- Drafting legal memoranda
- Reviewing legal memoranda for technical requirements
- Checking the citations in memoranda
- Reviewing legal memoranda from opposing counsel

Whatever your responsibilities are, realize that the attorney always expects accuracy and thoroughness. The attorney often relies on your research when advising clients or when arguing matters in court. Even if your job responsibilities do not include working as a research associate for an attorney, if you work in a law office, you often need to perform legal research for your own benefit. Legal research, analysis, and writing skills contribute greatly to your success in a law office.

A Point to Remember

A paralegal or a law clerk cannot give legal advice. To do so is the unauthorized practice of law and is unethical, not to mention illegal. Paralegals or clerks who do legal research should report their findings to a supervising attorney. All legal advice to a client must come from an attorney.

1-4 LEGAL PUBLICATIONS

Law is found in the same types of materials as any other information, that is, books, periodicals such as magazines or newspapers, and electronic media. Published law is called either a **primary source** of law or a **secondary source** of law. The former is a work that contains the law itself, such as publications of constitutions, statutes, administrative regulations, and cases. Publications of statutes are sometimes called **code books.** Publications of cases are called **case reporters.** Secondary sources of law are publications that explain or discuss the law, for example, legal encyclopedias and journals. Secondary sources are helpful in finding and understanding the primary law. The goal of legal research is to find a primary source of law that controls your factual situation or answers your legal question.

Until recently, the term *law publication* referred to books or magazines. Today, a broader definition is necessary. Primary and secondary sources of law are found not only in books, but also in electronic form. **CD-ROM libraries** containing both primary and secondary sources are common. Furthermore, legal researchers can read primary and secondary sources of the law through online services such as **LEXIS, Westlaw,** and the Internet.

As you become more experienced with legal research materials, you will note that two major publishers are responsible for most legal publications. These publishers are Thomson/West and Lexis Law Publishing and they produce many materials in both print and electronic format. Each of these publishers adds helpful editorial features to their legal publications to assist the researcher. As you proceed through this text, you will be introduced to these features.

primary source. A work that contains the law itself.

secondary source. A tool used to help understand the law; one such tool is a legal encyclopedia that explains the law.

code books. Books that contain codes or statutes.

case reporters. Books that contain case decisions from the courts.

CD-ROM libraries. Legal materials, either primary or secondary sources, stored on CD-ROM.

LEXIS. A computer-assisted legal research service.

Westlaw. A computer-assisted legal research service.

1-5 THE LAW LIBRARY

Traditional Law Libraries

One of the prerequisites to doing legal research is familiarity with the **law library,** which is a library dedicated to legal resource material. Many law firms maintain their own law libraries. These libraries vary in size and content and may contain small collections of basic law books or extensive collections of legal research material. Some larger law firms even employ law librarians to maintain their libraries.

If you need a comprehensive legal library, you might use a county law library or that of a nearby law school. These libraries generally contain primary and secondary sources related to the laws of your state as well as materials related to the

law library. A library that is dedicated to legal resource material.

A Point to Remember

You should make every effort to become familiar with your firm's law library as soon as possible. Knowing what resources are immediately available can save you time and worry.

Case Reporters	Large sets of books containing written case decisions or opinions from state and federal courts
Code Books	Sets of books containing either federal or state statutory law organized in a topical order; also may contain copies of the federal or state constitution
Encyclopedias	Multivolume sets of books that explain the law; they are organized alphabetically by topic; some explain American law in general, others are limited to explanations of laws in a single state
Digests	Multivolume sets of books that act as a detailed topical index to case reporters; are organized topically and contain short summaries of cases
Looseleaf Service	A type of legal work, usually concerning a single legal topic (such as family law), where the written material is kept in a pull-apart binder. The material is continually updated. When laws are changed the publisher sends replacement pages to the subscribers of the service. Pages with the old law are removed and replaced with new pages that reflect the changes in the law.
Treatises	Usually single books published on one legal subject
Form Books	Books containing forms that lawyers use to prepare legal documents; sometimes referred to as *practice books*
Legal Periodicals	Magazines, journals, and newspapers related to the practice of law; included are law reviews and journals published regularly by law schools

FIGURE 1-1 Types of Legal Materials

laws of the United States. Most likely, these libraries also contain primary and secondary sources concerning the laws of other states and of foreign nations. County law libraries are often open to the public. Law school libraries, on the other hand, may only be available to you if your law firm has a special arrangement with the school.

See Figure 1-1 for a list of the specific types of books found in most law libraries. Many law libraries also provide electronically stored information. Today legal materials are found not only in print, but also on disk and CD-ROM, and many law libraries make these available to researchers.

In addition to law libraries, you often find legal collections in many general libraries, although these collections are not as comprehensive as those found in law libraries. Your local public library may have copies of your state codes, federal

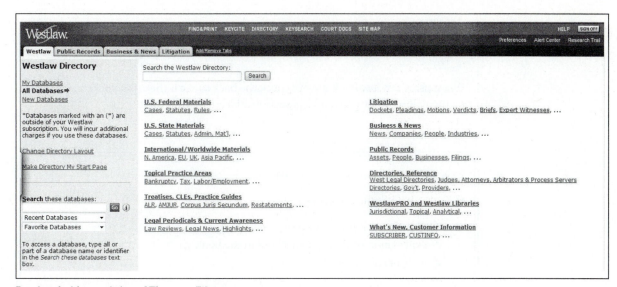

Reprinted with permission of Thomson/West

FIGURE 1-2 Screen Shot of Westlaw Directory

codes, or case law. Many university or college libraries contain a wide array of legal materials.

Virtual Law Libraries

In addition to the traditional law library, today's researcher has access to vast legal materials through online subscription sources such as LEXIS and Westlaw. The same books that are accessed in traditional libraries can be accessed and searched through these online services. For a list of some of the materials found on Westlaw, see Figure 1-2. Selected research materials are also available through many free Internet sites. In fact, both West and LEXIS sponsor free Web sites with *limited* legal materials. A researcher can almost always find primary law (i.e., constitutions, codes, and cases) for free. However, because of copyright issues, only limited secondary source materials are available.

In a virtual law library researchers can find legal material from the convenience of their own desk at almost any time of the day or night. All that is needed is a computer and Internet connection. If researchers want to access either Westlaw or LEXIS, they also need a subscription.

Features of Legal Publications

Learning to do legal research requires a great deal of time and effort. However, in some respects, legal research is similar to general research and law books and periodicals are often similar to nonlegal materials. Most law books (except for case reporters) have an extensive **table of contents** and index. The table of contents, like that of any book, is an outline of the material covered in the book. The index is a list of words and phrases that reflect the topics covered. Using both enables you to find any particular topic in the book. When using legal periodicals, you can locate specific topics in indexes that resemble the *Reader's Guide to Periodical Literature* that you probably used when writing research papers in high school and college.

table of contents. An outline of the material covered in the book or document.

A Point to Remember

When using any law book, always check the back to see if there is a pocket part supplement. If so, be sure to read any section addressing your topic.

BOX 1-2   COMMON FEATURES OF LAW BOOKS

Most Law Publications Contain:

- ✓ directions for using the book or set
- ✓ explanation of abbreviations used in the book
- ✓ table of contents
- ✓ index
- ✓ table of cases
- ✓ table of statutes
- ✓ supplements

---

table of cases. A common feature of legal publications containing the names of all cases cited in the book or document.

table of statutes. A common feature of legal publications containing a list of all statutes or codes that are referenced in the book.

table of abbreviations. A common feature of legal publications containing an explanation of all abbreviations found in the book.

pocket part. A removable supplement; includes all changes or additions to the material contained in the hardbound volume.

federalism. A system of government in which the people are regulated by both federal and state governments.

Many law books contain various tables, either in the front or the back, such as a **table of cases,** a **table of statutes,** and a **table of abbreviations.** These generally include references cited within the book.

One aspect of law books is fairly unique, however; they must be current. Because the law is constantly changing, law books must reflect those changes. Many law books are therefore supplemented regularly by **pocket part** supplements that contain recent changes in the law and slip into an opening on the inside of the back binding.

1-6 FEDERALISM AND LEGAL PUBLICATIONS

In the United States, government operates under a principle called **federalism,** which means that two separate governments, federal and state, regulate citizens. Each government is responsible for making its own laws. When researching an issue, you are therefore faced with different sets of laws for each state and for the federal government. A key feature of legal publications is that separate publications often exist for federal law and for that of each individual state. Even though some secondary sources attempt to discuss all laws, many legal publications (especially primary sources of law) contain law related only to a specific jurisdiction, that is, only federal law, or only the law of one state. When you begin your research you can save time, and be more accurate, if you focus on publications that contain the proper law. Read the problems in Box 1-3 and see if you know whether federal or state law applies. As you continue with your legal education, your ability to do this will improve.

In some cases your research may show that both state and federal laws apply. For example, consider the Meyers case mentioned at the beginning of the chapter. In this

BOX 1-3   TEST YOURSELF

Are the following situations controlled by federal law, by state law, or by both?

(1) Jackson is arrested for possession of narcotics. The drugs were found after Jackson was stopped for speeding. The officer states that as he was writing a ticket for Jackson, the officer noted the smell of marijuana, ordered the driver out of the car, searched the vehicle, and found the drugs. Jackson is charged with possession of marijuana, a state crime. The case is filed in state court. Which law controls?

(2) Adams, a resident of Texas, is involved in an automobile accident with Brown, a resident of California. The accident is Adams's fault and Brown is injured. Brown wants to sue. The accident occurred in California. In which court should the lawsuit be filed and which law should apply?

Answers

(1) Here, Jackson was arrested by local police so state law controls the question of whether a crime was committed. However, if Jackson's attorney claims that the search was unconstitutional, the state court must look at federal law regarding the legality of the search, because this involves a constitutional right. If the search is legal under the U.S. Constitution, the state will also consider Jackson's rights under the state constitution.

(2) Normally lawsuits arising out of automobile accidents are filed in state court and are governed by that state's law regarding negligence. However, in this case, Brown could file a lawsuit to recover his damages in federal court because the federal courts have jurisdiction when the lawsuit is between citizens of different states and the plaintiff is claiming more than $75,000 in damages. This is known as *diversity of citizenship*. However, although the case will be tried in a federal court, the state substantive law (i.e., the law of negligence) applies.

BOX 1-4   RESEARCH CHECKLIST

Before You Begin

✓ Review the factual situation.

✓ Determine if the factual situation is controlled by federal law, by state law, or by both.

✓ Use research materials that contain the proper law.

case, the defendant is charged with the crime of murder. This is a state crime and the case will be heard in a state court. However, the question of the legality of a search is controlled by the Fourth Amendment to the U.S. Constitution, which prohibits unreasonable searches and seizures. To complicate matters, the state in which Meyers resides may also have constitutional provisions regulating unreasonable searches by police. Researching this type of case can be difficult. Keep in mind that, where a conflict exists between state and federal law, federal law controls. This is because of the "Supremacy Clause" of the Constitution (Article VI): "This Constitution, and the Laws of the United States which shall be made in Pursuance thereof . . . shall be the supreme Law of the Land; and the Judges in every State shall be bound thereby, any

Thing in the Constitution or Laws of any State to the Contrary notwithstanding." When a state passes a law that conflicts with the Constitution, the U.S. Supreme Court has the power to declare that state law unconstitutional and unenforceable.

1-7 SOURCES OF U.S. LAW

Whether you research state law or federal law, you find some basic similarities because in both systems the laws come from the same types of sources. All governments, state and federal, have constitutions that are published in numerous sources. Other laws generally come from our legislatures, courts, and administrative agencies. Both the federal and state legislatures enact statutory laws. As a researcher, you most often use code books of the appropriate jurisdiction to find these laws. Federal courts and state courts are responsible for case law found in case reporters. Administrative agencies exist on both federal and state levels from which we derive administrative rules or regulations. U.S. law is thus found in four sources: constitutions, statutes, administrative rules or regulations, and case law decisions. Separate sources exist for the federal government and for each of the states.

Constitutional Law

The federal government and all states have constitutions, documents whose primary purpose is to establish the government and define its functions and obligations in relation to the people. The U.S. Constitution establishes and defines the role of the federal government and its relation to the people of the United States. The U.S. Constitution applies only to the federal government, unless expressly made applicable to individual states. Each state constitution establishes and defines the role of state government and its relationship to citizens of that state. The various constitutions are published in numerous ways, often with the statutory law for the jurisdiction. The U.S. Constitution can be found with the U.S. Codes and state constitutions are usually found with the state codes.

Statutory Law

Statutory law results from legislative action. The federal and state legislatures enact laws that are then sent to the chief executive (the president or governor) for approval. After they are signed (or a veto properly overridden), the laws are organized and published in codes. The code for the United States is known as the *United States Code*. Legislatures also empower the courts to enact rules, known as *rules of court*, which govern practice in the courts. In addition, local governing bodies (cities and counties) enact laws, often known as *local ordinances* or *municipal codes*.

Administrative Regulations

In order for government to perform all of its tasks, legislatures created various agencies to handle specific jobs. For example, Congress created the Securities Exchange Commission (S.E.C.) to handle corporate stock transactions. Agencies generally have the power to make necessary rules or regulations. These are known as *administrative regulations*. Administrative agencies exist in the federal government as well as in each state.

Case Law

U.S. law is based primarily on the English **common law,** a system in which laws developed through the courts and through case decisions. The common law was based on the concept of **precedent** or *stare decisis.* It was *not* based on a set of written laws or rules enacted by the government. Until a factual dispute arose and was resolved in the courts, there was no rule or law that controlled. When parties had a legal problem, their dispute was presented to a judge who decided the case. The decision became precedent. Then, if the same type of factual dispute was presented to a court in the future, the judge followed the decision of the first case. Precedent is also referred to as *stare decisis.* In the U.S. legal system, case law results from selected decisions made by various *appellate* courts, including the U.S. Supreme Court. It does not come from trial court decisions.

common law. Body of law developed through the courts.

precedent. The example set by the decision of an earlier court for similar cases or similar legal questions that arise in later cases.

stare decisis. "It stands decided"; another term for precedent.

Relationship Between Sources of Law

When you research an issue, you often find that more than one primary source of law applies. In the U.S. legal system, the courts have the power to interpret the U.S. Constitution, state constitutions, federal and state codes, and federal and state administrative regulations. Thorough research requires that when you find constitutional or statutory law (including administrative regulations), you must also determine if any case law interprets these laws.

BOX 1-5   PRIMARY SOURCES OF LAW

Federal Law

    U.S. Constitution

    United States Codes

    Federal Administrative Regulations

    Federal Cases

State Law

    State Constitution

    State Codes

    State Administrative Regulations

    State Cases

Online Legal Research

The Internet provides access to a great deal of legal information, both free and fee-based. Some of this information is useful and accurate. However, some information is outdated and inaccurate. Anyone can create and maintain his or her own Web page and legal information can be posted by anyone. Using a general search engine such as Google may lead you to unreliable sites. Be careful to evaluate the source of the information you locate. Always check to see who publishes the information you find and when it was last updated. One very reliable source is the law library Web site of the Library of Congress (http://www.loc.gov/law/public/law.html). This site provides extensive information about the U.S. legal system, as well as links to numerous sources of law. Here you will also find guides to the legislative and judicial process of the United States (Link to Guide to Law Online.) Especially helpful to beginning researchers are the links to pamphlets, How our Laws are Made and Understanding the Federal Courts.

It is impossible to provide a complete and accurate list of great legal research sites. However, this text suggests certain Web sites and provides tips to help you navigate the Internet successfully. The following sites lead you to virtual libraries, where you can access different legal sources without cost.

http://www.gpoaccess.gov/index.html	U.S. Government Printing Office
www.findlaw.com	FindLaw (A free Web site sponsored by West)
www.lexisone.com	lexisONE (A free Web site sponsored by LEXIS)

The following law school Web sites also offer substantial legal materials through the Internet without cost. Law schools are often tremendous sources of accurate information.

www.law.cornell.edu
www.law.indiana.edu
www.washburnlaw.edu

CITATION MATTERS

WHY LEGAL CITATION MATTERS

The term *citation* refers to special information provided by the author of a document. A legal citation shows the reader the origin of the cited authority. Everyone is familiar with the use of quotations. When you use a quote, you must indicate the origin of the quote. Generally, the citation to the original material follows the quoted language. The same is true in legal writing, only we take it a bit further. Most legal writing is designed to inform or convince. The best way to do that is to show the reader where the ideas originated, whether or not a quote is used.

Case law provides good examples of citation use in legal writing. Sometimes it seems as though every sentence has a citation following it. That can make reading legal material tedious and slow. But because legal citations alert the reader to the origin of the material, they are a critical element of legal writing. When a judge writes a decision in a case, that judge strives to explain the reasons for that decision. Often, these reasons are based on previously decided cases and citations to these cases are included.

When attorneys write legal memoranda, they are expected to provide legal authority for the statements they make. Previous cases carry what we call a "weight of authority"—something that personal opinion does not carry. A court is not interested in personal opinions. It is interested in the legal authority that supports the opinion. Courts and other attorneys sometimes need to read the authorities that are cited in memoranda or briefs. It is essential, therefore, that citations be accurate.

In your legal writing, you should strive to cite carefully and completely. Appendix B provides a basic overview of citation. Read it carefully and begin to learn the basic rules of legal citation. Review the use of legal citations below:

> The United States Constitution guarantees the right to trial by jury in order to prevent oppression by the government. U.S. CONST. amend.VI and XIV; *Duncan v. State of La.,* 391 U.S. 145, 194 (1968).

This sentence is a statement of law, not an opinion: "The United States Constitution guarantees the right to trial by jury in order to prevent oppression by the government." The writer shows his audience that the guarantee of a jury trial is found in the U.S. Constitution under Amendments Six and Fourteen. This same statement is further supported by the citation to a U.S. Supreme Court case. Notice that the two citations are separated by a semicolon and followed by a period. The second sentence is called a *citation sentence.*

The *name* of the case is *Duncan v. State of La.* The name of a case is italicized or underlined, never both.

This case is found in the United States Reports. *U.S.* is the proper abbreviation for the *official reporter* of U.S. Supreme Court case law.

This case is located in *volume* 391, and the *first page* of the case is 145. The writer also provided a "pinpoint cite" for the page in the case where the Court addresses the right to trial by jury. The pinpoint cite is to page 194.

The *year of the decision* is 1968. Notice that the year is placed at the end of the citation, and it must be placed in parentheses.

The citation manual used in the preparation of this text is THE BLUEBOOK: A UNIFORM SYSTEM OF CITATION (Columbia Law Review Ass'n et al. eds., 18th ed. 2000).

CHAPTER SUMMARY

Legal research usually involves finding the law that applies to a specific factual question. Because lawyers must know the current law in their jurisdiction, even the most experienced legal practitioners do research before advising a client or arguing a matter before a court. Paralegals and law clerks often do legal research; indeed many nonlegal professionals find this competency to be an important tool.

The total process of legal research involves identifying the factual issue, finding the law, applying the law to the factual situation, and communicating these findings. While paralegals and law clerks often perform the research, they should do so under the supervision of a lawyer. Accuracy and thoroughness are essential. Paralegals and other non-attorneys must be careful not to give legal advice to a client because to do so constitutes the unauthorized practice of law and is unethical and illegal.

Legal publications include primary and secondary sources of the law. A primary source includes the law itself (constitutions, cases, statutes, and administrative regulations). Secondary sources, such as legal encyclopedias and journals, help explain and find the primary source of law. Legal publications are found in printed as well as in electronic format.

Legal research is usually conducted in law libraries found in most law offices. Counties and law schools also maintain large law libraries. Materials there resemble materials found in any library. Law books contain many of the same features found in reference books, such as a table of contents and an index. In addition, many law books contain tables of cases, tables of statutes, and tables of abbreviations used in the book. Many books also include pocket part supplements that keep the work up-to-date.

Before you begin any legal research you must understand the U.S. legal system. This system is founded on the principle of federalism, which means that two separate governments, federal and state, regulate citizens. The laws of each government are usually found in separate publications. When you research a factual issue, it is generally controlled by either federal or state law, although at times both may apply. Determining which law applies to a factual question is one of the first decisions a researcher must make.

All laws, whether state or federal, are found in constitutions, statutes or codes, administrative regulations, and cases. Case law stems from the English Common Law, a system in which laws were developed through the courts and through case decisions. The common law was based on the concept of precedent or *stare decisis*, which means that once a court decided a factual dispute, the same factual dispute in the future had to be decided in the same way. In the United States today, case law results from decisions from the appellate and supreme courts in the federal and state systems.

TERMS TO REMEMBER

legal dictionary	case reporters	table of statutes
legal thesaurus	CD-ROM libraries	table of abbreviations
index	LEXIS	pocket part
legal citations	Westlaw	federalism
primary source	law library	common law
secondary source	table of contents	precedent
code books	table of cases	*stare decisis*

QUESTIONS FOR REVIEW

1. Explain the process of legal research, analysis, and writing.
2. Discuss the various sources of U.S. law.
3. What is the difference between a primary source of law and a secondary source?
4. What types of legal materials are found in law libraries?

5. Describe some of the common features of legal publications.

6. Explain the concept of federalism and how it affects legal research.

7. What are the primary sources of law in the United States?

CAN YOU FIGURE IT OUT?

1. Refer to Figure 1-1, Types of Legal Materials. One of the most famous cases decided by the U.S. Supreme Court is the case of *Miranda v. Arizona*. In which type of legal material would you expect to find that case? In which type of legal materials would you expect to find discussions or analysis of that case?

2. Refer to Figure 1-2, Screen Shot of Westlaw Directory. The directory contains general categories of materials (i.e., U.S. Federal Materials, U.S. State Materials, etc.). In which general categories of material would you expect to find the case of *Miranda v. Arizona*? In which general categories would you expect to find discussions or analysis of that case?

BUILDING YOUR RESEARCH SKILLS: ASSIGNMENTS AND ACTIVITIES

1. Using a legal dictionary, define the terms in Table 1-1.

2. Using a legal thesaurus, find different words for each of the terms in Table 1-1.

3. Visit the law library that you will use to do your legal research assignments. Locate the following legal sources:

The United States Codes
A case reporter containing decisions from the U.S. Supreme Court
Your state code
Case reporters containing case law from your state

Review the list of common features of law books found in Box 1-2 earlier in the chapter. Which of these features is found in each of the above-listed legal sources?

BUILDING YOUR ANALYSIS SKILLS: ASSIGNMENTS AND EXERCISES

1. Consider the following questions and state whether you would begin your research in state or federal sources.

   a. Can a client who filed bankruptcy five years ago file for bankruptcy again?

   b. If a person took $10,000 from an employer without permission, but paid it back when discovered, could that person be charged with any crime?

   c. What are the elements of the crime of counterfeiting?

   d. Mary's boss told her that if she did not have sex with him, she would not get a raise. What are Mary's options?

   e. Terry is a word processor and developed carpal tunnel syndrome. Terry's doctor says it is a result of Terry's job. What rights does Terry have?

2. In Appendix G find the case of *Ohio v. Robinette,* a U.S. Supreme Court case dealing with the questions of federalism and how federal and state law interact. Read the case and answer the following questions.
   a. Did federal drug laws apply to this case? Why or why not?
   b. What primary source of law is the Court interpreting in this case?
   c. Is there a conflict between the state and federal search and seizure laws in this case?
   d. If you were researching a similar search and seizure issue in your state, would you rely on the case of *Ohio v. Robinette* if (a) the issue revolved around your state's constitution or if (b) the issue revolved around the meaning of the U.S. Constitution?

BUILDING YOUR ONLINE RESEARCH SKILLS: ASSIGNMENTS AND EXERCISES

Review the Web sites listed in this chapter (in the Online Legal Research feature).

1. Which of these sources, if any, provide access to your state's constitution?
2. Which of these sources, if any, provide access to your state codes?
3. Which of these sources, if any, provide access to your state cases? If they do provide access to your state cases, for what years are cases provided?

CASE PROJECT

Select one hypothetical case from those found in Appendix A. (Your instructor may assign a specific case.) Read the facts carefully and make a list of all legal terms found in the factual scenario. Which of these terms appear in Table 1-1? Define all legal terms found in the factual situation.

CHAPTER 2

THE STARTING POINT: ANALYZING FACTS AND IDENTIFYING LEGAL ISSUES

S KILL OBJECTIVES FOR CHAPTER 2

When you complete this chapter you should be able to

- State and describe the three basic factual categories.
- Explain how to compare case law facts with a client's factual situation.
- Describe how to identify legal issues in a client's factual situation.
- Describe how to identify legal issues in a reported case law decision.
- Provide examples of good issue statements.

FROM THE DESK OF W. J. BRYAN, ESQ.

TO: Research Assistant

The office just received additional information on the Meyers murder case. We now have copies of the search warrant and a copy of the transcript from the grand jury hearing that resulted in Mr. Meyers's indictment for murder. The search warrant allows the police to search our client's house for drugs and drug paraphernalia. During their search, the police found and seized a bloody rag. Forensic evidence indicates that the blood belongs to a murder victim. Carefully read all the new documents, and identify and summarize all facts that are relevant to legality of the search and seizure. After you do that, try to find case law that will help our client.

2-1 INTRODUCTION

As described in the previous chapter, the legal research process consists of finding law, analyzing the law and the facts of your case, and communicating the results of your research and analysis to interested parties. This process usually begins with determining the important facts in your client's case and then identifying the legal question or issues in that case. This chapter discusses the importance of the facts and legal issues to the research process and provides some methods of analyzing the facts and identifying the issues.

At the beginning of the research process, a clear understanding of the facts involved in a client's situation is essential. No legal research is productive until the researcher acquires a good picture of the client's facts. A good client interview produces a factually rich picture of the events and people involved in the client's situation. Sometimes, additional interviews and investigation are necessary. Before any legal research begins, all *relevant* facts must be acquired and placed into perspective. Students who are new to the law may be tempted to begin research projects prior to establishing a clear picture of the events involved in the case. This is a time-consuming error. Until the facts are well established, researching the law is impossible. Contrary to what one might initially think, the facts determine the area of law to be researched. Facts are found in many places: client interviews, witness interviews, relevant documents, depositions, and other discovery. A thorough understanding of the facts enables the researcher to focus on those most significant, thereby leading the researcher to pinpoint the area of law to be reviewed.

2-2 KNOW AND ANALYZE THE FACTS

The attorney handling the Meyers case wants his research assistant to find case law that helps his client. In his note, Attorney Bryan gives an important instruction to his assistant. Before researching the law, the relevant facts must be identified. Research is usually performed as a direct result of a set of facts: The facts come first, then the law is applied to those facts. The researcher must begin by categorizing or analyzing the known facts. Obviously, some are more important than others. Your subsequent research assists you in determining which ones are *most* relevant. There are three basic fact categories:

- Relevant facts
- Explanatory facts
- Legally unimportant facts

Once you gather all of the known facts, the next step is to place them into one of these categories. However, determining relevant facts requires that the researcher have at least a general understanding of the legal principles governing the case. You cannot determine what facts are legally important if you are totally unfamiliar with the law. For example, if you know nothing about the criminal law, you might not know whether the contents of a search warrant are important. If you are unfamiliar with the area of law, you must perform some general legal research first. Become familiar with the basic legal principles and then analyze your client's facts. As your research continues, you might also have to reevaluate how to categorize the facts.

Relevant Facts: Relevant facts are absolutely essential; they cannot be ignored. They are legally and factually important. There may be several ways to identify them in a factual situation: (1) remove the fact and ask yourself if it *significantly* changes the situation; (2) change the fact and ask yourself if it *significantly* changes the situation. If either alters the fact situation, it is probably a relevant fact.

Explanatory Facts: Explanatory facts clarify the relevant facts. They enable the researcher to grasp the entire picture of the events by supplementing and explaining the relevant facts. They often provide color or depth of understanding to the situation.

Legally Unimportant Facts: Legally unimportant facts should be put aside during legal research. They play no real role in the legal situation. There are several ways to identify them: (1) remove the fact and ask yourself if it significantly changes the situation; (2) change the fact and ask yourself if it significantly changes the situation. If the answer to either question is "no, it does not alter the fact situation," the fact is probably legally unimportant.

2-3 HOW TO SORT THE FACTS OF A CLIENT'S CASE

Categorizing your client's facts helps you focus your research. Remember from the previous chapter, when you research you look for primary law (case law, statutory law, and constitutional law). Because of the rule of *stare decisis*, relevant case law

A Point to Remember

The relevant and explanatory facts are the focal points for the researcher. The key here is to recognize and put aside the legally unimportant facts. Sorting the facts enables you to zoom in on the relevant facts and highlight missing facts.

includes cases where the courts have decided the same or similar factual questions. Relevant statutory law includes laws or rules that can be applied to your factual situation. In any event, the relevant facts in your client's case must be identified.

The ultimate sorting of the facts is best left to those trained in the law. Clients are often ill equipped to categorize facts. What is important to a client may be legally irrelevant. However, always let the client tell the entire story. Do not encourage a client to edit the facts. Sometimes facts that appear unimportant initially take on special significance as the litigation or the case moves forward.

2-4 HOW TO COMPARE CASE LAW FACTS WITH YOUR CLIENT'S FACTS

If your research is focused on case law, you must compare your client's factual situation with those found in published cases. Before determining that specific cases apply to your client's situation, you must determine that the nature of the dispute or the issue is similar. The researcher looks for factually and legally similar cases to compare to the client's case. Identifying issues is discussed later in this chapter.

A process of comparison of relevant facts is a good starting place in the legal analysis process. Factual comparison usually takes place after the researcher clarifies the client facts and locates case law that may be applicable to the client's legal situation. The effective legal researcher works to locate **case law** that is as factually similar to the client facts as possible. Because our legal system is based on **precedent**, the sorting and comparison of facts are essential **legal analysis** skills.

case law. A collection of reported cases.

precedent. The example set by the decision of an earlier court for similar cases or similar legal questions that arise in later cases.

legal analysis. The process of comparing and contrasting facts and legal issues.

SORTING THE FACTS

Consider the following factual situation.

Rimma was traveling at 40 miles per hour on a city street when Emerson, moving at 65 miles per hour, ran into the back of Rimma's vehicle. Emerson's vehicle was a new black Jeep Cherokee. Rimma was driving a four-year-old green Volvo. Emerson did not notice that traffic was slowing and that Rimma's brake lights were on. Emerson was talking on a cellular phone and was in a hurry to get to his office. He was returning from an appointment with his physician. Emerson took a strong sedative about 30 minutes prior to the accident. He has been under a great deal of stress recently. Rimma's car was badly damaged and she was injured. As a result of the accident Rimma could not get to her job that evening, due to lack of transportation. Rimma is a twenty-two-year-old exotic dancer. She had a contract for a special engagement that evening, which would have paid her $1,000.00. Emerson is an automobile salesperson. Your office represents Rimma in an action against Emerson.

It is not always clear in which category a particular fact belongs. What is most important is that you begin to sort them. You are not discarding them, only sorting them. As research continues, the researcher may move the facts from one category to another.

Sort the facts above into the three categories.

Relevant Facts

1. Emerson was driving under the influence of a narcotic.
2. Emerson was exceeding a safe driving speed under the conditions.
3. Emerson's vehicle struck Rimma's vehicle.
4. Rimma's vehicle was damaged as a result of Emerson's actions.
5. Rimma lost wages as a result of Emerson's actions.

Explanatory Facts

1. Emerson was hurrying while returning to his office.
2. Emerson was talking on his cellular phone.
3. Emerson was returning from a visit to his physician.
4. Emerson was traveling at 65 mph while Rimma slowed to 40 mph.
5. Emerson did not notice that traffic was slowing down and did not see Rimma's brake lights.

Legally Unimportant Facts

1. Rimma is an exotic dancer.
2. Emerson is a car salesperson.
3. Rimma's car is a green Volvo.
4. Emerson's car is a new black Jeep Cherokee.

The fact category for any given fact may change if the fact pattern is altered. For example: Does the fact pattern change if Emerson's car was malfunctioning and the accelerator was stuck? Does the fact pattern change if Rimma is traveling 40 miles per hour in a 65 mile per hour zone and she is legally intoxicated? Obviously, the answer to both questions is "of course that changes the situation." You can see that changes in the facts may change the overall factual analysis of the case.

Factual comparison may at first seem confusing and somewhat arbitrary. However, once you establish a process, the confusion dissolves. When you compare the client's facts with those of a reported case, look for the following:

- Factual similarities
- Factual unknowns
- Factual differences

	Client's Case	*Published Case*
Factual Similarities:		
Factual Unknowns:		
Factual Differences:		

This chart enables you to easily compare and contrast the facts of your client's case with those of a reported case. A good number of similarities of relevant facts indicates that the case *may* apply in your client's situation. Conversely, a good number of differences in the relevant facts indicates that the case *may not* apply. When there are significant gaps or unknown facts, the reported case probably does not apply to your client's case. As a legal researcher, you are looking for cases that are factually and legally very similar to the one you are researching.

2-5 LEGAL ISSUES

Once the client's factual situation is clear, you can consider what the issues may be. Ask yourself the following question as you begin each legal research assignment: Do I understand the client's problems? If the answer is yes, you are ready to attempt to identify the issues or problems presented by the client's facts. If you are unclear on the legal issues, ask your supervisor for guidance.

Legal issues are specific questions raised by the facts. Think of it this way: An incident occurs, and now you need to give the factual situation a legal label. Properly identifying these "legal labels" helps you locate relevant law. After careful review of a fact pattern, the legal researcher must begin to identify the area of law involved. Once this is known (e.g., contract law, tort law, or family law), identification of the issues must occur. Review the factual situation in the case of *Rimma v. Emerson* described earlier in this chapter. This case involves the general area of tort law. The issue is therefore related to tort law. In very general terms, a question raised by these facts is "Did Emerson commit a tort?" This question or issue is much too broad and will not help you in your research. It must be more specifically identified and stated. A specific area of law involved here is negligence, a part of tort law. However, asking "Was Emerson negligent?" is also too broad. The issue must be more specifically stated in relationship to the facts of the case. A better way to state the issue might be "Was Emerson negligent when he drove his car on a city street at 65 miles per hour while he was under the influence of drugs, and rear-ended a vehicle driven by Rimma, damaging the car and injuring Rimma?" This is a more complete issue statement. To simply ask "Was Emerson negligent?" is not enough; the facts are missing.

Another way to think of issues is that they are the questions the parties to a lawsuit bring to the court for resolution. The court resolves the legal issues. Sometimes issues are also called **questions presented**—meaning the questions presented to the court for resolution.

2-6 HOW TO IDENTIFY THE LEGAL ISSUES

Issues in Your Client's Case

If **pleadings** have been filed in a case, go to the pleadings and read about the causes of action involved to help establish the issues. Issues are found in **causes of action** or **affirmative defenses** in pleadings. For example, if you read the complaint filed by Rimma against Emerson, you would probably find a cause of action labeled "negligence." When you read this cause of action, you see that Rimma claims (1) that Emerson was driving his car on a public road, (2) that he drove negligently in that he was under the influence of drugs and was not paying attention to traffic, (3) that he rear-ended the vehicle driven by Rimma, and (4) that he caused damage to the car and injury to Rimma. In this type of civil lawsuit, one of the questions the court is asked to decide is whether Emerson was negligent, if Rimma's claims are true.

questions presented. A statement of the legal issue presented to the court for resolution.

pleadings. The formal written allegations filed with the court by both sides to a lawsuit; claims and defenses are clearly set out so that both parties are placed on notice of the position of the opposing party.

causes of action. The basis upon which a lawsuit may be brought to the court.

affirmative defenses. Defenses raised by the defendant in the answer; reasons why the plaintiff should not recover even if all of the allegations of the complaint are true.

Let's look again at this issue statement: "Was Emerson negligent when he drove his car on a city street at 65 miles per hour while he was under the influence of drugs, and rear-ended a vehicle driven by Rimma, damaging the car and injuring Rimma?" Note how the claims or allegations in a cause of action relate to the way a proper issue statement is phrased. Of course, not all legal issues relate to the existence of a cause of action. Sometimes procedural problems or questions of the admissibility of evidence may also be a legal issue in a case. If you are in doubt about the specific legal issue you are asked to research, always ask your supervisor for initial guidance. As with your analysis of relevant facts, your specific legal questions may change as you do more research and find out more about the relevant law.

Issues in a Reported Case

Once you identify the issues in your client's case, you must look for case law dealing with the same issue and similar fact pattern. In reported cases, the court explains the legal issues. Usually, the issues are stated after the court has explained the factual background of the case and the **judicial history** of the case. The court in some instances actually states "The first issue is . . . " or "The question before this court involves. . . ." This is the clearest indication of the issue. Many cases involve more than one issue. The court usually indicates when it is moving from one issue to the next. The excerpt from the *Lopez* case that follows provides a typical example of the way in which a court introduces issues.

judicial history. The legal (courtroom) history of a case.

A Point to Remember

Case law is often written to instruct the legal community. It is written not so much for the parties involved in the litigation as for those who will read it in search of case law relevant to their client's situation. The parties to the litigation are primarily concerned with the outcome of the case. The legal researcher is concerned with the legal reasoning or legal analysis provided by the court.

2-7 HOW ISSUE STATEMENTS ARE WRITTEN

An issue statement sets forth the legal question *and* it provides the reader with the most significant facts. The issue is often stated as a question. Remember, it is the question presented to the court for resolution.

For example: John is the second baseman of the Hidden Valley Ranger softball team. He is its best hitter. After striking out, he carelessly tosses the wooden bat sixteen feet behind him, hitting and injuring Rachael, a ten-year-old spectator. The Rangers lost the final game of the season due to John's striking out.

Your initial research tells you that a cause of action for negligence has four **elements:** (1) a duty on the part of the defendant to act in a safe manner, (2) breach of the duty to behave in a safe manner, (3) causation (of the injury or damage), and (4) damage to the plaintiff. On a very basic level, the question in the fact pattern above is this: "Was John negligent?" However, this question does not provide the reader with enough information. A better, more specific issue statement is this: "Was John negligent when he carelessly tossed a wooden baseball bat into the crowd

elements. The components of a cause of action or of a statute.

prima facie case. On first view or on its face; for example, the plaintiff presented a strong *prima facie* case for establishing the negligence of the defendant.

injuring a spectator standing sixteen feet away?" This question or issue statement provides the reader with a clear picture of what happened. By placing the most relevant facts into the issue, the reader may easily look at the four elements of negligence and decide whether or not the plaintiff makes a *prima facie* **case** for negligence.

Read the excerpt from the *Lopez* case, looking for facts and issues.

CASE EXCERPT

United States v. Lopez,
514 U.S. 549 (1995)

OPINION: CHIEF JUSTICE REHNQUIST delivered the opinion of the Court.

In the Gun-Free School Zones Act of 1990, Congress made it a federal offense "for any individual knowingly to possess a firearm at a place that the individual knows, or has reasonable cause to believe, is a school zone." 18 U.S.C. § 922 (q)(1)(A) (1988, Supp. V). The Act neither regulates a commercial activity nor contains a requirement that the possession be connected in any way to interstate commerce. We hold that the Act exceeds the authority of Congress "to regulate Commerce . . . among the several States. . . ." U.S. Const., Art. I, § 8, cl. 3.

On March 10, 1992, respondent, who was then a 12th-grade student, arrived at Edison High School in San Antonio, Texas, carrying a concealed .38 caliber handgun and five bullets. Acting upon an anonymous tip, school authorities confronted respondent, who admitted that he was carrying the weapon. He was arrested and charged under Texas law with firearm possession on school premises. *See* Tex. Penal Code Ann. § 46.03(a)(1) (Supp. 1994). The next day, the state charges were dismissed after federal agents charged respondent by complaint with violating the Gun-Free School Zones Act of 1990. 18 U.S.C. § 922(q)(1)(A) (1988, Supp. V).

A federal grand jury indicted respondent on one count of knowing possession of a firearm at a school zone, in violation of § 922(q). Respondent moved to dismiss his federal indictment on the ground that § 922(q) "is unconstitutional as it is beyond the power of Congress to legislate control over our public schools." The District Court denied the motion, concluding that § 922(q)

"is a constitutional exercise of Congress' well-defined power to regulate activities in and affecting commerce, and the 'business' of elementary, middle and high schools affects interstate commerce." App. to Pet. for Cert. 55a. Respondent waived his right to a jury trial. The District Court conducted a bench trial, found him guilty of violating Section 922(q), and sentenced him to six months' imprisonment and two years' supervised release.

On appeal, respondent challenged his conviction based on his claim that Section 922(q) exceeded Congress' power to legislate under the Commerce Clause. The Court of Appeals for the Fifth Circuit agreed and reversed respondent's conviction. It held that, in light of what it characterized as insufficient congressional findings and legislative history, "section 922(q), in the full reach of its terms, is invalid as beyond the power of Congress under the Commerce Clause." 2 F.3d 1342, 1367–1368 (1993). Because of the importance of the issue, we granted *certiorari,* 511 U.S. _____ (1994), and we now affirm.

*   *   *

We have identified three broad categories of activity that Congress may regulate under its commerce power. *Perez v. United States, supra,* at 150; *see also Hodel v. Virginia Surface Mining & Reclamation Assn., supra,* at 276–277. First, Congress may regulate the use of the channels of interstate commerce. *See,* e.g., *Darby,* 312 U.S., at 114; *Heart of Atlanta Motel, supra,* at 256 (" 'The authority of Congress to keep the channels of interstate commerce free from immoral and injurious uses has been frequently sustained, and is no longer open to question.'" (*quoting Caminetti v. United States,* 242 U.S. 470, 491 (1917)). Second, Congress is empowered to regulate and protect the instrumentalities of interstate commerce, or persons or things in interstate commerce, even though the threat may come only from intrastate activities. *See,* e.g., *Shreveport Rate Cases,* 234 U.S. 342 (1914); *Southern R. Co. v. United States,* 222 U.S. 20 (upholding amendments to Safety Appliance Act as applied to vehicles used in intrastate commerce); *Perez, supra,* at 150 ("For example, the destruction of an aircraft (18 U.S.C. § 32), or thefts from interstate shipments (18 U.S.C. Section 659)"). Finally, Congress' commerce authority includes the power to regulate those activities having a substantial relation to interstate commerce, *Jones & Laughlin Steel,* 301 U.S., at 37, i.e., those activities that substantially affect interstate commerce. *Wirtz, supra,* at 196, n. 27.

Within this final category, admittedly, our case law has not been clear whether an activity must "affect" or "substantially affect" interstate commerce in order to be within Congress' power to regulate it under the Commerce Clause. *Compare Preseault v. ICC,* 494 U.S. 1, 17 (1990), with *Wirtz, supra,* at 196 (the Court has never declared that "Congress may use a relatively trivial impact on commerce as an excuse for broad general regulation of state or private activities."). We conclude, consistent with the great weight of our case law, that the proper test requires an analysis of whether the regulated activity "substantially affects" interstate commerce.

We now turn to consider the power of Congress, in light of this framework, to enact § 922(q). The first two categories of authority may be quickly disposed of: § 922(q) is not a regulation of the use of the channels of interstate commerce, nor is it an attempt to prohibit the interstate transportation of a commodity through the channels of commerce; nor can § 922(q) be justified as a regulation by which Congress has sought to protect an instrumentality of interstate commerce or a thing in interstate commerce. Thus, if Section 922(q) is to be sustained, it must be under the third category as a regulation of an activity that substantially affects interstate commerce.

*   *   *

Section 922(q) is a criminal statute that by its terms has nothing to do with "commerce" or any sort of economic enterprise, however broadly one might define those terms. Section 922(q) is not an essential part of a larger regulation of economic activity, in which the regulatory scheme could be undercut unless the intrastate activity were regulated. It cannot, therefore, be sustained under our cases upholding regulations of activities that arise out of or are connected with a commercial transaction, which viewed in the aggregate, substantially affects interstate commerce.

[T]to the extent that congressional findings would enable us to evaluate the legislative judgment that the activity in question substantially affected interstate commerce, even though no such substantial effect was visible to the naked eye, they are lacking here.

For the foregoing reasons the judgment of the Court of Appeals is affirmed.

Online Legal Research

At times we need information but we are not sure about how to locate it. A library provides several options: the computerized filings of the library collection, the card catalog, and the librarian. The Internet also provides choices. Sometimes you want to perform a search but are not sure which sites lead to good information.

The following list represents some of the major search engines that lead to legal information. These search engines search many Web sites at one time and then provide you with a great many options. Caution: Practice writing your searches. A poorly written search results in a great deal of unwanted information or no information at all. A search with carefully chosen terms produces finely focused information.

Choose your search terms only after you have identified the relevant facts and issues. A list of relevant facts and a statement of your issue will suggest search terms. Practice with creating searches is essential. Many search engines and Web sites provide help with how to use their site. Always check this information; you may be amazed at what is new since the last time you used the resource. Some search engines also provide opportunities for conducting "advanced searches." These features are often similar to search methods used in the legal databases of Westlaw and LEXIS.

Two of the major search engines are:

www.google.com   Google
www.yahoo.com   Yahoo!

CITATION MATTERS

LEGAL DICTIONARIES

THE BLUEBOOK—RULE 15.8

A legal dictionary requires a special citation form.
Black's Law Dictionary 657 (7th ed. 1999).
Ballentine's Law Dictionary 243 (3d ed. 1969).

Dictionary Citation Analyzed

title	page	edition and year
↓	↓	↓
Black's Law Dictionary	657	(7th ed. 1999).

The *title* of the dictionary is placed first.

The *page* from where the material was borrowed comes next. Notice there is no comma used here.

The *edition* is placed in parentheses at the end of the citation sentence. There is a space between the *3d* and the *ed.* There is also a space before the year.

A good legal dictionary is an essential research tool. All students of law need one. If you use a definition from the dictionary, you need to place a citation behind the definition.

Researchers also need a good legal thesaurus. These tools are often used together. If you look up your term in both resources, you are much more likely to understand it. Law libraries make legal dictionaries and legal thesauri available. These are resources you need to acquire for your personal use.

CHAPTER SUMMARY

The identification of relevant facts is an essential step in both reading the law and researching the law. Understanding the facts is the first step toward analysis of the legal problem. Until the facts are known and understood, no research should begin. Facts may be categorized as relevant, explanatory, or legally unimportant. Once this categorization takes place, you are ready to determine the legal issues. Factual analysis arises in two frameworks. First, one must analyze the client's facts. The second involves categorizing the facts in a reported case. When you compare your client's facts with the facts in a reported case, look for similarities, unknowns (gaps), and differences. The legal issues are stated as questions. A good issue statement contains a legal question surrounded by the relevant facts.

TERMS TO REMEMBER

case law	pleadings	judicial history
precedent	causes of action	elements
legal analysis	affirmative defenses	*prima facie* case
questions presented		

QUESTIONS FOR REVIEW

1. Why is the client's factual situation important?
2. State and describe the three basic fact categories.
3. Explain the process for factual comparison.
4. What is a legal issue?
5. How do you identify the issues in a case in which pleadings have been filed?
6. How do you identify the issues in a case in which no pleadings have been filed?
7. How do you identify the issues in a reported case?
8. What does a good issue statement contain?

CAN YOU FIGURE IT OUT?

1. Using the *United States v. Lopez* case (located in this chapter), can you find the name of Title 18 of the United States Code § 922?

BUILDING YOUR RESEARCH SKILLS: ASSIGNMENTS AND ACTIVITIES

1. Create a chart of relevant, explanatory, and legally unimportant facts for the *United States v. Lopez* case.
2. State the issue in the *United States v. Lopez* case. Remember to include the legal question and the key facts.

BUILDING YOUR ANALYSIS SKILLS: ASSIGNMENTS AND EXERCISES

1. Read the documents in the Meyers case file found in Appendix A. Summarize the relevant and explanatory facts regarding the legality of the search and seizure of the bloody rag.

2. Consider the following hypothetical case: Ms. Grace Sanchez, your client, was recently dismissed from her position as Day Manager of Helman's, a large local department store. Ms. Sanchez is sixty-four-years old. She was with the company for over thirty years. She began her career at Helman's as a clerk in the jewelry department. Ms. Sanchez believes Helman's dismissed her because she is approaching retirement age and they do not want to pay her a pension. Also read the case of *Cancellier v. Federated Department Stores*, 672 F.2d 1312 (9th Cir. 1981) found in Appendix G.

   a. Create a chart of the relevant, explanatory, and legally unimportant facts for the Sanchez fact pattern.
   b. What is the legal issue in the Sanchez case?
   c. What was the legal issue in the *Cancellier* case?

BUILDING YOUR ONLINE RESEARCH SKILLS: ASSIGNMENTS AND EXERCISES

1. Review the facts and issues in the case of Rimma v. Emerson found earlier in the chapter. Using the search features on both Google and Yahoo, look for information about applicable law. From your search results, select two Web sites and summarize the information you find. For each Web site, identify who prepared the site and the date of the latest revision of the site.

2. Repeat the assignment in question 1 for the Sanchez case, described above.

3. Repeat the assignment in question 1 for the Meyers's case (the search and seizure issue).

CASE PROJECT

Review the hypothetical case you selected in Chapter 1. Try to identify the relevant facts, explanatory facts, and legally unimportant facts. Also, try to identify the legal issues. Remember that this may change after you have researched the case.

FINDING AND ANALYZING CASE LAW

When you complete this chapter you should be able to
- List where case law may be located.
- Explain the purpose of case law.
- Explain the elements of a case law citation.
- List the print publications containing U.S. Supreme Court case law.
- Explain the differences between the official publication of U.S. Supreme Court case law and the unofficial publications of the same material.
- List other federal reporters.
- Explain the purpose of a regional reporter.
- List and define the components of a case.
- Compare and contrast the facts of a reported case with a client's factual situation.

FROM THE DESK OF W. J. BRYAN, ESQ.

TO: Research Assistant

The office needs to begin case law research in the Meyers case. Look for California and U.S. Supreme Court case law to support our client's position regarding the admissibility of the bloody handkerchief. Review the file before you begin. (The case file is found in Appendix A, Problem 10.) Please check with me if you need clarification. Create a list of the cases you locate and include a brief summary of each case on your list.

3-1 OVERVIEW OF CASE LAW AND THE CONCEPT OF *STARE DECISIS*

primary authority. The resources that provide the actual law; laws are found in constitutions, statutes, case law, and some administrative materials.

decision. The formal written resolution of a case; it explains the legal and factual issues, the resolution of the case, and the law used by the court in reaching its resolution.

opinion. A decision is sometimes referred to as an opinion.

Case law is **primary authority.** Cases are written by judges. Once a case is presented to the court and the legal and factual issues are resolved, the judge writes a **decision,** sometimes called an **opinion.** This written decision is case law. At the state and federal level decisions are reported for many appellate and all supreme court cases. At the federal level even some of the trial court cases are reported. Once you become familiar with case citations, you will know the level of the court deciding the case with just a glance at the reporter abbreviation in the case citation. Case law is based on the concept of *stare decisis,* which means "it stands decided." Case law is also known as precedent. This concept, which is the basis of English Common Law, means that once a court has decided a particular factual dispute, other courts should follow the same ruling when presented with the same facts. It is meant to give stability and uniformity to the legal system. Case law in the United States follows this idea, with some qualifications:

- First, *stare decisis* applies only to published case decisions that come from appellate or supreme courts. Decisions from trial courts, even if they are published, do not create case law that other courts must follow.

- Second, as a general rule, *stare decisis* applies only to cases within the same jurisdiction. For example, if the California Supreme Court decides a case, that decision is not binding, or *stare decisis*, in the other 49 states. Of course, if, in deciding a case, the United States Supreme Court interprets a federal law or the United States Constitution, that interpretation is binding in all states.

- Third, *stare decisis* requires that courts follow case decisions of *higher* courts. For example, if a court of appeals decides a particular dispute, all of the trial courts within that jurisdiction must follow the decision. Other appellate courts in that jurisdiction do not have to follow the decision.

When a case is truly *stare decisis*, lower courts in the same jurisdiction must follow the decision. The case is **mandatory authority,** sometimes called **binding authority.** However, this does not mean that a court cannot consider published cases from other courts. In fact, many courts consider nonbinding case law when deciding an issue. Nonbinding case law is sometimes called **persuasive authority.**

mandatory authority. Case law that must be followed by a court.

binding authority. Another term for *mandatory authority*.

persuasive authority. Nonbinding case law that nevertheless is considered by a court.

The Appeal Process

Because all case law comes from appellate courts, before reading case law you should be familiar with the appeal process (see Box 3-1). An appeal results when one party to an action is dissatisfied with the result and asks a higher court to review the trial. In general, in a civil case either party has the right to appeal. In a criminal trial, however, only the defendant has the right to appeal because of the **double jeopardy** clause of the Constitution. An appeal usually takes place only after a final judgment in the trial court. Appellate rules are very technical and the appeal process is very limited. However, in some instances, parties are allowed to seek appellate review from a higher court through proceedings known as writs. The courts hear petitions or requests for many types of writs including:

double jeopardy. Clause in the U.S. Constitution that generally prevents the government from trying a person more than once for the same offense.

Petition for writ of mandate	A request that the appellate court order the lower court to do something or to refrain from doing something
Petition for writ of habeas corpus	A request that the court order the release of one who is imprisoned or otherwise confined

Case law can result from both appeals and petitions for writs. In rendering its decision, the appellate court can **affirm** the decision, **reverse** the decision, or reverse and **remand** the decision. When the court affirms the decision, it lets the lower court decision stand. When it reverses the case, it overturns or changes the lower court decision. When it reverses and remands the case, it overturns the lower court decision, but sends it back to the trial court for a retrial. In any case, the appellate court always renders a written decision in which it explains its reasons. It discusses the claims made by each of the parties and also reviews and analyzes the various primary legal authorities cited by the parties.

affirm. To uphold: in connection with an appeal to uphold the lower court's decision.

reverse. To change.

remand. To send back.

In the federal legal system and in many states, a supreme court also exists. This court plays a role in the appellate process. If a party is still not satisfied after a hearing in the appellate court, parties can petition the highest court in their legal system for a hearing. If a case was originally tried in the state courts, the parties can petition

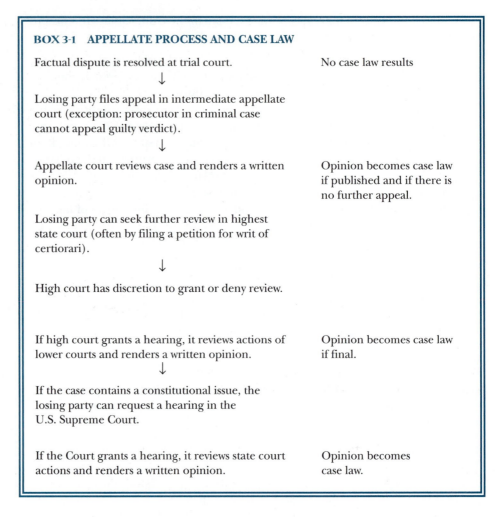

BOX 3-1 APPELLATE PROCESS AND CASE LAW

Factual dispute is resolved at trial court.   No case law results
↓

Losing party files appeal in intermediate appellate
court (exception: prosecutor in criminal case
cannot appeal guilty verdict).
↓

Appellate court reviews case and renders a written   Opinion becomes case law
opinion.   if published and if there is
                                                             no further appeal.

Losing party can seek further review in highest
state court (often by filing a petition for writ of
certiorari).
↓

High court has discretion to grant or deny review.

If high court grants a hearing, it reviews actions of   Opinion becomes case law
lower courts and renders a written opinion.   if final.
↓

If the case contains a constitutional issue, the
losing party can request a hearing in the
U.S. Supreme Court.

If the Court grants a hearing, it reviews state court   Opinion becomes
actions and renders a written opinion.   case law.

for a hearing in the U.S. Supreme Court if a federal issue is involved. Such a request is called a *petition for a writ of certiorari.*

The basis for any appeal is a legal error. This means that at the trial court, the law was not followed. Often this stems from the trial judge's ruling regarding the admissibility of evidence, or from the instructions given to the jury by the judge at the end of the trial. Legal errors can also stem from the court's ruling on various **motions** that attorneys make in the case. When you read case law, always be sure that you understand the nature of the proceedings in the trial court. If the appellate court describes unfamiliar procedures, be sure to use a dictionary or other resource.

motion. A request for an order from the court.

3-2 WHERE TO FIND CASE LAW

Cases are published by several publishers and may be located in a number of resources. Each state publishes, or arranges to have published, its appellate and supreme court cases. States such as New York, Texas, Florida, New Jersey, Washington, California, and many others publish their opinions in what are known as official publications of their case law. Other states arrange with the West Group to publish their case law in the appropriate **regional reporters**. A concise guide to the appropriate resources is found in the ***Uniform System of Citation*** (*The Bluebook*). In addition to the traditional paper publications, most state case law is available on various CD-ROM products and through the online legal databases of LEXIS and Westlaw. Most state's official Web sites also provide this data. Increasing collections of state and federal case law are found at various sites on the Internet.

Case Law Reporters

Case law reporters are books filled with decisions. They exist for most states; in addition, there are large sets of books known as *regional reporters* that publish selected case law from a geographical region of the United States. Those are discussed in Section 3-6.

LEXIS and Westlaw

LEXIS and Westlaw are huge online legal databases. Use of these services is through contract with the publishers. Both services should be used only by persons trained to search in large legal databases. Case law is only one of the many resources they provide.

CD-ROM Products

Several publishers offer case law on CD-ROM. These products often combine the ease of using books with the speed of using an online database.

Internet

There are Internet sites for case law retrieval. Many of these are provided in the On-line Legal Research boxes provided in each chapter. Because the Internet is growing and changing at a rapid rate, it is difficult to offer a reliable list of research sites. Some law schools continue to maintain consistently reliable Web sites. Try the following Internet site for U.S. Supreme Court case law: http://www.law.cornell.edu/.

3-3 WHAT IS A CASE?

A case is a decision, sometimes called an *opinion*, written by a judge (the court). Judges write opinions designed to inform and instruct those who read the decisions. The parties to most litigation are interested in the outcome of the case. But they may not be interested in the court's legal reasoning, although on appeal that may be important.

In the course of legal research, we read case law to attempt to understand the factual and legal issues and a court's resolution of those issues. Judges rely on previous decisions, the Constitution, statutory law, and administrative regulations in rendering decisions and writing opinions. Judges are acutely aware that legal researchers read reported case law looking for opinions that may apply to their client's situation. That is why judges are so careful to provide detailed facts and lengthy analysis of the factual and legal issues. It is not enough for a court to state, "Plaintiff, you win; defendant, you lose."

The importance of case law is apparent when we recall that the U.S. legal system relies on precedent. The court must look to past decisions to aid it in making current decisions. Therefore, researchers must do the same to locate case law similar to the factual and legal situation being researched.

---

regional reporters. A set of published volumes of cases by courts in specific regions of the United States; for example, the *Pacific Reporter* or the *North Eastern Reporter*.

Uniform System of Citation. A reference manual; it contains the rules for proper citation format; often called *The Bluebook.*

case law reporters. Sets of published volumes of cases decided by various courts.

When you read a case decision, keep in mind that the decision usually comes from a panel of judges. At the appellate level, three justices hear and decide a case; at the Supreme Court level, nine justices hear and decide a case. In many instances, the decision of the court is not unanimous. One or more justices may disagree entirely with the decision. In such a case, that justice may write a dissenting opinion in which the justice explains his or her position. Sometimes one or more justices may agree with the ultimate result of the case but not with the reasoning of the majority. That justice may write a concurring opinion, an opinion in which the justice explains his or her reasoning. Although concurring and dissenting opinions are published with the majority opinion, they do not result in "case law." Case law is found only in the majority opinion.

3-4 CASE CITATIONS

The name of the case is either italicized or underlined and placed at the beginning of any case law citation, which is arranged in the following format. The volume number is first, the abbreviation for the name of the reporter is next, and the page on which the case begins follows the reporter abbreviation. The year of the decision is placed either at the very end of the citation or in some instances just after the name of the case (see Figure 3-1).

FIGURE 3-1

> *Marvin v. Marvin* (1976) 18 Cal. 3d 660, 557 P. 2d.106, 134 Cal. Rptr. 815
>
> or
>
> *Marvin v. Marvin,* 18 Cal. 3d 660, 557 P. 2d.106, 134 Cal. Rptr. 815 (1976)

The year is always placed in parentheses. The *Uniform System of Citation (The Bluebook)* provides a comprehensive guide to proper citation format. Check your state citation rules for the proper placement of the year. Appendix B provides a Basic Citation Reference Guide.

A Point to Remember

When looking in a case reporter, check the very top of the first full page of the case for the proper case citation. This is the proper abbreviation of the case name. (See Figure 3-2.) *Illinois v. Gates,* 462 U.S. 213 (1983) is the accepted citation for this case. Usually it is shorter than the full names of all of the parties. Compare the full names of the parties in the *Texas v. Johnson* case with the short version at the top of the page (Figures 3-3 through 3-5).

official citation. This is the citation to the official publication of case law for a particular jurisdiction (this is usually a government publication); the official citation includes the name of the case, volume number in which the case is located, the first page of the case, and the year of the decision.

Sometimes, a case is reported in several publications. It is the same case, just different publishers. The **official citation** is always listed first; this is followed by the parallel (and unofficial) citations. For example, the *United States Reports,* abbreviated as U.S., is the official reporter of all U.S. Supreme Court case law. There are, however, other publishers of all U.S. Supreme Court case law. This is discussed in Section 3-5.

A Point to Remember

Sometimes in **secondary sources** the citations are incomplete. For example, the year may be omitted or the reporter abbreviation may differ from that suggested in the *Uniform System of Citation* or your state **style manual**. Once the case is retrieved, you are able to complete and, if necessary, correct the citation.

secondary sources. Tools used to understand the law; one such tool is a legal encyclopedia, which explains the law.

style manual. A manual illustrating the proper citation format for a particular state.

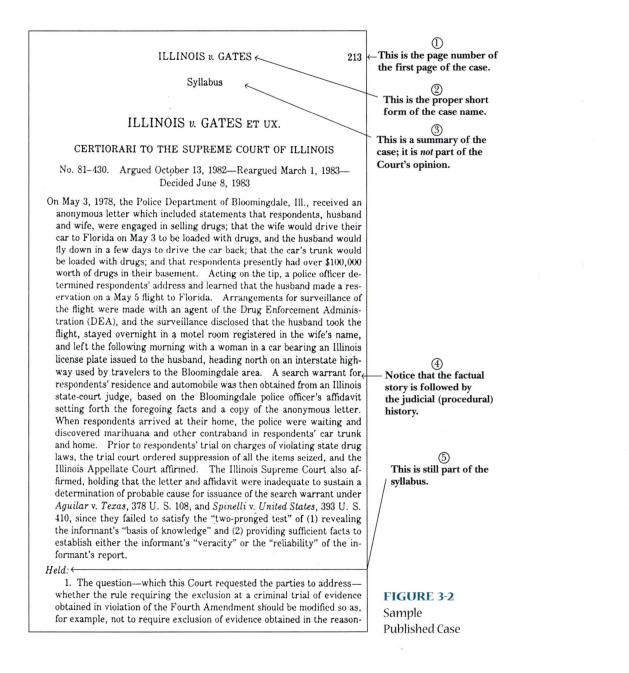

ILLINOIS *v.* GATES ← 213 ←

① This is the page number of the first page of the case.

Syllabus ←

② This is the proper short form of the case name.

③ This is a summary of the case; it is *not* part of the Court's opinion.

ILLINOIS *v.* GATES ET UX.

CERTIORARI TO THE SUPREME COURT OF ILLINOIS

No. 81–430.   Argued October 13, 1982—Reargued March 1, 1983— Decided June 8, 1983

On May 3, 1978, the Police Department of Bloomingdale, Ill., received an anonymous letter which included statements that respondents, husband and wife, were engaged in selling drugs; that the wife would drive their car to Florida on May 3 to be loaded with drugs, and the husband would fly down in a few days to drive the car back; that the car's trunk would be loaded with drugs; and that respondents presently had over $100,000 worth of drugs in their basement.   Acting on the tip, a police officer determined respondents' address and learned that the husband made a reservation on a May 5 flight to Florida.   Arrangements for surveillance of the flight were made with an agent of the Drug Enforcement Administration (DEA), and the surveillance disclosed that the husband took the flight, stayed overnight in a motel room registered in the wife's name, and left the following morning with a woman in a car bearing an Illinois license plate issued to the husband, heading north on an interstate highway used by travelers to the Bloomingdale area.   A search warrant for respondents' residence and automobile was then obtained from an Illinois state-court judge, based on the Bloomingdale police officer's affidavit setting forth the foregoing facts and a copy of the anonymous letter. When respondents arrived at their home, the police were waiting and discovered marihuana and other contraband in respondents' car trunk and home.   Prior to respondents' trial on charges of violating state drug laws, the trial court ordered suppression of all the items seized, and the Illinois Appellate Court affirmed.   The Illinois Supreme Court also affirmed, holding that the letter and affidavit were inadequate to sustain a determination of probable cause for issuance of the search warrant under *Aguilar* v. *Texas*, 378 U. S. 108, and *Spinelli* v. *United States*, 393 U. S. 410, since they failed to satisfy the "two-pronged test" of (1) revealing the informant's "basis of knowledge" and (2) providing sufficient facts to establish either the informant's "veracity" or the "reliability" of the informant's report.

④ Notice that the factual story is followed by the judicial (procedural) history.

⑤ This is still part of the syllabus.

Held: ←

1. The question—which this Court requested the parties to address— whether the rule requiring the exclusion at a criminal trial of evidence obtained in violation of the Fourth Amendment should be modified so as, for example, not to require exclusion of evidence obtained in the reason-

FIGURE 3-2
Sample
Published Case

Syllabus   462 U. S.

① **This is the volume number of the *United States Reports*.**

able belief that the search and seizure at issue was consistent with the Fourth Amendment will not be decided in this case, since it was not presented to or decided by the Illinois courts. Although prior decisions interpreting the "not pressed or passed on below" rule have not involved a State's failure to raise a defense to a federal right or remedy asserted below, the purposes underlying the rule are, for the most part, as applicable in such a case as in one where a party fails to assert a federal right. The fact that the Illinois courts affirmatively applied the federal exclusionary rule does not affect the application of the "not pressed or passed on below" rule. Nor does the State's repeated opposition to respondents' substantive Fourth Amendment claims suffice to have raised the separate question whether the exclusionary rule should be modified. The extent of the continued vitality of the rule is an issue of unusual significance, and adhering scrupulously to the customary limitations on this Court's discretion promotes respect for its adjudicatory process and the stability of its decisions, and lessens the threat of untoward practical ramifications not foreseen at the time of decision. Pp. 217–224.

② **Pages 217–224 of this case present the material covered in the first section of the Syllabus.**

2. The rigid "two-pronged test" under *Aguilar* and *Spinelli* for determining whether an informant's tip establishes probable cause for issuance of a warrant is abandoned, and the "totality of the circumstances" approach that traditionally has informed probable-cause determinations is substituted in its place. The elements under the "two-pronged test" concerning the informant's "veracity," "reliability," and "basis of knowledge" should be understood simply as closely intertwined issues that may usefully illuminate the common-sense, practical question whether there is "probable cause" to believe that contraband or evidence is located in a particular place. The task of the issuing magistrate is simply to make a practical, common-sense decision whether, given all the circumstances set forth in the affidavit before him, there is a fair probability that contraband or evidence of a crime will be found in a particular place. And the duty of a reviewing court is simply to ensure that the magistrate had a substantial basis for concluding that probable cause existed. This flexible, easily applied standard will better achieve the accommodation of public and private interests that the Fourth Amendment requires than does the approach that has developed from *Aguilar* and *Spinelli*. Pp. 230–241.

3. The judge issuing the warrant had a substantial basis for concluding that probable cause to search respondents' home and car existed. Under the "totality of the circumstances" analysis, corroboration of details of an informant's tip by independent police work is of significant value. Cf. *Draper* v. *United States*, 358 U. S. 307. Here, even standing alone, the facts obtained through the independent investigation of the Bloomingdale police officer and the DEA at least suggested that

FIGURE 3-2
(continued)

① **Name of the case.**

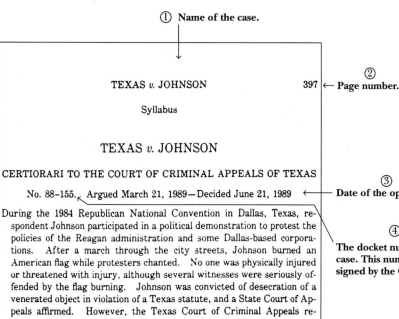

TEXAS *v.* JOHNSON   397 ← **Page number.** ②

Syllabus

TEXAS *v.* JOHNSON

CERTIORARI TO THE COURT OF CRIMINAL APPEALS OF TEXAS

No. 88-155.   Argued March 21, 1989—Decided June 21, 1989   ← **Date of the opinion.** ③

④
The docket number of the case. This number is assigned by the Court.

During the 1984 Republican National Convention in Dallas, Texas, respondent Johnson participated in a political demonstration to protest the policies of the Reagan administration and some Dallas-based corporations.   After a march through the city streets, Johnson burned an American flag while protesters chanted.   No one was physically injured or threatened with injury, although several witnesses were seriously offended by the flag burning.   Johnson was convicted of desecration of a venerated object in violation of a Texas statute, and a State Court of Appeals affirmed.   However, the Texas Court of Criminal Appeals reversed, holding that the State, consistent with the First Amendment, could not punish Johnson for burning the flag in these circumstances. The court first found that Johnson's burning of the flag was expressive conduct protected by the First Amendment.   The court concluded that the State could not criminally sanction flag desecration in order to preserve the flag as a symbol of national unity.   It also held that the statute did not meet the State's goal of preventing breaches of the peace, since it was not drawn narrowly enough to encompass only those flag burnings that would likely result in a serious disturbance, and since the flag burning in this case did not threaten such a reaction.   Further, it stressed that another Texas statute prohibited breaches of the peace and could be used to prevent disturbances without punishing this flag desecration.

Held: Johnson's conviction for flag desecration is inconsistent with the First Amendment.   Pp. 402–420.

(a) Under the circumstances, Johnson's burning of the flag constituted expressive conduct, permitting him to invoke the First Amendment. The State conceded that the conduct was expressive.   Occurring as it did at the end of a demonstration coinciding with the Republican National Convention, the expressive, overtly political nature of the conduct was both intentional and overwhelmingly apparent.   Pp. 402–406.

(b) Texas has not asserted an interest in support of Johnson's conviction that is unrelated to the suppression of expression and would therefore permit application of the test set forth in *United States* v. *O'Brien*, 391 U. S. 367, whereby an important governmental interest in regulating nonspeech can justify incidental limitations on First Amendment freedoms when speech and nonspeech elements are combined in the same course of conduct.   An interest in preventing breaches of the peace is not implicated on this record.   Expression may not be prohib-

FIGURE 3-3   *Texas v. Johnson,* from *U.S. Reports*

① **Page Number.**

② **Volume number and reporter.** (*United States Reports*)

③ **End of Syllabus.**

④ **List of justices participating in the opinion.**

⑤ **Lawyers.**

⑥ **Footnote.**

FIGURE 3-3
(continued)

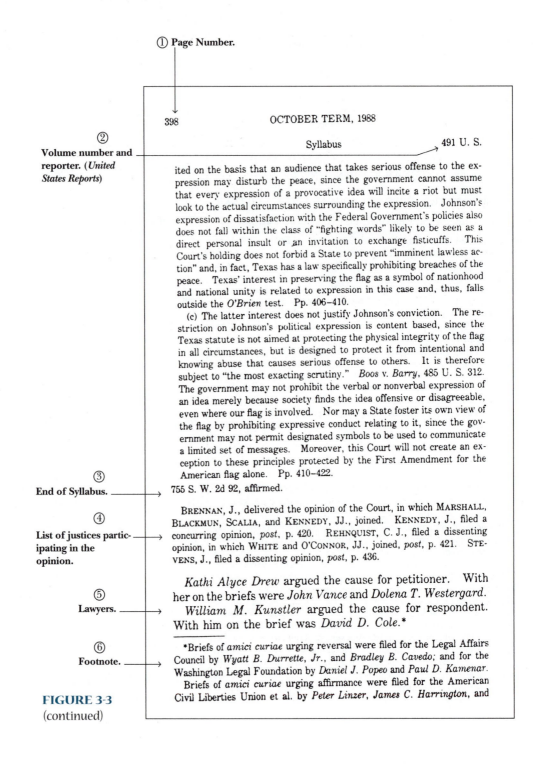

398   OCTOBER TERM, 1988

Syllabus   491 U. S.

ited on the basis that an audience that takes serious offense to the expression may disturb the peace, since the government cannot assume that every expression of a provocative idea will incite a riot but must look to the actual circumstances surrounding the expression. Johnson's expression of dissatisfaction with the Federal Government's policies also does not fall within the class of "fighting words" likely to be seen as a direct personal insult or an invitation to exchange fisticuffs. This Court's holding does not forbid a State to prevent "imminent lawless action" and, in fact, Texas has a law specifically prohibiting breaches of the peace. Texas' interest in preserving the flag as a symbol of nationhood and national unity is related to expression in this case and, thus, falls outside the *O'Brien* test. Pp. 406–410.

(c) The latter interest does not justify Johnson's conviction. The restriction on Johnson's political expression is content based, since the Texas statute is not aimed at protecting the physical integrity of the flag in all circumstances, but is designed to protect it from intentional and knowing abuse that causes serious offense to others. It is therefore subject to "the most exacting scrutiny." *Boos v. Barry*, 485 U. S. 312. The government may not prohibit the verbal or nonverbal expression of an idea merely because society finds the idea offensive or disagreeable, even where our flag is involved. Nor may a State foster its own view of the flag by prohibiting expressive conduct relating to it, since the government may not permit designated symbols to be used to communicate a limited set of messages. Moreover, this Court will not create an exception to these principles protected by the First Amendment for the American flag alone. Pp. 410–422.

755 S. W. 2d 92, affirmed.

BRENNAN, J., delivered the opinion of the Court, in which MARSHALL, BLACKMUN, SCALIA, and KENNEDY, JJ., joined. KENNEDY, J., filed a concurring opinion, *post*, p. 420. REHNQUIST, C. J., filed a dissenting opinion, in which WHITE and O'CONNOR, JJ., joined, *post*, p. 421. STEVENS, J., filed a dissenting opinion, *post*, p. 436.

Kathi Alyce Drew argued the cause for petitioner. With her on the briefs were *John Vance* and *Dolena T. Westergard*.

William M. Kunstler argued the cause for respondent. With him on the brief was *David D. Cole*.*

*Briefs of *amici curiae* urging reversal were filed for the Legal Affairs Council by *Wyatt B. Durrette, Jr.,* and *Bradley B. Cavedo;* and for the Washington Legal Foundation by *Daniel J. Popeo* and *Paul D. Kamenar.*

Briefs of *amici curiae* urging affirmance were filed for the American Civil Liberties Union et al. by *Peter Linzer, James C. Harrington,* and

TEXAS *v.* JOHNSON   399

397   Opinion of the Court

JUSTICE BRENNAN delivered the opinion of the Court.

After publicly burning an American flag as a means of political protest, Gregory Lee Johnson was convicted of desecrating a flag in violation of Texas law.   This case presents the question whether his conviction is consistent with the First Amendment.   We hold that it is not.

I

While the Republican National Convention was taking place in Dallas in 1984, respondent Johnson participated in a political demonstration dubbed the "Republican War Chest Tour."   As explained in literature distributed by the demonstrators and in speeches made by them, the purpose of this event was to protest the policies of the Reagan administration and of certain Dallas-based corporations.   The demonstrators marched through the Dallas streets, chanting political slogans and stopping at several corporate locations to stage "die-ins" intended to dramatize the consequences of nuclear war.   On several occasions they spray-painted the walls of buildings and overturned potted plants, but Johnson himself took no part in such activities.   He did, however, accept an American flag handed to him by a fellow protestor who had taken it from a flagpole outside one of the targeted buildings.

The demonstration ended in front of Dallas City Hall, where Johnson unfurled the American flag, doused it with kerosene, and set it on fire.   While the flag burned, the protestors chanted: "America, the red, white, and blue, we spit on you."   After the demonstrators dispersed, a witness to the flag burning collected the flag's remains and buried them in his backyard.   No one was physically injured or threatened with injury, though several witnesses testified that they had been seriously offended by the flag burning.

Steven R. Shapiro; for the Christic Institute et al. by *James C. Goodale;* and for Jasper Johns et al. by *Robert G. Sugarman* and *Gloria C. Phares.*

① Page number.

② The opinion begins here. All material before this is prefatory and *not* written by one of the justices.

③ Always pay attention to how the Court organizes the opinion.

FIGURE 3-3
(continued)

② This is the unofficial reporter citation for the *Supreme Court Reporter.*

③ Page number in the *Supreme Court Reporter.*

①
This is the offi- → **491 U.S. 397**
cial citation for
this case.

TEXAS v. JOHNSON
Cite as 109 S.Ct. 2533 (1989)

2533

trial court originally sentenced the defendant only to the term of imprisonment. When the court realized its mistake five hours later, it recalled the defendant for resentencing and imposed the $100 fine as well. We held that the resentencing did not violate the defendant's rights under the Double Jeopardy Clause. There, as in *DiFrancesco*, the defendant could not argue

④
Case name.

that his *legitimate* expectation of finality in the original sentence had been violated, because he was charged with knowledge that the court lacked statutory authority to impose the subminimum sentence in the first instance. See 330 U.S., at 166, 167, 67 S.Ct., at 648, 649. See also *United States v. Arrellano–Rios*, 799 F.2d 520, 524 (CA9 1986) (stating that defendant can have no legitimate expectation of finality in an illegal sentence); *United States v. Edmondson*, 792 F.2d 1492, 1496, n. 4 (CA9 1986) (same).

Applying *DiFrancesco* and *Bozza* here, it seems to me respondent must prevail. There is no doubt that the court had *authority* to impose the 15–year sentence, and respondent therefore had a legitimate expectation of its finality. There are only two grounds on which that could possibly be contested: (1) that the court had authority to impose a 15–year sentence, but not *both* a 15–year sentence and life, or (2) that his legitimate expectation was not necessarily 15 years, but rather *either* 15 years (on the one sentence) *or* life (on the other sentence). But at least where, as here, the one sentence has been fully served, these alternative approaches to defining his legitimate expectation are ruled out by *Bradley*. There also it could have been said that the court had no authority to impose both the $500 fine and the six months' imprisonment; and there also it could have been said that the defendant's legitimate expectation was not necessarily a $500 fine, but either a $500 fine or six months' imprisonment. But we in effect rejected those approaches, holding that once the fine had been paid a subsequent proceeding could

not replace₃₉₆ it with the alternative penalty. There is simply no basis for departing from that holding here.

The Double Jeopardy Clause is and has always been, not a provision designed to assure reason and justice in the particular case, but the embodiment of technical, prophylactic rules that require the Government to turn square corners. Whenever it is applied to release a criminal deserving of punishment it frustrates justice in the particular case, but for the greater purpose of assuring repose in the totality of criminal prosecutions and sentences. There are many ways in which these technical rules might be designed. We chose one approach in *Bradley*—undoubtedly not the only possible approach, but also not one that can be said to be clearly wrong. (The fact that it produces a "windfall" separates it not at all from other applications of the double jeopardy guarantee.) With technical rules, above all others, it is imperative that we adhere strictly to what we have stated the rules to be. A technical rule with equitable exceptions is no rule at all. Three strikes is out. The State broke the rules here, and must abide by the result.

For these reasons, I believe the Court of Appeals was correct to set aside respondent's life sentence. I would therefore affirm the judgment of the Court of Appeals, and respectfully dissent from the Court's disposition of this case.[*]

⑤
In the West reporters, a key symbol is used to mark the end of one case and the beginning of the next case.

491 U.S. 397, 105 L.Ed.2d 342

⌊₃₉₇TEXAS, Petitioner

v.

Gregory Lee JOHNSON.

No. 88–155.

Argued March 21, 1989.

Decided June 21, 1989.

⑥
References to the *Lawyers' Edition* citation for this case, an unofficial reporter citation.

→ Defendant was convicted in the County Criminal Court No. 8, Dallas County, John

State could not resentence or retry respondent for a non-jeopardy-barred lesser included of-

[*] I agree with the Court, *ante,* at 2527, n. 3, that the Court of Appeals erred in saying that the

⑦ The beginning of the West editor's summary, an editorial enhancement.

① Reference to the volume and name of the reporter.

2534　　　　　109 SUPREME COURT REPORTER　　　　491 U.S. 397

C. Hendrik, J., of desecration of venerated object, and he appealed. The Dallas Court of Appeals, Fifth Supreme Judicial District, 706 S.W.2d 120, Vance, J., affirmed, and defendant petitioned for discretionary review. The Texas Court of Criminal Appeals, 755 S.W.2d 92, Campbell, J., reversed and remanded, and certiorari was granted. The Supreme Court, Justice Brennan, held that: (1) defendant's act of burning American flag during protest rally was expressive conduct within protection of First Amendment, and (2) State could not justify prosecution of defendant based on interest in preventing breaches of peace or to preserve flag as symbol of nationhood and national unity.

Affirmed.

Justice Kennedy concurred and filed an opinion.

Chief Justice Rehnquist dissented and filed an opinion in which Justice White and Justice O'Connor joined.

Justice Stevens dissented and filed an opinion.

1. Constitutional Law ⚖90(1), 274.1(1)

Conduct may be sufficiently imbued with elements of communication to fall within scope of First and Fourteenth Amendments. U.S.C.A. Const.Amends. 1, 14.

2. Constitutional Law ⚖90.1(1)

In deciding whether particular conduct possesses sufficient communicative elements to bring First Amendment into play, it is necessary to determine whether there was an intent to convey a particularized message and whether likelihood was great that message would be understood by those who viewed it. U.S.C.A. Const. Amend. 1.

fense, see *Morris v. Mathews,* 475 U.S. 237, 106 S.Ct. 1032, 89 L.Ed.2d 187 (1986). Since it is undisputed, however, that the State has made

3. Constitutional Law ⚖90.1(1)

Any action taken with respect to American flag is not automatically expressive; rather, in characterizing such action for First Amendment purposes, Supreme Court considers context in which conduct occurred. U.S.C.A. Const.Amend. 1.

4. Constitutional Law ⚖90.1(2)

In prosecution for desecration of venerated object, defendant's burning of American flag as part of political demonstration that coincided with convening of political party and renomination of incumbent for President was expressive conduct subject to First Amendment protection. U.S.C.A. Const.Amend. 1; V.T.C.A., Penal Code § 42.09(a)(3).

5. Constitutional Law ⚖90(3)

Government generally has freer hand in restricting expressive conduct than it has in restricting written or spoken word, but it may not proscribe particular conduct because it has expressive elements; law directed at communicative nature of conduct must, like law directed at speech itself, be justified by substantial showing of need that First Amendment requires. U.S.C.A. Const.Amend. 1.

6. Constitutional Law ⚖90(1)

Principal function of free speech under our system of government is to invite dispute; it may indeed best serve its high purpose when it induces condition of unrest, creates dissatisfaction with conditions as they are, or even stirs people to anger. U.S.C.A. Const.Amend. 1.

7. Constitutional Law ⚖90.1(2)
United States ⚖5½

State's interest in preventing breaches of peace did not justify defendant's conviction for violation of Texas flag desecration

no attempt to do that, that portion of the Court of Appeals' opinion was the purest dictum, and no basis for reversal of its judgment.

② End of editor's summary.

③ This is West digest topic and corresponding key numbers. These are editorial enhancements. These digest topics and key numbers are called *headnotes.*

FIGURE 3-4
(continued)

491 U.S. 397 **TEXAS v. JOHNSON** **2535**
Cite as 109 S.Ct. 2533 (1989)

statute when he burned American flag as part of protest; no actual breach of peace occurred at time of flag burning or in response to flag burning, and mere potential for breach of peace could not serve to justify prosecution. U.S.C.A. Const. Amend. 1; V.T.C.A., Penal Code § 42.-09(a)(3).

8. Constitutional Law ⟜90.1(2)

In prosecution for violation of Texas flag desecration statute based on defendant's burning of American flag during protest rally, state's asserted interest in preserving special symbolic character of American flag would be subject to the most exacting scrutiny since defendant's political expression was restricted by prosecution because of content and message he conveyed. U.S.C.A. Const.Amend. 1; V.T.C.A., Penal Code, § 42.09(a)(3).

9. Constitutional Law ⟜90(1)

If there is a bedrock principle underlying the First Amendment, it is that government may not prohibit expression of an idea simply because society finds idea itself offensive or disagreeable. U.S.C.A. Const. Amend. 1.

10. Constitutional Law ⟜90.1(2)

State of Texas could not justify criminal prosecution under flag desecration statute of defendant who burned American flag at protest rally based on interest in preserving flag as symbol of nationhood and national unity. U.S.C.A. Const.Amend. 1; V.T.C.A., Penal Code § 42.09(a)(3).

→ *Syllabus* *

During the 1984 Republican National Convention in Dallas, Texas, respondent Johnson participated in a political demonstration to protest the policies of the Reagan administration and some Dallas-based

---

* The syllabus constitutes no part of the opinion of the Court but has been prepared by the Reporter of Decisions for the convenience of the

corporations. After a march through the city streets, Johnson burned an American flag while protesters chanted. No one was physically injured or threatened with injury, although several witnesses were seriously offended by the flag burning. Johnson was convicted of desecration of a venerated object in violation of a Texas statute, and a State Court of Appeals affirmed. However, the Texas Court of Criminal Appeals reversed, holding that the State, consistent with the First Amendment, could not punish Johnson for burning the flag in these circumstances. The court first found that Johnson's burning of the flag was expressive conduct protected by the First Amendment. The court concluded that the State could not criminally sanction flag desecration in order to preserve the flag as a symbol of national unity. It also held that the statute did not meet the State's goal of preventing breaches of the peace, since it was not drawn narrowly enough to encompass only those flag burnings that would likely result in a serious disturbance, and since the flag burning in this case did not threaten such a reaction. Further, it stressed that another Texas statute prohibited breaches of the peace and could be used to prevent disturbances without punishing this flag desecration.

Held: Johnson's conviction for flag desecration is inconsistent with the First Amendment. Pp. 2538–2548.

(a) Under the circumstances, Johnson's burning of the flag constituted expressive conduct, permitting him to invoke the First Amendment. The State conceded that the conduct was expressive. Occurring as it did at the end of a demonstration coinciding with the Republican National Convention, the expressive, overtly political nature of the conduct was both intentional and overwhelmingly apparent. Pp. 2538–2540.

---

reader. See *United States v. Detroit Lumber Co.,* 200 U.S. 321, 337, 26 S.Ct. 282, 287, 50 L.Ed. 499.

The Syllabus, provided, by the *United States Reports,* follows the headnotes.

FIGURE 3-4
(continued)

2536   **109 SUPREME COURT REPORTER**   491 U.S. 397

(b) Texas has not asserted an interest in support of Johnson's conviction that is unrelated to the suppression of expression and would therefore permit application of the test set forth in *United States v. O'Brien*, 391 U.S. 367, 88 S.Ct. 1673, 20 L.Ed.2d 672, whereby an important governmental interest in regulating nonspeech can justify incidental limitations on First Amendment freedoms when speech and nonspeech elements are combined in the same course of conduct. An interest in preventing breaches of the peace is not implicated on this record. Expression may not be prohibited₃₉₈ on the basis that an audience that takes serious offense to the expression may disturb the peace, since the government cannot assume that every expression of a provocative idea will incite a riot but must look to the actual circumstances surrounding the expression. Johnson's expression of dissatisfaction with the Federal Government's policies also does not fall within the class of "fighting words" likely to be seen as a direct personal insult or an invitation to exchange fisticuffs. This Court's holding does not forbid a State to prevent "imminent lawless action" and, in fact, Texas has a law specifically prohibiting breaches of the peace. Texas' interest in preserving the flag as a symbol of nationhood and national unity is related to expression in this case and, thus, falls outside the *O'Brien* test. Pp. 2540–2542.

(c) The latter interest does not justify Johnson's conviction. The restriction on Johnson's political expression is content based, since the Texas statute is not aimed at protecting the physical integrity of the flag in all circumstances, but is designed to protect it from intentional and knowing abuse that causes serious offense to others. It is therefore subject to "the most exacting scrutiny." *Boos v. Barry*, 485 U.S. 312, 108 S.Ct. 1157, 99 L.Ed.2d 333. The government may not prohibit the verbal or nonverbal expression of an idea merely because society finds the idea offensive or disagreeable, even where our flag is

involved. Nor may a State foster its own view of the flag by prohibiting expressive conduct relating to it, since the government may not permit designated symbols to be used to communicate a limited set of messages. Moreover, this Court will not create an exception to these principles protected by the First Amendment for the American flag alone. Pp. 2542–2548.

755 S.W.2d 92, (Tex.Cr.App.1988), affirmed.

BRENNAN, J., delivered the opinion of the Court, in which MARSHALL, BLACKMUN, SCALIA, and KENNEDY, JJ., joined. KENNEDY, J., filed a concurring opinion, *post*, p. 2548. REHNQUIST, C.J., filed a dissenting opinion, in which WHITE and O'CONNOR, JJ., joined, *post*, p. 2549. STEVENS, J., filed a dissenting opinion, *post*, p. 2556.

———

Kathi Alyce Drew, Dallas, Tex., for petitioner.

William M. Kunstler, New York City, for respondent.

⌐₃₉₉Justice BRENNAN delivered the opinion of the Court.

After publicly burning an American flag as a means of political protest, Gregory Lee Johnson was convicted of desecrating a flag in violation of Texas law. This case presents the question whether his conviction is consistent with the First Amendment. We hold that it is not.

I

While the Republican National Convention was taking place in Dallas in 1984, respondent Johnson participated in a political demonstration dubbed the "Republican War Chest Tour." As explained in literature distributed by the demonstrators and

① Page 398, in the *United States Reports* begins here: "ited."

② ⊥ 399 indicates where page 399 in the *United States Reports* begins (official reporter).

③ The Court's opinion begins here.

FIGURE 3-4
(continued)

① **The volume and reporter.** (*Lawyers' Edition 2d.*)

② **Full name designation of parties.** Look at the top of the next page for the proper short name of the case. Always cite the case using the short name.

③ **Summary of the case, written by an editor.**

④ **References to supplemental material available at the end of this volume.**

⑤ **The briefs filed with the Court are available to the researcher in *this* publication.**

U.S. SUPREME COURT REPORTS   105 L Ed 2d

[491 US 397]
TEXAS, Petitioner

v

GREGORY LEE JOHNSON

491 US 397, 105 L Ed 2d 342, 109 S Ct 2533

[No. 88-155]

Argued March 21, 1989. Decided June 21, 1989.

Decision: Conviction of protester for burning American flag as part of political demonstration held to violate Federal Constitution's First Amendment.

SUMMARY

While the 1984 Republican National Convention was taking place in Dallas, Texas, a group of people staged a political demonstration in Dallas to protest the policies of the President of the United States, who was being nominated by the Convention for re-election, and of certain Dallas-based corporations. During the course of that demonstration, one of the protesters (1) accepted an American flag handed to him by a fellow protester, who had taken the flag from a pole outside one of the targeted buildings, (2) doused the flag with kerosene, and (3) set the flag on fire. While the flag burned, the protesters chanted, "America, the red, white, and blue, we spit on you." The protester who allegedly had burned the flag was subsequently prosecuted in a Texas trial court for that act and was convicted of violating a state statute which (1) prohibited the desecration of, among other things, a state or national flag, and (2) defined desecration as the physical mistreatment of such objects in a way which the actor knows will seriously offend one or more persons likely to observe or discover the act. Several witnesses testified that they had been seriously offended by the flag burning. The defendant protester appealed his conviction on the ground, among others, that the application of the state statute violated his right to freedom of speech under the Federal Constitution's First Amendment. In affirming the conviction, the Court of Appeals for the Fifth District of Texas at Dallas ruled that the defendant protester's flag burning constituted symbolic speech requiring First Amendment scrutiny, but concluded that the desecration statute nevertheless could be upheld as a legitimate and constitutional means of (1)

SUBJECT OF ANNOTATION

Beginning on page 809, infra

Supreme Court's views as to constitutionality of laws prohibiting, or of criminal convictions for, desecration, defiance, disrespect, or misuse of American flag

---

Briefs of Counsel, p 807, infra.

342

FIGURE 3-5   *Texas v. Johnson,* from *Lawyers' Edition*

① Short name of case.

TEXAS v JOHNSON
(1989) 491 US 397, 105 L Ed 2d 342, 109 S Ct 2533 ←

② List of all three citations to the *Texas v. Johnson* case.

protecting the public peace, because acts of flag desecration are, of themselves, so inherently inflammatory that the state may act to prevent breaches of the peace, and (2) realizing the state's legitimate and substantial interest in protecting the flag as a symbol of national unity (706 SW2d 120). The Court of Criminal Appeals of Texas, however, held that the desecration statute as applied violated the defendant protester's First Amendment rights, because the statute (1) was too broad for First Amendment purposes as it related to breaches of the peace, and (2) was not adequately supported by the state's purported interest in preserving a symbol of unity; therefore, the court reversed the decisions below and remanded the case to the trial court with instructions to dismiss the information (755 SW2d 92).

On certiorari, the United States Supreme Court affirmed. In an opinion by BRENNAN, J., joined by MARSHALL, BLACKMUN, SCALIA, and KENNEDY, JJ., it was held that the conviction of the defendant protester was inconsistent with the First Amendment under the particular circumstances presented, because (1) the protester's conduct was sufficiently imbued with elements of communication to implicate the First Amendment, given that this flag burning was the culmination of a political demonstration and that the state conceded that the protester's conduct was expressive; (2) the state's interest in preventing breaches of the peace was not implicated on the record in this case, since (a) no disturbance of the peace actually occurred or threatened to occur because of the flag burning, (b) it cannot be presumed that an audience which takes serious offense at a particular expression is necessarily likely to disturb the peace, and (c) the flag burning does not fall within the small class of "fighting words" that are likely to provoke the average person to retaliation and thereby cause a breach of the peace; and (3) the state's asserted interest in preserving the flag as a symbol of nationhood and national unity does not justify the conviction, since (a) the attempted restriction on expression is content-based, and thus subject to the most exacting scrutiny, given that the flag-desecration statute is aimed not at protecting the physical integrity of the flag in all circumstances, but only against impairments that would cause serious offense to others, and is aimed at protecting onlookers from being offended by the ideas expressed by the prohibited activity, and (b) although the state has a legitimate interest in encouraging proper treatment of the flag, it may not foster its own view of the flag by prohibiting expressive conduct relating to it and by criminally punishing a person for burning the flag as a means of political protest.

KENNEDY, J., concurred, expressing the view that the First Amendment compels the result reached in this case, regardless of how distasteful that result may be to the Justices who announce it, because the defendant protester's acts were speech in both the technical and the fundamental meaning of the Federal Constitution.

REHNQUIST, Ch. J., joined by WHITE and O'CONNOR, JJ., dissented, expressing the view that (1) the Texas statute is not invalid under the First Amendment as applied in this case, because (a) the American flag has come to be the visible symbol embodying our nation and is not simply another

③ Page number.

343

FIGURE 3-5
(continued)

idea or point of view competing for recognition in the marketplace of ideas, and (b) the public burning of the American flag in this case was no essential part of any exposition of ideas and had a tendency to incite a breach of the peace, for flag burning is the equivalent of an inarticulate grunt or roar that is most likely to be indulged in not to express any particular idea, but to antagonize others, and the statute thus deprived the defendant protester of only one rather inarticulate symbolic form of protest—a form of protest that was profoundly offensive to many—and left him with a full panoply of other symbols and every conceivable form of verbal expression to express his deep disapproval of national policy; and (2) the statute is not unconstitutionally vague or overbroad.

STEVENS, J., dissented, expressing the view that (1) sanctioning the desecration of the flag will tarnish its value as a national symbol, a tarnish which is not justified by the trivial burden on free expression that is occasioned by requiring that alternative modes of expression be employed; (2) the flag-desecration statute does not prescribe orthodox views or compel any conduct or expression of respect for any idea or symbol; and (3) the defendant protester in this case was prosecuted not for his criticism of government policies, but for the method he chose to express those views, and a prohibition against that method is supported by a legitimate interest in preserving the quality of an important national asset.

FIGURE 3-5
(continued)

TEXAS v JOHNSON

(1989) 491 US 397, 105 L Ed 2d 342, 109 S Ct 2533

HEADNOTES

Classified to U.S. Supreme Court Digest, Lawyers' Edition

Constitutional Law §§ 934, 935, 960; Evidence § 419 — free speech — flag burning — provoking public disturbance — presumption

1a-1i. The conviction of a protester for burning an American flag, in violation of a state statute which prohibits the desecration of the flag and which defines desecration as physical mistreatment which the actor knows will seriously offend one or more persons likely to observe or discover the action, is inconsistent with the free speech guarantee of the Federal Constitution's First Amendment under the particular circumstances presented, where (1) the protester's conduct is sufficiently imbued with elements of communication to implicate the First Amendment, given that this flag burning was the culmination of a political demonstration protesting the policies of a President of the United States who was then being nominated for re-election in the city where the demonstration occurred, and the policies of various corporations based in

TOTAL CLIENT-SERVICE LIBRARY® REFERENCES

12 Am Jur 2d, Breach of Peace and Disorderly Conduct § 8; 16A Am Jur 2d, Constitutional Law §§ 507-511, 513, 514, 516; 35 Am Jur 2d, Flag §§ 3-5

USCS, Constitution, Amendment 1

US L Ed Digest, Constitutional Law §§ 934, 935, 960

Index to Annotations, Breach of Peace and Disorderly Conduct; Fighting Words; Flags; Freedom of Speech and Press

Auto-Cite®: Cases and annotations referred to herein can be further researched through the Auto-Cite® computer-assisted research service. Use Auto-Cite to check citations for form, parallel references, prior and later history, and annotation references.

ANNOTATION REFERENCES

Supreme Court's view as to the protection or lack of protection, under the Federal Constitution, of the utterance of "fighting words." 39 L Ed 2d 925.

The Supreme Court and the right of free speech and press. 93 L Ed 1151, 2 L Ed 2d 1706, 11 L Ed 2d 1116, 16 L Ed 2d 1053, 21 L Ed 2d 976.

What constitutes violation of flag desecration statutes. 41 ALR3d 502.

345

FIGURE 3-5
(continued)

U.S. SUPREME COURT REPORTS 105 L Ed 2d

that city, and given that the state conceded that the protester's conduct was expressive; (2) the interest in preventing breaches of the peace, asserted by the state as justifying the individual's conviction, is not implicated on the record in this case, because (a) no disturbance of the peace actually occurred or threatened to occur because of the flag burning, (b) the only evidence as to onlookers' reactions was the testimony of several persons who were seriously offended by the flag burning, (c) it cannot be presumed that an audience which takes serious offense at a particular expression is necessarily likely to disturb the peace, and (d) the flag burning does not fall within the small class of "fighting words" that are likely to provoke the average person to retaliation and thereby cause a breach of the peace; and (3) the state's asserted interest in preserving the flag as a symbol of nationhood and national unity does not justify the protester's conviction, since (a) the attempted restriction on expression is content-based, and thus subject to the most exacting scrutiny, given that the flag-desecration statute is aimed not at protecting the physical integrity of the flag in all circumstances, but only against impairments that would cause serious offense to others, and is aimed at protecting onlookers from being offended by the ideas expressed by the prohibited activity, and (b) although the state has a legitimate interest in encouraging proper treatment of the flag, it may not foster its own view of the flag by prohibiting expressive conduct relating to it and by criminally punishing a person for burning the flag as a means of political protest. (Rehnquist, Ch. J., and White, O'Connor, and Stevens, JJ., dissented from this holding.)

346

[See annotation p 809, infra]

Appeal § 1600; Constitutional Law § 960; Trial § 288 — free speech — flag burning — related speech — instruction on aiding and abetting — reversible error

2a, 2b. Although the jury, in the state court prosecution of a protester for burning the American flag—in violation of a state statute which makes it a crime to desecrate the flag, but does not on its face permit conviction for remarks critical of the flag or its referents—was instructed in accordance with the state's law of parties that a person is criminally responsible for an act committed by another if he or she solicits, encourages, directs, aids, or attempts to aid the other person to commit the offense with the intent of promoting or assisting the commission of the offense, this instruction could not have led the jury, in violation of the individual's rights under the Federal Constitution's First Amendment, to convict the protester solely for his words in leading chants denouncing the flag while it burned, where (1) this instruction was offered by the prosecution, because the individual's defense was that he was not the person who had burned the flag in question, (2) the instruction does not permit a conviction merely for the pejorative nature of the individual's words, and (3) the words themselves —"America, the red, white, and blue, we spit on you"—do not encourage the burning of the flag as the instruction seems to require; given the additional fact that the bulk of the prosecutor's argument, which mentioned that the individual had led this chant, was premised on the individual's culpability as a sole actor, it is too unlikely that the jury

FIGURE 3-5
(continued)

TEXAS v JOHNSON
(1989) 491 US 397, 105 L Ed 2d 342, 109 S Ct 2533

convicted the individual on the basis of this alternative theory for the conviction to be reversed on this ground.

Appeal § 732 — United States Supreme Court — review of state court decision — validity of state statute

3a, 3b. Although an individual who has been convicted in a state court of desecrating the American flag by burning it raises a claim that the state statute under which he was convicted violates on its face the free speech provisions of the Federal Constitution's First Amendment, the United States Supreme Court, in reviewing the individual's conviction on certiorari, will address only the alternative claim that the statute violates the First Amendment as applied to political expression like that engaged in by the individual—who allegedly burned the flag, to the accompaniment of the chant "America, the red, white, and blue, we spit on you," in the course of a demonstration protesting the policies of the incumbent President of the United States, who was then being nominated for a second term in the city where the demonstration was held, and of various corporations based in that city—because (1) although one violates the statute, according to its terms, only if one knows that one's physical mistreatment of the flag will seriously offend one or more persons likely to observe or discover this action, this does not necessarily mean that the statute applies only to expressive conduct protected by the First Amendment; (2) the prosecution of a person who had not engaged in expressive conduct would pose a different case; and (3) the case can be disposed of on narrower grounds.

Constitutional Law § 934 — free speech — regulation of expressive conduct

4. Under the Federal Constitution's First Amendment, the government generally has a freer hand in restricting expressive conduct than it has in restricting the written or spoken word, but it may not proscribe particular conduct because that conduct has expressive elements; a law directed at the communicative nature of conduct must, like a law directed at speech itself, be justified by the substantial showing of need that the First Amendment requires; in short, it is not simply the verbal or nonverbal nature of the expression, but the governmental interest at stake, that helps to determine whether a restriction on that expression is valid.

Appeal § 1662 — effect of decision on other grounds

5a, 5b. The United States Supreme Court—in reviewing on certiorari the state court criminal conviction of an individual who is charged with desecrating an American flag by burning it and who claims that his act was expressive conduct protected by the Federal Constitution's First Amendment—need not consider the individual's argument that the state's interest in preventing breaches of the peace, asserted as justifying the conviction, is related to the suppression of free expression in that the violent reaction to flag burnings feared by the state would be the result of the message conveyed by them, where the Supreme Court finds that this interest is not implicated on the particular facts of the case.

Constitutional Law § 934 — free speech — prosecution for expressive conduct

6. Under the Federal Constitu-

347

FIGURE 3-5
(continued)

U.S. SUPREME COURT REPORTS   105 L Ed 2d

tion's First Amendment, where a court is confronted with a case of prosecution for the expression of an idea through activity, the court must examine with particular care the interests advanced to support the prosecution.

Constitutional Law §§ 935, 960 — free speech — flag burning — audience reaction

7a, 7b. For purposes of the free speech clause of the Federal Constitution's First Amendment, there is no distinction of constitutional significance between (1) a state flag-desecration statute which is violated only when one physically mistreats the American flag in a way that he or she "knows" will offend others—so that a conviction for flag burning under that statute purportedly does not depend on onlookers' actual reactions, but on the actor's intent—and (2) a statute which depends on actual audience reaction.
[See annotation p 809, infra]

Constitutional Law § 935 — free speech — offensiveness

8. Under the Federal Constitu-

tion's First Amendment, the government may not prohibit the expression of an idea simply because society finds the idea itself offensive or disagreeable.

Constitutional Law §§ 925, 961 — freedom of speech and religion

9. Under the Federal Constitution, no official, high or petty, can prescribe what shall be orthodox in politics, nationalism, religion, or other matters of opinion or force citizens to confess by word or act their faith therein.

Constitutional Law § 934 — free speech — regulation — mode of expression

10. The rule, under the Federal Constitution's First Amendment, that the government may not prohibit expression simply because it disagrees with its message, is not dependent on the particular mode in which one chooses to express an idea.

SYLLABUS BY REPORTER OF DECISIONS

During the 1984 Republican National Convention, respondent Johnson participated in a political demonstration to protest the policies of the Reagan administration and some Dallas-based corporations. After a march through the city streets, Johnson burned an American flag while protesters chanted. No one was physically injured or threatened with injury, although several witnesses were seriously offended by the flag burning. Johnson was convicted of desecration of a venerated object in violation of a Texas statute, and a state court of appeals affirmed. However, the Texas Court of Criminal Appeals reversed, holding that the

State, consistent with the First Amendment, could not punish Johnson for burning the flag in these circumstances. The court first found that Johnson's burning of the flag was expressive conduct protected by the First Amendment. The court concluded that the State could not criminally sanction flag desecration in order to preserve the flag as a symbol of national unity. It also held that the statute did not meet the State's goal of preventing breaches of the peace, since it was not drawn narrowly enough to encompass only those flag burnings that would likely result in a serious disturbance, and since the flag burning in this case

FIGURE 3-5
(continued)

TEXAS v JOHNSON
(1989) 491 US 397, 105 L Ed 2d 342, 109 S Ct 2533

did not threaten such a reaction. Further, it stressed that another Texas statute prohibited breaches of the peace and could be used to prevent disturbances without punishing this flag desecration.

Held: Johnson's conviction for flag desecration is inconsistent with the First Amendment.

(a) Under the circumstances, Johnson's burning of the flag constituted expressive conduct, permitting him to invoke the First Amendment. The State conceded that the conduct was expressive. Occurring as it did at the end of a demonstration coinciding with the Republican National Convention, the expressive, overtly political nature of the conduct was both intentional and overwhelmingly apparent.

(b) Texas has not asserted an interest in support of Johnson's conviction that is unrelated to the suppression of expression and would therefore permit application of the test set forth in United States v O'Brien, 391 US 367, 20 L Ed 2d 672, 88 S Ct 1673, whereby an important governmental interest in regulating nonspeech can justify incidental limitations on First Amendment freedoms when speech and nonspeech elements are combined in the same course of conduct. An interest in preventing breaches of the peace is not implicated on this record. Expression may not be prohibited on the basis that an audience that takes serious offense to the expression may disturb the peace, since the Government cannot assume that every expression of a provocative idea will incite a riot but must look to the actual circumstances surrounding the expression. Johnson's expression of dissatisfaction with the Federal Government's policies also does not fall within the class of "fighting

words" likely to be seen as a direct personal insult or an invitation to exchange fisticuffs. This Court's holding does not forbid a State to prevent "imminent lawless action" and, in fact, Texas has a law specifically prohibiting breaches of the peace. Texas' interest in preserving the flag as a symbol of nationhood and national unity is related to expression in this case and, thus, falls outside the O'Brien test.

(c) The latter interest does not justify Johnson's conviction. The restriction on Johnson's political expression is content based, since the Texas statute is not aimed at protecting the physical integrity of the flag in all circumstances, but is designed to protect it from intentional and knowing abuse that causes serious offense to others. It is therefore subject to "the most exacting scrutiny." Boos v Barry, 485 US 312, 99 L Ed 2d 333, 108 S Ct 1157. The Government may not prohibit the verbal or nonverbal expression of an idea merely because society finds the idea offensive or disagreeable, even where our flag is involved. Nor may a State foster its own view of the flag by prohibiting expressive conduct relating to it, since the Government may not permit designated symbols to be used to communicate a limited set of messages. Moreover, this Court will not create an exception to these principles protected by the First Amendment for the American flag alone.

755 SW2d 92, affirmed.

Brennan, J., delivered the opinion of the Court, in which Marshall, Blackmun, Scalia, and Kennedy, JJ., joined. Kennedy, J., filed a concurring opinion. Rehnquist, C.J., filed a dissenting opinion, in which White and O'Connor, JJ., joined. Stevens, J., filed a dissenting opinion.

349

FIGURE 3-5
(continued)

APPEARANCES OF COUNSEL

Kathi Alyce Drew argued the cause for petitioner.
William M. Kunstler argued the cause for respondent.
Briefs of Counsel, p 807, infra.

OPINION OF THE COURT

[491 US 399]

Justice **Brennan** delivered the opinion of the Court.

[1a] After publicly burning an American flag as a means of political protest, Gregory Lee Johnson was convicted of desecrating a flag in violation of Texas law. This case presents the question whether his conviction is consistent with the First Amendment. We hold that it is not.

I

While the Republican National Convention was taking place in Dallas in 1984, respondent Johnson participated in a political demonstration dubbed the "Republican War Chest Tour." As explained in literature distributed by the demonstrators and in speeches made by them, the purpose of this event was to protest the policies of the Reagan administration and of certain Dallas-based corporations. The demonstrators marched through the Dallas streets, chanting political slogans and stopping at several corporate locations to stage "die-ins" intended to dramatize the consequences of nuclear war. On several occasions they spray-painted the walls of buildings and overturned potted plants, but Johnson himself took no part in

such activities. He did, however, accept an American flag handed to him by a fellow protestor who had taken it from a flag pole outside one of the targeted buildings.

The demonstration ended in front of Dallas City Hall, where Johnson unfurled the American flag, doused it with kerosene, and set it on fire. While the flag burned, the protestors chanted, "America, the red, white, and blue, we spit on you." After the demonstrators dispersed, a witness to the flag burning collected the flag's remains and buried them in his backyard. No one was physically injured or threatened with injury, though several witnesses testified that they had been seriously offended by the flag burning.

[491 US 400]

Of the approximately 100 demonstrators, Johnson alone was charged with a crime. The only criminal offense with which he was charged was the desecration of a venerated object in violation of Tex Penal Code Ann § 42.09(a)(3) (1989).[1] After a trial, he was convicted, sentenced to one year in prison, and fined $2,000. The Court of Appeals for the Fifth District of Texas at Dallas affirmed Johnson's conviction, 706 SW2d 120 (1986), but the Texas Court of Criminal Appeals reversed, 755 SW2d 92

---

1. Tex Penal Code Ann § 42.09 (1989) provides in full:

"§ 42.09. Desecration of Venerated Object

"(a) A person commits an offense if he intentionally or knowingly desecrates:

"(1) a public monument;

"(2) a place of worship or burial; or

"(3) a state or national flag.

"(b) For purposes of this section, 'desecrate' means deface, damage, or otherwise physically mistreat in a way that the actor knows will seriously offend one or more persons likely to observe or discover his action.

"(c) An offense under this section is a Class A misdemeanor."

350

---

① **The Court's opinion begins here.**

② **Page 400 in the *United States Reports* begins here.**

③ **Courts do not always follow *The Bluebook* Citation Format.**

FIGURE 3-5
(continued)

3-5 FEDERAL CASE LAW

Cases decided by federal courts are published in various federal case law reporters. For example, U.S. Supreme Court cases are available in written format from several publishers.

United States Supreme Court Case Law

This is a Supreme Court case citation with **parallel citations**:

Meritor Sav. Bank, FSB v. Vinson, 477 U.S. 57, 106 S.Ct. 2399, 91 L. Ed. 2d 49 (1986)

United States Reports

This is the official publication of all U.S. Supreme Court case law. It is published by the federal government. The proper citation format for the *United States Reports* is U.S. Figure 3-3 is the first page of the *Texas v. Johnson* case as it appears in the *United States Reports*.

Supreme Court Reporter

This is an **unofficial publication** of all Supreme Court case law. It is published by West Group. The cases are identical to those published in the *United States Reports*. The only differences are in the format in which the cases are published and the **editorial enhancements**. The primary editorial enhancement worth noting in all West case reporter publications is the inclusion of **digest topics** and **key numbers**. Digests are discussed in Chapter 8. These tools enable the researcher to quickly and easily expand the research. The West publications are linked together through the use of the digest topics and the key numbers. The proper citation format for the *Supreme Court Reporter* is S. Ct. Notice the different format of the *Supreme Court Reporter* publication of *Texas v. Johnson* (Figure 3-4) starting in the second column on page 40.

Lawyers' Edition

This is also an unofficial publication of all Supreme Court cases published by Lexis Law Publishing. It was previously published by Lawyers' Cooperative Publishing. The case law is identical to that in the *United States Reports* and the *Supreme Court Reporter*. Again, the differences involve format and editorial comments. The proper citation format for the *Lawyers Edition* is L. Ed. Always be sure to include the edition of the report for example, 91 L. Ed. 2d 49. Compare the *Lawyers' Edition* publication of *Texas v. Johnson* with the other versions. It is the same case; the differences lie in publication format and editorial enhancements. Over time, you will develop a preference for one publication over the other two. (See Figure 3-5.)

These are the three most common printed sources in which a researcher may locate all United States Supreme Court case law. The text of the opinion, what the justices wrote, is identical in each source. The differences are the editorial enhancements and the speed of publication. The official reporter, the *United States Reports*, is published later than all other reporters.

Other Federal Reporters

There are several reporters publishing federal case law. Most important to the beginning legal researcher are the *Federal Reporter* and the *Federal Supplement*. The

parallel citations. Many case citations include references to unofficial publications as well as the official citation. These additional references are parallel citations; simply stated—you may find the exact case in more than one publication.

United States Reports. Official publication of all United States Supreme Court case law; published by the federal government.

unofficial publication. Material not published by a government entity or a government designee.

editorial enhancements. Helpful information included in many unofficial publications; the enhancements assist the researcher to understand the material. Most official publications have little or no editorial enhancements.

digest topics. Topics included in an index (digest) to reported case law, arranged by subject.

key numbers. A research aid unique to the West Group materials; these numbers allow a researcher to quickly access specific material in a digest.

Supreme Court Reporter. Printed by West Group, this is an unofficial publication of all United States Supreme Court case law.

Lawyers' Edition. Lexis Law Publishing publishes this unofficial (nongovernment) printing of all U.S. Supreme Court case law.

Federal Reporter. The set containing all of the federal appellate decisions.

Federal Supplement. The set containing the cases argued and determined in the United States District Courts, the United States Court of International Trade, and the rulings of the Judicial Panel on Multidistrict Litigation.

Federal Reporter publishes the United States Circuit Court of Appeals opinions. The *Federal Supplement* includes cases from the U.S. District Courts and some special courts.

Federal Reporter   West's *Federal Reporter* is a set of federal appellate decisions. Because it is published by West Group, it uses the Key Number Digest System. There is also a specific digest for federal decisions. You will learn more about the Key Number Digest System and digests in general in Chapter 8. Figure 3-6 is a sample cover page from the *Federal Reporter*.

Federal Rules Decisions.
The set containing federal opinions, decisions, and rulings involving the Federal Rules of Civil Procedure and the Federal Rules of Criminal Procedure.

Federal Rules Decisions   West's *Federal Rules Decisions* collects federal opinions, decisions, and rulings involving the Federal Rules of Civil Procedure and the Federal Rules of Criminal Procedure. Figure 3-7 is a sample cover page from *Federal Rules Decisions*.

Federal Supplement   The *Federal Supplement* reports the cases argued and determined in the U.S. District Courts (trial courts), the United States Court of International Trade, and the rulings of the Judicial Panel on Multidistrict Litigation. This is a very large set, also published by West Group. Decisions from the *Federal Supplement* are digested in the *Federal Digest*. Figure 3-8 is a cover page from the *Federal Supplement*.

Specialized Reporters

specialized reporters.
Collections of cases grouped by specific topics rather than by level of court or jurisdiction.

West also publishes numerous **specialized reporters**. For example, the *Military Justice Reporter* provides opinions of the United States Courts of Appeals for the Armed Forces and selected opinions of the Courts of Criminal Appeals. Figure 3-9 is a cover page from this reporter. The *Bankruptcy Reporter* includes bankruptcy cases decided in the United States Bankruptcy Courts, the United States Bankruptcy Appellate Panels, the United States District Courts, the United States Courts of Appeals, and the Supreme Court of the United States. Figure 3-10 is a sample cover page from this reporter.

LEXIS and Westlaw

All U.S. Supreme Court case law may be found in either LEXIS or Westlaw. These large legal databases make retrieval of case law fast and extremely simple. The researcher may locate a case by its name, its citation, or its facts and legal issues. Computer Assisted Legal Research is addressed in Chapter 10.

Internet   U.S. Supreme Court case law is readily available on the Internet. New sites appear rapidly; look for changes and additions to the sites you already frequent. Cornell Law School's Legal Information Institute offers U.S. Supreme Court decisions on the day the decision is handed down. You may visit this site at http://www.law.cornell.edu. Another good site is http://www.findlaw.com.

3-6 STATE CASE LAW

State court cases are published in state and regional reporters. For example, in California, state cases are printed in the official reporters, *California Reports* (California Supreme Court case law) or *California Appellate Reports*, and in the unofficial reporter, *California Reporter*. In addition, selected cases are found in the regional

West's FEDERAL REPORTER

Third Series
A Unit of the National Reporter System

Volume 311 F.3d

Cases Argued and Determined
in the

UNITED STATES COURTS OF APPEALS

THOMSON

WEST ™

Mat # 40121287

FIGURE 3-6
Cover Page,
Federal Reporter

West's
FEDERAL RULES
DECISIONS

A Unit of the National Reporter System

Volume 210

Opinions, Decisions and Rulings
involving the

FEDERÁL RULES OF CIVIL PROCEDURE
AND
FEDERAL RULES OF CRIMINAL PROCEDURE

THOMSON
WEST

FIGURE 3-7
Cover Page, *Federal Rules Decisions*

Mat # 40119221

Reprinted with permission of Thomson/West

West's
FEDERAL
SUPPLEMENT

Second Series
A Unit of the National Reporter System

Volume 228 F.Supp.2d

Cases Argued and Determined
in the

UNITED STATES DISTRICT COURTS

UNITED STATES COURT OF INTERNATIONAL TRADE

and Rulings of the

JUDICIAL PANEL ON MULTIDISTRICT LITIGATION

Mat # 40121564

FIGURE 3-8   Cover Page, *Federal Supplement*

West's
MILITARY JUSTICE
REPORTER

A Unit of the National Reporter System

Volume 56

OPINIONS OF THE UNITED STATES COURT
OF APPEALS FOR THE ARMED FORCES

AND

SELECTED OPINIONS OF THE COURTS OF
CRIMINAL APPEALS

THOMSON

WEST

Mat # 18217538

FIGURE 3-9
Cover Page, *Military
Justice Reporter*

West's

BANKRUPTCY REPORTER

A Unit of the National Reporter System

Volume 285

Covering

285 West's Bankruptcy Reporter
123 S.Ct. 477–583
309 F.3d 1 to 311 F.3d 424

Bankruptcy Cases Decided in the

UNITED STATES BANKRUPTCY COURTS
UNITED STATES BANKRUPTCY APPELLATE PANELS
UNITED STATES DISTRICT COURTS
UNITED STATES COURTS OF APPEALS
SUPREME COURT OF THE UNITED STATES

THOMSON
—————*—————
WEST

Mat # 40119654

FIGURE 3-10
Cover Page,
*Bankruptcy
Reporter*

reporter, the *Pacific Reporter*, which includes cases from a number of western states, including California. Therefore, in California, all cases are found in at least two reporters, and some are found in a third.

Regional Reporters

There are seven regional reporters, each of which covers the case law of a specific region of the United States. For example, the following states are included in the Pacific Region:

PACIFIC REGION

Alaska, Arizona, California, Colorado, Hawaii, Idaho, Kansas, Montana, Nevada, New Mexico, Oklahoma, Oregon, Utah, and Washington.

Official Reporters

official reporters. Sets of case law published by the government or the designee of the government.

Some states, such as Missouri, do not have a state **official reporter**. For such states, *all* cases are reported in the appropriate regional reporter. These states contract with West Group to print all of their cases. In this way, the state avoids the expense and delay of a government publication. Other states print their own official reports. In these instances, West Group publishes only the state Supreme Court cases in the regional reporter. Figures 3-11 and 3-12 show sample cover pages from two of the regional reporters.

Unofficial Reporters

unofficial reporters. Collections of printed decisions that are not government publications.

headnote. Editorial enhancement added to the front material of a case; useful summary of most of the legal topics addressed in the case.

Unofficial reporters are collections of printed decisions, usually from a specific state, that are not government publications and are not authorized by the government. The publisher cannot change the text of the decision, but it adds useful information, which often includes a short summary of the facts of the case, the legal issue, and the outcome. In addition, **headnotes** are added to assist the researcher to find additional case law on a given topic. For these reasons, researchers often find these unofficial reporters extremely helpful.

A Point to Remember

At first, the concept of headnotes may be confusing. However, as your research skills improve and the importance of a digest becomes clear, you will find headnotes to be an important research aid. Always read them and the summary provided by the editors; this information is designed to help you understand the case you are about to read. The information is there to provide focus. However, you may not quote from the editorial material. All quotes must originate within the actual opinion of the court.

Remember, wherever you locate the case, no matter who published it, the actual language in the decision is *identical* in every source. Go back and look at the *Texas v. Johnson* case. Once the opinion begins, the language is identical.

West's PACIFIC REPORTER

Third Series
A Unit of the National Reporter System

Volume 57 P.3d

*Cases Argued and Determined
in the Courts of*

ALASKA	**MONTANA**
ARIZONA	**NEVADA**
CALIFORNIA	**NEW MEXICO**
COLORADO	**OKLAHOMA**
HAWAI'I	**OREGON**
IDAHO	**UTAH**
KANSAS	**WASHINGTON**
	WYOMING

THOMSON
★
WEST ™

Mat # 40122566

Reprinted with permission of Thomson/West

FIGURE 3-11
Cover Page, *Pacific Reporter*

West's
SOUTH EASTERN
REPORTER

Second Series
A Unit of the National Reporter System

Volume 571 S.E.2d

Cases Argued and Determined
in the Courts of

GEORGIA   **SOUTH CAROLINA**
NORTH CAROLINA   **VIRGINIA**
WEST VIRGINIA

THOMSON
—★—™
WEST

Mat # 40037910

FIGURE 3-12   Cover Page, *South Eastern Reporter*

Reprinted with permission of Thomson/West

Other Sources

State case law is also available on LEXIS and Westlaw. Some may be found on the Internet. Some states publish their case law on CD-ROM disks.

A Point to Remember

When performing legal research, one must be conscious of the jurisdiction in which the cause of action (the client's legal problem) arose. In general, if your client lives in Florida and the cause of action arose in Florida, your research usually takes place in the Florida codes, cases, and practice guides. Similarly, if the cause of action involves a federal issue, all research is performed in the federal research sources.

3-7 HOW TO READ A CASE

Most cases are compiled in a similar format; this format becomes familiar as one reads more case law. Knowing what to expect and looking for the basic components of a case helps you to read a case once rather than over and over in a seemingly vain attempt to master the court's reasoning.

Components of a Case

Initially, some students find case law difficult to read and understand. Each case must be approached with a plan. Case law contains each of the following components.

Facts   The key facts, provided by the court, are essential to the researcher. In legal research, you read case law to locate those cases that are similar, factually and legally, to your client's case. Without the facts, no effective comparisons may take place. Many judges provide the reader with the facts at the very beginning of the case.

Judicial History   The judicial history explains the prior proceedings—what happened in the lower court(s). This component is usually included early in the case.

Issues   Issues are the legal questions before the reviewing court.

Rules   Rules are the primary law relied upon by the court in the analysis or reasoning component of the case.

Analysis   The analysis or reasoning component of most cases will be the longest section. It usually follows the facts, judicial history, and a basic statement of the issues. This component contains a discussion of the facts, issues, and appropriate rules or laws relied upon by the court.

Conclusion   The conclusion—the holding of the court—is the legal outcome of the case.

Many students of the law learn to read cases looking for issues, rules, analysis, and a conclusion. Known as the *IRAC method*, it prepares the researcher to effectively summarize or "brief" the case. Add the relevant facts and the basic judicial history and you have a complete summary.

Each paragraph of a case includes one or more of these six components: (1) judicial history, (2) facts, (3) issues, (4) rules, (5) analysis, and (6) conclusion. As you read, identify the components of every paragraph. This allows you to focus and sort out the case while you read, rather than going back and rereading. Some of the paragraphs contain more than one element; for example, paragraphs of analysis almost always contain rules/law and possibly some relevant facts.

Reading Topic Sentences—An Approach to Reading Case Law

In good writing, the author opens each paragraph with a topic sentence (or sometimes a transition sentence). These topic sentences let the reader know the basic content of the body of the paragraph. We do not read case law as we might a work of fiction. In fiction we expect to be surprised or even confused. This is not true of reading legal writing.

Before you sit down to read a case from start to finish, try this: Read nothing but the first sentence of each paragraph. Do not take notes; do not underline; just read the first sentences. In most instances, this provides a great overview of the case. Good writers lead us through their documents.

Locate the *Illinois v. Caballas* case found on page 67. When we try this with the eleven paragraphs in the *Illinois v. Caballas* case, this is what we read:

1. Illinois State Trooper Daniel Gillette stopped respondent for speeding on an interstate highway.

2. Respondent was convicted of a narcotics offense and sentenced to 12 years' imprisonment and a $256,136 fine.

3. The question on which we granted certiorari, [citation omitted] is narrow: "Whether the Fourth Amendment requires reasonable, articulable suspicion to justify using a drug-detection dog to sniff a vehicle during a legitimate traffic stop."

4. Here, the initial seizure of respondent when he was stopped on the highway was based on probable cause, and was concededly lawful.

5. In the state-court proceedings, however, the judges carefully reviewed the details of Officer Gillette's conversations with respondent and the precise timing of his radio transmissions to the dispatcher to determine whether he had improperly extended the duration of the stop to enable the dog sniff to occur.

6. Despite this conclusion, the Illinois Supreme Court held that the initially lawful traffic stop became an unlawful seizure solely as a result of the canine sniff that occurred outside respondent's stopped car.

7. Official conduct that does not "compromise any legitimate interest in privacy" is not a search subject to the Fourth Amendment. [citation omitted]

8. Accordingly, the use of a well-trained narcotics-detection dog—one that "does not expose non-contraband items that otherwise would remain hidden from public view," during a lawful traffic stop, generally does not implicate legitimate privacy interests. [citation omitted]

9. This conclusion is entirely consistent with our recent decision that the use of a thermal-imaging device to detect the growth of marijuana in a home constituted an unlawful search. [citation omitted]

10. The judgment of the Illinois Supreme Court is vacated, and the case is remanded for further proceedings not inconsistent with this opinion.

After reading only these eleven sentences we have a good picture of the facts, the issue, some of the rules (law), and the outcome of the case. Now, we are ready to seriously read the case. The second reading involves marking the case and taking margin notes.

A Method for Reading and Color Highlighting a Legal Decision

Reading case law and looking for rules often feels like looking for a needle in a haystack. Decisions may contain more than a simple, direct explanation of the court's opinion. A court may take the opportunity to show the flaws of the argument of one or both parties. In addition, a court may show distinctions or differences between the current proceedings and past decisions. It can be difficult to sort through all of this.

Color highlighting a decision may help you better visualize the various components of the case. You need, at least, four color markers.

For example:

Pink: for facts

Blue: for the issue(s)

Green: for the rules (law) and the citation connected to the rules

Yellow: for the court's analysis

For the purposes of this process you do not need to color the judicial history or the court's holding. In general, these sections are not terribly difficult to identify.

First (pink): Shade all of the facts with the pink marker. The key facts are usually located near the beginning of the case. Courts often open with either the facts or the judicial history. Look for the information where the court is telling a story about people before trial. Above in *Caballas*, sentences 1 and 2 are factual.

Second (blue):   Shade the issue. A court often helps the reader with sentences that begin with language similar to:

> The question before this Court is whether . . . ; or
>
> The issue presented today is . . . ; or
>
> This Court must decide whether. . . .

The word *whether* is often the best clue that the issue is about to make an appearance. The issue is often stated just after the facts and judicial history. Not all cases follow this pattern, but many well-written decisions do follow this format. Topic sentence number 3 in *Caballas* is the issue statement.

Third (green): First, shade each citation. Second, look at the sentence directly preceding the citation. It is often this sentence that contains a rule of law. The rule can stand alone. This means that the rule may be applied in many cases; it is not unique to the case before the court. Third, as you search for the rules or the rule of law relied upon by the court look for statements that can stand alone, that is, statements that do not directly connect to the case under consideration. Notice that in the *Caballas* case topic sentence numbers 7 and 8 are rules that can stand alone (topic sentence number 9 contains the holding of a previous case and is not being used for its content here). The basic rules, in topic sentences 7 and 8, can be used in any number of situations.

Fourth (yellow): The most difficult information to identify may be the court's analysis. There are clues, however, for the reader. Paragraphs containing citations to law are usually paragraphs containing the court's analysis. When you see the green citations and the rules connected to those citations, you are probably looking at a paragraph containing the court's analysis. Think of the "analysis" as the court's reasoning or the court's explanation of the holding in the case. Courts want readers to understand how and why decisions are reached. The court cites, when applicable, to the constitution, statutes, rules and regulations, and case law. The court's analysis involves the application of the rule to the case before the court. The analysis is usually the long portion of any case. This includes the reasons the court did not hold for the other party. Topic sentence number 4 contains a statement of general analysis. At this point, you should not be surprised to find that the *Caballas* Court's analysis is generally found in the body of the paragraphs, rather than in the topic sentences. Court's usually explain the rule of law, then apply the rule of law.

After you complete this process, you should see a very colorful version of the case, one in which it is easy to identify the components you shaded with the color markers. To check yourself, the analysis paragraphs tend to be green and yellow. Fact paragraphs are mostly pink. Many times the blue-shaded issue opens an analysis paragraph. This is not an exact science, but it does provide a framework for reading and thinking about case law. In the *Caballas* example above, topic sentences 5 and 6 contain judicial history and topic sentence number 10 is the holding of the Court. After reading only the topic sentences, you are prepared to read and understand the case. You know the outcome of the case and some basic facts; now you must read the case to understand *why* the Court reached the decision contained in topic sentence number 10.

A Point to Remember

It is not possible, nor is it prudent, to give only one label to each paragraph of a decision. But remember: Each paragraph must contain at least one of the six components listed above. Do not become frustrated if you find four elements in one paragraph. Rather, congratulate yourself on careful analysis.

The *Illinois v. Caballas* case follows. The margin notes identify the components of the case. Try using color-coded markers as described above to mark the text.

CASE 3-1

Illinois v. Caballas,
543 U.S. 405 (2004)

JUSTICE STEVENS delivered the opinion of the Court

Illinois State Trooper Daniel Gillette stopped respondent for speeding on an interstate highway. When Gillette radioed the police dispatcher to report the stop, a second trooper, Craig Graham, a member of the Illinois State Police Drug Interdiction Team, overheard the transmission and immediately headed for the scene with his narcotics-detection dog. When they arrived, respondent's car was on the shoulder of the road and respondent was in Gillette's vehicle. While Gillette was in the process of writing a warning ticket, Graham walked his dog around respondent's car. The dog alerted at the trunk. Based on that alert the officers searched the trunk, found marijuana, and arrested respondent. The entire incident lasted less than 10 minutes.

Respondent was convicted of a narcotics offense and sentenced to 12 years' imprisonment and a $256,136 fine. The trial judge denied his motion to suppress the seized evidence and to quash his arrest. He held that the officers had not unnecessarily prolonged the stop and that the dog alert was sufficiently reliable to provide probable cause to conduct the search. Although the Appellate Court affirmed, the Illinois Supreme Court reversed, concluding that because the canine sniff was performed without any "'specific and articulable facts'" to suggest drug activity, the use of the dog "unjustifiably enlarg[ed] the scope of a routine traffic stop into a drug investigation." 207 Ill. 2d 504, 510, 802 N.E.2d 202, 205, 280 Ill. Dec. 277 (2003).

The question on which we granted certiorari, 541 U.S. 972, 159 L. Ed. 2d 84, 124 S. Ct. 2219 (2004), is narrow: "Whether the Fourth Amendment requires reasonable, articulable suspicion to justify using a drug-detection dog to sniff a vehicle during a legitimate traffic stop." Pet. for Cert. i. Thus, we proceed on the assumption that the officer conducting the dog sniff had no information about respondent except that he had been stopped for speeding; accordingly, we have omitted any reference to facts about respondent that might have triggered a modicum of suspicion.

Here, the initial seizure of respondent when he was stopped on the highway was based on probable cause, and was concededly lawful. It is nevertheless clear that a seizure that is lawful at its inception can violate the Fourth Amendment if its manner of execution unreasonably infringes interests protected by the Constitution. *United States v. Jacobsen,* 466 U.S. 109, 124, 80 L. Ed. 2d 85, 104 S. Ct. 1652 (1984). A seizure that is justified solely by the interest in issuing a warning ticket to the driver can become unlawful if it is prolonged beyond the time reasonably required to complete that mission. In an earlier case involving a dog sniff that occurred during an unreasonably prolonged traffic stop, the Illinois Supreme Court held that use of the dog and the subsequent discovery of contraband were the product of an unconstitutional seizure. *People v. Cox,* 202 Ill. 2d 462, 782 N.E.2d 275, 270 Ill. Dec. 81 (2002). We may assume that a similar result would be warranted in this case if the dog sniff had been conducted while respondent was being unlawfully detained.

In the state-court proceedings, however, the judges carefully reviewed the details of Officer Gillette's conversations with respondent and the precise timing of his radio transmissions to the dispatcher to determine whether he had improperly extended the duration of the stop to enable the dog sniff to occur. We have not recounted those details because we accept the state court's

1. Facts (what happened before court proceedings)

2. Judicial History (activity in lower court (s))

3. Issue (question before this Court—note that the Issue opens with the term "whether")

4. Analysis (rules and citations to law are part of the Court's analysis)

5. Analysis cont.

6. Analysis cont.

7. Analysis cont.

8. Analysis cont.

9. Analysis cont.

10. Holding (outcome of the case—this is sometimes called the "conclusion" but when a case is remanded this decision is not truly a *conclusion* to the case)

conclusion that the duration of the stop in this case was entirely justified by the traffic offense and the ordinary inquiries incident to such a stop.

Despite this conclusion, the Illinois Supreme Court held that the initially lawful traffic stop became an unlawful seizure solely as a result of the canine sniff that occurred outside respondent's stopped car. That is, the court characterized the dog sniff as the cause rather than the consequence of a constitutional violation. In its view, the use of the dog converted the citizen-police encounter from a lawful traffic stop into a drug investigation, and because the shift in purpose was not supported by any reasonable suspicion that respondent possessed narcotics, it was unlawful. In our view, conducting a dog sniff would not change the character of a traffic stop that is lawful at its inception and otherwise executed in a reasonable manner, unless the dog sniff itself infringed respondent's constitutionally protected interest in privacy. Our cases hold that it did not.

Official conduct that does not "compromise any legitimate interest in privacy" is not a search subject to the Fourth Amendment. *Jacobsen*, 466 U.S., at 123, 80 L. Ed. 2d 85, 104 S. Ct. 1652. We have held that any interest in possessing contraband cannot be deemed "legitimate," and thus, governmental conduct that *only* reveals the possession of contraband "compromises no legitimate privacy interest." *Ibid.* "This is because the expectation that certain facts will not come to the attention of the authorities" is not the same as an interest in "privacy that society is prepared to consider reasonable." *Id.*, at 122, 80 L. Ed. 2d 85, 104 S. Ct. 1652 (punctuation omitted). In *United States v. Place*, 462 U.S. 696, 77 L. Ed. 2d 110, 103 S. Ct. 2637 (1983), we treated a canine sniff by a well-trained narcotics-detection dog as "*sui generis*" because it "discloses only the presence or absence of narcotics, a contraband item." *Id.*, at 707, 77 L. Ed. 2d 110, 103 S. Ct. 2637; see also *Indianapolis v. Edmond*, 531 U.S. 32, 40, 148 L. Ed. 2d 333, 121 S. Ct. 447 (2000). Respondent likewise concedes that "drug sniffs are designed, and if properly conducted are generally likely, to reveal only the presence of contraband." Brief for Respondent 17. Although respondent argues that the error rates, particularly the existence

of false positives, call into question the premise that drug-detection dogs alert only to contraband, the record contains no evidence or findings that support his argument. Moreover, respondent does not suggest that an erroneous alert, in and of itself, reveals any legitimate private information, and, in this case, the trial judge found that the dog sniff was sufficiently reliable to establish probable cause to conduct a full-blown search of the trunk.

Accordingly, the use of a well-trained narcotics-detection dog—one that "does not expose non-contraband items that otherwise would remain hidden from public view," *Place*, 462 U.S., at 707, 77 L. Ed. 2d 110, 103 S. Ct. 2637—during a lawful traffic stop, generally does not implicate legitimate privacy interests. In this case, the dog sniff was performed on the exterior of respondent's car while he was lawfully seized for a traffic violation. Any intrusion on respondent's privacy expectations does not rise to the level of a constitutionally cognizable infringement.

This conclusion is entirely consistent with our recent decision that the use of a thermal-imaging device to detect the growth of marijuana in a home constituted an unlawful search. *Kyllo v. United States*, 533 U.S. 27, 150 L. Ed. 2d 94, 121 S. Ct. 2038 (2001). Critical to that decision was the fact that the device was capable of detecting lawful activity—in that case, intimate details in a home, such as "at what hour each night the lady of the house takes her daily sauna and bath." *Id.*, at 38, 150 L. Ed. 2d 94, 121 S. Ct. 2038. The legitimate expectation that information about perfectly lawful activity will remain private is categorically distinguishable from respondent's hopes or expectations concerning the non-detection of contraband in the trunk of his car. A dog sniff conducted during a concededly lawful traffic stop that reveals no information other than the location of a substance that no individual has any right to possess does not violate the Fourth Amendment.

The judgment of the Illinois Supreme Court is vacated, and the case is remanded for further proceedings not inconsistent with this opinion.

It is so ordered.

The Chief Justice took no part in the decision of this case.

A Point to Remember

While you are learning to read case law effectively, make a copy of the case, highlight the components, and note in the margins the components found in each paragraph. This helps you to remain focused while you read.

Official and Unofficial Publications

When citing to case law, always cite to the official citation first; the parallel/unofficial citation follows the official. In most citation formats the year follows the last parallel citation.

A Point to Remember

Sometimes the unofficial publishers go to press so quickly that they publish cases a court later decides to **de-publish** in whole or in part. When a case is de-published, it cannot be used as case precedent. Always check to make sure that the case has an official citation. One good method to ensure that you do not miss a de-published case is to carefully *Shepardize* all cases you research. *Shepardizing* will be presented in detail in Chapter 9.

de-publish. In rare instances, a court will decide a case, write and release a decision, *but before it is published in the official reporter*, the court decides not to publish some or all of the case decision. A de-published case cannot be used as precedent.

3-8 HOW TO USE CASE LAW

Compare and Contrast the Facts of a Reported Case with Your Client's Facts

The doctrine of precedent mandates that, when you use case law, you must show factual similarities between your client's situation and the case law found in your research.

First

Compare the facts of the cases you locate in your research with those of your client's situation. If both sets are similar, or easily analogous, the case *may* be considered precedent.

Second

Contrast the facts of the cases you research with those of your client's situation. Significant factual differences probably mean that the case should *not* be used in an attempt to support your client's position.

After comparison of the facts, compare the legal issues. Ask yourself: Are my client's problems the same as, or similar to, the problems in the case I located? If the answer is yes, the case *may* be considered precedent.

Consider the following fact pattern:

Our client Mr. Mark Thelle was arrested for possession of a large amount of marijuana. He was stopped on a local freeway because he was driving well below the speed limit. He was returning from the auto repair shop where he had work done on his brakes. After leaving the repair shop, he merged onto the freeway, but when he tried to accelerate to join traffic, his car started to slow down. He put his warning flashers on and was heading for the first possible exit when a patrol car pulled him over. When the officer asked for his license, he just handed it over without trying to explain his situation. After about five minutes, while the officer was checking on his license, his partner exited the patrol car, with his drug detection dog. When the dog reached the back passenger door, he alerted. The officer opened the door and pulled out a duffle bag filled with bags of marijuana. Mr. Thelle was arrested for possession of an illegal substance. Based on the *Caballas* case what advice is your firm likely to give Mr. Thelle?

A Point to Remember

In legal research, never lose sight of the fact that you are researching on behalf of a client. The more you understand about the client's factual situation, the better you are able to focus the research.

Online Legal Research

The major law schools often provide access to some case law. Try these sites:

www.law.cornell.edu

www.law.indiana.edu

www.washburnlaw.edu

This is only a starting place. Explore as your time permits.
You will find court opinions on the following sites:

www.findlaw.com/casecode/supreme.html (Great resource for U.S. Supreme Court case law)

www.findlaw.com/casecode/courts/index.html (Federal circuit court opinions)

www.statelocalgov.net/index.cfm (Directory to state court case law)

www.usscplus.com (Database of U.S. Supreme Court case law)

Note: Each Circuit also has its own Web site. These sites are usually maintained by a law school in the Circuit.

Searching for case law on the Internet is most likely to be successful if you are looking for U.S. Supreme Court cases, very recent cases, or cases of high interest. The very best sources of online accurate case law are LEXIS and Westlaw. However, these are not free resources. You may visit their Web sites to read about their services and try some of their resources. There are other pay-per-view providers of case law. You see most of them advertised in legal newspapers, bar journals, and legal periodicals.

www.lexis.com

www.westlaw.com

C ITATION MATTERS

UNITED STATES SUPREME COURT CASE LAW

THE BLUEBOOK—RULE 8

Capitalize "Court" when referring to the United States Supreme Court.

> The Court stated that all immigrants are entitled to due process. (referring to the United States Supreme Court)

THE BLUEBOOK—RULE 10

United States Supreme Court Case Law Citation Analyzed

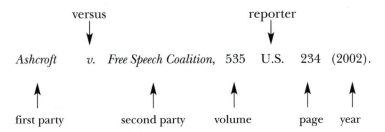

This is a *citation sentence* and a period is placed at the end.

THE BLUEBOOK—TABLE 1 (T.1)

Cite to the *U.S. Reports* unless the official citation is not yet assigned. This is often the situation with very new cases. When there is no U.S. citation, cite to the *Supreme Court Reporter* (S. Ct.), *Lawyer's Edition* (L. Ed., L. Ed. 2d), or *United States Law Week* (U.S.L.W.), in that order of preference.

The *U.S. Reports* is the official reporter of United States Supreme Court case law. It is "official" because it is published by the federal government. The *Supreme Court Reporter, Lawyer's Edition,* and *United States Law Week* are all unofficial reporters of United States Supreme Court case law. That simply means these collections of U.S. Supreme Court case law are not published by the federal government. The *case law decisions* in these sets are identical. The differences are found in the editorial enhancements. Chapter 4 explains some of the features found in the unofficial publications. Take a trip to your local law library. Locate the following volumes.

491 U.S. 397
109 S. Ct. 2533
105 L. Ed. 2d 342

Open all of them to the first page of the *Texas v. Johnson* case. Remember, the first number is the volume number, the second number is the first page of the case. Notice that the prefatory material varies from one publication to the next. You may use any of these volumes during your research.

However, you must cite to the official publication (the U.S.). Notice that the unofficial publications indicate the page breaks for the *U.S. Reports*. That means it is not necessary to actually read the official publication because you can easily cite to it from the unofficial publications.

Look at Figure 3-4 on page 43. Notice that in the first column the word *prohibited* is broken with what looks like an upside down T. It is breaking the word *prohibited*, and there is a number following *ited*. This shows that page 398, in the official reporter (U.S.), begins with "ited on the basis that . . . ."

Look at Figure 3-5 on page 44. Notice that the first column opens with "[491 US 397]." This publication lets the reader know that the material following the bracketed citation is the beginning of page 399 in the official reporter. Remember, this is done so that the researcher may use the unofficial publications and still cite to the official publication.

A researcher may quote from material *in* the opinion. A researcher should never quote from anything added by a publisher. That material (the editorial enhancements) is there to help, but it is not part of the decision, so it cannot be cited.

OTHER FEDERAL REPORTERS

The *Federal Reporter* publishes the United States Court of Appeals cases for the Federal Circuits. This is an example of a *Federal Reporter* citation:

Free Speech Coalition v. Reno, 220 F.3d 1113 (9th Cir. 2000).

There is no space between the F. and 3d.

The *Federal Supplement* publishes the United States trial court cases for the Federal Districts. This is an example of a *Federal Supplement* citation:

EEOC v. Rotary Corp., 297 F. Supp. 2d 643 (N.D.N.Y. 2003).

There is a space between F. and Supp.

Other reporters of federal case law are listed in Table 1 (T.1) of *The Bluebook*.

STATE CASE LAW

THE BLUEBOOK—RULE 10

The Bluebook—Table 1 (T.1)

State case law is cited in the same basic format that the U.S. Supreme Court cases are cited. In many instances, state case law is published in two or three reporters. Some states publish their own case law reporters; those are the official reporters. Unofficial reporters also publish these cases. For example, in California the state authorizes one publication of all California Supreme Court and Appellate Court cases. All California cases are also published in the *California Reporter* (unofficial). In addition, the California Supreme Court cases are included in the *Pacific Reporter*, the regional reporter for California (this is also an unofficial reporter). Be sure to check Table 1 to review the publications and proper abbreviations for the state case law you need to cite.

CHAPTER SUMMARY

Case law is primary authority. Cases are presented to the court. Once the legal and factual issues are resolved by the court, the judge writes a decision, often called an *opinion*. The concept of *stare decisis*, or precedent, requires that courts look to what other courts in the same jurisdiction have done with the same or similar legal and factual issues.

Case law is published in large sets of books often referred to as *reporters*. Most states publish their own case law. In addition to the government publications (official reporter), several independent publishers (unofficial reporters) quickly add editorial enhancements and publish well ahead of the government publications. Case law is also easily located on LEXIS, Westlaw, and the Internet.

Learning to cite the law properly is essential. Review of a style manual or the *Uniform System of Citation* is required of anyone citing to legal references. Many citations contain official and unofficial references. All citations must include the short name of the case followed by the volume, the abbreviation for the reporter, the number of the first page of the case, and the year of the decision.

All U.S. Supreme Court cases are published in three separate publications. The official reporter is the *United States Reports* (U.S.). The two unofficial reporters are the *Supreme Court Reporter* (S. Ct.) and the *Lawyers' Edition* (L. Ed.). Other federal case law is found in the *Federal Reporter, Federal Rules Decisions, Federal Supplement,* and various specialized reporters. The Internet is also a good resource for some case law.

State case law is usually published by the state government; this is the official reporter. There is also a regional reporter system, which breaks up the United States into geographic regions.

As you read a case, always focus on the six components of a decision: (1) facts, (2) judicial history, (3) issues, (4) rules, (5) analysis, and (6) conclusion. In your research, remain focused on the doctrine of precedent. When you use or cite case law, you must show factual similarities between your client's situation and the case law found in your research.

TERMS TO REMEMBER

primary authority	regional reporters	key numbers
decision	*Uniform System of Citation*	*Supreme Court Reporter*
opinion	LEXIS	*Lawyers' Edition*
precedent	Westlaw	*Federal Reporter*
stare decisis	case law reporters	*Federal Supplement*
mandatory authority	official citation	*Federal Rules Decisions*
binding authority	secondary sources	specialized reporters
persuasive authority	style manual	official reporters
double jeopardy	parallel citations	unofficial reporters
affirm	*United States Reports*	headnote
reverse	unofficial publication	de-publish
remand	editorial enhancements	
motion	digest topics	

QUESTIONS FOR REVIEW

1. Discuss the importance of precedent or *stare decisis*.
2. What is a case law reporter?
3. Explain what is meant by "official citation."
4. Discuss the differences between the three publishers of United States Supreme Court case law.
5. What is a parallel citation?
6. Why will a researcher choose to read an unofficial reporter?
7. List, with brief explanations, the various publications of federal case law.
8. What is a regional reporter?
9. List, with brief explanations, the six components of a case.
10. Why is factual analysis so important?

CAN YOU FIGURE IT OUT?

1. Which regional reporter reports Virginia state case law (Figure 3-12)?
2. What cases are reported in the *Military Justice Reporter* (Figure 3-9)?
3. Which reporter listed in the *Marvin v. Marvin* case citation is the official cite (Figure 3-1)?
4. State four highly relevant facts from *Illinois v. Caballas*.
5. State the factual similarities between the fact pattern in Section 3-8 and *Illinois v. Caballas*.

BUILDING YOUR RESEARCH SKILLS: ASSIGNMENTS AND ACTIVITIES

1. Locate the following U.S. Supreme Court cases, preferably in a library, in print. For each case, write the name of the case (the short form of the name), the official citation, and the year. Use the *Uniform System of Citation* format:

   Gideon v. Wainwright, 372 U.S. 335 (1963).

   Cases to be located:
   491 U.S. 274
   387 U.S. 1
   367 U.S. 568
   384 U.S. 436
   471 U.S. 1
2. Locate and read *Kyllo v. United States*, 533 U.S. 27 (2001). Summarize the case using the components set forth in Section 3-7 of this chapter.

BUILDING YOUR ANALYSIS SKILLS: ASSIGNMENTS AND EXERCISES

1. Locate the following case: *Arizona v. Hicks*, 480 U.S. 321 (1980). Read and summarize the case using the components in Section 3-7.
2. Compare the facts of the Justin Meyers case with the facts of *Arizona v. Hicks*.

A Point to Remember

When you receive instructions, be sure to complete each part of the assignment. For example, under Building Your Analysis Skills above, items 1 and 2 ask you to complete more than one task. In fact, you are asked to do several separate tasks: (1) read the *Hicks* case; (2) summarize the case; and (3) compare the facts of the Meyers case with the facts of the *Hicks* case.

Your completed written project should clearly set out the summary and the factual comparison. Avoid making your reader guess what is coming next. Use simple titles or headings (these are called Point Headings). Make your written work very easy to follow. Always write for your audience.

BUILDING YOUR ONLINE RESEARCH SKILLS: ASSIGNMENTS AND EXERCISES

1. List at least two online locations where you can locate United States Supreme Court cases.

2. Locate the following cases online. For each case provide the proper name of the case and the year. Following the citation, state the name of the justice who wrote the opinion. If there are concurrences or dissents, list the name of the justice and the type (concurrence or dissent) of opinion he or she wrote.
   a. 466 U.S. 109
   b. 462 U.S. 696
   c. 531 U.S. 32
   d. 533 U.S. 27

CASE PROJECT

Review the hypothetical case you selected in Chapter 1. List the numerous case reporters that contain mandatory authority for the situation.

HOW TO BRIEF A CASE

S KILL OBJECTIVES FOR CHAPTER 4

When you complete this chapter you should be able to

- Explain the purpose of a case brief.
- List the components of a case brief.
- Describe the components of a case brief.
- Explain how to systematically approach a daunting project.

FROM THE DESK OF W. J. BRYAN, ESQ.

TO: Research Assistant

Please read *Minnesota v. Dickerson* (copy attached) and brief it for me. This is a U.S. Supreme Court decision; I have not had time to get to this and we need to be familiar with the legal reasoning in this case. For now, just read and summarize the case. Later we will compare and contrast the *Dickerson* case with our client's facts in the Meyers situation.

4-1 PURPOSE OF A CASE BRIEF

Simply stated, a **case brief** is a short summary of a **reported case**. It serves several purposes. Students of the law write case briefs to summarize the cases they read for class in an effort to keep track of the large number of cases they are required to read and analyze. During legal research, case briefs serve to help the researcher keep track of the cases read and analyzed, and may serve as the foundation for legal arguments in **trial briefs** or other documents filed with the court. An attorney may hear about a case and ask a research assistant to read and brief or summarize the case. The overall purpose is to concisely summarize the components of a case.

 Recall from Chapter 3 that case law is written by judges to inform and educate the legal community. If we focus on the purpose of case law, it is easier to understand the purpose of a case brief. A well-written case brief simplifies and condenses the reported case. Most case law is written in a basic simple format using certain components. Once you realize that all cases contain the same or very similar components, the mystery of reading cases begins to fade.

case brief. A short summary of a reported case.

reported case. A published judicial decision.

trial brief. A document submitted to the court; the trial brief contains a statement of facts, the issues, the party's legal argument, and the holding.

4-2 THE COMPONENTS OF A CASE BRIEF

A judge, writing to inform the legal community, has certain goals in every reported case. It is important that the reader of any case understand the following.

Who are the parties?

What happened in the lower court(s)—if the case is an appeal?

What happened to bring these parties into court in the first place?

What is the legal question before *this* court?

What rules (primary law) did the court rely on in reaching its decision?

How did the court analyze the facts in light of the legal question and the rules?

How did the court resolve the dispute?

 These questions lay the foundation for the components of a case brief.

A Point to Remember

Whenever possible, make a copy of the case you plan to brief. Note in the margins, for each paragraph, which component (or components) of the brief is included in that paragraph. This technique helps you focus as you read and provides organization as you begin writing the brief. Remember that highlighting the various components helps you visualize the different case components.

These components may be divided into the following elements: name and citation of the case, judicial history, facts, issue(s), rule(s), analysis/reasoning, and holding.

Name and Citation of the Case

The name of the case, the citation, and the year are essential. Always provide the name and full citation of the case at the beginning of the case brief.

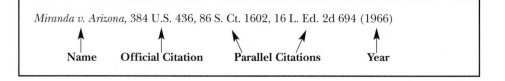

Miranda v. Arizona, 384 U.S. 436, 86 S. Ct. 1602, 16 L. Ed. 2d 694 (1966)

Name   **Official Citation**   **Parallel Citations**   **Year**

When you cite a U.S. Supreme Court case, you need only give the official citation. However, in a case brief you may want to include the full citation, including parallel citations. This way a reader may use any one of the three publications of U.S. Supreme Court case law.

Judicial History

The judicial history explains how the case traveled through the courts. The reader of the brief needs to know who sued whom and why. Let the reader know what happened in each of the courts. Avoid explaining why each court made certain decisions. The focus of a case brief must be on what this reviewing court decides.

Facts

Include only the facts that are relevant to the court's reasoning and decision. Tell a story about what happened to bring these parties before the court. If possible, tell a story about people. Leave the legal terminology *out* of this section.

Issue(s)

The issue is the question presented to this court for resolution. Each should be one sentence long and is best written as a question. Most cases have judicial history. This means that lower courts already adjudicated this case. The case you are briefing is probably an appeal of what the lower court decided. Many times the issue is stated in the format of "Did the lower court err when it held . . . ?" This issue asks: "Did the last court to hear this case make one or more mistakes in its resolution of the legal issues?" Many times courts begin the issue statement with the word *whether*.

Rule(s)

The rules section is usually a listing of the laws the court relied on in the analysis or reasoning. This might include statutes, case law, articles or amendments from the Constitution, or other **primary sources** of the law. This section does not include every source discussed by the court, just the relevant primary sources. Each

primary sources. A work that contains the law.

constitutional reference and statute, and the cases most relied upon by the court, should receive a very brief statement including the title of the constitutional reference, the topic of the statute, and the relevance of the case law cited.

Analysis or Reasoning

This is the lengthiest and also the most important section of most case briefs. The analysis *incorporates* much of the information from the facts, issues, and rules into a focused discussion. If you are asked to read and brief a case for someone else, that person did not read the case. The reader must understand why the court resolved the issues as it did. This section never includes the writer's personal analysis or opinions. Think of the analysis as a summary of how the court analyzed the facts and issues. Notice the laws used or discussed by the court. All of this provides the court's **rationale** or reasoning supporting its ultimate holding or conclusion.

rationale. The reasoning or explanation for the court's ultimate resolution of the case.

Holding

The conclusion or **holding** is the court's answer to the issue or question presented and the action taken by the court. Each issue has an answer. It is easiest to list each issue with its answer. Keep this section short and to the point. This is not a discussion section.

holding. The legal principle to be taken from the court's decision.

A Point to Remember

A case brief does not include the writer's personal opinion. The brief is a summary of (1) what the court held, and (2) why the court held as it did. There is no room for the pronoun 'I' in a good case brief. Pay close attention to the facts stressed by the court. Notice when one or more facts are discussed at length or in more than one context. This is a clue for the reader that the court views these facts as relevant; they are essential to an overall understanding of the case.

Apply the notes-in-the-margin technique from Chapter 3 with the *Gideon v. Wainwright* case. As you read the case, locate the following:

The name and the citation of the case: Name of litigants and correct legal citation for this reported case.

The judicial history: What happened in the lower court(s)?

The facts: What happened to bring the parties before the Court?

The issues: What is the legal question before *this* Court?

The rules: What rules (primary law) did the court rely on in reaching its decision?

The analysis: How did the court analyze the facts in light of the legal question and the rules?

The holding: How did the Court resolve the dispute?

When we look only at the topic sentences for *Gideon v. Wainwright*, the case condenses to this:

- Petitioner was charged in a Florida state court with having broken and entered a poolroom with intent to commit a misdemeanor.

- "The COURT: Mr. Gideon, I am sorry, but I cannot appoint Counsel to represent you in this case."

- "The DEFENDANT: The United States Supreme Court says I am entitled to be represented by Counsel."

- Put to trial before a jury, Gideon conducted his defense about as well as could be expected from a layman.

- The facts upon which Betts claimed that he had been unconstitutionally denied the right to have counsel appointed to assist him are strikingly like the facts upon which Gideon here bases his federal constitutional claim.

- "Asserted denial [of due process] is to be tested by an appraisal of the totality of facts in a given case."

- Treating due process as a "concept less rigid and more fluid than those envisaged in other specific and particular provisions of the Bill of Rights," the Court held that refusal to appoint counsel under the particular facts and circumstances in the *Betts* case was not so "offensive to the common and fundamental ideas of fairness" as to amount to a denial of due process.

- The Sixth Amendment provides, "In all criminal prosecutions, the accused shall enjoy the right . . . to have the Assistance of Counsel for his defense."

- We think the Court in *Betts* had ample precedent for acknowledging that those guarantees of the Bill of Rights which are fundamental safeguards of liberty immune from federal abridgment, are equally protected against state invasion by the Due Process Clause of the Fourteenth Amendment.

- We accept *Betts v. Brady*'s assumption, based as it was on our prior cases, that a provision of the Bill of Rights, which is "fundamental and essential to a fair trial," is made obligatory upon the States by the Fourteenth Amendment.

- "We concluded that certain fundamental rights, safeguarded by the first eight amendments against federal action, were also safeguarded against state action by the due process of law clause of the Fourteenth Amendment, and among them the fundamental right of the accused to the aid of counsel in a criminal prosecution."

- And again in 1938 this Court said: "[The assistance of counsel] is one of the safeguards of the Sixth Amendment deemed necessary to insure fundamental human right of life and liberty. . . . The Sixth Amendment stands as a constant admonition that if the constitutional safeguards it provides be lost, justice will not 'still be done.'"

- In light of these and many other prior decisions of this Court, it is not surprising that the *Betts* Court, when faced with the contention that "one charged with crime, who is unable to obtain counsel, must be furnished counsel by the State," conceded that "expressions in the opinions of this court lend color to the argument. . . ."

- "The right to be heard would be, in many cases, of little avail if it did not comprehend the right to be heard by counsel."

- The Court in *Betts v. Brady* departed from the sound wisdom upon which the Court's holding in *Powell v. Alabama* rested.

- The judgment is reversed and the cause is remanded to the Supreme Court of Florida for further action non inconsistent with this opinion.

A review of the topic sentences provides an excellent overview and introduction to the case. Notice how many of the six case components are touched upon in the topic sentences. You are now ready to read and fully understand *Gideon v. Wainwright.*

CASE 4-1

Gideon V. Wainwright
372 U.S. 335 (1963)

SYLLABUS:
Charged in a Florida State Court with a non-capital felony, petitioner appeared without funds and without counsel and asked the Court to appoint counsel for him; but this was denied on the ground that the state law permitted appointment of counsel for indigent defendants in capital cases only. Petitioner conducted his own defense about as well as could be expected of a layman; but he was convicted and sentenced to imprisonment. Subsequently, he applied to the State Supreme Court for a writ of *habeas corpus*, on the ground that his conviction violated his rights under the Federal Constitution. The State Supreme Court denied all relief.

Held:
The right of an indigent defendant in a criminal trial to have the assistance of counsel is a fundamental right essential to a fair trial, and petitioner's trial and conviction without the assistance of counsel violated the Fourteenth Amendment. *Betts v. Brady*, 316 U.S. 455.

OPINION: MR. JUSTICE BLACK delivered the opinion of the Court.
Petitioner was charged in a Florida state court with having broken and entered a poolroom with intent to commit a misdemeanor. This offense is a felony under Florida law. Appearing in court without funds and without a lawyer, petitioner asked the court to appoint counsel for him, whereupon the following colloquy took place:

"The COURT: Mr. Gideon, I am sorry, but I cannot appoint Counsel to represent you in this case. Under the laws of the State of Florida, the only time the Court can appoint Counsel to represent a Defendant is when that person is charged with a capital offense. I am sorry, but I will have to deny your request to appoint Counsel to defend you in this case."

"The DEFENDANT: The United States Supreme Court says I am entitled to be represented by Counsel."

Put to trial before a jury, Gideon conducted his defense about as well as could be expected from a layman. He made an opening statement to the jury, cross-examined the State's witnesses, presented witnesses in his own defense, declined to testify himself, and made a short argument "emphasizing his innocence to the charge contained in the Information filed in this case." The jury returned a verdict of guilty, and petitioner was sentenced to serve five years in the state prison. Later, petitioner filed in the Florida Supreme Court this *habeas corpus* petition attacking his conviction and sentence on the ground that the trial court's refusal to appoint counsel for him denied him rights "guaranteed by the Constitution and the Bill of Rights by the United States Government." Treating the petition for *habeas corpus* as properly before it, the State Supreme Court, "upon consideration thereof" but without an opinion, denied all relief. Since 1942, when *Betts v. Brady*, 316 U.S. 455, was decided by a divided Court, the problem of a defendant's federal constitutional right to counsel in a state court has been a continuing source of controversy and litigation in both state and federal courts. To give this problem another review here, we granted *certiorari*. 370 U.S. 908. Since Gideon was proceeding *in forma pauperis*, we appointed counsel to represent him and requested both sides to discuss in their briefs and oral arguments the following: "Should this Court's holding in *Betts v. Brady*, 316 U.S. 455, be reconsidered?"

I.

The facts upon which Betts claimed that he had been unconstitutionally denied the right to have counsel appointed to assist him are strikingly like the facts upon which Gideon here bases his federal constitutional claim. Betts was indicted for robbery in a Maryland state court. On arraignment, he told the trial judge of his lack of funds to hire a lawyer and asked the court to appoint one for him. Betts was advised that it was not the practice in that country to appoint counsel for indigent defendants except in murder and rape cases. He then pleaded not guilty, had witnesses summoned, cross-examined the State's witnesses, examined his own, and chose not to testify himself. He

was found guilty by the judge, sitting without a jury, and sentenced to eight years in prison. Like Gideon, Betts sought release by *habeas corpus*, alleging that he had been denied the right to assistance of counsel in violation of the Fourteenth Amendment. Betts was denied any relief, and on review this Court affirmed. It was held that a refusal to appoint counsel for an indigent defendant charged with a felony did not necessarily violate the Due Process Clause of the Fourteenth Amendment, which for reasons given the Court deemed to be the only applicable federal constitutional provision. The Court said:

"Asserted denial [of due process] is to be tested by an appraisal of the totality of facts in a given case. That which may, in one setting, constitute a denial of fundamental fairness, shocking to the universal sense of justice, may, in other circumstances, and in the light of other considerations, fall short of such denial." 316 U.S. at 462.

Treating due process as "a concept less rigid and more fluid than those envisaged in other specific and particular provisions of the Bill of Rights," the Court held that refusal to appoint counsel under the particular facts and circumstances in the *Betts* case was not so "offensive to the common and fundamental ideas of fairness" as to amount to a denial of due process. Since the facts and circumstances of the two cases are so nearly indistinguishable, we think the *Betts v. Brady* holding if left standing would require us to reject Gideon's claim that the Constitution guarantees him the assistance of counsel. Upon full reconsideration we conclude that *Betts v. Brady* should be overruled.

II.

The Sixth Amendment provides, "In all criminal prosecutions, the accused shall enjoy the right . . . to have the Assistance of Counsel for his defense." We have construed this to mean that in federal courts counsel must be provided for defendants unable to employ counsel unless the right is competently and intelligently waived. Betts argued that this right is extended to indigent defendants in state courts by the Fourteenth Amendment. In response the Court stated that, while the Sixth Amendment laid down "no rule for the conduct of the States, the question recurs whether the constraint laid by the Amendment upon the national courts expresses a rule so fundamental and essential to a fair trial, and so, to due process of law, that it is made obligatory upon the States by the Fourteenth Amendment." 316 U.S. at 465. In order to decide whether the Sixth Amendment's guarantee of counsel is of this fundamental nature, the Court in *Betts* set out and considered "relevant data on the subject . . . afforded by constitutional and statutory provisions subsisting in the colonies and the States prior to the inclusion of the Bill of Rights in the national Constitution, and in the constitutional, legislative, and judicial history of the States to the present date." 316 U.S. at 465. On the basis of this historical data the Court concluded that "appointment of counsel is not a fundamental right, essential to a fair trial." 316 U.S. at 471. It was for this reason the *Betts* Court refused to accept the contention that the Sixth Amendment's guarantee of counsel for indigent federal defendants was extended to or, in the words of that Court, "made obligatory upon the States by the Fourteenth Amendment." Plainly, had the Court concluded that appointment of counsel for an indigent criminal defendant was "a fundamental right, essential to a fair trial," it would have held that the Fourteenth Amendment requires appointment of counsel in a state court, just as the Sixth Amendment requires in a federal court.

We think the Court in *Betts* had ample precedent for acknowledging that those guarantees of the Bill of Rights which are fundamental safeguards of liberty immune from federal abridgment are equally protected against state invasion by the Due Process Clause of the Fourteenth Amendment. This same principle was recognized, explained, and applied in *Powell v. Alabama*, 287 U.S. 45 (1932), a case upholding the right of counsel, where the Court held that despite sweeping language to the contrary in *Hurtado v. California*, 110 U.S. 516 (1884), the Fourteenth Amendment "embraced" those "fundamental principles of liberty and justice which lie at the base of all our civil and political institutions," even though they had been "specifically dealt with in another part of the federal Constitution." 287 U.S. at 67. In many cases other than *Powell* and *Betts*, this Court has looked to the fundamental nature of original Bill of Rights guarantees to decide whether the Fourteenth Amendment makes them obligatory on the States.

Explicitly recognized to be of this "fundamental nature" and therefore made immune from state invasion by the Fourteenth, or some part of it, are the First Amendment's freedoms of speech, press, religion, assembly, association, and petition for redress of grievances. For the same reason, though not always in precisely the same terminology, the Court has made obligatory on the States the Fifth Amendment's command that private property shall not be taken for public use without just compensation, the Fourth Amendment's prohibition of unreasonable searches and seizures, and the Eighth's ban on cruel and unusual punishment. On the other hand, this Court in *Palko v. Connecticut*, 302 U.S. 319 (1937), refused to hold that the Fourteenth Amendment made the double jeopardy provision of the Fifth Amendment obligatory on the States. In so refusing, however, the Court, speaking through Mr. Justice Cardozo, was careful to emphasize that "immunities that are valid as against the federal government by force of the specific pledges of particular amendments have been found to be implicit in the concept of ordered liberty, and thus, through the Fourteenth Amendment, become valid as against the states" and that guarantees "in their origin . . . effective against the federal government alone" had by prior cases "been taken over from the earlier articles of the federal bill of rights and brought within the Fourteenth Amendment by a process of absorption." 302 U.S. at 324–325, 326.

We accept *Betts v. Brady's* assumption, based as it was on our prior cases, that a provision of the Bill of Rights which is "fundamental and essential to a fair trial" is made obligatory upon the States by the Fourteenth Amendment. We think the Court in *Betts* was wrong, however, in concluding that the Sixth Amendment's guarantee of counsel is not one of these fundamental rights. Ten years before *Betts v. Brady*, this Court, after full consideration of all the historical data examined in *Betts*, had unequivocally declared that "the right to the aid of counsel is of this fundamental character." *Powell v. Alabama*, 287 U.S. 45, 68 (1932). While the Court at the close of its *Powell* opinion did by its language, as this Court frequently does, limit its holding to the particular facts and circumstances of that case, its conclusions about the fundamental nature of the right to counsel are unmistakable. Several years later, in 1936, the Court reemphasized what it had said about the fundamental nature of the right to counsel in this language:

"We concluded that certain fundamental rights, safeguarded by the first eight amendments against federal action, were also safeguarded against state action by the due process of law clause of the Fourteenth Amendment, and among them the fundamental right of the accused to the aid of counsel in a criminal prosecution." 297 U.S. 233, 243–244 (1936).

And again in 1938 this Court said:

"[The assistance of counsel] is one of the safeguards of the Sixth Amendment deemed necessary to insure fundamental human rights of life and liberty. . . . The Sixth Amendment stands as a constant admonition that if the constitutional safeguards it provides be lost, justice will not 'still be done.'" *Johnson v. Zerbst*, 304 U.S. 458, 462 (1938). To the same effect, *see Avery v. Alabama*, 308 U.S. 444 (1940), and *Smith v. O'Grady*, 312 U.S. 329 (1941).

In light of these and many other prior decisions of this Court, it is not surprising that the *Betts* Court, when faced with the contention that "one charged with crime, who is unable to obtain counsel, must be furnished counsel by the State," conceded that "expressions in the opinions of this court lend color to the argument. . . ." 316 U.S. at 462–463. The fact is that in deciding as it did—that "appointment of counsel is not a fundamental right, essential to a fair trial"—the Court in *Betts v. Brady* made an abrupt break with its own well-considered precedents. In returning to these old precedents, sounder we believe than the new, we but restore constitutional principles established to achieve a fair system of justice. Not only these precedents but also reason and reflection require us to recognize that in our adversary system of criminal justice, any person haled into court, who is too poor to hire a lawyer, cannot be assured a fair trial unless counsel is provided for him. This seems to us to be an obvious truth. Governments, both state and federal, quite properly spend vast sums of money to establish machinery to try defendants accused of crime. Lawyers to prosecute are everywhere deemed essential to protect the public's interest in an orderly society. Similarly, there are few defendants charged with crime, few indeed, who fail to hire the best lawyers they can get to prepare and present their defenses. That government hires lawyers to prosecute and defendants who have the money hire lawyers to defend are the strongest indications of the widespread belief that lawyers in criminal courts are necessities, not luxuries. The right of one charged with crime to counsel may not be deemed fundamental and essential to fair trials in some countries, but it is in ours. From the very beginning, our state and national consititutions and laws have laid great emphasis on procedural and substantive safeguards designed to assure fair trials before impartial tribunals in which every defendant stands equal before the law. This noble ideal cannot be realized if the poor man charged with crime has to face his accusers without a lawyer to assist him. A defendant's need for a lawyer is nowhere better stated than in the moving words of Mr. Justice Sutherland in *Powell v. Alabama:*

"The right to be heard would be, in many cases, of little avail if it did not comprehend the right to be heard by counsel. Even the intelligent and educated layman has small and sometimes no skill in the science of law. If charged with crime, he is incapable, generally, of determining for himself whether the indictment is good or bad. He is unfamiliar with the rules of evidence. Left without the aid of counsel he may be put on trial without a proper charge, and convicted upon incompetent evidence, or evidence irrelevant to the issue or otherwise inadmissible. He lacks both the skill and knowledge adequately to prepare his defense, even though he have a perfect one. He requires the guiding hand of counsel at every step in the proceedings against him. Without it, though he be not guilty, he faces the danger of conviction because he does not know how to establish his innocence." 287 U.S. at 68–69.

The Court in *Betts v. Brady* departed from the sound wisdom upon which the Court's holding in *Powell v. Alabama* rested. Florida, supported by two other States, has asked that *Betts v. Brady* be left intact. Twenty-two States, as friends of the Court, argue that Betts was "an anachronism when handed down" and that it should now be overruled. We agree.

The judgment is reversed and the cause is remanded to the Supreme Court of Florida for further action not inconsistent with this opinion.

Reversed.

4-3 HOW TO WRITE A CASE BRIEF

Each component should be set forth as a separate section of the case brief. Paragraphs explaining the component follow each section heading. The analysis, or reasoning, section combines or synthesizes much of what is included in the facts, issues, and rules sections. As a writer, you may detect that there is a certain degree of redundancy.

A brief or summary of the *Gideon* case might look like this:

Gideon v. Wainwright, 372 U.S. 335 (1963)

Judicial History

The trial court denied Gideon's request for appointment of defense counsel. As a result of this denial, he conducted his own defense. The jury found him guilty. The Florida State Supreme Court denied Gideon's request for relief.

Facts

Gideon was charged with breaking and entering a poolroom. He appeared for trial without counsel. He asked the court to appoint counsel for him, his request was denied. Gideon conducted his own defense.

Issues

1. Were Gideon's rights under the Fourteenth Amendment violated when, as an indigent defendant in a state criminal trial, he was denied assistance of counsel?

2. Should *Betts v. Brady* be overruled? (This issue was raised by the Court. Both parties were asked to argue this issue.)

Rules

Fourteenth Amendment: Due Process Clause

Sixth Amendment: "In all criminal prosecutions, the accused shall enjoy the right . . . to have the Assistance of Counsel for his defense."

Betts v. Brady, 316 U.S. 455 (1942): "appointment of counsel is not a fundamental right, essential to a fair trial. . . ." (*Betts* is reconsidered by the Court in *Gideon* and overruled.)

Powell v. Alabama, 287 U.S. 45 (1932): the right to counsel is fundamental and essential to a fair trial. (Followed in *Gideon*.)

Analysis

The facts of the *Gideon* case are very similar to the facts of the *Betts v. Brady* case. The *Betts* case held that "a refusal to appoint counsel for an indigent defendant charged with a felony did not necessarily violate the due process clause of the Fourteenth Amendment." The Court overruled *Betts v. Brady*. Relying on the Sixth Amendment, the Court held that "counsel must be provided for defendants unable to employ counsel unless the right is competently and intelligently waived." The fundamental safeguards of liberty are protected by the due process clause of the Fourteenth Amendment. The Sixth Amendment guarantee of counsel is one of these fundamental safeguards. The Court cites the sound wisdom upon which the *Powell v. Alabama* case was decided. In *Powell*, the Court explained that a criminal defendant needs the "guiding hand of counsel at every step in the proceedings against him."

Conclusion

The judgment of the Florida State Supreme Court was reversed. The cause was remanded to the Florida courts for "further action not inconsistent with this opinion." *Betts v. Brady* was overruled.

This is only one approach to briefing the *Gideon* case. No two people will write exactly the same brief, and the actual format for the brief may differ, but the information contained generally falls into the categories set forth in this sample brief. The following case brief contains the same basic information, but it is arranged differently.

Gideon v. Wainwright, **372 U.S. 335 (1963)**

Facts

Gideon was charged with breaking and entering a poolroom. He appeared for trial without counsel. He asked the court to appoint counsel for him, his request was denied. Gideon conducted his own defense. The jury found him guilty. The Florida State Supreme Court denied Gideon's request for relief.

Issues

1. Were Gideon's rights under the Fourteenth Amendment violated when, as an indigent defendant in a state criminal trial, he was denied assistance of counsel?

2. Should *Betts v. Brady* be overruled? (This issue was raised by the Court. Both parties were asked to argue this issue.)

Holding

The judgment of the Florida State Supreme Court was reversed. The cause was remanded to the Florida courts for "further action not inconsistent with this opinion." *Betts v. Brady* was overruled.

Rationale

The facts of the *Gideon* case are very similar to the facts of the *Betts v. Brady*, 316 U.S. 455 (1942) case. The *Betts* case held that "a refusal to appoint counsel for an indigent defendant charged with a felony did not necessarily violate the due process clause of the Fourteenth Amendment." The Court overruled *Betts v. Brady*. Relying on the Sixth Amendment, the Court found that "counsel must be provided for defendants unable to employ counsel unless the right is competently and intelligently waived." The fundamental safeguards of liberty are protected by the due process clause of the Fourteenth Amendment. The Sixth Amendment guarantee of counsel is one of these fundamental safeguards. The Court cites the sound wisdom upon which the *Powell v. Alabama*, 287 U.S. 45 (1932) case was decided. In *Powell*, the Court explained that a criminal defendant needs the "guiding hand of counsel at every step in the proceedings against him."

A Point to Remember

Some cases include concurring opinions and dissenting opinions. You need to include a section explaining the concurrence or dissent only if there is something of importance that your reader needs to know. Read *Minnesota v. Dickerson*. Take notes on the judicial history, facts, issues, rules, analysis, and conclusion/holding. Color highlight the six components of a case to help you visualize the patterns in the decision.

CASE 4-2

Minnesota v. Dickerson,
508 U.S. 366 (1993)

JUSTICE WHITE delivered the opinion of the Court.

In this case, we consider whether the Fourth Amendment permits the seizure of contraband detected through a police officer's sense of touch during a protective patdown search.

I

On the evening of November 9, 1989, two Minneapolis police officers were patrolling an area on the city's north side in a marked squad car. At about 8:15 p.m., one of the officers observed respondent leaving a 12-unit apartment building on Morgan Avenue North. The officer, having previously responded to complaints of drug sales in the building's hallways and having executed several search warrants on the premises, considered the building to be a notorious "crack house." According to testimony credited by the trial court, respondent began walking toward the police but, upon spotting the squad car and making eye contact with one of the officers, abruptly halted and began walking in the opposite direction. His suspicion aroused, this officer watched as respondent turned and entered an alley on the other side of the apartment building. Based upon respondent's seemingly evasive actions and the fact that he had just left a building known for cocaine traffic, the officers decided to stop respondent and investigate further.

The officers pulled their squad car into the alley and ordered respondent to stop and submit to a patdown search. The search revealed no weapons, but the officer conducting the search did take an interest in a small lump in respondent's nylon jacket. The officer later testified:

"As I pat-searched the front of his body, I felt a lump, a small lump, in the front pocket. I examined it with my fingers and it slid and it felt to be a lump of crack cocaine in cellophane." Tr. 9 (Feb. 20, 1990).

The officer then reached into respondent's pocket and retrieved a small plastic bag containing one fifth of one gram of crack cocaine. Respondent was arrested and charged in Hennepin County District Court with possession of a controlled substance.

Before trial, respondent moved to suppress the cocaine. The trial court first concluded that the officers were justified under *Terry v. Ohio*, 392 U.S. 1, 20 L. Ed. 2d 889, 88 S. Ct. 1868 (1968), in stopping respondent to investigate whether he might be engaged in criminal activity. The court further found that the officers were justified in frisking respondent to ensure that he was not carrying a weapon. Finally, analogizing to the "plain-view" doctrine, under which officers may make a warrantless seizure of contraband found in plain view during a lawful search for other items, the trial court ruled that the officers' seizure of the cocaine did not violate the Fourth Amendment:

"To this Court there is no distinction as to which sensory perception the officer uses to conclude that the material is contraband. An experienced officer may rely upon his sense of smell in DWI stops or in recognizing the smell of burning marijuana in an automobile. The sound of a shotgun being racked would clearly support certain reactions by an officer. The sense of touch, grounded in experience and training, is as reliable as perceptions drawn from other senses. 'Plain feel,' therefore, is no different than plain view and will equally support the seizure here." App. to Pet. for Cert. C-5.

His suppression motion having failed, respondent proceeded to trial and was found guilty. On appeal, the Minnesota Court of Appeals reversed. The court agreed with the trial court that the investigative stop and protective patdown search of respondent were lawful under *Terry* because the officers had a reasonable belief based on specific and articulable facts that respondent was engaged in criminal behavior and that he might be armed and dangerous. The court concluded, however, that the officers had overstepped the bounds allowed by *Terry* in seizing the cocaine. In doing so, the Court of Appeals "decline[d] to adopt the plain feel exception" to the warrant requirement. 469 N.W.2d 462, 466 (1991).

The Minnesota Supreme Court affirmed. Like the Court of Appeals, the State Supreme Court held that both the stop and the frisk of respondent were valid under *Terry*, but found the seizure of the cocaine to be unconstitutional. The court expressly refused "to extend the plain view doctrine to the sense of touch" on the grounds that "the sense of touch is inherently less immediate and less reliable than the sense of sight" and that "the sense of touch is far more intrusive into the personal privacy that is at the core of the Fourth Amendment." 481 N.W.2d 840, 845 (1992). The court thus appeared to adopt a categorical rule barring the seizure of any contraband detected by an officer through the sense of touch during a patdown search for weapons. The court further noted that "even if we recognized a 'plain feel' exception, the search in this case would not qualify" because "the pat search of the defendant went far beyond what is permissible under *Terry.*" *Id.* at 843, 844, n.1. As the State Supreme Court read the record, the officer conducting the search ascertained that the lump in respondent's jacket was contraband only after probing and investigating what he certainly knew was not a weapon. *See id.*, at 844.

We granted certiorari, 506 U.S. 814 (1992), to resolve a conflict among the state and federal courts over whether contraband detected through the sense of touch during a patdown search may be admitted into evidence. We now affirm.

II

A

The Fourth Amendment, made applicable to the States by way of the Fourteenth Amendment, *Mapp v. Ohio*, 367 U.S. 643, 6 L. Ed. 2d 1081, 81 S. Ct. 1684 (1961), guarantees "the right of the people to be secure in their persons, houses, papers, and effects, against unreasonable searches and seizures." Time and again, this Court has observed that searches and seizures "'conducted outside the judicial process, without prior approval by judge or magistrate,

are *per se* unreasonable under the Fourth Amendment—subject only to a few specifically established and well delineated exceptions.'" *Thompson v. Louisiana*, 469 U.S. 17, 19–20, 83 L. Ed. 2d 246, 105 S. Ct. 409 (1984) *(per curiam)* (quoting *Katz v. United States*, 389 U.S. 347, 357, 19 L. Ed. 2d 576, 88 S. Ct. 507 (1967) (footnotes omitted)); *Mincey v. Arizona*, 437 U.S. 385, 390, 57 L. Ed. 2d 290, 98 S. Ct. 2408 (1978); *see also United States v. Place*, 462 U.S. 696, 701, 77 L. Ed. 2d 110, 103 S. Ct. 2637 (1983). One such exception was recognized in *Terry v. Ohio*, 392 U.S. 1, 20 L. Ed. 2d 889, 88 S. Ct. 1868 (1968), which held that "where a police officer observes unusual conduct which leads him reasonably to conclude in light of his experience that criminal activity may be afoot . . . ," the officer may briefly stop the suspicious person and make "reasonable inquiries" aimed at confirming or dispelling his suspicions. *Id.*, at 30; *see also Adams v. Williams*, 407 U.S. 143, 145–146, 32 L. Ed. 2d 612, 92 S. Ct. 1921 (1972).

Terry further held that "when an officer is justified in believing that the individual whose suspicious behavior he is investigating at close range is armed and presently dangerous to the officer or to others," the officer may conduct a patdown search "to determine whether the person is in fact carrying a weapon." 392 U.S. at 24. "The purpose of this limited search is not to discover evidence of crime, but to allow the officer to pursue his investigation without fear of violence . . . ." *Adams, supra*, at 146. Rather, a protective search—permitted without a warrant and on the basis of reasonable suspicion less than probable cause—must be strictly "limited to that which is necessary for the discovery of weapons which might be used to harm the officer or others nearby." *Terry, supra*, at 26; see also *Michigan v. Long*, 463 U.S. 1032, 1049, 77 L. Ed. 2d 1201, 103 S. Ct. 3469, and 1052, n.16 (1983); *Ybarra v. Illinois*, 444 U.S. 85, 93–94, 62 L. Ed. 2d 238, 100 S. Ct. 338 (1979). If the protective search goes beyond what is necessary to determine if the suspect is armed, it is no longer valid under *Terry* and its fruits will be suppressed. *Sibron v. New York*, 392 U.S. 40, 65–66, 20 L. Ed. 2d 917, 88 S. Ct. 1889 (1968).

These principles were settled 25 years ago when, on the same day, the Court announced its decisions in *Terry* and *Sibron*.

The question presented today is whether police officers may seize nonthreatening contraband detected during a protective patdown search of the sort permitted by *Terry*. We think the answer is clearly that they may, so long as the officers' search stays within the bounds marked by *Terry*.

B

We have already held that police officers, at least under certain circumstances, may seize contraband detected during the lawful execution of a *Terry* search. In *Michigan v. Long, supra*, for example, police approached a man who had driven his car into a ditch and who appeared to be under the influence of some intoxicant. As the man moved to reenter the car from the roadside, police spotted a knife on the floor-board. The officers stopped the man, subjected him to a patdown search, and then inspected the interior of the vehicle for other weapons. During the search of the passenger compartment, the police discovered an open pouch containing marijuana and seized it. This Court upheld the validity of the search and seizure under *Terry*. The Court held first that, in the context of a roadside encounter, where police have reasonable suspicion based on specific and articulable facts to believe that a driver may be armed and dangerous, they may conduct a protective search for weapons not only of the driver's person but also of the passenger compartment of the automobile. 463 U.S. at 1049. Of course, the protective search of the vehicle, being justified solely by the danger that weapons stored there could be used against the officers or bystanders, must be "limited to those areas in which a weapon may be placed or hidden." *Ibid.* The Court then held: "If, while conducting a legitimate *Terry* search of the interior of the automobile, the officer should, as here, discover contraband other than weapons, he clearly cannot be required to ignore the contraband, and the Fourth Amendment does not require its suppression in such circumstances." *Id.* at 1050; accord, *Sibron*, 392 U.S. at 69–70 (WHITE, J., concurring); *id.*, at 79 (Harlan, J., concurring in result).

The Court in *Long* justified this latter holding by reference to our cases under the "plain-view" doctrine. *See Long, supra*, at 1050; *see also United States v. Hensley*, 469 U.S. 221, 235, 83 L. Ed. 2d 604, 105 S. Ct. 675 (1985) (upholding plain-view seizure in context of *Terry* stop). Under that doctrine, if police are lawfully in a position from which they view an object, if its incriminating character is immediately apparent, and if the officers have a lawful right of access to the object, they may seize it without a warrant. *See Horton v. California*, 496 U.S. 128, 136–137, 110 L. Ed. 2d 112, 110 S. Ct. 2301 (1990); *Texas v. Brown*, 460 U.S. 730, 739, 75 L. Ed. 2d 502, 103 S. Ct. 1535 (1983) (plurality opinion). If, however, the police lack probable cause to believe that an object in plain view is contraband without conducting some further search of the object—*i.e.*, if "its incriminating character [is not] 'immediately apparent,'" *Horton, supra*, at 136—the plain-view doctrine cannot justify its seizure. *Arizona v. Hicks*, 480 U.S. 321, 94 L. Ed. 2d 347, 107 S. Ct. 1149 (1987).

We think that this doctrine has an obvious application by analogy to cases in which an officer discovers contraband through the sense of touch during an otherwise lawful search. The rationale of the plain-view doctrine is that if contraband is left in open view and is observed by a police officer from a lawful vantage point, there has been no invasion of a legitimate expectation of privacy and thus no "search" within the meaning of the Fourth Amendment—or at least no search independent of the initial intrusion that gave the officers their vantage point. *See Illinois v. Andreas*, 463 U.S. 765, 771, 77 L. Ed. 2d 1003, 103 S. Ct. 3319 (1983); *Texas v. Brown, supra*, at 740. The warrantless seizure of contraband that presents itself in this manner is deemed justified by the realization that resort to a neutral magistrate under such circumstances would often be impracticable and would do little to promote the objectives of the Fourth Amendment. *See Hicks, supra*, at 326–327; *Coolidge v. New Hampshire*, 403 U.S. 443, 467–468, 469–470, 29 L. Ed. 2d 564, 91 S. Ct. 2022 (1971) (opinion of Stewart, J.). The same can be said of tactile discoveries of contraband. If a police officer lawfully pats down a suspect's outer clothing and feels an object whose contour or mass makes its identity immediately apparent, there has been no invasion of the suspect's privacy beyond that already authorized by the officer's search for weapons; if the object is contraband, its warrantless seizure would be justified by the same practical considerations that inhere [SIC] in the plain-view context.

The Minnesota Supreme Court rejected an analogy to the plain-view doctrine on two grounds: first, its belief that "the sense of touch is inherently less immediate and less reliable than the sense of sight," and second, that "the sense of touch is far more intrusive into the personal privacy that is at the core of the Fourth Amendment," 481 N.W.2d at 845. We have a somewhat different view. First, *Terry* itself demonstrates that the sense of touch is capable of revealing the nature of an object with sufficient reliability to support a seizure. The very premise of *Terry*, after all, is that officers will be able to detect the presence of weapons through the sense of touch and *Terry* upheld precisely such a seizure. Even if it were true that the sense of touch is generally less reliable than the sense of sight, that only suggests that officers will less often be able to justify seizures of unseen contraband. Regardless of whether the officer detects the contraband by sight or by touch, however, the Fourth Amendment's requirement that the officer have probable cause to believe that the item is contraband before seizing it ensures against excessively speculative seizures. The court's second concern—that touch is more intrusive into privacy than is sight—is inapposite in light of the fact that the intrusion the court fears has already been authorized by the lawful search for weapons. The seizure of an item whose identity is already known occasions no further invasion of privacy. *See Soldal v. Cook County*, 506 U.S. 56, 66, 121 L. Ed. 2d 450, 113 S. Ct. 538 (1992); *Horton, supra*, at 141; *United States v. Jacobsen*, 466 U.S. 109, 120, 80 L. Ed. 2d 85, 104 S. Ct. 1652 (1984). Accordingly, the suspect's privacy interests are not advanced by a categorical rule barring the seizure of contraband plainly detected through the sense of touch.

III

It remains to apply these principles to the facts of this case. Respondent has not challenged the finding made by the trial court and affirmed by both the Court of Appeals and the State Supreme Court that the police were justified under *Terry* in stopping him and frisking him for weapons. Thus, the dispositive question before this Court is whether the officer who conducted the search was acting within the lawful bounds marked by *Terry* at the time he gained probable cause to believe that the lump in respondent's jacket was contraband. The State District Court did not make precise findings on this point, instead finding simply that the officer, after feeling "a small, hard object wrapped in plastic" in respondent's pocket, "formed the opinion that the object . . . was crack . . . cocaine," App. to Pet. for Cert. C-2. The District Court also noted that the officer made "no claim that he suspected this object to be a weapon," *id.* at C-5, a finding affirmed on appeal, *see* 469 N.W.2d at 464 (the officer "never thought the lump was a weapon"). The Minnesota Supreme Court, after "a close examination of the record," held that the officer's own testimony "belies any notion that he 'immediately'" recognized the lump as crack cocaine. *See* 481 N.W.2d at 844. Rather, the court concluded, the officer determined that the lump was contraband only after "squeezing, sliding and otherwise manipulating the contents of the defendant's pocket"—a pocket which the officer already knew contained no weapon. *Ibid.*

Under the State Supreme Court's interpretation of the record before it, it is clear that the court was correct in holding that the police officer in this case overstepped the bounds of the "strictly circumscribed" search for weapons allowed under *Terry. See Terry*, 392 U.S. at 26. Where, as here, "an officer who is executing a valid search for one item seizes a different item," this Court rightly "has been sensitive to the danger . . . that officers will enlarge a specific authorization, furnished by a warrant or an exigency, into the equivalent of a general warrant to rummage and seize at will." *Texas v. Brown*, 460 U.S. at 748 (STEVENS, J., concurring in judgment). Here, the officer's continued exploration of respondent's pocket after having concluded that it contained no weapon was unrelated to "the sole justification of the search [under *Terry*:] . . . the protection of the police officer and others nearby." 392 U.S. at 29. It therefore amounted to the sort of evidentiary search that *Terry* expressly refused to authorize, *see id.*, at 26, and that we have condemned in subsequent cases. *See Michigan v. Long*, 463 U.S. at 1049, n.14; *Sibron*, 392 U.S. at 65–66.

Once again, the analogy to the plain-view doctrine is apt. In *Arizona v. Hicks*, 480

U.S. 321, 94 L. Ed. 2d 347, 107 S. Ct. 1149 (1987), this Court held invalid the seizure of stolen stereo equipment found by police while executing a valid search for other evidence. Although the police were lawfully on the premises, they obtained probable cause to believe that the stereo equipment was contraband only after moving the equipment to permit officers to read its serial numbers. The subsequent seizure of the equipment could not be justified by the plain-view doctrine, this Court explained, because the incriminating character of the stereo equipment was not immediately apparent; rather, probable cause to believe that the equipment was stolen arose only as a result of a further search—the moving of the equipment—that was not authorized by a search warrant or by any exception to the warrant requirement. The facts of this case are very similar. Although the officer was lawfully in a position to feel the lump in respondent's pocket, because *Terry* entitled him to place his hands upon respondent's jacket, the court below determined that the incriminating character of the object was not immediately apparent to him. Rather, the officer determined that the item was contraband only after conducting a further search, one not authorized by *Terry* or by any other exception to the warrant requirement. Because this further search of respondent's pocket was constitutionally invalid, the seizure of the cocaine that followed is likewise unconstitutional. *Horton*, 496 U.S. at 140.

IV.
The judgment is affirmed.

Case Questions

1. Summarize the facts in the *Dickerson* case.
2. What are the legal issues?
3. Which rules/law did the Court rely upon most?

4-4 ANALYSIS AND THE CASE BRIEF

The brief or summary of a reported case is only the starting point. The legal researcher reads law looking for primary law that is applicable to a client's situation. When you begin serious research, you are armed with the facts of your client's case. These facts provide the initial foundation for your research and your research plan or strategy. The facts help the researcher identify and articulate the legal issues involved in the client's case. Always attempt to identify the most relevant facts involved in your client's situation.

When researching, you search for primary law containing facts that are similar to the facts of your client's case. In Chapter 2 you learned to separate facts into the following categories:

Relevant

Explanatory

Legally unimportant

Once the facts of a case you researched are categorized, you are ready to compare and contrast the facts of the reported decision with those of your client's situation. This process of comparing the facts of a client's case with those of a reported case is an essential analytical skill. As you begin the comparison process, be sure to look for the following:

Similarities

Differences

Unknowns (gaps)

4-5 AN APPROACH TO A DAUNTING PROJECT

Briefing cases is often part of a larger research project. Sometimes this larger project is daunting. If so, try the following approach.

1. Reread the ***directions.*** Ask yourself:

   Do I fully understand what I have been asked to do?
   > If not, get clarification.

   Do I have a mental picture of the document I must create?
   > If not, get an example.

   Do I have a deadline?

   Do I have special instructions?

2. Begin the project *only* after framing clear answers to the preceding questions.

3. Begin the project in a ***logical fashion.***

   Create an outline of the material to be covered. Leave plenty of space between the sections. Do this on the word processor. In this way, the project officially begins.

   Fill in the outline with key words and phrases.

   Make a separate list of problem areas.

   Identify the easy parts of the project.
   > Consider doing these portions first.

   Identify the difficult part of the project.
   > Create a special approach for this part of the project.

4. Choose one section of the project and begin writing. Do not worry about spelling, grammar, consistency, or anything else at this point. Just get your ideas on paper. You will proofread and edit later. Remember, your computer software will do much of this simple proofing for you.

5. Complete one section before you move on to another section of the project. Try to accomplish closure of small portions of the project. This will serve you well in the workplace. Because it is easy to show your supervisor small portions of a project, the supervisor has the opportunity to see that you are organized and proceeding in a logical fashion.

6. Consider this: Will placing material into a chronology help you? Will the chronology help the reader? If it helps you, do it in an effort to get your ideas on paper. If a chronology will not be particularly helpful to the reader, do not use it in the final copy.

   A chronology may help the writer sort out a large number of facts or events. Creation of a "list" is often helpful. This list probably does not belong in the final written product, but it is a good outlining tool during the drafting stage. As you look at a long, often very detailed list, you often see where you may combine facts or events. Or you may see a pattern emerge.

   For example: If you have a series of judicial events, think about lumping them into a time frame, **or** addressing the happenings at each court level, **or** saying "Petitioner's various motions to re-open the case were repeatedly denied" **or** "Defendant's motions were heard favorably in the appellate court, but the State Supreme Court was not so lenient. . . ."

   Remember, not all judicial events are equal in importance; even the number of hearings or trials may not be significant. In a summary, the writer cannot possibly cover everything in the original document and therefore must make choices based on knowledge and analytical skill. Such choices are learned through practice.

7. If you are summarizing a document, is there a specific format or order in which it is written?

   If there is a specific format or order, adopt it if at all possible.

   Until you fully understand the document, you will not be able to create an effective summary.

   Ask yourself the following questions:
   On what does the author of the document focus?
   On what does the author spend the most time?
   What seems most critical to the author of the document? (*not* what do *you* think is most important?)

   Follow the lead of the original document.

8. Remember, a summary should *reflect* the original. Think about this. A summary synthesizes or condenses the original document.

9. Avoid creating confusion. We are often our own worst enemies.

10. Go back to the directions. Are you still focused?

    Have you done what you were asked to do?

    Is your document clear and concise?

    Is it in the appropriate format?

    When is the deadline?

11. At this point, put your draft away for 24 to 48 hours. Just let it sit; avoid even thinking about it.

    Then: a) Get out a bright color pen (felt pen edits are hard to ignore).

    b) Re-read the directions (yes, again).

    c) Start reading at the beginning, marking as you go.

       Proofread for simple errors (spelling, grammar, etc.).
       Edit for passive voice (use active voice, if possible).
       Edit for long sentences (count the words!).
       Edit for topic sentences (make sure you have them).
       Edit for format consistency.
       Edit for internal consistency.
       Edit for vagueness.
       Edit for redundancy.

12. At this point, all sorts of potential changes (improvements) are identified. Make the necessary corrections and put the document aside. You are done. Going over and over a document is not realistic. Of course, we all strive for some degree of perfection, but the sheer reality of the working world often precludes perfection in all aspects of every project. Remember: Sometimes our changes are just changes, not improvements. You can overthink and overedit your work.

13. Closure is a good thing!

Online Legal Research

There are a growing number of large, inclusive showcases on the Web. These mega search engines search groups of other search engines. The following sites represent only two of the more successful mega search engines.

www.hg.org

www.dogpile.com

A caution: Searching a large group of search engines is a great idea and often works reasonably well. But remember, the form in which you write a search for one site or search engine may vary from others. This variation could cause you to miss otherwise available information. Sometimes valuable information may not be retrieved because not all of the search engines used by these inclusive showcases are able to understand or properly assimilate the search request. When you do not retrieve appropriate data you should try again. Change your search terms and target reliable search engines.

CITATION MATTERS

QUOTATIONS

THE BLUEBOOK—RULE 5

Quotations are an important part of legal writing. When you quote, you *must* alert the reader that you are using quoted language. This means, in most instances, you need quotation marks. A citation must follow a quote. This citation lets the reader know where the borrowed material originated.

Quotations of fifty words or more are *blocked* and no quotation marks are used. A blocked quote is single spaced and slightly indented on the left and right margins. The citation that follows a blocked quote is placed on the line below the last line of the blocked quote and it is drawn all the way over to the left margin. Good examples are included under *The Bluebook* Rule 5.

Example of a blocked quote:

> The *Ferber* case upheld a prohibition on the distribution and sale of child pornography, as well as its production, because these acts were "intrinsically related" to the sexual abuse of children in two ways. *New York v. Ferber*, 458 U.S. 747, 759 (1982). First, as a permanent record of a child's abuse, the continued circulation itself would harm the child who had participated. *See id.* Second, because the traffic in child pornography was an economic motive for its production, the State had an interest in closing the distribution network.

Id. at 760.

Quotes of forty-nine words or fewer should be placed in quotation marks, but not set off from the remainder of the text. Place periods and commas inside the quotation marks. Other punctuation is placed inside the quotation marks *only* if it is part of the quoted excerpt.

CHAPTER SUMMARY

A case brief is a summary of a reported case. Briefs serve many purposes: Some are written as a reminder for the writer; others for someone who did not read the case. A good case brief simplifies and condenses the reported case. It must be broken down into components that enable the reader to follow the information easily. The most common components of a case brief are (1) name of the case, (2) judicial history, (3) facts, (4) issues, (5) rules, (6) analysis or reasoning, and (7) conclusion or holding. Making notes in the margin while reading the case is an effective method of initial summarization. Color highlighting the components of the case is also helpful in acquiring a good understanding of the case.

Analysis of your client's situation involves placing facts into categories. Facts should be categorized as (1) relevant, (2) explanatory, and (3) legally unimportant. Then you can compare and contrast them.

A daunting project requires advance planning. A logical approach to the project saves time and helps the writer create the structure of the document early in the drafting process. Editing your own work is a skill you should work on with every document you produce.

TERMS TO REMEMBER

case brief	primary sources	holding
trial brief	rationale	reported case

QUESTIONS FOR REVIEW

1. Discuss the various uses of case law briefs.
2. What is the purpose of a case brief?
3. What questions lay the foundation for the components of a case brief?
4. List and explain the components of a case brief.
5. What clues might a court provide as to which facts are most important?
6. When comparing facts, what categories help in the compare and contrast process?

CAN YOU FIGURE IT OUT?

1. Use your citation manual to define the following.
   Cf.
   Id. at 847
   Cert. Denied
2. What is the first page of the *Miranda v. Arizona* case in the official reporter (United States Reports—U.S.)? (Refer to box on page 78.)
3. What is the first page of the *Miranda v. Arizona* case in the *Supreme Court Reporter?* (Refer to box on page 78.)

BUILDING YOUR RESEARCH SKILLS: ASSIGNMENTS AND ACTIVITIES

1. Find the *Terry v. Ohio*, 392 U.S. 1 (1968) case in your local law library. Search for the two unofficial reporters that also publish this case. Cite them. (*Hint:* You are looking for the Supreme Court Reporter—S. Ct. and the Lawyer's Edition—L. Ed.)

2. Find the *Map v. Ohio*, 367 U.S. 643 (1961) case. Summarize the facts of this case.

BUILDING YOUR ANALYSIS SKILLS: ASSIGNMENTS AND EXERCISES

1. Write a brief of the *Minnesota v. Dickerson* case. Use the six components of a case brief.

2. Compare and contrast the Meyers case with the *Dickerson* case. Identify and discuss the factual similarities, differences, and gaps. Discuss whether the *Dickerson* precedent should apply to the Meyers case.

3. Consider the following situation: Our client, Mr. Nguyen, was arrested three weeks ago under the following circumstances: Mr. Nguyen rents one-half of a duplex on North 15th Street. Apparently, Mr. Nguyen's residence was under surveillance for several days prior to the arrest that took place three weeks ago. The police received a tip that large numbers of automatic weapons were being sold out of Mr. Nguyen's residence. The officers believe that the sale and purchase of the weapons is gang-related. A search warrant was obtained for the residence several hours prior to the arrest. Two uniformed officers, armed with a properly executed search warrant, approached the residence while other officers positioned themselves around the duplex. As the officers stepped onto the porch, Mr. Nguyen's brother opened the front door; upon seeing the officers, he began to yell over his shoulder and retreated into the home. Without announcing their intent or purpose, five officers rushed the doors of the duplex at that time. The front and back doors were broken down and the officers entered the duplex. Many weapons were seized and our client was arrested. Apply the *Richards v. Wisconsin* decision to Mr. Nguyen's situation. Write a short memorandum explaining the application of the *Richards* precedent to the Nguyen situation. *Richards v. Wisconsin*, 520 U.S. 385 (1997) is printed in Appendix G.

4. Reread the *Illinois v. Caballas* case, found in Chapter 3. Complete the missing sections (facts, analysis, holding) of the following case brief.

Judicial History

Respondent Caballas was charged with possession of cannibis in the Illinois state court. In the trial court he moved to suppress the cannibis and the motion was denied. Subsequently, he was convicted and appealed the conviction. The Illinois appellate court affirmed the conviction. The Illinois Supreme Court heard the Respondent's appeal and reversed the conviction. The State of Illinois filed a petition for writ of *certiorari* to the U.S. Supreme Court and the Court granted a hearing.

Facts

Issue

Does the Fourth Amendment require reasonable, articulable suspicion to justify using a drug-detection dog to sniff a vehicle during a legitimate traffic stop, where the vehicle stop is not unreasonably prolonged?

Rules
1. Fourth Amendment to U.S. Constitution—right to be free from unreasonable search or seizures.
2. *People v. Cox*, 202 Ill. 2d 462, 270 Ill. Dec. 81, 782 N.E.2d 275 (2002): contraband discovered through a dog sniff that occurred during an unreasonably prolonged traffic stop, was the product of an unconstitutional seizure.
3. *United States v. Jacobsen*, 466 U.S. 109, 124, 104 S. Ct. 1652, 80 L. Ed. 2d 85 (1984): a seizure that is lawful at its inception can violate the Fourth Amendment if its manner of execution unreasonably infringes interests protected by the Constitution.
4. *United States v. Place*, 462 U.S. 696, 103 S. Ct. 2637, 77 L. Ed. 2d 110 (1983): the use of a well-trained narcotics-detection dog during a lawful traffic stop, generally does not implicate legitimate privacy interests.

Analysis

Conclusion

BUILDING YOUR ONLINE RESEARCH SKILLS: ASSIGNMENTS AND EXERCISES

1. Try the following search on Google: seizing evidence not listed in a search warrant. Summarize the information in the first few "hits." Did you find any information that might be helpful in the Meyers case regarding the bloody handkerchief found and seized by the police?
2. Using a site such as www.find.law or www.lawcornell.edu, search for cases and other information on illegal police searches. Explain your online research results.

CONSTITUTIONS, STATUTES, AND ADMINISTRATIVE REGULATIONS

S KILL OBJECTIVES FOR CHAPTER 5

When you complete this chapter you should be able to

- Explain how federal statutory law is enacted.
- Discuss the differences between public laws and private laws.
- Find a section of the United States Code with a citation to the United States Code, the United States Code Service, or the United States Code Annotated.
- Use a pocket part supplement.
- Locate a law within the *Statutes at Large* and explain the relationship of the *Statutes at Large* to the codes.
- Discuss the differences between the *Code of Federal Regulations* and the *United States Code.*
- Find administrative regulations and rules of court.
- Use an index to locate applicable constitutional or statutory law.

FROM THE DESK OF W. J. BRYAN, ESQ.

TO: Research Assistant

After reading the cases you found for the Meyers case, I decided that the bloody handkerchief and our client's subsequent statements in the patrol car were illegally obtained. I need to make a proper motion in court to have this evidence suppressed. Please check the state codes for any law regarding search warrants. Also, check the code and rules of Court to see what type of motion we should make. Finally find and summarize the procedures we must follow in making the motion.

5-1 INTRODUCTION

Although the legal system in the United States relies heavily on common law principles, case law is not the only source of law in this country. Constitutions, statutes, and administrative regulations are other sources as well. The U.S. legal system relies on these various rules and regulations. Unlike case law, these rules are not created after disputes arise. They are in place and provide guidelines to parties *before* a dispute arises. When disputes arise between parties, courts look to constitutional provisions, statutory law, or administrative regulations in deciding how to resolve the dispute. If appropriate law exists, the court must apply it to the factual dispute.

5-2 CONSTITUTIONS

The United States Constitution, the supreme law of the land, provides the framework for the establishment of the federal government. It describes governmental powers and the limits of that power. The United States Constitution also sets out rights that people have in relationship to the federal government. This part of the Constitution is referred to as the **Bill of Rights**.

Bill of Rights. First ten amendments to United States Constitution.

The Constitution has three main parts: the preamble, the articles, and the amendments. In addition to the preamble, the original Constitution consists of seven articles that are subdivided into clauses and sections. For example, consider the following excerpt from Article II of the Constitution:

Article II

Section 1

Clause 1: The executive Power shall be vested in a President of the United States of America. He shall hold his Office during the Terms of four Years and, together with the Vice President, chosen for the same Term, be elected, as follows

Clause 2: Each State shall appoint, in such Manner as the Legislature thereof may direct a Number of Electors, equal to the whole Number of Senators and representatives to which the State may be entitled in the Congress: but no Senator or Representative, or Person holding an Office of Trust or Profit under the United States, shall be appointed Elector.

The amendments are changes or additions to the original Constitution. At present there are twenty-seven amendments. In some publications the amendments are referred to as articles. Knowing the article or amendment number allows a researcher to easily locate a specific provision in the Constitution. See Figure 5-1 for examples of the various parts of the Constitution.

The United States Constitution is published in numerous sources. It is published as a single pamphlet and in connection with other works, including the *United States Code Annotated* and *United States Code Service*, which are discussed later in this chapter. For legal researchers, these publications are important for two reasons. First, the Constitution is **indexed** with the Code. This enables researchers to locate appropriate provisions of the Constitution when researching a specific topic. Second, it is published in an **annotated** format, with the annotated codes discussed below. In an annotated format, the publisher provides not only the exact text of the Constitution but also references to cases that interpret the Constitution. See Figure 5-2 for an example of an annotated Constitutional provision. An annotated U.S. Constitution can also be found on the Internet at www.gpoaccess.gov/constitution/index.html. This document was prepared under the direction of the Library of Congress. A copy is also found on www.findlaw.com.

index. A list of words and phrases that reflect the topics covered in the book.
annotated. A brief summary of a statute or a case added to explain or clarify.

Each state has a constitution. Like the U.S. Constitution, state constitutions are published either separately or with the state codes. They may also be found on the Internet, generally through the state's official homepage.

CONSTITUTION OF THE UNITED STATES OF AMERICA—1787[1]

① ←——— **Preamble**

WE THE PEOPLE of the United States, in Order to form a more perfect Union, establish Justice, insure domestic Tranquility, provide for the common defence, promote the general Welfare, and secure the Blessings of Liberty to ourselves and our Posterity, do ordain and establish this Constitution for the United States of America.

② ARTICLE. I.

SECTION 1. All legislative Powers herein granted shall be vested in a Congress of the United States, which shall consist of a Senate and House of Representatives.

SECTION. 2. [1]The House of Representatives shall be composed of Members chosen every second Year by the People of the several States, and the Elector in each State shall have the Qualifications requisite for Electors of the most numerous Branch of the State Legislature.

[2]No Person shall be a Representative who shall not have attained to the Age of twenty five Years, and been seven Years a Citizen of the United States, and who shall not, when elected, be an Inhabitant of that State in which he shall be chosen.

[3]Representatives and direct Taxes shall be apportioned among the several States which may be included within this Union, according to their respective Numbers, which shall be determined by adding to the whole Number of free Persons, including those bound to Service for a Term of Years, and excluding Indians not taxed, three fifths of all other Persons.[2] The actual Enumeration shall be made within three Years after the first Meeting of the Congress of the United States, and within every subsequent Term of ten Years, in such Manner as they shall by Law direct. The Number of Representatives shall not exceed one for every thirty Thousand, but each State shall have at Least one Representative; and until such enumeration shall be made, the State of New Hampshire shall be entitled to chuse three, Massachusetts eight, Rhode-Island and Providence Plantations one, Connecticut five, New-York six, New Jersey four, Pennsylvania eight, Delaware one, Maryland six, Virginia ten, North Carolina five, South Carolina five, and Georgia three.

[4]When vacancies happen in the Representation from any State, the Executive Authority thereof shall issue Writs of Election to fill such Vacancies.

SECTION 4. The President, Vice President and all civil Officers of the United States, shall be removed from Office on Impeachment for, and Conviction of, Treason, Bribery, or other high Crimes and Misdemeanors.

ARTICLE. II.

SECTION. 1.

CLAUSE 1: The executive Power shall be vested in a President of the United States of America. He shall hold his Office during the Term of four Years, and, together with the Vice President, chosen for the same Term, be elected, as follows

CLAUSE 2: Each State shall appoint, in such Manner as the Legislature thereof may direct a Number of Electors, equal to the whole Number of Senators and representatives to which the State may be entitled in the Congress: but no Senator or Representative, or Person holding an Office of Trust or Profit under the United States, shall be appointed an Elector.

——— **Articles**

CLAUSE 3: The Electors shall meet in their respective States, and vote by Ballot for two Persons, of whom one at least shall not be an Inhabitant of the same State with themselves. And they shall make a List of all the Persons voted for, and of the Number of Votes for each; which List they shall sign and certify, and transmit sealed to the Seat of the Government of the United States, directed to the President of the Senate. The President of the Senate shall, in the Presence of the Senate and House of Representatives, open all the Certificates, and the Votes shall then be counted. The Person having the greatest Number of Votes shall be the President, if such Number be a Majority of the whole Number of Electors appointed; and if there be more than one who have such Majority, and have an equal Number of Votes, then the House of Representatives shall immediately chuse by Ballot one of them for President; and if no Person have a Majority, then from the five highest on the List the said House shall in like Manner chuse the President. But in chusing the President, the Votes shall be taken by States, the Representation from each State having one Vote: A quorum for this Purpose shall consist of a Member or Members from two thirds of the States, and a Majority of all the States shall be necessary to a Choice. In every Case, after the Choice of the President, the Person having the greatest Number of Votes of the Electors shall be the Vice President. But if there should remain two or more who have equal Votes, the Senate shall chuse from them by Ballot the Vice President.

CLAUSE 4: The Congress may determine the Time of chusing the Electors, and the Day on which they shall give their Votes; which Day shall be the same throughout the United States.

CLAUSE 5: No Person except a natural born Citizen, or a Citizen of the United States, at the time of the Adoption of this Constitution, shall be eligible to the Office of the President; neither shall any Person be eligible to that Office who shall not have attained to the Age of thirty five Years, and been fourteen Years a Resident within the United States.

CLAUSE 6: In Case of the Removal of the President from Office, or of his Death, Resignation, or Inability to discharge the Powers and Duties of the said Office *(See Note 9)* the Same shall devolve on the Vice President, and the Congress may by Law provide for the Case of Removal, Death, Resignation or Inability, both of the President and Vice President,

FIGURE 5-1
U.S. Constitution

declaring what Officer shall then act as President, and such Officer shall act accordingly, until the Disability be removed, or a President shall be elected.

CLAUSE 7: The President shall, at stated Times, receive for his Services, a Compensation, which shall neither be encreased nor diminished during the Period for which he shall have been elected, and he shall not receive within that Period any other Emolument from the United States, or any of them.

CLAUSE 8: Before he enter on the Execution of his Office, he shall take the following Oath or affirmation:—"I do solemnly swear (or affirm) that I will faithfully execute the Office of President of the United States, and will to the best of my Ability, preserve, protect and defend the Constitution of the United States."

SECTION. 2.

CLAUSE 1: The President shall be Commander in Chief of the Army and Navy of the United States, of the Militia of the several States, when called into the actual Service of the United States; he may require the Opinion, in writing, of the principal Officer in each of the executive Departments, upon any Subject relating to the Duties of their respective Offices, and he shall have Power to grant Reprieves and Pardons for Offences against the United States, except in Cases of Impeachment.

CLAUSE 2: He shall have Power, by and with the Advice and Consent of the Senate, to make Treaties, provided two thirds of the Senators present concur; and he shall nominate and by and with the Advice and Consent of the Senate, shall appoint Ambassadors, other public Ministers and Consuls, Judges of the supreme Court, and all other Officers of the United States, whose Appointments are not herein otherwise provided for, and which shall be established by Law: but the Congress may by Law vest the Appointment of such inferior Officers, as they think proper, in the President alone, in the Courts of Law, or in the Heads of Departments.

CLAUSE 3: The President shall have Power to fill up all Vacancies that may happen during the Recess of the Senate, by granting Commissions which shall expire at the End of their next Session.

SECTION. 3.

He shall from time to time give to the Congress Information of the State of the Union, and recommend to their Consideration such Measures as he shall judge necessary and expedient; he may, on extraordinary Occasions, convene both Houses, or either of them, and in Case of Disagreement between them, with Respect to the Time of Adjournment, he may adjourn them to such Time as he shall think proper; he shall receive Ambassadors and other public Ministers; he shall take Care that the Laws be faithfully executed, and shall Commission all the Officers of the United States.

SECTION. 4.

The President, Vice President and all civil Officers of the United States, shall be removed from Office on Impeachment for, and Conviction of, Treason, Bribery, or other high Crimes and Misdemeanors.

ARTICLE. III.

SECTION. 1. The judicial Power of the United States, shall be vested in one supreme Court, and in such inferior Courts as the Congress may from time to time ordain and establish. The Judges, both of the supreme and inferior Courts, shall hold their Offices during good Behaviour, and shall, at stated Times, receive for their Services, a Compensation, which shall not be diminished during their Continuance in Office.

SECTION. 2. [1]The judicial Power shall extend to all Cases, in Law and Equity, arising under this Constitution, the Laws of the United States, and Treaties made, or which shall be made, under their Authority;—to all Cases affecting Ambassadors, other public Ministers and Consuls;—to all Cases of admiralty and maritime Jurisdiction;—to Controversies to which the United States shall be a Party;—to Controversies between two or more States;—between a State and Citizens of another State; [10]—between Citizens of different States,—between Citizens of the same State claiming Lands under Grants of different States, and between a State, or the Citizens thereof, and foreign States, Citizens or Subjects.

[2]In all Cases affecting Ambassadors, other public Ministers and Consuls, and those in which a State shall be Party, the supreme Court shall have original Jurisdiction. In all the other Cases before mentioned, the supreme Court shall have appellate Jurisdiction, both as to Law and Fact, with such Exceptions, and under such Regulations as the Congress shall make.

[3]The Trial of all Crimes, except in Cases of Impeachment, shall be by Jury; and such Trial shall be held in the State where the said Crimes shall have been committed; but when not committed within any State, the Trial shall be at such Place or Places as the Congress may by Law have directed.

SECTION. 3. [1]Treason against the United States, shall consist only in levying War against them, or in adhering to their Enemies, giving them Aid and Comfort. No Person shall be convicted of Treason unless on the Testimony of two Witnesses to the same overt Act, or on Confession in open Court.

[2]The Congress shall have Power to declare the Punishment of Treason, but no Attainder of Treason shall work Corruption of Blood, or Forfeiture except during the Life of the Person attainted.

ARTICLE. IV.

SECTION. 1. Full Faith and Credit shall be given in each State to the public Acts, Records, and judicial Proceedings of every other State. And the Congress may by general Laws prescribe the Manner in which such Acts, Records and Proceedings shall be proved, and the Effect thereof.

SECTION. 2. [1]The Citizens of each State shall be entitled to all Privileges and Immunities of Citizens in the several States.

[2]A Person charged in any State with Treason, Felony, or other Crime, who shall flee from Justice,

FIGURE 5-1
(continued)

and be found in another State, shall on Demand of the executive Authority of the State from which he fled, be delivered up, to be removed to the State having Jurisdiction of the Crime.

[3]No Person held to Service or Labour in one State, under the Laws thereof, escaping into another, shall, in Consequence of any Law or Regulation therein, be discharged from such Service or Labour, but shall be delivered up on Claim of the Party to whom such Service or Labour may be due.[11]

SECTION. 3. [1]New States may be admitted by the Congress into this Union; but no new State shall be formed or erected within the Jurisdiction of any other State; nor any State be formed by the Junction of two or more States, or Parts of States, without the Consent of the Legislatures of the States concerned as well as of the Congress.

[2]The Congress shall have Power to dispose of and make all needful Rules and Regulations respecting the Territory or other Property belonging to the United States; and nothing in this Constitution shall be so construed as to Prejudice any Claims of the United States, or of any particular State.

SECTION. 4. The United States shall guarantee to every State in this Union a Republican Form of Government, and shall protect each of them against Invasion; and on Application of the Legislature, or of the Executive (when the Legislature cannot be convened) against domestic Violence.

ARTICLE. V.

The Congress, whenever two thirds of both Houses shall deem it necessary, shall propose Amendments to this Constitution, or, on the Application of the Legislatures of two thirds of the several States, shall call a Convention for proposing Amendments, which, in either Case, shall be valid to all Intents and Purposes, as Part of this Constitution, when ratified by the Legislatures of three fourths of the several States, or by Conventions in three fourths thereof, as the one or the other Mode of Ratification may be proposed by the Congress; Provided that no Amendment which may be made prior to the Year One thousand eight hundred and eight shall in any Manner affect the first and fourth Clauses in the Ninth Section of the first Article; and that no State, without its Consent, shall be deprived of its equal Suffrage in the Senate.

ARTICLE. VI.

[1]All Debts contracted and Engagements entered into, before the Adoption of this Constitution, shall be as valid against the United States under this Constitution, as under the Confederation.

[2]This Constitution, and the Laws of the United States which shall be made in Pursuance thereof; and all Treaties made, or which shall be made, under the Authority of the United States, shall be the supreme Law of the Land; and the Judges in every State shall be bound thereby, any Thing in the Constitution or Laws of any State to the Contrary notwithstanding.

[3]The Senators and Representatives before mentioned, and the Members of the several State Legislatures, and all executive and judicial Officers, both of the United States and of the several States, shall be bound by Oath or Affirmation, to support this Constitution; but no religious Test shall ever be required as a Qualification to any Office or public Trust under the United States.

ARTICLE. VII.

The Ratification of the Conventions of nine States, shall be sufficient for the Establishment of this Constitution between the States so ratifying the Same.

DONE in Convention by the Unanimous Consent of the States present the Seventeenth Day of September in the Year of our Lord one thousand seven hundred and Eighty seven and of the Independence of the United States of America the Twelfth IN WITNESS whereof We have hereunto subscribed our Names,

G.° WASHINGTON—*Presid[t].*
and deputy from Virgina

[Signed also by the deputies of twelve States.]

New Hampshire
JOHN LANGDON
NICHOLAS GILMAN

Massachusetts
NATHANIEL GORHAM
RUFUS KING

Connecticut
W[M]. SAM[L.] JOHNSON
ROGER SHERMAN

New York
ALEXANDER HAMILTON

New Jersey
WIL: LIVINGSTON
DAVID BREARLEY.
W[M]. PATERSON.
JONA: DAYTON

Pennsylvania
B FRANKLIN
THOMAS MIFFLIN
ROB[T] MORRIS
GEO. CLYMER
THO[S]. FITZSIMONS
JARED INGERSOLL
JAMES WILSON.
GOUV MORRIS

Delaware
GEO: READ
GUNNING BEDFORD jun
JOHN DICKINSON
RICHARD BASSETT
JACO: BROOM

FIGURE 5-1
(continued)

Maryland

JAMES MᶜHENRY

DAN OF Sᵀ THOˢ. JENIFER

DANᴸ CARROLL.

Virginia

JOHN BLAIR—

JAMES MADISON JR.

North Carolina

Wᴹ BLOUNT

RICHᴰ. DOBBS SPAIGHT.

HU WILLIAMSON

South Carolina

J. RUTLEDGE

CHARLES COTESWORTH PINCKNEY

CHARLES PINCKNEY

PIERCE BUTLER.

Georgia

WILLIAM FEW

ABR BALDWIN

Attest   WILLIAM JACKSON *Secretary*

ARTICLES IN ADDITION TO, AND AMEND-MENT OF, THE CONSTITUTION OF THE UNITED STATES OF AMERICA, PROPOSED BY CONGRESS, AND RATIFIED BY THE LEGISLATURES OF THE SEVERAL STATES, PURSUANT TO THE FIFTH ARTICLE OF THE ORIGINAL CONSTITUTION[12]

③ ARTICLE [I.][13] ← ————————————————— **Amendments**

Congress shall make no law respecting an es-tablishment of religion, or prohibiting the free exer-cise thereof; or abridging the freedom of speech, or of the press; or the right of the people peaceably to as-semble, and to petition the Government for a redress of grievances.

ARTICLE [II.]

A well regulated Militia, being necessary to the security of a free State, the right of the people to keep and bear Arms, shall not be infringed.

ARTICLE [III.]

No soldier shall, in time of peace be quartered in any house, without the consent of the owner, nor in time of war, but in a manner to be prescribed by law.

ARTICLE [IV.]

The right of the people to be secure in their per-sons, houses, papers, and effects, against unreason-able searches and seizures, shall not be violated, and no Warrants shall issue, but upon probable cause, supported by oath or affirmation, and particularly de-scribing the place to be searched, and the persons or things to be seized.

ARTICLE [V.]

No person shall be held to answer for a capital, or otherwise infamous crime, unless on a present-ment or indictment of a Grand Jury, except in cases arising in the land or naval forces, or in the Militia, when in actual service in time of War or public dan-ger; nor shall any person be subject for the same of-fence to be twice put in jeopardy of life or limb; nor shall be compelled in any criminal case to be a wit-ness against himself, nor be deprived of life, liberty, or property, without due process of law; nor shall pri-vate property be taken for public use, without just compensation.

ARTICLE [VI.]

In all criminal prosecutions, the accused shall enjoy the right to a speedy and public trial, by an im-partial jury of the State and district wherein the crime shall have been committed, which district shall have been previously ascertained by law, and to be in-formed of the nature and cause of the accusation; to be confronted with the witnesses against him; to have compulsory process for obtaining witnesses in his favor, and to have the Assistance of Counsel for his defence.

ARTICLE [VII.]

In Suits as common law, where the value in con-troversy shall exceed twenty dollars, the right of trial by jury shall be preserved, and no fact tried by a jury, shall be otherwise re-examined in any Court of the United States, than according to the rules of the com-mon law.

ARTICLE [VIII.]

Excessive bail shall not be required, nor exces-sive fines imposed, nor cruel and unusual punish-ments inflicted.

ARTICLE [IX.]

The enumeration in the Constitution, of certain rights, shall not be construed to deny or disparage others retained by the people.

ARTICLE [X.]

The powers not delegated to the United States by the Constitution, nor prohibited by it to the States, are reserved to the States respectively, or to the people.

ARTICLE [XI.]

The Judicial power of the United States shall not be construed to extend to any suit in law or equity, commenced or prosecuted against one of the United States by Citizens of another State, or by Citizens or Subjects of any Foreign State.

PROPOSAL AND RATIFICATION

The eleventh amendment to the Constitution of the United States was proposed to the legislatures of the several States by the Third Congress, on the 4th of March 1794; and was declared in a message from the President to Congress, dated the 8th of January, 1798, to have been ratified by the legislatures of three-fourths of the States. The dates of ratification

FIGURE 5-1   (continued)

Preamble to →
Constitution

PREAMBLE

WE THE PEOPLE of the United States, in Order to form a more perfect Union, establish Justice, insure domestic Tranquility, provide for the common defence, promote the general Welfare, and secure the Blessings of Liberty to ourselves and our Posterity, do ordain and establish this CONSTITUTION for the United States of America.

Editorial →
enhancement

WESTLAW ELECTRONIC RESEARCH

WESTLAW supplements your legal research in many ways, Westlaw allows you to

• update your research with the most current informantion
• expand your library with additional resources
• retrieve current, comprehensive history citing references to a case with KeyCite

For more information on using Westlaw to supplement your research, see the Westlaw Electronic Research Guide, which follows the explanation

Annotations →

NOTES OF DECISIONS

Formation of more perfect Union   3
Nature and function of Preamble   1
Ordainment and establishment of Constitution   6

Promotion of general welfare   4
Securing of liberty   5
United States of America   7
We the People   2

PREAMBLE

1. Nature and function of Preamble

The Preamble can never be resorted to, to enlarge the powers confided to the general government and can never be the legitimate source of any implied power, when otherwise drawn from the Constitution; its true office is to expound the nature, extent, and application of the powers actually conferred by the Constitution and not substantively to create them. U.S. v. Boyer, W.D.Mo.1898, 85 F. 425.

2. We the People

In our system, while sovereign powers are delegated to the agencies of government, sovereignty itself remains with the people, by whom and for whom all government exists and acts. Yick Wo v. Hopkins, U.S.Cal.1886, 6 S.Ct. 1064, 118 U.S. 356, 30 L.Ed. 220.

The Constitution of the United States was made by, and for the protection of, the people of the United States. League v. De Young, U.S.Tex.1850, 52 U.S. 185, 11 How. 185, 13 L.Ed. 657.

The Constitution was ordained and established by the people of the United States for themselves, for their own government and not for the government of the individual states; the people of the United States framed such a government for the United States as they supposed best adapted to their situation and best calculated to promote their interests.

Lessee, U.S.Va.1816, 14 U.S. 304, 4 L.Ed. 97, 1 Wheat. 304.

Under the Constitution we see the people acting as sovereigns of the whole country; and in the language of sovereignty, establishing a constitution by which it was their will that the state governments should be bound, and to which the state constitutions should be made to conform. Chisholm v. Georgia, U.S.Ga. 1793, 2 U.S. 419, 2 Dall. 419, 1 L.Ed. 440.

3. Formation of more perfect Union

The separate governments of the separate states, bound together by the Articles of Confederation alone, were not sufficient for the promotion of the general welfare of the people in respect to foreign nations, or for their complete protection as citizens of the confederated states; for this reason, the people of the United States, "in order to form a more perfect union, establish justice, insure domestic tranquillity, provide for the common defense, promote the general welfare, and secure the blessings of liberty" to themselves and their posterity, ordained and established the government of the United States, and defined its powers by a Constitution, which they adopted as its fundamental law and made its rule of action. U.S. v. Cruikshank, U.S.La.1875, 92 U.S. 542, 2 Otto 542, 23 L.Ed. 588.

The Federal Constitution created not a confederacy of states, but a government of individuals assumed that the govern-

FIGURE 5-2 Annotated Constitution (Preamble) as published in U.S.C.A.

Barron v. City of Baltimore, U.S.Md. 1833, 32 U.S. 243, 7 Pet. 243, 8 L.Ed. 672.

The Constitution emanated from the people, and was not the act of sovereign and independent states. M'Culloch v. State, U.S.Md.1819, 17 U.S. 316, 4 L.Ed. 579, 4 Wheat. 316.

The Constitution of the United States was ordained and established not by the states in their sovereign capacities, but emphatically, as the preamble of the Constitution declares, by "the people of the United States; there can be no doubt that it was competent to the people to invest the general government with all the powers which they might deem proper and necessary, to extend or restrain these powers according to their own good pleasure, and to give them a paramount and supreme authority. Martin v. Hunter's

ment and the Union which it created, and the states which were incorporated into the Union, would be indestructible and perpetual; as far as human means could accomplish such a work, it intended to make them so. White v. Hart, U.S.Ga. 1871, 80 U.S. 646, 20 L.Ed. 685, 13 Wall. 646.

The Constitution of the United States established a government, and not a league, compact, or partnership, and it was constituted by the people. Legal Tender Cases, U.S.Tex.1870, 79 U.S. 457, 20 L.Ed. 287, 12 Wall. 457. See, also, U.S., v. Cathcart, C.C.Ohio 1864, 1 Bond 556, 25 Fed.Cas. No. 14,756.

The union of the states began among the colonies, and grew out of common origin, mutual sympathies, kindred principles, similar interests, geographical relations, and received definite form, and character, and sanction from the Articles

FIGURE 5-2
(continued)

Reprinted with permission of Thomson/West

A Point to Remember

State constitutions should always be reviewed when researching a constitutional question. Remember that when you research an issue controlled by the Bill of Rights, your state constitution may give an individual more rights than he or she has under the U.S. Constitution. If this is the case, your research must focus on your state constitution and on cases that interpret your state constitution, as well as on the U.S. Constitution.

5-3 FEDERAL STATUTORY LAW

Enactment of Statutory Law

In the U.S. system of government, legislative bodies have the power to make laws. These laws are described as **statutory law**. Unlike case law, statutory law is not enacted to resolve a specific factual dispute. Instead, legislative bodies make rules or laws that apply to society in general. Statutory law governs many aspects of our lives, including traffic, domestic relations, criminal and civil liability, corporate operation, immigration, and homeland security. Statutory law comes from federal, state, and local governing bodies.

Federal statutory law includes those laws enacted by the United States Congress. Congress meets for two-year terms, each separate term given a number. For example, the Congress for the years 2007–2008 is referred to as the 110th Congress. Each year of Congress constitutes a separate session. One of the primary responsibilities of each Congress is the enactment of new legislation, which consists of the following steps.

statutory law. Law enacted through the legislative process.

Legislation Proposed   All federal laws begin with a proposal, known as a **bill.**

Bill Introduced   The bill is introduced into either the House of Representatives or the Senate and immediately assigned a number. This number is preceded by "H.R." if the bill is introduced into the House of Representatives, or "S" if the bill is introduced into the Senate. The bill retains this number throughout the legislative process. These numbers are important when researching the **legislative history** of any statute. Legislative histories are discussed later in this chapter.

Bill Referred to Committee   After a bill is introduced, it is referred to the appropriate committee for consideration. Both the House and the Senate have a number of standing committees that concentrate on certain matters. Once the bill is referred, the proper committee reviews and discusses the proposal, sometimes holding public hearings on the bill. If a committee looks favorably on a bill, it prepares a committee report with its recommendations and analysis of the bill.

Vote by Legislators   If a report is issued, the whole house then considers the bill and votes on it. If it receives a majority vote of approval, it is passed and sent to the other house.

Action by Other House   When referred to the other house, the bill goes through much the same process again. If the bill is amended or changed, a joint conference from both houses may convene to work out differences. Both houses must approve the same bill before it can be submitted to the president. Once passed by both houses, the bill is sent to the president for approval.

Executive Action   The president has the power to approve or to veto the bill. If the president does nothing with the bill, it is deemed approved after ten days unless Congress should adjourn within that ten-day period. If this happens, the bill is considered vetoed (pocket veto). If the president vetoes a bill, it can still be enacted as law if a two-thirds majority of each house votes to override the veto.

Initial Publication of Statutes

Laws enacted by Congress are categorized as either public laws or private laws. **Public laws** are those that concern the general public. For example, read the following code section:

bill.   Proposed legislation.

legislative history.   The proceedings that relate to a bill before it becomes law.

public laws.   Laws enacted by Congress that affect the public in general.

Title 50—War and National Defense

Sec. 403-4b. Transformation of Central Intelligence Agency

The Director of the Central Intelligence Agency shall, in accordance with standards developed by the Director in consultation with the Director of National Intelligence—

1. enhance the analytic, human intelligence, and other capabilities of the Central Intelligence Agency;

2. develop and maintain an effective language program within the Agency;

3. emphasize the hiring of personnel of diverse backgrounds for purposes of improving the capabilities of the Agency;

> **4.** establish and maintain effective relationships between human intelligence and signals intelligence within the Agency at the operational level; and
>
> **5.** achieve a more effective balance within the Agency with respect to unilateral operations and liaison operations.

(Pub. L. 108–458, title I, Sec. 1011(c), Dec. 17, 2004, 118 Stat. 3661.)

private laws. Laws enacted by Congress that affect only selected individuals.

slip law. First publication of a law; usually in pamphlet form.

code. A topical organization of statutes.

It is a public law because it regulates an agency that affects the general public.

Private laws are those that concern single individuals or groups. Private laws usually deal with matters such as naturalization or settlement of a claim by the government. See Figure 5-3 for an example of a private law. This law affects a specifically named individual, Orlando Wayne Naraysingh, regarding his specific immigration status.

After a bill completes the legislative process and is signed by the president (or a veto properly overridden), the law is labeled as either a public law or a private law and assigned a number. The number includes the number of the Congress and the chronological number of the bill. Thus, the first public law enacted by the 110th Congress is identified as Public Law 110-1. Remember that, at this point, the legislation has two numerical references: the original number of the bill (i.e., H.R. 1234) and the public or private law number assigned after passage.

As each law is passed, it is published by the government in pamphlet form, known as a **slip law.** At the end of each session of Congress, all of these laws are published in a book referred to as the *Statutes at Large.* The *Statutes at Large* publishes laws in chronological order. They are not organized according to topic or subject matter. As a result, the *Statutes at Large* (and slip laws) is extremely difficult to research. In order to alleviate this problem, federal statutes are codified (put into codes). A **code** is an organization by subject matter of all of the public laws found in statutes. Because of the way Congress works, it is not uncommon for one statute to contain many different kinds of laws that end up in different code sections. In recent years, when *Statutes at Large* is published, it contains margin references to the codes where the section of the statute will be included. See Figure 5-4 for a sample of a law found in the *Statutes at Large.* Note the different code sections affected by the one statute. Box 5-1 outlines the numerical history of the publication of 50 U.S.C. Section 403-4b, the federal statute located earlier in this Section.

5-4 UNITED STATES CODES

The United States Codes contain a consolidation of the general and permanent laws of the United States arranged topically. (Private laws are not included in the code.) The laws are organized according to subject matter in fifty separate title headings. For example, all laws regarding bankruptcy are arranged under the general topical heading of bankruptcy or Title 11 (see Table 5-1 for a list of subject matter headings). The general topics are arranged alphabetically. However, the titles are officially referred to numerically rather than by the topical name. Titles are further divided into sections. Each section is a separate law. Laws are referred to and cited by title and section.

For example, if you refer to the code section at the beginning of the chapter, you say, "Title 18, section 242 of the *United States Code.*" Of course, in speaking,

PRIVATE LAW 103-7—OCT. 22, 1994   108 STAT. 506

Private Law 103–6
103d Congress

An Act

FOR THE RELIEF OF ORLANDO WAYNE NARAYSINGH.   Oct. 22, 1994
[H.R. 2266]

*Be it enacted by the Senate and House of Representatives of the United States of America in
Congress assembled,*

SECTION I. IMMEDIATE RELATIVE STATUS FOR ORLANDO WAYNE NARAYSINGH.

(a) IN GENERAL.—Orlando Wayne Naraysingh shall be classified as a child under section
101(b)(1)(E) of the Immigration and Nationality Act for purposes of approval of a relative visa
petition filed under section 204 of such Act by his adoptive parent and the filing of an application for an immigrant visa or adjustment of status.

(b) ADJUSTMENT OF STATUS.—If Orlando Wayne Naraysingh enters the United States before the filing deadline specified in subsection (c), he shall be considered to have entered and
remained lawfully and shall, if otherwise eligible, be eligible for adjustment of status under section 245 of the Immigration and Nationality Act as of the date of the enactment of this Act.

(c) DEADLINE FOR APPLICATION AND PAYMENT OF FEES.—Subsections (a) and (b) shall
apply only if the petition and the application for issuance of an immigrant visa or the application for adjustment of status are filed with appropriate fees within 2 years after the date of the
enactment of this Act.

(d) REDUCTION OF IMMIGRANT VISA NUMBER.—Upon the granting of an immigrant visa
or permanent residence to Orlando Wayne Naraysingh, the Secretary of State shall instruct the
proper officer to reduce by 1, for the current or next following fiscal year, the worldwide level
of family-sponsored immigrants under section 201(c)(1)(A) of the Immigration and Nationality Act.

(e) DENIAL OF PREFERENTIAL IMMIGRATION TREATMENT FOR CERTAIN RELATIVES.—
The natural parents, brothers, and sisters of Orlando Wayne Naraysingh shall not, by virtue of
such relationship, be accorded any right, privilege, or status under the Immigration and Nationality Act.

Approved October 22, 1994.

Private Law 103–7
103d Congress

An Act

For the relief of Leteane Clement Monatei.   Oct. 22, 1994
[H.R. 2411]

*Be it enacted by the Senate and House of Representatives of the United States of America in
Congress assembled,*

SECTION I. IMMEDIATE RELATIVE STATUS FOR LETEANE CLEMENT MONATSI

(a) IN GENERAL.—Leteane Clement Monatsi shall be classified as a child under section
101(b)(1)(E) of the Immigration and Nationality Act for purposes of approval of a relative visa

**Note that private
← law applies only to
named individual.**

FIGURE 5-3
Private Law

lawyers often refer to the various codes by their more popular names, such as the
Bankruptcy Code. The code books contain popular name indexes so that researchers can find code sections by their common or popular name.

In researching statutory law, legal researchers generally search the codes rather
than the *Statutes at Large.* This is because the organization and indexing make the
codes much easier to use. When statutory law is organized and put into appropriate

codes, differences between the language of the statute and the language of the code occasionally occur. The law is the language that was approved by Congress. To eliminate confusion, Congress enacted several code titles as law. This allows researchers to rely on the code rather than the difficult-to-use *Statutes at Large*. Once approved, the code, rather than the statute at large, becomes the law and is called **positive law**. Code titles not reenacted are considered *evidence* of what the law is. That means that you can cite the code sections to a court.

positive law. Codes that were enacted into law by Congress.

PUBLIC LAW 103-322—SEPT. 13, 1994   ① 108 STAT. 1970

① **Note two references to same law.**

"(1) for murder, by death or life imprisonment, or a fine of not more than $250,000, or both; and for kidnapping, by imprisonment for any term of years or for life, or a fine of not more than $250,000, or both;".

(13) GENOCIDE.—Section 1091(b)(1) of title 18, United States Code, is amended by striking " a fine of not more than $1,000,000 or imprisonment for life," and inserting ", where death results, by death or imprisonment for life and a fine of not more than $1,000,000, or both;".

(14) CARJACKING.—Section 2119(3) of title 18, United States Code, is amended by striking the period after "both" and inserting ", or sentenced to death."; and by striking ", possessing a firearm as defined in section 921 of this title, and inserting ", with the intent to cause death or serious bodily harm". (b) CONFORMING AMENDMENT TO FEDERAL AVIATION ACT OF 1954.—Chapter 465 of title 49, United States Code, is amended—

(1) in the chapter analysis by striking "Death penalty sentencing procedure for aircraft piracy" and inserting "Repealed"; and

(2) by striking section 46503.

SEC. 60004. APPLICABILITY TO UNIFORM CODE OF MILITARY JUSTICE.

18 USC 3591 note

Chapter 228 of title 18, United States Code, as added by this title, shall not apply to prosecutions under the Uniform Code of Military Justice (10 U.S.C. 801).

SEC. 60005. DEATH PENALTY FOR MURDER BY A FEDERAL PRISONER.

(a) IN GENERAL.—Chapter 51 of title 18, United States Code, is amended by adding at the end the following new section:

"§ 1118. Murder by a Federal prisoner

"(a) OFFENSE.—A person who, while confined in a Federal correctional institution under a sentence for a term of life imprisonment, commits the murder of another shall be punished by death or by life imprisonment.

"(b) DEFINITIONS.—In this section—

"'Federal correctional institution' means any Federal prison, Federal correctional facility, Federal community program center, or Federal halfway house.

"'murder' means a first degree or second degree murder (as defined in section 1111).

"'term of life imprisonment' means a sentence for the term of natural life, a sentence commuted to natural life, an indeterminate term of a minimum of at least fifteen years and a maximum of life, or an unexecuted sentence of death.".

(b) TECHNICAL AMENDMENT.—The chapter analysis for chapter 51 of title 18, United States Code, is amended by adding at the end the following new item:

"1118. Murder by a Federal prisoner.".

SEC. 60006. DEATH PENALTY FOR CIVIL RIGHTS MURDERS.

(a) CONSPIRACY AGAINST RIGHTS.—Section 241 of title 18, United States Code, is amended by striking the period at the end of the last sentence and inserting ", or may be sentenced to death.".

(b) DEPRIVATION OF RIGHTS UNDER COLOR OF LAW.—Section 242 of title 18, United ← States Code, is amended by striking the period at the end of the last sentence and inserting ", or may be sentenced to death.".

This section amends 18 USC § 242.

FIGURE 5-4   Pages from *Statutes at Large*, Volume 108, pages 1970 and 1971

108 STAT. 1970   PUBLIC LAW 103-322—SEPT. 13, 1994

(c) FEDERALLY PROTECTED ACTIVITIES.— Section 245(b) of title 18, United States Code, is amended in the matter following paragraph (5) by inserting ", or may be sentenced to death" after "or for life".

(d) DAMAGE TO RELIGIOUS PROPERTY; OBSTRUCTION OF THE FREE EXERCISE OF RELIGIOUS RIGHTS.—Section 247(c)(1) of title 18, United States Code, is amended by inserting ", or may be sentenced to death" after "or both".

SEC. 60007. DEATH PENALTY FOR THE MURDER OF FEDERAL LAW ENFORCEMENT OFFICIALS.

Section 1114 of title 18, United States Code, is amended by striking "punished as provided under sections 1111 and 1112 of this title," and inserting "punished, in the case of murder, as provided under section 1111, or, in the case of manslaughter, as provided under section 1112."

Drive-By Shooting Prevention Act of 1994. 18 USC 36 note.

SEC. 60008. NEW OFFENSE FOR THE INDISCRIMINATE USE OF WEAPONS TO FURTHER DRUG CONSPIRACIES.

(a) SHORT TITLE.—This section may be cited as the "Drive-By Shooting Prevention Act of 1994".

(b) IN GENERAL.—Chapter 2 of title 18, United States Code, is amended by adding at the end the following new section:

"§ 36. Drive-by-shooting

"(a) DEFINITION.—In this section, 'major drug offense' means—

"(1) a continuing criminal enterprise punishable under section 403(c) of the Controlled Substances Act (21 U.S.C. 848(c));

"(2) a conspiracy to distribute controlled substances punishable under section 406 of the Controlled Substances Act (21 U.S.C. 846) section 1013 of the Controlled Substances Import and Export Control Act (21 U.S.C. 963); or

"(3) an offense involving major quantities of drugs and punishable under section 401(b)(1)(A) of the Controlled Substances Act (21 U.S.C. 841(b)(1)(A)) or section 1010(b)(1) of the Controlled Substances Import and Export Act (21 U.S.C. 960(b)(1)).

"(b) OFFENSE AND PENALTIES.—(1) A person who, in furtherance or to escape detection of a major drug offense and with the intent to intimidate, harass, injure, or maim, fires a weapon into a group of two or more persons and who, in the course of such conduct, causes grave risk to any human life shall be punished by a term of no more than 25 years, by fine under this title, or both.

"(2) A person who, in furtherance or to escape detection of a major drug offense and with the intent to intimidate, harass, injure, or maim, fires a weapon into a group of 2 or more persons and who, in the course of such conduct, kills any person shall, if the killing—

"(A) is a first degree murder (as defined in section 1111(a)), be punished by death or imprisonment for any term of years or for life, fined under this title, or both; or

"(B) is a murder other than a first degree murder (as defined in section 1111(a)), be fined under this title, imprisoned for any term of years or for life, or both."

FIGURE 5-4
(continued)

BOX 5-1 NUMERICAL HISTORY OF A CODE SECTION

Public Law 108-458	The initial publication of the law in pamphlet format
118 Stat. 3661 (Volume 118 of the *Statutes at Large,* page 3661)	The publication of the law at the end of the session of Congress, along with all public laws enacted during the same session; Laws are published in chronological order
50 U.S.C. §403-4b (Title 50 of the *United States Code,* section 403-4b)	The publication of the law in the *United States Codes* where laws are topically organized

TABLE 5-1   Title Headings for U.S. Code and Administrative Regulations

U.S. Code	*Code of Federal Regulations*
Topic Heading	Topic Heading
1. General Provisions	1. General Provisions
2. The Congress	2. The Congress (reserved)
3. The President	3. The President
4. Flag and Seal, Seat of Government, and the States	4. Accounts
5. Government Organization and Employees	5. Administrative Personnel
6. Domestic Security	6. Homeland Security
7. Agriculture	7. Agriculture
8. Aliens and Nationality	8. Aliens and Nationality
9. Arbitration	9. Animals and Animal Products
10. Armed Forces	10. Energy
11. Bankruptcy	11. Federal Elections
12. Banks and Banking	12. Banks and Banking
13. Census	13. Business Credit and Assistance
14. Coast Guard	14. Aeronautics and Space
15. Commerce and Trade	15. Commerce and Foreign Trade
16. Conservation	16. Commercial Practices
17. Copyrights	17. Commodity and Securities Exchange
18. Crimes and Criminal Procedure	18. Conservation of Power and Water Resources
19. Customs Duties	19. Customs Duties
20. Education	20. Employees' Benefits
21. Food and Drugs	21. Food and Drugs
22. Foreign Relations and Intercourse	22. Foreign Relations
23. Highways	23. Highways
24. Hospitals and Asylums	24. Housing and Urban Development
25. Indians	25. Indians
26. Internal Revenue Code	26. Internal Revenue
27. Intoxicating Liquors	27. Alcohol, Tobacco Products, and Firearms
28. Judiciary and Judicial Procedure	28. Judicial Administration
29. Labor	29. Labor
30. Mineral Lands and Mining	30. Mineral Resources
31. Money and Finance	31. Money and Finance: Treasury
32. National Guard	32. National Defense
33. Navigation and Navigable Waters	33. Navigation and Navigable Waters
34. Navy (eliminated by the enactment of Title 10)	34. Education
35. Patents	35. Panama Canal (reserved)
36. Patriotic and National Observances, Ceremonies, and Organizations	36. Parks, Forests, and Public Property
37. Pay and Allowances of the Uniformed Services	37. Patents, Trademarks and Copyrights
38. Veterans' Benefits	38. Pensions, Bonuses, and Veterans' Relief
39. Postal Service	39. Postal Service
40. Public Buildings, Property, and Works	40. Protection of the Environment
41. Public Contracts	41. Public Contracts and Property Management

TABLE 5-1 *(continued)*

U.S. Code	Code of Federal Regulations
42. The Public Health and Welfare	42. Public Health
43. Public Lands	43. Public Lands: Interior
44. Public Printing and Documents	44. Emergency Management and Assistance
45. Railroads	45. Public Welfare
46. Shipping	46. Shipping
47. Telegraphs, Telephones, and Radio-telegraphs	47. Telecommunications
48. Territories and Insular Possessions	48. Federal Acquisition Regulations System
49. Transportation	49. Transportation
50. War and National Defense	50. Wildlife and Fisheries

Legislative Histories

Once in a while, a legal dispute arises regarding the meaning of a particular code section. When this happens in connection with a factual dispute, the court is called upon to interpret the code section. The court gives great weight to the **legislative intent** behind the law. The legislative intent is what the legislature intended to accomplish by passing the law. While no one can absolutely prove what was in the minds of all the legislators when the law was enacted, various documents help the court make this determination. The original language of the bill and changes made to that language often provide evidence of intent. Transcripts of committee hearings and transcripts of debates on the bill also help.

legislative intent. The purpose of the legislature in passing a law.

Rather than seeking the originals of these records, a researcher can use *United States Code and Congressional and Administrative News* (U.S.C.C.A.N.). This contains the legislative history of statutes, federal regulations, and court rules. It contains bills in their original format, changes, and committee hearings and discussions. Determining the meaning of any code section is more involved than simply looking at legislative intent. The following chapter discusses this in more detail.

United States Code Publications

There are three main publications of the Unites States Code: the *United States Code*, published by the Government Printing Office, the *United States Code Annotated*, published by Thomson/West, and the *United States Code Service*, now published by Lexis Law Publishing. The *United States Code* (abbreviated U.S.C.) contains only the statutory language of the code. On the other hand, both *United States Code Annotated* (abbreviated U.S.C.A.) and the *United States Code Service* (abbreviated U.S.C.S.) are annotated editions of the code. An annotated version of a code contains references to cases that interpret the code section along with references to other legal sources that explain the code section. The annotations that are not part of the code are added by the publisher and are intended to assist the researcher. See Figures 5-5A, 5-5B, and 5-5C for examples of a code section found in each of these three sources.

There is, however, one difference between the *United States Code Annotated* and the *United States Code Service*. The U.S.C.A. uses the exact language found in the *United States Code*. The U.S.C.S. uses the exact language found in the *Statutes at Large*. In most cases, this presents no problem to the researcher who can usually use either source. All versions of the United States Code can be found online. The U.S.C.A. is

CHAPTER 13—CIVIL RIGHTS

Sec.
241.   Conspiracy against rights.
242.   Deprivation of rights under color of law.
243.   Exclusion of jurors on account of race or color.
244.   Discrimination against person wearing uniform of armed forces.
245.   Federally protected activities.
246.   Deprivation of relief benefits.
247.   Damage to religious property; obstruction of persons in the free exercise of religious beliefs.
248.   Freedom of access to clinic entrances.

AMENDMENTS

1994—Pub. L. 103–322, title XXXIII, § 330023(a)(1), Sept. 13, 1994, 108 Stat. 2150, substituted "Freedom of access to clinic entrances" for "Blocking access to reproductive health services" in item 248.

Pub. L. 103–259, § 4, May 26, 1994, 108 Stat. 697, added item 248.

1988—Pub. L. 100–690, title VII, § 7018(b)(2), Nov. 18, 1988, 102 Stat. 4396, struck out "of citizens" after "rights" in item 241.

Pub. L. 100–346, § 3, June 24, 1988, 102 Stat. 645, added item 247.

1976—Pub. L. 94–453, § 4(b), Oct. 2, 1976, 90 Stat. 1517, added item 246.

1968—Pub. L. 90–284, title I, § 102, Apr. 11, 1968, 82 Stat. 75, added item 245.

§ 241. Conspiracy against rights

If two or more persons conspire to injure, oppress, threaten, or intimidate any person in any State, Territory, or District in the free exercise or enjoyment of any right or privilege secured to him by the Constitution or laws of the United States, or because of his having so exercised the same; or

If two or more persons go in disguise on the highway, or on the premises of another, with intent to prevent or hinder his free exercise or enjoyment of any right or privilege so secured—

They shall be fined under this title or imprisoned not more than ten years, or both; and if death results from the acts committed in violation of this section or if such acts include kidnapping or an attempt to kidnap, aggravated sexual abuse or an attempt to commit aggravated sexual abuse, or an attempt to kill, they shall be fined under this title or imprisoned for any term of years or for life, or both, or may be sentenced to death.

(June 25, 1948, ch. 645, 62 Stat. 696; Apr. 11, 1968, Pub. L. 90–284, title I, § 103(a), 82 Stat. 75; Nov. 18, 1988, Pub. L. 100–690, title VII, § 7018(a), (b)(1), 102 Stat. 4396; Sept. 13, 1994, Pub. L. 103–322, title VI, § 60006(a), title XXXII, §§ 320103(a), 320201(a), title XXXIII, § 330016(1)(L), 108 Stat. 1970, 2109, 2113, 2147.)

HISTORICAL AND REVISION NOTES

Based on title 18, U.S.C., 1940 ed., § 51 (Mar. 4, 1909, ch. 321, § 19, 35 Stat. 1092).

Clause making conspirator ineligible to hold office was omitted as incongruous because it attaches ineligibility to hold office to a person who may be a private citizen and who was convicted of conspiracy to violate a specific statute. There seems to be no reason for imposing such a penalty in the case of one individual crime, in view of the fact that other crimes do not carry such a severe consequence. The experience of the Department of Justice is that this unusual penalty has been an obstacle to successful prosecutions for violations of the act.

Mandatory punishment provision was rephrased in the alternative.

Minor changes in phraseology were made.

AMENDMENTS

1994—Pub. L. 103–322, § 320201(a), substituted "person in any State" for "inhabitant of any State" in first par.

Pub. L. 103–322, §§ 320103(a)(1), 330016(I)(L), amended section identically, substituting "They shall be fined under this title" for "They shall be fined not more than $10,000" in third par.

Pub. L. 103–322, § 320103(a)(2)–(4), in third par., substituted "results from the acts committed in violation of this section or if such acts include kidnapping or an attempt to kidnap, aggravated sexual abuse or an attempt to commit aggravated sexual abuse, or an attempt to kill, they shall be fined under this title or imprisoned for any term of years or for life, or both" for "results, they shall be subject to imprisonment for any term of years or for life".

Pub. L. 103–322, § 60006(a), substituted ", or may be sentenced to death." for period at end of third par.

1988—Pub. L. 100–690 struck out "of citizens" after "rights" in section catchline and substituted "inhabitant of any State, Territory, or District" for "citizen" in text.

1968—Pub. L. 90–284 increased limitation on fines from $5,000 to $10,000 and provided for imprisonment for any term of years or for life when death results.

CROSS REFERENCES

Action for neglect to prevent, see section 1986 of Title 42, The Public Health and Welfare.

Conspiracy to commit offense or to defraud United States, see section 371 of this title.

Conspiracy to interfere with civil rights, see section 1985 of Title 42, The Public Health and Welfare.

Proceedings in vindication of civil rights, see section 1988 of Title 42.

§ 242. Deprivation of rights under color of law

Whoever, under color of any law, statute, ordinance, regulation, or custom, willfully subjects any

U.S. Code provides amendments and cross annotations but no case decisions.

Note amendment from Pub. L 103–322 (Figure 5-4).

FIGURE 5-5A
U.S.C. (United States Code)

person in any State, Territory, or District to the deprivation of any rights, privileges or immunities secured or protected by the Constitution or laws of the United States, or to different punishments, pains, or penalties, on account of such person being an alien, or by reason of his color, or race, than are prescribed for the punishment of citizens, shall be fined under this title or imprisoned not more than one year, or both; and if bodily injury results from the acts committed in violation of this section or if such acts include the use, attempted use, or threatened use of a dangerous weapon, explosives, or fire, shall be fined under this title or imprisoned not more than ten years, or both; and if death results from the acts committed in violation of this section or if such acts include kidnapping or an attempt to kidnap, aggravated sexual abuse, or an attempt to commit aggravated sexual abuse, or an attempt to kill, shall be fined under this title, or imprisoned for any term of years or for life, or both, or may be sentenced to death.

(June 25, 1948, ch. 645, 62 Stat. 696; Apr. 11, 1968, Pub. L. 90–284, title I, § 103(b), 82 Stat. 75; Nov. 18, 1988, Pub. L. 100–690, title VII, § 7019, 102 Stat. 4396; Sept. 13, 1994, Pub. L. 103–322, title VI, § 60006(b), title XXXII, §§ 320103(b), 320201(b), title XXXIII, § 330016(1)(H), 108 Stat. 1970, 2109, 2113, 2147.)

HISTORICAL AND REVISION NOTES

Based on title 18, U.S.C., 1940 ed., § 52 (Mar. 4, 1909, ch. 321, § 20, 35 Stat. 1092).

Reference to persons causing or procuring was omitted as unnecessary in view of definition of "principal" in section 2 of this title.

A minor change was made in phraseology.

AMENDMENTS

1994—Pub. L. 103–322, § 320201(b), substituted "any person in any State" for "any inhabitant of any State" and "on account of such person" for "on account of such inhabitant".

Pub. L. 103–322, §§ 320103(b)(1), 330016(1)(H), amended section identically, substituting "shall be fined under this title" for "shall be fined not more than $1,000" after "citizens,".

Pub. L. 103–322, § 320103(b)(2)–(5), substituted "bodily injury results from the acts committed in violation of this section or if such acts include the use, attempted use, or threatened use of a dangerous weapon, explosives, or fire, shall be fined under this title or imprisoned not more than ten years, or both; and if death results from the acts committed in violation of this section or if such acts include kidnapping or an attempt to kidnap, aggravated sexual abuse, or an attempt to commit aggravated sexual abuse, or an attempt to kill, shall be fined under this title, or imprisoned for any term of years or for life, or both" for "bodily injury results shall be fined under this title or imprisoned nor more than ten years, or both; and if

death results shall be subject to imprisonment for any term of years or for life".

Pub. L. 103–322, § 60006(b), inserted before period at end ", or may be sentenced to death".

1988—Pub. L. 100–690 inserted "and if bodily injury results shall be fined under this title or imprisoned not more than ten years, or both;" after "or both;".

1968—Pub. L. 90–284 provided for imprisonment for any term of years or for life when death results.

CROSS REFERENCES

Civil action for deprivation of rights, see section 1983 of Title 42, The Public Health and Welfare.

Equal rights under the law, see section 1981 of Title 42.

Minor offenses tried by United States magistrate judges as excluding offenses punishable under this section, see section 3401 of this title.

Proceedings in vindication of civil rights, see section 1988 of Title 42, The Public Health and Welfare.

§ 243. Exclusion of jurors on account of race or color

No citizen possessing all other qualifications which are or may be prescribed by law shall be disqualified for service as grand or petit juror in any court of the United States, or of any State on account of race, color, or previous condition of servitude; and whoever, being an officer or other person charged with any duty in the selection or summoning of jurors, excludes or fails to summon any citizen for such cause, shall be fined not more than $5,000.

(June 25, 1948, ch. 645, 62 Stat. 696.)

HISTORICAL AND REVISION NOTES

Based on section 44 of title 8, U.S.C., 1940 ed., Aliens and Nationality (Mar. 1, 1875, ch. 114, §4, 18 Stat 336).

Words "be deemed guilty of a misdemeanor, and" were deleted as unnecessary in view of definition of misdemeanor in section 1 of this title.

Words "on conviction thereof" were omitted as unnecessary, since punishment follows only after conviction.

Minimum punishment provisions were omitted. (See reviser's note under section 203 of this title.)

Minor changes in phraseology were made.

FEDERAL RULES OF CIVIL PROCEDURE

Jurors, see rule 47, Title 28, Appendix, Judiciary and Judicial Procedure.

FEDERAL RULES OF CRIMINAL PROCEDURE

Grand jury, see rule 6, Appendix to this title.
Trial jurors, see rule 24.

FIGURE 5-5A
(continued)

Bribery of public officials and witnesses, see section 201 of this title.

Civil rights generally, see section 1981 et seq. of Title 42, The Public Health and Welfare.

Exclusion or excuse from jury service, see section 1863 of Title 28, Judiciary and Judicial Procedure.

Grand jurors, number of and summoning additional jurors, see section 3321 of this title.

Juries generally, see section 1861 et seq. of Title 28, Judiciary and Judicial Procedure.

Manner of drawing jurors, see section 1864 of Title 28.

Qualifications of jurors, see section 1861 of Title 28.

Summoning jurors, see section 1867 of Title 28.

§ 244. Discrimination against person wearing uniform of armed forces

Whoever, being a proprietor, manager, or employee of a theater or other public place of entertainment or amusement in the District of Columbia, or in any Territory, or Possession of the United States, causes any person wearing the uniform of any of the armed forces of the United States to be discriminated against because of that uniform, shall be fined under this title.

(June 25, 1948, ch. 645, 62 Stat. 697; May 24, 1949, ch. 139, §5, 63 Stat. 90; Sept. 13, 1994, Pub. L. 103–322, title XXXIII, § 330016(1)(G), 108 Stat. 2147.)

Historical and Revision Notes

1948 Act

Based on title 18, U.S.C., 1940 ed., § 523 (Mar. 1, 1911, ch. 187, 36 Stat. 963; Aug. 24, 1912, ch. 387, § 1, 37 Stat. 512; Jan. 28, 1915, ch. 20, § 1, 38 Stat. 800).

Words "guilty of a misdemeanor", following "shall be", were omitted as unnecessary in view of definition of "misdemeanor" in section 1 of this title. (See revisioner's note under section 212 of this title.)

Changes were made in phraseology.

1949 Act

This section [section 5] substitutes, in section 244 of title 18, U.S.C., "any of the armed forces of the United States" for the enumeration of specific branches and thereby includes the Air Force, formerly part of the Army. This clarification is necessary because of the establishment of the Air Force as a separate branch of the Armed Forces by the act of July 26, 1947.

Amendments

1994—Pub. L. 103–322 substituted "fined under this title" for "fined not more than $500".

1949—Act May 24, 1949, substituted "any of the armed forces of the United States" for enumeration of the specific branches.

Cross References

Uniforms, wearing without authority, see section 702 of this title.

FIGURE 5-5A
(continued)

---

18 § 241
Note 64

CRIMES   Part 1

repetition in testimony and to properly restrict examination of witnesses by multiple counsel and were not prejudicial. Posey v. U. S., C.A.5 (Miss.) 1969, 416 F.2d 545, certiorari denied 90 S.Ct. 964, 397 U.S. 946, 25 L.Ed.2d 127, rehearing denied 90 S.Ct. 1267, 397 U.S. 1031, 25 L.Ed.2d 544, certiorari denied 90 S.Ct. 965, 397 U.S. 946, 25 L.Ed.2d 127, certiorari denied 90 S.Ct. 966, 397 U.S. 946, 25 L.Ed.2d 127.

In prosecution for conspiracy against citizens' rights in violation of election laws, that prosecution cross-examined adverse witness regarding statements which he had given to federal bureau of investigation during investigation preceding prosecution did not require reversal of convictions where at time statements were read defendants made no objection or any suggestion that it was inadmissible and court had instructed that what the witness had said in court was her evidence. Fields v. U.S., C.A.4 (Va.) 1955, 228 F.2d 544, certiorari denied 76 S.Ct. 468, 350 U.S. 982, 100 L.Ed. 850.

victed of conspiracy to oppress laborers in enjoyment of their federal right to be free from involuntary servitude resulting in the death of one laborer, and only one conspiracy had been charged and proven at trial, since verdict with regard to first defendant was a legally unassailable product of jury lenity. U.S. v. Harris, C.A.4 (N.C.) 1983, 701 F.2d 1095, certiorari denied 103 S.Ct. 3554, 463 U.S. 1214, 77 L.Ed.2d 1400.

In prosecution of members of "special" investigations unit of White House for conspiracy to violate constitutional rights of psychiatrist by burglarizing psychiatrist's office in search of records on patient who had allegedly "leaked" classified government documents, the court reversed a conviction on the ground that the trial judge had erred in applying the general rule that mistake of law is not a defense, and had failed to permit consideration by the jury under one of the exceptions to that rule; Judge Wilkey, on the theory of reasonable and good faith

FIGURE 5-5B
U.S.C.A. (United States Code Annotated)

65. Reversal

Conviction of one defendant of conspiracy to oppress laborers in enjoyment of their federal right to be free from involuntary servitude not resulting in death was not subject to reversal even though defendant's two coconspirators were convicted on the theory of action in reliance on the apparent authority of an official by citizens recruited to aid him on a special assignment, and Judge Merhige, on the theory of action in reliance on a government official's misstatement of the law. U. S. v. Barker, C.A.D.C. 1976, 546 F.2d 940, 178 U.S.App.D.C. 174.

§ 242. Deprivation of rights under color of law

Whoever, under color of any law, statute, ordinance, regulation, or custom, willfully subjects any person in any State, Territory, Commonwealth, Possession, or District to the deprivation of any rights, privileges, or immunities secured or protected by the Constitution or laws of the United States, or to different punishments, pains, or penalties, on account of such person being an alien, or by reason of his color, or race, than are prescribed for the punishment of citizens, shall be fined under this title or imprisoned not more than one year, or both; and if bodily injury results from the acts committed in violation of this section or if such acts include the use, attempted use, or threatened use of a dangerous weapon, explosives, or fire, shall be fined under this title or imprisoned not more than ten years, or both; and if death results from the acts committed in violation of this section or if such acts include kidnapping or an attempt to kidnap, aggravated sexual abuse, or an attempt to commit aggravated sexual abuse, or an attempt to kill, shall be fined under this title, or

770

Ch. 13 CIVIL RIGHTS   18 § 242 ← ① The top of each page in U.S.C.A. contains a header identifying the title and section.

imprisoned for any term of years or for life, or both, or may be sentenced to death.

(June 25, 1948, c. 645, 62 Stat. 696; Apr. 11, 1968, Pub.L. 90–284, Title I, § 103(b), 82 Stat. 75; Nov. 18, 1988, Pub.L. 100–690, Title VII, § 7019, 102 Stat. 4396; Sept. 13, 1994, Pub.L. 103–322, Title VI, § 60006(b), Title XXXII, §§ 320103(b), 320201(b), Title XXXIII, § 330016(1)(H), 108 Stat. 1970, 2109, 2113, 2147; Oct. 11, 1996, Pub.L. 104–294, Title VI, §§ 604(b)(14)(B), 607(a), 110 Stat. 3507, 3511.)

HISTORICAL AND STATUTORY NOTES

Revision Notes and Legislative Reports

1948 Acts. Based on Title 18, U.S.C., 1940 ed., § 52 (Mar. 4, 1909, c. 321, § 20, 35 Stat. 1092 [Derived from R.S. § 5510]).

Reference to persons causing or procuring was omitted as unnecessary in view of definition of "principal" in § 2 of this title.

A minor change was made in phraseology. 80th Congress House Report No. 304.

1968 Acts. Senate Report No. 721, see 1968 U.S. Code Cong. and Adm. News, p. 1837.

vation of any rights, privileges, or immunities secured or protected by the Constitution or laws of the United States, or to different punishments, pains, or penalties, on account of such inhabitant being an alien, or by reason of his color, or race, than are prescribed for the punishment of citizens, shall be fined not more than $1,000 or imprisoned not more than one year, or both; and if bodily injury results shall be fined under this title or imprisoned not more than ten years, or both; and if death results, shall be subject to imprisonment for any term of years or for life." See Repeals note set out under this section.

FIGURE 5-5B
(continued)

1988 Acts. For Related Reports, see 1988 U.S. Code Cong. and Adm. News, p. 5937.

1994 Acts. House Report Nos. 103–324 and 103–489, and House Conference Report No. 103–711, see 1994 U.S. Code Cong. and Adm. News, p. 1801.

1996 Acts. House Report No. 104–788, see 1996 U.S. Code Cong. and Adm. News, p. 4021.

Amendments

1996 Amendments. Pub.L. 104–294, § 604(b)(14)(B), repealed duplicative amendment by section 320103(b)(1) of Pub.L. 103–322, which required no change in text. See Repeals and Effective Date notes under this section.

Pub.L. 104–294, § 607(a), substituted "any State, Territory, Commonwealth, Possession, or District" for "any State, Territory, or District".

1994 Amendments. Pub.L. 103–322, §§ 60006(b), 320103(b), 320201(b), amended section generally. Prior to amendment section read as follows: "Whoever, under color of any law, statute, ordinance, regulation, or custom, willfully subjects any inhabitant of any State, Territory, or District to the depri-

Pub.L. 103–322, § 330016(1)(H), directed that, in text, the phrase "under this title" be substituted for the phrase "not more than $1,000" after "punishment of citizens, shall be fined". Identical amendment was made by section 320103(b)(1) of Pub.L. 103–322.

1988 Amendments. Pub.L. 100–690 inserted "and if bodily injury results shall be fined under this title or imprisoned not more than ten years, or both;" after "or both;".

1968 Amendments. Pub.L. 90–284 provided for imprisonment for any term of years or for life when death results.

Effective and Applicability Provisions

1996 Acts. Amendment by section 604 of Pub.L. 104–294 effective Sept. 13, 1994, see section 604(d) of Pub.L. 104–294, set out as a note under section 13 of this title.

Repeals

Pub.L. 103–322, Title XXXII, § 320103(b)(1), Sept. 13, 1994, 108 Stat. 2109, appearing in the credit of this section, was repealed by Pub.L. 104–294, Title VI, § 604(b)(14)(B), Oct. 11, 1996, 110 Stat. 3507.

---

18 § 242   CRIMES   Part 1

CROSS REFERENCES

Civil action for deprivation of rights, see 42 USCA § 1983.
Equal rights under the law, see 42 USCA § 1981.
Misdemeanors tried by United States magistrates as excluding offenses punishable under this section, see 18 USCA § 3401.
Proceedings in vindication of civil rights, see 42 USCA § 1988.

FEDERAL SENTENCING GUIDELINES

See Federal Sentencing Guidelines §§ 2H1.4, 2H2.1, 18 USCA.

LIBRARY REFERENCES

Administrative Law

Civil liability of local officials, see West's Federal Administrative Practice § 12124.
Voting rights, see West's Federal Administrative Practice § 12281 et seq.

American Digest System

Conspiracy ⟂29.5.

Encyclopedias

Conspiracy, see C.J.S. § 57(1).
RICO (Racketeer Influenced and Corrupt Organizations), see C.J.S. § 12.
Police Misconduct Litigation—Plaintiff's Remedies, 15 Am Jur Trials, p. 555.

Law Review and Journal Commentaries

Balancing the Fourth Amendment scales: The bad-faith "exception" to exclusionary rule limitations. George C. Thomas III, and Barry S. Pollack 45 Hastings L.J. 21 (1993).
Blue by day and white by [k]night: Regulating the political affiliations of law enforcement and military personnel. Robin D. Barnes, 81 Iowa L.Rev. 1079 (1996).
Criminalization of employer fraud against alien employees? A national priority. Roshani M. Gunewardene, 25 New Eng.L.Rev. 795 (1991).
Decertification of police: An alternative to traditional remedies for police misconduct. Roger Goldman and Steven Puro, 15 Hastings Const.L.Q. 51 (1987)

FIGURE 5-5B
(continued)

Texts and Treatises

Civil rights—deprivation under color of state law, see Devitt and Blackmar § 27.01 et seq.

Construction of under color of law by courts, see Wright, Miller & Cooper Jurisdiction § 3573.

Illegally seized evidence, exclusionary rule, see LaFave and Israel § 3.1.

Mistake or ignorance of law as defense, see Robinson § 62.

Civil Rights, 6 Fed Proc L Ed §§ 11:954, 955, 957, 960, 961, 963, 972.

WESTLAW ELECTRONIC RESEARCH

Conspiracy cases: 9·1k[add key number].

See WESTLAW guide following the Explanation pages of this volume.

Notes of Decisions

Admissibility of evidence 44
Amendment of indictment 32
Arrest, deprivation of rights 13
Assault and battery, deprivation of rights 14
Bill of particulars 35
Bodily injury, deprivation of rights 15
Burden of proof 42

Civil remedies 28
Color of law 21
Conspiracy 22
Constitutionality 1
Construction 2
Construction with other laws 3
Contraband 24
Cross-examination 46

Ch 13 CIVIL RIGHTS	18 § 242
	Note 1

Defenses 23
Deprivation of rights 12-19
   Generally 12
   Arrest 13
   Assault and battery 14
   Bodily injury 15
   Education 16
   Elections 17
   Homicide 18
   Particular acts 19
Double jeopardy 26
Education, deprivation of rights 16
Elections deprivation of rights 17
Elements of offense 6
Evidentiary hearing 38
Fair warning requirement 25
Harmless or prejudicial error 51
Homicide, deprivation of rights 18
Indictment 31-33
   Generally 31
   Amendment of indictment 32
   Sufficiency of indictment 33
Information 34
Inhabitants 11
Instructions 48
Judicial notice 43
Jurisdiction 30
Jury trial 41
Knowledge 8
Limitations 27
Mistrial 49
Motion to dismiss 37
New trial 50
Official witnesses 10
Particular acts, deprivation of rights 19
Persons liable 9
Pretrial suspension 39
Private right of action 29
Purpose 5
Questions for jury 47
Res judicata 40
Review 53
Selective prosecution 20
State criminal laws 4

1951, 71 S.Ct. 576, 341 U.S. 97, 95 L.Ed. 774.

Amendments to criminal statutes prohibiting conspiracies to deprive another person of his civil rights and proscribing actual deprivation of civil rights of another person, to set punishment in instances in which "death results," did not have effect of creating new "death resulting" crimes having similar elements, but were intended to add "death resulting" as factor that would justify enhanced sentences; victim's death was not element of either offense, but simply aggravating circumstance, which gave district court authority to impose harsher punishment. Catala Fonfrias v. U.S., C.A.1 (Puerto Rico) 1991, 951 F.2d 423, certiorari denied 113 S.Ct. 105, 506 U.S. 834, 121 L.Ed.2d 64.

This section making it a crime to, under color of law, subject a person to the deprivation of any federal right, privilege or immunity on account of said person's color or race is not unconstitutionally vague in further providing "* * * if death results shall be subject to imprisonment for any term of years or for life," notwithstanding defendant's argument that the law does not provide any means to follow the causal connections between the death and the acts of violating civil rights. U. S. v. Hayes, C.A.5 (Tex.) 1979, 589 F.2d 811, rehearing denied 591 F.2d 1343, certiorari denied 100 S.Ct. 93, 444 U.S. 847, 62 L.Ed.2d 60.

The states, in adopting U.S.C.A.Const. Amend. 14, expressly delegated to Congress the power to provide for the enforcement of its provisions by appropriate legislation, and former § 52 of this title [now this section] was enacted in the exercise of such power. Culp v. U. S., C.C.A.8 (Ark.) 1942. 131 F.2d 93.

FIGURE 5-5B
(continued)

---

1 Constitutionality

This section, as applied to sustain a conviction for obtaining a confession by use of force and violence by private detective acting under semblance of policeman's power, was not unconstitutional on theory that no specific standard of guilt was provided. Williams v. U.S., U.S.Fla.

A right or immunity, whether created by federal constitution or only guaranteed thereby, even without any express delegation of power, may be protected by Congress. Culp v. U. S., C.C.A.8 (Ark.) 1942, 131 F 2d 93.

Actions of 400-pound correctional officer in stepping on prison inmate's penis on three separate occasions did not constitute de minimis application of force and were of nature repugnant to conscience of mankind, satisfying objective element of Eighth Amendment violation necessary to conviction for criminal violation of rights under color of law, where

18 § 242	CRIMES Part 1
Note 19	

denied 85 S.Ct. 649, 379 U.S. 972, 13 L.Ed.2d 564.

No duty existed on part of Florida state attorney, either by statute or any principle of common law, to make application to trial judge for release of prisoner after directed verdict of not guilty on charge of murder, following which the prisoner was detained until state should prepare information charging him as an accessory after the facts, and thus the failure of the state attorney to procure the release of the prisoner did not subject the state attorney to a prosecution under this section. U. S. v. Hunter, C.A.5 (Fla.) 1954, 214 F.2d 356, certiorari denied 75 S.Ct. 208, 348 U.S. 888, 99 L.Ed. 698.

Town officers did not have duty to disperse crowd of more than thirty white persons assembled at apartment building located in area inhabited by white persons, and in which a Negro had rented an apartment, regardless of danger to themselves, even though it appeared that there was reasonable cause to fear that persons assembled would create a disturbance of peace, it being duty of officers under statute to go among persons assembled, or as near to them as was safe, and to command crowd to disperse, and if crowd did not. disperse, to command assistance of all persons present in arresting persons unlawfully assembled. U. S. v. Konovsky, C.A.7 (Ill.) 1953, 202 F.2d 721.

Where deputy sheriff undertook active and unwarranted steps to subject victims to affirmative indignities solely by reason of their membership in a religious sect and their practices founded on their beliefs and failed to protect the victims from group violence or to arrest members of mob who insulted the victims, the acts of the deputy sheriff constituted a violation of his common-law duty, and his dereliction in such respect was violation of former § 52 of this title [now this section]. Catlette v. U. S., C.C.A.4 (W.Va.) 1943, 132 F.2d 902.

Information describing in detail a statewide conspiracy against "Freedom Rid-

dom Riders" to travel interstate had been detected and that information should have been transmitted to Department of Justice. Bergman v. U. S., W.D. Mich 1983, 565 F.Supp. 1353.

Violation of F.S.A. § 925.05 by a prison officer in inflicting illegal punishment on a state prisoner for alleged violation of prison regulations does not subject such officer to prosecution under this section U. S. v. Walker, N.D.Fla. 1954, 121 F.Supp. 458, reversed 216 F 2d 683, certiorari denied 75 S.Ct. 450, 348 U.S. 959 99 L.Ed. 748.

20. Selective prosecution

Statistics revealing some selectivity in enforcement of the law do not alone establish that defendant is victim of selective prosecution. U. S. v. Carson, D.C.Conn.1977, 434 F.Supp. 806.

21. Color of law

To act "under color" of law for purposes of this section prohibiting, under color of law, willfully subjecting any inhabitant of any state to deprivation of any rights, privileges or immunities secured or protected by Constitution or laws of United States does not require that accused be officer of state and it is enough that he is a willful participant in joint activity with state or its agents. U. S. v. Price, U.S.Miss.1966, 86 S.Ct. 1152, 383 U.S. 787, 16 L.Ed.2d 267.

Private persons, jointly engaged with state officials in prohibited action, are acting "under color of law" for purposes of this section prohibiting, under color of law, willfully subjecting any inhabitant of any state to deprivation of any rights, privileges or immunities secured or protected by Constitution or laws of United States. U. S. v. Price, U.S.Miss.1966, 86 S.Ct. 1152, 383 U.S. 787, 16 L.Ed.2d 267.

If release of three men from county jail, interception of them on highway and assault and murder of them was joint activity of state officers and nonofficial defendants, nonofficial defendants were acting,

FIGURE 5-5B
(continued)

ers" which relied heavily upon involvement of individuals acting under color of state law and working in concert with Federal Bureau of Investigation informant should have apprised Federal Bureau of Investigation, in reasonable and prudent exercise of its duty to detect and prosecute crimes against United States, that conspiracy to violate rights of "Free-

under color of law, in violation of this section providing punishment for whoever, under color of law, subjects any inhabitant of any state to deprivation of rights, privileges, or immunities secured or protected by Constitution or laws of United States. U. S. v. Price, U.S.Miss. 1966, 86 S.Ct. 1152, 383 U.S. 787, 16 L.Ed.2d 267.

Ch. 13 CIVIL RIGHTS	18 § 242
	Note 21

Where detective hired by lumber company to ascertain identity of thieves held special police officer's card issued by city, and took suspects to shack on company's premises and obtained confessions by forcing a suspect to look at bright light, by repeatedly hitting him with rubber hose and sash cord, by knocking another from chair and hitting him in the stomach, by beating, threatening and punishing suspects, and by flashing his badge and city policeman sent by his superior was present to lend authority to the proceedings, jury could properly find that detective was acting under "color of law" within this section. Williams v. U.S., U.S.Fla.1951, 71 S.Ct. 576, 341 U.S. 97, 95 L.Ed. 774.

Under this section, "color of law" includes misuse of power possessed by virtue of state law and made possible only because wrongdoer is clothed with authority of state law. Williams v. U.S., U.S.Fla.1951, 71 S.Ct. 576, 341 U.S. 97, 95 L.Ed. 774.

Misuse of power, possessed by virtue of state law and made possible only because the wrongdoer is clothed with the authority of state law, is action taken "under color of law" within former § 52 of this title. U. S. v. Classic, U.S.La.1941, 61 S.Ct. 1031, 313 U.S. 299, 85 L.Ed. 1368, rehearing denied 62 S.Ct. 51, 314 U.S. 707, 86 L.Ed. 565. See, also, Catlette v. U.S., C.C.A.W.Va.1943, 132 F.2d 902; Culp v. U.S., C.C.A.Ark.1942, 131 F.2d 93.

"Color of law" requirement for conviction for willfully subjecting person to deprivation of federal rights while acting under color of state law was satisfied when defendant, although not on duty and as result of arrestee's derogatory comments directed to defendant personally, obtained key to cell in which arrestee was placed, removed arrestee from cell and beat him and also threatened to arrest him in future, given that actions occurred in restricted area of jail to which defendant had access only due to his status as police officer, which also gave him access to key, authority to remove arrestee from cell, and authority to threaten future arrests. U.S. v. Colbert, C.A.8 (Mo.) 1999, 172 F.3d 594.

Evidence was sufficient to show that defendant, a deputy sheriff, acted under color of law for purposes of statutes prohibiting deprivation of rights secured by

the Constitution and laws of the United States under color of law; although deputy claimed he was acting as a jealous husband, not as police officer, when he assaulted his wife's former lover in his own home, he claimed during assault to have special authority for his actions by virtue of his official status, and that he could kill victim because he was an officer of the law, he summoned another police officer to scene and identified him as a fellow officer, and then proceeded with the other officer to run victim out of town in their squad car. U.S. v. Tarpley, C.A.5 (Tex.) 1991, 945 F.2d 806, rehearing denied, certiorari denied 112 S.Ct. 1960, 504 U.S. 917, 118 L.Ed.2d 562.

Fact that privately employed railroad policemen who were accused of denying civil rights to persons whom they beat might have taken the same action had they not been cloaked with color of state law did not preclude finding that their actions were taken under color of state law. U. S. v. Hoffman, C.A.7 (Ill.) 1974, 498 F.2d 879.

"Under color of law" within this section means under pretense of law, as affecting the question of state action, and includes misuse of power possessed by virtue of state law made possible only because the wrongdoer is clothed with authority of state law. U. S. v. Ramey, C.A.4 (W.Va.) 1964, 336 F.2d 512, certiorari denied 85 S.Ct. 649, 379 U.S. 972, 13 L.Ed.2d 564.

A defendant who was charged with a violation of this section acted under "color of law", within such act where he went to home of victim as a constable and officer of a state, and arrested and had incarcerated victim knowing warrant under which the arrest was affected to be illegal, groundless of fictitious. U. S. v. Ramey, C.A.4 (W.Va.) 1964, 336 F.2d 512, certiorari denied 85 S.Ct. 649, 379 U.S. 972, 13 L.Ed.2d 564.

State prison guard, who beat prisoner, was, in so doing, acting under color of state law, within this section. U. S. v. Jackson, C.A.8 (Ark.) 1956, 235 F.2d 925.

Under this section providing that whoever, under "color of any law", willfully subjects any inhabitant of any state, territory or district to deprivation of any rights secured or protected by U.S.C.A.Const. Amend. 14, shall be subject to prescribed penalty, quoted term means pretense of law, and it may in-

FIGURE 5-5B
(continued)

Evidence of victims' reactions to cross-burning, including photographs of security measures they took afterwards and son's testimony he began to sleep with baseball bat, was admissible, since it was probative of defendant's intent under 18 USCS §§ 241 and 844. United States v Magleby (2001, CA10 Utah) 241 F3d 1306.

73. —Sufficiency

Evidence that defendants resorted to acts which are not constitutionally protected, including bottle throwing, brandishing knives and verbally threatening, in order to prevent black persons from using public park was sufficient to prove violation of 18 USCS § 241. United States v McDermott (1994, CA8 Iowa) 29 F3d 404.

Evidence was sufficient to prove that defendant intended to threaten victims of cross burning with physical violence, where he made racial derogatory statements while constructing cross and testified at trial that his purpose was to scare victims so they would move out of town, in addition to which victim testified that she and her children felt physically threatened. United States v Pospisil (1999, CA8 Mo) 186 F3d 1023, reh en banc, den (1999, CA8) 1999 US App LEXIS 22128.

Evidence was sufficient to convict defendant of conspiring to violate 18 USCS § 241, despite fact that he did not directly participate in cross burning, where on afternoon of cross burning men waited to discuss defendant's altercation with victim until defendant arrived, defendant not only knew about, discussed, and encouraged action but initiated it, defendant was informed when mission was accomplished, and his credibility was suspect. United States v Whitney (2000, CA 10 Kan) 229 F3d 1296, 2000 Colo J C A R 5742.

Jury could infer that defendant intended to oppress, threaten, and intimidate victims in free exercise of their federal right to occupy property, where

he, understanding meaning of burning cross to general public, had placed one in their yard. United States v Magleby (2001, CA10 Utah) 241 F3d 1306.

Juvenile delinquents are guilty beyond reasonable doubt of violation of 18 USCS § 241, where they were all active members of skinhead group New Dawn Hammerskins, which desecrated several Jewish temples and vandalized car of Jewish teacher, because U.S. has proven that defendants had specific intent to interfere with federal right of Jewish inhabitants to hold and use property. United States v Three Juveniles (1995, DC Mass) 886 F Supp 934.

75. Instructions

In prosecution of police officers for alleged use of excessive force in making arrests, jury instructions did not constructively amend indictment, which could be read in due process terms, whereas instruction alleged Fourth Amendment violation, since proof was same and defendants' substantial rights were not affected; instructions adequately distinguished specific intent and violation of constitutional rights as elements of proof. United States v Reese (1993, CA9 Cal) 2 F3d 870, 93 CDOS 5642, 93 Daily Journal DAR 9617, petition for certiorari filed (Oct 28, 1993) and (among conflicting authorities noted in United States v Lilly (CA1) 1994 US App LEXIS 69).

District court did not err in instructing jury that, while victim's reaction to cross-burning was not conclusive evidence of defendant's intent in burning cross in yard of Afro-American, it could be considered as some evidence of it. United States v Hartbarger (1998, CA7 Ind) 148 F3d 777, 49 Fed Rules Evid Serv 783, reh en banc, den (1998, CA7 Ind) 1998 US App LEXIS 177724.

District court properly instructed jury that victims' reactions to cross-burning could be considered by trier of fact as relevant evidence of defendant's intent under 18 USCS § 241. United States v Magleby (2001, CA10 Utah) 241 F3d 1306.

Same code as U.S.C. but features are added

§ 242. Deprivation of rights under color of law

Whoever, under color of any law, statute, ordinance, regulation, or custom, willfully subjects any person in any State, Territory, Commonwealth, Possession, or District to the deprivation of any rights, privileges, or immunities secured or protected by the Constitution or laws of the United States, or to different punishments, pains, or penalties, on account of such person being an alien, or by reason of his color, or race, than are prescribed for the punishment of citizens, shall be fined under this title or imprisoned not more than one year, or both; and if bodily injury results from the acts committed in violation of this section or if such acts include the use, attempted use, or threatened use of a dangerous weapon, explosives, or fire, shall be fined under this title or imprisoned not more than ten years or both; and if death results from the acts committed in violation of this section or if such acts include kidnapping or an attempt to kidnap, aggravated sexual abuse, or an attempt to commit aggravated sexual abuse, or an attempt to kill, shall be fined under this title, or imprisoned for any term of years or for life, or both, or may be sentenced to death.

(As amended Sept. 13, 1994, P. L. 103-322, Title VI, § 60006(b), Title XXXII, Subtitle A, § 320103(b), Subtitle B, § 320201(b), Title XXXIII, § 330016(1)(H), 108 Stat. 1970, 2109, 2113, 2147; Oct. 11, 1996, P. L. 104-294, Title VI, §§ 604(b)(14)(B), 607(a), 110 Stat. 3507, 3511.)

CRIMES

HISTORY; ANCILLARY LAWS AND DIRECTIVES

Amendments:

1994. Act Sept. 13, 1994, substituted "person in" for "inhabitant of", substituted "such person" for "such inhabitant", and inserted ", or may be sentenced to death".

Section 320103(b), as amended by Act Oct. 11, 1996 (effective on 9/13/94, pursuant to § 604(d) of such Act, which appears as 18 USCS § 13 note), inserted "from the acts committed in violation of this section or if such acts include the use, attempted use, or threatened use of a dangerous weapon, explosives, or fire", inserted "from the acts committed in violation of this section or if such acts include kid-

FIGURE 5-5C
U.S.C.S. (United States Code Service)

napping or an attempt to kidnap, aggravated sexual abuse, or an attempt to commit aggravated sexual abuse, or an attempt to kill, shall be fined under this title, or", substituted "imprisoned" for "shall be subject to imprisonment", and inserted ", or both".

Section 330016(1)(H) of such Act substituted "under this title" for "not more than $1,000". 1996, Act Oct 11, 1996 (effective on 9/13/94, pursuant to § 604(d) of such Act, which appears at 18 USCS § 13 note) (amended § 320103(b) of Act Sept. 13, 1994, which amended this section.

Such Act further substituted "any State, Territory, Commonwealth, Possession, or District" for "any State, Territory, or District".

CROSS REFERENCES

Sentencing Guidelines for the United States Courts, 18 USCS Appx §§ 2H1.1, 2H2.1.

RESEARCH GUIDE

Publisher added features or enhancements to code

Federal Procedure:
12 Fed Proc L Ed, Evidence § 33:209.

Am Jur:
15 Am Jur 2d, Civil Rights §§ 205–215.
29 Am Jur 2d, Evidence § 441.

Immigration:
1 Immigration Law and Procedure (Matthew Bender rev. ed.), Aliens' Rights, Privileges and Liabilities § 6.02.
6 Immigration Law and Procedure (Matthew Bender rev. ed.), Procedure in Deportation Cases § 72.03.
8 Immigration Law and Procedure (Matthew Bender rev. ed.), Judicial Review § 104.11.

Annotations:
Validity, construction, and application of 18 USCS §§ 241 and 242 (and similar predecessor provisions), providing criminal liability for conspiring to deprive, or depriving, person of civil rights—Supreme Court cases. 137 L Ed 2d 1091.

Law Review Articles:
To serve and protect: police civil liability. 41 Fed B News & June 1994.
Fink; Rohr. Scylla and Charybdis: charting a course for law enforcement officers caught between 42 U.S.C. § 1983 and 18 U.S.C. §§ 241 and 242. 41 Fed B News & J, June 1994.

INTERPRETIVE NOTES AND DECISIONS

I. IN GENERAL

1. Generally

There is no private right of action under either 18 USCS § 242 or 18 USCS § 1385. Robinson v Overseas Military Sales Corp. (1994, CA2, NY) 21

right only if, in light of pre-existing law, unlawfulness under Constitution is apparent; where unlawfulness is apparent, constitutional requirement of fair warning of § 242 liability is satisfied; single standard for fair warning does not point a single level of specificity, for (1) in some circumstances, as when earlier case expressly leaves open whether general rule applies to conduct at issue, very high degree of prior factual particularity may be necessary, while (2) in other instances, general constitutional rule already identified in decisional law may apply with obvious clarity to conduct in question, even though conduct has not previously been held unlawful. United States v Lanier (1997, US) 137 L Ed 2d 432, S Ct 1219, 97 CDOS 2350, 97 Daily Journal DAR 4168, 10 FLW Fed S 388.

7. Relationship with other laws

General terms of 18 USCS § 242 incorporate constitutional law by reference, in lieu of describing specific conduct forbidden, and thus, neither statute nor good many of its constitutional references delineate range of forbidden conduct with particularity.

8. Civil liability

Former federal employee's 18 USCS §§ 242 and 371 claims against federal judges were dismissed because it was impermissible to bring private cause of action under those statutes. Rockefeller v United States Court of Appeals Office (2003, DC Dist Col) 248 F Supp 2d 17.

F3d 502, 64 BNA FEP Cas 638, 64 CCH EPD ¶ 42973.

6. Construction, generally

Criminal liability may be imposed under 18 USCS § 242 for deprivation of federal constitutional

II. ELEMENTS OF CRIME

10. Deprivation of rights protected by Federal Constitution or laws

Test of whether officers violated arrestees' or detainees' Fourth Amendment rights by use of excessive force—as distinct from determination of specific intent—is objective one. United States v Reese (1993, CA9 Cal) 2 F3d 870, 93 CDOS 5642, 93 Daily Journal DAR 9617, petition for certiorari filed (Oct 28, 1993) and (among conflicting authorities noted in United States v Lilly (CA1) 1994 US App LEXIS 69). United States v Lanier (1997, US) 137 L Ed 2d 432, 117 S Ct 1219, 97 CDOS 2350, 97 Daily Journal DAR 4168, 10 FLW Fed S 388.

Because 18 USCS § 242 is merely criminal analog of 42 USCS § 1983, and because Congress intended both statutes to apply similarly in similar situations, civil precedents are equally persuasive in criminal context. United States v Mohr (2003, CA4 Md) 318 F3d 613.

Double jeopardy does not bar federal prosecution of former police officer for violation of 18 USCS § 242, where he allegedly used excessive force and assaulted person while attempting to arrest him, even though he was found guilty of criminally negligent homicide in state trial, because (1) § 242 and state crime require proof of different elements and (2) doctrine of dual sovereignty allows federal indictment charging conduct that was previously subject of state prosecution. United States v Livoti (1998, SD NY) 8 F Supp 2d 246.

FIGURE 5-5C
(continued)

available on Westlaw. The U.S.C.S is available on LEXIS and the U.S.C. is available through the Web site for the government printing office www.gpoaccess.gov.

BOX 5-2   COMMON FEATURES OF AN ANNOTATED CODE

- History of law
- Cross reference to similar laws
- References to secondary authorities
- References to case decisions

Pocket Part Supplements

pocket part supplement.
A removable supplement; includes all changes or additions to the material contained in the hard-bound volume.

repeal. To undo; to declare a law no longer in effect.

amend. To change.

Laws change every year and code publications must be kept up-to-date to reflect these changes. This is done by the use of **pocket part supplements**. These are replaced each year and contain all changes to the law. When a code is **repealed** or **amended**, that change is found in the pocket part supplement. In annotated codes, the pocket part supplement also contains the latest cases to interpret the statute. Thus, even if a code section has not changed, you must check the pocket part supplement to see if any recent case decisions affect the interpretation of the law. Occasionally, supplemental material becomes too voluminous for a pocket part supplement. When this happens, a separately bound volume known as a *bound supplement* is produced. Every six years, new editions of the code are published. See Figure 5-6 for an example of a pocket part supplement.

5-5 STATE STATUTORY LAW

Every state has statutory law enacted by the state legislature and then codified. Because state governments are largely patterned after the federal government, the legislative process is similar.

Publication of state laws is similar to that of federal law. In general, statutes are published first as slip laws. At the end of the state congressional session, all laws are published in chronological fashion in works similar to the *Statutes at Large*. Although differences exist from state to state in what these works are called, they are often referred to as **session laws**. Finally, state laws are organized and arranged topically in a code.

session laws. Laws from state legislatures, published in chronological order.

Differences exist from state to state regarding the names of the codes. In some states individual codes are assigned separate names and are cited by those names, for example, California Penal Code §187. On the other hand, some states follow the federal pattern and refer to the codes only by the state name and section number. Citation manuals such as the *The Bluebook* explain how state codes are cited. Also, like the United States Codes, state codes are published in both annotated and unannotated form.

State codes are kept up-to-date by the use of pocket part supplements. In addition to publications that contain the entire state code, many publishers produce books containing selected titles from the total code, for example, the state's penal code. These are particularly useful to lawyers or paralegals who specialize in an area of law and want easy access to frequently needed codes. However, these are usually not annotated and not supplemented. Instead, each year a new volume is published and the old volume is discarded.

18 § 241   CRIMES AND CRIMINAL PROCEDURE

Note 62

defendants were threatened after they were incarcerated. U.S. v. LaVallee. C.A.10 (Colo.) 2006, 439 F.3d 670. Sentencing And Punishment ⊨ 860

§ 242. Deprivation of rights under color of law

Notes of Decisions

1. Constitutionality

De minimus injuries suffered by inmates when they were attacked by defendants while defendants were working as prison guards could support conviction for deprivation of Eighth Amendment rights under color of law; defendants could not beat inmates so long as the resulting injuries were neither permanent nor required medical attention. U.S. v. LaVallee, C.A.10 (Colo.) 2006, 439 F.3d 670. Civil Rights ⊨ 1808

Embodied in the Fourteenth Amendment right to bodily integrity is the right to be free from unauthorized and unlawful physical abuse at the hands of the state by a state official acting or claiming to act under color of law, when the alleged conduct is of such a nature as to shock one's conscience. U.S. v. Giordano, D.Conn. 2002, 260 F.Supp.2d 477. Constitutional Law ⊨ 274(2)

3. Construction with other laws

The offense of a deprivation of rights under color of law resulting in bodily injury or involving a dangerous weapon was a "crime of violence" for purposes of the offense of carrying a firearm during and in relation to any crime of violence. U.S. v. Acosta, C.A.2 (N.Y.) 2006, 470 F.3d 132. Weapons ⊨ 4

6. Elements of offense

Mayor's federal criminal conviction for two counts of acting under color of law to deprive minor of constitutional right to be free from unwanted sexual abuse did not have collateral estoppel effect, in two minors' §§ 1983 action against mayor in his individual capacity, where jury had been instructed in criminal action that it could convict mayor if it found each element of the offense with respect to either of the two victims; jury did not necessarily find each element of the offense was established as to both victims or as to one victim. Doe v. City of Waterbury, D.Conn.2006, 453 F.Supp.2d 537. Judgment ⊨ 648

9. Persons liable

County corrections supervisor's conviction for being accessory after the fact to conspiracy to deprive inmate of his right to be free from cruel and unusual punishment and for substantive crime of depriving inmate of his right to be free from cruel and unusual punishment was collaterally estopped from disputing his § 1983 liability for conspiracy to violate inmate's Eighth Amendment rights. Pizzuto v. County of Nassau, E.D.N.Y.2003, 239 F.Supp.2d 301. Judgment ⊨ 648

13. —— Arrest, deprivation of rights

Defendant's conviction of depriving victim of her civil rights by falsely arresting her was proper, although immigration law was subsequently changed to allow municipal police officers to arrest people whom they reasonably

suspect of being illegal aliens, where record showed that defendant did not arrest victim because he had probable cause to believe she was an illegal alien, but rather, he arrested her so he could rape her. U.S. v. Contreras, S.D.Tex.2000, 134 F.Supp.2d 820. Civil Rights ⊨ 472.1

14. —— Assault and battery, deprivation of rights

County corrections officers who pleaded guilty to depriving inmate of his right to be free from cruel and unusual punishment were collaterally estopped from disputing their § 1983 liability for battery in violation of inmate's Eighth Amendment rights. Pizzuto v. County of Nassau, E.D.N.Y.2003, 239 F.Supp.2d 301. Judgment ⊨ 648

19. —— Particular acts, deprivation of rights

Gunshot that police officer fired into vehicle of driver being pursued for traffic violation was "seizure" under Fourth Amendment, in that officer thereby applied physical force and show of authority which caused fleeing driver to stop; therefore, officer's conduct in firing gunshot supported his conviction for willfully depriving person of constitutional rights under color of law based on use of excessive force to effect arrest. U.S. v. Bradley, C.A.7 (Ill.) 1999, 196 F.3d 762. Arrest ⊨ 68(4)

21. Color of law

Federal district court exceeded its authority following guilty plea on obstruction of justice charge by denying government's motion to dismiss accompanying count charging deprivation of civil rights under color of law, and by appointing special prosecutor for civil rights count, warranting mandamus relief; in refusing to dismiss, for stated reason that obstruction count alone did not reflect gravity of offense, court was telling government which crimes to prosecute. In re U.S., C.A.7 (Wis.) 2003, 345 F.3d 450. Criminal Law ⊨ 303.15

Corrections officer's acts of stepping on inmate's penis were under color of state law, as required to support his conviction for violating inmate's constitutional rights; fact that defendant was corrections officer, in charge of supervising, caring for, and disciplining inmate, provided defendant with access and opportunity to exercise his power over inmate, and defendant, on duty and in full uniform, was acting within his authority to supervise and care for inmates under his watch when assaults occurred. U.S. v. Walsh, C.A.2 (N.Y.) 1999, 194 F.3d 37. Civil Rights ⊨ 472.1

Although actions by a state official in pursuit of personal matters is not conduct under color of law, an official's action need not remain within the precise bounds of his or her legal authority in order to constitute action under color of law, for purposes of offense of willfully depriving

All of these cases were decided after the main volume was published

FIGURE 5-6   Pocket Part Supplement for U.S.C.A.

FIGURE 5-6
(continued)

federal investigators were free from any taint, as federal investigators had no knowledge of officer's statements, or their existence at time when reports were prepared. U.S. v. Daniels, C.A.5 (La.) 2002, 281 F.3d 168, certiorari denied 122 S.Ct. 2313, 535 U.S. 1105, 152 L.Ed.2d 1067. Criminal Law ☞ 42

33. —— Sufficiency of indictment

Under *Apprendi,* the statute setting forth the offense of deprivation of a person's rights under

dant's statements and the testimony of numerous other witnesses, showed defendant deprived victim of federal rights and caused her to engage in sexual acts through force. U.S. v. Simmons, C.A.5 (Miss.) 2006, 470 F.3d 1115. Civil Rights ☞ 1809

Evidence was sufficient to prove that defendant acted under color of law, as required to support convictions for depriving minors of their due process right to be free from sexual abuse;

Reprinted with permission of Thomson/West

BOX 5-3   FEDERAL STATUTORY RESEARCH MATERIAL

- *Slip Laws*: publication of single statute in pamphlet form
- *Statutes at Large*: cumulative chronological publication of laws enacted by Congress during a congressional session
- *United States Code*: topical organization of public statutory law
- *United States Code Annotated*: topical organization of public statutory law with references to related legal materials
- *United States Code Service*: topical organization of public statutory law with references to related legal materials

---

5-6 LOCAL ORDINANCES

The right to make laws belongs not only to federal and state governments but also to local governing bodies. These municipal or county laws, sometimes called ordinances or codes are not as widely published as state and federal codes. Generally, they can be located in the local county law library or in the local public libraries. Many local ordinances are now online.

5-7 ADMINISTRATIVE REGULATIONS

Much of the work of the federal government is done through the creation of boards or agencies, known as *administrative agencies*. These agencies are empowered by Congress to make rules or regulations to carry out their functions. As administrative rules and regulations are adopted, they are printed in the *Federal Register*. The *Federal Register* is a daily government publication (except for weekends and holidays) that keeps the public informed of actions taken by administrative agencies. Included in the publication are the following:

1. Enacted or amended rules or regulations
2. Proposed rules
3. Notices of administrative hearings
4. Presidential proclamations

Like the *Statutes at Large*, the *Federal Register* is a chronological organization of rules and notices and therefore difficult to use. In order to allow easier access to administrative rules, like the statutes, the administrative rules or regulations are topically organized in the *Code of Federal Regulations* (abbreviated C.F.R.). This code is organized in a manner similar to the United States Codes. There are fifty titles, whose topics closely parallel the topics of the fifty titles of the United States Codes. See Table 5-1 for a comparison of the title topics.

A major difference between the *Code of Federal Regulations* and the *United States Code* is how the laws are updated. The *United States Code* is updated with pocket part supplements. The *Code of Federal Regulations* is not. Checking the current state of administrative regulations is a cumbersome process. You must use a separate publication titled "LSA-List of CFR Sections Affected." This is a monthly update of federal regulations that tells you if any section of the *Code of Federal Regulations* was changed. The LSA only tells you *if* the section was changed. It refers you to the *Federal Register* where you can see *what* the change is.

Because states have administrative agencies, administrative rules and regulations are also found at the state level.

The *Federal Register,* the *Code of Federal Regulations,* and the "List of Sections Affected" can be accessed online through the Web site for the Government Printing Office:

http://www.gpoaccess.gov/fr/index.html   Federal Register

http://www.gpoaccess.gov/cfr/index.htm   1 C.F.R.

http://www.gpoaccess.gov/lsa/index.html   LSA

5-8 COURT RULES

Congress gives the courts the right to make rules for practice within the courts. These are known as court rules or **rules of court**. The federal court has adopted several rules for practice in the federal courts, including the following.

rules of court. Procedural rules adopted by all courts regulating practice in the court.

Federal Rules of Civil Procedure

Federal Rules of Bankruptcy Practice

Federal Rules of Evidence

Federal Rules for Appellate Procedure

Federal Rules of Criminal Procedure

The rules of court are published with the codes. The Federal Rules can also be accessed online through the Web site for the United States Courts at http://www.uscourts.gov/rules/. In addition to the rules of court that apply in all federal courts, each court is allowed to adopt its own **local rules of court**. These local rules are generally found on the Web site for the specific court.

local rules of court. Procedural rules adopted by an individual court for practice in that specific court.

State courts also have state rules of court as well as local rules of court for individual courts. You will probably find state rules of court with your state codes. A local law library should have copies of the local rules of court. These are often kept at the reference desk. You also find most local rules of court on the Web sites for the individual courts.

5-9 UNIFORM LAWS AND MODEL CODES

Because each state makes its own laws, a number of differences exist in the law from state to state. In order to promote more uniformity among the states, representatives from the states to draft proposed laws known as *uniform laws* and *model codes.* The most noted uniform law is the Uniform Commercial Code, a code that regulates contracts for the sale of goods. There are over 175 proposed uniform laws. A uniform law or model code, however, is *not* law in any state unless it was enacted by the state's legislature. The **uniform laws** and **model codes** are published in an annotated form by West (*Uniform Laws Annotated*). These books closely resemble other code books. The case annotations to uniform laws come from all jurisdictions. To read more about uniform codes and to see the uniform laws your state has adopted, go to http://www.nccusl.org/Update/, the Web site for the National Conference of Commissioners on Uniform State Laws.

When researching statutory law, you must refer to your state's code and not the uniform law or model code. If your state has enacted a uniform law or model code, you can check the annotations in the uniform laws to find case law that controls your factual situation. Remember, however, if you find a case and it does not come from your state, it is only persuasive authority.

uniform laws. Similar laws that are enacted by the legislatures of different states (i.e., Uniform Commercial Code); intended to create uniformity in the law.

model codes. A collection of sample laws; created for the states to adopt in whole or in part; helps to create uniformity in law.

5-10 FINDING CONSTITUTIONAL PROVISIONS, STATUTORY LAW, ADMINISTRATIVE REGULATIONS, AND RULES OF COURT

Finding the Law

If you are using a print source, locating a constitutional provision, code section, or rule of court when you have the citation is an easy task. Consider the following citations:

U.S. Const. art. II, § 2, cl. 3

18 U.S.C. § 242

Locating the constitutional provision listed above requires only that you locate a copy of the U.S. Constitution. Since all of the parts of the Constitution are labeled, you simply look for Article II, Section 2, clause 3. Refer to Figure 5-1 found earlier in this chapter and you see that this provision of the Constitution deals with the power of the president to make appointments during congressional recesses.

Locating the citation to the United States Codes is also straight forward. Although the U.S. Codes consist of several volumes, the outside binding clearly

A Point to Remember

Indexes are prepared by the publishers of the works and differ from edition to edition. If you are not successful in one index, check another.

If you are using an online version of the code, you will probably find that there is no index. (Westlaw is an exception to this.) Search methods for online resources are discussed in Chapter 10.

A Point to Remember

Before you start researching, try to determine if your factual situation is governed by federal law or by state law. Federal and state laws are published separately.

U.S. Code (Laws made by the U.S. Congress)

Search the U.S. Code by Title and Section :
If you already know which Title and Section of the U.S. Code you want to retrieve, fill in the following boxes. (Example: If you are looking for 42 USC 1395, fill in Title 42, Section 1395)

Title: [ ]   **Section:** [ ]   [Search]

Search the U.S. Code by keyword:
[   ]   [Search]

FIGURE 5-7
Findlaw: Template for Finding Code Section

Reprinted with permission of Findlaw a Thomson business

identifies the code sections contained in each volume. To find this citation, first look for the volume containing Title 18, then for the volume also containing Section 242.

If you are using an online source rather than a print source, your research task is probably even easier. Most online sources provide an easy template for finding specific code sections. Figure 5-7 provides an example from the popular Web site Findlaw.

The more difficult research problem is locating the *proper* law when you have a factual situation or problem and are looking for an answer to the problem. A number of different methods can be used to do this. Probably the most common way when searching print sources is to use the index at the end of the code. The *United States Code,* the *United States Code Annotated,* and the *United States Code Service* all contain topical indexes that refer the reader to code sections that deal with the topic. The key here is to properly identify the topics and vocabulary used in the index. A legal dictionary and thesaurus can help. See Figure 5-8 for an example of an index.

In addition to topical indexes, the various print editions of the code contain popular name tables, as do many of the online publications of the code. When laws are passed, many of them have popular names, such as "Civil Rights Act of 1968." By checking this name in the table of popular names, you learn the proper citation and are able to find the law. (See Figure 5-9.) In addition to indexes, statutory law is located using secondary sources. These are discussed in Chapters 7 and 8.

BOX 5-4   RESEARCH CHECKLIST: FINDING THE CODES

- Analyze factual situation and identify key words or terms.
- Consider synonyms and/or related terms for key words.
- Check index to code for words or terms.
- If unsuccessful, check index to alternate publication of code.
- Read code section.
- Check pocket part and any bound supplement.

BOX 5-5   ADMINISTRATIVE REGULATIONS—RESEARCH MATERIAL

- *Code of Federal Regulations:* topical organization of federal administrative regulations
- LSA—List of Sections Affected: publication containing list of all administrative regulations that have changed
- *Federal Register:* monthly publication of all changes and proposed changes to administrative regulations

←— **18 U.S.C. § 242 contains the terms "under color of law" and "deprivation of civil rights."**

FIGURE 5-8   Index to Code

Civil Liberties Act Amendments of 1992

Pub. L. 102–371, Sept. 27, 1992, 106 Stat. 1167

Civil Obedience Act of 1968

Pub. L. 90–284, title X, Apr. 11, 1968, 82 Stat. 90 (Title 18, §§ 231–233)

Civil Relief Act (Soldiers and Sailors)

See Soldiers' and Sailors' Civil Relief Acts of 1918 and 1940

Civil Rights Acts

See Title 42, §§ 1971 et seq., 1981 et seq.

Apr. 9, 1866, ch. 31, 14 Stat. 27

May 31, 1870, ch. 114, 16 Stat. 140

Feb. 28, 1871, ch. 99, 16 Stat. 433

Apr. 20, 1871, ch. 22, 17 Stat. 13

Mar. 1, 1875, ch. 114, §§ 3–5, 18 Stat. 336, 337

Civil Rights Act of 1957

Pub. L. 85–315, Sept. 9, 1957, 71 Stat. 634 (Title 28, §§ 1343, 1861; Title 42, §§ 1971, 1971 note, 1975–1975e, 1995)

Pub. L. 86–383, title IV, § 401, Sept. 28, 1959, 73 Stat. 724

Pub. L. 86–449, May 6, 1960, titles IV, VI, 74 Stat. 89, 90

Pub. L. 87–264, title IV, Sept. 21, 1961, 75 Stat. 559

Pub. L. 88–152, § 2, Oct. 17, 1963, 77 Stat. 271

Pub. L. 88–352, title V, July 2, 1964, 78 Stat. 249

Pub. L. 90–198, § 1, Dec. 14, 1967, 81 Stat. 582

Pub. L. 91–521, Nov. 25, 1970, 84 Stat. 1356

Pub. L. 92–64, Aug. 4, 1971, 85 Stat. 166

Pub. L. 92–496, Oct. 14, 1972, 86 Stat. 913

Pub. L. 94–292, § 2, May 27, 1976, 90 Stat. 524

Pub. L. 95–132, § 2, Oct. 13, 1977, 91 Stat. 1157

Pub. L. 95–444, §§ 2–7, Oct. 10, 1978, 92 Stat. 1067, 1068

Pub. L. 96–81, §§ 2, 3, Oct. 6, 1979, 93 Stat. 642

Pub. L. 96–447, § 2, Oct. 13, 1980, 94 Stat. 1894

Civil Rights Act of 1960

Pub. L. 86–449, May 6, 1960, 74 Stat. 86 (Title 18, §§ 837, 1074, 1509; Title 20, §§ 241, 640; Title 42, §§ 1971, 1974–1974e, 1975d)

Civil Rights Act of 1964

Pub. L. 88–352, July 2, 1964, 78 Stat. 241 (Title 28, § 1447; Title 42, §§ 1971, 1975a–1975d, 2000a et seq.)

Pub. L. 92–261, §§ 2–8, 10, 11, 13, Mar. 24, 1972, 86 Stat. 103–113

Pub. L. 92–318, title IX, § 906(a), June 23, 1972, 86 Stat. 375

Pub. L. 93–608, § 3(1), Jan. 2, 1975, 88 Stat. 1972

Pub. L. 94–273, § 3(24), Apr. 21, 1976, 90 Stat. 377

Pub. L. 95–251, § 2(a)(11), Mar. 27, 1978, 92 Stat. 183

Pub. L. 95–555, § 1, Oct. 31, 1978, 92 Stat. 2076

Pub. L. 95–598, title III, § 330, Nov. 6, 1978, 92 Stat. 2679

Pub. L. 95–624, § 5, Nov. 9, 1978, 92 Stat. 3462

Pub. L. 96–191, § 8(g), Feb. 15, 1980, 94 Stat. 34

Pub. L. 100–259, § 6, Mar. 22, 1988, 102 Stat. 31

Pub. L. 102–166, title I, §§ 104, 105(a), 106–108, 109(a), (b)(1), 110(a), 111, 112, 113(b), 114, Nov. 21, 1991, 105 Stat. 1074–1079

Pub. L. 102–411, § 2, Oct. 14, 1992, 106 Stat. 2102

Pub. L. 103–382, title III, § 391(q), Oct. 20, 1994, 108 Stat. 4024

Civil Rights Act of 1968

Pub. L. 90–284, Apr. 11, 1968, 82 Stat. 73–92 (Title 18, §§ 231–233, 241, 242, 245, 1153, 2101, 2102; Title 25, § 1301 et seq.; Title 28, § 1360 note; Title 42, §§ 1973j, 3533, 3535, 3601 et seq.)

Pub. L. 93–265, Apr. 12, 1974, 88 Stat. 84

Pub. L. 93–383, title VIII, § 808(b), Aug. 22, 1974, 88 Stat. 729

Pub. L. 100–430, §§ 4, 5, 6(a), (b)(1), (2), (c)–(e), 7–10, 15, Sept. 13, 1988, 102 Stat. 1619–1636

Pub. L. 101–511, title VIII, § 8077(b), (c), Nov. 5, 1990, 104 Stat. 1892

Civil Rights Act of 1991

Pub. L. 102–166, Nov. 21, 1991, 105 Stat. 1071

Pub. L. 102–392, title III, § 316, Oct. 6, 1992, 106 Stat. 1724

Pub. L. 103–50, § 1204(a), July 2, 1993, 107 Stat. 268

Pub. L. 103–283, title III, § 312(f)(1)–(3), July 22, 1994, 108 Stat. 1446

Civil Rights Attorney's Fees Awards Act of 1976

Pub. L. 94–559, Oct. 19, 1976, 90 Stat. 2641 (Title 42, §§ 1981 note, 1988)

Civil Rights Commission Act of 1978

Pub. L. 95–444, Oct. 10, 1978, 92 Stat. 1067 (Title 42, §§ 1975 note, 1975b–1975e)

Civil Rights Commission Act of 1983

Pub. L. 98–183, Nov. 30, 1983, 97 Stat. 1301 (title 42, § 1975 et seq.)

Pub. L. 101–180, § 2, Nov. 28, 1989, 103 Stat. 1325

Pub. L. 102–167, §§ 2–5, Nov. 26, 1991, 105 Stat. 1101

Pub. L. 102–400, § 2, Oct. 7, 1992, 106 Stat. 1955

Pub. L. 103–419, § 2, Oct. 25, 1994, 108 Stat. 4338

Civil Rights Commission Amendments Act of 1994

Pub. L. 103–419, Oct. 25, 1994, 108 Stat. 4338

---

18 U.S.C. § 242 is popularly called "Civil Rights Act of 1968." If you know that, you check the popular name and it refers you to 18 U.S.C. § 242.

FIGURE 5-9 Popular Name Index

After locating the code section in the main volume of a print resource, remember to check any pocket part or bound supplement. This tells you if any changes in the law have occurred. It also gives you citations to new cases interpreting the statute. Online versions of the code or rules of court are not usually supplemented in the same way as print resources. If you are using an online version of the code or rules of court, be sure to check the date to verify that you are reading a current version of the law.

Finding Administrative Regulations and Rules of Court

Finding a particular topic in the *Code of Federal Regulations* is similar to finding a topic in the U.S. Codes. That is, words or phrases describing the topic are located in an index. The index then directs you to appropriate titles and sections of the regulations. Verifying that the law is current, however, cannot be done as it is with the codes. Unfortunately, the *Code of Federal Regulations* is not regularly supplemented with pocket part supplements. Checking for revisions or changes is a two-step process. First, refer to the "LSA: List of CFR Sections Affected," a monthly publication listing regulations that have changed and telling you where to find the change in the *Federal Register*. Second, refer to the *Federal Register* to see how the regulation was changed.

Finding a constitutional provision, code section, administrative regulation, or court rule is only the beginning of your research. These laws must also be analyzed, interpreted, and applied to your factual situation before your research is complete. That process is discussed in the next chapter.

Online Legal Research

Federal, state, and local statutory and regulatory materials are easily located on the Internet. Remember, however, that free Internet sources do not contain annotations such as case notations. Also remember to carefully check the date of any statutory or legislative material found on the Internet. The following are some free Web sites for locating statutory and regulatory information:

For comprehensive federal and state materials:

www.findlaw.com	Findlaw
www.law.cornell.edu/	Cornell University Law School

For comprehensive federal materials:

www.gpoaccess.gov/index.html	Government Printing Office

For individual state materials:

www.multistate.com	Multistate Associates
http://www.statelocalgov.net/	State and Local Governments on the Net State homepage

For local government materials:

http://municipalcodes.lexisnexis.com/	LexisNexis™ Municipal Codes

CITATION MATTERS

UNITED STATES CONSTITUTION AND UNITED STATES CODE

THE BLUEBOOK—RULE 11

This is the correct format for a citation to the Fourteenth Amendment to the United States Constitution:

U.S. CONST. amend. XIV.

United States Constitution Citation Analyzed

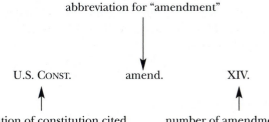

abbreviation for "amendment"

U.S. CONST.   amend.   XIV.

abbreviation of constitution cited   number of amendment cited

Other examples:

U.S. CONST. amend. XIV, § 2.

U.S. CONST. art. I, § 9, cl. 2.

When you refer to one of the constitutional amendments, it is best to use the number spelled out. The number and the term *amendment* are capitalized, for example, Fourteenth Amendment.

THE UNITED STATES CODE

THE BLUEBOOK—RULE 12

18 U.S.C. § 242 (2000)

Occupational Safety and Health Act (OSHA) of 1970, 29 U.S.C. § 651 (1988 & Supp. V 1993)

The *United States Code* (U.S.C.) is the official federal code. There are two popular unofficial federal codes. They are the *United States Code Service* (U.S.C.S) and the *United States Code Annotated* (U.S.C.A.). You should cite to the official code when possible.

United States Code Citation Analyzed

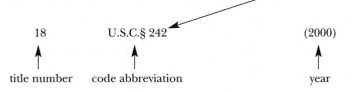

section sign and specific code section

18   U.S.C.§ 242   (2000)

title number   code abbreviation   year

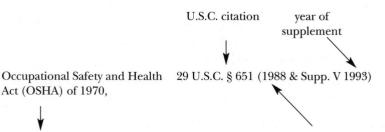

Occupational Safety and Health   29 U.S.C. § 651 (1988 & Supp. V 1993)
Act (OSHA) of 1970,

title of the act   year on bound
                                                         volume

The Bluebook rules for citing the United States Code are detailed and complex. However, between Rule 12 and Table 1 (T.1), most situations are addressed.

STATE CODES

THE BLUEBOOK—RULE 12

The Bluebook—Table 1 (T.1)

State codes are cited in much the same way the federal codes are cited. Each state has its own code. Each state has a specific format and special abbreviations. Look up the state in Table 1; examples are provided.

COURT RULES

THE BLUEBOOK—RULE 12.8.3

This is the correct format for a citation to Rule 26 of the Federal Rules of Civil Procedure:

FED. R. CIV. P. 26

This is the correct format for a citation to Rule 6 of the Federal Rules of Criminal Procedure:

FED. R. CRIM. P. 6

This is the correct format for a citation to Rule 301 of the Federal Rules of Evidence:

FED. R. EVID. 301

CHAPTER SUMMARY

In addition to case law, primary law is found in constitutions, statutes or codes, administrative regulations, and court rules. All of these sources exist on the federal and state level. The United States Constitution, the supreme law of the land, can be located in numerous sources, including publications of the *United States Code*. In these sources the Constitution is indexed. The Constitution that is published with the annotated codes is also annotated, containing references to cases interpreting the various constitutional provisions or amendments.

Laws enacted by legislative bodies are known as *statutory laws.* Federal statutory law results from action by the United States Congress. Congress enacts both public laws and private laws. Public laws affect the general population. Private laws affect only named individuals or groups. When federal statutory law is enacted, it is first published in pamphlet form and is known as *slip law.* At the end of each session of Congress, all of the public laws are published in chronological order in *Statutes at Large,* and then topically organized and published as a code known as the *United States Code.* The *United States Code* is also published in annotated form by two private publishers, West, which publishes the *United States Code Annotated,* and Lexis Law Publishing, which now publishes the *United States Code Service.* In annotated format, the codes contain references to other legal resources, including cases that help with understanding the code. All codes are indexed and kept up-to-date by the use of pocket part supplements. All states have statutory law found in state codes. Many local governments enact statutory law often known as *municipal ordinances* or *codes.*

Federal administrative agencies, created by Congress, often enact rules or regulations to carry out their functions. They are authorized by Congress to make these rules. Administrative rules or regulations are first published in the *Federal Register,* a monthly publication of the U.S. Government. The regulations are topically organized and published in the *Code of Federal Regulations.* Courts are empowered by Congress to make rules for practice within the courts. These are known as *rules of court* and are published with the United States Codes. States also have administrative regulations and rules of court.

Finding sections of the Constitution, codes, administrative regulations, or court rules requires that you know the citation. The citation can be found by analyzing your factual situation and identifying topics and key words. Those terms are then checked in a general index, which gives you the citation you need to find the law.

TERMS TO REMEMBER

Bill of Rights	private laws	amend
index	slip law	session laws
annotated	code	rules of court
statutory law	positive law	local rules of court
bill	legislative intent	uniform laws
legislative history	pocket part supplement	model codes
public laws	repeal	

QUESTIONS FOR REVIEW

1. What are the three parts of the U.S. Constitution?
2. Where will you find publications of the U.S. Constitution?
3. Describe the steps in the enactment of statutory law.
4. What do the following abbreviations mean?
   a. H.R. 346
   b. S. 123
   c. Public Law 104–398
5. What is a slip law?

6. What is contained in the *Statutes at Large?*
7. What are the similarities and differences among the *United States Code,* the *United States Code Annotated,* and the *United States Code Service?*
8. Explain the concept of positive law.
9. What is the importance of a pocket part supplement?
10. Describe the *Federal Register,* the *Code of Federal Regulations,* and "LSA—List of Sections Affected."
11. What are court rules?
12. How do you find a code section if you do not have the citation?

CAN YOU FIGURE IT OUT?

1. Refer to Figure 5-1 (U.S. Constitution).
   a. What does Article IV, Section 1 provide?
   b. What does the Ninth Amendment provide?
2. Refer to Figure 5-2 (annotated Constitution). Does the preamble to the Constitution give powers to the federal government? Give the source of your answer.
3. Refer to Figure 5-3.
   a. What is the subject matter of Private Law 103-6?
   b. Was this act first introduced in the House of Representatives or the Senate? How do you know?
4. Refer to Figure 5-4.
   a. Give the *Statutes at Large* citation for Public Law 103-322.
   b. Give the citation for the code sections affected by Public Law 103-322.
5. Refer to Figure 5-5A.
   a. What is the number of the Public Law from the 103rd Congress that amended 18 U.S.C. §242?
   b. How did Public Law 103-322 §60006(b) amend this law?
   c. What is the year of this amendment?
   d. What is the code section for a civil lawsuit based on a deprivation of rights?
6. Refer to Figure 5-5B.
   a. Cite a 1991 case discussing the constitutionality of 18 U.S.C.A. § 242.
   b. Cite one case that explains the phrase *color of law.*
7. Refer to Figure 5-5C. Give a citation to a 1998 case that discusses 18 U.S.C.S. § 242.
8. Refer to Figure 5-8.
   a. What is the main topic indexed in this figure?
   b. Look at the subtopic "Desegregation." Under this, it states, "Public education, post, this heading." What does this mean?
   c. Look under the subtopic "Counselors." Here it states, "Attorneys and counselors, generally, ante, this heading." What does this mean?
   d. Look at the subtopic "Courts of Appeals." Here it says, "this index." What does this mean?
   e. What code section deals with obstruction of court orders?
9. Refer to Figure 5-9. Give the Public Law number and *Statutes at Large* citation for the Civil Rights Attorneys Fee Awards Act of 1976.

BUILDING YOUR RESEARCH SKILLS: ASSIGNMENTS AND ACTIVITIES

1. Find the following sections of the law. Summarize each in your own words.
   a. 18 U.S.C. § 6002
   b. 2 U.S.C. § 192
   c. 11 U.S.C. § 541

2. Using the U.S. Codes, answer the following questions and cite the source of your answer.
   a. Can a television news crew accompany and tape a search made by a federal law enforcement officer who is searching pursuant to a warrant?
   b. Can a court award costs and attorney fees to successful litigants in a copyright infringement case?
   c. Can one place an advertisement on the U.S. flag in Washington, D.C.?
   d. Can a state impose income tax on retirement income of an individual who is not a resident or domicile of that state?
   e. Which governmental entity or entities have the right to regulate the importation of honeybees into the United States? Why is it regulated? What is the punishment for unlawful importation?
   f. When is failure to pay child support a federal crime?
   g. Using the Popular Name table, find the Home Health Care and Alzheimer Disease Amendment of 1990. Where is this found in the U.S. Code? Is this a public law or a private law? How do you know?

3. Using an annotated U.S. Code answer the following.
   a. What code section makes it a crime for anyone to desecrate the flag? How has the Supreme Court considered this statute? Give the name and citation of a Supreme Court case or cases.
   b. What is the punishment for counterfeiting? Review annotations in the U.S.C.S. and answer the following questions, providing full case citations using *The Bluebook*.
      1. Can states also have counterfeiting laws?
      2. Is it counterfeiting to insert a black-and-white photocopy of a $1 bill into a coin change machine?

4. Using the United States Constitution, answer the following questions.
   a. What does U.S. Const. art. IV, § 1 provide?
   b. What does U.S. Const. art. 1, § 2, cl.2 provide?
   c. What does U.S. Const. amend. XXV provide?
   d. How often must Congress assemble and when does the meeting begin? Give the authority for your answer.
   e. Who has the power of impeachment? Give the authority for your answer.

5. Use the Rules of Court and the *Code of Federal Regulations* to answer the following.
   a. Summarize the following.
      1. Fed. R. Civ. Proc. 56
      2. Fed. R Crim. Proc. 6
      3. 27 C.F.R. § 555.180
   b. Which federal rule sets out the requirement for the use of interrogatories in civil cases?
   c. Can a deposition be used in a criminal case in federal court? Cite your authority.

BUILDING YOUR ANALYSIS SKILLS: ASSIGNMENTS AND EXERCISES

1. Review the Meyers case. Assume that charges were brought against Meyers in your state court and you are asked to find the procedure for suppressing evidence in that court. Create a list of terms that you might check in an index to the state codes or rules of court to begin this research task.

2. Locate 18 U.S.C. § 36. Compare this code section with the similar provision found in Figure 5-4 (Public Law 103-322). How does §36 (a)(1) of the U.S. Code compare with the same section found in the Public Law (Figure 5-4)?

3. Write a short paragraph summarizing each of the code sections listed above in question 1, Building Your Research Skills.

BUILDING YOUR ONLINE RESEARCH SKILLS: ASSIGNMENTS AND EXERCISES

1. Access the Web site for the government printing office, www.gpoaccess.gov. Make a list of legislative and executive statutory and regulatory resources.

2. Access an annotated version of the U.S. Constitution, using a site such as www.findlaw.com.
   a. What right does the Seventh Amendment establish?
   b. Does the right mentioned in the Seventh Amendment generally apply in state courts? Cite cases to support your answer.
   c. Conduct a Keyword Search for due process. Which constitutional amendment expressly refer to this term?

3. Using any of the relevant Web sites listed in the chapter, find the following code sections and give the title of each:
   a. 21 U.S.C. § 801
   b. 15 U.S.C. § 1172
   c. 42 U.S.C. § 3543
   d. 8 C.F.R 232.2
   e. 6 C.F.R §25.9
   f. Federal Rules of Evidence 802

CASE PROJECT

Research federal and/or state codes for your Appendix A hypothetical case. List any relevant code sections and give a short summary of any code sections you find. List all terms that you checked in the index to the codes.

STATUTORY AND CONSTITUTIONAL ANALYSIS

CHAPTER OUTLINE

S KILL OBJECTIVES FOR CHAPTER 6

When you complete this chapter you should be able to

- Explain why it is helpful to outline statutory language.
- Discuss why it is helpful to review case law that interprets code provisions.
- Explain the importance of legislative history.
- List the four steps used in the IRAC approach.
- Analyze a code section by identifying the statutory requirements or elements.
- Analyze a factual situation controlled by statutory law, using the IRAC method.
- Discuss how to determine whether the U.S. Constitution or a state constitution applies to a factual situation arising under state law.

FROM THE DESK OF W. J. BRYAN, ESQ.

TO: Research Assistant

Please write a brief memo explaining how the Fourth Amendment to the U.S. Constitution applies to the Meyers case and our motion to suppress the bloody handkerchief. Also, please summarize and explain the code sections you found that deal with search warrants.

6-1 INTRODUCTION

In the previous chapter you read about the Constitution and the different types of statutory law and administrative regulations. You also learned how to locate this type of law. However, researching constitutions, statutes, and administrative regulations requires more than merely locating code sections, constitutional provisions, or specific regulations, just as researching case law requires more than just finding a case. Researchers must understand and be able to explain how the law applies to a client's factual situation. This requires legal analysis.

As you read in Chapter 2, all legal analysis starts with identifying your client's legal issue and relevant facts. If your research produces case law, you start by comparing your client's factual situation with the facts of the cases you find. If your client's factual situation and issue are the same as that in the cases, and the cases are controlling in your jurisdiction, then the holdings or rules of law found in the cases apply to your case. However, legal analysis involving constitutions, statutes, and administrative rules and regulations is different. Unlike case law, these sources of law contain general rules that are not stated in reference to a specific factual situation.

After identifying your client's issue and key facts, you should begin constitutional or statutory analysis by examining the language of the law. Administrative regulations are analyzed in the same way. In this chapter you will see how to analyze statutory and constitutional law.

6-2 CONSTITUTIONAL ANALYSIS

Article VI of the U.S. Constitution states that the Constitution is the supreme law of this land. "This Constitution, and the Laws of the United States which shall be made in Pursuance thereof . . . shall be the supreme Law of the Land; and the Judges in every State shall be bound thereby, any Thing in the Constitution or Laws of any State to the Contrary notwithstanding." It is therefore important to determine if a matter is controlled by any provision in the Constitution.

Many of the words and phrases found in the Constitution are not precise and are subject to various interpretations. Consider phrases such as "unreasonable search and seizure," "due process," and "equal protection." When faced with a research problem requiring interpretation and analysis of any provision in the U.S. Constitution, you must research case law that interprets that provision. The United States Supreme Court has the final say on what the U.S. Constitution means.

Constitutional research and analysis, however, sometimes presents an additional consideration. Many constitutional research problems deal with an individual's constitutional rights under the Bill of Rights (the first ten amendments) and under the Due Process and Equal Protection Clauses of the Fourteenth Amendment. Consider the Meyers case. Recall from earlier chapters that local police searched Meyers's residence pursuant to a search warrant. Meyers was suspected of drug dealing. During the search officers found and seized a bloody handkerchief. This evidence leads to criminal charges of murder against Meyers. These charges are filed in a state court. Meyers's attorney decides to make a motion to suppress the evidence of the bloody handkerchief on the grounds that it was an unreasonable search and seizure and violated the safeguards found in the Fourth Amendment to the U.S. Constitution. You are asked to help with the research.

You are faced with an important initial research question here. Should you begin your research in state sources or in federal sources? This is a state crime prosecuted in a state court. In all probability, this state has a state constitutional provision also regulating the area of search and seizure. However, the U.S. Constitution gives all individuals certain rights. Should your research focus on the state constitution and state cases or on the U.S. Constitution and Supreme Court cases? Recall that one of the first steps in legal analysis of constitutional (and statutory) law requires that you determine that a law applies to your case. In the Meyers case, therefore, you must determine whether federal or state constitutional law applies. This requires that you understand the concept of federalism and the relationship between state and federal governments.

Federalism—The Relationship Between Federal and State Government

In the United States, government operates under a principle called federalism. **Federalism** means that citizens are regulated by two separate governments: federal and state. The federal government has *limited* power over all fifty states. State governments have power only within their state boundaries. Additionally, states cannot make laws that conflict with the laws of the federal government.

Because there are areas of **concurrent jurisdiction,** conflicts sometimes exist between federal laws and state laws. Where a conflict exists, federal law controls. This is because of the **Supremacy Clause** of the Constitution mentioned above. When a state passes a law that conflicts with the Constitution, the United States Supreme Court has the power to declare the state law unconstitutional and unenforceable.

federalism. A system of government in which the people are regulated by both federal and state governments.

concurrent jurisdiction. Jurisdiction or power exercised by two different entities.

Supremacy clause. Clause in the U.S. Constitution providing that the U.S. Constitution is the supreme law of the land.

However, the fact that both state and federal governments regulate an area does not necessarily create a conflict. For example, if a defendant kidnaps a victim and takes the victim across state lines, both federal and state laws are violated and the defendant could be tried in either the state or federal court (or both) for the crime. Furthermore, in this situation the federal court has no priority over the state court.

In determining if a conflict between state and federal law exists, a particular problem arises in the area of criminal procedure. If an individual is arrested for a state crime, such as murder, that individual is tried in the state courts. States are allowed to formulate their own procedural rules and safeguards for this process. However, states are also bound by the Fourteenth Amendment to the Constitution, which provides in part, "nor shall any State deprive any person of life, liberty, or property, without due process of law." The United States Constitution does not set out specific rights that states must respect. Rather, it sets out a *minimum standard* that all states must follow, that is, due process. The Supreme Court decides what due process means. But remember that it is a minimum standard. States can grant more rights to criminal defendants and not be in conflict with federal law. On the other hand, once the Supreme Court sets forth a specific minimum standard, states cannot take away a right. States may make laws in this area as long as those laws do not violate due process.

A conflict does not necessarily exist just because the state and federal rules differ. When you research such a problem, you must read Supreme Court cases to determine the minimum standard. You must then review state cases to determine how the state constitution has been interpreted. If the state constitution affords more rights, it controls. If it affords fewer rights, then the United States Constitution and the cases decided by the U.S. Supreme Court control.

A Point to Remember

Where conflicts exist between federal and state laws, the federal law controls. However, not all differences result in a conflict. Do not assume that federal law always controls. In determining if a difference results in a conflict, first determine if the federal law preempted the area of law. If it has, then the federal law controls. If the federal law did not preempted the area, then read the federal law carefully to determine its meaning. You must understand the federal law to determine if a conflict exists in the state law.

6-3 ANALYZING STATUTES AND REGULATIONS

Determine If Law Applies

Just as with constitutional law, before analyzing a statute or regulations, you must first determine that the law applies to your client's factual situation. Sometimes the words of the statute answer this question. Other times, you find clues in the organization of the laws. For example, a rule setting forth motion procedures found in the Federal Rules of Criminal Procedure would not apply to a motion made in a civil case. Sometimes only part of a statute or regulation applies. Codes and rules are sometimes written to cover numerous types of factual situations. For example, consider Rule 4 of the Federal Rules of Civil Procedure—the rule that establishes the methods of serving a civil complaint in a lawsuit. This rule is very long and consists of several subparts. The titles of some of the subparts are the following:

(e) Serving an Individual within a Judicial District of the United States.

(f) Service upon Individuals in a Foreign Country.

(g) Serving a Minor or an Incompetent Person.

(h) Serving a Corporation, Partnership, or Association.

(i) Serving the United States, ITS Agencies, Corporations, Officers, or Employees.

(j) Serving a Foreign, State, or Local Government.

Under each of these subparts are directions for service of the complaint and summons. If you were asked to find the rules for serving a corporation doing business within the United States, you would read and follow the procedures found in subsection (h), not those found in any of the other subsections.

Outline Statutory or Regulatory Language

After identifying a client's issue and relevant facts, and after you determine that a statute or rule applies to your facts, legal analysis requires that you determine the meaning of the relevant law. This is not always easy. Unfortunately, statutory language is often cumbersome and confusing. To be understood, statutes must be carefully read. Although different types of code sections require different approaches to analysis, outlining the language of the law is usually helpful. One type of code or rule is one that sets forth court procedures that must be followed. Outlining the procedures protects you from missing an essential step in the procedures. For example, in researching the procedure for making a motion to suppress evidence, the research associate working on the Meyers case might find a state law similar to Rule 47 of the Federal Rules of Criminal Procedure, which provides the following.

Rule 47. Motions and Supporting Affidavits

(a) In General. A party applying to the court for an order must do so by motion.

(b) Form and Content of a Motion. A motion—except when made during a trial or hearing—must be in writing, unless the court permits the party to make the motion by other means. A motion must state the grounds on which it is based and the relief or order sought. A motion may be supported by affidavit.

(c) Timing of a Motion. A party must serve a written motion—other than one that the court may hear ex parte—and any hearing notice at least 5 days before the hearing date, unless a rule or court order sets a different period. For good cause, the court may set a different period upon ex parte application.

(d) Affidavit Supporting a Motion. The moving party must serve any supporting affidavit with the motion. A responding party must serve any opposing affidavit at least one day before the hearing, unless the court permits later service.

(As amended Apr. 29, 2002, eff. Dec. 1, 2002.)

An outline of this section might look something like the following:

A. Form and Content of the Motion

  1. Must be in writing, unless court says otherwise

  2. Must state the grounds for the motion

  3. Must state the relief requested

  4. Must be supported by affidavits

B. Timing of Service
   1. 5 days service of written notice required
   2. Court can set different time by order or by court rule

C. Supporting and Opposing Affidavits
   1. Affidavits supporting motion must be served with motion
   2. Affidavits opposing motion must be served 1 day prior to court hearing
   3. Court can permit later service

Rather than setting forth procedures to be followed, many statutes establish rights, liabilities, and obligations. This type of statute usually identifies requirements that must be met before the rights, liabilities, or obligations arise. For example, consider Research Problem 9 in Appendix A, *The Rambeaux Matter*. This case arises from a traffic stop made by an off-duty police officer who was still in uniform. Individuals in the vehicle claim that the officer used excessive force during the stop and made racial slurs. The federal prosecutor is considering filing criminal charges against the officer for a civil rights violation under 18 U.S.C. § 242. That section provides:

Whoever, under color of any law, statute, ordinance, regulation, or custom, willfully subjects any person in any State, Territory, Commonwealth, Possession, or District to the deprivation of any rights, privileges, or immunities secured or protected by the Constitution or laws of the United States, or to different punishments, pains, or penalties, on account of such person being an alien, or by reason of his color, or race, than are prescribed for the punishment of citizens, shall be fined under this title or imprisoned not more than one year, or both; and if bodily injury results from the acts committed in violation of this section or if such acts include the use, attempted use, or threatened use of a dangerous weapon, explosives, or fire, shall be fined under this title or imprisoned not more than ten years, or both; and if death results from the acts committed in violation of this section or if such acts include kidnapping or an attempt to kidnap, aggravated sexual abuse, or an attempt to commit aggravated sexual abuse, or an attempt to kill, shall be fined under this title, or imprisoned for any term of years or for life, or both, or may be sentenced to death.

statutory requirements.
Various requirements or elements of a statute that must be met before the statute applies to a situation.

This statute creates criminal liability if certain requirements are met. These are sometimes called **statutory requirements** or sometimes the statutory elements. By outlining the code section, the researcher can determine that the law requires the following elements before any criminal responsibility exists:

1. Someone must act under color of law *and*
2. Act willfully *and*
3. Deprive another of rights granted under the Constitution *or* the laws of U.S.
4. *Or* subject another to different punishments, pains or penalties, *and* do this because of race *or* color *or* because of being an alien.

To analyze a statute, you must pay close attention to all "connectors" and "qualifiers" such as *shall, and, or, except, unless,* and *provided that.* These tell you if all or only some of the elements or requirements must be met before a statute applies to a set of facts.

Before listing the elements of a statute you should identify the research issue or question. The above elements answer the question "When does basic criminal responsibility occur?" If your question is different, your analysis is different. For example, suppose your research question is "What is Rambeaux's potential punishment?" To answer this question you must include the punishment described in the statute.

Outlining a statute or regulation is only one step in the process of analysis. Words or phrases in statutes and regulations are sometimes unclear or ambiguous. Solving these ambiguities or uncertainties is the job of the researcher. This is done in different ways.

Review Case Law That Interprets Code or Regulatory Provisions

If case law explains a statute or regulation and that case law is controlling law in the jurisdiction, the rule of *stare decisis* requires that the court's interpretation be followed. Reading the annotations following the statute helps you locate relevant cases. Consider again the Rambeaux case and the criminal liability statute. A number of questions arise depending on the facts of the case. For example, what does the phrase "under color of any law" mean? Does it include a police officer? What if Rambeaux is off duty at the time of the shooting? Is he still acting under color of law? Also, consider the clause "on account of such person being an alien, or by reason of his color, or race." Does this clause require a racial motivation if an action is based on a deprivation of constitutional rights, or does this clause relate only to a situation where an individual is subject to "different punishments, pains, or penalties"? To answer these questions, it is necessary to see how the courts interpret the statute. Look at Figure 6-1, and a copy of some of the annotations following 18 U.S.C.S. § 242. Looking at the annotations in Figure 6-1 you see that case law provides interpretations. Of course, you cannot rely on reading only the annotation. You must read the entire case.

stare decisis. "It stands decided"; another term for precedent.

A Point to Remember

When using a print resource, always check the pocket part or bound supplement. Even if a code section was not amended, new case decisions may add to the interpretation of the statute.

Even if you think that the words of a statute are clear and that your facts obviously fit the language of the statute, your research should include case law. If courts have applied a particular code section to a factual situation that parallels your factual dispute, this gives added support to your analysis.

Review Other Code Sections

Sometimes terms used in one code section are defined in another section of the same code. For example, Title 6 of the United States Code deals with the Homeland Security Organization. One of the first sections within that title, section 101, provides definitions of several terms that apply in the chapter. See Box 6-1 for a copy of that code section. Note the numerous terms that are defined.

In addition, many codes provide general rules to aid in the interpretation of the language of the code. For example, the following are two basic rules to help us understand the language of the statute.

1. Statutes are to be read as promoting the common law.
2. Particular or specific provisions control over general statements.

18 USCS § 242, n 9

lowing elements must be established by government, namely: (1) that defendants' acts must have deprived someone of right secured or protected by Constitution or laws of United States; (2) that defendants' illegal acts must have been committed under color of law; (3) that person deprived of his rights must have been inhabitant of state, territory, or district; and (4) that defendants must have acted willfully. United States v Shafer (1974, DC Ohio) 384 F Supp 496.

Elements of offense under 18 USCS § 242 are (1) that action was taken under color of state law, (2) wilfully to deprive rights protected by Constitution and laws of United States, (3) from inhabitant of any state of United States. United States v Fleming (1975, ED Mo) 399 F Supp 77, revd on other grounds (1975, CA8 Mo) 526 F2d 191, cert dismd (1976) 423 US 1082, 47 L Ed 2d 93, 96 S Ct 872.

10. Deprivation of rights protected by Federal Constitution or laws

Predecessor of 18 USCS § 242 making it federal offense wilfully to deprive any person under color of law of any rights, privileges, or immunities secured or protected by Constitution and laws of United States, does not come into play merely because law under which officer purports to act is violated, but is applicable only when some one is deprived of Federal right by such action. Screws v United States (1945) 325 US 91, 89 L Ed 1495, 65 S Ct 1031, 162 ALR 1330.

Both 18 USCS § 241, which makes conspiracy to interfere with citizen's free exercise or enjoyment of any right or privilege secured to him by Constitution or laws of United States federal offense, and 18 USCS § 242, which makes it federal offense wilfully to deprive any person under color of law of same rights, include, presumably, all of Constitution and laws of United States. United States v Price (1966) 383 US 787, 16 L Ed 2d 267, 86 S Ct 1152 (ovrld on other grounds by Adickes v S. H. Kress & Co. (1970) 398 US 144, 26 L Ed 2d 142, 90 S Ct 1598) as stated in Gresham Park Community Organization v Howell (1981, CA5 Ga) 652 F2d 1227.

Federal court had jurisdiction where defendant was charged with depriving named person of rights and privileges under Constitution of United States, even though acts of defendants also violated laws of state. Williams v United States (1950, CA5 Fla) 179 F2d 656, affd (1951) 341 US 97, 95 L Ed 774, 71 S Ct 576.

18 USCS § 242 is concerned only with deprivation of rights guaranteed by federal law or Constitution. United States v O'Dell (1972, CA6 Tenn) 462 F2d 224.

Once due process right has been defined and made specific by court decisions, right is encompassed by 18 USCS § 242. United States v Hayes

(1979, CA5 Tex) 589 F2d 811, reh den (1979, CA5 Tex) 591 F2d 1343 and cert den (1979) 444 US 847, 62 L Ed 2d 60, 100 S Ct 93.

Acts done under color of state law do not violate federal law if only local rights are involved, since constitutional right must be violated before federal law is involved. Arkansas use of Temple v Central Surety & Ins. Corp. (1952, DC Ark) 102 F Supp 444.

11. Illegal act committed under color of law, generally

Predecessor to 18 USCS § 242 required actions under color of state law. United States v Powell (1909) 212 US 564, 53 L Ed 653, 29 S Ct 690.

It is immaterial, for purposes of predecessor to 18 USCS § 242, whether acts committed under color of state law are authorized by state law. Guinn v United States (1915) 238 US 347, 59 L Ed 1340, 35 S Ct 926.

Misuse of power, possessed by virtue of state law and made possible only because wrongdoer is clothed with authority of state law, is action taken "under color of" state law, within meaning of predecessor of 18 USCS § 242 making it offense to deprive inhabitant of state of his constitutional rights "under color of" any law. United States v Classic (1941) 313 US 299, 85 L Ed 1368, 61 S Ct 1031, reh den (1941) 314 US 707, 86 L Ed 565, 62 S Ct 51 and (ovrld on other grounds by Monell v Department of Social Services (1978) 436 US 658, 56 L Ed 2d 611, 98 S Ct 2018, 17 BNA FEP Cas 873, 16 CCH EPD ¶ 8345) as stated in Scott v Rosenberg (1983, CA9 Cal) 702 F2d 1263, cert den (1984) 465 US 1078, 79 L Ed 2d 760, 104 S Ct 1439, later proceeding (1984, CA9 Cal) 739 F2d 1464, 39 FR Serv 2d 1295 and later proceeding (1984, CA9 Cal) 746 F2d 1377.

Question was not whether state law had been violated but whether inhabitant of state had been deprived of federal right by one who acted under color of any law. Screws v United States (1945) 325 US 91, 89 L Ed 1495, 65 S Ct 1031, 162 ALR 1330.

Phrase "under color of any statute, ordinance, regulation, or custom" should be accorded same construction in both 18 USC § 242, which provides for criminal punishment of, and Rev Stat § 1979 (42 USC § 1983), which gives right of action against, person who, "under color of" state law, subjects another to deprivation of any rights, privileges, or immunities secured by Federal Constitution. Monroe v Pape (1961) 365 US 167, 5 L Ed 2d 492, 81 S Ct 473 (ovrld on other grounds by Monell v Department of Social Services (1978) 436 US 658, 56 L Ed 2d 611, 98 S Ct 2018, 17 BNA FEP Cas 873, 16 CCH EPD ¶ 8345) and (ovrld on other grounds by Ingraham v Wright (1977) 430 US 651, 51 L Ed 2d 711, 97 S Ct 1401) as stated

452

Annotations from Main Volume and Supplement.

FIGURE 6-1 18 U.S.C.S. § 242

CRIMES   **18 USCS § 242, n 16**

identically in four other provisions of Title 18, namely, 18 USCS §§ 831, 1365(h)(4), 1515(a)(5, 1864(d)(2), as (A) cut, abrasion, bruise, burn, or disfigurement; (B) physical pain; (C) illness; (D) impairment of a/the function of bodily member, organ, or mental faculty; or (E) any other injury to body, no matter how temporary. United States v Bailey (2005, CA1 Mass) 405 F3d 102.

10. Deprivation of rights protected by Federal Constitution or laws

Test of whether officers violated arrestees' or detainees' Fourth Amendment rights by use of excessive force—as distinct from determination of specific intent—is objective one. United States v Reese (1993, CA9 Cal) 2 F3d 870, 93 CDOS 5642, 93 Daily Journal DAR 9617, cert den (1994) 510 US 1094, 127 L Ed 2d 220, 114 S Ct 928 and (criticized in United States v Farrow (1999, CA6 Ohio) 198 F3d 179, 1999 FED App 409P).

11. Illegal act committed under color of law, generally

Government need not prove that police officers who allegedly used excessive force acted for ostensible government purpose rather than for personal reasons, since their acts were committed "under color of law." United States v Reese (1993, CA9 Cal) 2 F3d 870, 93 CDOS 5642, 93 Daily Journal DAR 9617, cert den (1994) 510 US 1094, 127 L Ed 2d 220, 114 S Ct 928 and (criticized in United States v Farrow (1999, CA6 Ohio) 198 F3d 179, 1999 FED App 409P).

Evidence was sufficient to show that town's mayor was acting "under color of law" when he invoked real or apparent power of his office to allegedly make continuing sexual abuse of two minor children possible in violation of 18 USCS § 242 because evidence established that mayor threatened minor children (and their mother/aunt) by invoking his "special authority" as mayor to undertake retaliatory action, and he used his authority to cause victims to submit to repeated abuse, by causing victims to fear that he would use his mayoral power to harm them if they reported abuse. United States v Giordano (2006, CA2) 442 F3d 30.

12. —Miscellaneous

Off-duty police officer who admitted to beating prisoner in city jail, using his official authority to get prisoner out of jail cell in order to attack him, and threatening to arrest prisoner every time he saw him in future was guilty of violating 18 USCS § 242 under color of state law, even though he was off-duty at time and his motivation was personal. United States v Colbert (1999, CA8 Mo) 172 F3d 594.

Convictions of police officer, drug dealer, and his associate for conspiracy to violate 18 USCS § 241 and violation of 18 USCS §§ 242, 1512 regarding murder of individual who filed complaint against police officer were for conduct "under color of state law," where officer abused his official power to access police station, police car, and police radio to plan, execute, and cover up murder, and his codefendants jointly engaged with him in these prohibited actions. United States v Causey (1999, CA5 La) 185 F3d 407, cert den (2000) 530 US 1277, 147 L Ed 2d 1010, 120 S Ct 2747 and cert den (2000) 530 US 1277, 147 L Ed 2d 1010, 120 S Ct 2747 and cert den (2000) 530 US 1277, 147 L Ed 2d 1010, 120 S Ct 2747 and (criticized in United States v Guadalupe (2005, CA3 Pa) 2005 US App LEXIS 5155).

Court affirmed defendant's conviction for felonious

deprivation of civil rights under color of law in violation of 18 USCS § 242; where defendant was in uniform and on duty and victim was in custody at jail, even if defendant did not participate in victim's arrest and victim was not in defendant's custody, there was sufficient evidence that defendant acted "under color of law" when he punched and kneed victim in face. United States v Christian (2003, CA7 Ind) 342 F3d 744, 62 Fed Rules Evid Serv 55, cert den (2004) 540 US 1126, 157 L Ed 2d 927, 124 S Ct 1095.

14. Willfulness; intent

In determining whether police officers assigned to special drug task force had specific intent to use excessive force in arresting and detaining individuals, it was not necessary to prove that they knew their conduct was unlawful. United States v Reese (1993, CA9 Cal) 2 F3d 870, 93 CDOS 5642, 93 Daily Journal DAR 9617, cert den (1994) 510 US 1094, 127 L Ed 2d 220, 114 S Ct 928 and (criticized in United States v Farrow (1999, CA6 Ohio) 198 F3d 179, 1999 FED App 409P).

In order to convict under 18 USCS § 242, government must show that defendant had particular purpose of violating protected right made definite by rule of law or recklessly disregarded risk that he would violate such right; government does not need to show that defendant knowingly violated any right. United States v Johnstone (1997, CA3 NJ) 107 F3d 200 (criticized in United States v Farrow (1999, CA6 Ohio) 198 F3d 179, 1999 FED App 409P).

"Willfulness" under 18 USCS § 242 essentially requires that defendant intended to commit unconstitutional act without necessarily intending to do that act for specific purpose of depriving another of constitutional right; in other words, to act "willfully" in § 242 sense, defendant must intend to commit act that results in deprivation of established constitutional right as reasonable person would understand that right. United States v Bradley (1999, CA7 Ill) 196 F3d 762.

Evidence that defendant, police officer, released defendant's police dog on another suspect at later date was probative of willfulness by suggesting that, at least on one other occasion, defendant used dog in reckless disregard of another's right to be free from excessive force and was admissible under FRE 404(b), and was not unduly prejudicial under FRE 403 merely because it was pointed out that suspect was African-American; defendant's conviction under 18 USCS § 242 was affirmed. United States v Mohr (2003, CA4 Md) 318 F3d 613, 60 Fed Rules Evid Serv 906.

Actions of 400-pound correctional officer in stepping on prison inmate's penis on 3 separate occasions were subjectively wanton and malicious, violating inmate's Eighth Amendment rights and satisfying subjective element of conviction of criminal deprivation of rights under color of law pursuant to 18 USCS § 242, since there was no need for application of force used, there was no threat reasonably perceived by officer given that inmate was in his cell, and officer made no effort to temper severity of his forceful response. United States v Walsh (1998, WD NY) 27 F Supp 2d 186, subsequent app (1999, CA2 NY) 194 F3d 37.

III. RIGHTS AND PRIVILEGES SECURED OR PROTECTED

16. Freedom from unlawful arrest

Criminal liability may be imposed on commanding police officer who failed to prevent use of excessive

157

These annotations are in a pocket-part supplement. Note the newer cases.

FIGURE 6-1
(continued)

BOX 6-1   6 U.S.C. § 101

In this chapter, the following definitions apply:

(1) Each of the terms "American homeland" and "homeland" means the United States.

(2) The term "appropriate congressional committee" means any committee of the House of Representatives or the Senate having legislative or oversight jurisdiction under the Rules of the House of Representatives or the Senate, respectively, over the matter concerned.

(3) The term "assets" includes contracts, facilities, property, records, unobligated or unexpended balances of appropriations, and other funds or resources (other than personnel).

(4) The term "critical infrastructure" has the meaning given that term in section 5195c(e) of Title 42.

(5) The term "Department" means the Department of Homeland Security.

(6) The term "emergency response providers" includes Federal, State, and local governmental and nongovernmental emergency public safety, fire, law enforcement, emergency response, emergency medical (including hospital emergency facilities), and related personnel, agencies, and authorities.

(7) The term "executive agency" means an executive agency and a military department, as defined, respectively, in sections 105 and 102 of Title 5.

(8) The term "functions" includes authorities, powers, rights, privileges, immunities, programs, projects, activities, duties, and responsibilities.

(9) The term "key resources" means publicly or privately controlled resources essential to the minimal operations of the economy and government.

(10) The term "local government" means—
    (A) a county, municipality, city, town, township, local public authority, school district, special district, intrastate district, council of governments (regardless of whether the council of governments is incorporated as a nonprofit corporation under State law), regional or interstate government entity, or agency or instrumentality of a local government;
    (B) an Indian tribe or authorized tribal organization, or in Alaska a Native village or Alaska Regional Native Corporation; and
    (C) a rural community, unincorporated town or village, or other public entity.

(11) The term "major disaster" has the meaning given in section 5122(2) of Title 42.

(12) The term "personnel" means officers and employees.

(13) The term "Secretary" means the Secretary of Homeland Security.

(14) The term "State" means any State of the United States, the District of Columbia, the Commonwealth of Puerto Rico, the Virgin Islands, Guam, American Samoa, the Commonwealth of the Northern Mariana Islands, and any possession of the United States.

(15) The term "terrorism" means any activity that—
    (A) involves an act that—
        (i) is dangerous to human life or potentially destructive of critical infrastructure or key resources; and
        (ii) is a violation of the criminal laws of the United States or of any State or other subdivision of the United States; and
    (B) appears to be intended—
        (i) to intimidate or coerce a civilian population;
        (ii) to influence the policy of a government by intimidation or coercion; or
        (iii) to affect the conduct of a government by mass destruction, assassination, or kidnapping.

> **BOX 6-1** **(Continued)**
> **(16)** **(A)** The term "United States", when used in a geographic sense, means any State of the United States, the District of Columbia, the Commonwealth of Puerto Rico, the Virgin Islands, Guam, American Samoa, the Commonwealth of the Northern Mariana Islands, any possession of the United States, and any waters within the jurisdiction of the United States.
> **(B)** Nothing in this paragraph or any other provision of this chapter shall be construed to modify the definition of "United States" for the purposes of the Immigration and Nationality Act [8 U.S.C.A. § 1101 et seq.] or any other immigration or nationality law.

Watch Your Dates

When a factual dispute is controlled by both statutory law and case law, differences may exist between the two sources of law. When this happens, it is important to check the dates of the statute and the case. To determine whether the statute or the case applies, use the following guidelines:

1. If the issue is constitutional, then the case probably controls, regardless of the dates, unless the Constitution was amended.
2. If a statute is passed after a case is decided, that statute probably controls over the case, unless the issue is constitutional.
3. If there is a constitutional amendment after a case decision, then the constitutional amendment controls.

Read Box 6-2. This sets out the development of the law in California regarding the liability of bar owners and social hosts for furnishing too much alcohol to someone who injures another.

> **BOX 6-2** **TEST YOURSELF**
> **CHANGES IN THE LAW—STATUTES AND CASES**
>
> **Reconciling Statutes and Case Law**
>
> **Research Question:** Is a person who furnishes alcohol to another liable to a third person who is injured by an intoxicated individual to whom alcohol was furnished?
>
> **Research Findings:** Prior to 1971, common law was followed. Common law provides that there is no liability on the part of the one who furnishes alcohol because that person is not the proximate cause of the injuries.
>
> 1971—State Supreme Court decides that the common law rule should not be followed as to commercial providers of alcohol (bars) and that they should be liable to third persons who are injured by one to whom alcohol was provided.
>
> 1978—State Supreme Court extends rule of liability to non-commercial providers of alcohol.
>
> 1978—State legislature amends statutes, expressly abrogates above holdings of State Supreme Court and provides that commercial and noncommercial providers

> **BOX 6-2   (Continued)**
>
> of alcohol to intoxicated persons are not the proximate cause of injuries suffered by a third person injured by the intoxicated individual.
>
> Based on the above case and statute, how would you answer the research question?
>
> **Answer:**
>
> Here, the statute eliminating liability of bars and other providers of alcohol was enacted after the California Supreme Court decision. Because this case does not involve any constitutional issue, the statute controls, not the case.

Legislative History

Another source used to aid in statutory interpretation is the legislative history of the statute. The legislative history helps the researcher determine the intent of the legislature in passing the law. A bill goes through several stages before becoming law. At each step there are records of what happened. These records include copies of the bill with deletions, additions, and changes noted. They might include transcripts of hearings and discussions on the bill. Rather than seeking the originals of these records, you can use a source such as *United States Code and Congressional and Administrative News* (U.S.C.C.A.N.). This contains the legislative history of statutes, federal regulations, and court rules. It contains bills in their original format, changes, and committee hearings and discussions. See Figure 6-2 for an example of the contents of U.S.C.C.A.N.

6-4 APPLYING STATUTORY LAW TO A FACT PATTERN

Statutory or regulatory analysis is not complete until you *explain* how a particular code section or rule controls your factual situation. When you explain a position, you should use the general IRAC approach in much the same way you do in using case law. (Review Chapters 3 and 4.) The IRAC approach consists of the following:

1. Stating your **I**ssue
2. Stating the **R**ule of law that applies
3. **A**nalyzing the situation by applying the law to your facts
4. Reaching a **C**onclusion

The issue is the question you are researching. The rule of law is the relevant code section. The analysis consists of applying your facts to the language of the law. The conclusion is the answer to your research question. Any factual situation may contain more than one issue. Each issue is analyzed separately using the IRAC approach. Consider the Rambeaux case mentioned earlier in the chapter. Assume you are working with the following facts.

Randy Rambeaux made a routine traffic stop on an automobile because the driver failed to signal when making a right-hand turn. The occupants of the vehicle were two Latino males in their late teens. According to the occupants, the following events occurred. Rambeaux approached the car and ordered the two out of the car. When the occupants asked why, Rambeaux opened the driver's door, and with his weapon drawn and pointed directly at the driver, again ordered them out of the car.

OKLAHOMA CITY NATIONAL MEMORIAL ACT OF 1997

PUBLIC LAW 105–58, see page 111 Stat. 1261

DATES OF CONSIDERATION AND PASSAGE

Senate: July 31, 1997

House: September 23, 1997

Cong. Record Vol. 143 (1997)

Senate Report (Energy and Natural Resources Committee)
No. 105–71, July 30, 1997
[To accompany S. 871]

House Report (Resources Committee)
No. 105–316, October 8, 1997
[To accompany H.R. 1849]

The Senate Report is set out below.

SENATE REPORT NO. 105–71

[page 1]

The Committee on Energy and Natural Resources, to which was referred the bill (S. 871) to establish the Oklahoma City National Memorial as a unit of the National Park System; to designate the Oklahoma City Memorial Trust, and for other purposes, having considered the same, reports favorably thereon without amendment and recommends that the bill do pass.

PURPOSE OF THE MEASURE

The purpose of S. 871 is to establish the Oklahoma City National Memorial as a unit of the National Park System and to establish the Oklahoma City Memorial Trust and to manage the Memorial.

BACKGROUND AND NEED

One hundred and sixty-eight Americans lost their lives and many more were injured on April 19, 1995, when a bomb was detonated at the Alfred P. Murrah Federal Building in Oklahoma City, Oklahoma. This tragedy constitutes the worst domestic terrorist incident in American history.

This legislation would create a memorial at the site of the Murray Federal Building in Oklahoma City on 5th Street, between Robinson and Harvey Streets and would also include the sites of the Water Resources Building and Journal Record Building.

Concepts for the memorial were solicited through a design competition that included 624 design submissions from all 50 states and 23 foreign countries. The design that was selected was created by Hans-Ekkehard Butzer, Torrey Butzer and Sven Berg, a German-based design team. The design includes 168 chairs in the Murrah Building footprint, a water element designed to reflect spirit of change, a survivor tree, envisioned to reflect hope and "gates of time" on each end of Fifth Street that focus the visitor's attention on memorial inscriptions and the other elements of the memorial. Torrey Butzer of the German team states, "We watched Oklahomans and the world respond to this terrible tragedy from afar. This is our way of giving something to honor the victims, survivors and the heros. This design will tell the story of all of us changed forever."

The memorial established pursuant to this Act would serve not only as a monument to those who died and were injured in the bombing on April 19th, but also as a symbol of the galvanization of 'assistance, courage and good will shown by local citizens and Americans across the country in their outpouring of aid following the incident.

The Oklahoma City National Memorial will be designated as a unit of the National Park System. It will be placed under the charge of a wholly-owned government corporation, to be known as the Oklahoma City National Trust (Trust). The Trust will be governed by a nine-member Board of Directors (Board) which will have the authority to appoint an executive director and other key staff. Interim staff are authorized for two years to assist in the development of the memorial. Permanent National Park service staff and the ability to retain staff from other Federal agencies are also provided for by this measure on a reimbursable basis.

S. 871 authorizes $5 million in Federal funds for construction and maintenance, but stipulates that any Federal expenditures must be matched by non-Federal funds, dollar for dollar. It is expected that matching fund sources will include the Oklahoma State legislature and private donations.

FIGURE 6-2

Sample Page from U.S.C.C.A.N.

LEGISLATIVE HISTORY

S. 871 was introduced June 10, 1997 by Senators Nickles and Inhofe and was referred to the Committee on Energy and Natural Resources. The Subcommittee on National Parks, Historic Preservation and Recreation held a hearing in Oklahoma City on July 3, 1997 and in Washington, D.C. on July 17, 1997.

COMMITTEE RECOMMENDATIONS AND TABULATION OF VOTES

The Committee on Energy and Natural Resources, in open business session on July 30, 1997, by a unanimous vote of a quorum present, recommends that the Senate pass S. 871 without amendment.

The rollcall vote on reporting the measure was 20 yeas, 0 nays, as follows:

YEAS	NAYS
Mr. Murkowski	
Mr. Domenici	
Mr. Nickles	
Mr. Craig	
Mr. Campbell[1]	
Mr. Thomas	
Mr. Kyl	
Mr. Grams	
Mr. Smith	
Mr. Gorton	
Mr. Burns[1]	
Mr. Bumpers	
Mr. Ford	
Mr. Bingaman[1]	
Mr. Akaka	
Mr. Dorgan	
Mr. Graham	
Mr. Wyden	
Mr. Johnson	
Ms. Landrieu[1]	

[1]Indicates voted by proxy.

SECTION-BY-SECTION ANALYSIS

Section 1 entitles the bill the "Oklahoma City National Memorial Act of 1997".

Section 2 sets forth Congressional findings and purpose. The purpose of the bill is to establish the Oklahoma City National Memorial as a unit of the National Park System and to further establish how the memorial will be developed and managed.

Section 3 defines certain terms in the bill.

Section 4(a) establishes the Oklahoma City National Memorial (Memorial) and further establishes the Memorial as a unit of the National Park System.

Subsection (b) references the official boundary map for the memorial and authorizes the Oklahoma City National Memorial Trust (the Trust) to make boundary revisions when necessary.

Section 5(a) establishes a wholly owned government corporation to be known as the Oklahoma City National Memorial Trust.

Section (b)(1) sets forth the membership of the Board of Directors (Board) for the Trust. The 9-member Board shall consist of the Secretary of the Interior (Secretary) or his designee and 8 additional members appointed by the President, but selected from lists of nominees submitted by the Governor of Oklahoma, the Mayor of Oklahoma City and the Oklahoma delegations from the United States House of Representatives and Senate. This section also directs that the President is to appoint the Board members within 90 days after the date of enactment.

Paragraph (b)(2) sets the terms of Board members at 4 years and limits consecutive terms to 8 years. The section also staggers the first series of appointments, with two members serving for 2 years and two members serving a term of 3 years.

Paragraph (b)(3) directs that 5 members shall constitute a quorum.

Paragraph (b)(4) directs that the Board shall organize itself in a manner it deems most appropriate and that members shall not receive compensation, but may be reimbursed for actual and necessary travel and subsistence associated with Trust duties.

Paragraph (b)(5) establishes that Board members will not be considered Federal employees except for the purposes of the Federal Tort Claims Act, the Ethics in Government Act and provisions of titles 11 and 18 of the United States Code.

FIGURE 6-2
(continued)

After the driver exited the vehicle, Rambeaux struck him on the head with the gun and, according to the two occupants, said, "Why don't you guys go back where you belong? This country is for Americans." The driver maintains that he did nothing to provoke the attack.

You are asked to research whether Rambeaux is criminally responsible under 18 U.S.C. § 242. This is an issue. The rule of law in this case is the code section 18 U.S.C. § 242. The analysis is accomplished by identifying the elements or requirements of the code section and then matching each element with the relevant facts. This should be done initially in an outline or table format. See Box 6-3 for an example of a table listing the statutory requirements of 18 U.S.C. § 242 and the related facts.

BOX 6-3

Requirements of 18 U.S.C. § 242	**Application to Client Facts**
1. Accused must act under color of authority.	Rambeaux is a police officer, performing a police function, that is, a traffic stop.
2. The action must be willful.	The incident was intentional, not accidental.
3. The action must either deprive a person of civil rights *or* impose different punishment, penalties, or pains because of race, and so on.	Rambeaux violated the Fourth Amendment to the Constitution: unreasonable arrest. Rambeaux beat the suspect; his comments about "going back" and "Americans" suggest racial bias.

A complete analysis requires that you find and discuss case law that interprets this code section. For example, suppose in the Rambeaux case that Rambeaux was off duty when the incident occurred. Under such circumstances, whether he was acting under color of authority is questionable and case law should be researched. This research might lead you to the case of *United States v. Tarpley*, 945 F.2d 806 (5th Cir. 1991). The *Tarpley* case discusses the meaning of color of law and helps to answer the question of whether an off-duty police officer can be acting under color of law. The case is found later in this chapter. After researching applicable case law you should revise your analysis outline or table. It should then look something like the table in Box 6-4.

BOX 6-4

Requirements of 18 U.S.C. § 242	**Case Law Interpretation of Statutory Provisions**	**Application to Client Facts**
1. Accused must act under color of authority.	*U.S. v. Tarpley:* Police officer was acting under color of law rather than as jealous husband where air of official authority pervaded entire assault incident.	Rambeaux is a police officer, performing a police function, that is, a traffic stop. The stop had the air of official authority.
2. The action must be willful.	(Here you include cases that discuss the meaning of willful.)	The incident was intentional, not accidental.

After outlining the statutory requirements, determining the meaning of these requirements by examining case law and then applying each element to your facts, you can reach a conclusion. The conclusion should answer the question you are researching. In this case, the conclusion tells whether Rambeaux violated the statute.

Your analysis is not complete until you communicate your findings in an appropriate manner. Subsequent chapters in this text describe the various types of documents used to accomplish this. However, Box 6-5 illustrates a preliminary draft of a statutory analysis using the IRAC method. Be sure to read the *Tarpley* case before reading Box 6-5.

CASE 6-1

United States v. Tarpley,
945 F.2d 806 (5th Cir. 1991)

A deputy sheriff appeals his conviction for violations of 18 U.S.C. §§ 241 and 242, which prohibit the deprivation of rights secured by the Constitution and laws of the United States under color of law. We find sufficient evidence to show that the defendant acted under color of law and conspired with another in doing so, and affirm.

I.

This is what happened, in the light most favorable to the government. In 1988, William Tarpley, deputy, Collingsworth County Sheriff's police force, learned of a past affair of his wife, Kathryn and Kerry Lee Vestal. Tarpley devised a plan to lure Vestal to the Tarpley home for the purpose of assaulting him.

Tarpley had his wife call Vestal and tell him that she had separated from her husband and that she wanted him to come pick her up. On the day that Vestal was to arrive,

Tarpley and another deputy, Michael Pena, made a pair of "sap gloves" in his office at the sheriff's station. These are gloves with rubber hosing filled with metal or lead shot attached to the fingers. Tarpley told Pena that he planned to have his wife call her boyfriend over and then use the sap gloves on him.

That evening, Tarpley parked his patrol car behind the house of another deputy so as not to alert Vestal that he was at home. When Vestal arrived at the Tarpley residence, Mrs. Tarpley opened the door and pulled him into the house. Mr. Tarpley immediately tackled Vestal and hit him repeatedly in the head. He also inserted his service pistol in Vestal's mouth. He told Vestal that he was a sergeant on the police department, that he would and should kill Vestal, and that he could get away with it because he was a cop. He repeated "I'll kill you. I'm a cop. I can." As he continued to beat and threaten Vestal, Mrs. Tarpley may have been taking pictures of the encounter.

Tarpley then had his wife telephone the sheriff's station and ask Pena to come to their house. She did, and when Pena arrived, Tarpley introduced him to Vestal as a fellow sergeant from the police department. Pena confirmed Tarpley's claims that Tarpley had shot people in the past.

Eventually, Tarpley let Vestal go, chasing him out of the house with threats to kill him if he reported the incident. Pena then gave Vestal his keys, and Vestal drove away, but not before Tarpley smashed the headlights on Vestal's truck. Pena and the Tarpleys followed Vestal in Pena's squad car until Vestal had left town. Pena also apparently radioed for another officer to meet up with them and that police car also followed Vestal to the edge of town.

A federal grand jury indicted Tarpley and Pena and "another individual known to the grand jury" for conspiracy to injure and oppress Vestal in the exercise of his constitutional rights, as well as willfully subjecting Vestal to a deprivation of his constitutional rights, in violation of 18 U.S.C. §§ 241 and 242. Jointly tried, Pena was acquitted on both counts and Tarpley was convicted on both counts. Defense counsel later learned that during the trial one of the jurors spoke with the juror's daughter, a legal secretary, about the difficulty he had understanding the nature of a conspiracy charge. There was also evidence that the juror's daughter had in turn contacted a lawyer about the matter. The district court held a hearing concerning these events at which both the lawyer and the juror's daughter testified. The court determined that no extrinsic evidence had reached the jury and that further investigation was not required.

Tarpley now appeals his conviction to this court.

II.

Tarpley was convicted of violating two statutes, both of which require that an individual act "under color of law." 18 U.S.C. §§ 241 and 242. Tarpley argues that the jury's finding that he acted "under color of law" was insufficiently supported by the evidence produced at trial. In reviewing the sufficiency of the evidence, this court "must view the evidence in the light most favorable to the verdict to determine whether any rational trier of fact could have found each element of the crime beyond a reasonable doubt." *United States v. Berisha*, 925 F.2d 791, 795 (5th Cir. 1991).

The Supreme Court has in two famous cases explained the concept of "under color of law." In *United States v. Classic*, 313 U.S. 299, 326 (1941), the court stated that "misuse of power, possessed by virtue of state law and made possible only because the wrongdoer is clothed with the authority of state law, is action taken 'under color of' state law." In *Screws v. United States*, 325 U.S. 91, 111 (1944), the court reaffirmed the classic formula and stated more simply that "under 'color' of law means under 'pretense' of law." The court in *Screws* also observed that "acts of officers who undertake to perform their official duties are included whether they hew to the line of their authority or overstep it." *Id.* However, "acts of officers in the ambit of their personal pursuits are plainly excluded."

This court and other courts of appeals have made clear that whether a police officer is acting under color of law does not depend on duty status at the time of the alleged violation. *Delcambre v. Delcambre*, 635 F.2d 407 (5th Cir. 1981) (*per curiam*); *Layne v. Sampley*, 627 F.2d 12, 13 (6th Cir. 1980). Nor does *Screws* mean that if officials act for purely personal reasons, they necessarily fail to act "under color of law." *Brown v. Miller*, 631 F.2d 408 (5th Cir. 1980); *United States v. Davila*, 704 F.2d 749 (5th Cir. 1983). Rather, *Screws* held simply that individuals pursuing private aims and not acting by virtue of state authority are not acting under color of law purely because they are state officers. *Brown*, 631 F.2d at 411. Tarpley argues that there is no evidence that he "misused power possessed by virtue of state law" or that his actions were "made possible only because" he was "clothed with state authority." According to Tarpley, he was acting as a jealous husband, not as a police officer. He assaulted Vestal in his own home under circumstances in which it was clear that the motive for his attack was the extramarital affair. That he told Vestal that he was a police officer, the argument continues, does not suggest that he was purporting to act under official authority. He never threatened to arrest Vestal. Vestal already knew he was a cop.

We are not persuaded. There was sufficient evidence in the record from which a rational juror could conclude that Tarpley was acting under color of law. Tarpley did more than simply use his service weapon and identify himself as a police officer. At several points during his assault of Vestal, he claimed to have special authority for his actions by virtue of his official status. He claimed that he could kill Vestal because he was an officer of the law. Significantly, Tarpley summoned another police officer from the sheriff's station and identified him as a fellow officer and ally. The men then proceeded to run Vestal out of town in their squad car. The presence of police and the air of official authority pervaded the entire incident. Under these circumstances, we are unwilling to say that no rational juror could find that Tarpley acted under color of law.

III.

The defendant also contends that he cannot be convicted on the conspiracy count after his alleged co-conspirator, Pena, was acquitted in the same proceeding. *The United States v. Klein*, 560 F.2d 1236, 1242 (5th Cir. 1977), *cert. denied*, 434 U.S. 1073 (1978), for the proposition that the conviction of only one defendant in a conspiracy prosecution will not be upheld if all other alleged co-conspirators are acquitted. Although this has long been the rule in this Circuit, *see, e.g., Herman v. United States*, 289 F.2d 362, 368 (5th Cir.1961); *United States v. Sheikh*, 654 F.2d 1057, 1062 (5th Cir. 1981), its continuing validity has recently come into question. We need not address this issue in this case, however, because there was a third potential co-conspirator not acquitted. The indictment alleged that "Tarpley and Pena, and another individual known to the grand jury, conspired to injure, threaten, oppress, and intimidate Kerry Vestal." The evidence is sufficient to support a conspiracy between Tarpley and this other individual, namely his wife. Mrs. Tarpley phoned Vestal and convinced him to come to the Tarpley home. She pulled Vestal into the house and apparently took pictures while her husband beat him. She contacted Pena at her husband's bidding and accompanied the two men as they followed Vestal out of town.

This court has held that even when named co-conspirators are acquitted, a person can be convicted of conspiring with unnamed individuals as long as the indictment refers to these individuals and the evidence supports their complicity. *United States v. Price*, 869 F.2d 801, 805 (5th Cir. 1989). It is also clear that "private persons, jointly engaged with state officials in the prohibited action, are acting 'under color' of law for purposes of the statute." *United States v. Price*, 383 U.S. 787, 794 (1996); *Adickes v. S.H. Kress & Co.*, 398 U.S. 144, 152 (1970).

IV.

The defendant argues next that the district court erred in its investigation of juror misconduct by failing to allow him to question the jurors or by failing to conduct its own voir dire. He relies on *United States v. Phillips*, 664 F.2d 971 (5th Cir.), *cert. denied*, 457 U.S. 1136 (1981), for the proposition that "any off-the-record contact with a jury is presumptively prejudicial and the Government bears a heavy burden of proving that such contact did not affect the jury; if the Government cannot meet this burden, a new trial is required." He argues that the government failed to carry its burden and that the district court effectively shifted the burden to him. We review the district court's decision not to grant a new trial for an abuse of discretion. *United States v. Sedigh*, 658 F.2d 1010, 1014 (5th Cir. 1981), *cert. denied*, 455 U.S. 921 (1982).

The defendant's argument is without merit. The district court here followed established procedure for addressing allegations of juror misconduct. This court has held that "the trial court should investigate the asserted impropriety to determine initially if and what extrinsic factual matter was disclosed to the jury." *Sedigh*, 658 F.2d at 1014. When the allegations remain speculative, the trial court need not inquire further. *Id.*

The district court in this case held a hearing at which the juror's daughter and the lawyer with whom she spoke testified. The juror's daughter testified that although her father had expressed uncertainty as to whether the crime of conspiracy required that both co-conspirators be convicted, she did not express any opinion on the matter. When she asked a lawyer about it, he told her that any communication with a juror on such issues was improper, and the juror's daughter had no further contact with the juror until after the verdict was rendered. The district court found that this testimony indicated beyond a reasonable doubt that extrinsic evidence was not disclosed to the jury. Consequently, further investigation was not required. The district court acted in accordance with standard procedures and did not abuse its discretion.

It is true that if the defendant had been able to demonstrate as a threshold matter that improper communication of extrinsic information had likely occurred, further investigation might have been required. *See United States v. Forrest*, 620 F.2d 446, 457–58 (5th Cir. 1980) (describing a two-part process under which voir dire is required upon a threshold showing of likely communication of extrinsic material). However in this case, the district court found that no extrinsic information had reached the jury. Contrary to defendant's assertions, it is not sufficient to trigger the requirement of further investigation that a juror have had contact with an outside source of information. Rather, the defendant must show "that extraneous prejudicial material had likely reached the jury." *Forrest*, 620 F.2d at 458. This showing was not made in the present case.

V.

Finally, the defendant argues that several sentences in the jury instructions were misleading. The standard for their review is "'whether the court's charge, as a whole, is a correct statement of the law and whether it clearly instructs the jurors as to the principles of law applicable to the factual issues confronting them.'" *United States v. Stacey*, 896 F.2d 75, 77 (5th Cir. 1990) [citations omitted].

Defendant's objections to the length and repetition in the jury instructions are without merit. Evaluated as a whole, the court's instructions stated the law. AFFIRMED.

BOX 6-5   STATUTORY ANALYSIS

Under the facts presented, Rambeaux probably committed a criminal offense as defined in 18 U.S.C. § 242. This section makes it a federal crime for anyone acting under color of authority to deprive any person of a constitutional right or to subject a person to different punishments, pains, or penalties because of that person's race or color. In order for Rambeaux to be found guilty of the federal crime, the following elements must be shown:

Issue
(The issue is found in the first sentence.)

1. That he acted under color of law;
2. That he acted willfully;
3. That he deprived someone of his constitutional rights or;
4. That he imposed different punishments, pains, or penalties and that he did this because of the person's race or color.

Rules
(Here you set out the statutory requirements.)

In this case, when Rambeaux made the traffic stop and ordered the occupants out of the car, he was off duty. Therefore, a question arises as to whether he was acting under color of law. In *United States v. Tarpley*, 945 F.2d 806 (5th Cir. 1991) a federal appellate court was faced with a similar situation. In the *Tarpley* case, defendant Tarpley, a deputy sheriff, learned of a past affair between his wife and another individual, Vestal. Tarpley assaulted Vestal by inserting his service revolver in Vestal's mouth and told him that he could get away with it because he was a police officer. Tarpley also enlisted the aid of another sheriff's deputy to threaten Vestal. When they finally released Vestal, the officers followed him in a police vehicle. Tarpley was arrested and charged with violating 18 U.S.C. § 242. He was found guilty and appealed, claiming that he was not acting under color of law because he was off duty at the time of these events. The court of appeals found that even though he was off duty, he was still acting under color of law because "the air of official authority pervaded the entire incident." *United States v. Tarpley*, 945 F.2d 806, 809. In like manner, the air of official authority pervades the Rambeaux incident. Rambeaux was doing what police officers routinely do—stopping traffic offenders. He was acting on behalf of the State, attempting to enforce state laws. Thus, Rambeaux was acting under color of law, meeting the first element of the statute.

Analysis
(Here you apply the language of the statute to your facts. You also compare facts of relevant cases to your client's facts.)

All of the actions in this case were clearly willful. Rambeaux knew what he was doing and intended to do what he did. This was no accident. [At this point bring in case law that interprets the word, willful.] Thus, the second element is met.

BOX 6-5   (Continued)

In making this traffic stop, Rambeaux violated the constitutional rights of the driver. The Constitution guarantees that all persons have the right to be free from unreasonable searches and seizures. In this case, Rambeaux made a traffic stop and in doing this "seized" the persons in the vehicle, even if only temporarily. While Rambeaux may have been justified in making the stop, his conduct during this seizure was clearly unreasonable. The use of physical force such as occurred here is not allowed in simple traffic stops where the offender neither uses any force nor threatens the officer with any the use of force. [At this point refer to case law that describes what force is constitutionally permissible during a traffic stop] Thus, the third element of the statute is met.

In addition to violating the victim's constitutional rights, the evidence also suggests that Rambeaux subjected him to different punishment or pain because of the victim's race. Rambeaux used unnecessary force, subjecting the victim to pain. While it may be difficult to prove racial motivation, the facts do suggest its existence. According to the witnesses, Rambeaux made the statement, "Why don't you guys go back where you belong? This country is for Americans." This is strong evidence that Rambeaux's actions were racially motivated, also fulfilling the third requirement of the statute. [At this point discuss case law that interprets this element of the statute.]

Conclusion   The facts of this case support the conclusion that Rambeaux violated the federal law.

BOX 6-6   STATUTORY ANALYSIS CHECKLIST

- Determine if statute applies.
- Outline statutory language, listing the elements or requirements of the law.
- Note the meaning of connectors such as *and, or,* etc.
- Determine meaning of statutory terms by referring to other code sections, case law, or legislative histories.
- Apply statutory law to factual situation using IRAC method.

Online Legal Research

The Internet provides access to many legal documents containing examples of statutory legal analysis. The following sites are valuable resources for sample documents:

www.usdoj.gov The Web site for the Department of Justice contains numerous briefs and memoranda. Reading these documents will help develop your analytic skills. To find the documents, go to the homepage and search for "legal cases and documents."

http://www.supremecourtus.gov/ The Web site for the U.S. Supreme Court provides a link to merits, briefs, and transcripts of oral arguments for cases heard by the Court.

http://supreme.lp.findlaw.com/supreme_court/briefs/index.html Findlaw publishes many of the briefs filed by the parties for Supreme Court cases.

CITATION MATTERS

CAPITALIZATION

THE BLUEBOOK—RULE 8

In titles and headings, capitalize the first word, the word following a colon, and all other words except articles, prepositions of four or fewer letters, and conjunctions of four or fewer letters. Capitalize nouns referring to groups or people only when they identify specific, groups, persons, government offices, or government bodies or groups:

> the President
>
> Congress
>
> the Agency
>
> the FBI

Capitalize *act* only when referring to a specific act:

> Labor Management Relations Act
>
> the Act

Capitalize *circuit* only when used with the circuit number:

> the Ninth Circuit

Capitalize *code* only when referring to the *specific* code:

> the 1956 and 1962 Codes

Capitalize *constitution* only when naming a constitution in full and when referring to the U.S. Constitution. Always capitalize components of the United States Constitution when using them in textual sentences:

> Fourteenth Amendment
>
> Supremacy Clause
>
> Article I, Section 8, Clause 17 of the Constitution

However, this is the proper capitalization in a *citation:*

> U.S. CONST. art I, & § 8, cl. 17

> Capitalize *judge* only when using the name of a specific justice or judge, or when referring to a United States Supreme Court Justice:

> Judge Murphy
>
> Justice Marshall
>
> the Justice (used as a reference to a United States Supreme Court Justice)

CHAPTER SUMMARY

Unlike case law, statutory law, administrative regulations, and constitutions contain general rules intended to apply to many different factual situations. Therefore, legal analysis based on these sources differs from analysis based on case law. Analyzing a legal question based on these sources requires that you determine the meaning of the law. When researching constitutional law, you must further determine whether the situation is governed by the state constitution or the U.S. Constitution. Statutory and regulatory analysis requires that you outline relevant provisions of the law by identifying the elements, sometimes referred to as *statutory requirements*. The various elements should then be applied to the facts of the case. Where the meaning of a word or phrase is unclear, you should review other statutory law, case law, or legislative history. A written analysis of a statute, administrative regulation, or constitution should follow the IRAC method. State the issue, give the rule, apply the rule to your facts, and reach a conclusion.

TERMS TO REMEMBER

federalism   Supremacy Clause   *stare decisis*

concurrent jurisdiction   statutory requirements

QUESTIONS FOR REVIEW

1. How do you determine whether the U.S. Constitution or a state constitution applies to a factual situation arising under state law?
2. How does statutory analysis differ from case law analysis?
3. What is meant by *statutory requirements*?
4. List the steps in analyzing a statute or administrative regulation
5. What sources can you consult to determine the meaning of a statute, administrative regulation, or constitutional provision?

CAN YOU FIGURE IT OUT?

1. The following abbreviations appear in the case found in this chapter. What do they mean?
   Per curiam
   Id.
   Cert. Denied
2. Refer to Figure 6-1.
   a. Can excessive force be the basis of an action under 18 U.S.C. § 242? Cite a case for your answer.
   b. How does the court define "willfulness" in *United States v. Bradley?*
   c. Does 18 U.S.C. § 242 require that the defendant be acting for a governmental rather than personal purpose? Cite a case for your answer.
3. Refer to Box 6-1. Does the phrase local government include a school district? Cite the section of the law that applies.
4. Refer to Figure 6-2.
   a. Who introduced the bill that led to The Oklahoma City National Memorial Act of 1997?
   b. What is the purpose of this Act?
   c. On what dates was the bill passed in both the Senate and the House of Representatives?

BUILDING YOUR ANALYSIS SKILLS: ASSIGNMENTS AND EXERCISES

1. Read 42 U.S.C. § 1983 and list the elements or requirements for finding a person liable for civil damages under this code section:

42 U.S.C. § 1983

Every person who, under color of any statute, ordinance, regulation, custom, or usage, of any State or Territory or the District of Columbia, subjects, or causes to be subjected, any citizen of the United States or other person within the jurisdiction thereof to the deprivation of any rights, privileges, or immunities secured by the Constitution and laws, shall be liable to the party injured in an action at law, suit in equity, or other proper proceeding for redress, except that in any action brought against a judicial officer for an act or omission taken in such officer's judicial capacity, injunctive relief shall not be granted unless a declaratory decree was violated or declaratory relief was unavailable. For the purposes of this section, any Act of Congress applicable exclusively to the District of Columbia shall be considered to be a statute of the District of Columbia.

2. Read the following code section.

Robbery defined: Robbery is the felonious taking of personal property in the possession of another, from his person or immediate presence, and against his will, accomplished by means of force or fear.

a. Complete the following list of the statutory elements.
  1. felonious taking
  2. personal property
  3.
  4.
  5.
  6.

b. Analyze the following factual situation and determine if the defendant committed a robbery.

Defendant points a gun at a victim and tells him to hand over his wallet. The victim does and defendant opens the wallet, looks inside, sees it is empty, and throws it on the ground.

Begin your analysis by completing the following chart.

Elements of Statute	*Factual Application*
1. Felonious taking →	1. D told V to "hand over" and V does
2. Personal property →	2. A wallet is personal property
3.	
4.	
5.	
6.	

Reach a Conclusion: Did Defendant commit a robbery?

c. Using the same chart and the same statute, analyze the following facts.
  1. X and Y were engaged. X gave Y his grandmother's ring as an engagement ring. They break up and X wants the ring back. Y refuses. X threatens Y and Y gives back the ring.
  2. X steals a saxophone from a store. A security guard from another establishment chases and is threatened.
  3. D and V know each other. He drugs her coffee. When she passes out, he steals her jewelry.

3. Read the following code section.

Subject to this division, the father and mother of a minor child have an equal responsibility to support their child in the manner suitable to the child's circumstances.

The duty of support imposed herein continues as to an unmarried child who has attained the age of 18 years, is a full-time high school student, and who is not self-supporting, until the time the child completes the 12th grade or attains the age of 19 years, whichever occurs first.

    a. Outline the statutory requirements for a parent to be responsible for supporting a child who is 18 years of age.

    b. Consider the following facts: Jeffrey turned 18 four months ago. He is a senior in high school, living at home, and will graduate in two months. He has a part-time job at a local fast-food restaurant and earns approximately $400 per month, most of which he spends on his car and entertainment. He is not married. Apply the code section to these facts, using the outline format found in Box 6-3. Are his parents obligated to support him? If so, for how long?

4. Read the following language from 18 U.S.C. § 1105.

Whoever—

assaults, kidnaps, or murders, or attempts or conspires to kidnap or murder, or threatens to assault, kidnap or murder a member of the immediate family of a United States official, a United States judge, a Federal law enforcement officer, with intent to impede, intimidate, or interfere with such official, judge, or law enforcement officer while engaged in the performance of official duties, or with intent to retaliate against such official, judge, or law enforcement officer on account of the performance of official duties, shall be punished as provided in subsection (b).

As used in this section, the term

"immediate family member" of an individual means—

    a. his spouse, parent, brother or sister, child or person to whom he stands in loco parentis; or

    b. any other person living in his household and related to him by blood or marriage;

Now consider the following facts: Judge Thomas Merkins, a United States District Court Judge, sentenced James Oakley to a lengthy prison term for a drug-related offense. Oakley's father, John, outraged at the sentence, vowed to get even with the judge. He hired two thugs to attack the judge's son-in-law. Police officials learned of this before any attack occurred. The judge's daughter and son-in-law are temporarily living with the judge. Consider if John Oakley can be punished under 18 U.S.C. § 115. Before reaching your conclusion, do the following.

    a. Outline the statutory elements or requirements under 18 U.S.C. § 115 for any person to be punished under the section.

    b. Prepare a statutory analysis of the facts in outline form, relating appropriate statutory language to relevant facts. (See Box 6-3.)

    c. Determine if there are any ambiguities or uncertainties that necessitate further research. If so, explain what research steps you would take.

5. Read the following amendments to the U.S. Constitution.

Amendment V:

No person shall be held to answer for a capital, or otherwise infamous crime, unless on a presentment or indictment of a Grand Jury, except in cases arising in the land or naval forces, or in the Militia, when in actual service in time of War or public danger; nor shall any person be subject for the same offence to be twice put in jeopardy of life or limb; nor shall be compelled in any criminal case to be a witness against himself, nor be deprived of life, liberty, or property, without due process of law; nor shall private property be taken for public use, without just compensation.

Amendment XIV:

All persons born or naturalized in the United States and subject to the jurisdiction thereof, are citizens of the United States and of the State wherein they reside. No State shall make or enforce any law which shall abridge the privileges or immunities of citizens of the United States; nor shall any State deprive any person of life, liberty, or property, without due process of law; nor deny to any person within its jurisdiction the equal protection of the laws.

a. List all terms in these amendments that could be considered ambiguous.

b. Keeping in mind that the Bill of Rights (the first ten amendments) applies only to the federal government, analyze the following factual situations in relation to the Fifth and Fourteenth Amendments. Prepare an outline of the appropriate constitutional language related to the relevant facts (Box 6-3) and answer the specific questions asked.

1) Financial support of elementary schools in Washington, D.C. that are predominantly composed of minority students is substantially less than the support given to elementary schools that are not minority-based.

   a. Is there a potential violation of the Fifth Amendment?

   b. Is there a potential violation of the Fourteenth Amendment?

   c. Are there any issues or questions you would want to research further? If so, list those questions and identify the sources you would consult.

2) A regional planning commission in the Lake Tahoe area imposed a three-year moratorium on all building near the lake. Jones, who owned lake-view property, was unable to build and therefore unable to use his land. He claimed that the government should compensate him for his property.

   a. Does Jones have any potential claims under the Fifth Amendment?

   b. Does Jones have any potential claims under the Fourteenth Amendment?

   c. Are there any issues or questions you would want to research further? If so, list those questions and identify the sources you would consult.

3) Write an analysis of the Rambeaux situation regarding Rambeaux's civil liability under 42 U.S.C. § 1983. Follow the example in Box 6-5.

4) Assume that you work as a research assistant for the attorney handling the Meyers case. In researching the codes you find the following penal code section:

1538.5. (a) (1) A defendant may move for the return of property or to suppress as evidence any tangible or intangible thing obtained as a result of a search or seizure on either of the following grounds:

(A) The search or seizure without a warrant was unreasonable.

(B) The search or seizure with a warrant was unreasonable because any of the following apply:

   (i) The warrant is insufficient on its face.

   (ii) The property or evidence obtained is not that described in the warrant.

   (iii) There was not probable cause for the issuance of the warrant.

   (iv) The method of execution of the warrant violated federal or state constitutional standards.

   (v) There was any other violation of federal or state constitutional standards.

Write a short paragraph explaining how this code section applies to the motion to suppress the bloody handkerchief in the Meyers case.

BUILDING YOUR ONLINE RESEARCH SKILLS: ASSIGNMENTS AND EXERCISES

1. Access a copy of the annotated U.S. Constitution, either through www.findlaw.com or through http://www.gpoaccess.gov/constitution/browse.html. Review the annotations to the Fourth Amendment. Locate and cite any cases that might help with the Meyers case. Explain how or why the cases help.

2. Using an online source (such as www.findlaw.com or www.law.cornell.edu) locate and read *Robinson v. Shell Oil Company*, 519 U.S. 337 (1997). Explain the steps that the Court went through in interpreting the term *employee*.

CASE PROJECT

In the previous chapter, you researched one of the hypothetical situations in Appendix A to determine what statutory law applied. Taking your results

a. identify the elements of any statutes,

b. write an outline of the statutory elements and the facts, and

c. write a statutory analysis using the facts of the hypothetical situation.

CHAPTER

7

SECONDARY SOURCES

CHAPTER OUTLINE

S KILL OBJECTIVES FOR CHAPTER 7

When you complete this chapter you should be able to

- Describe and use the common features of secondary source materials.
- Research a legal question using legal encyclopedias.
- Research a legal question using the *American Law Reports*.
- Evaluate the advantages and disadvantages of using treatises and periodicals to research a legal issue.
- Describe the features of a looseleaf service and explain its purpose.
- Explain the relevance and limitations of the *Restatement of Law* as a research tool.
- Explain why pattern jury instructions and form books are useful research tools.

FROM THE DESK OF W. J. BRYAN, ESQ.

TO: Research Assistant

Yesterday, a pretrial conference was held in the Meyers case and the judge ordered us to file all pretrial motions within the next 30 days. We need to file a motion to suppress the bloody handkerchief. I think we also have grounds to suppress statements Meyers made to the police while they were transporting him to jail. Review the Grand Jury Transcript and Search Warrant and conduct some preliminary research concerning our basis for making this motion to suppress. Write a brief memo summarizing your findings. Try to find a treatise that deals exclusively with criminal procedure but if you do not find one, try a legal encyclopedia. Either of these should give you a good overview of the law.

7-1 INTRODUCTION

Usually, the goal of legal research is to find primary law that controls a factual dispute or question. As you saw in previous chapters, you can locate constitutional provisions and relevant code sections by using the index to the codes. You can locate case law through the case notes in an annotated code. However, there are other, and often easier, ways to find all the relevant law.

To facilitate the legal research process many publishers produce works generally known as *secondary sources*. A **secondary source of law** is not the law itself. It is someone's interpretation or explanation of the law. However, most secondary sources provide references or citations to the **primary source of law**. Using secondary sources in the initial research process is very helpful because it provides an overview of the relevant area of law and enables you to identify the key facts and legal issues of the research problem. Once you identify the precise issue, a secondary source leads you to the relevant primary law. If both statutory law and case law apply to a situation, the secondary source refers you to each. Secondary sources include multivolume

secondary source of law. Tool we use to help us understand the law; one such tool is a legal encyclopedia that explains the law.

primary source of law. A work that contains the law itself.

A Point to Remember

A secondary source is someone's interpretation of the primary law. It is not the law and you should never rely on a secondary source as authority. You should always read the primary law and cite to it.

works, single books, and periodicals. Many are available on disk, CD-ROM, or through online services such as LEXIS or Westlaw. This chapter covers some of the more common types of secondary sources.

7-2 FEATURES OF SECONDARY SOURCE MATERIALS

Finding specific information in secondary source materials is facilitated by several editorial features added to the text materials. Most secondary source materials have some, if not all, of the following features.

- **Descriptive Word Index**—An alphabetized list of words or phrases describing subjects discussed in the text. The index directs you to the page or section in the text where the material is covered; it is usually located at the end of the secondary source material. Multivolume works often contain separate volumes located at the end of the set containing the index. By identifying key words in your research problem, you are able to check these terms in an index and find the appropriate sections in the secondary source. See Figure 7-1.
- **Table of Contents**—A detailed list of topics covered in the text that precedes the text material. This is organized in the same order as the material appears in the text; similar and related topics are usually grouped together. A table of contents provides an overview of the material covered.
- **Table of Statutes Cited**—A list of statutes or codes discussed in the text. This is usually arranged alphabetically by the name of the code and then numerically within each titled code. If the code has no name, it is arranged numerically. The table of statutes tells you where in the text material the code section is found. If you know of a code section that applies to your research problem, you can check the table of statutes cited to find a section of the text in which the code section is cited. See Figure 7-2.
- **Table of Cases Cited**—A list of cases cited in the text material, arranged alphabetically by the plaintiff's name; sometimes also arranged alphabetically by the defendant's name. This table normally provides the case citation and a reference to the page or section in the text material where the case appears; sometimes called "Plaintiff/Defendant Index" or "Defendant/Plaintiff Index." See Figure 7-3.
- **Table of Abbreviations**—A list of all abbreviations used in the text including those used for case reporters and other legal sources. This is an important feature to check because many secondary sources do not use standard or approved abbreviations for legal sources.

- **Preface**—A description of the contents and purpose of the material; often contains an explanation of how to use the material.
- **Parallel Reference Tables**—Tables included in works that are published in more than one series or edition. These tables show the reader how to find in the new editions material contained in the original editions.
- **Pocket Part Supplement**—Many print versions of secondary sources are supplemented in the way that codes are, that is, with pocket part supplements. (Online versions of secondary sources incorporate supplemental material with the initial publication.)

AMERICAN JURISPRUDENCE 2d

SHERIFFS, POLICE, AND CONSTABLES—Cont'd
Defects and irregularities
  arrests, defective or improper, Sheriffs § 49
  levy on property, below
  surety's liability on official bonds, below
Defenses
  generally, CrimLaw § 290; Sheriffs §§ 61-66
  amercement, Sheriffs § 114
  answers, Sheriffs § 124
  bonds, defenses of sureties, Sheriffs § 71
  failure to levy process, Sheriffs § 65
  failure to make return, Sheriffs § 66
  governmental immunity, Sheriffs § 62
  indemnity, Sheriffs § 96
  instructions to officer, Sheriffs § 63
  justification under writ, Sheriffs § 64
  official bonds, defenses of sureties in actions on, Sheriffs § 71
  return, failure to make, Sheriffs § 66
Definitions, Sheriffs §§ 1-6
Delay
  levy on property, Sheriffs § 48
  return or execution of process, Sheriffs § 48
Demand
  actions against officers, demand or notice of, Sheriffs § 100
  license, demand for display of, Autos § 112
Deputies
  generally, Sheriffs § 6
  actions against officer for wrongful acts of deputy
    generally, Sheriffs §§ 54-60
    arrest, acts in connection with, Sheriffs § 58
    civil rights, deprivation of, Sheriffs § 59
    damages, Sheriffs § 149
    execution, defective, Sheriffs § 57
    failure to supervise, train, or discipline deputy, Sheriffs § 56
    imprisonment, acts in connection with, Sheriffs § 58
    levy, defective, Sheriffs § 57
    motor vehicles, operation of, Sheriffs § 60
  pleadings, Sheriffs § 121
  presumptions and burden of proof, Sheriffs § 132
  return, defective, Sheriffs § 57
  sale, defective, Sheriffs § 57
  statutory provisions, Sheriffs § 55
  surety's liability on official bonds, below
  appointment, Sheriffs § 13
  elections, Sheriffs § 13
  imputed negligence. Actions against

SHERIFFS, POLICE, AND CONSTABLES—Cont'd
Deputies—Cont'd
    officer for wrongful acts of deputy, above in this group
    powers and duties, Sheriffs § 32
    property rights in office, Sheriffs § 17
    surety's liability on official bonds, below
  United States Marshals (this index)
  vicarious liability. Actions against officer for wrongful acts of deputy, above in this group
Directions from traffic officers, Autos § 887
Disbursements, Sheriffs § 44
Discovery (this index)
Discretion, Sheriffs § 31
Documentary evidence, police records and reports, generally, Evidence §§ 1158, 1316, 1360-1362
Drugs and narcotics, DrugsEtc § 194
Elections
    generally, Sheriffs § 12
    deputy sheriffs, Sheriffs § 13
Elevators, Elevators § 28
Eligibility, Sheriffs §§ 7-11
Embezzlement, criminal liability for, Sheriffs § 155
Escape, Prison Breaking, and Rescue (this index)
Evidence
    generally, Sheriffs §§ 125-139
    admissibility of evidence, Sheriffs §§ 125-129
    documentary evidence, Evidence §§ 1158, 1316, 1360-1362
    habit or routine practice (rule 406), Evidence § 40
    levy, wrongful, Sheriffs § 129
    misconduct, effect of exclusionary rule in deterring, Evidence § 590
    presumptions and burden of proof, below
    removal from office, Sheriffs § 28
    return as evidence, Sheriffs §§ 127, 128
    search for defendant as showing flight, Evidence § 533
    seizure of property, Sheriffs § 126
    weight and sufficiency of evidence, Sheriffs § 139
Exclusion of evidence, deterring misconduct, Evidence § 590
Execution of process
    generally, Sheriffs § 39
    actions against officers
      generally, Sheriffs § 47
      delay, Sheriffs § 48
      deputy, liability for defective levy by, Sheriffs § 57
      failure to execute process, below in this group
      limitation of actions, Sheriffs § 118
      omissions, Sheriffs § 48

SHERIFFS, POLICE, AND CONSTABLES—Cont'd
Execution of process—Cont'd
    actions against officers—Cont'd
      surety's liability on official bonds, Sheriffs § 90
    civil arrest, defective, improper, or failure to make, Sheriffs § 49
    deputy, liability for defective levy by, Sheriffs § 57
    failure to execute process
      civil arrest, defective, improper, or failure to make, Sheriffs § 49
      damages, Sheriffs § 143
      pleadings, Sheriffs § 122
      presumptions and burden of proof, Sheriffs § 133
      omissions. Failure to execute process, above in this group
    sale of property, below
    surety's liability on official bonds, Sheriffs § 90
Expenses, Sheriffs § 44
Expiration of term of office, Sheriffs § 37
Explosions and Explosives (this index)
Extraterritorial powers, Sheriffs § 36
Failure of officer to sign as principal, Sheriffs § 72
Failure to enforce laws, Sheriffs § 46
Failure to execute process. Execution of process, above
Failure to make civil arrest, Sheriffs § 49
Failure to make levy. Levy on property, below
Failure to make return. Return of process, below
Failure to pay over money, liability of sureties on official bonds, Sheriffs § 81
Failure to safeguard property, presumptions and burden of proof, Sheriffs § 135
Failure to supervise, train, or discipline deputy, Sheriffs § 56
Fair Labor Standards Act (this index)
False returns, damages, Sheriffs § 147
Federal Bureau of Investigation (FBI) (this index)
Federal Employers' Liability and Compensation Act (FELCA) (this index)
Federal marshals. United States Marshals (this index)
Federal Tort Claims Act (this index)
Fees, Sheriffs § 43
Force and violence
    Assault and Battery (this index)
    Obstruction of Justice (this index)
Fraud and deceit, false returns, damages, Sheriffs § 147
Fugitives, testimony as to search for defendant, Evidence § 533
Governmental immunity, Sheriffs § 62
Home rule, MuncCorp § 119
Identification materials. Police Identification

For assistance using this Index, call 1-800-328-4880

288

To find general information about a police officer's failure to enforce laws, go to the Topic "Sheriffs" in Am. Jr. 2d and read section 46.

Instead of looking under "SHERIFFS AND POLICE" go to "Marshals" in the index

FIGURE 7-1
American Jurisprudence 2d, Index Page

Reprinted with permission of Thomson/West

AMERICAN JURISPRUDENCE 2d

UNITED STATES CODE ANNOTATED—Continued

18 U.S.C.A.	Sec.
210	BRIBERY: 2
211	BRIBERY: 2, 15
212	BRIBERY: 2
213	BRIBERY: 2
215	BANKS: 431; BRIBERY: 2
215(a)(1)	BANKS: 433
215(a)(2)	BANKS: 433
215(d)	BANKS: 433
216	LABOR: 1918; PUBLICOFF: 378, 379, 384
216(b)	PUBLICOFF: 319, 415, 417
216(c)	PUBLICOFF: 415
224	EXTORTION: 120
224(a)	BRIBERY: 22
224(b)	BRIBERY: 22
224(c)(1)	BRIBERY: 22
224(c)(2)	BRIBERY: 22
224(c)(3)	BRIBERY: 22
228	COMMERCE: 41; DESERTION: 1, 29, 32
228(a)	DESERTION: 32
228(a)(1)	DESERTION: 32
228(a)(2)	DESERTION: 32
228(a)(3)	DESERTION: 27, 32
228(c)(1)	DESERTION: 32
228(c)(2)	DESERTION: 32
228(d)	DESERTION: 32
228(e)(1)	DESERTION: 32
228(e)(2)	DESERTION: 32
228(e)(3)	DESERTION: 32
232(5)	EXPLOS: 5
232(5)(A)	EXPLOS: 5
232(5)(B)	EXPLOS: 5
232(5)(C)	EXPLOS: 5
241	CIVILRGHTS: 197, 199 to 204; ELECTIONS: 458; GRANDJURY: 32; INVOLSERV: 4
242	ALIENS: 1841; CIVILRGHTS: 90, 205 to 215; EVIDENCE: 441
245	CIVILRGHTS: 216 to 222
245(a)(1)	CIVILRGHTS: 219
245(a)(2)	CIVILRGHTS: 219
245(b)	CIVILRGHTS: 216, 218, 221, 222, 521; EVIDENCE: 439
245(b)(1)	CIVILRGHTS: 216
245(b)(2)	CIVILRGHTS: 216
245(b)(2)(B)	CIVILRGHTS: 222

18 U.S.C.A.	Sec.
245(b)(2)(C)	JOBDISCRIM: 2802
245(b)(2)(E)	CIVILRGHTS: 521
247	ARSON: 4
248	ABORTION: 96, 109, 115; COMMERCE: 41; INJUNCTION: 82
248(a)	ABORTION: 75, 83, 114, 122
248(a)(1)	ABORTION: 83, 114
248(a)(3)	ABORTION: 83
248(b)	ABORTION: 122
248(c)(1)(A)	ABORTION: 114
248(c)(1)(B)	ABORTION: 114
248(c)(2)(A)	ABORTION: 115
248(c)(2)(B)	ABORTION: 115
248(c)(3)(A)	ABORTION: 115
248(c)(3)(B)	ABORTION: 115
248(d)	ABORTION: 97
248(e)(4)	ABORTION: 99
248(e)(5)	ABORTION: 100
285	FALSEPR: 10, 87
286	FALSEPR: 81
287	FALSEPR: 80; FEDTAXENF: 1198, 1215
288	FALSEPR: 87; POST: 92, 93, 100
289	FALSEPR: 87; VETERANS: 147, 149
290	FALSEPR: 87
291	FALSEPR: 87
292	FALSEPR: 87
331	MONEY: 60
332	EMBEZZLE: 6, 67
333	MONEY: 60
334	BANKS: 431
336	MONEY: 32
341 et seq.	CARRIERS: 34
342	ALIENS: 22
351	HOMICIDE: 2
371	ABDUCTION: 16, 46; ALIENS: 1569; ATTNYS: 93; BANKRUPTCY: 417; BROKERS: 26; CONSPIRACY: 1, 15, 45; CORAMNOBIS: 8; ELECTIONS: 458; FEDTAXENF: 1198, 1215; MILITARY: 151; OBSTRUCT: 4; RECEIVSTOL: 38, 39, 45; ROBBERY: 99; SECURITIES: 1731; SEDITION: 12, 20, 38, 42; WELFARE: 41
401	BAIL: 159; CONTEMPT: 29, 44, 55, 62, 65, 118, 126, 147, 173, 196, 203, 206; JOBDISCRIM: 2797; LABOR: 3530; OBSTRUCT: 5
401(1)	CONTEMPT: 29, 50

① 18 U.S.C.A § 242 is mentioned in several Am. Jur. 2d topics and sections; it is mentioned in section 1841 of the topic Aliens, Sections 90 and 205 to 215 of the topic Civil Rights and section 441 of the topic Evidence.

FIGURE 7-2 Table of Statutes Cited

178

CASES CITED IN ALR FEDERAL

Urquhart v Lockhart (1983, ED Ark) 557 F Supp 1334
   75 ALR Fed 9, § 26

Urrutia, In re (1990, DC Puerto Rico) 137 BR 363
   140 ALR Fed 1, §§ 43, 45

Urrutia v United States (1958, CA5 Fla) 253 F2d 501
   38 ALR Fed 617, §§ 3, 4

Ursic v. Bethlehem Mines, 719 F.2d 670, 4 Employee Benefits Cas. (BNA) 2297, 14 Fed. R. Evid. Serv. 395 (3d Cir. 1983)
   172 ALR Fed 571, § 4

Cruz v. Callahan, 965 F. Supp. 324, 53 Soc. Sec. Rep. Serv. 605, Unempl. Ins. Rep. (CCH) ¶ 15780B (N.D.N.Y. 1997)
   165 ALR Fed 203, §§ 3-5, 9, 10, 20, 24, 25, 28, 31

Urwyler v Reece (1987, ED Cal) 87-1 USTC P 9298, 59 AFTR 2d 87-843
   99 ALR Fed 700, § 4

Urwyler v United States (1989, ED Cal) 90-1 USTC P 50016, 71A AFTR 2d 93-5338
   117 ALR Fed 75, §§ 16, 18, 34

Ury v Santee (1969, ND Ill) 303 F Supp 119
   66 ALR Fed 750, §§ 6, 12

U.S. v. 1,380.09 Acres of Land, More or Less, Situated In Caldwell Parish, State of La., 574 F.2d 238 (5th Cir. 1978)
   172 ALR Fed 507, § 24

U.S. v. 2,116 Boxes of Boned Beef, Weighing Approximately 154,121 Pounds, 726 F.2d 1481 (10th Cir. 1984)
   173 ALR Fed 465, §§ 7, 10

U.S. v. 2,200 Paper Back Books, 565 F.2d 566 (9th Cir. 1977)
   172 ALR Fed 239, § 3

U.S. v. 4.18 Acres of Land, More or Less, in Idaho County, State of Idaho, 542 F.2d 786 (9th Cir. 1976)
   172 ALR Fed 507, §§ 2, 4

U.S. v. 5,555.80 Acres of Land, More or Less, in Concordia Parish, State of La., 451 F. Supp. 220 (W.D. La. 1978)
   172 ALR Fed 507, § 5

U.S. v. 12 200-Foot Reels of Super 8mm. Film, 413 U.S. 123, 93 S. Ct. 2665, 37 L. Ed. 2d 500 (1973)
   172 ALR Fed 239, § 2

U.S. v. 25,000 Magazines, Entitled "Revue", 254 F. Supp. 1014 (D. Md. 1966)
   172 ALR Fed 239, § 3

U.S. v. 31 Photographs, 156 F. Supp. 350 (S.D.N.Y. 1957)
   172 ALR Fed 239, §§ 3, 5

U.S. v 35 M.M. Motion Picture Film "Language of Love", 432 F.2d 705 (2d Cir. 1970)
   172 ALR Fed 239, § 4

U.S. v. 40.00 Acres of Land, More or Less, in Henry County, Mo., 427 F. Supp. 434 (W.D. Mo. 1976)
   172 ALR Fed 507, § 6

U.S. v. 122.00 Acres of Land, More or Less, Located in Koochiching County, Minn., 850 F.2d 56 (8th Cir. 1988)
   172 ALR Fed 507, §§ 4, 10

U.S. v. 127,295 Copies of Magazines, More or Less, Entitled "Amor", 295 F. Supp. 1186 (D. Md. 1968)
   172 ALR Fed 239, § 3

U.S. v. 243,538 Acres of Land, More or Less, In Maui County, State of Hawaii, 509 F. Supp. 981 (D. Haw. 1981)
   172 ALR Fed 507, §§ 4, 10, 15, 16, 20, 21, 28

U.S. v. 329.73 Acres of Land, Situated in Grenada and Yalobusha Counties, State of Miss., 704 F.2d 800, 20 Env't. Rep. Cas. (BNA) 1025 (5th Cir. 1983)
   172 ALR Fed 507, § 2

U.S. v. 341.45 Acres of Land, More or Less, Located in the County of St. Louis, State of Minn., 751 F.2d 924 (8th Cir. 1984)
   172 ALR Fed 507, § 2

U.S. v. 410.69 Acres of Land, More or Less in Escambia County, State of Fla., 608 F.2d 1073 (5th Cir. 1979)
   172 ALR Fed 507, § 4

U.S. v. 431.60 Acres of Land, More or Less, in Richmond County, State of Ga., 355 F. Supp. 1093 (S.D. Ga. 1973)
   172 ALR Fed 507, §§ 2, 10, 15, 26, 28

U.S. v. 640.00 Acres of Land, More or Less, In Dade County, State of Fla., 756 F.2d 842 (11th Cir. 1985)
   172 ALR Fed 507, § 2

U.S. v. 1500 Cases, More or Less, etc., 249 F.2d 382 (7th Cir. 1957)
   173 ALR Fed 465, §§ 7, 10

U.S. v. A Motion Picture Film Entitled "I Am Curious-Yellow", 404 F.2d 196 (2d Cir. 1968)
   172 ALR Fed 239, § 4

U.S. v. Abod, 770 F.2d 1293 (5th Cir. 1985)
   173 ALR Fed 613, §§ 2, 4, 5, 9

U.S. v. ACB Sales & Service, Inc., 590 F. Supp. 561 (D. Ariz. 1984)
   173 ALR Fed 223, § 7

U.S. v. Adler, 52 F.3d 20 (2d Cir. 1995)
   173 ALR Fed 667, § 3

U.S. v. Ailsworth, 948 F. Supp. 1485 (D. Kan. 1996)
   173 ALR Fed 1, § 61

U.S. v. Al-Cantara, 978 F.2d 1256 (4th Cir. 1992)
   173 ALR Fed 613, § 9

U.S. v. Alessi, 638 F.2d 466, 7 Fed. R. Evid. Serv. 909 (2d Cir. 1980)
   173 ALR Fed 613, § 9

U.S. v. Alexander, 48 F.3d 1477, 41 Fed. R. Evid. Serv. 774 (9th Cir. 1995)
   173 ALR Fed 1, § 24

U.S. v. Alkins, 925 F.2d 541 (2d Cir. 1991)
   172 ALR Fed 109, §§ 3-5, 18

U.S. v. American Cyanamid Co., 427 F. Supp. 859, 1 Fed. R. Evid. Serv. 672 (S.D.N.Y. 1977)
   173 ALR Fed 1, § 28

U.S. v. American Tel. and Tel. Co., 516 F. Supp. 1237, 8 Fed. R. Evid. Serv. 893 (D.D.C. 1981)
   173 ALR Fed 1, §§ 26, 28, 46, 95

U.S. v. American Tel. and Tel. Co., 1981-1 Trade Cas. (CCH) ¶ 63938, 1981 WL 2047 (D.D.C. 1981)
   173 ALR Fed 1, §§ 7, 95

U.S. v. Ames Sintering Co., 927 F.2d 232 (6th Cir. 1990)
   172 ALR Fed 109, § 3

U.S. v. Antelope, 430 U.S. 641, 97 S. Ct. 1395, 51 L. Ed. 2d 701 (1977)
   172 ALR Fed 1, §§ 2, 23

U.S. v. Arduin, 19 F.3d 177, 73 A.F.T.R.2d 94-1799, 73 A.F.T.R.2d 94-2432 (5th Cir. 1994)
   173 ALR Fed 667, § 4

U.S. v. Armstrong, 517 U.S. 456, 116 S. Ct. 1480, 134 L. Ed. 2d 687 (1996)
   172 ALR Fed 1, § 26

U.S. v. Articles of Food Clover Club Potato Chips, 67 F.R.D. 419 (D. Idaho 1975)
   173 ALR Fed 465, § 10

U.S. v. Atkins, 558 F.2d 133, 2 Fed. R. Evid. Serv. 296 (3d Cir. 1977)
   173 ALR Fed 1, § 6

U.S. v. Atkins, 618 F.2d 366, 6 Fed. R. Evid. Serv. 166 (5th Cir. 1980)
   173 ALR Fed 1, § 57

U.S. v. Azure, 801 F.2d 336, 21 Fed. R. Evid. Serv. 801 (8th Cir. 1986)
   173 ALR Fed 1, § 64

U.S. v. Azure, 845 F.2d 1503, 25 Fed. R. Evid. Serv. 1053 (8th Cir. 1988)
   173 ALR Fed 1, § 64

U.S. v. Bachsian, 4 F.3d 796, 39 Fed. R. Evid. Serv. 1091 (9th Cir. 1993)
   173 ALR Fed 1, §§ 3, 7, 22

U.S. v. Bailey, 581 F.2d 341, 3 Fed. R. Evid. Serv. 371 (3d Cir. 1978)
   173 ALR Fed 1, §§ 5, 6

U.S. v. Bailin, 1990 WL 114741 (N.D. Ill. 1990)
   172 ALR Fed 109, § 5

U.S. v. Bajakajian, 524 U.S. 321, 118 S. Ct. 2028, 141 L. Ed. 2d 314, 172 A.L.R. Fed. 705 (1998)
   172 ALR Fed 389, §§ 3, 5-7, 12

U.S. v. Balfany, 965 F.2d 575, 35 Fed. R. Evid. Serv. 990 (8th Cir. 1992)
   173 ALR Fed 1, § 64

U.S. v. Banner, 226 F. Supp. 904, 64-1 U.S. Tax Cas. (CCH) ¶ 9264, 13 A.F.T.R.2d 579 (N.D.N.Y. 1963)
   173 ALR Fed 465, §§ 27, 28

U.S. v. Barnes, 12 M.J. 614 (N.M.C.M.R. 1981)
   173 ALR Fed 1, § 71

U.S. v. Barnes, 586 F.2d 1052, 3 Fed. R. Evid. Serv. 1278 (5th Cir. 1978)
   173 ALR Fed 1, § 57

U.S. v. Barrett, 8 F.3d 1296, 38 Fed. R. Evid. Serv. 398 (8th Cir. 1993)
   173 ALR Fed 1, § 67

U.S. v. Barrett, 598 F. Supp. 469 (D. Me. 1984)
   173 ALR Fed 1, §§ 4, 39

U.S. v. Barretto, 708 F. Supp. 577, 89-2 U.S. Tax Cas. (CCH) ¶ 9046, 64 A.F.T.R.2d 89-5623 (S.D.N.Y. 1989)
   173 ALR Fed 465, § 26

U.S. v. Bell, 36 F.3d 1164 (9th Cir. 1996)
   173 ALR Fed 1, § 60

U.S. v. Beltran, 761 F.2d 1, 18 Fed. R. Evid. Serv. 40 (1st Cir. 1985)
   173 ALR Fed 1, § 83

For assistance, call 1-800-328-4880   465

U.S. v. Ames Sintering Co. is cited in section 3 of the article starting on page 109 in volume 172 of *A.L.R. Fed.*

Reprinted with permission of Thomson/West

FIGURE 7-3   Cases Cited in *A.L.R. Federal*

7-3 LEGAL ENCYCLOPEDIAS: *AMERICAN JURISPRUDENCE 2D* AND *CORPUS JURIS SECUNDUM*

Nonlegal encyclopedias are multivolume works containing thorough discussions of a variety of subjects arranged alphabetically. **Legal encyclopedias** are multivolume works containing comprehensive and thorough discussions of a variety of *legal* topics arranged alphabetically. For example, you might find such broad topics as "aliens and citizens," "arrest," "civil rights," "job discrimination," "federal courts," "negligence," "space law," and "computers and the Internet." Each broad topic is divided into many specific subtopics. For example, under the general topic of "aliens and citizens" you find such subtopics as "immigration laws," and "ports of entry to the United States; border crossings." In addition to a discussion and analysis of legal principles, each article in the encyclopedia refers you to relevant primary sources of law.

> **legal encyclopedia.** A collection of legal information arranged alphabetically by topic; a secondary source of the law.

Two major legal encyclopedias cover the entirety of U.S. law. These are *American Jurisprudence 2d (Am. Jur. 2d)* and *Corpus Juris Secundum (C.J.S.)*. These encyclopedias discuss legal topics of both state and federal law. Other encyclopedias are state specific, covering only the law of that particular state. Articles in print versions of encyclopedias are generally kept current with pocket part supplements.

Using Legal Encyclopedias

Because material in a legal encyclopedia is organized by general topic, the first step in using a legal encyclopedia is to identify that topic for your specific research question. Fortunately, all encyclopedias contain descriptive word indexes to help you do this. For example, suppose the question you are researching is as follows: "Does a police officer who uses excessive force in making an arrest incur criminal or civil liability under federal law?" At this point you should proceed as follows.

1. Go to the index found at the end of the set of books.
2. Identify key terms or words to check in the index. Do this by reviewing the known facts. For example, since your research question relates to police officers, you might check for the word *police*. Other key words for this research question might include *excessive force* or *arrest*. When you locate the word *police*, the index directs you to another phrase in the index, "Sheriffs and Police." When you locate this phrase in the index, you find several subtopics. See Figure 7-1 for a portion of this index topic.
3. Review the subtopics found under the main topic. Some of the subtopics will lead you directly to a specific article in the encyclopedia. For example, the subtopic "Failure to Enforce Laws" directs you to section 46 of the general topic Sheriffs and Police. (It is abbreviated as Sheriff in the index.) Other subtopics direct you to other parts of the index. Eventually you will be directed to an article and section in the encyclopedia.

A Point to Remember

If you have trouble finding the right term in an index, go back to your problem and make a list of all key words. If necessary, use a legal thesaurus.

When you read an encyclopedia article, consider the issues of mandatory and persuasive authority discussed in earlier chapters. Both *Am. Jur. 2d* and *C.J.S.* provide cites to authorities in many different states. If the topic is one that is controlled by state law, first look for authorities from your state, as only these are binding. Other authorities are persuasive. Also, always check the pocket part supplement for any changes or additions to the law. Remember to check the pocket part supplement to the index. Sometimes new topics or subtopics are added to reflect changes in the law.

For an example of an encyclopedia article from *American Jurisprudence 2d*, see Figure 7-4. *American Jurisprudence 2d* and *Corpus Juris Secundum* are available in print and online through the Westlaw and/or LEXIS databases.

BOX 7-1   USING ENCYCLOPEDIAS

(*American Jurisprudence 2d* and *Corpus Juris Secundum*)

✓ Review your research question and identify:
General legal topic
Specific legal topic
All descriptive words

✓ Look up descriptive words in the index to locate the proper encyclopedia topic.

✓ Retrieve the alphabetically arranged volume containing the relevant topic.

✓ Read the article and make note of primary law from your jurisdiction.

✓ Check pocket part supplement for updates.

7-4 AMERICAN LAW REPORTS

American Law Reports (A.L.R.) and *American Law Reports Federal (A.L.R. Fed.)*, now published by Thomson/West, are other important secondary sources used by legal researchers. *American Law Reports* covers American law as found in the various states, and *American Law Reports Federal* covers federal law. Like encyclopedias, *American Law Reports* provides citations to primary law from all states. You must, therefore, consider the issues of mandatory and persuasive authorities in relying on cases cited within the annotations.

In print format *A.L.R.* contains both leading cases and articles or annotations discussing and analyzing the legal issues raised in those cases. The online versions, found on both Westlaw and LEXIS, contain only the annotations. (The cases are available online through other sources.) Figure 7-5 shows a portion of an annotation from *A.L.R. Fed. 2d.*

American Law Reports was first published in 1919 and is currently in its sixth edition or series. The various series are referred to as *A.L.R., A.L.R.2d, A.L.R.3d, A.L.R.4th, A.L.R.5th,* and *A.L.R.6th.* The federal series is in its second series and is known as *A.L.R. Fed.* and *A.L.R. Fed. 2d.*

The legal topics that form the basis of each article in *American Law Reports* are much more specific than those found in encyclopedias. For example, look at the title of the annotation reprinted in Figure 7-5. This article deals with one issue involving the war on terror. Articles in encyclopedias tend to be much more expansive in coverage. A second major difference between *A.L.R.* and encyclopedias is the arrangement of topics. *A.L.R.* does not arrange alphabetically. Rather, the arrangement is dependent on the date of the case law that leads to the article.

his deputy's failure to make return of an execution within the time required by statute.[64]

If a deputy is negligent in the performance of his duties in regard to the notification, the mode of conducting sale, the title to be given the purchaser, and the return of his precept, the principal is liable to persons injuriously affected.[65] Constables and sheriffs have also been held liable for false returns made by deputies,[66] but the plaintiffs alleging that a deputy sheriff had made a false return of service have the burden of establishing that service of civil process was within the deputy's authority.[67]

§ 155. Acts in connection with arrest or imprisonment

A sheriff may be liable for the wrongful acts of his deputy in making an arrest,[68] including alleged violations of the suspect's civil rights,[69] using excessive force to capture persons committing a crime,[70] and escaping prisoners,[71] or for false imprisonment,[72] where such acts are done by virtue of his office as deputy and within the scope of his authority. For the act to have that character, it must have been done under a warrant or under circumstances which authorized the deputy to make an arrest without warrant. If the deputy makes an arrest in any other way it is not authorized by law and is consequently his individual, and not his official, act. But where the deputy acts under a warrant and abuses that process in making the arrest, the sheriff will be liable.[73] An arrest made in any other way is not authorized by law and

---

64. Rogers v Anderson (Tenn) 580 SW2d 782.

65. Sexton v Nevers, 37 Mass 451.

66. Houser v Hampton, 29 NC 333.

Under a statute providing that the official acts of a deputy sheriff shall be deemed to be those of the sheriff himself, the sheriff alone, and not the deputy, is liable for a deputy's failure to take bail from a person arrested on civil process or for his false return that he has taken bail. Liability may not exist, however, where the plaintiff has directed the deputy not to take bail. Ordway v Bacon, 14 Vt 378.

67. Karr v Dow (App) 84 NM 708, 507 P2d 455, cert den 84 NM 696, 507 P2d 443.

68. Miles v Wright, 22 Ariz 73, 194 P 88, 12 ALR 970.

Practice Aids.—Complaint in action against deputy, sheriff, and sheriff's surety for wounding by sheriff's deputy. 22 Am Jur Pl & Pr Forms (Rev) Sheriffs, Police, and Constables, Form 133.

Police Misconduct Litigation—Plaintiff's Remedies. 15 Am Jur Trials 555 §§ 21-25.

69. § 156.

70. Widow stated cause of action against sheriff for death of husband killed in exchange of gun fire between sheriff's deputies and fleeing felons who had taken husband as hostage where complaint alleged that sheriff's deputies were negligent in failing to engage in proper police practices, in engaging in close pursuit and thus placing husband's life in jeopardy, and in failing to retreat despite fact that husband's life was endangered. Michel v Hometown Super Markets, Inc. (La App 4th Cir) 352 So 2d 557.

71. Andry v Orleans (La App 4th Cir) 309 So 2d 814, later app (La App 4th Cir) 358 So 2d 334 (holding that under a statute providing that no sheriff nor his surety shall be liable for any act or tort committed by one of his deputies beyond the amount of the bond or limits of liability insurance furnished by the deputy sheriff, unless the deputy sheriff in the commission of the said tort acts in compliance with a direct order of, and in the personal presence of, the sheriff, at the time the act or tort is committed, a sheriff would not be liable individually for excessive force allegedly used by his deputy sheriff to apprehend a prisoner during an escape attempt, but a cause of action existed against the sheriff in his official capacity).

As to means permissible in recapturing prisoners, generally, see 27 Am Jur 2d, Escape, Prison Breaking, and Rescue § 26.

72. Abbott v Cooper, 218 Cal 425, 23 P2d 1027.

73. Miles v Wright, 22 Ariz 73, 194 P 88, 12 ALR 970; Ivy v Osborne, 152 Tenn 470, 279 SW 384.

343

Volume 70 of *American Jurisprudence Second*, page 343, section 155; the main topic here is "SHERIFFS, POLICE AND CONSTABLES"

Cases and other supporting authorities are cited in footnotes.

FIGURE 7-4   Text Material, Am Jur 2d

consequently is not the deputy's official act, but his individual act, for which his superior is then not liable.[74]

A chief of police sued for false imprisonment for the acts of police officers in which he did not participate has been held entitled to the benefit of the general rule that with respect to governmental functions a municipal officer performing duties strictly public is not liable for negligent acts of misfeasance of persons employed by the municipality who are under his general direction and authority.[75] But if superior officers order that an arrest be made, their actions may be so intertwined with that of the officer making the arrest that the liability of all must be considered together.[76]

Although it is frequently held that where a superior officer has not authorized nor consented to the wrongful act of his deputy, no liability will attach,[77] lack of knowledge of the wrongful acts has also been held not to prevent a finding of liability.[78]

---

74. Where plaintiff was arrested without any process, warrant, or other legal authority, by one not a deputy sheriff, who turned him over to the deputy sheriff in charge of the jail, and the deputy then imprisoned the plaintiff, such imprisonment was a usurpation of power by the deputy, for which the sheriff could not be held liable. Swenson v Cahoon, 111 Fla 788, 152 So 203.

Where the petition and the evidence negate every state of facts under which the deputy constable might have made a lawful arrest, it follows that he was acting in his individual capacity, and not in his official capacity, and the surety on the bond of the constable is not liable under a statute providing that a constable and his sureties shall be liable on the bond for the acts and omissions of his deputy. Fidelity & Deposit Co. v Hall, 215 Ky 36, 284 SW 426.

Arrest by a deputy without a warrant for an alleged offense beyond the view of the deputy is without color of authority and is a personal wrong committed by the deputy for which he alone would be liable, in accordance with the general rule that public officers are not liable to third persons for the extraofficial acts of their deputies. Ivy v Osborne, 152 Tenn 470, 279 SW 384.

75. Wommack v Lesh, 180 Kan 548, 305 P2d 854.

Practice Aids.—Complaint in action against peace officers for assault and battery on prisoner. 22 AM JUR PL & PR FORMS (Rev), SHERIFFS, POLICE, AND CONSTABLES, Form 132.

76. Nesmith v Alford (CA5 Ala) 318 F2d 110, reh den (CA5 Ala) 319 F2d 859, and cert den 375 US 975, 11 L Ed 2d 420, 84 S Ct 489.

77. Kangieser v Zink (1st Dist) 134 Cal App 2d 559, 285 P2d 950; Klam v Boehm, 72 Idaho 259, 240 P2d 484.

Where an arrest is made by a deputy sheriff without warrant and the prisoner is incarcerated in a jail for the management of which the sheriff was responsible without the knowledge of the sheriff, the sheriff would not be responsible for such arrest or imprisonment. McBeath v Campbell (Tex Com App) 12 SW2d 118.

A police captain who receives a call to the effect that trouble may be brewing and assigns an officer to investigate is not, without other evidence, liable for a false arrest by the investigating official. Nesmith v Alford (CA5 Ala) 318 F2d 110, reh den (CA5 Ala) 319 F2d 859, and cert den 375 US 975, 11 L Ed 2d 420, 84 S Ct 489.

A sheriff may be held liable for the brutality and mistakes of his deputies only if the sheriff knew of and participated in the torts, ratified the tortious conduct, or if the tortious conduct had persisted for such an extended period that the sheriff is, factually or legally, charged with knowledge. Dean v Gladney (SD Tex) 451 F Supp 1313, affd in part and revd in part (CA5 Tex) 621 F2d 1331, cert den 450 US 983, 67 L Ed 2d 819, 101 S Ct 1521.

78. A chief of police who was made keeper of the city prison by the city charter would be liable for the conduct of the persons immediately in charge of the prison, notwithstanding that he might not have participated in or known of such conduct. Ulvestad v Dolphin, 152 Wash 580, 278 P 681, distinguishing Pavish v Meyers, 129 Wash 605, 225 P 633, 34 ALR 561, on the ground that in the Ulvestad Case there was a city charter making the chief of police the keeper of the city prison.

If a deputy sheriff were acting in his capacity as deputy sheriff at the time of an alleged false arrest, he and a surety on his bond, and a sheriff and a surety on his bond, would be proper and necessary parties to the action based on the cause of action for the alleged false arrest. State ex rel. Cain v Corbett, 235 NC 33, 69 SE2d 20.

FIGURE 7-4
(continued)

70 Am Jur 2d   SHERIFFS, POLICE, AND CONSTABLES   § 156

The provisions of applicable statutes have also been determinative of liability.[79] The acts of deputy sheriffs in shooting a person while attempting to arrest him for an offense committed in their presence are "official acts" within a statute making a sheriff responsible for the official acts of his deputies.[80]

▐▐▐▐ *Practice guide:* In such a case, the plaintiff should allege that the deputy's act was done not in the lawful exercise of his authority, but while he was pretending or professing to act by virtue of his office, that is, under color of his office.[81] However, if the evidence fails to show that the offense for which the deputies were attempting to make an arrest was committed in their presence or that they were acting under a warrant, a case of "official acts" is not made out so as to render the sheriff liable.[82]

§ 156. Deprivation of civil rights

In general the federal courts have rejected the concept of imposing vicarious liability upon a public officer, such as a sheriff or police commissioner, for his deputy's civil rights violations[83] under the applicable federal statute.[84] Exceptions to the general rule rejecting vicarious liability for civil rights violations have been recognized where the sheriff participated directly in, was present at, or otherwise authorized the actions of his deputy;[85] absent such involvement, however, the sheriff escapes liability.[86] Some cases holding that absent overt

---

79. Under a statute making the sheriff and his surety liable for any misconduct of his deputy, they were held liable for his act in killing one arrested under a warrant for a misdemeanor, since he was acting by virtue of his office, and what he did was done as an official act. Brown v Weaver, 76 Miss 7, 23 So 388.

80. Brown v Wallis, 100 Tex 546, 101 SW 1070.

81. Harwell v Morris, 255 Ala 344, 51 So 2d 511.

82. Brown v Wallis, 100 Tex 546, 101 SW 1070.

83. Jennings v Davis (CA8 Mo) 476 F2d 1271 (neither chief of police nor board of police commissioners of a major city were to be liable under respondeat superior for civil rights violations of police officers); Kroes v Smith (ED Mich) 540 F Supp 1295 (deputy county sheriff charged with civil rights violations in beating plaintiff and subjecting him to strip search after stopping automobile following high speed chase by police; county could not be liable for acts of deputy sheriffs under respondeat superior); Painter v Baltimore County (DC Md) 535 F Supp 321 (dismissing action against chief of police for vicarious liability regarding assault by police officer); Dunkin v Lamb (DC Nev) 500 F Supp 184 (granting sheriff's motion for summary judgment since action attempting to make sheriff liable through agency theory and effect was not permissible under civil rights act); Schweiker v Gordon (ED Pa) 442 F Supp 1134 (police commissioner; no vicarious liability under respondeat superior for police offi-

cer's civil rights violations); Delaney v Dias (DC Mass) 415 F Supp 1351 (police commissioner not charged with personal involvement in the alleged civil rights violations of his subordinates; respondeat superior inapplicable to impose vicarious liability); Manfredonia v Barry (ED NY) 401 F Supp 762 (no vicarious liability; plaintiffs acknowledged that the police commissioner had neither ordered the offending acts nor participated in their execution, but sought to impose liability on the theory that the commissioner's failure to undo the acts thereafter should constitute ratification thereof); Runnels v Parker (CD Cal) 263 F Supp 271 (chief of police could not be liable for false arrest of plaintiffs by police officers because of departmental policy requiring arrests and transportation to the police station of suspects whose interrogation would take more than ½ hour; no liability for chief of police unless he was present, directed such acts, or personally cooperated in them).

Annotation: 51 ALR Fed 285 § 3; 61 ALR Fed 7.

84. 42 USCS § 1983.

85. Campbell v Buckles (DC Tenn) 448 F Supp 288.

86. Harris v Pirch (CA8 Mo) 677 F2d 681 (action under 42 USCS § 1983 will not lie against police supervisory officers for failure to prevent police misconduct absent a showing of direct responsibility therefor; Hopper v Hayes (DC Idaho) 573 F Supp 1368 (although a city police officer was deputized to act as a deputy sheriff, the county sheriff could not be held

345

FIGURE 7-4
(continued)

acts, the statute does not authorize recovery of monetary damages through respondeat superior, recognize other exceptions to the rule, and a sheriff may be held liable, without necessarily having participated therein or authorized such acts, for the actions of his appointed deputies, over whom he has control, in certain circumstances.[87]

A number of courts have held that regardless of whether concepts of vicarious liability may be inherently within the scope of the federal statute itself, superiors sued under that statute for civil rights violations committed by their subordinates may be vicariously liable where state law imposes liability without personal fault on the particular superior for the wrong of his subordinates in the scope of employment. Hence, state law may require that a sheriff be found liable for the civil rights violations committed by a deputy.[88] Conversely, in a state which absolves the sheriff from vicarious liability for the acts of his deputy, the state rule applies to bar liability for the deputy's civil rights violations.[89] Without precisely declaring that a state law imposing vicarious liability on a superior public official for wrongs committed by his subordinates in the course of their employment would serve to impose such liability for civil rights violations by such subordinates in an action under the federal civil rights acts, the courts of one circuit have supported such a view.[90] Other courts have specifically stated that liability of a superior for civil rights violations by his subordinates cognizable under the federal statute cannot be imposed by reference to state laws imposing vicarious liability on such superiors for subordinates' wrongs.[91]

§ 157. Operation of motor vehicle

The liability of a sheriff or other peace officer for damages resulting to a third person from the operation of a motor vehicle by a deputy or other subordinate of the peace officer depends heavily upon the circumstances presented. Factors considered in determining such liability have included whether or not the subordinate was proceeding toward or returning from the spot where his actual official duty was performed,[92] whether or not the person

---

liable for the shooting of a plaintiff by the city police officer absent any specific request or authorization that the city police officer so act on the day in question or in relation to the incident).

87. Taylor v Gibson (CA5 Ala) 529 F2d 709 (recognizing rule; court did not specify circumstances, and declined to determine whether derivative liability would be supported under the broad allegations of the complaint).

88. Scott v Vandiver (CA4 SC) 476 F2d 238; Hesselgesser v Reilly (CA9 Wash) 440 F2d 901; Whited v Fields (WD Va) 581 F Supp 1444; Knipp v Weikle (ND Ohio) 405 F Supp 782.

The sheriff could be held liable for the alleged unlawful arrest and beating of the plaintiff by his deputies, on the basis of state law establishing such liability independent of 42 USCS § 1983. Brunson v Hyatt (DC SC) 409 F Supp 35.

346

Annotation: 51 ALR Fed 285 § 4.

89. Johnson v Duffy (CA9 Cal) 588 F2d 740; Dudley v Bell, 50 Mich App 678, 213 NW2d 805.

90. McDaniel v Carroll (CA6 Tenn) 457 F2d 968, cert den 409 US 1106, 34 L Ed 2d 687, 93 S Ct 897; Sandlin v Pearsall (ED Tenn) 427 F Supp 494.

91. Marks v Lyon County Bd. of County Comrs. (DC Kan) 590 F Supp 1129; Love v Davis (WD La) 353 F Supp 587 (notwithstanding the existence of a state law imposing liability on a sheriff for the wrongful acts of his deputy acting in the scope of employment, liability under the federal civil rights acts must be premised on personal culpability).

92. Usrey v Yarnell, 181 Ark 804, 27 SW2d 988.

Annotation: 15 ALR3d 1189 § 2[a].

A marshal is not liable for the negligence of his deputy where, having served a writ in a

---

FIGURE 7-4
(continued)

16 A.L.R. Fed. 2d 257
Admissibility of Evidence Procured by Torture or Alleged Torture—Global Cases

16 A.L.R. Fed. 2d 257 (Originally published in 2007)

American Law Reports
ALR Federal 2d
The ALR databases are made current by the weekly addition of relevant new cases.

Admissibility of Evidence Procured by Torture or Alleged Torture—Global Cases

Kurtis A. Kemper, J.D.

The admissibility of a confession or other statement (including a statement procured by torture or alleged torture) in judicial proceedings depends on whether it was made voluntarily. In U.S. v. Abu Ali, 395 F. Supp. 2d 338, 16 A.L.R. Fed. 2d 683 (E.D. Va. 2005), the defendant moved to suppress certain statements he made to Saudi Arabian authorities, claiming, inter alia, that the statements were inadmissible because he was tortured and the statements in question were involuntary. Denying the motion based on a finding that the government demonstrated by a preponderance of the evidence that any incriminating statements made by the defendant were voluntary and admissible, the court recognized its solemn duty to uphold the human rights guarantees of United States Constitution and those international documents on human rights to which the United States is a signatory. Note also that the United Kingdom House of Lords in A v. Secretary of State for the Home Department, 2005 WL 3299089 (HL 2005), held broadly that it would give a very clear negative answer to the question of whether evidence obtained by torturing another human being may lawfully be admitted against a party to proceedings in a British court, irrespective of where, by whom, or on whose authority the torture was inflicted. This annotation collects and analyzes those global cases which have considered the admissibility of evidence procured by torture or alleged torture.

TABLE OF CONTENTS

ARTICLE OUTLINE

FIGURE 7-5 *A.L.R.*
Annotation as it
appears on Westlaw

INDEX

[index terms omitted]

Table of Cases

[case citations omitted]

I. Preliminary Matters

§ 1. Scope

This annotation collects and analyzes the state and federal cases from the United States, as well as cases reported in the English language from the United Kingdom and the former and present British Commonwealth countries, in which the courts discussed the admissibility of evidence procured by torture or alleged torture.[FN1]

Some opinions discussed in this annotation may be restricted by court rule as to publication and citation in briefs; readers are cautioned to check each case for restrictions. A number of jurisdictions may have rules, regulations, constitutional provisions, or legislative enactments directly bearing upon this subject. These provisions are discussed herein only to the extent and in the form that they are reflected in the court opinions that fall within the scope of this annotation. The reader is consequently advised to consult the appropriate statutory or regulatory compilations to ascertain the current status of all statutes discussed herein.

§ 2. Summary and comment

According to the United States Supreme Court, it is axiomatic that a defendant in a criminal case is deprived of due process if his or her conviction is founded, in whole or in part, on an involuntary confession, without regard for the truth or falsity of the confession.[FN2] It was recognized by an English court, in an often cited case decided in 1783, that "A confession forced from the mind by the flattery of hope or by the torture of fear comes in so questionable a shape, when it is to be considered as evidence of guilt, that no credit ought to be given to it."[FN3]

FIGURE 7-5
(continued)

The Supreme Court in <u>Lyons v. State of Okl., 322 U.S. 596, 64 S. Ct. 1208, 88 L. Ed. 1481 (1944)</u>, recognized that declarations procured through torture are not premises from which a civilized forum will infer guilt. The requirement that statements obtained through torture must be excluded from judicial proceedings is recognized internationally. Under § 15 of the United Nations Convention Against Torture and Other Cruel, Inhuman or Degrading Treatment or Punishment, a treaty to which the United States in a signatory, state parties are required to ensure that any statement which is established to have been made as a result of torture shall not be invoked as evidence in any proceedings, except against a person accused of torture as evidence that the statement was made.[FN4]

In the context of criminal trials, the courts have held that statements obtained by government agents through torture or alleged torture of the defendant (whether physical, nonphysical, or threatened) are admissible in evidence where the evidence failed to establish the involuntary nature of the statement (§§ <u>4</u>, <u>6</u>). Conversely, where sufficient evidence was presented to show the involuntary nature of a statement allegedly obtained by physical, nonphysical, or threatened torture of the defendant by government agents, the courts have held such statements inadmissible (§§ <u>5</u>, <u>7</u>). The courts have also addressed the admissibility of statements of persons other than the defendant which were obtained by torture or alleged torture of government agents (<u>§ 8</u>). Similarly, where a statement was the result of torture or alleged torture by agents of a foreign government or by individuals not associated with a government, the courts have held the statement inadmissible where it was established that the statement was involuntarily made (<u>§ 10</u>), but not where there was insufficient evidence to establish that issue (<u>§ 9</u>). When a criminal defendant challenges a state court conviction in federal court on the ground that his or her confession was procured by torture, involuntary, and inadmissible in evidence, relief may be granted only on a showing that the circumstances under which the confession was received violated those fundamental principles of liberty and justice protected by the Fourteenth Amendment against infraction by the state.[FN5] With respect to direct appeals from a state appellate court decision affirming a defendant's conviction, the Supreme Court has found the evidence sufficient to show that admission of a statement obtained through torture or alleged torture at trial constituted a violation of the defendant's constitutional rights under the circumstances of some cases (<u>§ 11</u>), but not under other circumstances (<u>§ 12</u>). In addition, where a collateral challenge to a state court conviction was based on the trial court's admission of a statement obtained by torture or alleged torture, the federal courts have considered whether the evidence sufficient to warrant relief or at least an evidentiary hearing on the defendant's claim (§§ <u>13</u>, <u>14</u>).

The admissibility of statements procured by torture or alleged torture has also arisen in contexts other than criminal trials. In extradition proceedings, such statements have been held admissible by the courts in some cases (<u>§ 15</u>), but not in other cases (<u>§ 16</u>). That issue was also addressed in court martial proceedings (<u>§ 18</u>). Recently, the courts in the United States and the United Kingdom have determined whether statements procured by torture or alleged torture may be admitted in proceedings related to the detention of persons for national security reasons (<u>§ 17</u>).

. . . . .

Section 1 Footnotes:
[FN1] The annotation at <u>Confession by one who has been subjected to or threatened with physical suffering, 24 A.L.R. 703</u>, need no longer be referenced with respect to cases expressly referring to confessions obtained by torture or alleged torture.

Section 2 Footnotes:

FIGURE 7-5
(continued)

> [FN2] Jackson v. Denno, 378 U.S. 368, 84 S. Ct. 1774, 12 L. Ed. 2d 908, 1 A.L.R.3d 1205 (1964).
> See Am. Jur. 2d, Evidence § 719 (due process requires that a confession be voluntarily made; confessions are admissible as evidence when they are voluntarily given, not as a result of threats, promises, violence, or other improper inducements or influences).
>
> [FN3] Rex v. Warickshall, 1 Leach 263 (1783).
>
> [FN4] See Construction and Application of United Nations Convention Against Torture and Other Cruel, Inhuman or Degrading Treatment, or Punishment, 184 A.L.R. Fed. 385.
>
> [FN5] Gallegos v. State of Neb., 342 U.S. 55, 72 S. Ct. 141, 96 L. Ed. 86 (1951).

FIGURE 7-5
(continued)

Reprinted with permission of Thomson/West

Using *A.L.R.*

The easiest way to find an article is to use the general *A.L.R. Index.* This is a descriptive word index that covers *A.L.R. 2d* through *A.L.R. 6th.* The first series of *A.L.R.* contains a separate index. A separate index also exists for *A.L.R. Fed.* The index refers you to specific articles. In addition to the index, *A.L.R.* contains a digest covering all of the topics found in *A.L.R. 3d* through *6th.* The digest organizes all law into over 400 legal topics. The digest arranges these in alphabetical order. To use the digest, you must first identify the proper legal topic. One advantage of the digest over the index is that the digest refers to other secondary sources.

All *A.L.R.* articles have similar features. Each article contains the following:

1. **Table of Contents**   describes what you will find in the annotation.
2. **Research References**   refers you to other legal resources that are related to your topic.
3. **Research Sources**   lists the sources used in compiling the article; later series include the **electronic search query** used by authors of the article as well as West Digest Key Numbers; the electronic search query is used to find information on Westlaw and LEXIS. This is discussed in Chapter 10.
4. **Article Descriptive Word Index**   helps you locate treatment of specific subjects within the article.
5. **Jurisdictional Table of Cited Statutes and Cases**   lists by jurisdiction all cases and statutes cited in the article.
6. **Scope**   states exactly what is covered in the article.
7. **Related Annotations**   lists other *A.L.R.* articles that are closely related.
8. **Summary and Comment**   summarizes the substantive part of the article.
9. **Practice Pointers**   hints to the best way to handle a case within the scope of the article.
10. **Substantive Sections**   discusses the legal topic thoroughly.

When you use an *A.L.R.* article, you must check to see if the article was updated or **supplemented**. The publishers update the articles by providing references to new cases and statutes that deal with the topic. In print form, the various series of A.L.R. are supplemented as follows:

A.L.R. (first series)	*A.L.R. Blue Book of Supplemental Decisions*
A.L.R. 2d	*A.L.R. 2d Later Case Service*
A.L.R. 3d through *6th*	Pocket part supplements

electronic search query. Words that constitute a search request when using electronically stored data, that is, information on the Internet or on a CD-ROM.

supplemented. Kept up-to-date.

BOX 7-2   USING *A.L.R.* OR *A.L.R. FED.*

✓ Determine if research question is one of state law or federal law.

✓ Review research question and identify descriptive words.

✓ Check general *A.L.R. Index* or *Digest* for a citation to an article if the question is one of state law.

✓ Check *A.L.R. Fed. Index* or *Digest* for a citation to an article if the question is one of federal law.

✓ Find appropriate article(s).

✓ Identify primary law from your jurisdiction.

✓ Check the pocket part supplement (or other supplement for early editions).

✓ Check the history of annotations table for superseded articles.

In addition to checking if your article was supplemented, check if the article was **superseded**. In some cases, the law changes so often that an older article is no longer valid or helpful. As a result, a new article is written, superseding the prior article. The last volume of the *A.L.R. Index* contains an annotation history table that provides this information. In an online format, supplements are incorporated with the main article.

superseded.   Replaced.

The publishers of *A.L.R.* offer some online features for users. Some of these features can be viewed even by nonsubscribers. Review the Web site http://west. thomson.com/alr/ and link to "access A.L.R. free resources."

A Point to Remember

Remember that an *A.L.R.* article is a secondary source. Do not cite it to a court as your only authority. Always give the court references to primary law.

7-5 TREATISES

A **treatise** is a publication covering a single legal topic, usually written by a legal scholar or practicing attorney who specializes in that area of law. It contains a thorough discussion and explanation of the law and provides cites to primary authority. Treatises may be a single volume or a multivolume set. Some are updated regularly, but others may never be supplemented. A well-known class of treatises is published by West and known as the **hornbook** series. These books are written primarily for law students but are useful to anyone. Hornbook series books are also often published in a condensed version called the **Nutshell Series**.

treatise.   Either one book or a multivolume series of books dealing with one legal topic.

hornbook.   Name given to books published by West that are a type of treatise; commonly used by law students.

Nutshell Series. Condensed versions of hornbooks.

Using a Treatise

If there is a treatise relating to your research question (and there probably is), you can locate it in a law library by checking the library catalogue. The catalogue contains an

> **BOX 7-3   USING A TREATISE**
>
> ✓ Identify the legal topic.
> ✓ Check the library catalog.
> ✓ Check the copyright date on the treatise.
> ✓ Determine if the treatise is supplemented.
> ✓ Use the index to find the specific topic.

alphabetical listing of legal topics and a list of all books relating to that topic that can be found in the library. Most treatises contain an index at the end of the book that is designed to help you locate your specific research issue. In using a treatise, be particularly careful to check the copyright date of the book, especially if there is no pocket part supplement. Some treatises found in law libraries are outdated.

7-6 PERIODICALS

periodical. Legal material, published at regular intervals, consisting of magazines, journals, and law reviews.

Numerous legal magazines and journals (**periodicals**) are published. Many professional associations publish magazines. For example, the American Bar Association publishes a monthly magazine, *The American Bar Journal.* Selected articles from the magazine are published online at abajournal.com. The state bar associations also publish regular magazines or journals for their members. Magazines containing articles on legal topics are published for paralegals, for example, *Legal Assistant Today.* National and local paralegal associations may also publish regular newsletters. Often, these newsletters contain articles on current legal topics.

law review. A type of legal periodical published by law schools containing articles on different legal topics.

One very important type of periodical publication is a **law review**. A law review is a publication from a law school. It contains scholarly articles by noted legal authorities, usually on current legal issues. It may also contain shorter articles written by law students. Most law schools publish law reviews at regular intervals. A law review article can be an excellent research source. If your research issue is the subject of a law review article, you will find a thorough discussion of the law including references to numerous primary authorities. The major disadvantage of law review articles (or most periodical literature) is that they are not supplemented or updated.

Guides to Periodicals

Two indexes to legal periodicals are published: *Current Law Index* and *Index to Legal Periodicals and Books.* These indexes resemble the *Readers Guide to Periodical Literature* and allow you to find information by subject matter or by author. They contain references to more than 1,000 different sources from the United States and several foreign jurisdictions.

> **BOX 7-4   USING PERIODICALS**
>
> ✓ Identify the legal topic or author.
> ✓ Check the *Index to Legal Periodicals* and/or *Current Law Index.*
> ✓ Locate the periodical.
> ✓ Check current status of the law.

7-7 LOOSELEAF SERVICES

The term **looseleaf service** is used to describe a type of secondary research material that is published in a binder format rather than as a bound book. Material concerning an area of law is printed on unbound, or "loose," pages and assembled in a binder. The purpose of these services is to allow frequent supplementation of the material without the use of the traditional pocket part supplement. As changes occur in the law, subscribers to the looseleaf service are sent the changes. These are printed on replacement pages for the binder. The subscribers remove the old page and replace it with a new page reflecting the current law.

Looseleaf services are commonly used for areas of law regulated by administrative rules or regulations. Recall from Chapter 5 that finding the latest updates for administrative regulations is a cumbersome process if you rely on the official publications. Looseleaf services are secondary sources that provide this information. Major publishers of looseleaf services are Commerce Clearing House (CCH), Prentice Hall, and Bureau of National Affairs (BNA).

looseleaf service. Legal material published in a binder format, regularly supplemented with replacement pages.

A Point to Remember

When replacement pages are sent to a looseleaf service subscriber, a preface page is included indicating the date of the latest page revisions. If you are responsible for updating the books, always file this page. If you are using the book, always check the date to make sure the material is current.

7-8 THE RESTATEMENT OF LAW

In reading case law, you have undoubtedly come across references to the "Restatement." This is a multivolume work compiled by The American Law Institute, and is the result of the efforts of well-known and respected legal scholars. U.S. law is largely the result of English Common Law. However, because of many court decisions and legislative changes, some of those principles evolved and changed. The Restatement is a "statement" of the many principles of U.S. law as those principles exist today. The work is organized by legal topic and each is known accordingly, for example, the *Restatement of the Law of Torts* and the *Restatement of the Law of Contracts*. The principles of law found in the Restatement look very similar to code sections. They are often followed by comments and examples. It is important to remember that the Restatement is *not* primary law. The statements of law found here may or may not reflect the law in your state. However, this is a well-respected source and it is often quoted by judges in written opinions. The Restatement and the comments are especially helpful when the law of your state is not clear. In such an instance, referring to the Restatement can help. Although, remember, this is only persuasive authority, not mandatory. See Figure 7-6 for sample pages from the *Restatement of Torts 2d.*

§ 70   TORTS, SECOND   Ch. 4

to inflict, as where his assailant is standing on the brink of a cliff or on a girder of a steel building under construction so that the actor should realize that the other's instinctive reaction to his threatening gesture may cause a serious fall. If such is the case, the actor may not be privileged even to threaten to inflict a harm which under ordinary circumstances he would be privileged to inflict, and certainly is not privileged to threaten a greater harm. It is frequently a matter for the jury to to determine, under proper instructions, whether the privilege exists in such a case.

§ 71. Force in Excess of Privilege

If the actor applies a force to or imposes a confinement upon another which is in excess of that which is privileged,

(a) the actor is liable for only so much of the force or confinement as is excessive;

(b) the other's liability for an invasion of any of the actor's interests of personality which the other may have caused is not affected;

(c) the other has the normal privilege stated in this Topic to defend himself against the actor's use or attempted use of excessive force or confinement.

See Reporter's Notes.

Comment on Clause (a):

a. While the actor is liable to another for any force or confinement which he applies or imposes upon the other which is in excess of that which he is privileged to impose, he is not liable for so much of the force or confinement as he is privileged to apply or impose, and so he does not become a "trespasser ab initio" by his abuse of his privilege.

b. While it is usually difficult to separate the harm done by the excess of force, it can sometimes be done, as where a confinement is continued longer than is necessary to prevent the commission of a battery. Where no such separation can be made, the actor is held liable for all of the harm inflicted by the use of the excessive force.

FIGURE 7-6
Restatement of
Torts 2nd

Ch. 4 SELF-DEFENSE § 71

Illustrations:

1. A inflicts an offensive contact upon B, and threatens to continue it. Being stronger than A, B could easily prevent a continuance of the contact by seizing and holding A, and does so. B then unnecessarily strikes A in the face, breaking A's nose. B is not liable for holding A, but is subject to liability to A for the broken nose.

2. A inflicts an offensive contact upon B, and threatens to continue it. B could easily prevent the continuance of the contact by striking A a light blow. Instead he strikes a heavy blow, which breaks A's nose. B is subject to liability to A for the blow and the harm done.

Comment on Clause (b):

c. If the actor applies a force to or imposes a confinement upon another which is in excess of that which is privileged, the other's liability for an invasion of any of the actor's interests of personality which the other may have caused is not affected. In such a case, the actor and the other have cross actions against one another; the actor for the "assault," "battery," or "false imprisonment" which the other committed before the actor abused his privilege by using excessive force, the other for the excess of force used by the actor. The other's violation of the actor's right is entirely independent of the actor's abuse of his privilege. So far from being caused by the actor's misconduct, the violation of the actor's right gives the privilege which he abuses. There is, therefore, no reason why the actor's misconduct should exonerate the other's independent violation of his right, nor should the actor be penalized for his abuse of his privilege by a forfeiture of his right of action which preceded and was the occasion for his abuse. The liability to answer for his excess of force is both a sufficient punishment for the actor's abuse of his privilege and a sufficient deterrent to such misconduct.

Illustration:

3. Under the circumstances given in Illustration 1, while B is liable to A for the harm which he has caused to A by the excess of force which he used in self-defense, A is subject to liability to B for the offensive contact which he has inflicted upon B.

FIGURE 7-6
(continued)

§ 71 TORTS, SECOND Ch. 1

Comment on Clause (c):

d. If the actor applies a force to, or imposes a confinement upon another which is in excess of that which is privileged, the other has the normal privilege stated in this Topic to defend himself against the actor's use, or attempted use, of excessive force or confinement. One who intentionally invades or attempts to invade any of another's interests of personality, does not by his wrongdoing forfeit his privilege to defend himself by any means which would be privileged were he innocent of wrongdoing against any excess of force which the other uses in self-defense. A fortiori, mere provocation by words or conduct does not deprive a man of his privilege to defend himself against an attack which another is thereby provoked into making upon him.

Illustration:

4. A attempts to slap B's face. Although B can easily prevent A from so doing by pushing A away, he attempts to protect himself by striking A with a heavy stick. A is privileged to defend himself by using appropriate force against B.

e. Withdrawal from combat. The aggressor may withdraw from the combat which he has initiated. If he does so, and makes clear by words or conduct his intention to discontinue the encounter, he may thereafter be privileged to defend himself against the man he has attacked. His original aggression does not justify retaliation, or acts no longer necessary for defense against him. Allowance must, however, be made for the excitement of the fight and the absence of time for reflection, and if under the circumstances the defendant reasonably believes that he is still under attack, he may be privileged to continue to act in self-defense, although the attack has in fact terminated.

Illustration:

5. A insults B. B attacks A, knocks him down and jumps on him, and inflicts a severe beating. B then abandons his attack and starts to walk away. A arises, pursues B, and strikes him a heavy blow. Whether A is liable to B depends upon whether, making allowance for A's disturbed state of mind and the absence of time for reflection, A should know that B has abandoned the attack.

FIGURE 7-6
(continued)

Reprinted with permission of American Law Institute

7-9 MISCELLANEOUS RESOURCES

Form Books

Form books are another type of research tool that lawyers and their assistants frequently utilize. The main purpose of these books, of course, is to provide sample forms for lawyers to follow. However, form books are a valuable secondary source of the law. In addition to containing sample forms, many form books provide explanations of the law related to the use of the form, including references to the controlling primary law. Form books are often multivolume sets and are published for practice in the federal courts, as well as for practice in state courts.

There are two major types of comprehensive form books: those that contain forms for use in connection with a lawsuit and those for use in connection with business or personal transactions. Forms for use in connection with lawsuits are often called **forms of pleading and practice**. In forms of pleading and practice you find sample complaints, responsive pleadings, motions, and other litigation forms. Forms for use in business or personal transactions are often called **transaction forms**. In transaction form books you find forms such as sample articles of incorporation, partnership agreements, and wills.

In your state research material you may find **practice books**. These are usually single-volume books (although some may be many volumes) that deal with one legal topic and contain both explanations and discussions of the law and sample forms related to the practice of that area of law.

forms of pleading and practice.
Form books containing forms for use in connection with ligitation.

transaction forms.
Form books containing forms for use in connection with business and personal transactions.

practice books.
Books for use in federal and state legal practice; these often contain discussions of an area of law and provide forms needed for practice in that legal area.

jury instructions.
Statements of the law read to the jury at the end of trial.

Pattern Jury Instructions

At the end of any jury trial, the judge must tell the jury what law applies to the evidence presented during trial. These statements of law are called **jury instructions**. Judges do not create new instructions every time they preside over a trial. Instead, they consult books containing approved statements of law or jury instructions, referred to as *pattern jury instructions*. Using these books, the judge and the attorneys develop a set of instructions to give the jury. However, the court is not limited to these approved jury instructions, and sometimes the judge or the attorneys write specific instructions for a case.

Books containing jury instructions can be valuable research tools for two reasons. First, each jury instruction provides a reference to the primary law from which it is taken. Second, unlike many other sources, these statements of law are written in easy-to-understand language because they are written for jurors, not lawyers.

Pattern jury instructions exist for practice in the state and federal courts. See Figure 7-7 for an example.

The Legal Dictionary and Legal Thesaurus

A legal dictionary and a legal thesaurus are essential tools for any legal researcher. A legal dictionary contains definitions of legal words and phrases. Because legal vocabulary is often unique, a beginning researcher can be very confused without the help of a legal dictionary. There are many legal dictionaries available for

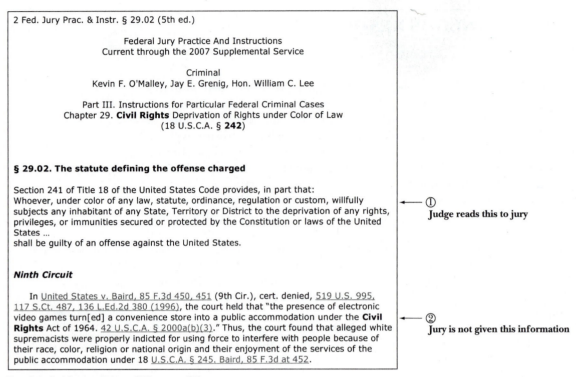

Reprinted with permission of Thomson/West

FIGURE 7-7   Jury Instructions—Sample Form

researchers: The most famous, and probably the most comprehensive, is *Black's Law Dictionary.* A legal thesaurus provides synonyms and antonyms for legal words. This tool is invaluable in helping you use an index to legal source material. A work that is somewhat similar to a legal dictionary is *Words and Phrases.* This set, published by West, contains numerous legal terms as they are defined in court opinions.

Box 7-5 is a list of several common secondary sources.

BOX 7-5   COMMON SECONDARY SOURCES

- *American Jurisprudence 2d*
- *Corpus Juris Secundum*
- *American Law Reports*
- Legal treatises
- Legal periodicals and law reviews
- Looseleaf services
- *Restatement*
- Form books
- Pattern jury instructions

Online Legal Research

Most of the traditional secondary resources and research tools, such as legal encyclopedias, pleading and practice sets, and legal specialty sets, are not available free over
the Internet. Many of these resources are easily located on LEXIS/NEXIS and Westlaw.
The Internet does provide other secondary source material without cost.
A researcher can "Google" any legal topic and probably find some information. When
using any of these sources, however, you must carefully consider the reliability and
the date of the information. Relying on this information alone is dangerous. If this
information cites primary authority, and sometimes it does, then you should read
the primary law.

Some reliable Web sites do provide some secondary source information. Law
school library Web sites are often valuable. (Always check for the .edu in the U.R.L.)
Review the following: http://www.law.cornell.edu/ and http://tarlton.law.utexas.edu/
vlibrary/.

Law librarians sometimes host valuable Web sites. One such site is http://www.
nocall.org/.

The Library of Congress also provides access to some secondary source materials. For example, you can access selected law reviews at http://www.loc.gov/law/
guide/lawreviews.html.

CITATION MATTERS

SECONDARY RESOURCES

The Bluebook—RULES 15, 16, 17, AND 18

Books, Periodical Materials, and Other Secondary Sources
Rules 15 through 18 provide numerous examples for citation format for
secondary sources. Set out below are common examples. If you cannot
find an example of the exact source you need to cite, find a very similar
resource and follow the general format for that citation.

EXAMPLES:

15 AM. JUR. 2D *Civil Rights* § 18 (1983) (legal encyclopedia)

23 C.J.S. *Contracts* § 33 (1977) (legal encyclopedia)

William B. Johnson, Annotation, *Use of Plea Bargain or Grant of
Immunity as Improper Vouching for Credibility of Witness in Federal Cases,* 76
A.L.R. FED. 409 (1986). (*The Bluebook* example for the *American Law
Reports* citation format.)

CHAPTER SUMMARY

Secondary sources are research tools that contain discussions and explanations of the primary law. They direct the researcher to the primary law by providing citations to relevant cases, statutes, and constitutional provisions. There are different types of secondary sources, but many have some, if not all, of the following features: descriptive word indexes, tables of contents, tables of statutes cited, tables of cases cited, tables of abbreviations, prefaces, parallel reference tables, and pocket part supplements.

One important type of secondary source is the legal encyclopedia. *American Jurisprudence 2d* and *Corpus Juris Secundum* are two national legal encyclopedias. In these works, hundreds of legal topics are arranged alphabetically. The encyclopedias contain discussions and explanations of those topics with references to relevant primary law. These books are updated with pocket part supplements. Some states have specific encyclopedias for legal topics in their jurisdictions.

Another important type of secondary source is *American Law Reports (A.L.R.)*. The publishers of *American Law Reports* publish annotations dealing with the legal issues of newly published cases. The annotations contain extensive discussions of the issues as well as references to other relevant primary law. *A.L.R.* annotations are now supplemented with pocket part supplements. Occasionally, because of extensive changes in the law, an annotation is superseded rather than supplemented.

Secondary source material also includes treatises and a variety of legal periodicals, including law reviews. These materials may not be supplemented.

Looseleaf services consist of material found in binders and often relate to areas of law controlled by administrative regulations. These materials are supplemented frequently by revised replacement pages.

The *Restatement of Law* is a well-respected legal source that discusses and explains the current state of U.S. law. References to primary law from all states are included. Although frequently cited in judicial opinions the Restatement is not primary law.

Form books are another valuable research tool for lawyers. Form books are found in comprehensive multivolume sets containing either forms for use in the courts (forms of pleading and practice) or for use in business or personal matters (transaction forms). Forms may be found in single-topic works, often referred to as *practice books*. Many form books provide not only sample forms, but explanations of the law related to the forms and reference the controlling primary law.

Also important are pattern jury instructions. These contain short, concise statements of law written for nonlawyers. Books containing pattern jury instructions reference the primary law from which the instruction was taken.

A legal dictionary and a legal thesaurus are essential tools for researchers. Legal dictionaries explain legal words and phrases. A legal thesaurus provides synonyms and antonyms for legal words and phrases.

TERMS TO REMEMBER

secondary source of law	treatise	forms of pleading and practice
primary source of law	hornbook	transaction forms
legal encyclopedia	Nutshell Series	practice books
electronic search query	periodical	jury instructions
supplemented	law review	
superseded	looseleaf service	

QUESTIONS FOR REVIEW

1. What is the purpose of a secondary source of law?
2. Describe some of the common features of secondary sources.
3. What is a legal encyclopedia?
4. How do you use a legal encyclopedia?
5. Describe the contents of *American Law Reports.*
6. How is *A.L.R.* kept up-to-date?
7. How does a treatise differ from a legal encyclopedia or *A.L.R.*?
8. What is a law review?
9. Why are pattern jury instructions a useful research tool?
10. What is the Restatement?

CAN YOU FIGURE IT OUT?

1. Refer to Figure 7-1. In which *Am. Jur. 2d* article (title and section) will you find a discussion of governmental immunity?
2. Refer to Figure 7-2. In which *Am.Jur.2d* article (title and section) will you find a discussion of 18 U.S.C.A. § 332?
3. Refer to Figure 7-4.
   a. Cite a case for the proposition that a sheriff may be liable for the wrongful acts of his deputy in making an arrest of an escaping prisoner.
   b. Where would you find a form for a complaint in an action against peace officers for wounding a prisoner?
4. Refer to Figure 7-5. In which section of this *A.L.R.* article do you find a discussion of cases in which physical torture of defendants resulted in admissible statements?
5. Refer to Figure 7-6. What does *Restatement of Torts 2d* § 71 (a) provide?

BUILDING YOUR RESEARCH SKILLS: ASSIGNMENTS AND ACTIVITIES

Part One: Using Encyclopedias: *American Jurisprudence 2d*

For each of the following, answer the questions and cite to the section in *Am. Jur. 2d* where you found the answer.

1. Can a state impound a lost animal considering it to be abandoned? Cite case authority for your answer.
2. What is the monetary liability of credit card owners for unauthorized use of their credit card? Cite statutory authority for your answer.
3. Can a child who is born illegitimate, but later legitimized, inherit from the natural father?
4. What is the test to determine whether a game is one of chance or one of skill?
5. Susan knowingly makes a false statement of fact under penalty of perjury. Later Susan changes the story to the truth. Does this excuse the perjury? What is the controlling federal statute?

6. Can a company that does interstate business refuse to hire a woman as vice president? Cite the controlling case.

7. Does the doctrine of *res ipsa loquitur* apply to test-firing of rockets by the federal government?

8. John married his cousin but believed that the marriage was void. After separating from his cousin, John later married Jill without obtaining a divorce from his first wife. Is John guilty of bigamy? Cite the controlling case.

Part Two: Using *A.L.R.*

9. Cite an *A.L.R.* annotation dealing with liability of property owners for injury caused by failure of an elevator to level at the floor.

10. What is the subject of the annotation found at 6 *A. L. R. 2d* 391? What issue is discussed in § 2 of this article?

11. Find and cite an *A.L.R.* annotation in *A.L.R. 4th* dealing with state laws that require a person who requests a jury trial in a civil case to pay costs associated with the jury.

12. Find and cite an *A.L.R.* annotation in *A.L.R. Fed.* dealing with the complexity of civil action as affecting the Seventh Amendment right to trial by jury.

13. What is the purpose of the annotation found at 24 *A.L.R. Fed.* 940? What is meant by the phrase "comity of nation" as used in the article?

14. Find and cite an *A.L.R.* annotation involving undue influence and nontestamentary gifts to clergymen, spiritual advisors, or the church.

15. Find and cite an *A.L.R.* annotation dealing with injury or property damage caused by lightning as a basis of tort liability.

Part Three: Periodicals and Law Reviews

16. Cite a 2007 law review article in the Columbia Law Review discussing the case of *Hamdan v. Rumsfeld*.

17. Find and cite a 1994 article in the *U.C.L.A. Law Review* dealing with lunar mining.

18. Find and cite an article in the *American Bar Association Journal* dealing with the legal aspects of artificial insemination.

Part Four: Restatement

19. Where in the *Restatement 2d* do you find a section dealing with undue influence by a third person rendering a transaction voidable at the request of the victim where the other contracting party knew of the undue influence?

20. Where in the *Restatement 2d* is negligence defined? What does comment "d" provide?

Part Five: State Research

21. Find out if your state has a state-specific encyclopedia. If so, what is its title and who is the publisher?

22. Identify at least one secondary source in your state that covers state law in general.

23. Identify at least three law reviews published in your state.

24. Find out if your state bar association publishes a journal. If so, what is its title?

BUILDING YOUR ANALYSIS SKILLS: ASSIGNMENTS AND EXERCISES

1. Read the portion of the *A.L.R.* annotation found in Figure 7-5 and write a paragraph summarizing the material.
2. Access the Web site abajournal.com. Summarize any recent article found online.
3. Review Research Problems 1, 2, and 3 in Appendix A. Assume that you are starting to research these questions in a secondary source such as an encyclopedia or treatise. For each fact pattern create a list of words or phrases that you might search for in a descriptive word index.

BUILDING YOUR ONLINE RESEARCH SKILLS: ASSIGNMENTS AND EXERCISES

1. Select a Research Fact Pattern from Appendix A. Using the Web sites listed in the Online Legal Research Feature, conduct preliminary research. Write a summary of your findings, including references to any primary law.
2. Conduct an online search of law schools in your state. Do any of these offer law reviews online?
3. Access the following Web site: http://www.loc.gov/law/guide/lawreviews.html. Here you find links to several law reviews.
   a. Select law reviews from one law school and list the titles of the articles found within one volume of the publication.
   b. Read and summarize one article found in a law review. (Hint: *Akron Law Review* provides full articles online.)

CASE PROJECT

Using the same case that you researched in previous chapters, find and cite articles in appropriate encyclopedias, periodicals, and the *A.L.R.* that relate to the issue. Read the articles and note cases and statutes that might apply to these issues. Write a brief summary of the articles and list cases and statutes that you should read. Read the cases and statutes and take notes.

DIGESTS

SKILL OBJECTIVES FOR CHAPTER 8

When you complete this chapter you should be able to

- Explain the relationship between case reporters and digests.
- Explain how headnotes are organized in a digest.
- Describe the West topic and key number system.
- Describe the West digest system.
- Use a descriptive word index in a digest to locate case law.
- Use a headnote from a case to find similar cases in a digest.
- Describe online search methods for Westlaw and LEXIS that utilize the digest concept.

FROM THE DESK OF W. J. BRYAN, ESQ.

TO: Research Assistant

I finished reading your recent memo on the Meyers case. I think the *Dickerson* case that you mention in the memo is very helpful. Please keep looking and see if you can find any similar cases. You might try looking in a digest.

8-1 INTRODUCTION

In addition to the secondary sources described in the previous chapter, an important legal resource to help you find case law is a **digest**. Unlike legal encyclopedias, *American Law Reports*, and treatises, digests do not explain or discuss the law. Nor do they refer you to constitutional or statutory law. Digests are a multivolume, special index to case reporters and are published by both West and Lexis Law Publishing to accompany their case reporters.

Digests contain hundreds of legal topics arranged alphabetically. However, unlike descriptive word indexes, each topic in a digest is followed by various case headnotes that relate to the topic. Although digests are found in print format, the concept behind digests plays an important role in finding cases on both Westlaw and LEXIS. This chapter discusses digests and how the digest concept influences online case searching.

digest. An index to reported cases, arranged by subject; a short summary of cases is provided.

8-2 HEADNOTES AND TOPICS

Digests are based on the headnotes that precede the cases. Recall from Chapter 3 that when cases are published in case reporters, the publishers add many features including **headnotes**. The headnotes are brief statements of the legal principles found in the case. Each legal principle is assigned a topic name and number. Because many cases deal with the same or similar subjects, several different cases found in the same reporter system often contain the same headnote topic and number. Also, because one case may contain a discussion of several legal topics, one case often has several different headnote topics and numbers. Review Figures 8-1 and 8-2. Here you see headnotes to the case, *Minnesota v. Dickerson* in both the *Supreme Court Reporter* and the *Lawyer's Edition*. Note the different headnote topics found in the different reporter publications of the same case. Also note that each reporter has several different headnotes for the same case.

headnotes. Editorial enhancement added to the front material of a case; useful summary of most of the legal topics addressed in the case.

In a digest, headnotes from different cases that contain the same topic names and numbers are combined and organized alphabetically by topic name. The headnotes are further organized by topic number. Refer to Figure 8-3 to see pages from the West digest for the *Supreme Court Reporter*. Note that this figure contains the same topic and key number as is found in Figure 8-1, the *Supreme Court Reporter* publication of *Dickerson*. Note how other cases involving the same topic are also referenced. Using the digest as a research tool enables you to locate cases containing the same legal principles as the *Dickerson* case. Also, compare the topics and key numbers in

2130   **113 SUPREME COURT REPORTER**   508 U.S. 365

I respectfully dissent and would affirm the judgment of the Court of Appeals.

○══ KEY NUMBER SYSTEM

508 U.S. 366, 124 L.Ed.2d 334

₃₆₆**MINNESOTA, Petitioner,**

v.

Timothy DICKERSON.

No. 91–2019.

Argued March 3, 1993.

Decided June 7, 1993.

Defendant's motion to suppress seizure of crack cocaine from defendant's person was denied by the District Court, Hennepin County, and defendant appealed. The Minnesota Court of Appeals, 469 N.W.2d 462, reversed. The State appealed. The Minnesota Supreme Court, 481 N.W.2d 840, affirmed. The State's petition for certiorari was granted. The Supreme Court, Justice White, held that: (1) police may seize nonthreatening contraband detected through the sense of touch during protective patdown search so long as the search stays within the bounds marked by *Terry*, and (2) search of defendant's jacket exceeded lawful bounds marked by *Terry* when officer determined that the lump was contraband only after squeezing, sliding and otherwise manipulating the contents of the defendant's pocket, which officer already knew contained no weapon.

Affirmed.

Justice Scalia filed a concurring opinion.

The Chief Justice filed an opinion concurring in part and dissenting in part, in

which Justice Blackmun and Justice Thomas joined.

1. Criminal Law ══1134(3)

Defendant's constitutional challenge to validity of patdown search was not moot even though, under Minnesota law, diversionary sentence would not be considered a conviction; there was possibility of reinstatement of the record of the charges in subsequent state or federal proceedings that would carry collateral legal consequences. U.S.C.A. Const.Amend. 4; M.S.A. § 152.18.

2. Arrest ══63.5(9)

A *Terry* protective search—permitted without a warrant and on basis of reasonable suspicion less than probable cause—must be strictly limited to that which is necessary for the discovery of weapons which might be used to harm the officer or others nearby. U.S.C.A. Const.Amend. 4.

3. Arrest ══63.5(9)

If the *Terry* protective search goes beyond what is necessary to determine if the suspect is armed, it is no longer valid and its fruits will be suppressed. U.S.C.A. Const. Amend. 4.

4. Arrest ══63.5(9)

Police officers may seize nonthreatening contraband detected during a patdown search for weapons so long as the officer's search stays within the bounds marked by *Terry*. U.S.C.A. Const.Amend. 4.

5. Searches and Seizures ══47.1, 49

Under "plain-view" doctrine, if police are lawfully in a position from which they view an object, if its incriminating character is immediately apparent, and if the officers have lawful right of access to the object, they may seize it without a warrant, but if the police lack probable cause to believe that an

ion circulated, hardly deserves acknowledgment, let alone comment. I had thought that this was a court of justice and that a criminal defendant in this country could expect to receive a genuine

analysis of the constitutional issues in his case rather than the dismissive and conclusory rhetoric with which Kevin Taylor is here treated. I adhere to my derided "constitutional stew."

Headnote from Supreme Court Reporter Publication *Minnesota v. Dickerson.* See how this figure relates to Figure 8-3.

FIGURE 8-1   Supreme Court Reporter Headnotes

508 U.S. 366   **MINNESOTA v. DICKERSON**   2131
Cite as 113 S.Ct. 2130 (1993)

object in plain view is contraband without conducting some further search of the object, i.e., if its incriminating character is not immediately apparent, the "plain-view" doctrine cannot justify its seizure. U.S.C.A. Const. Amend. 4.

6. Searches and Seizures ⬅47.1

"Plain-view" doctrine has obvious application by analogy to cases in which an officer discovers contraband through the sense of touch during an otherwise lawful search. U.S.C.A. Const.Amend. 4.

7. Searches and Seizures ⬅16

Rationale of "plain-view" doctrine is that if contraband is left in open view and is observed by police officer from lawful vantage point, there has been no invasion of legitimate expectation of privacy and thus no "search" within meaning of the Fourth Amendment. U.S.C.A. Const.Amend. 4.

8. Searches and Seizures ⬅47.1

Warrantless seizure of contraband that is in plain view is deemed justified by realization that resort to neutral magistrate under such circumstances would often be impracticable and would do little to promote objectives of Fourth Amendment. U.S.C.A. Const.Amend. 4.

9. Searches and Seizures ⬅47.1, 49

If police officer lawfully pats down a suspect's outer clothing and feels an object whose contour or mass makes its identity immediately apparent, there has been no invasion of the suspect's privacy beyond that already authorized by the officer's search for weapons; if the object is contraband, its warrantless seizure would be justified by the same practical considerations that inhere in the plain view context. U.S.C.A. Const. Amend. 4.

10. Searches and Seizures ⬅49

Regardless of whether during *Terry* stop and patdown search the officer detects the contraband by sight (plain-view) or by touch (plain-feel), the Fourth Amendment's requirement that the officer have probable cause to believe that the item is contraband before seizing it ensures against excessively speculative seizures. U.S.C.A. Const.Amend. 4.

11. Searches and Seizures ⬅49

The seizure during *Terry* patdown search of an item whose identity is already known occasions no further invasion of privacy and thus suspect's privacy interests are not advanced by categorical rule barring seizure of contraband plainly detected through sense of touch. U.S.C.A. Const.Amend. 4.

12. Arrest ⬅63.5(9)

Police officer overstepped lawful bounds marked by *Terry* when officer determined that lump in pocket of defendant's jacket was contraband crack cocaine only after squeezing, sliding and otherwise manipulating the contents of the defendant's pocket, a pocket which the officer already knew contained no weapon. U.S.C.A. Const.Amend. 4.

13. Searches and Seizures ⬅47.1, 147.1

Where an officer who is executing a valid search for one item seizes a different item, Supreme Court is sensitive to the danger that officers will enlarge specific authorization, furnished by warrant or an exigency, into the equivalent of a general warrant to rummage or seize at will. U.S.C.A. Const. Amend. 4.

14. Arrest ⬅63.5(9)

Searches and Seizures ⬅49

Although police officer was lawfully in a position to feel lump in defendant's jacket pocket, because *Terry* entitled him to place his hands upon defendant's jacket, the incriminating character of the object was not immediately apparent to officer and was determined to be contraband only after officer conducted further search, one not authorized by *Terry* or by any other exception to the warrant requirement, and thus further search of defendant's pocket was constitutionally invalid; seizure of the cocaine that followed was likewise unconstitutional.

FIGURE 8-1
(continued)

Reprinted with permission of Thomson/West

HEADNOTES

Classified to United States Supreme Court Digest, Lawyers' Edition

Search and Seizure §§ 11, 11.5, 25 — patdown search of pocket — warrant requirement — seizure of cocaine

1a, 1b. The Federal Constitution's Fourth Amendment does not permit the seizure of a small plastic bag containing one fifth of one gram of

---

TOTAL CLIENT-SERVICE LIBRARY® REFERENCES

68 Am Jur 2d, Searches and Seizures §§ 51, 78, 161, 191

8 Federal Procedure, L Ed, Criminal Procedure § 22:210

7 Federal Procedural Forms, L Ed, Criminal Procedure §§ 20:611, 20:612, 20:624

22 Am Jur Pl & Pr Forms (Rev), Searches and Seizures, Forms 81, 84, 85, 86, 91, 106

44 Am Jur Proof of Facts 2d 229, Lack of Probable Cause for Warrantless Arrest

USCS, Constitution, Amendment 4

L Ed Digest, Search and Seizure §§ 11, 11.5, 25

L Ed Index, Investigation and Investigators; Search and Seizure; Stop and Frisk

ALR Index, Investigations and Interrogations; Search and Seizure; Stop and Frisk

Auto-Cite®: Cases and annotations referred to herein can be further researched through the Auto-Cite® computer-assisted research service. Use Auto-Cite to check citations for form, parallel references, prior and later history, and annotation references.

ANNOTATION REFERENCES

Applicability of "plain view" doctrine and its relation to Fourth Amendment prohibition against unreasonable searches and seizures—Supreme Court cases. 110 L Ed 2d 704.

Law enforcement officer's authority, under Federal Constitution's Fourth Amendment, to stop and briefly detain, and to conduct limited protective search of or "frisk," for investigative purposes, person suspected of criminal activity—Supreme Court cases. 104 L Ed 2d 1046.

Admissibility of evidence obtained by illegal search and seizure—Supreme Court cases. 93 L Ed 1797, 96 L Ed 145, 98 L Ed 581, 100 L Ed 239, 6 L Ed 2d 1544.

When criminal case becomes moot so as to preclude review of or attack on conviction or sentence. 1 L Ed 2d 1876.

Lawfulness of nonconsensual search and seizure without warrant, prior to arrest. 89 ALR2d 715.

FIGURE 8-2
Minnesota v. Dickerson
Lawyers' Edition
Headnotes

MINNESOTA v DICKERSON
(1993) 508 US 366, 124 L Ed 2d 334, 113 S Ct 2130

crack cocaine, which was detected through a police officer's sense of touch during a protective patdown search of a person for weapons which was justified under Terry v Ohio (1968) 392 US 1, 20 L Ed 2d 889, 88 S Ct 1868, where (1) the officer determined that a small lump in the front pocket of the person's nylon jacket was contraband only after squeezing, sliding, and otherwise manipulating the contents of the pocket, which the officer already knew contained no weapon; and (2) because the officer's further search of the pocket was constitutionally invalid in that it was not authorized by Terry v Ohio or any other exception to the Fourth Amendment's warrant requirement, the seizure of the cocaine that followed likewise is unconstitutional.

Search and Seizure §§ 11.5, 25 — patdown search for weapons — seizure of nonthreatening contraband — warrant requirement

2a-2d. Consistent with the Federal Constitution's Fourth Amendment, a police officer may seize nonthreatening contraband detected during a protective patdown search of a person whom the officer has briefly stopped based on the officer's reasonable conclusion that criminal activity may be afoot with respect to such person, where the officer is justified in believing that the person is armed and presently dangerous to the officer or to others nearby, so long as the officer's search is strictly limited to that which is necessary for the discovery of weapons which might be used to harm the officer or others, because (1) the "plain-view" doctrine—under which police officers may seize an object without a warrant if the officers are lawfully in a position from which they view the object, its in-

criminating character is immediately apparent, and the officers have a lawful right of access to the object—has an obvious application by analogy to cases in which an officer discovers contraband through the sense of touch during an otherwise lawful search; (2) if a police officer lawfully pats down a suspect's outer clothing and feels an object whose contour or mass makes its identity immediately apparent, there has been no invasion of the suspect's privacy beyond that already authorized by the officer's search for weapons, and the warrantless seizure of the object if it is contraband is justified by the realization that resort to a neutral magistrate under such circumstances would often be impractical and would do little to promote the objectives of the Fourth Amendment; and (3) a suspect's privacy interests are not advanced by a categorical rule barring the warrantless seizure of contraband plainly detected through the sense of touch, since (a) the sense of touch is capable of revealing the nature of an object with sufficient reliability to support a seizure, (b) even if it were true that the sense of touch is generally less reliable than the sense of sight, such fact suggests only that officers will less often be able to justify seizures of unseen contraband, (c) the Fourth Amendment's requirement that officers have probable cause to believe that an item is contraband before seizing it insures against excessively speculative seizures, and (d) the seizure of an item whose identity is already known occasions no further invasion of privacy.

Appeal § 1662 — mootness — criminal case

3a, 3b. The possibility of a crimi-

FIGURE 8-2
(continued)

nal defendant's suffering collateral legal consequences from a sentence already served precludes a finding of mootness with respect to appellate review of such defendant's case.

Appeal § 1662 — mootness — dismissal of charges against defendant

4a, 4b. A live controversy remains in a case before the United States Supreme Court, on certiorari to review a decision by a state's highest court, where an accused was found guilty on a state drug possession charge, but such charge was dismissed after the accused was sentenced to probation under a diversionary sentencing statute, and therefore such case is not moot, where reinstatement of the record of the charge against the accused—by way of its use in (1) determining the merits of subsequent proceedings against the accused, and (2) calculating the accused's criminal history category in the event of a subsequent federal conviction—would carry collateral legal consequences.

Search and Seizure § 25 — necessity of warrant

5. Searches and seizures conducted outside the judicial process, without prior approval by judge or magistrate, are per se unreasonable under the Federal Constitution's Fourth Amendment, subject to only a few specifically established and well-delineated exceptions.

Search and Seizure § 11.5 — brief stop of suspicious person

6. Where a police officer observes unusual conduct which leads the officer reasonably to conclude in light of the officer's experience that criminal activity may be afoot, the officer may, under the Federal Constitution's Fourth Amendment, briefly stop the suspicious person and make reasonable inquiries aimed at confirming or dispelling the officer's suspicions.

Evidence § 681; Search and Seizure §§ 11.5, 25 — patdown search for weapons — scope — fruits where invalid — necessity of warrant

7. When a police officer is justified in believing that the individual whose suspicious behavior the officer is investigating at close range is armed and presently dangerous to the officer or to others, the officer may, under the Federal Constitution's Fourth Amendment, conduct a patdown search to determine whether the person is in fact carrying a weapon; such protective search—permitted without a warrant and on the basis of reasonable suspicion less than probable cause—must be strictly limited to that which is necessary for the discovery of weapons which might be used to harm the officer or others nearby; if the protective search goes beyond what is necessary to determine if the suspect is armed, the search is no longer valid and its fruits will be suppressed.

Search and Seizure §§ 2.7, 25 — plain-view doctrine — necessity of warrant

8a, 8b. Under the "plain-view" doctrine, police officers may seize an object without a warrant if (1) the officers are lawfully in a position from which they view the object, (2) the object's incriminating character is immediately apparent, and (3) the officers have a lawful right of access to the object; if contraband is left in open view and is observed by a police officer from a lawful vantage point, there has been no invasion of

FIGURE 8-2
(continued)

MINNESOTA v DICKERSON
(1993) 508 US 366, 124 L Ed 2d 334, 113 S Ct 2130

a legitimate expectation of privacy and thus no "search" within the meaning of the Federal Constitution's Fourth Amendment, or at least no search independent of the initial intrusion that gave the officers their vantage point; however, the plain-view doctrine cannot justify the seizure of an object in plain view if the police lack probable cause to believe that the object is contraband without conducting some further search of the object, that is, if its incriminating character is not immediately apparent.

Appeal § 1673 — affirmance — invalid seizure of cocaine

9. The United States Supreme Court will affirm the judgment of a state's highest court which held that a police officer's seizure of cocaine violated the Federal Constitution's Fourth Amendment, where (1) the state's highest court (a) appeared to adopt a categorical rule barring the seizure of any contraband detected by an officer through the sense of touch during a patdown search for weapons, and (b) noted that even if a "plain feel" exception was recognized, the incriminating character of a small lump of cocaine detected in the front pocket of an accused's nylon jacket during a patdown search was not immediately apparent to the officer, based on the officer's testimony that after feeling the lump, the officer examined it with his fingers, and "it slid and it felt to be a lump of crack cocaine in cellophane"; and (2) the Supreme Court rules that (a) a police officer may seize nonthreatening contraband detected during a patdown search strictly limited to that which is necessary for the discovery of weapons, but (b) the state's highest court was correct under its interpretation of the record in holding that the officer overstepped such limits. (Rehnquist, Ch. J., and Blackmun and Thomas, JJ., dissented from this holding.)

SYLLABUS BY REPORTER OF DECISIONS

Based upon respondent's seemingly evasive actions when approached by police officers and the fact that he had just left a building known for cocaine traffic, the officers decided to investigate further and ordered respondent to submit to a patdown search. The search revealed no weapons, but the officer conducting it testified that he felt a small lump in respondent's jacket pocket, believed it to be a lump of crack cocaine upon examining it with his fingers, and then reached into the pocket and retrieved a small bag of cocaine. The state trial court denied respondent's motion to suppress the cocaine, and he was found guilty of possession of a controlled substance. The Minnesota Court of Appeals reversed. In affirming, the State Supreme Court held that both the stop and the frisk of respondent were valid under Terry v Ohio, 392 US 1, 20 L Ed 2d 889, 88 S Ct 1868, but found the seizure of the cocaine to be unconstitutional. Refusing to enlarge the "plain-view" exception to the Fourth Amendment's warrant requirement, the court appeared to adopt a categorical rule barring the seizure of any contraband detected by an officer through the sense of touch during a patdown search. The court further noted that, even if it recognized such a "plain-feel" exception, the search in this case would not qualify because it went far beyond what is permissible under Terry.

FIGURE 8-2
(continued)

☞42.1 SEARCHES & SEIZURES

For later cases, see same Topic and Key Number in Pocket Part

cause of a generalized urgency of law enforcement. U.S.C.A.Const. Amend. 4.

> Torres v. Com. of Puerto Rico, 99 S.Ct. 2425, 442 U.S. 465, 61 L.Ed.2d 1.

U.S.Utah 1977. Facts of the instant case, involving seizures of property in partial satisfaction of income tax assessments, did not fall under the "exigent circumstances" exception to the warrant requirement, as was clear from the internal revenue agents' own delay in making entry of office in which records were seized. 26 U.S.C.A. (I.R.C.1954) § 6331; U.S.C.A.Const. Amend. 4.

> G. M. Leasing Corp. v. U. S., 97 S.Ct. 619, 429 U.S. 338, 50 L.Ed.2d 530, on remand 560 F.2d 1011, certiorari denied 98 S.Ct. 1485, 435 U.S. 923, 55 L.Ed.2d 516.

☞43. —— Pursuit.

For other cases see the Decennial Digests and WESTLAW.

☞44. —— Presence of probable cause.

U.S.Dist.Col. 1948. Where officers heard adding machines which they knew were frequently used in the numbers operation and saw defendants busily engaged in their lottery venture, the officers had adequate grounds for seeking a search warrant and inconvenience of officers and delay in preparing papers and getting before magistrate was not a justification for search without warrant. U.S.C.A.Const. Amend. 4.

> McDonald v. U.S., 69 S.Ct. 191, 335 U.S. 451, 93 L.Ed. 153.

U.S.Ill. 1992. When "operational necessities" exist, seizures can be justified on less than probable cause.

> Soldal v. Cook County, Ill., 113 S.Ct. 538, 506 U.S. 56, 121 L.Ed.2d 450, on remand 986 F.2d 1425, on remand 1993 WL 199050.

U.S.N.H. 1971. No amount of probable cause can justify a warrantless search or seizure, in absence of exigent circumstances. (Per Mr. Justice Stewart with three Justices concurring and one Justice concurring in the judgment.) U.S.C.A.Const. Amends. 4, 14.

> Coolidge v. New Hampshire, 91 S.Ct. 2022, 403 U.S. 443, 29 L.Ed.2d 564, rehearing denied 92 S.Ct. 26, 404 U.S. 874, 30 L.Ed.2d 120.

U.S.N.Y. 1980. Probable cause for belief that certain articles subject to seizure are in dwelling cannot alone justify search without warrant. U.S.C.A.Const. Amend. 4.

> Payton v. New York, 100 S.Ct. 1371, 445 U.S. 573, 63 L.Ed.2d 639, on remand People v. Payton, 433 N.Y.S.2d 61, 51 N.Y.2d 169, 412 N.E.2d 1288.

☞45. —— Likely escape or loss of evidence.

U.S.Cal. 1966. In view of fact that time had to be taken to bring accused to hospital from scene of accident where he had been arrested for driving automobile while under influence of intoxicating liquor and that percentage of alcohol in blood of accused would begin to diminish shortly after his drinking stopped, officer might reasonably have believed that he was confronted with emergency in which delay necessary to obtain search warrant threatened destruction of evidence and attempt, without warrant to secure evidence of blood-alcohol content by officer's directing physician in hospital to take blood sample from accused was an appropriate incident to accused's arrest. U.S.C.A.Const. Amend. 4; West's Ann.Cal.Vehicle Code, § 23102(a).

> Schmerber v. California, 86 S.Ct. 1826, 384 U.S. 757, 16 L.Ed.2d 908.

☞46–47. *For other cases see the Decennial Digests and WESTLAW.*

Library references

C.J.S. Searches and Seizures.

☞47. Plain view from lawful vantage point.

☞47.1. —— In general.

U.S.Ariz. 1987. "Plain view" doctrine may legitimate actions beyond scope of original exigencies that justified warrantless search; clarifying *Mincey v. Arizona*, 437 U.S. 385, 98 S.Ct. 2408, 57 L.Ed.2d 290. U.S.C.A. Const.Amend. 4.

> Arizona v. Hicks, 107 S.Ct. 1149, 480 U.S. 321, 94 L.Ed.2d 347.

Absent special operational necessities, any seizure that is unrelated to original exigencies that justified officers' warrantless entry onto premises must itself be supported by probable cause, even though object seized is located in plain view on premises. U.S.C.A. Const.Amend. 4.

> Arizona v. Hicks, 107 S.Ct. 1149, 480 U.S. 321, 94 L.Ed.2d 347.

Officer's actions, in moving stereo equipment in order to locate serial numbers and determine if equipment was stolen, had to be supported by probable cause, notwithstanding that officer was lawfully present in apartment where equipment was located in plain view. U.S.C.A. Const.Amend. 4.

> Arizona v. Hicks, 107 S.Ct. 1149, 480 U.S. 321, 94 L.Ed.2d 347.

U.S.Cal. 1990. If article is already in plain view, neither its observation nor its seizure would involve any invasion of privacy for Fourth Amendment purposes; seizure of article, however, would invade owner's possessory interest. U.S.C.A. Const.Amend. 4.

> Horton v. California, 110 S.Ct. 2301, 496 U.S. 128, 110 L.Ed.2d 112.

See how topic (Searches and Seizures) and key number (47.1) match headnote number 5 in figure 8-1.

FIGURE 8-3   *West Supreme Court Digest*

For references to other topics, see Descriptive-Word Index

It is essential predicate to any valid warrantless seizure of incriminating evidence under plain-view doctrine that police officer not violate Fourth Amendment in arriving at place from which evidence could be plainly viewed. U.S.C.A. Const.Amend. 4.

Horton v. California, 110 S.Ct. 2301, 496 U.S. 128, 110 L.Ed.2d 112.

To justify warrantless seizure of item in plain view, not only must item be in plain view, its incriminating character must be immediately apparent. U.S.C.A. Const.Amend. 4.

Horton v. California, 110 S.Ct. 2301, 496 U.S. 128, 110 L.Ed.2d 112.

To justify warrantless seizure of item in plain view, not only must police officer be lawfully located in place from which object can be plainly seen, but he or she must also have lawful right or access to object itself. U.S.C.A. Const.Amend. 4.

Horton v. California, 110 S.Ct. 2301, 496 U.S. 128, 110 L.Ed.2d 112.

Seizure of object in plain view does not involve intrusion on privacy. U.S.C.A. Const. Amend. 4.

Horton v. California, 110 S.Ct. 2301, 496 U.S. 128, 110 L.Ed.2d 112.

U.S.Cal. 1986. Mere fact that individual has taken measures to restrict some views of his activities does not preclude police officer's observations from public vantage point where he has right to be and which renders activities clearly visible. U.S.C.A. Const.Amend. 4.

California v. Ciraolo, 106 S.Ct. 1809, 476 U.S. 207, 90 L.Ed.2d 210, rehearing denied 106 S.Ct. 3320, 478 U.S. 1014, 92 L.Ed.2d 728.

U.S.Dist.Col. 1968. Objects falling in plain view of officer who has right to be in position to have that view are subject to seizure and may be introduced in evidence. U.S.C.A.Const. Amend. 4.

Harris v. U. S., 88 S.Ct. 992, 390 U.S. 234, 19 L.Ed.2d 1067.

U.S.Fla. 1980. Even though some circumstances—for example, if the results of a private search are in plain view when materials are turned over to the government—may justify the government's reexamination of the materials, the government may not exceed the scope of the private search unless it has the right to make an independent search. (Per Mr. Justice Stevens, with one Justice joining, two Justices concurring in part and in the judgment, and the one Justice concurring in the judgment.)

Walter v. U.S., 100 S.Ct. 2395, 447 U.S. 649, 65 L.Ed.2d 410, on remand U.S. v. Sanders, 625 F.2d 1311.

U.S.Ill. 1992. Absent consent or warrant, "plain view" seizures can be justified only if they meet probable cause standard and if they are unaccompanied by unlawful trespass because, in the absence of a privacy interest notwithstanding, seizure would obviously invade owners' possessory interests. U.S.C.A. Const. Amend. 4.

Soldal v. Cook County, Ill., 113 S.Ct. 538, 506 U.S. 56, 121 L.Ed.2d 450, on remand 986 F.2d 1425, on remand 1993 WL 199050.

Plain view doctrine merely reflects application of Fourth Amendment's central requirement of reasonableness of law governing seizures of property. U.S.C.A. Const.Amend. 4.

Soldal v. Cook County, Ill., 113 S.Ct. 538, 506 U.S. 56, 121 L.Ed.2d 450, on remand 986 F.2d 1425, on remand 1993 WL 199050.

If officers' presence in home itself entailed violation of Fourth Amendment, no amount of probable cause to believe that item in plain view is incriminating evidence will justify its seizure. U.S.C.A. Const.Amend. 4.

Soldal v. Cook County, Ill., 113 S.Ct. 538, 506 U.S. 56, 121 L.Ed.2d 450, on remand 986 F.2d 1425, on remand 1993 WL 199050.

U.S.Ill. 1983. Plain view doctrine authorizes seizure of illegal or evidentiary item visible to a police officer whose access to item has some prior Fourth Amendment justification and who has probable cause to suspect that item is connected with criminal activity. U.S.C.A. Const.Amend. 4.

Illinois v. Andreas, 103 S.Ct. 3319, 463 U.S. 765, 77 L.Ed.2d 1003.

U.S.Md. 1932. Search of garage and seizure of whisky without warrant after officers smelled whisky odor and saw cardboard cases through small opening held unreasonable. U.S.C.A. Const.Amend. 4.

Taylor v. U. S., 52 S.Ct. 466, 286 U.S. 1, 76 L.Ed. 951.

U.S.Minn. 1993. Under "plain-view" doctrine, if police are lawfully in a position from which they view an object, if its incriminating character is immediately apparent, and if the officers have lawful right of access to the object, they may seize it without a warrant, but if the police lack probable cause to believe that an object in plain view is contraband without conducting some further search of the object, i.e., if its incriminating character is not immediately apparent, the "plain-view" doctrine cannot justify its seizure. U.S.C.A. Const.Amend. 4.

Minnesota v. Dickerson, 113 S.Ct. 2130, 508 U.S. 366, 124 L.Ed.2d 334.

Note the reference to *Minnesota v. Dickerson* and citations to several other cases.

FIGURE 8-3
(continued)

this digest to the headnotes in Figure 8-2. Figure 8-2 shows headnotes from the Lexis Law publication of Supreme Court cases (*Lawyer's Edition*). Note how the topics and sections for these headnotes do not match the topics and sections in the West digest.

A Point to Remember

Each publisher uses topics that *it* selects. Thus, the same legal principle may be identified by different topic names in different publications.

In assigning a topic to the headnotes, the editors of case reporters use lists of topics previously created. Figure 8-4 shows the lists of topics used by Thomson/West. Other publishers use different terms. If you refer to Figure 8-1, you see that the topic of headnote number one, "Criminal Law," deals with the issue of "mootness." Compare this to headnote numbers 3 and 4 in Figure 8-2. Here, a similar legal principle is found in the topic "Appeal."

8-3 WEST DIGESTS

Thomson/West, a major publisher of case reporters, publishes numerous digests. A comprehensive digest system from West, the American Digest System, covers annotations to *all* state and federal cases. Other West digests contain case annotations to United States Supreme Court cases, to selected state cases, to federal district court and appellate court cases, and to cases found in various specialty court reporters.

topic and key number.
System used by West Group to integrate its various primary and secondary resource materials.

Like other West publications, the West digests use the **topic and key number** system. In selecting its digest topics, West started with seven main divisions of law: persons, property, contracts, torts, crimes, remedies, and government. More than 400 topics are now created under these categories. (Refer to Figure 8-4 for a list of these topics.) The topics describe different aspects of U.S. law. Each topic is then divided into more specific subjects that are assigned a number, called a key number. For example, one general topic used by West is "Searches and Seizures." One specific section of this topic deals with police executing a search warrant and seizing evidence not identified in the warrant. This section is assigned the key number 147.1. In print versions of the case reporters, the headnote number is preceded by a key symbol. (Refer to Figure 8-1.) In the online system, Westlaw, the headnote number is preceded by a "k." (In Westlaw, the main topic is also assigned a number. This number comes before the "k." See Figure 8-5.)

The American Digest System   The largest digest available to researchers is the *American Digest System,* published by West. This digest system is based on the headnotes found in case reporters in the West reporter system and is a topical arrangement of headnotes of *all* state and federal cases published in any of the national reporters. *The American Digest System,* first published at the end of the 1800s, includes case references to every state and dates back to 1658! When first published, it consisted of 50 volumes and was called the *Century Digest*. The *Century Digest* contains case annotations for the years 1658 to 1896. After the publication of the *Century Digest*, West updated the set with the publication of *Decennial Digests*. As the name suggests, these digests were published every ten years, and are known as *First Decennial Digest*, *Second Decennial Digest*, and so on. These are now published every five

Century Digest.
Part of the American Digest System; contains case annotations for the years 1658 to 1896.

Decennial Digest.
Updates to the *Century Digest*, published every five years.

years, and are referred to as Part I and Part 2 of that *Decennial Digest.* Each decennial digest contains case annotations for the ten-year period it serves and consists of many volumes.

OUTLINE OF THE LAW

Digest Topics are arranged for your convenience by Seven Main Divisions of Law. Complete alphabetical list of Digest Topics with topic numbers follows this section.

---

1. PERSONS
2. PROPERTY
3. CONTRACTS
4. TORTS
5. CRIMES
6. REMEDIES
7. GOVERNMENT

1. PERSONS

RELATING TO NATURAL PERSONS IN GENERAL

Civil Rights
Dead Bodies
Death
Domicile
Food
Health
Holidays
Intoxicating Liquors
Names
Seals
Signatures
Sunday
Time
Weapons

PARTICULAR CLASSES OF NATURAL PERSONS

Absentees
Aliens, Immigration, and Citizenship
Chemical Dependents
Children Out-of Wedlock
Convicts
Indians
Infants
Mental Health
Slaves
Spendthrifts

PERSONAL RELATIONS

Adoption
Attorney and Client
Child Custody
Child Support
Executors and Administrators
Guardian and Ward
Husband and Wife
Labor and Employment
Marriage
Parent and Child
Principal and Agent
Workers' Compensation

ASSOCIATED AND ARTIFICIAL PERSONS

Associations
Beneficial Associations
Building and Loan Associations
Clubs
Colleges and Universities
Corporations
Exchanges
Joint-Stock Companies and Business Trusts
Limited Liability Companies
Partnership
Religious Societies

PARTICULAR OCCUPATIONS

Accountants
Agriculture
Antitrust and Trade Regulation
Auctions and Auctioneers
Aviation
Banks and Banking
Bridges
Brokers
Canals
Carriers

IX

FIGURE 8-4 West's Key Number System: Alphabetical List of Digest Topics

1. PERSONS — Cont'd

PARTICULAR OCCUPATIONS — Cont'd

Commerce
Consumer Credit
Credit Reporting Agencies
Detectives
Electricity
Explosives
Factors
Ferries
Gas
Hawkers and Peddlers
Innkeepers
Insurance
Licenses
Manufactures
Pilots
Public Amusement and Entertainment
Railroads
Seamen
Shipping
Steam
Telecommunications
Towage
Turnpikes and Toll Roads
Urban Railroads
Warehousemen
Wharves

2. PROPERTY

NATURE, SUBJECTS, AND INCIDENTS OF OWNERSHIP IN GENERAL

Abandoned and Lost Property
Accession
Adjoining Landowners
Confusion of Goods
Improvements
Property

PARTICULAR SUBJECTS AND INCIDENTS OF OWNERSHIP

Animals
Annuities
Automobiles
Boundaries
Cemeteries
Common Lands
Copyrights and Intellectual Property
Crops
Fences
Fish

Fixtures
Franchises
Game
Good Will
Logs and Logging
Mines and Minerals
Monopolies
Navigable Waters
Party Walls
Patents
Public Lands
Trademarks
Waters and Water Courses
Woods and Forests

PARTICULAR CLASSES OF ESTATES OR INTERESTS IN PROPERTY

Charities
Condominium
Dower and Curtesy
Easements
Estates in Property
Joint Tenancy
Landlord and Tenant
Life Estates
Perpetuities
Powers
Remainders
Reversions
Tenancy in Common
Trusts

PARTICULAR MODES OF ACQUIRING OR TRANSFERRING PROPERTY

Abstracts of Title
Adverse Possession
Alteration of Instruments
Assignments
Chattel Mortgages
Conversion
Dedication
Deeds
Descent and Distribution
Escheat
Fraudulent Conveyances
Gifts
Lost Instruments
Mortgages
Pledges
Secured Transactions
Wills

x

FIGURE 8-4
(continued)

3. CONTRACTS

NATURE, REQUISITES, AND INCIDENTS OF AGREEMENTS IN GENERAL

Contracts
Customs and Usages
Frauds, Statute of
Interest
Usury

PARTICULAR CLASSES OF AGREEMENTS

Bailment
Bills and Notes
Bonds
Breach of Marriage Promise
Champerty and Maintenance
Compromise and Settlement
Covenants
Deposits and Escrows
Exchange of Property
Gaming
Guaranty
Implied and Constructive Contracts
Indemnity
Joint Adventures
Lotteries
Principal and Surety
Public Contracts
Rewards
Sales
Subscriptions
Vendor and Purchaser

PARTICULAR CLASSES OF IMPLIED OR CONSTRUCTIVE CONTRACTS OR QUASI CONTRACTS

Account Stated
Contribution
Implied and Constructive Contracts

PARTICULAR MODES OF DISCHARGING CONTRACTS

Novation
Payment
Release
Subrogation
Tender

4. TORTS

Assault and Battery
Collision
Conspiracy
False Imprisonment
Forcible Entry and Detainer
Fraud
Libel and Slander
Malicious Prosecution
Negligence
Nuisance
Products Liability
Seduction
Torts
Trespass
Trover and Conversion
Waste

5. CRIMES

Abortion and Birth Control
Adulteration
Adultery
Arson
Bigamy
Breach of the Peace
Bribery
Burglary
Compounding Offenses
Controlled Substances
Counterfeiting
Criminal Law
Disorderly Conduct
Disorderly House
Disturbance of Public Assemblage
Embezzlement
Escape
Extortion and Threats
False Personation
False Pretenses
Fires
Forgery
Homicide
Incest
Insurrection and Sedition
Kidnapping
Larceny
Lewdness
Malicious Mischief
Mayhem
Neutrality Laws
Obscenity
Obstructing Justice
Perjury
Prostitution
Racketeer Influenced and Corrupt Organizations
Rape
Receiving Stolen Goods
Rescue
Riot

XI

FIGURE 8-4
(continued)

5. CRIMES—Cont'd

Robbery
Sodomy
Suicide
Treason
Unlawful Assembly
Vagrancy

6. REMEDIES

REMEDIES BY ACT OR AGREEMENT OF PARTIES

Accord and Satisfaction
Alternative Dispute Resolution
Submission of Controversy

REMEDIES BY POSSESSION OR NOTICE

Liens
Lis Pendens
Maritime Liens
Mechanics' Liens
Notice
Salvage

MEANS AND METHODS OF PROOF

Acknowledgment
Affidavits
Estoppel
Evidence
Oath
Records
Witnesses

CIVIL ACTIONS IN GENERAL

Action
Declaratory Judgment
Election of Remedies
Limitation of Actions
Parties
Set-Off and Counterclaim
Venue

PARTICULAR PROCEEDINGS IN CIVIL ACTIONS

Abatement and Revival
Appearance
Costs
Damages
Execution
Exemptions
Homestead
Judgment

Jury
Motions
Pleading
Pretrial Procedure
Process
Reference
Stipulations
Trial

PARTICULAR REMEDIES INCIDENT TO CIVIL ACTIONS

Arrest
Assistance, Writ of
Attachment
Bail
Deposits in Court
Garnishment
Injunction
Judicial Sales
Ne Exeat
Receivers
Recognizances
Sequestration
Undertakings

PARTICULAR MODES OF REVIEW IN CIVIL ACTIONS

Appeal and Error
Audita Querela
Certiorari
Exceptions, Bill of
New Trial
Review

ACTIONS TO ESTABLISH OWNER-SHIP OR RECOVER POSSESSION OF SPECIFIC PROPERTY

Detinue
Ejectment
Entry, Writ of
Interpleader
Possessory Warrant
Quieting Title
Real Actions
Replevin
Trespass to Try Title

FORMS OF ACTIONS FOR DEBTS OR DAMAGES

Account, Action on
Action on the Case
Assumpsit, Action of
Covenant, Action of
Debt, Action of

XII

FIGURE 8-4
(continued)

6. REMEDIES—Cont'd

ACTIONS FOR PARTICULAR FORMS OR SPECIAL RELIEF

Account
Cancellation of Instruments
Debtor and Creditor
Divorce
Partition
Reformation of Instruments
Specific Performance

CIVIL PROCEEDINGS OTHER THAN ACTIONS

Habeas Corpus
Mandamus
Prohibition
Quo Warranto
Scire Facias
Supersedeas

SPECIAL CIVIL JURISDICTIONS AND PROCEDURE THEREIN

Admiralty
Bankruptcy
Equity
Federal Civil Procedure

PROCEEDINGS PECULIAR TO CRIMINAL CASES

Double Jeopardy
Extradition and Detainers
Fines
Forfeitures
Grand Jury
Indictment and Information
Pardon and Parole
Penalties
Searches and Seizures
Sentencing and Punishment

7. GOVERNMENT

POLITICAL BODIES AND DIVISIONS

Counties
District of Columbia
Municipal Corporations
States
Territories
Towns
United States

SYSTEMS AND SOURCES OF LAW

Administrative Law and Procedure
Common Law
Constitutional Law
International Law
Parliamentary Law
Statutes
Treaties

LEGISLATIVE AND EXECUTIVE POWERS AND FUNCTIONS

Bounties
Census
Commodity Futures Trading Regulation
Customs Duties
Drains
Eminent Domain
Environmental Law
Highways
Inspection
Internal Revenue
Levees and Flood Control
Pensions
Postal Service
Private Roads
Public Contracts
Public Utilities
Schools
Securities Regulation
Social Security and Public Welfare
Taxation
Unemployment Compensation
Weights and Measures
Zoning and Planning

JUDICIAL POWERS AND FUNCTIONS, AND COURTS AND THEIR OFFICERS

Amicus Curiae
Clerks of Courts
Contempt
Court Commissioners
Courts
Federal Courts
Judges
Justices of the Peace
Removal of Cases
Reports
United States Magistrates

CIVIL SERVICE, OFFICERS, AND INSTITUTIONS

Ambassadors and Consuls
Asylums and Assisted Living Facilities

XIII

FIGURE 8-4
(continued)

FIGURE 8-4
(continued)

7. GOVERNMENT—Cont'd	
CIVIL SERVICE, OFFICERS, AND INSTITUTIONS—Cont'd	Registers of Deeds Sheriffs and Constables United States Marshals
Attorney General Coroners District and Prosecuting Attorneys Elections Newspapers Notaries Officers and Public Employees Prisons	**MILITARY AND NAVAL SERVICE AND WAR** Armed Services Military Justice Militia War and National Emergency

Reprinted with permission of Thomson/West

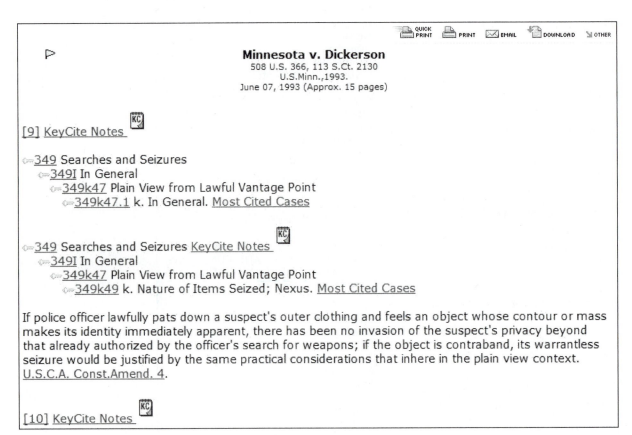

Reprinted with permission of Thomson/West

FIGURE 8-5   *Minnesota v. Dickerson,* Westlaw Headnote

A Point to Remember

Each decennial digest is *not* a cumulative supplement of case annotations. It covers only a ten-year period.

In addition to the *Century Digest* and the *Decennial Digests*, the American Digest System contains a set known as the **General Digest**. This set contains volumes that update the latest *Decennial Digest*.

General Digest. Updates to the *Decennial Digest.*

State Digests   West publishes digests for cases from most states. In addition, digests are available for the regional reporters: *Atlantic Reporter, Pacific Reporter, North Western Reporter*, and *South Western Reporter*.

Federal and Supreme Court Digests   West digests exist for cases published in federal reporters. The *United States Supreme Court Digest* is tied to the *Supreme Court Reporter* and contains annotations to United States Supreme Court cases. West's *Federal Practice Digest* contains references to published federal district court, court of appeals, and Supreme Court cases. Earlier editions of the *Federal Practice Digest* are known as the *Federal Digest* and *Modern Federal Practice Digest*.

Specialty Digests   Digests also exist for certain special case reporters. Examples include West's *Bankruptcy Digest* and *United States Court of Claims Digest*. See Box 8-1 for an overview of the West Digest System.

BOX 8-1   WEST DIGEST SYSTEM

The American Digest System

Century Digest (1658 through 1896)

Decennial Digest (10 years increments beginning in 1897)

General Digest (updates to Decennial Digest)

Supreme Court Digest

Federal Practice Digest

Atlantic Digest

North Western Digest

Pacific Digest

South Eastern Digest

State Digests

Specialty Digests

8-4 OTHER DIGESTS

Lexis Law Publishing produces a digest to accompany its case reporter, *United States Supreme Court Cases, Lawyers' Edition.* This is known as the *United States Supreme Court Reports Digest, Lawyers' Edition.* (Until recently, this case reporter and digest were published by Lawyers Cooperative Publishing Company.) The organization and features of this digest are similar to the West digest. The topic names, however, differ.

State-specific digests, accompanying state reporters, are also published. See Box 8-2 for a list of case reporters and corresponding digests.

BOX 8-2

If You Are Using This Case Reporter:	Then Use This Digest:
Lawyers' Edition	*Supreme Court Digest, Lawyers' Edition*
Supreme Court Reporter	*Supreme Court Digest*
Federal Reporter	*Federal Practice Digest*
Atlantic Reporter	*Atlantic Digest*
North Western Reporter	*North Western Digest*
Pacific Reporter	*Pacific Digest*
South Eastern Reporter	*South Eastern Digest*
Any West Reporter	*American Digest*

8-5 USING DIGESTS

A digest is most effectively used in legal research once you find a case dealing with your research issue. (Using an encyclopedia or other secondary source helps you to do this.) Once a case is found, identify the headnote or headnotes dealing with your issue. At this point, take the topic and number of the headnote, go to the appropriate digest, and find the topic and number. Here you find references to other cases dealing with the same issue.

Although not recommended, digests can be used as a starting point in your research. All digests contain descriptive word indexes just like other secondary sources. Once you review and analyze your research question, you can identify key words or phrases that are likely to be found in a **descriptive word index**. This index will help you identify the topic and number that is relevant to your research.

When using a digest, check the latest updates or supplements. Digests might be supplemented by bound volumes, by pocket part supplements, or by supplemental pamphlets. In addition, when using a digest, you must check to see what years are covered in the particular series you are using. Later series of digests are not usually cumulative. For example, if you use the *Federal Practice Digest 4th*, you will see that it does not contain references to cases that were summarized in *Federal Practice Digest 3d.* This information is found in the **prefatory material** and should always be checked.

descriptive word index. An alphabetical listing of words describing the topics contained in a book or set of books; refers the researcher to the volume and page where the topic is discussed.

prefatory material. Material found in the front of a book or set of books describing such matters as the purpose of the book and directions for using the book.

One special and very helpful feature found in digests is the table of cases. This table alphabetically lists all cases found in the digest by both the plaintiff's name and the defendant's name. Thus, if you know only a case name, you can find the citation.

Whenever you use a digest, pay attention to a few matters. Be careful about which digest you use. If you have a topic and number from a West case reporter, you cannot locate that information in any digest not published by West. Also use care in relying on all cases you find in a digest. The American Digest System and the regional digests contain case references from several states. When researching an issue of state law, remember that only cases from your state are binding authority. Using a digest that is specific to a state reporter (if available) is the way to begin. If you find cases dealing with the legal issue from your state, there is no need to use a larger digest. See Boxes 8-3 and 8-4 for a checklist for using digests.

BOX 8-3 USING DIGESTS

Starting with a Known Case

✓ Identify headnotes relevant to your issue.

✓ Note the topic and number of those headnotes.

✓ Find the digest corresponding to the case reporter.

✓ Locate the topic and number in digest.

✓ Note citations to other cases under the topic and number.

✓ Read the other cases.

BOX 8-4 USING DIGESTS

Starting with Issue or Facts, but No Known Cases

✓ Identify key words in facts and issues.

✓ Locate key words in the descriptive word index.

✓ Identify the proper topic and numbers from the index.

✓ Locate the topic and number in the digest.

✓ Note the case citations under the topic and number.

✓ Read the cases.

8-6 WESTLAW, LEXIS, AND DIGESTS

Neither LEXIS nor Westlaw provides direct access to the digests. However, the digest concept of finding cases, that is, finding cases with similar headnotes, affects search features on these legal databases. Both online legal databases provide features that allow the researcher to perform digest-type searches. Because of the increased power of online searching, using these features often produces better search results than using the digest in its print format. Cases reported in both LEXIS and Westlaw contain headnotes with topics and subtopics. In both legal databases, the researcher can use these headnotes to find additional cases with the same headnote topics and subtopic.

To see how this is done on LEXIS, refer to Figure 8-6, which shows a LEXIS headnote from *Minnesota v. Dickerson*. Note the topics assigned to the headnotes. There are two ways to perform a digest-type search. First, note the small box next to the headnote "Constitutional Law." This link eventually leads you to "all headnotes and additional cases on this topic." Prior to completing the search, the researcher has the opportunity to limit the search by jurisdiction and date, thus retrieving more relevant results.

A second way of conducting a digest-type search on LEXIS is by following the link stating "more like this headnote." Again, refer to Figure 8-6. If you follow this link, you retrieve the window that allows you to limit your search and narrow your results.

Westlaw utilizes its key number system for headnotes. By using these numbers to search, you retrieve cases containing the same key numbers. There are two easy ways to do this type of search using the headnotes from the case. Refer to Figure 8-7, a copy of the headnotes from *Minnesota v. Dickerson*. You can link from either the key number or the hyperlinked phrase, "most cited cases." In either event, you retrieve a new search box, entitled "Custom Digest." See Figure 8-8. Here you can limit and refine your search by jurisdiction or by date. You can also retrieve the most current cases or the most cited cases. You also have the opportunity to add search terms to the key number to even further individualize or customize your search.

An additional feature on Westlaw utilizes the data found in the West Digest system. The "keysearch" feature allows you to browse several topics selected by West and based on their digest topics (although the topics are not identical). See Figure 8-9 for the initial keysearch screen. Your search is conducted by recognizing and then linking to relevant terms. For example, if you were researching an issue similar to that in *Minnesota v. Dickerson*, you might click on Search and Seizure

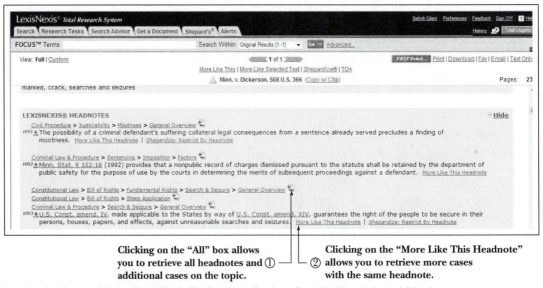

Clicking on the "All" box allows you to retrieve all headnotes and ① additional cases on the topic.

Clicking on the "More Like This Headnote" ② allows you to retrieve more cases with the same headnote.

Reprinted with permission of LexisNexis. Further reproduction of any kind is strictly prohibited.

FIGURE 8-6   *Minnesota v. Dickerson,* LEXIS Headnote

Reprinted with permission of Thomson/West

FIGURE 8-7   *Minnesota v. Dickerson,* Westlaw Headnote

Reprinted with permission of Thomson/West

FIGURE 8-8   Custom Digest on Westlaw

found under the general topic of Criminal Justice. (Refer to Figure 8-9.) Eventually you are asked to specify a jurisdiction for your search. Rather than searching
for case law, you have the option to retrieve various secondary sources.

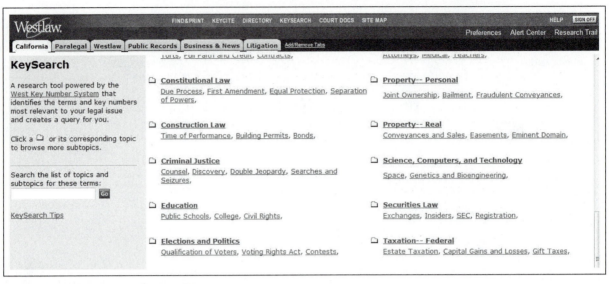

Reprinted with permission of Thomson/West

FIGURE 8-9   KeySearch on Westlaw (Digest Topics)

Online Legal Research

Without access to Westlaw or LEXIS it is difficult to perform an efficient digest-type search online. However, using some online sources can help you in using digests in print form or searching on Westlaw or LEXIS. An essential step in using digests is identifying the topic. Unless you have already found a case headnote on point, identifying a digest topic first requires that you analyze your research questions and identify key words that can be located in a descriptive word index. A dictionary and a legal thesaurus help you to identify relevant terms. The following Web sites provide access to these two valuable tools:

Legal Dictionaries

    www.lectlaw.com/ref.html

    http://dictionary.law.com/

    http://dictionary.lp.findlaw.com/

Dictionaries

    www.m-w.com/ (Webster)

    www.onelook.com/ (links to dozens of dictionaries)

Thesaurus

    www.thesaurus.com/

    www.m-w.com/

      You can also find information about using digests and the Westlaw keysearch feature through the Westlaw site, www.westlaw.com. This information does not require that you access the Westlaw database and is available to anyone.

Free Web sites containing reported cases often allow the researcher to search by topic. However, search results generally contain a list of case names. You do not retrieve headnote summaries (since these are copyright protected by the publishers). To determine the relevance of retrieved cases, you are required to read the entire text of the case. One site that allows case searching by providing a list of preselected topics is www.law.cornell.edu. On this site you can search archived Supreme Court opinions from 1990 forward by topic (http://www.law.cornell.edu/supct/index.html).

C ITATION MATTERS

BOOKS

THE BLUEBOOK—RULE 15

Rule 15 states: "Cite books, pamphlets, and other nonperiodic materials by volume, if more than one (rule 3.2(a)); author, editor, and/or translator (rule 15.1); title (rule 15.2); serial number, if any (rule 15.3); page, section, or paragraph (rules 3.3 and 3.4), if only part of a volume is cited; edition, if more than one has appeared; publisher, if not the original one; and date (rule 15.4). Cite prefaces or forewords according to rule 15.6, supplements according to rule 3.2(c), and appendices according to rule 3.5."

THE BLUEBOOK provides the following examples:

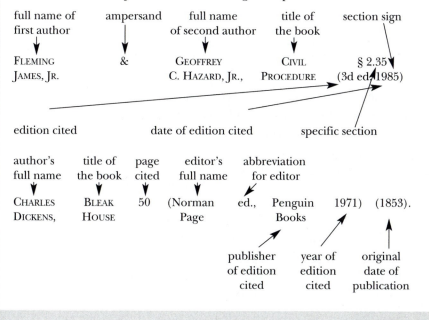

CHAPTER SUMMARY

An important research tool used to find case law is the digest. A digest is an alphabetical arrangement of topics found in headnotes with references to the cases where the headnotes are found. The publishers of the various case reporters publish digests corresponding to the case reporters. You can use a digest to find case law if you already have one case that relates to your issue or if you have identified key words from your facts and issues. If you have a known case, you note the appropriate headnotes, locate them in the digest that accompanies the case reporter you are using, and then find other cases on the same topic. If you do not have a known case, check the key terms in the descriptive word index. The index directs the researcher to various topics in the digest.

Although online services of LEXIS and Westlaw do not provide direct access to the digest, both contain features that allow the researcher to perform digest-type searches. On both sites, the researcher can link from the headnote of one case to similar headnotes in other cases. Additionally, Westlaw offers the "keysearch" feature. This feature allows the researcher to search a database containing all of the West topics and key numbers.

TERMS TO REMEMBER

digest   *Century Digest*   descriptive word index
headnotes   *Decennial Digest*   prefatory material
topic and key number   *General Digest*

QUESTIONS FOR REVIEW

1. What is a digest?
2. How are headnotes organized in a digest?
3. Describe the West topic and key number system.
4. How do key numbers in print sources differ from key numbers in Westlaw?
5. If you have a known case and are using a digest to find more cases, why is it important to use the digest published by the company that published the case reporter where you found the case?
6. What types of cases are found in West's American Digest System?
7. What is a table of cases and why is it useful?
8. How do you use a digest if you do not have any case law related to your issue?
9. How are digests kept up-to-date?
10. Describe features on both LEXIS and Westlaw that are based on the digest-concept of searching headnotes.

CAN YOU FIGURE IT OUT?

1. List the legal topics and key numbers for the headnotes found in Figure 8-1.
2. List the legal topics and section numbers for the headnotes found in Figure 8-2.
3. Refer to Figure 8-3. Find key number 43. Which other sources should be checked?
4. Refer to Figure 8-3. Cite cases other than *Dickerson* that deal with the topic Searches and Seizures and key number 47.1.

BUILDING YOUR RESEARCH SKILLS: ASSIGNMENTS AND ACTIVITIES

1. Using the *10th Decennial Digest—Part I*, answer the following.
   a. Cite a case in which Dannon Yogurt is a defendant.
   b. What is the specific topic of Patents 16.29?
      1. What is the name of a New York federal case, found in this section, dealing with a patent from the United Kingdom?
      2. Locate the case described in "a." What case headnote corresponds to this digest entry?
   c. Using the descriptive word index, which civil rights section deals with arrest as a deprivation of constitutional rights?
2. Using the *11th Decennial Digest—Part 2*, answer the following.
   d. Find the topic and key number, Searches and Seizures 47.1.
      1. Give the name and citation for a Ninth Circuit Federal case decided in 2003 related to this issue.
      2. Give the name and citation for a 2004 case from Rhode Island regarding this issue.
   e. Assume that you are researching the following question, "Is it a violation of the freedom of speech to prohibit students from saying prayers at a high school graduation ceremony?" Use the descriptive word index to find digest topics that cover this issue. Answer the following.
      1. What topics and key numbers provide case law relevant to the following topic: freedom of speech generally in schools?
      2. What topics and key numbers provide case law relevant to the following topic: prayers at graduation ceremonies?

BUILDING YOUR ANALYSIS SKILLS: ASSIGNMENTS AND EXERCISES

1. Select one research problem from Appendix A and read it carefully. Find at least five topics in Figure 8-4 that apply to the situation.

BUILDING YOUR ONLINE RESEARCH SKILLS: ASSIGNMENTS AND EXERCISES

1. Access the following site: http://www.law.cornell.edu/supct/index.html. Search archived Supreme Court opinions by topic.
   a. If you are searching for cases similar to *Minnesota v. Dickerson*, which topics would you select? (Consider the headnote topics you saw in Figures 8-1 and 8-2.)
   b. Select a topic and then search for more cases dealing with the specific area of plain view searches? What did you find?
2. Perform an advanced "Google" search for legal digests. Limit your search to documents in a Microsoft PowerPoint format. What did you find?
3. If you have access to Westlaw, do the following:
   Access *Hamdi v. Rumsfeld*, 542 U.S. 507, 124 S.Ct. 2633 (2004).
   a. What is the specific topic and key number for the first West headnote?
   b. What is the most cited case for the legal topic found in the first headnote?
4. If you have access to LEXIS, do the following:
   Access *Hamdi v. Rumsfeld*, 542 U.S. 507, 159 L. Ed. 2d (2004).
   a. What is the topic of headnote 1?
   b. Click on More Like This Headnote and check for Supreme Court cases only. How many cases did you retrieve?

CASE PROJECT

Using the same case that you researched in previous chapters, check the appropriate digest for topics relating to the issues. Begin by making a list of terms to check in the index to the digest. Make a list of relevant digest topics and cases. Read the cases and take notes.

CHAPTER

9

VALIDATING YOUR RESEARCH: USING *SHEPARD'S*, KEYCITE, AND OTHER CITATORS

CHAPTER OUTLINE

S KILL OBJECTIVES FOR CHAPTER 9

When you complete this chapter you should be able to

- Explain the purpose of a citator.
- List the types of authorities that can be Shepardized.
- Shepardize a case using print and online resources.
- Explain the difference between the history of the case and the treatment of the case.
- Explain how *Shepard's* uses headnote numbers.
- Shepardize a statute using print and online resources.
- KeyCite case law and other legal authorities.
- Discuss the differences between *Shepard's* online and other online citators.
- "Cite check" a document.

FROM THE DESK OF W. J. BRYAN, ESQ.

TO: Research Assistant

Attached is a copy of the memorandum of points and authorities that I plan to file in support of our motion to suppress evidence in the Meyers case. Please Shepardize all the cases cited in the memo to verify that they are still good law. Also, check all cites in the document and correct any citation problems.

9-1 INTRODUCTION TO CITATORS

U.S. law is in a constant state of change. Although case law is founded on the concept of *stare decisis*, courts occasionally overrule or modify prior case law to meet the needs of justice in a changing society. Statutory law likewise undergoes changes. Statutes are commonly amended and repealed, or given new interpretations by courts. Sometimes courts declare that statutes are unconstitutional and therefore unenforceable. Your research is never complete until you verify that your authorities are still **good law.**

good law. Law that is still in effect or valid and can be cited as authority.

Determining that an authority is good law requires the use of special research material. Case reporters and code books do not provide complete up-to-date information on the cases and codes found in the books. When you read a case in a case reporter, you cannot tell if that case was overruled or criticized in later cases. Published codes provide better information, but even they are not totally up-to-date. While most codes contain pocket part supplements, these supplements are replaced only once a year. Because most legislative changes take effect at the beginning of the year rather than when they are enacted, supplementing once a year is usually sufficient to provide the latest statutory language. However, some legislation is considered to be "emergency legislation" and takes effect immediately. This is not found in a yearly supplement. Furthermore, if you rely on case notes in an annotated code, you may miss important new relevant case law.

The research materials used to update or **validate** legal authorities are known as **citators**, the most familiar of which is *Shepard's Citations*. *Shepard's* is available in print and online through LEXIS. LEXIS provides two other means of cite checking, Auto-cite and Lexcite. Another important citator is KeyCite, available online through Westlaw.

validate. To verify that an authority is still good law.

citators. Research materials used to update or "validate" legal authorities.

9-2 *SHEPARD'S CITATIONS*

Shepard's Citations is a popular collection that researchers use to validate their research. When you use any *Shepard's* citator to check a legal citation, you are said to be **"Shepardizing"** your authority. The legal citation you are Shepardizing is called the **cited authority**. New law found when Shepardizing is referred to as the **citing authority**. While *Shepard's* is most commonly used to check case law, it is also used to check other authorities, such as constitutions, statutory law, administrative regulations, selected law review articles, *A.L.R.* annotations, court rules, and approved jury instructions. *Shepard's* includes specialized citators for areas of law such as bankruptcy and patents. See Box 9-1.

Shepardize. To check the validity of a citation in one of the *Shepard's* citations.

cited authority. The authority you are Shepardizing.

citing authority. Authorities you are referred to when you Shepardize.

BOX 9-1   YOU CAN SHEPARDIZE THESE AUTHORITIES

Case law

Statutory law

Constitutions

Administrative regulations

Selected law reviews and *A.L.R.*s

Court rules

Approved jury instructions

The primary reason for Shepardizing any authority is to verify that the law found is still good law. However, *Shepard's* provides such extensive information regarding the cited authority that it can be used as a research tool. Citations to other cases and secondary authorities often help the researcher.

Shepard's Case Citators in Print

Shepard's includes separate case citators for cases from different courts. For federal cases, *Shepard's* publishes the following:

- *Shepard's United States Citations* for Shepardizing United States Supreme Court cases
- *Shepard's Federal Citations* for Shepardizing federal district court and appellate court decisions (*Federal Supplement* and *Federal Reporters*)

Additionally, *Shepard's* publishes citators for each of the regional reporters as well as citators for state case reporters.

Cases listed in *Shepard's* are organized first by reporter and series then numerically by volume and page number of the case. See Figure 9-1 for an example of a page from a *Shepard's* case citator in print. On this page you see *Shepard's* reports for three cases found in volume 316 of the *U.S. Reports*. The three cases start on pages 447, 450, and 455. (Note how all reports include citations to other authorities.)

A Point to Remember

When you use a state-specific case citator, you can only Shepardize cases (cited authorities) from the selected jurisdiction. However, citing authorities may be from all jurisdictions.

Because case citators are published for all major case reporters, researchers are able to Shepardize a case with either the official citation or with a parallel citation. It is advisable to Shepardize all citations to the same case, though, because citing authorities are different, especially secondary authorities. (This is not the case if you Shepardize online.) See Figures 9-2 and 9-3 for examples of pages from *Shepard's* showing the parallel cites for the same case as in Figure 9-1.

A Point to Remember

When you Shepardize a case, you must check all parallel cites to obtain references to all citing authorities.

Analyzing Information   Once you find a case in *Shepard's*, you must analyze or interpret your findings. Shepardizing a case provides two types of information concerning your case (the cited case): the history of the case and the treatment of the case. The history of the case provides the published background of the *same* case you are checking. If you are Shepardizing a U.S. Supreme Court case, *Shepard's* provides the cite to published opinions of the same case from lower courts. If you are Shepardizing an appellate court case, *Shepard's* tells you if a higher court has granted a hearing. The treatment of the case provides citations to *other* authorities mentioning your case. In some instances, by the use of short abbreviations preceding the cite, it tells you how these other authorities viewed your case. Some of the more important facts that *Shepard's* tells you are whether a case was:

- Overruled by a subsequent case
- Criticized by a subsequent case
- Approved by a subsequent case
- Questioned by a subsequent case
- Cited in the dissent of a subsequent case

Shepard's also tells you if a case was cited in *A.L.R.* or law review articles. See Figure 9-4 for an illustrative page from *Shepard's* showing the various case treatments and corresponding abbreviations.

When you Shepardize a case using *Shepard's* in print, you also find the following:

- The first time a case appears in *Shepard's*, you see the case name.
- The first time a case appears in *Shepard's*, you find parallel citations in parentheses at the beginning of the citations.
- References to authorities are chronological (oldest cases first) within the following categories: U.S. Supreme Court cases, federal court cases, state court cases, and secondary sources. Citing references are not listed in order of importance.

See Figure 9-5 for an illustration from *Shepard's* case citations showing this.

FIGURE 9-1

Shepard's United States Reports

Vol. 316		UNITED STATES REPORTS		
75McL527	400F2d823	12A2.363n	q) 369US519	111FS418
65MnL80	270FS939	12A2.368n	q) 369US520	123FS443
80MnL1451	Cir. 7	12A2.370n	370US908	124FS37
83MnL1224	160FS328	12A2.371n	372US337	141FS606
85MnL1437	Cir. 8	—455—	o) 372US339	332FS834
72NwL26	266F2d69	Betts v Brady	372US348	377FS1341
57TxL540	69F3d1407	1942	e) 372US349	432FS115
64TxL12	Cir. 9	(86LE1595)	372US478	q) 253FS2d33
77TxL167	172FS938	(62SC1252)	j) 375US3	Cir. 2
60VaL197	Cir. 10	s) 315US791	q) 378US6	e) 137F2d1010
83YLJ433	80FS344	317US24	j) 378US26	190F2d253
85YLJ45	Cir. DC	317US276	j) 378US407	221F2d629
94LE377n	707F2d561	321US115	q) 379US80	d) 250F2d354
94LE378n	Cir. Fed.	j) 322US495	q) 380US414	263F2d943
47LE851n	856F2d172	322US602	j) 381US512	292F2d323
171AR773n	CCPA	324US46	381US590	303F2d885
171AR788n	j) 359F2d885	324US764	j) 381US616	d) 313F2d460
16ARF429n	ClCt	324US768	384US469	315F2d866
	36FedCl 33	325US95	e) 385US399	j) 319F2d318
—447—	38FedCl 667	325US97	385US564	330F2d304
National Broad-	CtCl	326US326	q) 386US43	q) 330F2d310
casting Co. v	375F2d838	327US85	j) 388US172	j) 330F2d315
United States	530F2d869	329US665	q) 389US134	332F2d891
1942	620F2d855	j) 332US83	395US794	q) 333F2d610
(86LE1586)	f) 47FS119	332US137	q) 395US795	398F2d985
(62SC1214)	e) 48FS358	j) 332US140	c) 405US484	q) 465F2d121
s) 319US190	55FS624	j) 332US141	j) 405US485	j) 611F2d421
s) 44FS688	60FS469	333US281	q) 407US31	694F2d22
s) 47FS940	f) 97CCL262	333US656	q) 407US65	e) 709F2d168
cc) 316US407	e) 99CCL570	333US659	408US287	113FS920
Cir. 7	99CCL571	333US660	q) 411US788	171FS561
95FS669	101CCL743	333US666	j) 419US255	177FS507
97CR840	104CCL122	333US676	422US807	184FS282
80MnL1451	179CCL610	j) 333US677	j) 422US844	184FS542
94LE377n	208CCL579	j) 333US679	q) 440US371	200FS907
94LE378n	223CCL430	334US684	j) 440US378	205FS514
47LE851n	4TCt216	j) 334US685	q) 452US25	209FS530
171AR773n	18TCt12	334US730	j) 452US35	210FS277
171AR788n	24TCt637	334US739	466US656	f) 210FS279
	29TCt271	335US441	469US394	212FS880
—450—	36TCt282	337US780	q) 492US12	212FS928
American	58TCt911	c) 337US782	j) 492US21	214FS646
Chicle Co. v	59TCt74	339US661	499US34	219FS153
United States	66TCt356	339US666	509US109	e) 219FS266
1942	77TCt63	342US64	q) 510US273	q) 219FS268
(86LE1591)	89TCt776	342US179	q) 511US493	261FS400
(62SC1144)	90TCt1306	d) 348US9	j) 511US738	q) 327FS546
s) 315US793	100TCt11	348US108	523US850	Cir. 3
s) 41FS537	103TCt470	349US391	j) 4LE292	130F2d657
s) 94CCL699	104TCt729	350US118	q) 159LE507	175F2d254
493US140	107TCt337	j) 351US36	j) 80SC315	203F2d426
505US73	Ala	354US77	q) 124SC2514	203F2d806
Cir. 1	503So2d303	355US159	9FRD348	224F2d508
61FS1016	Mass	j) 356US83	24FRD79	224F2d512
Cir. 2	378Mas273	d) 357US441	33FRD424	f) 310F2d724
158F2d161	391NE263	j) 357US442	33FRD438	j) 310F2d735
306F2d827	Okla	358US636	33FRD454	e) 329F2d858
199FS458	780P2d668	361US246	38FRD463	q) 334F2d529
199FS466	P R	j) 361US255	39FRD284	355F2d313
Cir. 3	74PRR922	j) 363US704	Cir. 1	j) 359F2d947
181F2d405	So C	j) 364US275	181F2d602	j) 430F2d469
Cir. 4	233SoC48	365US117	d) 191F2d965	752F2d921
205F2d342	103SE427	q) 365US119	203F2d935	j) 782F2d455
Cir. 5	78CR1659	j) 365US208	204F2d362	994F2d1016
562F2d978	92HLR1646	j) 366US158	96FS707	74FS848
Cir. 6	122PaL348	368US459	f) 101FS165	81FS870
151F2d1000	153AR1189n	369US517	f) 105FS529	81FS871
229F2d698				

22

① The reporter and volume number appear at the top of the page.

② Here you find *Shepard's* analysis of *Betts v. Brady*, 316 U.S. 455 (1942). Parallel citations are found in other parts of *Shepard's*. This is the cited authority.

③ All of the following cases are the citing authority. These cases all cite *Betts v. Brady*.

This page analyzes *Betts v. Brady*, if you have the *Lawyers' Edition* citation 86 L. Ed. 1595 (1942).

FIGURE 9-2

Shepard's United States Supreme Court Reports, Lawyers' Edition

Vol. 86	UNITED STATES SUPREME COURT REPORTS, LAWYERS' EDITION			
38FedCl[1] 667	90LE[6]108	q) 17LE[4]721	q) 330F2d[7]310	130F2d[4]881
CtCl	90LE[2]548	j) 18LE[9]1121	j) 330F2d[7]315	133F2d477
375F2d[1]838	j) 91LE[4]1925	q) 19LE[8]340	332F2d[7]891	155F2d[4]5
530F2d869	91LE[4]1958	q) 23LE[6]716	q) 333F2d[4]610	198F2d[4]471
620F2d855	j) 91LE[4]1960	23LE[7]716	398F2d[7]985	280F2d[7]539
f) 47FS[1]119	92LE[4]698	c) 31LE[8]382	q) 465F2d[8]121	280F2d[9]539
e) 48FS[1]358	92LE[9]995	j) 31LE[4]383	j) 611F2d421	280F2d[6]541
55FS[1]624	92LE[7]997	j) 31LE[8]387	694F2d[8]22	294F2d[9]396
60FS[2]469	92LE[8]997	q) 32LE[6]535	e) 709F2d[9]168	294F2d[6]609
f) 97CCL262	92LE[6]1000	q) 32LE[8]554	113FS[6]920	297F2d853
e) 99CCL570	92LE[4]1001	33LE377	171FS[9]561	d) 299F2d[4]173
99CCL571	j) 92LE[4]1006	q) 36LE[7]665	177FS[2]507	j) 310F2d[6]917
101CCL743	j) 92LE[6]1006	j) 42LE[4]428	184FS[7]282	315F2d[7]644
104CCL122	j) 92LE[8]1006	j) 42LE[6]428	184FS[9]542	315F2d[8]644
179CCL610	j) 92LE[9]1006	45LE[5]566	200FS[7]907	q) 319F2d[9]2
208CCL579	j) 92LE[7]1007	j) 45LE587	205FS[9]514	q) 319F2d[9]4
223CCL430	92LE[4]1655	j) 45LE[4]587	209FS[4]530	q) 319F2d[8]772
4TCt216	j) 92LE[4]1655	q) 59LE[8]387	210FS[6]277	c) 368F2d298
18TCt12	92LE[4]1686	j) 59LE392	f) 210FS[6]279.	375F2d628
24TCt637	92LE[4]1692	q) 68LE[8]648	212FS[8]880	c) 381F2d[6]641
29TCt271	93LE[4]131	j) 68LE655	212FS[4]928	c) 415F2d1325
36TCt282	93LE[9]1691	80LE666	214FS[7]646	f) 443F2d[8]1095
58TCt911	c) 93LE1692	83LE828	219FS[7]153	j) 443F2d[4]1100
59TCt74	94LE1190	q) 106LE[9]12	e) 219FS[7]266	447F2d[4]57
66TCt356	94LE[7]1192	j) 106LE18	q) 219FS[9]268	483F2d[4]655
77TCt63	96LE[9]94	113LE[6]30	q) 220FS[9]892	j) 166F3d283
89TCt776	d) 99LE[4]9	125LE94	261FS[8]400	47FS[2]366
90TCt1306	99LE[6]138	q) 127LE123	q) 327FS[4]546	165FS[6]24
100TCt11	99LE[7]1174	q) 128LE[5]526	Cir. 3	176FS[4]954
103TCt470	100LE[9]130	j) 128LE762	130F2d[7]657	201FS[9]447
104TCt729	j) 100LE[6]908	140LE[7]1060	175F2d254	206FS[9]302
107TCt337	1LE[7]1197	q) 159LE507	203F2d[8]426	q) 216FS[8]290
Ala	2LE[9]171	9FRD348	203F2d[4]806	227FS[2]
503So2d303	j) 2LE[9]627	24FRD79	224F2d[7]508	q) 227FS[8]3
Mass	d) 2LE1455	33FRD424	224F2d[8]512	251FS[7]665
378Mas273	j) 2LE[4]1456	33FRD438	f) 310F2d[7]724	e) 257FS[4]808
391NE263	3LE[4]560	33FRD454	j) 310F2d[7]735	q) 307FS[4]206
Okla	4LE[7]276	38FRD463	329F2d[7]858	j) 310FS[7]563
780P2d668	j) 4LE[4]292	39FRD284	e) 329F2d[8]858	q) 312FS[7]310
P R	j) 4LE[6]1505	Cir. 1	q) 334F2d[6]529	324FS[7]697
74PRR922	j) 4LE[8]1716	181F2d[6]602	355F2d[4]313	355FS[5]344
So C	5LE[6]451	d) 191F2d[9]965	j) 359F2d[4]947	Cir. 5
233SoC48	q) 5LE[6]452	203F2d[4]935	j) 430F2d469	158F2d[4]617
103SE427	j) 5LE[6]517	204F2d[4]362	752F2d[4]921	194F2d[4]865
78CR1659	j) 6LE[6]182	96FS[7]707	j) 782F2d455	205F2d[6]668
92HLR1646	7LE[9]454	f) 101FS[7]165	994F2d1016	j) 205F2d[7]675
122PaL348	8LE[7]78	f) 105FS[9]529	74FS[2]848	224F2d[7]905
153AR1189n	q) 8LE[7]79	111FS[6]418	74FS[6]848	228F2d[9]659
12AL363n	q) 8LE[7]80	123FS[6]443	74FS[8]848	228F2d[4]664
12AL368n	8LE403	124FS[6]37	81FS[6]870	250F2d[6]647
12AL370n	9LE[9]801	141FS[7]606	81FS[9]871	258F2d[9]941
12AL371n	o) 9LE802	332FS[8]834	84FS[6]940	j) 258F2d[4]944
—1595—	9LE[9]807	377FS[9]1341	85FS[7]787	261F2d[4]233
Betts v Brady	e) 9LE[9]808	432FS[7]115	88FS[6]780	j) 263F2d744
1942	9LE[9]894	q) 253FS2d33	97FS[9]939	j) 263F2d[9]46
(316US455)	j) 11LE[9]42	Cir. 2	148FS[9]684	330F2d[7]525
(62SC1252)	q) 12LE[9]658	e) 137F2d[2]1010	187FS[6]715	341F2d[7]98
s) 86LE1194	j) 12LE[7]670	190F2d[9]253	196FS[6]53	c) 341F2d[9]776
87LE[2]10	j) 12LE[6]933	221F2d[7]629	208FS[9]639	341F2d[8]780
87LE[4]273	q) 13LE136	d) 250F2d[4]354	226FS[6]420	e) 353F2d[6]107
j) 88LE[7]1415	q) 13LE[6]932	263F2d[6]943	q) 226FS[9]582	366F2d[7]27
88LE[7]1485	j) 14LE[7]532	292F2d[7]323	243FS[4]700	q) 400F2d[5]596
89LE[4]1352	14LE[6]585	303F2d[7]885	271FS[7]409	410F2d[9]335
89LE[2]1354	j) 14LE[6]600	d) 313F2d460	207F2d2d347	j) 416F2d[5]1027
89LE[7]1499	16LE[7]720	315F2d[7]866	Cir. 4	422F2d[7]301
89LE[4]1500	e) 17LE473	j) 319F2d[6]318	128F2d[4]1013	430F2d[8]1117
89LE[4]1742	17LE[7]614	330F2d[7]304	129F2d[4]110	496F2d[7]1058

Vol. 62	SUPREME COURT REPORTER			
Ore	30LE835n	j) 80SC[10]315	Cir. 1	e) 329F2d[8]858
170Ore596	30LE839n	j) 80SC1319	181F2d602	q) 334F2d529
214Ore318	37LE1139n	j) 80SC[8]1470	d) 191F2d[7]965	355F2d[10]313
21OrA761	103LE966n	81SC418	203F2d[10]935	j) 359F2d[10]947
135P2d757	141AR1031n	q) 81SC419	204F2d[10]362	j) 430F2d[8]469
330P2d22	146AR109n	j) 81SC495	96FS[6]707	752F2d[10]921
537P2d125	147AR699n	j) 81SC977	f) 101FS[6]165	j) 782F2d455
Pa	93A2117n	82SC[7]507	f) 105FS[7]529	994F2d[9]1016
149PaS181	65A3514n	82SC[6]891	111FS418	74FS[2]848
153PaS434		q) 82SC[6]892	123FS443	74FS[8]848
27A2d669	—1252—	82SC1259	124FS37	81FS870
34A2d169	Betts v Brady	83SC[7]770	141FS[6]606	81FS[7]871
R I	1942	83SC[7]793	332FS[9]834	84FS940
121RI545	(316US455)	o) 83SC794	332FS[11]834	85FS787
401A2d445	(86LE1595)	83SC[7]799	377FS[11]341	88FS780
So C	s) 62SC639	e) 83SC[7]799	432FS[6]115	97FS[10]939
204SoC343	s) 62SC1252	j) 84SC[7]81	q) 253FS2d33	148FS[7]684
239SoC148	63SC[2]9	q) 84SC[7]1492	Cir. 2	187FS715
29SE541	63SC[10]240	j) 84SC[6]1503	e) 137F2d[2]1010	196FS53
122SE211	64SC[10]449	j) 84SC1797	190F2d[7]253	208FS[7]639
S D	j) 64SC[6]1085	q) 85SC[4]218	221F2d[6]629	226FS420
69SD471	64SC[6]1212	q) 85SC1073	d) 250F2d[10]354	q) 226FS[7]582
11NW525	65SC[10]520	85SC1663	263F2d943	243FS[10]700
Tenn	65SC[10]980	j) 85SC1677	292F2d[6]323	271FS[6]409
188Ten25	65SC[2]982	j) 85SC[6]1697	303F2d[6]885	207FS2d347
216SW711	65SC[6]1032	86SC[6]1625	d) 313F2d460	Cir. 4
529SW58	65SC[10]1033	e) 87SC547	315F2d[6]866	128F2d[10]1013
Tex	66SC163	87SC[6]653	j) 319F2d318	129F2d[10]110
j) 913SW502	66SC[2]453	q) 87SC[10]837	330F2d304	130F2d[10]881
j) 975SW584	67SC[7]597	j) 87SC[7]2000	q) 330F2d[6]310	133F2d[4]477
Va	j) 67SC[10]1692	q) 88SC[7]256	j) 330F2d[6]315	155F2d[10]5
186Va845	67SC[10]1718	89SC[6]2062	332F2d[6]891	198F2d[10]471
44SE412	j) 67SC[10]1719	q) 89SC[6]2063	q) 333F2d[10]610	280F2d[6]539
Wash	j) 67SC[10]1720	c) 92SC[8]1020	398F2d[6]985	280F2d[7]539
16Wsh2d380	68SC[10]511	j) 92SC[10]1020	q) 465F2d[10]121	280F2d541
51Wsh2d770	68SC[7]771	j) 92SC[8]1023	j) 611F2d421	294F2d[7]396
6WAp98	68SC[6]773	q) 92SC[8]2009	694F2d[8]22	294F2d609
133P2d807	68SC[8]773	q) 92SC[6]2026	e) 709F2d[8]168	297F2d853
322P2d848	68SC776	92SC2751	113FS920	d) 299F2d[10]173
492P2d241	68SC[10]781	q) 93SC[8]1763	171FS[7]561	j) 310F2d917
Wyo	j) 68SC782	j) 95SC[6]471	177FS[2]507	315F2d[6]644
71Wyo94	j) 68SC[7]782	j) 95SC[10]471	184FS[6]282	315F2d[8]644
254P2d200	j) 68SC[8]782	95SC[5]2527	184FS[7]542	q) 319F2d[7]2
42CLA662	j) 68SC[10]782	j) 95SC2545	200FS[6]907	q) 319F2d[7]4
61Cor966	j) 68SC[6]783	j) 95SC[10]2546	205FS[7]514	q) 319F2d[8]772
74CR377	68SC[10]1254	q) 99SC[11]1161	209FS[10]530	c) 368F2d298
82CR1099	68SC[10]1257	j) 99SC1164	210FS277	375F2d628
99CR173	68SC[10]1276	q) 101SC[6]2158	f) 210FS279	c) 381F2d[11]641
90McL225	j) 68SC[10]1277	j) 101SC2164	212FS[8]880	c) 415F2d1325
95McL334	69SC[10]186	104SC2045	212FS[10]928	f) 443F2d[7]1095
67MnL545	69SC[7]1250	105SC835	214FS[6]646	f) 443F2d[8]1095
49NYL815	c) 69SC1251	q) 109SC[7]2772	219FS[6]153	j) 443F2d[8]1100
150PaL119	70SC911	j) 109SC2776	e) 219FS[6]266	447F2d[7]57
36StnL683	70SC[6]913	111SC1051	q) 219FS[7]268	447F2d[8]57
55TxL1160	72SC[7]147	113SC2524	q) 220FS[7]892	483F2d[4]655
62TxL409	72SC[7]213	q) 114SC813	261FS[8]400	q) 561F2d[11]542
64TxL829	d) 75SC[10]4	q) 114SC[8]1737	q) 327FS[8]546	j) 166F3d283
64TxL831	75SC147	j) 114SC1934	Cir. 3	47FS[2]366
74TxL1297	75SC[6]823	118SC[11]1719	130F2d[6]657	165FS24
77VaL749	76SC[7]225	q) 124SC2514	175F2d[4]254	176FS[10]954
87VaL781	j) 76SC599	9FRD348	203F2d[8]426	201FS[7]447
88VaL485	77SC[6]1262	24FRD79	203F2d[10]806	206FS[7]302
90YLJ745	78SC[7]194	33FRD424	224F2d[6]508	q) 216FS[8]290
91YLJ1292	j) 78SC[7]589	33FRD438	224F2d[8]512	227FS[8]2
93LE1160n	d) 78SC[7]1292	33FRD454	f) 310F2d[6]724	q) 227FS[8]3
93LE1182n	j) 78SC[10]1293	38FRD463	j) 310F2d[6]735	251FS[6]665
96LE977n	79SC[10]435	39FRD284	329F2d[6]858	e) 257FS[10]808
	80SC[6]303			

1466

This page analyzes the *Supreme Court Reporter* version of *Betts v. Brady*, 62 S. Ct. 1252 (1942).

FIGURE 9-3

Shepard's Analysis of a *Supreme Court Reporter* citation

CASE ANALYSIS–ABBREVIATIONS

HISTORY OF CASES

cc	(Connected Case)	The citing case is related to the case you are *Shepardizing*, arising out of the same subject matter or involving the same parties.
m	(Modified)	On appeal, reconsideration or rehearing, the citing case modifies or changes in some way, including affirmance in part and reversal in part, the case you are *Shepardizing*.
r	(Reversed)	On appeal, reconsideration or rehearing, the citing case reverses the case you are *Shepardizing*.
S	(Superseded)	On appeal, reconsideration or rehearing, the citing case supersedes or is substituted for the case you are *Shepardizing*.
s	(Same Case)	The citing case involves the same litigation as the case you are *Shepardizing*, but at a different stage of the proceedings.
US reh den	(Rehearing Denied)	The citing order by the United States Supreme Court denies rehearing in the case you are *Shepardizing*.
US reh dis	(Rehearing Dismissed)	The citing order by the United States Supreme Court dismisses rehearing in the case you are *Shepardizing*.
v	(Vacated)	The citing case vacates or withdraws the case you are *Shepardizing*.

TREATMENT OF CASES

c	(Criticized)	The citing opinion disagrees with the reasoning/result of the case you are *Shepardizing*, although the citing court may not have the authority to materially affect its precedential value.
ca	(Conflicting Authorities)	Among conflicting authorities as noted in cited case
d	(Distinguished)	The citing case differs from the case you are *Shepardizing*, either involving dissimilar facts or requiring a different application of the law.
e	(Explained)	The citing opinion interprets or clarifies the case you are *Shepardizing* in a significant way.
f	(Followed)	The citing opinion relies on the case you are *Shepardizing* as controlling or persuasive authority.
h	(Harmonized)	The citing case differs from the case you are *Shepardizing*, but the citing court reconciles the difference or inconsistency in reaching its decision.
j	(Dissenting Opinion)	A dissenting opinion cites the case you are *Shepardizing*
L	(Limited)	The citing opinion restricts the application of the case you are *Shepardizing*, finding its reasoning applies only in specific limited circumstances.
o	(Overruled)	The citing case expressly overrules or disapproves the case you are *Shepardizing*.

(continued)

FIGURE 9-4
Shepard's Case Analysis Abbreviations

op	(Overruled or in Part)	Ruling in the cited case overruled partially or on other grounds with other qualifications.
q	(Questioned)	The citing opinion questions the continuing validity or precedential value of the case you are *Shepardizing* because of intervening circumstances, including judicial or legislative overruling.
qab	(Abrogated as stated in)	The citing opinion states that the decision that you are Shepardizing has been reversed, vacated, abrogated or invalidated by an earlier decision.
qabp	(Abrogated in part as stated in)	The citing opinion states that the decision that you are Shepardizing has been reversed, vacated, abrogated or invalidated in part by an earlier decision.
qo	(Overruled as Stated in)	The citing opinion notes that the continuing validity of an earlier opinion you are *Shepardizing* is in question because it has been overruled in an earlier decision.
qop	(Overruled in Part as Stated in)	The citing opinion notes that the continuing validity of an earlier opinion you are *Shepardizing* is in question because it has been overruled in part in an earlier decision.
su	(Superseded)	Superseded by statute as stated in cited case.

OTHER

SPECIAL SYMBOL FOR CONCURRING OPINIONS

| ~ | (Concurring Opinion) | A concurring opinion cites the statute, rule or regulation you are *Shepardizing*. This designation may appear in conjunction with other Judicial Treatment abbreviations listed on these pages. |

SPECIAL SYMBOLS FOR CALIFORNIA CASES

| # | | The citing case is of questionable precedential value because review or rehearing has been granted by the California Supreme Court and/or the citing case has been ordered depublished pursuant to Rule 976 of the California Rules of Court. (Publication status should be verified before use of the citing case in California.) |

FIGURE 9-4
(continued)

A Point to Remember

If you see the following abbreviations, stop:

"o" (overruled): If a case was overruled, you cannot use the case as authority. This means it is no longer good law. However, sometimes only part of a case is overruled. You can use the case if your issue is not overruled.

"Grtd" (hearing granted): If a hearing was granted in a higher court, you cannot use your citation as authority. It is not a final decision. If the higher court has issued a published opinion, you can use that cite.

"c" (criticized): If a case was criticized, you can still use it as authority, but it would be better to find other authorities following your decision.

"q" (questioned): If a case was questioned, you can still use it as authority, but it would be better to find other authorities following your decision.

"r" (reversed): If a case was reversed by a higher court, you cannot cite it.

"S" (superseded): The decision in the case was superseded or replaced by another decision. Do not cite it.

"v" (vacated): Your case is no longer law. Do not cite it.

A Point to Remember

When a case is cited by numerous authorities, you must read the list of *all* of the citing authorities carefully. A citing authority overruling your case may appear in the middle of several pages of citations. Other than the abbreviation "o," nothing distinguishes this cite. Examine Figures 9-1, 9-2, and 9-3. Note the placement of the overruling case. Also, see Box 9-2.

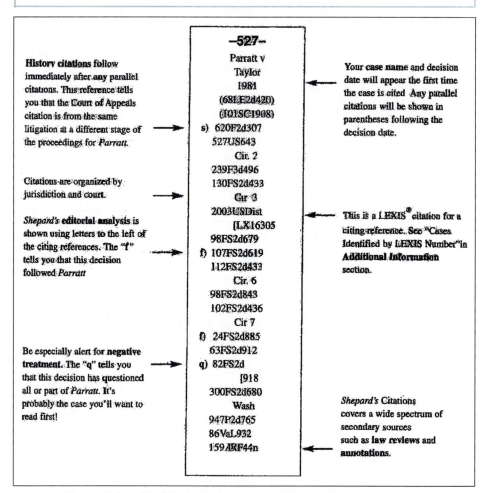

FIGURE 9-5
Shepard's Illustrative Citations

Reproduced by permission of LexisNexis. Further reproduction of any kind is strictly prohibited.

BOX 9-2   SHEPARDIZING CASE LAW: INFORMATION PROVIDED

- ✓ Parallel cites for the cited authority
- ✓ Cites to the same case (if there are prior or subsequent reported decisions in the same action)
- ✓ Cites to all other cases discussing your citation
- ✓ Description of how other cases have considered your case citation
- ✓ Cites to selected secondary sources discussing your citation

Abbreviations *Shepard's* in print relies heavily on the use of abbreviations. The cited and citing references are abbreviated in a way that is unique to *Shepard's*. In describing the history and treatment of a particular case, one or two letter abbreviations are used. Often, although not always, the abbreviation is the first letter of the word. Each volume of *Shepard's* contains tables of abbreviations for cited cases, citing cases, history of the case, and treatment of the case. See Figure 9-6. *Shepard's* uses an unusual method of abbreviating the different series of case reporters. The series number is superimposed on the abbreviation for the case reporter.

Headnotes When an opinion in any case is written, the court often discusses different points of law within the opinion. For example, a court might discuss issues relating to the hearsay rule of evidence and the tort of strict liability in the same case. Cases that later citing to this case might be citing it because of what the court said about the hearsay rule or because of what it said about strict liability. When Shepardizing, your only concern might be to verify that what the court said about strict liability is still good law. How other courts have viewed this court's interpretation of hearsay might be irrelevant to you. *Shepard's* helps you to make this type of distinction by using the headnote numbers from your cited authority (the case you are Shepardizing). Review Figure 9-3 to see how this is done.

A Point to Remember

Each publisher of case reporters uses different headnotes and headnote numbers. The headnotes referred to when you Shepardize a *Lawyers' Edition* cite relate only to those headnotes found in the *Lawyers' Edition* publication of the case. When you Shepardize parallel cites, be sure not to confuse headnote numbers.

Updating *Shepard's* Legal researchers expect *Shepard's* to be as current as possible. In order to assure that this happens, *Shepard's* in print is continually supplemented. When you Shepardize, you must check all books containing references to your cited authority. Normally this includes the following:

1. The main citator. This volume indicates on the spine what years it covers. Sometimes there is more than one volume.
2. A cumulative supplement (a red-covered paperback).
3. An annual or semiannual supplement (a gold-covered paperback).
4. White pamphlet-type supplements called Advance Sheets. (These are usually a few weeks old before they reach a library shelf.)

Shepard's helps you recognize what books and supplements you need to check, by printing on the cover "What your library should contain . . ." Before you Shepardize any authority you must be sure that you have all the relevant books and supplements. (Most often the problem you will encounter in a library is that the librarians failed to remove a supplement that was replaced. This will not cause any serious research problems for you, although it might lead you to check more books than necessary.)

TABLES OF ABBREVIATIONS

A2d—Atlantic Reporter, Second Series
ADC—Appeal Cases, District of Columbia
    Reports
AkA—Arkansas Appellate Reports
A5—American Law Reports, Fifth Series
ARF—American Law Reports, Federal
ARF2d—American Law Reports, Federal,
    Second Series
ALR6—American Law Reports, Sixth Series
Ark—Arkansas Reports
Az—Arizona Reports
Bankr LX—United States Bankruptcy
    Court & United States District Court
    Bankruptcy Cases LEXIS Documents
BRW—Bankruptcy Reporter
CAAF LX—U.S. Court of Appeals for the
    Armed Forces LEXIS Documents
CCA LX—U.S. Military Courts of Criminal
    Appeals LEXIS Documents
C4th—California Supreme Court Reports,
    Fourth Series
CA4th—California Appellate Reports, Fourth
    Series
CA4S—California Appellate Reports, Fourth
    Series, Supplement
CaL—California Law Review
CaR2d—California Reporter, Second Series
CaR3d—California Reporter, Third Series
ChL—University of Chicago Law Review
CIT—United States Court of International
    Trade
CLA—University of California at
    Los Angeles Law Review
Cor—Cornell Law Review
CR—Columbia Law Review
CS—Connecticut Supplement
Ct—Connecticut Reports
CtA—Connecticut Appellate Reports
DC4d—Pennsylvania District and County
    Reports, Fourth Series
DPR—Decisiones de Puerto Rico
F3d—Federal Reporter, Third Series
FCCR—Federal Communications
    Commission Record
Fed Appx—Federal Appendix
FedCl—Federal Claims Reporter
FRD—Federal Rules Decisions

FS2d—Federal Supplement, Second Series
Ga—Georgia Reports
GaA—Georgia Appeals Reports
Geo—Georgetown Law Journal
Haw—Hawaii Reports
HLR—Harvard Law Review
Ida—Idaho Reports
Il2d—Illinois Supreme Court Reports
    Second Series
IlA—Illinois Appellate Court Reports, ◄─── Notice how the abbreviation
    Third Series   for "Third Series" (3rd)
IlCCl—Illinois Court of Claims Reports   is superimposed on the "A".
IlLR—University of Illinois Law Review
JTS—Jurisprudencia del Tribunal Supremo
    de Puerto Rico
KA2d—Kansas Court of Appeals Reports,
    Second Series
Kan—Kansas Reports
LCP—Law and Contemporary Problems
LE—United States Supreme Court Reports,
    Lawyers' Edition, Second Series
MaA—Massachusetts Appeals Court
    Reports
MADR—Massachusetts Appellate Division
    Reports
Mas—Massachusetts Reports
McA—Michigan Court of Appeals Reports
Mch—Michigan Reports
McL—Michigan Law Review
Md—Maryland Reports
MdA—Maryland Appellate Reports
MJ—Military Justice Reporter
MnL—Minnesota Law Review
Mt—Montana Reports
NC—North Carolina Reports
NCA—North Carolina Court of Appeals
    Reports
NE—Northeastern Reporter, Second Series
Neb—Nebraska Reports
NebA—Nebraska Advance Reports
Nev—Nevada Reports
NH—New Hampshire Reports
NJ—New Jersey Reports
NJS—New Jersey Superior Court Reports
NJT—New Jersey Tax Court Reports
NM—New Mexico Reports
NVAdv—Nevada Advance Reports

(continued)

FIGURE 9-6   Tables of Abbreviations

NW—Northwestern Reporter, Second
Series
NwL—Northwestern University Law Review
NY—New York Court of Appeals Reports,
Second Series
NY—New York Court of Appeals Reports,
Third Series
NYAD—New York Appellate Division
Reports, Second Series
NYAD—New York Appellate Division
Reports, Third Series
NYL—New York University Law Review
NYM—New York Miscellaneous
Reports, Second Series
NYM—New York Miscellaneous
Reports, Third Series
NYS2d—New York Supplement, Second
Series
OA3d—Ohio Appellate Reports, Third Series
OhM2d—Ohio Miscellaneous Reports,
Second Series
OrA—Oregon Court of Appeals Reports
Ore—Oregon Reports
OS3d—Ohio State Reports, Third Series
P3d—Pacific Reporter, Third Series
Pa—Pennsylvania State Reports
PaL—University of Pennsylvania Law Review
SC—Supreme Court Reporter
SE—Southeastern Reporter, Second Series
So2d—Southern Reporter, Second Series
SoC—South Carolina Reports

StnL—Stanford Law Review
SW—Southwestern Reporter, Second Series
SW—Southwestern Reporter,
Third Series
TCt—Tax Court of the United States
Reports; United States Tax Court Reports
TPR—Official Translations of the Opinions
of the Supreme Court of Puerto Rico
TxL—Texas Law Review
UCR2d—Uniform Commercial Code
Reporting Service, Second Series
US—United States Reports
USApp LX—United States Court of
Appeals LEXIS Documents
USClaims LX—United States Court of
Federal Claims LEXIS Documents
USDist LX—United States District Court
LEXIS Documents
US LX—United States Supreme Court
LEXIS Documents
Va—Virginia Reports
VaA—Virginia Court of Appeals Reports
VaL—Virginia Law Review
VCO—Virginia Circuit Court Opinions
Vt—Vermont Reports
WAp—Washington Appellate Reports
Wis2d—Wisconsin Reports, Second Series
WLR—Wisconsin Law Review
Wsh2d—Washington Reports, Second Series
WV—West Virginia Reports
YLJ—Yale Law Journal

COURT ABBREVIATIONS

Cir. (number)—United States Court of
Appeals, United States District Court
Cir. DC—United States Court of Appeals,
DC Circuit, United States District Court,
DC Circuit
Cir. Fed.—United States Court of Appeals,
Federal Circuit
ClCt—United States Claims Court and
United States Court of Federal Claims

CuCt—Unifed States Customs Court
CIT—United States Court of
International Trade
CCPA—Court of Customs and Patent Appeals
ECA—Temporary Emergency Court
of Appeals
ML—Judicial Panel on Multidistrict Litigation
RRR—Special Court Regional Rail
Reorganization Act of 1973

FIGURE 9-6 (continued)

A Point to Remember

If you are Shepardizing a relatively new case, it might not appear in the main citator. Always pay attention to the date of any case being Shepardized and start the Shepardizing process with the volume that first covers that time period. You can tell if you are in the right book if you see the case name and parallel cites for the case, as these only appear the first time the cite is mentioned.

If you use all of the *Shepard's* supplements that are in print, you are still missing recent case decisions. *Shepard's* therefore has a "Daily Update" service that provides you with information that is no more than 24 to 48 hours old. This service is accessed through the Internet, by fax, or by telephone.

Shepard's Case Citations Online

Shepard's is available through the online service LEXIS. *Shepard's* Online is much easier to use than *Shepard's* in print and offers many advantages. Some of these advantages include the following:

- Information is current so there is no need to check supplements or updates.
- Information provided under all parallel citations is the same so a case must be checked only once.
- Negative information, such as overruling, is highlighted at the beginning.
- Citing information can be displayed selectively (i.e., only negative treatment).
- Treatment of the case is explained in normal terminology rather than abbreviations.
- Hyperlinks to citing authorities are provided.
- *Shepard's* can be accessed by hyperlinking from the LEXIS online version of the case.

Because of the numerous advantages and greater reliability of information, *Shepard's* Online is by far the preferred method of Shepardizing a case or other authority. See Figures 9-7 and 9-8 for examples of *Shepard's* Online.

Shepard's Statutory Citators

In addition to its case citators, *Shepard's* publishes citators that allow you to Shepardize constitutions, statutes or codes, and administrative rules or regulations, including the Code of Federal Regulations. These citators are similar to case citators in many respects. When you Shepardize this type of material, you find information about the history of the law, that is, if it was amended or repealed. You also find citations to cases and secondary authorities that discuss the law. See Box 9-3. Again, in print *Shepard's* uses abbreviations and special terms to describe how cases have interpreted the written law. The terms and abbreviations *Shepard's* uses to describe the treatment of statutory law differ from the terms *Shepard's* uses to describe the treatment of cases. See Figure 9-9 for a list of these abbreviations and Figure 9-10 for an example

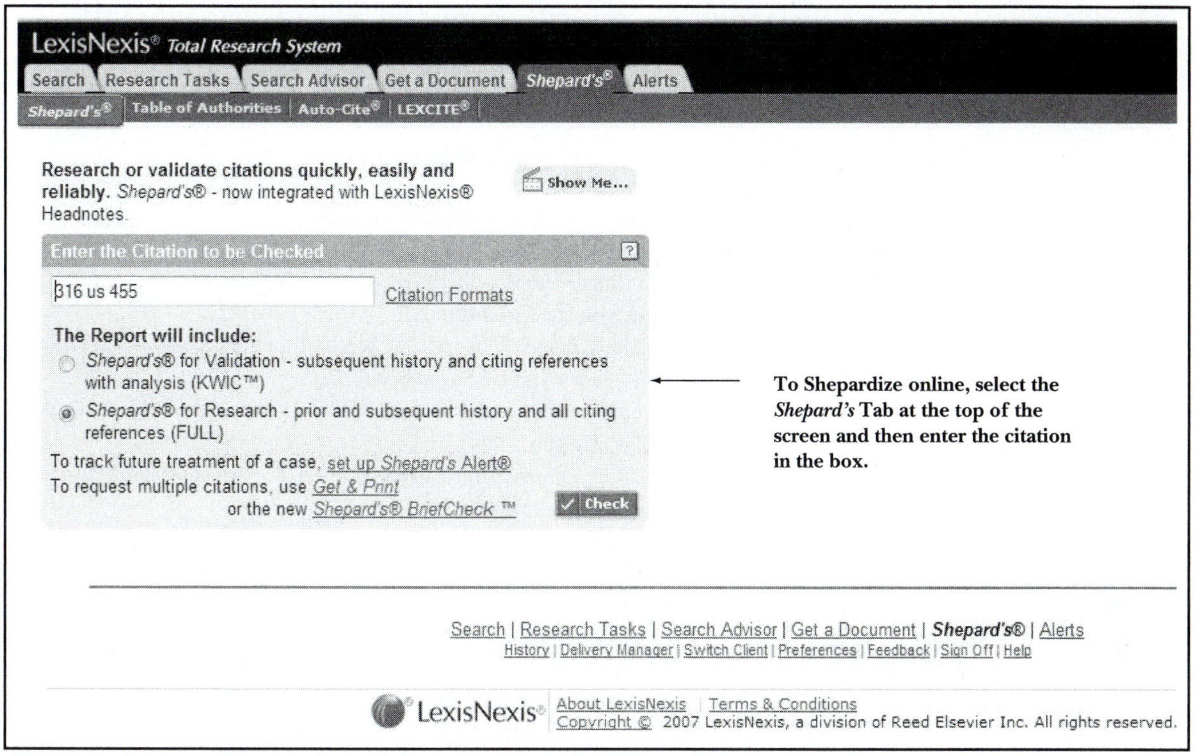

FIGURE 9-7   *Shepard's* Online (LEXIS): Retrieving a Case

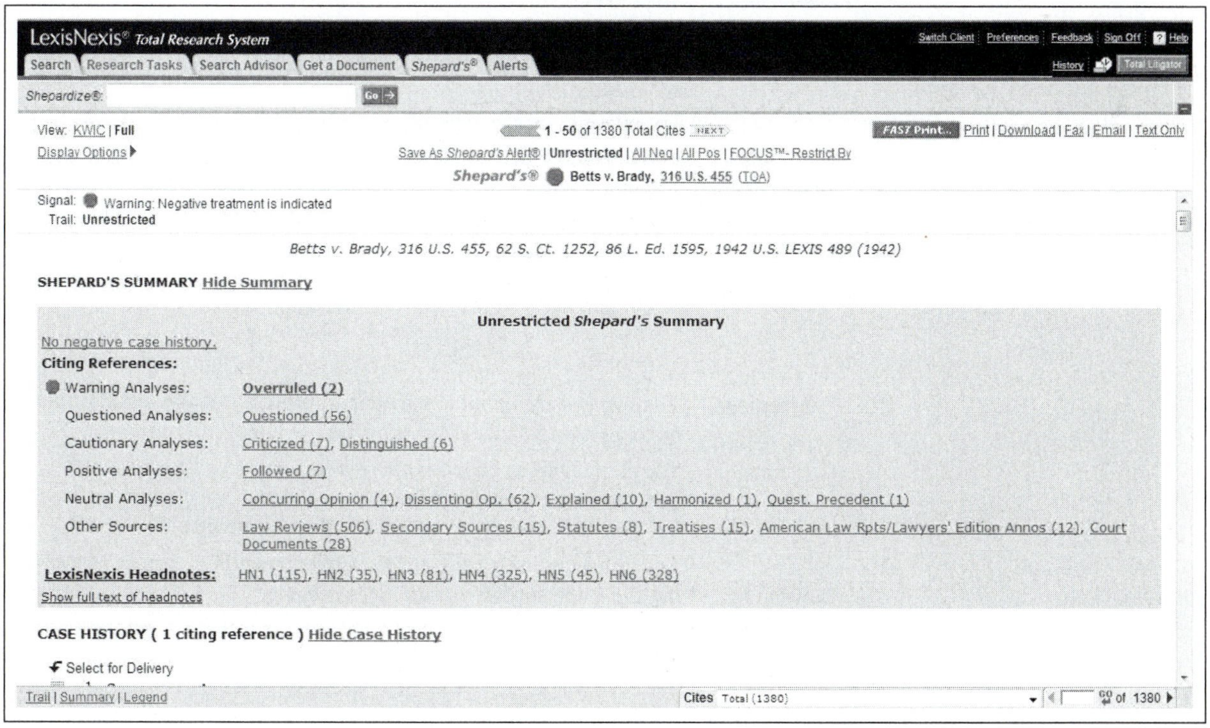

FIGURE 9-8   *Shepard's* Online (LEXIS): History and Treatment

ANALYSIS OF STATUTES, RULES, REGULATIONS AND ORDERS–ABBREVIATIONS

LEGISLATIVE

A	(Amended)	The citing reference, typically a session law, amends or alters the statute you are *Shepardizing*.
Ad	(Added)	The citing reference, typically a session law, adds new matter to the statute you are *Shepardizing*.
E	(Extended)	The citing reference extends the scope of, or the time period specified in, the statute you are *Shepardizing*.
L	(Limited)	The citing reference refuses to extend the provisions of the statute you are *Shepardizing*.
R	(Repealed)	The citing reference, typically a session law, repeals or abrogates the statute you are *Shepardizing*.
Re-en	(Re-enacted)	The citing reference, typically a session law, re-enacts the statute you are *Shepardizing*.
Rn	(Renumbered)	The citing reference, typically a session law, renumbers the statute you are *Shepardizing*.
Rp	(Repealed in Part)	The citing reference, typically a session law, repeals or abrogates in part the statute you are *Shepardizing*.
Rs	(Repealed & Superseded)	The citing reference, typically a session law, repeals and supersedes the statute you are *Shepardizing*.
Rv	(Revised)	The citing reference, typically a session law, revises the statute you are *Shepardizing*.
S	(Superseded)	The citing reference, typically a session law, supersedes the statute you are *Shepardizing*.
Sd	(Suspended)	The citing reference, typically a session law, suspends the statute you are *Shepardizing*.
Sdp	(Suspended in Part)	The citing reference, typically a session law, suspends in part the statute you are *Shepardizing*.
Sg	(Supplementing)	The citing reference, typically a session law, supplements the statute you are *Shepardizing*.
Sp	(Superseded in Part)	The citing reference, typically a session law, supersedes in part the statute you are *Shepardizing*.

JUDICIAL

C	(Constitutional)	The citing case upholds the constitutionality of the statute, rule or regulation you are *Shepardizing*.
cr	(Criticized)	The citing opinion criticizes the statute, rule or regulation you are Shepardizing in some significant way, although the citing court may not have the authority to materially affect its precedential value.
DG	(Decision for Gov't)	The citing decision holds for the Government in a dispute concerning the Code section you are *Shepardizing*.

FIGURE 9-9

Shepard's Tables of Abbreviations (Statutes)

DGp	(Decision for Gov't in Part)	The citing decision holds in part for the Government in a dispute concerning the Code section you are *Shepardizing.*
DT	(Decision for Taxpayer)	The citing decision holds for the taxpayer in a dispute concerning the code section you are *Shepardizing.*
DTp	(Decision for Taxpayer in Part)	The citing decision holds in part for the taxpayer in a dispute concerning the code section you are *Shepardizing.*
f	(Followed)	The citing opinion expressly relies on the statute, rule or regulation you are *Shepardizing* as controlling authority.
i	(Interpreted)	The citing opinion interprets the statute, rule or regulation you are *Shepardizing* in some significant way, often including a discussion of the statute's legislative history.
j	(Dissenting Opinion)	A dissenting opinion cites the statute, rule or regulation you are *Shepardizing.*
na	(Not Applicable)	The citing opinion expressly finds the statute, rule or regulation you are *Shepardizing* inapplicable to the legal or factual circumstances of the citing case.
rt	(Retroactive/ Prospective)	The citing opinion discusses retroactive or prospective application of the statute, rule or regulation you are *Shepardizing.*
U	(Unconstitutional)	The citing case declares unconstitutional the statute, rule or regulation you are *Shepardizing.*
Up	(Unconstitutional in Part)	The citing case declares unconstitutional in part the statute, rule or regulation you are *Shepardizing.*
V	(Void or Invalid)	The citing case declares void or invalid the statute, rule, regulation or order you are *Shepardizing* because it conflicts with an authority that takes priority.
Va	(Valid)	The citing case upholds the validity of the statute, rule, regulation or order you are *Shepardizing.*
Vp	(Void or Invalid in Part)	The citing case declares void or invalid part of the statute, rule, regulation, or order you are *Shepardizing* because it conflicts with an authority that takes priority.

SPECIAL SYMBOL FOR CONCURRING OPINIONS

~	(Concurring Opinion)	A concurring opinion cites the statute, rule or regulation you are *Shepardizing.*

SPECIAL SYMBOL FOR CALIFORNIA CASES

#	The citing case is of questionable precedential value because review or rehearing has been granted by the California Supreme Court and/or the citing case has been ordered depublished pursuant to Rule 976 of the California Rules of Court. (Publication status should be verified before use of the citing case in California.)

SPECIAL SYMBOLS FOR DATES OF UNITED STATES CODE AND CFR PROVISIONS

*****	followed by a year refers to the United States Code or CFR edition, when year is cited.
Δ	followed by a year indicates the date of the citing reference, when year is not cited.

FIGURE 9-9
(continued)

UNITED STATES CODE 1988 and 1994 Eds.   **TITLE 18 § 700**

857F2d523
937F2d461
945F2d1075
969F2d775
9F3d68
11F3d120
22F3d942
C 40F3d1000
59F3d940
661FS723
789FS346
918FS1383

Cir. 10
799F2d619
53F3d1108
64F3d1515
79F3d994
814FS1528
149FRD647

Cir. 11
905F2d352
907FS402

§ 666 (a)

Cir. 2
4F3d108

Cir. 4
874F2d217

Cir. 5
841F2d575
930F2d1091
987F2d1136
659FS834
687FS1049
727FS1069
C 816FS1136

Cir. 6
63F3d463

Cir. 7
957F2d1393
982F2d1105

Cir. 10
53F3d1110

§ 666 (a) (1)

Cir. 6
63F3d462
66F3d129

§ 666 (a) (1)
(A)

Cir. 2
979F2d936
55F3d723
784FS63

Cir. 5
987F2d1137
80F3d1055
C 816FS1134

Cir. 6
966F2d186

Cir. 9
11F3d121
40F3d1001

§ 666 (a) (1)
(A) (1)

Cir. 3
990F2d101

Cir. 5
727FS1070

Cir. 6
63F3d462
66F3d127

§ 666 (a) (1)
(A) (2)

Cir. 5
727FS1070

Cir. 6
63F3d462

Cir. 9
40F3d1001

§ 666 (a) (1)
(B)

Cir. 2
996F2d18
4F3d104
37F3d849
57F3d172
73F3d485
795FS1268
809FS1002
809FS1010
833FS204

Cir. 3
938F2d443
10F3d981

Cir. 5
841F2d577
987F2d1137
80F3d1055

Cir. 6
966F2d188

Cir. 7
913F2d1259
46F3d27

Cir. 9
937F2d463

§ 666 (a) (2)

Cir. 1
983F2d1153

Cir. 2
909F2d63
996F2d19
4F3d104
42F3d99
57F3d169
57F3d172
784FS63

794FS530
842FS1535
913FS704

Cir. 4
11F3d430

Cir. 5
889F2d1369
687FS1048
781FS1183
C 816FS1134

Cir. 7
777FS1397

Cir. 10
36F3d946

Cir. 11
C 907FS402

§ 666 (b)

Cir. 2
986F2d33
4F3d104
55F3d729
784FS63
794FS530
913FS705

Cir. 3
874F2d180
938F2d443

Cir. 4
11F3d434

Cir. 5
841F2d574
846F2d968
889F2d1369
930F2d1091
987F2d1136
659FS834
687FS1048
727FS1070
C 816FS1137

Cir. 6
63F3d462

Cir. 8
977F2d1232

Cir. 9
857F2d521
937F2d463
11F3d121
40F3d1000

§ 666 (c)

Cir. 2
979F2d936
C 987F2d896
996F2d21
4F3d104
651FS1035
815FS619
913FS711

Cir. 5
987F2d1137

727FS1072
C 816FS1137

Cir. 6
63F3d465

Cir. 7
868F2d936

Cir. 8
915FS1477

Cir. 9
11F3d121
40F3d1000

Cir. 10
799F2d619

§ 666 (d)

Cir. 2
4F3d109

Cir. 9
857F2d523

Cir. 10
799F2d620

§ 666 (d) (1)

Cir. 2
851FS508

Cir. 3
990F2d101

Cir. 9
40F3d1001

§ 666 (d) (2)

Cir. 2
913FS707

Cir. 5
987F2d1137
727FS1070

Cir. 9
857F2d523

Cir. 10
799F2d620

§ 666 (d) (3)

Cir. 10
799F2d620

§ 666 (d) (4)

Cir. 2
851FS508

Cir. 4
11F3d434

Cir. 9
857F2d523
969F2d775

Cir. 10
799F2d620

§ 666 (d) (5)

Cir. 2
897FS113

Cir. 6
63F3d463

§ 667
Ad 98St2149

§ 687
487US255
101LE237
108SC2373

§ 688
122LE222
113SC865

§ 700
et seq.

Cir. 1
531F2d1087

§ 700
Ad 82St291
394US604
459US949
Up 496US312
22LE592
74LE207
U 110LE292
129LE520
89SC1372
103SC267
U 110SC2406
114SC2461
128FRD300
136FRD238

Cir. DC
445F2d226
511F2d1312
U 731FS1125

Cir. 1
343FS165
397FS263

Cir. 2
324FS1278

Cir. 3
765FS188

Cir. 4
313FS49
317FS138
322FS593

Cir. 5
479F2d1177

Cir. 8
C 897F2d918

Cir. 9
462F2d96
C 302FS1112
U 731FS416
790FS221

Cir. 11
758F2d1481
560FS546
105LE812n
105LE816n

41A3504n

§ 700 (a)
415US582
491US427
496US314
39LE617
105LE369
U 110LE293
94SC1251
109SC2551
U 110SC2407

Cir. DC
445F2d226
C 454F2d972

Cir. 2
324FS1278
385FS167

Cir. 5
479F2d1179
407FS497

Cir. 9
C 462F2d96

Cir. 11
739F2d571
571FS1025

§ 700 (a) (1)
496US317
U 110LE295
U 110SC2409

Cir. DC
U 731FS1125

Cir. 9
U 731FS417

§ 700 (a) (2)
496US317
U 110LE295
U 110SC2409

Cir. DC
U 731FS1125

Cir. 9
U 731FS417

§ 700 (b)
496US314
U 110LE294
U 110SC2407

Cir. DC
445F2d226
U 731FS1125

Cir. 9
C 462F2d96
U 731FS417

§ 700 (c)
394US598
22LE588
89SC1369

Cir. 4
322FS585

521

FIGURE 9-10

Shepard's United States Code 1988 and 1994 Eds.

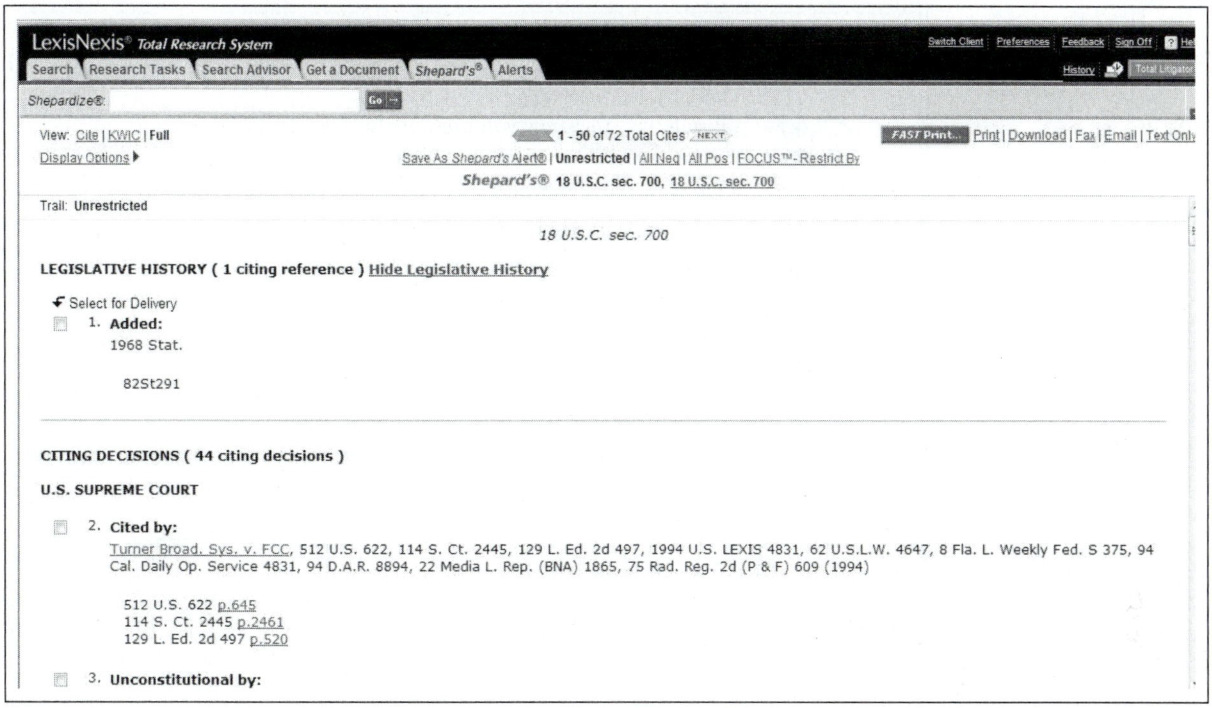

Reproduced by permission of LexisNexis

FIGURE 9-11 *Shepard's* Online 18 U.S.C. § 700

of a page from a statutory citator. Like *Shepard's* case citators, statutory citators are available in print and online through LEXIS. See Figure 9-11 for an example of a statutory report from *Shepard's* Online.

BOX 9-3 SHEPARDIZING STATUTORY LAW: INFORMATION PROVIDED

- Whether the statute was amended or repealed
- Cites to case law discussing the statute
- Description of how case law considered the statute
- Cites to selected secondary sources discussing the citation

---

A Point to Remember

Shepard's provides excellent explanations of how to use its resources along with complete tables of abbreviations. This is found in the preface if you are using *Shepard's* in print. This information is found in the "Help" menu on the online service. You can also find out more about *Shepard's* by visiting the Web site at http://law.lexisnexis.com/shepards.

BOX 9-4   SHEPARDIZING IN PRINT

✓ Note the citation to be Shepardized.

✓ Locate all relevant *Shepard's* volumes, including supplements and advance sheets.

✓ Check "What your library should contain . . ." on the cover of supplements.

✓ Locate the first appearance of your authority in *Shepard's.*

✓ Check your citation in all supplements and advance sheets.

✓ Interpret or analyze your findings.

✓ Review the tables of abbreviations in the front of books, if necessary.

✓ If Shepardizing case law, repeat this process with all parallel cites.

✓ Use Daily Update Service.

BOX 9-5   SHEPARDIZING ONLINE

✓ Note the citation to be Shepardized and access LEXIS.

✓ Access *Shepard's* Online service or access the case or other authority to be Shepardized.

✓ Enter the citation in the search box or hyperlink to *Shepard's* from the cited authority.

✓ Use the "Help" feature, if necessary.

✓ Analyze or interpret the results.

9-3 KEYCITE

KeyCite is the online citator available through Westlaw. Since *Shepard's* is not available through the Westlaw site, researchers must use KeyCite to validate legal authorities. As with *Shepard's,* you can use KeyCite to check a case, statute, administrative decision, or regulation to determine if it is still good law. The basic information about the validity of any legal authority is the same on *Shepard's* and KeyCite. Some terminology and icons may differ, however. For example, rather than the warning signs used on *Shepard's,* KeyCite uses warning "flags" to alert the researcher to problems with the case. See Figure 9-12. As with *Shepard's,* the researcher using KeyCite can find:

- Parallel cites
- Cites to the same case (if there are prior or subsequent reported decisions in the same action)
- Cites to all other cases discussing your citation
- Description of how other cases have considered your case citation
- Cites to selected secondary sources discussing your citation

For statutory law, KeyCite provides the following information about the citation:

- Whether the statute has been amended or repealed
- Cites to case law discussing the statute

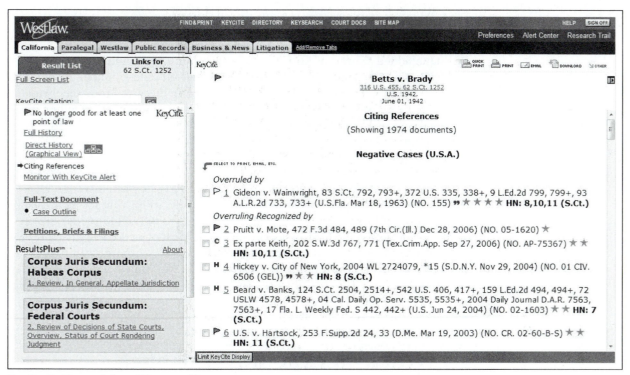

Reprinted with permission of Thomson/West.

FIGURE 9-12 KeyCite

Reprinted with permission of Thomson/West.

FIGURE 9-13 KeyCite

- Description of how case law considered the statute
- Cites to selected secondary sources discussing the citation

One added feature of KeyCite is an evaluation of the citing authorities (the cases citing the cite you are Keyciting). This is reflected in the number of "depth of treatment stars" assigned to each of the citing cases. In this way, a researcher can tell if the cited case was merely mentioned in the citing authority or whether it was discussed and analyzed in great detail. (One star indicates the cited authority is just mentioned; two stars indicate some discussion; three stars indicate substantial discussion; and four stars indicate extensive discussion.)

KeyCite can be accessed in different ways. Once you are signed on to the Westlaw database you can select the feature, KeyCite. When you enter your citation, the KeyCite analysis appears. Alternatively, when you access a case or statute, you can link from any KeyCite warning flag to the full KeyCite analysis. A third way of accessing KeyCite is through the West-owned Web site, Findlaw. When you retrieve a case, a screen appears offering KeyCite. You can enter your case citation and access the KeyCite feature—however, unless you are a Westlaw subscriber, you must pay for this feature. See Figures 9-12 and 9-13 for examples of KeyCite screens.

9-4 OTHER ELECTRONIC CITATORS

In addition to *Shepard's*, several other citators are found through the online services of Westlaw and LEXIS. These citators include the following:

Auto-Cite: A case citator found on the LEXIS service; this citator provides parallel citations, the history of the case, and negative treatment of the case. It does not refer you to all cases that have cited your authority in a positive manner.

Lexcite: Lexcite is a LEXIS feature that allows you to search the LEXIS case databases for every case that has cited your authority. Your search results reveal those authorities without any editorial comment or evaluation.

9-5 CITE CHECKING A DOCUMENT

Before any legal memorandum or brief is filed with a court, the document is normally reviewed and all citations are checked. This task is one that is often assigned to a research assistant such as a paralegal or law clerk. When a document is "cite-checked," the following items must be verified.

1. **Citation Format:** Courts generally require that cites in legal memoranda or briefs comply with the format set out in *The Bluebook* or other approved style manual. Some states have adopted a style manual for use within the state. All citations in a document to be filed with a court must be reviewed to make certain they are in proper format. (See Appendix B for an introduction to the use of *The Bluebook.*)

2. **Citation Accuracy:** Obviously, attorneys and courts are concerned with the accuracy of the citation. A wrong volume number, a wrong page, or a wrong series in a case cite can make it impossible for a judge or other attorney to find

a case cited in a brief. Checking for citation accuracy requires that you physically check the primary source, either in print or online, to make sure that the cite is correct in all aspects.

3. **Validity of Authorities:**   This involves Shepardizing or otherwise verifying the cited authority is still good law.

4. **Accuracy of Authority:**   In addition to checking for the accuracy of the citation, cite checking sometimes requires that you check the accuracy of the authority itself. Does a case or code section really support the statements of law made in the brief? This requires that the person doing the cite checking actually read and analyze the law.

5. **Citation of Quotation:**   Pages where quotations appear must be verified. If parallel citations are used, page numbers must be verified in those citations.

6. **Accuracy of Quotations:**   Quotations must also be checked for accuracy. Any language quoted in a brief must match exactly the language found in a quoted case or statute.

It is a long and tedious job to cite check a memorandum or brief by referring to original sources entirely in print. The online services of Westlaw and LEXIS can make this a much easier and quicker task. In addition, both Westlaw and LEXIS provide free downloadable software to automate much of the cite checking process. This software detects all of the citations in your Microsoft Word documents and then verifies the citations by using either KeyCite or *Shepard's*. Without requiring the use of either KeyCite or *Shepard's*, the software also checks the format of citations and creates a table of authorities. Some of the features of the software can be used without accessing either Westlaw or LEXIS. However, the more powerful features require that the user subscribe to the databases. (Review the following Web sites for information about this software, as well as for links to download some software: http://law.lexisnexis.com/shepards-brief-suite or http://west.thomson.com/software/default.asp.)

Online Legal Research

Extensive information about *Shepard's* can be found at the following:

http://www.lexisnexis.com/shepards/

http://law.lexisnexis.com/lexis/brochures

Information about KeyCite can be found at:

http://west.thomson.com/store/

On both sites look for brochures, user guides, or online tutorials. Also, search the site for information regarding software downloads that can be use to automatically cite check documents.

If you can access either Westlaw or LEXIS, use the "Help" features to learn more about using KeyCite or *Shepard's*.

C ITATION MATTERS

INTRODUCTORY SIGNALS

THE BLUEBOOK—RULE 1.2

The purpose of a signal is to alert the reader to something. Signals are used to show support, suggest a comparison, indicate a contradiction, and indicate background materials. These signals must be italicized. However, when a signal is used as a verb in a sentence, it is not italicized.

Examples of signals used to *show support:*

- *No signal*—indicates the cited authority (a) directly states the proposition, (b) shows the source of quoted language, or (c) identifies the authority cited in the text.

- *E.g.,*—is used to show that the cited material states the proposition presented in the sentence; other materials also state the same proposition, but a citation to them is not helpful or is not necessary. This signal is often used in combination with other signals, for example: *See, e.g.,*.

- *See*—is used instead of "no signal" when the proposition presented is not *exactly* stated by the authority cited, but it clearly follows from it. This signal alerts the reader that there is an *inferential step* between the proposition and the cited authority.

- *See Also*—is used to show that the cited authority is additional support for the proposition presented.

- *Cf.*—is used when the writer needs the reader to understand that the cited authority provides material that is analogous with the main proposition.

Example of a signal used to suggest a *comparison:*

- *Compare*—is used to show that comparison of the authorities offers support for the proposition presented. Parenthetical explanations often follow these authorities.

Examples of signals that indicate a *contradiction:*

- *Contra*—is used to show that the cited authority *states* the contrary of the proposition.

- *But see*—is used to show that the cited authority *supports* a position that is contrary to the writer's main position.

Example of a signal that indicates *background material:*

- *See generally*—is used to show that the cited authority offers background information related to the proposition.

Example of a signal used as a *verb:*

- *See Wisconsin v. Mitchell,* 508 U.S. 476 (1993). (*See* used as a signal.)

- See *Wisconsin v. Mitchell,* 508 U.S. 476 (1993) for an explanation of what made the statute at issue unconstitutionally overbroad. (See used as a verb.)

CHAPTER SUMMARY

Citators are a type of legal research material that allows the researcher to determine if certain legal authorities are still good law. Citators lead the researcher to additional authorities dealing with the same legal issues. The most well-known citators are published by *Shepard's*. *Shepard's* publishes citators for all jurisdictions and for many different types of legal authorities including cases, constitutions, statutes, and selected secondary sources. *Shepard's* is available in print and online. An alternative citator, KeyCite, is available online through Westlaw. KeyCite has many of the same features as *Shepard's*. Auto-Cite and Lexcite, features found on LEXIS, are sometimes used to determine if a case is still good law. Researchers often use citators to help cite check a memorandum or brief that is to be filed with the court. In addition to checking whether an authority is still good law, cite checking requires that one check citation format, citation accuracy, accuracy of the authority, and accuracy of quotations.

TERMS TO REMEMBER

good law	citator	cited authority
validate	Shepardize	citing authority

QUESTIONS FOR REVIEW

1. What is a citator?
2. What types of authorities can be Shepardized?
3. What information is found in *Shepard's* case citators?
4. What is the difference between cited authority and citing authority?
5. If a case has parallel cites, is it necessary to Shepardize all cites? Explain.
6. What is the difference between the history of the case and the treatment of the case?
7. How does *Shepard's* use headnote numbers in its case citators?
8. What are AutoCite and Lexcite?
9. What is KeyCite?
10. What must a person do to cite check a document?

CAN YOU FIGURE IT OUT?

1. Refer to Figures 9-1 and 9-4. Find the case of *Betts v. Brady*.
   a. What is the cite for the U.S. Supreme Court case to overrule *Betts v. Brady*?
   b. Do any cases in the *Federal Reporter 2d* from the Third Circuit cite this case in dissenting opinions?
   c. What are the reporter citations for all the cases Shepardized on this page?
2. Refer to Figure 9-2. Find the case of *Betts v. Brady*.
   a. What is the Lawyer's Edition citation for this case?
   b. This same case appears on a different page in the same volume. What is that cite?

    c. What are the parallel cites for the case?

    d. Give the *Lawyers' Edition* cite for the U.S. Supreme Court case that over-ruled *Betts v. Brady.*

    e. Give cites of all cases in the *Federal Reporter 2d* from the Third Circuit to discuss the issues found in headnote number 4 of *Betts v. Brady* (published in the *Lawyers' Edition*).

3. Refer to Figure 9-3. Find the case of *Betts v. Brady.*

    a. What is the cite for the Supreme Court Reporter cite for the U.S. Supreme Court case to overrule *Betts v. Brady?*

    b. List the cites of all cases in the *Federal Reporter 2d* from the Third Circuit to discuss headnote number 4. Compare these cites with those found in Figure 9-2. Why are they different?

4. Refer to Figure 9-10.

    a. Find 18 U.S.C. § 700. What has the U.S. Supreme Court said about this section?

    b. Give the *Lawyers' Edition* cite for a case to discuss 18 U.S.C. § 700 (c).

BUILDING YOUR RESEARCH SKILLS: ASSIGNMENTS AND ACTIVITIES

1. Shepardize *United States v. Bramblett*, 348 U.S. 503 (1955). Answer the following questions.

    a. What are the parallel cites?

    b. What are the lower court citations for this case?

    c. Give all parallel cites for the case that overruled *Bramblett.*

    d. What is the full name of the *Bramblett* case?

    e. What is the citation for the case from the Eighth Circuit that questioned *Bramblett?*

    f. What is the citation for an *A.L.R.* annotation where the case is mentioned?

2. Shepardize the case at 279 U.S. 263.

    a. What is the case name?

    b. What are the parallel cites?

    c. Give all the parallel cites for the case that overruled it.

    d. Give the cite of a case from the Ninth Circuit that harmonized with the cite.

    e. Give the cite to a *Stanford Law Review* that mentioned the case.

3. Shepardize 18 U.S.C. § 242.

    a. Give the citations for the *Statutes at Large* in which this section was amended.

    b. Give the citation for the U.S. Supreme Court case in volume 515 of the *U.S. Reports* that mentions this section.

    c. Give the cites for California cases that list this section as questionable precedent.

4. All of the following contain problems—Shepardize and identify the problem.

    a. *Ford Motor Co. v. Department of Treasury of Indiana*, 323 U.S. 459 (1945).

    b. *Penry v. Lynaugh*, 492 U.S. 302 (1989).

    c. *Walton v. Arizona*, 497 U.S. 639 (1990).

    d. *Bowers v. Hardwick*, 478 U.S. 186 (1986).

    e. *Ohio v. Roberts*, 448 U.S. 56 (1980).

    f. Va. Code Ann. § 18.2-423.

BUILDING YOUR ANALYSIS SKILLS: ASSIGNMENTS AND EXERCISES

1. Review Boxes 9-2 and 9-3. What information would be helpful in using *Shepards* as a research tool? Explain.

BUILDING YOUR ONLINE RESEARCH SKILLS: ASSIGNMENTS AND EXERCISES

1. If you can access KeyCite or *Shepard's* answer the following:
  a. 514 U.S. 549
    1. What is the name of this case?
    2. Why is there a warning sign for this case?
    3. Is the case still good law?
  b. 18 U.S.C. § 922 (q)
    1. When was this law last amended?
    2. What is the name of the 2005 U.S. Supreme Court Case to cite this statute in a dissenting opinion?

CASE PROJECTS

1. Shepardize any cases and statutes that you found previously in working on the case project. Have any cases are overruled? Make a list of any cases that question or criticize your cases. Read these.

2. Cite check the following Memorandum of Points and Authorities. Check each cite for format and accuracy. Also check each quotation for accuracy. Refer to Appendix B for proper citation format.

ATLAS INSURANCE COMPANY, A corporation,	))	
Plaintiff,	)	No. 12345
	)	
v.	)	MEMORANDUM OF
		POINTS &
	)	AUTHORITIES
SAVAGE RIDER, et al.	)	
Defendants	)	

Facts

The defendant was involved in a motor vehicle accident on June 23 of the previous year with an uninsured vehicle. Defendant Rider was operating a motorcycle owned by his roommate Motorcycle Murphy. This vehicle was not covered by insurance either. However, Rider did have a policy of automobile insurance, which policy is the subject of this lawsuit. The insurance policy in question covers Rider while he is operating another vehicle, as long as that vehicle is not owned by a "member of his household."

From the deposition testimony it is clear that Rider and Murphy had a typical roommate relationship. They shared rent on an apartment. However, they each led their own social lives and had their own friends. Murphy in fact had a girlfriend and spent much of his time with her, away from the apartment. Meals were seldom shared by the defendant and his roommate.

Issue

Are roommates, who are unrelated and live separate lives, "members of the same household" under the exclusion provision of an insurance policy?

Argument

1. A "HOUSEHOLD" REQUIRES A FAMILIAL BOND, NOT JUST A JOINT RESIDENCE

In their complaint, plaintiffs state that the basis of the controversy is the fact that Savage Rider was driving a vehicle owned by a member of his household. The courts in various jurisdictions, including California, have clearly held that the mere fact that two persons reside under the same roof does not make them members of the same household. Rather a more familial or social bond is required. See *Island v. Fireman's Fund Indemnity Co.*, 30 C.2d 540 at 547–8. As the Supreme Court has stated, "Persons who dwell together as a family constitute a 'household.'" *Arthur v. Morton* 112 U.S. 495, 500.

A case on point with the one here is *Bartholet v. Berkness* (Minn.), 189 N.W. 2d 410. In this case the court held that two unmarried and unrelated men, dwelling in the same living quarters and sharing expenses but having separate and independent social lives, were not members of the same household. And in a Texas case, the court stated:

> A rather unreasonable and ridiculous result follow from an attempt to ascribe to the term "household" in the phrase under consideration the meaning of a building or structure, or to ascribe to the term resident a meaning which would embrace any and all persons who sleep within or take meals at such structure. . . .

> This court reached the conclusion that similar use of the term "household" connoted a "family" or a group of persons who habitually reside under one roof and form one domestic circle.

State Farm Mutual Automobile Insurance Company v. Walker et al. (1960, Tex. Civ. App.) 334 S.W.2d 458, 463–464. See also *Giakares v. Kincade* (1961. Mo.) 330 S.W.2d 633 wherein a grandmother was held not to be a member of the same household as her grandchildren even though living under the same roof.

2. ANY AMBIGUITY IN THE INSURANCE POLICY MUST BE INTERPRETED AGAINST THE INSURANCE COMPANY AND IN FAVOR OF THE INSURED

Clearly, in the common, ordinary meaning of the words, as well as by judicial interpretation of them, "members or residents of the same household" must have more than a relationship than just "roommates." At most in the case at hand plaintiffs could contend that there is some ambiguity as to the meaning of the words. However, even if that were true, plaintiff could not prevail. It is a cardinal rule that where any ambiguity exists in an insurance policy it must be resolved in favor of the policy holder, not the insurance company. *Island v. Fireman's Fund Indemnity Co.*, 184 Pac. 153 at 159. See also *Juzefsky v. Western Cas. & Surety Co.*, 324 Pac. 2d 929.

Conclusion

In conclusion, the purpose of an exclusionary provision in an insurance policy such as the one here is to avoid multiple coverage of several vehicles owned by members of the same family, who, by their close intimacy, might be expected to use each other's vehicles without hindrance and with or without the permission of another, thus increasing the liability of the insurer without benefit or added premium. The facts of this case show that the defendant, Rider, and his roommate, Murphy, led very separate and independent lives. Murphy's vehicle was not made freely available for Rider's use. In fact, Rider had only used it once, the day of the accident. Further, the motorcycle was generally kept at the house of Murphy's parents. In addition, there was no way that Rider could have obtained insurance for the motorcycle, as he had no insurable interest therein. Thus, the objectives of the exclusionary provisions would not be properly served by applying the exclusion to the instant case.

CHAPTER 100

COMPUTER-ASSISTED LEGAL RESEARCH (CALR)

C HAPTER OUTLINE

S KILL OBJECTIVES FOR CHAPTER 10

When you complete this chapter you should be able to

- List and describe the types of computer-assisted legal research.
- Distinguish Boolean searching from plain English searching.
- Effectively use online search aids such as templates, menus, and search boxes.
- Discuss the benefits of full-text searching.
- Develop a search query for a legal research question.
- Identify and access legal Web sites that are free and reliable.
- Retrieve a document using LEXIS.
- Retrieve a document using Westlaw.
- List the steps the researcher should follow when preparing to perform computer-assisted legal research.
- Construct a search query that avoids some common problems with a computer search.

FROM THE DESK OF W. J. BRYAN, ESQ.

TO: Research Assistant

Attached is a copy of the memorandum of points and authorities to be filed in support of our motion to suppress evidence in the Meyers case. Before I file it, I want to be sure I am complying with all of the local rules of court. Please check these rules for me. You can probably find the rules of court on the court's Web site or on LEXIS or Westlaw.

There is a second matter I want you to research. Motions in criminal cases are heard by only two judges in the local court, Judge Susan Templeton or Judge R. J. Guzman. Please see what you can find out about them. You can do a judicial profile on Westlaw.

10-1 INTRODUCTION

In previous chapters, you read about the case reporters, code books, and various other materials used by legal researchers. For many years these materials were available only in print. As a result, if lawyers wanted quick and easy access to the law, they maintained substantial legal libraries in their offices. The alternative was to complete one's legal research at a law school or county law library. Modern technology and the Internet provide another alternative. Fee-based Web sites such as LEXIS and Westlaw and numerous free Web sites provide access to both federal and state law. Lawyers are no longer required to keep hundreds, or in some cases, thousands, of volumes of legal books in their offices. Nor are they limited to standard library hours in which to accomplish their research. Furthermore, these online sources offer search methods and capabilities that are impossible using traditional methods of legal research. In addition to the Internet, the publication of legal materials on CD-ROM is also popular. CD-ROMs allow attorneys to store voluminous materials in small spaces and provide the enhanced capabilities of computer search methods. Some firms also maintain legal **databases** on a network accessible only by a specific group, usually firm members and clients. This is known as an **intranet.**

Because online databases and CD-ROM are accessed with a computer, searching materials in these formats is often referred to as **computer-assisted legal research (CALR).** The computer adds a great deal of flexibility and convenience to the research process. It also gives the researcher access to many materials not otherwise available. On the other hand, computer-assisted legal research is not without its difficulties. This chapter discusses online search methodology, various legal Web sites, the use of CD-ROMs and intranets, and some of the advantages and disadvantages of CALR.

database. Compilation of electronically stored information.

intranet. A secure database set up and accessible by a specific group, such as a law firm.

computer-assisted legal research (CALR). Legal research done with the use of a computer; includes the use of CD-ROM, online services such as LEXIS and Westlaw, the Internet, and intranets.

10-2 COMMON ONLINE SEARCH METHODS

Search methods for individual Web sites are determined by the creator of the Web site. However, many sites employ similar methods and search features. Some of the common Web site features that help online researchers are menus, templates, search boxes, and tables of contents. Many legal Web sites consist of multiple types of legal materials. For example, a Web site might provide access to federal and state cases, federal and state codes, as well as a variety of other legal sources. A menu supplies a list of items, or materials, allowing the researcher to select and link to a desired type of material so that the ultimate search is more efficient. For example, see Figure 10-1, a copy of a menu from the Law Library of Congress.

The list of items or materials is a menu. By clicking on a menu item you go directly to the desired source.

FIGURE 10-1 Menu from Library of Congress

```
┌─────────────────────────────────────────────────┐
│ Browsing                                         │
│                                                  │
│     U.S. Supreme Court Decisions: by volume, by year │
│     Recent Decisions                             │
│     2006 Decisions                               │
│     2005 Decisions                               │
│     2004 Decisions                               │
│     2003 Decisions                               │
│     2002 Decisions                               │
│     2001 Decisions                               │
│     2000 Decisions                               │
│     1999 Decisions                               │
│                                                  │
│     Opinion Summaries Archive: September 2000 - Present │
│                                                  │
│ Citation Search                                  │
│                                                  │
│     [      ]  U.S.  [      ] [get it] e.g. 410 U.S. 113. │
└─────────────────────────────────────────────────┘
```

The case template provides the abbreviation for the reporter (*U.S. for United States Reports*) and provides boxes in which you insert the volume and the page.

FIGURE 10-2   Case Template from Findlaw

Reprinted with permission of Findlaw, a Thomson publication.

Many sites also provide templates to assist the researcher. Templates simplify the search process when you have a citation to a case or code section and want to retrieve it. Using a template to find a code section or a case allows you to avoid problems caused by citation formats. See Figure 10-2 and Figure 10-3 for examples of templates used for retrieving cases and codes.

Most Web sites provide some type of "search" box that allows the researcher to search part or all of the material on the Web site. In order to conduct a search, you must first formulate a **query.** A search query consists of key words that relate to your research question. There are two different ways to formulate or phrase your search question. One is by using **Boolean** logic, often referred to as "terms and connectors." The other is by phrasing your question in a normal question format. This is sometimes called a plain English search or a "natural language search." Refer to Figure 10-3.

query. Words that constitute a search request when using CD-ROM or online materials.

Boolean. A special logic used in computerized legal research; utilizes the use of connective words.

Boolean Searching

One major advantage of computer-assisted legal research is the ability to do a **full-text search.** Full-text searching involves searching the text of the legal material rather than relying on an index. For example, full-text searching of case law means searching the actual opinions of all cases found in the database in which you are working. If you were searching case law in print form, you would not be able to do this. You would need to use a digest, an annotated code, or some secondary source to lead you to a case.

Boolean searching allows you to search the full text of primary and secondary sources of material by searching for specified combinations of words in a document. This is done by using connective words or **connectors** between **key words.** Key words are generally descriptive nouns, adjectives, or verbs. Words such as "a," "the," "of," "when," or "where" should not be included in a Boolean search query. (Sometimes

Full–text search. Legal research method utilized in computer assisted legal research, in which all documents in a database are searched for certain words.

connectors. Words such as *and* or *or* used in a search query to show the relationship between key words or terms.

key word. Words that describe important aspects of a research question.

Search the United States Code

Office of the Law Revision Counsel

To view a section or group of sections, specify the title and section or other subdivision, leaving the search words blank. To search for a phrase, enclose it in single quotes. You can use boolean and proximity connectors and parentheses. Upper/lower case does not matter. Additional search options (e.g., concept, fuzzy) appear below. Or click help for more detail.

Search Word(s): ②

You may limit your search to part of the Code using any of the following fields. ①

Title: Section: [Search]

Appendix: ☐   [Reset Form]

Subtitle: Division:

Chapter: Part:

Subchapter: Subpart:

Rule: Form:

② A search box is provided for doing a full-text search. Note the instructions above about formulating your search query.

① You only need to insert the title and section of the U.S. Code section that you want to retrieve.

FIGURE 10-3   U.S. Code Template from Law Revision Counsel

these are called "noise" words.) The most common connectors are the words *and* and *or*. For example, consider the following research questions: What is the liability of a police department when innocent bystanders are hurt as a result of a high-speed car chase? Using a Boolean search method to find case law, you must formulate a query or search terms consisting of words you expect to see in cases dealing with this issue. You must then join these words with the proper connectors. In this case, you might be looking for cases that contain all of the following key terms: *police, liability, bystander, hurt, car*, and *chase*. Because you want to find cases containing all of these terms, you could connect them with *and*. On the other hand, you may not be sure if a case uses the term *hurt* instead of *injured* or *automobile* instead of *car*. In that case, you could search for hurt *or* injured, and car *or* automobile. In any one search query, you can combine different connectors. Using only the *and* and *or* connectors, your search query could read as follows:

Police and liability and bystander and hurt or injured and car or automobile and chase

Most Web sites that allow Boolean searching provide instructions for its use. Because the specifics of this type of searching differ from site to site, it is important to review these instructions. The instructions tell you

- what connecting terms can be used in your search query,
- whether connecting words or terms can be abbreviated, and
- whether a "wildcard" can be substituted for letters within search terms.

For example, one Web site might allow you to search for words or terms within the same sentence and instruct you to use a "/s" as an abbreviation for this. Another site might allow you to search for words "near" one another. Many Web sites also allow you to search for variations of words without typing in each and every variation. Two characters, the asterisk (*) and the exclamation mark (!), are frequently used as the "wildcards" or "universal character." A more detailed discussion of Boolean searching on LEXIS and Westlaw follows later in the chapter. See Figure 10-4 for an example of the type of search help found on the Library of Congress Web site.

Natural Language Searching

As an alternative to Boolean searches, some sites allow you to formulate a search using plain English. This is often known as a "natural language search." A natural language search for the search question mentioned above might read:

> Is a police department liable for damages suffered by a bystander when police are chasing a suspect in an automobile?

When you use natural language, the computer program converts your question into Boolean language.

Searching Through a Table of Contents

Searching codes and secondary sources is sometimes done by searching the table of contents. The researcher can either browse the full table of contents or conduct a word

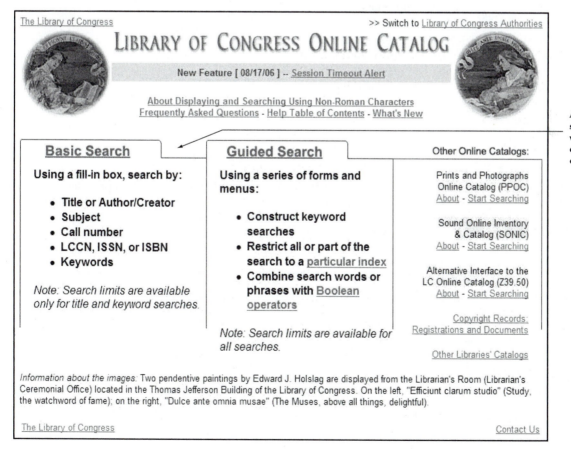

As with many Web sites, you are provided with instructions for conducting different types of searches.

FIGURE 10-4   Search help on library of Congress Web Site

Concept	Search Examples	Retrieval Formula
AND	rodgers **AND** hammerstein children **AND** poverty "civil war" **AND** virginia	Retrieves only records containing both terms.
OR	sixties **OR** 60s **OR** 1960s labor **OR** labour email **OR** e-mail **OR** "electronic mail"	Retrieves records containing either one or more terms.
NOT	caribbean **NOT** cuba jockey **NOT** disc "civil war" **NOT** american	Excludes records containing the second term.
NESTING	fruit **AND** (banana **OR** apple) (women **OR** woman) **AND** basketball ((color **OR** colour) **AND** (decorate **OR** decoration)) **NOT** (art **OR** architecture)	Use parentheses ( ) to group portions of boolean queries for more complex searches.

Here you are provided with the Boolean connectors used on the Library of Congress site along with an explanation of their use.

Use the browser's [Back] button to resume searching.

FIGURE 10-4   (continued)

search within the table of contents. This method of searching often provides narrower results than a full-text search and is therefore more efficient. See Figure 10-5 for an example of a screen containing a table of contents. For a summary of the procedures for full-text searching, see Box 10-1.

BOX 10-1   PROCEDURE FOR FULL-TEXT SEARCHING

✓ Determine contents of available databases.

✓ Select database(s) containing law of proper jurisdiction.

✓ Select database(s) containing relevant source of law (i.e., case law, codes, etc.).

✓ Identify relevant words and phrases.

✓ Formulate search query.

✓ Review results.

✓ Validate results.

Office of the Law Revision Counsel

Click a title for a further breakdown.

- Organic Laws
- Title 1, General Provisions
- Title 2, The Congress
- Title 3, The President
- Title 4, Flag and Seal, Seat of Government, and the States
- Title 5, Government Organization and Employees; and Appendix
- Title 6, Domestic Security
- Title 7, Agriculture
- Title 8, Aliens and Nationality
- Title 9, Arbitration
- Title 10, Armed Forces; and Appendix
- Title 11, Bankruptcy; and Appendix
- Title 12, Banks and Banking
- Title 13, Census
- Title 14, Coast Guard
- Title 15, Commerce and Trade
- Title 16, Conservation
- Title 17, Copyrights
- Title 18, Crimes and Criminal Procedure; and Appendix
- Title 19, Customs Duties
- Title 20, Education

You can browse the table of contents of the Code to find a topic. When you select a specific topic, that topic list expands and you can find a specific section. Eventually you link to the code section itself.

FIGURE 10-5   U.S. Code Table of Contents

10-3 PREPARING TO SEARCH

If you are engaged in computer-assisted legal research, you must prepare to research just as you do when researching materials in print. This is even more important when researching on a fee-based service where you may be charged for the time you spend on the service. Your research process for using computer-assisted legal research should include the following steps.

- Understand your research assignment.
- Review all available facts.
- Identify all key facts.
- Identify legal issues.
- List words describing your key facts and legal issues.
- Consider synonyms, antonyms, and variations of all words listed.
- Consider the relationship among the words (i.e., should two or more words appear in the same sentence, the same paragraph, etc.).
- Develop your search question.
- Choose the type of material to be searched (i.e., federal or state cases or codes).

As with all legal research, adequate preparation will make your research much more efficient and successful.

10-4 INTERNET LEGAL RESEARCH

The Internet provides access to the law as well as access to the electronic version of print materials used by legal researchers. Access to the electronic version of print materials (i.e., the West or LexisNexis case reporters, the annotated codes, encyclopedias such as *American Jurisprudence* 2d) is generally limited to fee-based services such as Westlaw or LEXIS. These materials are not found in free Web sites. However, much of the *law* that we find in print is freely available online, especially primary law. In most instances, primary law found on free Internet sites is not annotated. Cases found on free sites do not have the West or LEXIS headnotes and codes do not have case annotations.

Although many free Web sites also provide discussions, explanations, or analysis of the law, great care must be taken before relying on that information. The researcher must ask two critical questions: (1) Who is responsible for the Internet site? and (2) How current is the information on the site? Government sites, law school sites, and sites maintained by reputable legal publishers are the most reliable, provided that the information is current.

A Point to Remember

Researchers must always verify that the information is current, even with reputable sources.

Government Web Sites (.gov)

Multiple Web sites maintained by federal and state governmental agencies provide access to virtually all primary law. The following are a few important sites.

www.gpoaccess.gov   A good starting point for federal law is the Web site for the government printing office. This office disseminates information from all three branches of government. A menu on the homepage allows you to easily find and link to the various types of federal primary law. See Figure 10-6. Here you see a menu that

GPO Access Resources by Branch

Legislative Resources
- View All
- Congressional Bills
- Congressional Record
- Public and Private Laws
- United States Code

Executive Resources
- View All
- Code of Federal Regulations
- Federal Register
- Presidential Materials

Judicial Resources
- View All
- Supreme Court Web Site

Catalog of U.S. Government Publications

FIGURE 10-6   GPO Access Menu

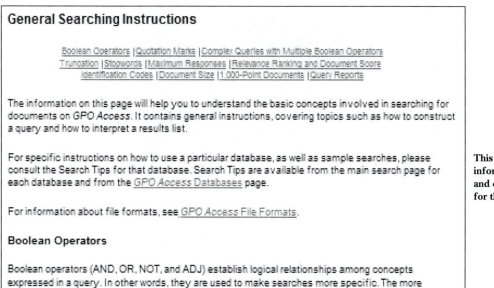

This page contains detailed information about Boolean and other search methods for the GPO Web site.

FIGURE 10-7   Introduction to GPO General Searching Instructions

leads you to the U.S. Codes, the Code of Federal Regulations, and Supreme Court cases. Numerous other federal publications can be directly accessed. This site also provides several "search tips" to help the researcher locate appropriate codes and regulations. See Figure 10-7 for an introduction to the search help offered by the site.

www.loc.gov/law/public/law.html   A second excellent Web site for access to U.S. and international law is the Law Library of Congress. This is a comprehensive site maintained by the Library of Congress. It provides access to international, federal, and state primary law. It also provides access to numerous law reviews. Again, a menu helps you find specific types of primary law. See Figure 10-8 for examples of the materials found on this site.

www.house.gov   The Web site for the House of Representatives leads you to a searchable version of the U.S. Code and selected legislative materials.

U.S. and State Court Web Sites   All federal and state courts maintain Web sites. Individual federal courts can be accessed through links provided by the Web site maintained by the Administrative Office of the Courts for the U.S. Courts (http://www.uscourts.gov/courtlinks/). In addition to links to all federal courts, this site also links to all the federal rules. See Figure 10-9. State courts can generally be found through a general search engine such as Google or through the homepage for the state. The Web site www.statelocalgov.net provides links to all state government homepages. From a state's homepage you can also generally find state constitutions, state codes, state cases, and state administrative regulations.

Law School Web Sites (.edu)

Many law school libraries provide excellent information through their Web sites. Often the sites have links to both federal and state primary law. Many also provide

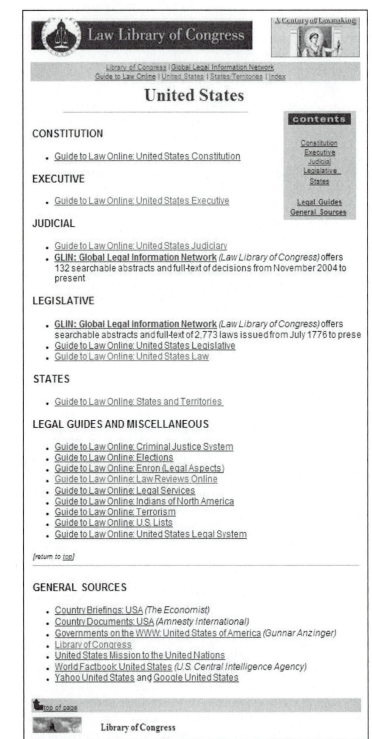

FIGURE 10-8 Law Library of Congress Menu

research guides with detailed information about the research process. A few well-recognized sites follow:

http://www.law.cornell.edu/   This is the site for the Legal Information Institute of Cornel Law School. It is a comprehensive legal database that provides access to federal and state constitutions, codes, cases, and administrative regulations. In most

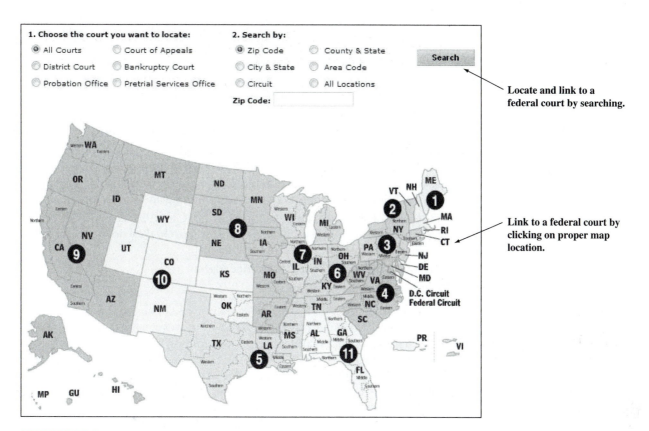

FIGURE 10-9 Page from www.uscourts.gov

instances, the databases are searchable using Boolean search methods. The site also contains information about several legal topics, much like a legal encyclopedia. On this site you can also find an introduction to basic legal citation based on both the ALWD and *The Bluebook.*

Other recognized law library Web sites include:

http://www.ll.georgetown.edu/ The Web site for Georgetown University Law Library

http://www.law.indiana.edu/lib/ The Web site for Indiana University School of Law Library

http://www.law.berkeley.edu/library/ The Web site for the University of California at Berkeley Law Library

Commercial Web Sites (.com)

Although you need to be careful when using a commercial Web site for legal research, several commercial sites provide reliable information. One of the most well-known commercial Web sites is www.findlaw.com. Findlaw is a comprehensive database of legal materials owned by West/Thomson. This site provides access to federal and state constitutions, codes, cases, and administrative rules and regulations. It also provides topical information about many substantive areas of law. Some of the valuable features on Findlaw are:

- An annotated version of the U.S. Constitution with a detailed table of contents and hyperlinks to cases that interpret the Constitution. (The U.S. Constitution is annotated by the Congressional Research Service of the Library of Congress and is thus a public document.)

- The U.S. Code, which can be searched or browsed by citation (a template is provided), by key word, by table of contents, or by popular name.
- The Code of Federal Regulations, which can be searched by citation (a template is provided) or by key word. (There is also a link to the search tips for the CFR found on the www.gpoacess.gov site.)
- A searchable version of the Federal Register
- Links to the Federal Rules of Civil Procedure, Criminal Procedure and Evidence
- Supreme Court Cases, which can be retrieved by citation (a template is provided), by a party name search or a full-text search using key words. Recent cases can also be browsed by year. (Findlaw also provides an explanation of query language, with information about Boolean searching and use of wildcards.)
- U.S. Court of Appeals cases dating from 1994 to 1997 depending on the circuit. The cases can be browsed by date, or searched by docket number, by party name, or by a key word full-text search.
- Selected information from U.S. district courts
- Links to state codes and cases

See Figure 10-10 for a look at an initial menu page from Findlaw.

Another popular commercial site is lexisONE (www.lexisone.com). LexisONE, owned by LexisNexis®, offers limited free case searching to its users. U.S. Supreme Court cases date back to 1790. However, other federal and state cases are available only for the past five years. LexisONE provides a very user-friendly search box with detailed instructions for searching. Because the search terms are similar to those found on LEXIS, this site provides a good opportunity for a researcher to develop skills that are easily transferable to LEXIS. See Figure 10-11 for a search box

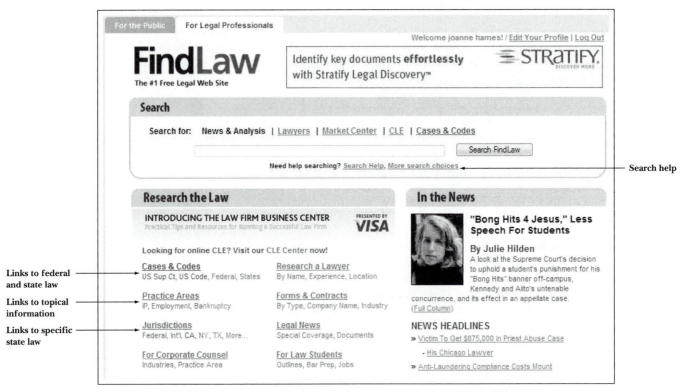

FIGURE 10-10   Findlaw Research Menu Page

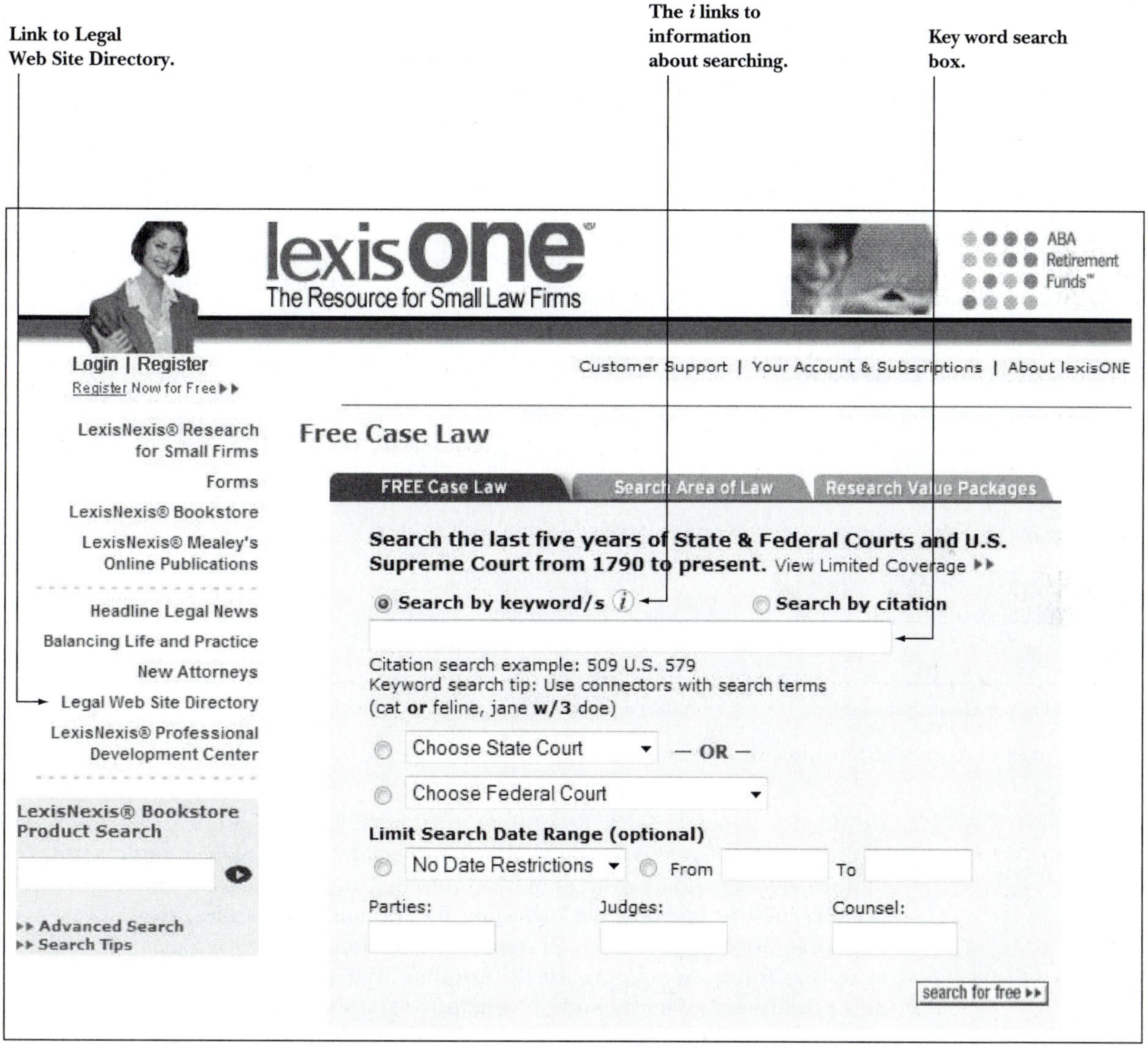

**Link to Legal
Web Site Directory.**

**The *i* links to
information
about searching.**

**Key word search
box.**

Reproduced by permission of LexisNexis. Further reproduction of any kind is strictly prohibited.

FIGURE 10-11   LexisOne Search Box

FIGURE 10-12   Legal Web Site Directory, LexisONE

provided on the lexisONE site. Another valuable feature on this site is the Legal Web Site Directory. This directory allows the researcher to link to countless primary and selected secondary sources of law. From this directory you can link to multiple areas related to law practice including federal and state codes, regulations and rules, extensive resources for all states, information about different practice areas as well as forms. See Figure 10-12. Another Web site maintained by LexisNexis also provides valuable research information. The site http://www.lexisnexis.com/ infopro/ provides important research information and tutorials for various LexisNexis products. In addition, from this site you can link to an online legal encyclopedia, *Zimmerman's Research Guide.*

Findlaw and lexisONE are only two of many Internet legal sources. Although you can find a great deal of information from these and other sources, the fee-based sites LEXIS and Westlaw are the most comprehensive and reliable databases on the Internet. It is not coincidental that the publishers of LEXIS and Westlaw are also the publishers of most legal materials in print form.

10-5 LEXIS

LEXIS is a subscription online service providing access to legal materials, news and business materials, and public records. Many of the legal print resources discussed in previous chapters can be accessed in electronic format through the LEXIS database. The database includes primary and secondary sources of law, but unlike free Internet sites, the primary law is editorially enhanced and the secondary sources are comprehensive. Cases on LEXIS contain LEXIS headnotes, case summaries, and a list of core terms to assist the researcher develop search queries. Code sections are annotated with case notes. See Figure 10-13.

Traditional legal encyclopedias, such as *American Jurisprudence Second*, multiple treatises and journals, including law reviews, are also found. In addition, news sources, business resources, and public records can also be accessed through LEXIS. When using LEXIS, you should consider that you are using the electronic version of the same books and legal materials that you use in print form in a library. See Figure 10-14 for a menu of many LEXIS materials. See Box 10-2 for a list of some of the materials found on LEXIS.

One of the most important databases on LEXIS is the *Shepard's Citator* system. LEXIS is the only online database that provides access to *Shepard's*.

Searching and Retrieving Documents on LEXIS

There are several ways to search the LEXIS database. Documents can be retrieved by citation, by a Boolean search, and by a natural language search. (The word **document** as used by online research databases such as LEXIS and Westlaw has a special meaning. It often refers to a case, a single code section, or a section in a secondary source.) Features of certain legal materials, such as tables of contents and statutory popular name indexes, can also be used to find information.

document. An identifiable item located in a database; can refer to a case or a single code section.

BOX 10-2

Primary Law	Secondary Sources	Public Records and News Sources
United States Constitution	Encyclopedias *(Am. Jur. 2d)*	Business information
United States Code	*A.L.R.*	Real property information
Federal cases	Treatises	Court records
Code of Federal Regulations	Practice books	Legal news publications
Federal Rules	Form books	Worldwide general news publications
State constitutions	Law reviews and journals	
State codes	The Restatement	
State cases		
State administrative regulations		
Selected international laws		

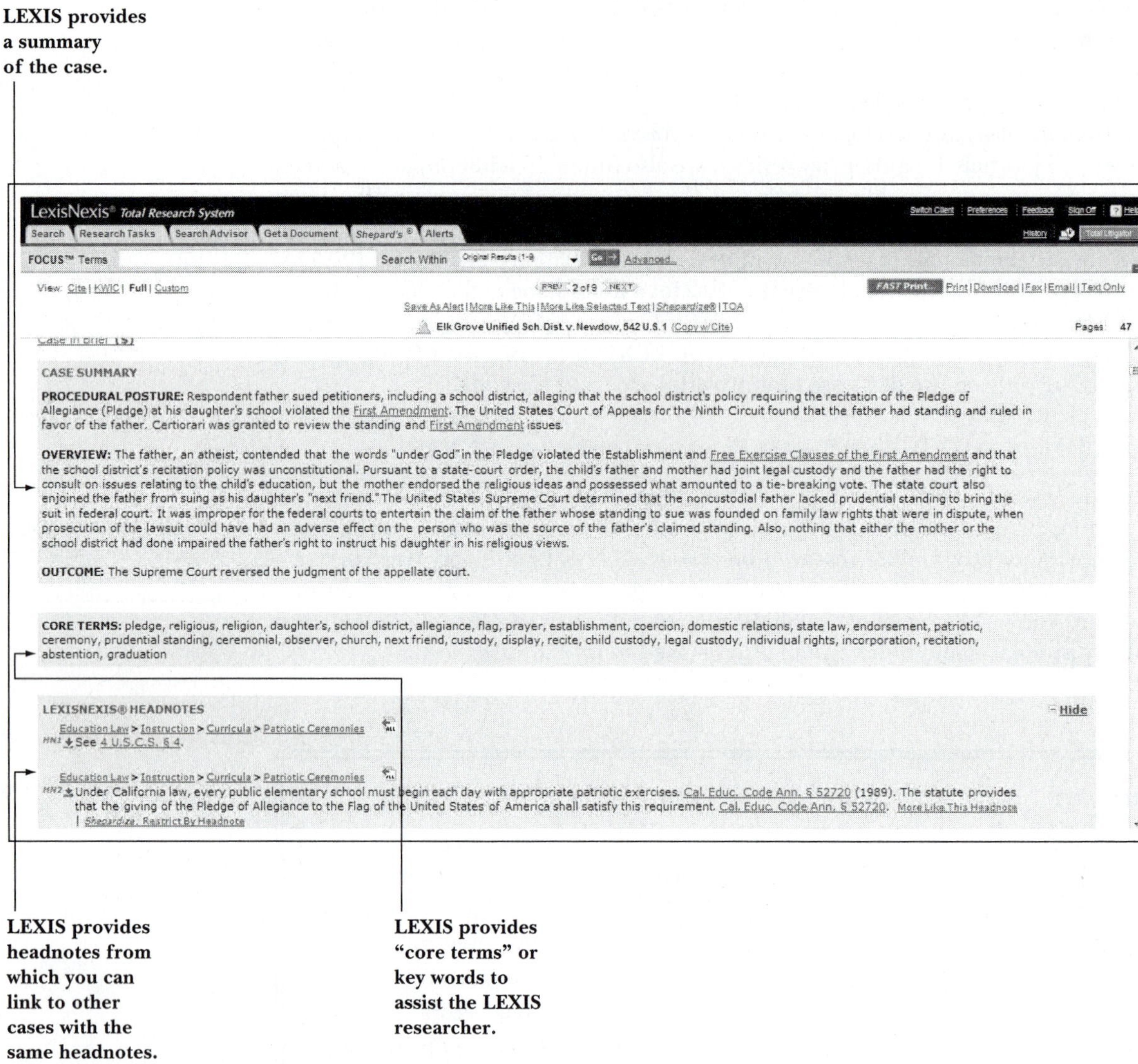

**LEXIS provides
a summary
of the case.**

**LEXIS provides
headnotes from
which you can
link to other
cases with the
same headnotes.**

**LEXIS provides
"core terms" or
key words to
assist the LEXIS
researcher.**

FIGURE 10-13   Editorially Enhanced Case on LEXIS

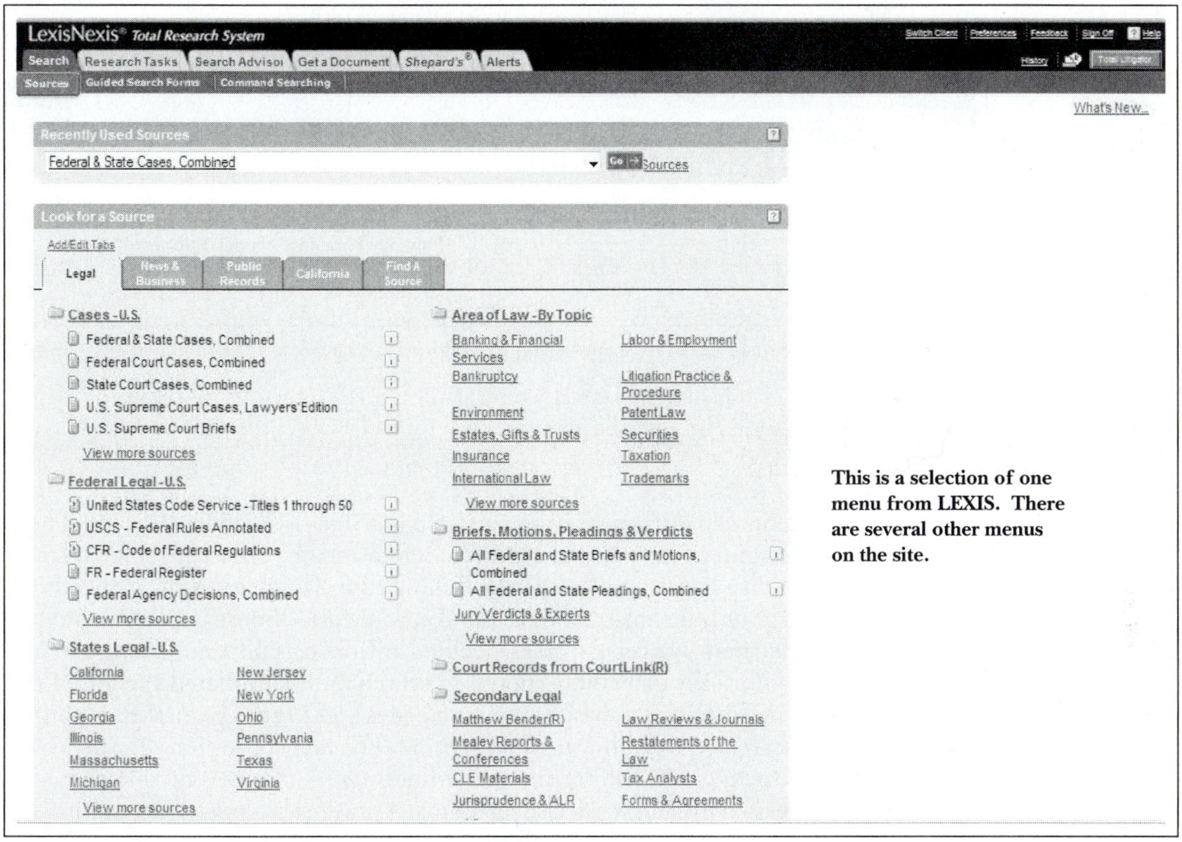

This is a selection of one menu from LEXIS. There are several other menus on the site.

FIGURE 10-14   Partial Menu of Legal Materials on LEXIS

Get a Document   The "Get a Document" feature allows the researcher to retrieve cases, codes, and selected secondary sources with a citation. LEXIS provides help if the researcher is uncertain of the proper citation format. This feature also allows the researcher to retrieve cases by party name or by docket number. See Figure 10-15 for an example of this feature.

Search   The search feature allows the researcher to do full-text searching using either "terms and connectors" (Boolean searching) or natural language. Prior to accessing this page you need to select the correct source from a LEXIS menu. The term *source* in LEXIS is used to describe a database containing specified types of legal materials. Sources may include one type of legal material, such as "Supreme Court Cases" or might include several different types of materials, such as "federal and state cases combined." (Refer back to Figure 10-14.) LEXIS contains more material than any traditional legal library and, in most cases, researchers have no need to search the entire database. The various sources appear in a menu format on the initial search page. Researchers can choose to search one or more sources simultaneously. To facilitate the research process, LEXIS allows the researcher to "customize" the list of sources that appears on the search page by selecting frequently used sources.

   After selecting the source, the researcher has the choice to proceed with either a Boolean type search (called "terms and connectors" on LEXIS) or a natural language search. Before searching, the researcher has the option to further limit the search. Although LEXIS searches can be full-text searches, you can limit a search to

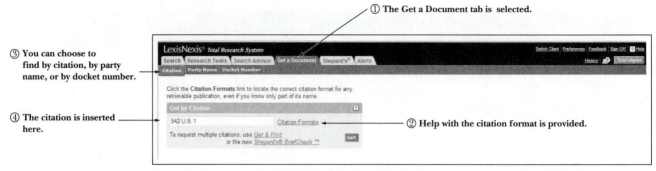

① The Get a Document tab is selected.

③ You can choose to find by citation, by party name, or by docket number.

④ The citation is inserted here.

② Help with the citation format is provided.

Reproduced by permission of LexisNexis. Further reproduction of any kind is strictly prohibited.

FIGURE 10-15 Get a Document Search Box on LEXIS

certain segments of a document or to certain dates. This is sometimes referred to as restricting by segment or restricting by date. (Occasionally, this is also referred to as a field restriction.) For example, when searching case law you can search only the title of the case or only the majority opinion. You could also choose to search opinions written by specified justices or cases decided within certain time frames. When searching statutory law you could choose to search an unannotated version of the code. When you search a database containing codes LEXIS gives you another option. Rather than searching the full-text you can browse the table of contents for the code.

In constructing a LEXIS "terms and connectors" search, several different connectors can be used to achieve precise searching. A universal character, an asterisk, (*) and a root expander (!) are also available. The universal character is used as a substitute for one letter within a word (e.g., wom*n includes woman and women). The root extender is placed at the end of a word that can end with several variations (e.g., liab! includes liability or liable). See Box 10-3 found later in the chapter for a list of both the LEXIS and Westlaw connecting terms.

See Figure 10-16 for the search page for Supreme Court cases.

Natural Language and Easy Search As an alternative to Boolean searching, LEXIS allows you to state your search query in plain English. Generally this type of search is not as precise as a Boolean search, but it often produces the desired result. Easy search is a relatively new feature. It allows the researcher to use only a few key words.

Other Search Methods LEXIS provides other ways of locating relevant documents. One way is by hyperlinking. When one authority cites another, LEXIS frequently allows you to hyperlink directly to the second authority. You can hyperlink from one case to another, from a statutory annotation to a case, or from a secondary authority to a case or code section. You can also use case headnotes to search for similar cases. LEXIS has features that allow you to retrieve cases with similar headnotes simply by following links.

Shepard's Citators

LEXIS is the only online service offering direct access to the various *Shepard's* citators. Not only can the researcher Shepardize authorities on LEXIS, but whenever a case is retrieved, it contains a *Shepard's* warning if there is any negative treatment of the case. LEXIS also provides software utilizing *Shepard's* citators to assist researchers

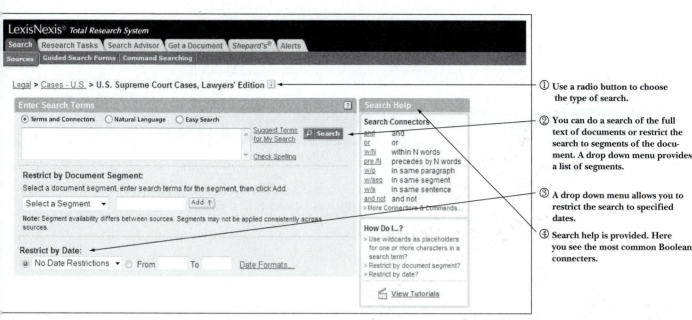

The figure shows a LexisNexis search box with the following callouts:

① Use a radio button to choose the type of search.

② You can do a search of the full text of documents or restrict the search to segments of the document. A drop down menu provides a list of segments.

③ A drop down menu allows you to restrict the search to specified dates.

④ Search help is provided. Here you see the most common Boolean connecters.

FIGURE 10-16   LEXIS Search Box

with preparing legal memoranda and briefs. The software automatically checks the accuracy and format of citations, warns of any negative treatment of cited authorities, and creates a table of authorities. See Figure 10-17. *Shepard's* online was discussed in more detail in Chapter 9.

Other Features

LEXIS has many features not mentioned above and continually adds new features. Fortunately, LEXIS provides online tutorial user guides explaining its numerous features and offering research tips. A subscription to the LEXIS service is not needed to access the tutorials. LEXIS also has an excellent "help" feature that can be accessed from within the LEXIS database.

10-6 WESTLAW

Westlaw is an online subscription service similar to LEXIS in the type of materials found and in the search methods used. As with LEXIS, on Westlaw the researcher has access to annotated constitutions, codes, and regulations. Case law contains case summaries and headnotes. In addition to primary law, numerous secondary sources, public records, and news sources are available through Westlaw. The Westlaw database allows the user to determine and personalize the start-up page so that frequently used sources and jurisdictions appear and can be immediately selected from a menu.

Searching and Retrieving Documents on Westlaw

Find and Print or Find by Citation   The Westlaw feature used to retrieve constitutional provisions, codes, cases, and selected secondary sources when you know the

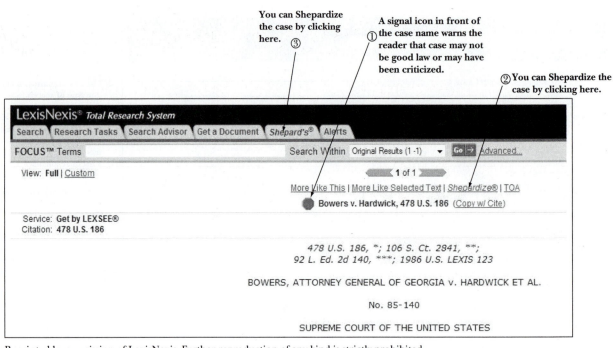

Reprinted by permission of LexisNexis. Further reproduction of any kind is strictly prohibited.

FIGURE 10-17   *Shepard's* Case Warning

citation is "Find and Print" or "Find by Citation." Within this feature you can retrieve documents by inserting a citation in a search box. To avoid citation problems Westlaw provides, for optional use, a template containing the proper abbreviation for the document. The researcher fills in the volume and page or title and section number. A case can also be found by using the feature, "find a case by party name." See Figure 10-18.

Shortcuts   Westlaw provides a "Shortcut Menu" providing several quick ways to find a particular document. The Shortcut menus provide an easy means to retrieve numerous documents including local rules of court, public records, continuing legal education materials, and profiles of judges or attorneys. A researcher can also use the Shortcut feature to access indexes to federal and state codes and tables of contents for numerous documents. The Shortcut menu also provides a quick means to cite-check a document using the KeyCite feature of Westlaw. See Figures 10-18 and 10-19.

Search   Again, as with LEXIS, the researcher can conduct a full-text search using either a Boolean or natural language search. Either search begins with selecting the proper database. If a Boolean search is selected, a terms and connector search query is constructed. For a list of connectors found on Westlaw, see Box 10-3. Westlaw also utilizes the asterisk (*) as a universal character and the exclamation point (!) as a root expander. Rather than conducting a full-text search, researchers can also choose to limit the search to certain segments or fields of a document. The search can also be limited by date. Rather than using a Boolean search, researchers can also construct a search query using plain English. See Figure 10-20 for a sample of a Westlaw search page.

Key Number Searching   One of the unique features of West publications—key numbers—is found on Westlaw and can be used as a basis for searching. Westlaw has

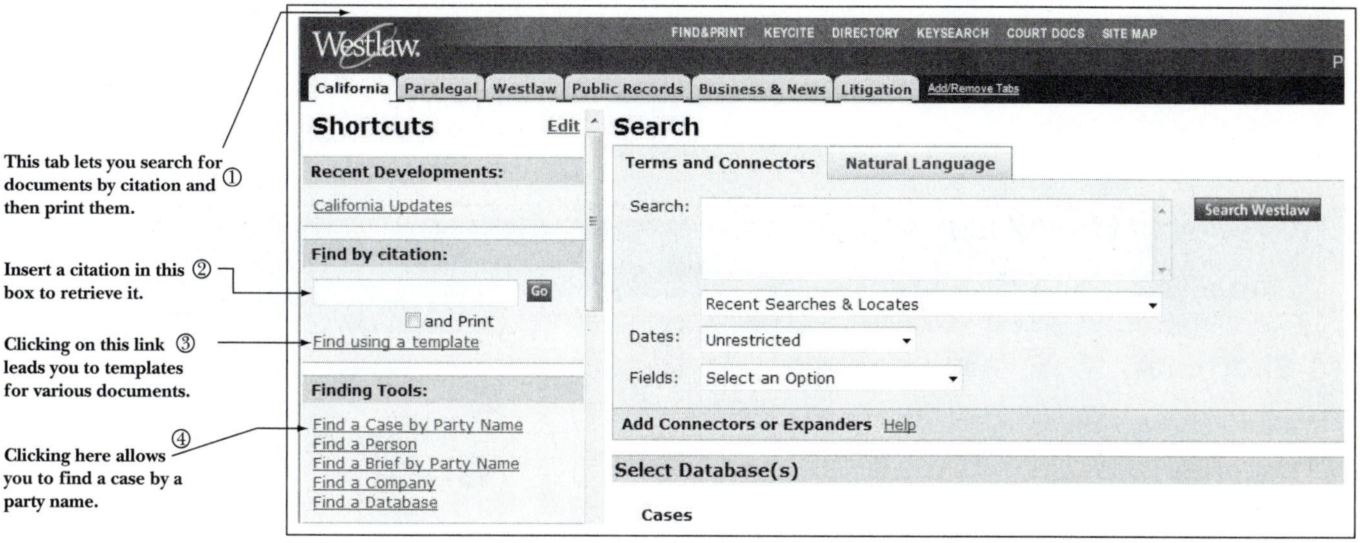

This tab lets you search for documents by citation and then print them. ①

Insert a citation in this box to retrieve it. ②

Clicking on this link leads you to templates for various documents. ③

Clicking here allows you to find a case by a party name. ④

Reprinted with permission of Thomson/West.

FIGURE 10-18   Westlaw Find Feature

a feature titled KeySearch. This allows you to browse the numerous topics and subtopics West includes in its key number system. After selecting a relevant topic you can retrieve cases or selected secondary sources discussing that topic. See Figures 10-21 and 10-22. In addition to using the KeySearch feature you can use the hyperlink feature with the key numbers found in the headnotes to the cases. This leads you to other cases with the same key number headnotes.

See Box 10-3 for a comparison of the connectors and expanders on LEXIS and Westlaw.

KeyCite

Rather than *Shepard's*, Westlaw provides a service called KeyCite to check the validity of legal sources. As described in the previous chapter, KeyCite is similar to *Shepard's* in the information provided. Westlaw also provides software utilizing KeyCite to assist researchers with preparing legal memoranda and briefs. The software automatically checks the accuracy and format of citations, warns of any negative treatment of cited authorities, and creates a table of authorities. As with LEXIS and *Shepard's*, when you access a case, Westlaw provides KeyCite information with warning signals. Westlaw also provides textual information regarding the KeyCite results. See Figure 10-23. KeyCite is discussed in more detail in Chapter 9.

Other Features

Westlaw has many other features to assist a legal researcher and, like LEXIS, continually updates and enhances its search capabilities. One recent addition is

① The Shortcut menu gives you easy access to many of Westlaw's features.

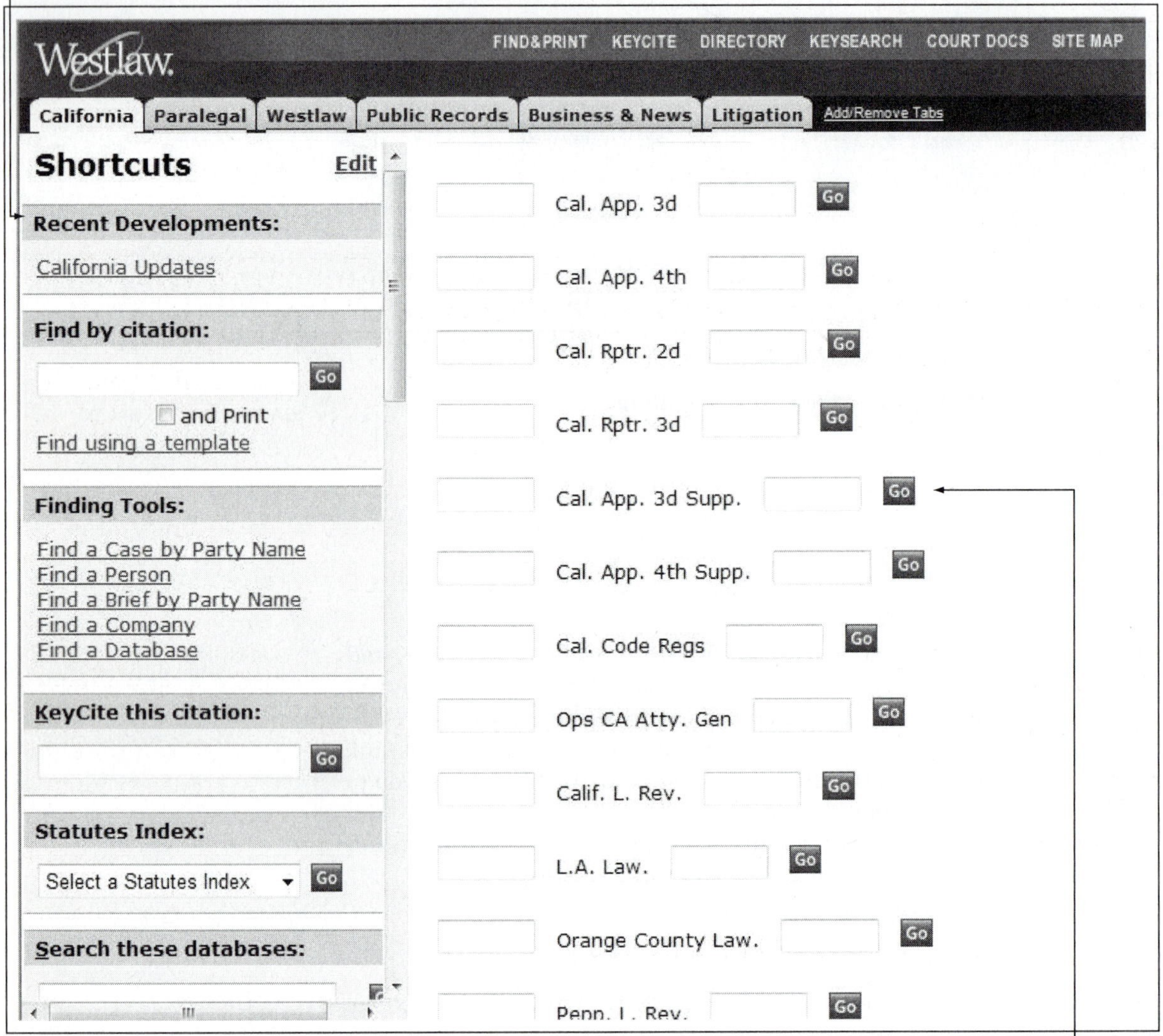

Reprinted with permission of Thomson/West.

FIGURE 10-19   Westlaw Shortcut Screen with Templates for Searching

② By inserting the appropriate volume and page in these templates, Westlaw allows you to retrieve documents with these abbreviations.

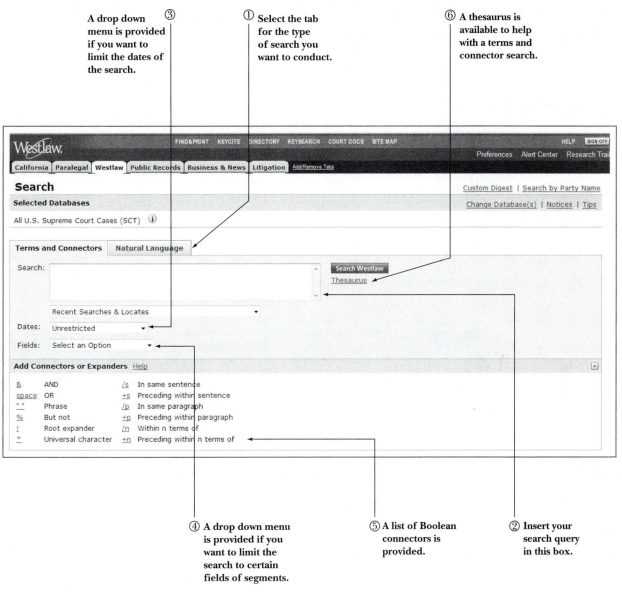

Reprinted with permission of Thomson/West.

FIGURE 10-20   Westlaw Search Box

① Use this tab to begin
a key number search.

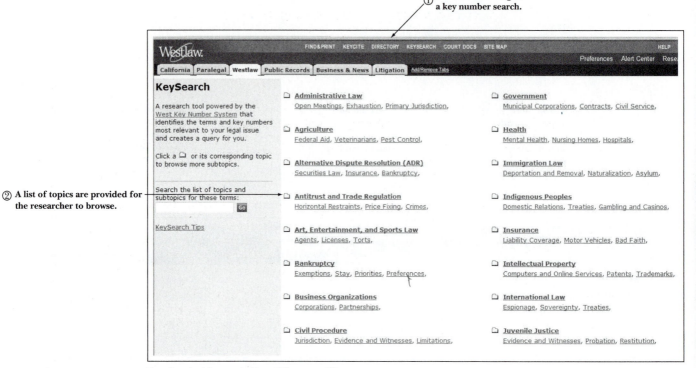

② A list of topics are provided for
the researcher to browse.

Reprinted with permission of Thomson/West.

FIGURE 10-21   Westlaw KeySearch, Initial Page for Browsing

After selecting a specific topic, you
are presented with this search screen.
This allows you to limit key number
search to selected sources and
jurisdictions. You can also add your
own key words in a search box.

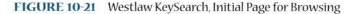

Reprinted with permission of Thomson/West.

FIGURE 10-22   Westlaw KeySearch, Final Search Page

BOX 10-3   CONNECTORS AND EXPANDERS ON LEXIS AND WESTLAW

LEXIS	**Westlaw**	
And	&, and	Finds documents containing all key words connected by and or &
Or	A space, or	Finds documents containing either key word
w/n, /n	/n	Finds documents with key terms separated by the specificied number of words, i.e., "search /3 unreasonable" would retrieve documents where the word search appears within 3 words of the term unreasonable
not w/n		Finds documents where two words do not occur within a specified range
pre w/n	+n, +p, +s	Finds documents where one term appears *before* another term within a specified number of words (pre w/n or +n), within the same paragraph (+p), or within the same sentence (+s)
w/p, /p	/p	Finds documents where two key words appear in the same paragraph
not w/p		Finds documents where two key words do not appear in the same paragraph
w/seg		Finds documents where two key words appear in the same segment
not w/seg		Finds documents where two key words do not appear in the same segment
w/s, /s	/s	Finds documents where two terms appear in the same sentence
not w/s		Finds documents where two terms do not appear in the same sentence
and not	%	Finds documents with the first term but not the second

A Point to Remember

When conducting a Boolean-type search, check the Web site help features for a list of connectors that can be used. They change from site to site and are not interchangeable.

a feature called "ResultsPlus." Whenever you retrieve a case or statute, a list of relevant secondary sources appears on the screen. You can link to any of these for additional research. Refer to Figure 10-23. Westlaw also provides several helpful user guides and pamphlets, which can be downloaded without cost from their Web site as well as providing online tutorials. You need not be a subscriber to access these aids.

For a summary of the benefits of LEXIS and Westlaw, see Box 10-4.

10-7 OTHER TYPES OF CALR

Computer-assisted legal research is not limited to the Web sites listed above. There are many other free sites and other fee-based sites, including Loislaw (www.losislaw.com), VersusLaw (www.versuslaw.com) and TheLaw.net (www.thelaw.net). These fee-based sites are not as powerful or as comprehensive as Westlaw or LEXIS, but they

② Westlaw provides a brief KeyCite description in a left pane when you access a case.

③ You can also access KeyCite from this tab.

① Westlaw provides a KeyCite warning flag when a case is treated negatively by subsequent case. By clicking on the signal you access KeyCite for this case.

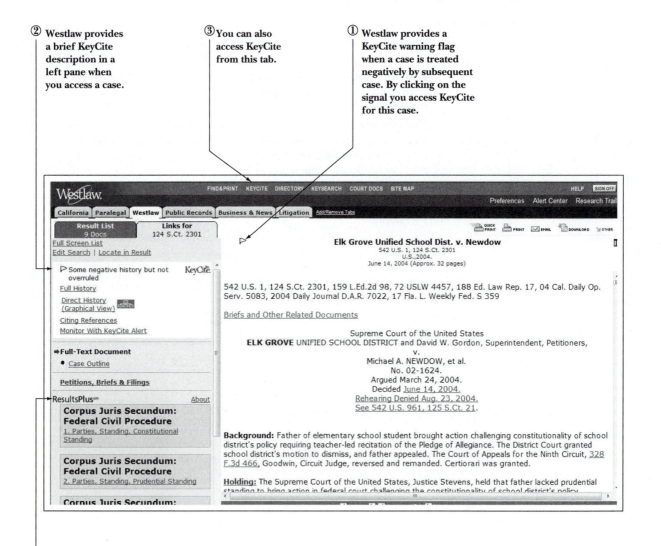

④ The ResultsPlus feature appears with cases and statutes. Note the references to *Corpus Juris Secundum.* The articles referenced here deal with issues related to the issues in this case.

Reprinted with permission of Thomson/West.

FIGURE 10-23   Westlaw KeyCite Case Warnings

BOX 10-4   LEXIS AND WESTLAW ALLOW YOU TO

✓ Search full text of case law and codes for specific words and phrases.

✓ Search numerous secondary sources (e.g., encyclopedias, *A.L.R.,* law reviews) for specific words and phrases.

✓ Search tables of contents for codes and numerous secondary sources.

✓ Retrieve documents (cases, codes, and secondary sources) with a citation.

✓ Search case opinions written by or mentioning specific justices.

✓ Search for cases within certain dates.

✓ Search numerous public documents (e.g., corporate and real estate documents).

✓ Search general news articles.

✓ Search selected foreign materials.

✓ Validate your research findings (using *Shepard's* or KeyCite).

---

offer a broader range of case law and more sophisticated searching than most free sites. They also provide limited secondary sources. In addition to the Internet, computer-assisted legal research occurs with the use of CD-ROMs. Many legal publications available in print format are also available on CD-ROM. The advantages to the use of CD-ROM are many. Much less physical space is needed to store volumes of materials. Materials that would normally fill all the shelves of a large library can be kept on a corner of an attorney's desk. Supplementing is much easier than it is with material in print. Pocket part supplements and separate supplement volumes are not necessary. Instead, the publishers supplement materials on CD-ROM with cumulative replacement CDs.

Another tool for computer-assisted legal research is an intranet. Intranets are databases set up and accessible by a specific group, such as a law firm. All members of the firm can access it. If a law firm has several branches in different localities, information on an intranet can be accessed by all of them. Intranets also provide the mechanism for setting up e-mail among the various users. Because an intranet is not part of the Internet, some of the security concerns associated with the Internet do not exist. In terms of legal research, intranets provide a vehicle for firms to index and maintain any legal memoranda they prepared. Before researching legal questions, lawyers can check this database to see if the research was done in connection with some other case in the office. Like the Internet, an intranet allows lawyers and their support staff to conduct online discussion groups.

10-8 SEARCH POSSIBILITIES AND PROBLEMS

Computer-assisted legal research opens search possibilities that do not exist with materials in print. Web sites such as LEXIS and Westlaw are often able to publish cases online the same day a decision is handed down, eliminating the need to search advance sheets or slip opinions. Full-text searching does not require the researcher to rely on secondary sources or digests. You can search a case database for the presence of any word or combinations of words. This allows you to search not only for legal issues and facts, but for names of individuals appearing in cases. Thus, you can search for appellate cases written by certain judges or for cases dealing with lower court decisions by certain judges. If you are presented with a question about possible biases of a certain judge, you could search case law databases to see if his or her name appears.

Other advantages of computer assisted legal research include:

- Ability to restrict a full-text search by factors such as date, author, jurisdiction
- Ability to locate a case with the name of one party and no case citation
- Ability to hyperlink to an authority cited within the document you are reading
- Ability to instantly cite-check a case you are reading by hyperlinking to *Shepard's* or KeyCite
- Ability to "copy and paste" language or citations into a word-processing document
- Availability of popular materials (especially practice books) to more than one person at a time

On the other hand, computer-assisted legal research is not without problems. Some of these include the following.

- Computers search literally; misspelled words or typographical errors will result in a failed search.
- Computers do not distinguish a different word usage; a search for RICO will produce references to the Rico Act as well as Puerto Rico.
- Computers do not automatically search for synonyms; a search for *vehicle* will not produce results containing the word *automobile.*
- A tendency to overuse hyperlinks can result in unorganized (and lost) research.
- The use of LEXIS and Westlaw can be costly.

Another potential problem with online services stems from the fact that the services contain some unpublished opinions and opinions that were vacated because a higher court granted a hearing. Most of these cases do not appear in printed case reporters. It is absolutely essential that any cite on these services be validated.

Whether you use print or online resources your legal research strategies are similar. The following is an overview of those strategies.

1. Create a vocabulary list based on your factual problem.
2. Formulate the issue.
3. Use a legal thesaurus and legal dictionary to complete your vocabulary list.
4. Create a research plan before going to a law library or accessing an online site.
5. Determine whether to begin in primary or secondary sources.
6. Take your research terms/vocabulary to indexes.
7. Add additional terms to your vocabulary list as suggested by the indexes.
8. Take notes whether using print or online sources.
9. Organize photocopied or downloaded material.

Read Appendix C for a more detailed overview of research strategies.

Online Legal Research

Legal research on the Internet is continually changing. One good Web site that helps you keep up to date is the Web site Internet for Lawyers located at http://www. netforlawyers.com/index.htm.

Another good guide to fee-based online sources is found at http://www. nyulawglobal.org/globalex/US_Fee-Based_Legal_Databases1.htm.

Other important resources can be found on the Westlaw and LexisNexis sites. Both provide excellent up-to-date information about their products. Try these Web sites:

http://west.thomson.com/westlaw/guides/

http://law.lexisnexis.com/communityportal/

When you use the Internet for legal research, you will undoubtedly find several favorite sites. Internet browsers, such as Internet Explorer, allow you to "bookmark" these sites and keep the Web addresses in a "favorites" file. This gives you easy access to frequently used sites.

CITATION MATTERS

INTERNET CITATIONS

THE BLUEBOOK—RULE 18

Electronic Media and Other Nonprint Resources

Rule 18 covers a multitude of citation requirements. Legal researchers who use the Internet must pay close attention to the new rules associated with citing to the Internet. A short list of the rules and what each rule covers follows.

Rule 18.2:	information about the authority being cited
Rule 18.2.2:	explanatory phrase indicating which source was used
Rule 18.2.2:	provider responsible for the Internet site (if not clear from URL)
Rule 18.2.1(a):	the URL
Rule 18.2.3(e):	a date parenthetical
Rule 18.2.2(c):	order of authorities and parentheticals
Rule 18.2.3(d):	pinpoint citations to Internet sources

LEXIS, WESTLAW, AND OTHER ELECTRONIC DATABASES

THE BLUEBOOK—RULE 18

Electronic Media and Other Nonprint Resources

LEXIS and Westlaw are large commercial electronic databases. There are other reliable and authoritative commercial databases as well. The rules covering citation to these resources are covered in the following rules.

CHAPTER SUMMARY

Legal researchers today use legal resource material in electronic format in addition to material in print. This type of research is known as *computer-assisted legal research*. Computer-assisted legal research consists of the use of free Internet Web sites, fee-based legal databases such as LEXIS and Westlaw, CD-ROMs, and intranets.

Legal Web sites offer a variety of methods for searching the site. Menus, templates, and tables of contents sometimes simplify an online search. An important method of searching online legal sources involves the use of Boolean logic. In a Boolean search, sometimes referred to as a terms and connector search, the researcher develops a search query based on key words found in the research question and certain connective words. On many sites, natural language or plain English can also be used to formulate a search query. Boolean and natural language searches allow the researcher to conduct full-text searches. A full-text search is a search of the actual documents rather than a search of an index.

Most primary law is available through free Internet sites, although generally it lacks editorial enhancements such as headnotes or annotations. Reliability is a key concern with free Internet sites. Reliable free Internet Web sites are established and maintained by governmental agencies, university law schools, and some commercial enterprises. In addition to free Internet sites, several fee-based sites are available. The two most well-known sites are LEXIS and Westlaw. These sites contain databases with extensive amounts of primary and secondary legal research material. In addition to legal research material, a researcher can also access public documents, records from popular current cases, and numerous news sources. Both sites also provide a system for validating research. *Shepard's* is found on LEXIS and KeyCite is found on Westlaw. Both sites provide numerous search methods as well as search help.

Legal publishers produce many legal materials in CD-ROM format. A CD-ROM is a compact disk holding thousands of pages of material. A CD-ROM provides many benefits. Less space is needed to store material, supplementing is easier, and search possibilities are greater.

The use of computer-assisted legal research offers search possibilities that do not exist otherwise. However, it is not without problems.

TERMS TO REMEMBER

database	query	connectors
intranet	Boolean	key word
computer-assisted legal research (CALR)	full-text search	document

QUESTIONS FOR REVIEW

1. What is computer-assisted legal research?
2. What is a Boolean search?
3. What is a plain English or natural language search?
4. What is a full-text search?
5. List examples of reliable government Web sites, educational Web sites, and commercial Web sites.
6. What types of materials can be found on LEXIS and Westlaw?
7. Describe the different types of search methods found on LEXIS and Westlaw.
8. List the steps in preparing to search online.
9. What are some of the advantages of a CD-ROM?
10. What are some of the problems with computer assisted legal research?

CAN YOU FIGURE IT OUT?

1. Refer to Figure 10-3. Assume you wanted to retrieve 18 U.S.C. §242. How would you complete the search screen?
2. Refer to Figure 10-5. Which title would you click on if you were looking for a code section dealing with homeland security?
3. Refer to Figure 10-6. Under which category (legislative, executive, or judicial) would you find the following?
   a. Federal Register
   b. Congressional Record
   c. Private Laws
4. Refer to Figure 10-9. If you wanted to link to the Court of Appeals for the circuit in which you live, what number on the map would you click on?
5. Refer to Figure 10-10. If you were looking for your state's code, which two menu items could you click on?
6. Refer to Figure 10-12. If you were looking for your state's codes, which materials in the directory might be relevant?
7. Refer to Figure 10-14. If you were researching case law from your state, which sources would you select?
8. Refer to Figure 10–14. If you were researching Supreme Court case law, which sources could you select?

BUILDING YOUR RESEARCH SKILLS: ASSIGNMENTS AND ACTIVITIES

1. Review problems 1 and 5 in Appendix A and Research Strategies in Appendix C. For each problem do the following:
   a. Create a vocabulary list of both factual and legal terms.
   b. Review a legal dictionary and legal thesaurus for additional terms.
   c. Create a list of primary and secondary print sources that might be helpful in your research.
   d. Determine whether you would start your research in a primary or secondary source and explain why.
   e. Explain how your research plan might change if you use electronic sources (such as LEXIS or Westlaw) rather than print sources.

BUILDING YOUR ANALYSIS SKILLS: ASSIGNMENTS AND EXERCISES

1. Review the problems in Appendix A.
   a. Draft queries for finding cases for each of the problems using Boolean logic. Use the LEXIS connectors.
   b. Do the same using the Westlaw connectors.
   c. Do the same using natural language.

BUILDING YOUR ONLINE RESEARCH SKILLS: ASSIGNMENTS AND EXERCISES

1. **Statutory Research on the Internet:** Find answers to the following questions using the Internet. (Try www.findlaw.com and http://uscode.house.gov/usc.htm.)
   a. What does 28 U.S.C. § 135 provide?
   b. What does 2 U.S.C. § 135 provide?
   c. Which section of the United States Code establishes the Department of Homeland Security?
   d. Where in the United States Code do you find the "Drive-by Shooting Prevention Act of 1994"?
   e. Which two constitutional amendments use the term *due process*?
2. **Case Law Research on the Internet:** Find answers to the following questions using the Internet. (Try www.findlaw.com and www.lexisone.com.)
   a. What U.S. Supreme Court cases prior to 2004 discuss the law regarding "enemy combatants"?
   b. Which 2003 U.S. Supreme Court case discusses the use of affirmative action in the admission process of a law school?
3. Using a general search engine such as www.google.com, search for information about employment discrimination. You should retrieve numerous sites. Would any of the first five sites help if you were doing legal research on this issue? Explain. Make a list of legal resources available through this site.

CASE PROJECT

Use the Internet to do further research on your case. Do the following.

   a. Conduct a general search of the main issues in your case.
   b. See if any of the cases or statutes you have found can be located on the Internet.
   c. See if the local rules of court for your jurisdiction are on the Internet.
   d. See if your local court has a homepage.

BASIC LEGAL WRITING TOOLS

S KILL OBJECTIVES FOR CHAPTER 11

When you complete this chapter you should be able to

- Discuss a researcher's initial consideration after completion of the research.
- Explain the purpose of a thesis paragraph.
- Write a thesis paragraph.
- Write a topic sentence.
- Describe the editing and revision processes.

FROM THE DESK OF W.J. BRYAN, ESQ.

TO: Research Assistant

Now that it has been a few days since you wrote the memorandum in the Meyers case, I would like you to take a final look at it. Edit for grammar and style. The judges who consider these motions are extremely busy. I want our document to be clear and concise.

11-1 INITIAL CONSIDERATIONS AFTER COMPLETION OF THE RESEARCH

Before you begin to write, go back to your initial instructions. Did you follow them?

- Did you answer the questions clearly and concisely?
- Did you respond to *all* of the questions?
- Can you honestly tell your supervisor that your research results are accurate, current, and valid?
- Were you as thorough as possible?

If your response to each of these questions is "yes," you are ready to begin the drafting process. After the research is complete, the note-taking and copying are replaced with analysis and writing. The questions and considerations below help organize your writing.

11-2 OVERVIEW OF A LEGAL RESEARCH AND WRITING PROJECT

These questions or considerations help the legal writer focus on the project and recognize problem areas.

1. What exactly is the research project or what is your goal?
2. Who is the reading audience?
3. What legal issues does the research explore?
4. How will the reading audience benefit from the results of the research?

5. List the most important points you must get across to your audience.

6. List the legal authority that supports each point listed in number 5 above.

7. Which citation manual must be followed?
   (*The Bluebook, A.L.W.D. Citation Manual*)

8. Is there a length restriction? If so, what is it?

9. What is the length of your current draft?

10. When must this project be completed?

These questions help the writer focus and provide structure to the process of research and writing.

11-3 THE THESIS PARAGRAPH

A well-written legal discussion lays a solid foundation for the reader. Before you begin to write, slow down and consider what your reader knows about the problem. You may have worked for many hours and become extremely familiar with all aspects of the problem, but the reader may have little or no knowledge.

A legal discussion or argument should begin with a **thesis paragraph** to introduce readers to your client's problem, the legal issues arising from the facts, the rules that govern the issues, and a legal conclusion. This paragraph sets the scene for the reader and provides a short overview of the internal organization of the argument section of a trial brief or the discussion section of a memorandum.

thesis paragraph. The thesis paragraph lays a solid foundation for the reader. This paragraph sets forth the client's problem, states the legal issue, briefly explains the legal rules governing the issues, and states the legal conclusion.

How to Arrange a Thesis Paragraph

1. State the legal issue

2. Briefly explain the rules of law governing the issues

3. State the legal conclusion (the thesis)

The thesis paragraph represents the writer's first opportunity to set the tone and educate the reader and is, therefore, very important. It also outlines the overall organization of the information. Clearly, the thesis paragraph cannot be written until the research is complete and the final analysis is performed.

The following paragraphs are taken from the Argument section of the Brief for the United States as Amicus Curiae Supporting Petitioner in *Minnesota v. Dickerson*, 508 U.S. 366 (1993). Notice that each paragraph follows the format set out above.

I. The Minnesota Supreme Court erred in holding that the police officer who searched respondent exceeded the scope of the protective pat-down search authorized under *Terry v. Ohio*. *Terry* authorizes a "careful exploration" of a suspect's outer clothing for weapons. 392 U.S. at 16. Officer Rose's brief and limited touching of the pocket of respondent's jacket was an appropriate part of the "careful" examination permitted under *Terry*. Officer Rose did not engage in the sort of prolonged and intrusive manipulation of clothing about which the state supreme court expressed concern. Nor does the record support the suggestion of the state supreme court that Rose made a discrete, conscious, decision to continue handling the object in respondent's pocket after concluding that the object was not a weapon. Instead, the officer's act of feeling the object was merely a continuation of a pat-down search indisputably justified at its inception. For that reason the officer's actions are distinguishable from the conduct found to constitute a separate, unauthorized search in *Arizona v. Hicks*, 480 U.S. 321 (1987).

When this paragraph is examined closely, it provides the following:

1. The client's legal issue:

> The Minnesota Supreme Court erred in holding that the police officer who searched respondent exceeded the scope of the protective pat-down search authorized under *Terry v. Ohio. Terry* authorizes a "careful exploration" of a suspect's outer clothing for weapons. 392 U.S. at 16.

2. A short explanation of the rule(s) of law:

> *Terry* authorizes a "careful exploration" of a suspect's outer clothing for weapons. 392 U.S. at 16. Officer Rose's brief and limited touching of the pocket of respondent's jacket was an appropriate part of the "careful" examination permitted under *Terry.* Officer Rose did not engage in the sort of prolonged and intrusive manipulation of clothing about which the state supreme court expressed concern. Nor does the record support the suggestion of the state supreme court that Rose made a discrete, conscious decision to continue handling the object in respondent's pocket after concluding that the object was not a weapon. Instead, the officer's act of feeling the object was merely a continuation of a pat-down search indisputably justified at its inception.

3. The legal conclusion:

> For that reason the officer's actions are distinguishable from the conduct found to constitute a separate, unauthorized search in *Arizona v. Hicks,* 480 U.S. 321 (1987).

II. The Minnesota Supreme Court also erred in holding that the sense of touch can never provide probable cause to believe that the object felt is contraband. This Court has recognized that probable cause can be acquired through senses other than the sense of sight. For example, in *United States v. Johns,* 469 U.S. 478 (1985), the Court held that the "distinct odor of marijuana" provided probable cause to believe that the vehicles from which the odor emanated contained contraband. Moreover, this Court's decision in *Terry* is premised on the ability of police officers to detect concealed firearms by touching the outside of a suspect's clothing. Many lower federal courts have held that the sense of touch may provide probable cause to believe that an item is contraband. In holding to the contrary, the court below mistakenly relied on the differences it perceived between the sense of sight and the sense of touch. Those differences do not warrant a categorical prohibition of the use of the sense of touch to acquire probable cause.

This paragraph also follows a logical format. When examined, it may be separated into the same three components.

1. The client's legal issue:

> The Minnesota Supreme Court also erred in holding that the sense of touch can never provide probable cause to believe that the object felt is contraband.

2. A short explanation of the rule(s) of law:

> This Court has recognized that probable cause can be acquired through senses other than the sense of sight. For example, in *United States v. Johns,* 469 U.S. 478 (1985), the Court held that the "distinct odor of marijuana" provided probable cause to believe that the vehicles from which the odor emanated contained contraband. Moreover, this Court's decision in *Terry* is premised on the ability of police officers to detect concealed firearms by touching the outside of a suspect's clothing. Many lower federal courts have held that the sense of touch may provide probable cause to believe that an item is contraband. In holding to the contrary, the court below mistakenly relied on the differences it perceived between the sense of sight and the sense of touch.

3. The legal conclusion:

> Those differences do not warrant a categorical prohibition of the use of the sense of touch to acquire probable cause.

Paragraphs in General

An effective paragraph is a grouping of related sentences that flow logically and that address one idea. It should be clear to the reader why a certain sentence is in a certain paragraph. Good paragraph construction takes time and patience. For each sentence, the writer must ultimately answer the question: Why is *this sentence* in *this paragraph*?

Legal writing, in the Discussion section of a **predictive office memorandum**, or in the Argument section of a **persuasive document** written to convince a court, generally follows a pattern of legal (rule) explanation paragraphs, followed by legal application paragraphs. Put another way, the rules of law are set out and explained. The following paragraphs apply the rules of law to the client's situation. A final paragraph usually reaches a conclusion based on the legal explanation and legal application paragraphs. This organization allows the reader to easily follow the discussion or argument.

The following Argument was taken from a brief filed with the United States Supreme Court in *Illinois v. Caballes*, 543 U.S. 405 (2005). Margin notes are provided to point out various legal writing details, and to identify the overall structure of the Argument.

predictive office memorandum. A predictive memorandum predicts the outcome of a legal issue, based upon legal research and analysis. This document does not "take sides" or try to convince the reader to adopt a position.

persuasive document. A persuasive document is drafted to persuade the reader to adopt the writer's legal analysis of a specific legal problem. The audience for most persuasive documents is a court (judge).

ARGUMENT

I. The Fourth Amendment Does Not Require Reasonable Suspicion To Use A Drug-Detection Dog To Sniff The Exterior Of A Vehicle During A Traffic Stop Justified By Probable Cause.

We begin with a matter that the majority below did not address: the status of canine sniffs under the Fourth Amendment. Settled precedent holds that a sniff by a drug-detection dog, in and of itself, is not a search. Given this premise, it does not violate the Fourth Amendment to conduct a canine sniff on the exterior of a vehicle during a traffic stop justified by probable cause.

In *United States v. Place*, 462 U.S. 696 (1983), an officer subjected the defendant's luggage to a canine sniff. *Id.* at 698–699. The dog alerted to the luggage, which later was found to contain cocaine. *Id.* at 699. In considering defendant's challenge to his conviction, this Court noted that if a canine sniff were a Fourth Amendment search, then the seizure of the luggage "could not be justified on less than probable cause." *Id.* at 706. The Court concluded, however, that a sniff by a drug-detection dog is not a search:

> The Fourth Amendment protects people from unreasonable government intrusions into their legitimate expectations of privacy. . . . A 'canine sniff' by a well-trained narcotics detection dog, however, does not require opening the luggage. It does not expose non-contraband items that otherwise would remain hidden from public view, as does, for example, an officer's rummaging through the contents of the luggage. Thus, the manner in which information is obtained through this investigative technique is much less intrusive than a typical search. Moreover, the sniff discloses only the presence or absence of narcotics, a contraband item. Thus, despite the fact that the sniff tells the authorities something about the contents of the luggage, the information obtained is limited. This limited disclosure also ensures that the owner of the property is not subjected to the embarrassment and inconvenience entailed in less discriminate and more intrusive investigative methods.

Id. at 707. After stating that it was "aware of no other investigative procedure that is so limited both in the manner in which the information is obtained and in the content of the information revealed by the procedure," the Court held that a canine sniff in a public place "does not constitute a 'search' within the meaning of the Fourth Amendment." *Ibid.*

The Court has never questioned *Place's* holding that canine sniffs are not searches. *See Soldal v. Cook County, Illinois*, 506 U.S. 56, 63 (1992) (noting that *Place* held "that subjecting luggage to a 'dog sniff' did not constitute a search for Fourth Amendment purposes because it did not compromise any privacy interest"); *United States v. Jacobsen*, 466 U.S. 109, 123–124 (1984) (same); *see also Kyllo v. United States*, 533 U.S. 27, 47 (2001) (Stevens, J., dissenting) ("in [*Place*], we held that a dog sniff that discloses only the presence or absence of narcotics does not constitute a search within the meaning of the Fourth Amendment") (internal quotations and citations omitted); *Bond v. United States*, 529 U.S. 334, 341 (2000) (Breyer, J., dissenting) (noting "the accepted police practice of using dogs to sniff for drugs hidden inside luggage").

In *City of Indianapolis v. Edmond*, 531 U.S. 32 (2000), the Court expressly reaffirmed *Place* with respect to canine sniffs of the exterior of a vehicle. *Edmond* considered a challenge to a drug-interdiction checkpoint where vehicles were subjected to a sniff by a drug-detection dog. The Court concluded that the checkpoint violated the Fourth Amendment because it was suspicionless and undertaken for an improper primary purpose. *Id.* at 41–44; *see also Illinois v. Lidster*, 540 U.S.———, 124 S. Ct. 885, 888 (2004) ("*Edmond* involved a checkpoint at which the police stopped vehicles to look for evidence of drug crimes committed by occupants of those vehicles.")

In so ruling, however, *Edmond* reaffirmed *Place's* holding that use of a drug-detection dog to sniff the exterior of a vehicle is not a Fourth Amendment search:

> It is well established that a vehicle stop at a highway checkpoint effectuates a seizure within the meaning of the Fourth Amendment. The fact that an officer walks a narcotics-detection dog around the exterior of each car at the Indianapolis checkpoints does not *transform* the seizure into a search. *See United States v. Place*, 462 U.S. 696, 707 (1983). Just as in *Place*, an exterior sniff of an automobile does not require entry into the car and is not designed to disclose any information other than the presence or absence of narcotics. Like the dog sniff in *Place*, a sniff by a dog that simply walks around a car is much less intrusive than a typical search. Rather, what principally [makes] these checkpoints [unlawful] is their primary purpose.

531 U.S. at 40 (emphasis added) (internal quotations and most citations omitted). Thus, the Fourth Amendment infirmity in *Edmond* was not that a dog sniff transformed a vehicular seizure into a search—the Court made clear that a sniff is not a search—but that the vehicles had been improperly seized in the first place. *Id.* at 40–44.

Because a sniff by a drug-detection dog is not a search, the Illinois Supreme Court erred in holding that reasonable suspicion is required to conduct a sniff of a vehicle already detained on probable cause that a traffic violation occurred. The reason is rooted in long-settled Fourth Amendment doctrine: When police officers, positioned at a lawful vantage point, discover incriminating facts without conducting an additional search or seizure, the discovery causes no intrusion on privacy or security and therefore does not violate the Fourth Amendment. *See Minnesota v. Dickerson*, 508 U.S. 366, 374–375 (1993); *Horton v. California*, 496 U.S. 128, 133 n.5, 141 (1990); *Arizona v. Hicks*, 480 U.S. 321, 325 (1987); *United States v. Hensley*, 469 U.S. 221, 235 (1985); *Michigan v. Long*, 463 U.S. 1032, 1050 (1983); *Illinois v. Andreas*, 463 U.S. 765, 771 (1983).

Thus, if Trooper Gillette, when requesting respondent's license and registration, had seen a bag of cocaine or a handgun on the passenger seat, that visual observation would not have been a search and therefore would not have violated the Fourth Amendment. *See Whren v. United States,* 517 U.S. 806, 808–809 (1996) (officer who pulled over vehicle for traffic violations observed bag of crack cocaine in driver's hands); *Hensley,* 469 U.S. at 224 (during investigatory stop of vehicle, officer observed butt of revolver protruding from underneath passenger's seat); *Long,* 463 U.S. at 1036 (during investigatory stop of vehicle, officer discovered bag of marijuana under arm rest). Likewise, if Trooper Graham, upon his arrival at the traffic stop, had smelled marijuana smoke coming from the passenger compartment or the scent of a corpse coming from the trunk, that olfactory observation would not have violated the Fourth Amendment. *See* 1 Wayne R. LaFave, Search and Seizure, § 2.2(a), at 403 (3d ed. 1996).

The same result obtains under the actual facts of this case. Because there was probable cause to stop respondent for speeding, Troopers Gillette and Graham were entitled to detain and approach respondent's car. The marijuana odors that caused the drug-detection dog to alert were present in the air surrounding the car. Respondent had no legitimate expectation of privacy in the air surrounding his car. *See New York v. Class,* 475 U.S. 106, 114 (1986) ("The exterior of a car, of course, is thrust into the public eye, and thus to examine it does not constitute a 'search.'"). He certainly had no legitimate expectation of privacy in the marijuana odors outside of his car. *See Jacobsen,* 466 U.S. at 123 ("[a] chemical test that merely discloses whether or not a particular substance is cocaine does not compromise any legitimate interest in privacy"); *Place,* 462 U.S. at 707. Thus, the canine sniff of respondent's car entailed no intrusion—more specifically, no intrusion beyond that already effected by its lawful seizure—on respondent's legitimate privacy and possessory interests. *See Dickerson,* 508 U.S. at 375–376. For that reason, the sniff did not violate the Fourth Amendment.

Two considerations might be advanced to support a contrary result, but neither has merit. The first consideration is that Trooper Graham used a dog, rather than his own faculties, to detect the odor of marijuana outside respondent's car. This consideration could not be squared with *Edmond* and *Place,* which held, respectively, that "an exterior sniff of an automobile . . . is not designed to disclose any information other than the presence or absence of narcotics," 531 U.S. at 40, and that a canine sniff "disclosing only the presence or absence of narcotics, a contraband item," invades no legitimate privacy interest, 462 U.S. at 707. *See also Jacobsen,* 466 U.S. at 123–124. Thus, it is of no Fourth Amendment moment that Trooper Graham used a dog's superior sense of smell, rather *than his own, to detect the odor of marijuana outside of respondent's vehicle. Compare Kyllo,* 533 U.S. at 38 (use of thermal imaging device "might disclose" intimate details of the home, such as "at what hour each night the lady of the house takes her daily sauna and bath").

It might also be argued that the sniff was unlawful because the dog's arrival at respondent's traffic stop was not inadvertent. *See* Pet. App. 4a ("In *Cox,* we concluded that evidence obtained by a canine sniff was properly suppressed because calling in a canine unit unjustifiably broadened the scope of an otherwise routine traffic stop into a drug investigation.") (citing *Cox,* 202 Ill. 2d at 469, 471, 782 N.E.2d at 280–281). Such a consideration could not be squared with *Horton v. California, supra.* In *Horton,* a police officer searched the defendant's home pursuant to a warrant; the warrant authorized a search for rings stolen during an armed robbery, but not for the weapons used in the robbery. 496 U.S. at 130–131. While conducting the search, the officer discovered the weapons in plain view. *Id.* at 131.

The defendant argued that the weapons should have been suppressed because the officer wanted to discover them. This Court disagreed, holding that the Fourth Amendment imposes no "inadvertence" requirement where the police discover incriminating evidence from a lawful vantage point without effecting any additional intrusion on the defendant's legitimate privacy interests. *Id.* at 141–142. Under *Horton*, it does not matter under the Fourth Amendment that Trooper Graham and his dog did not inadvertently stumble upon the scene of respondent's traffic stop.

For these reasons, conducting a canine sniff during the course of respondent's traffic stop did not violate the Fourth Amendment. The Illinois Supreme Court's contrary ruling should be reversed.

A Point to Remember

While drafting, try not to slow yourself down worrying about small writing errors. Get your ideas on the screen or page. You must allow time to go back and edit your work. Sometimes valuable ideas are lost because we try to make our first draft absolutely perfect. Draft the document. Go back to edit and proofread.

The Role of Topic Sentences

topic sentence. A topic sentence introduces the issues or subissues and connects back to the thesis paragraph.

Most paragraphs begin with a special type of sentence, a **topic sentence.** A good topic sentence introduces issues or subissues and connects back to the thesis paragraph. It creates unity within the paragraph by summarizing the point made in the paragraph. It forces the writer to articulate clearly. Its function is to set forth the relationship at the very beginning of the paragraph.

Take a look at how the topic sentences work in the Argument from the *Caballes* case. As you read, ask yourself if these sentences provide a good road map for the reader.

ARGUMENT

The Fourth Amendment Does Not Require Reasonable Suspicion To Use A Drug-Detection Dog To Sniff The Exterior Of A Vehicle During A Traffic Stop Justified By Probable Cause. [point heading]

1. We begin with a matter that the majority below did not address: the status of canine sniffs under the Fourth Amendment.
2. In *United States v. Place*, 462 U.S. 696 (1983), an officer subjected the defendant's luggage to a canine sniff.
3. The Court has never questioned *Place's* holding that canine sniffs are not searches.
4. In *City of Indianapolis v. Edmond*, 531 U.S. 32 (2000), the Court expressly reaffirmed *Place* with respect to canine sniffs of the exterior of a vehicle.
5. In so ruling, however, *Edmond* reaffirmed *Place's* holding that use of a drug-detection dog to sniff the exterior of a vehicle is not a Fourth Amendment search:

   It is well established that a vehicle stop at a highway checkpoint effectuates a seizure within the meaning of the Fourth Amendment. The fact that an officer walks a narcotics-detection dog around the exterior of each car at the Indianapolis checkpoints does not transform the seizure into a search. *See United States v. Place*, 462 U.S. 696, 707 (1983). Just as in *Place*, an exterior sniff of an automobile does not require entry into the car and is not designed to disclose any information other than the presence or absence of narcotics. Like the dog sniff in *Place*, a sniff by a dog that simply walks around a car is much less intrusive than a typical search. Rather, what principally [makes] these checkpoints [unlawful] is their primary purpose.

6. Because a sniff by a drug-detection dog is not a search, the Illinois Supreme Court erred in holding that reasonable suspicion is required to conduct a sniff of a vehicle already detained on probable cause that a traffic violation occurred.
7. Thus, if Trooper Gillette, when requesting respondent's license and registration, had seen a bag of cocaine or a handgun on the passenger seat, that visual observation would not have been a search and therefore would not have violated the Fourth Amendment.
8. The same result obtains under the actual facts of this case.
9. Two considerations might be advanced to support a contrary result, but neither has merit.
10. It might also be argued that the sniff was unlawful because the dog's arrival at respondent's traffic stop was not inadvertent.
11. For these reasons, conducting a canine sniff during the course of respondent's traffic stop did not violate the Fourth Amendment.

The reader of this document should notice that the author (the advocate) opens with the issue, follows with the legal explanation paragraphs, then uses the rules of law in the legal application paragraphs, and ultimately reaches a conclusion. This is one way for you to test your documents. When you pull out the topic sentences, they should provide a logical road map to your legal conclusions.

A Point to Remember

Topic sentences may be added after the paragraph is drafted in rough format. If you find that writing good topic sentences slows you down or even stops the flow of your writing, add them during the revision process.

In general avoid placing a citation in the topic sentence. Readers are distracted by citations, and may miss the actual emphasis of the sentence.

During the revision process, make an outline using only the first sentences, the topic and transition sentences of each paragraph. Review this outline; does it flow? Can you easily follow the information? Topic sentences are a good way to check the internal organization of most legal documents.

These are the topic sentences from the two paragraphs taken from one of the briefs filed in the *Minnesota v. Dickerson* case.

The Minnesota Supreme Court erred in holding that the police officer who searched respondent exceeded the scope of the protective pat-down search authorized under *Terry v. Ohio.*

> The Minnesota Supreme Court also erred in holding that the sense of touch can never provide probable cause to believe that the object felt is contraband.

Both sentences introduce the topic of the paragraph. Each topic sentence is clear and concise.

Construction of a Well-Written Paragraph

Consider the type of analysis to be used in the paragraph before drafting the body of the paragraph. A good paragraph does not assume too much knowledge on the reader's part; it is self-explanatory. Various analytical tools are available to the legal writer. A well-constructed paragraph may use a chronological narration of the facts, or comparison and contrast, or cause and effect to present the information.

The following paragraphs are from the *Minnesota v. Dickerson* decision. Notice the Court's use of detail and simple chronology. Each paragraph opens with a simple topic sentence that sets the scene for the information in the remainder of the paragraph.

> On the evening of November 9, 1989, two Minneapolis police officers were patrolling an area on the city's north side in a marked squad car. At about 8:15 p.m., one of the officers observed respondent leaving a 12-unit apartment building on Morgan Avenue North. The officer, having previously responded to complaints of drug sales in the building's hallways and having executed several search warrants on the premises, considered the building to be a notorious "crack house." According to testimony credited by the trial court, respondent began walking toward the police but, upon spotting the squad car and making eye contact with one of the officers, abruptly halted and began walking in the opposite direction. His suspicion aroused, this officer watched as respondent turned and entered an alley on the other side of the apartment building. Based upon respondent's seemingly evasive actions and the fact that he had just left a building known for cocaine traffic, the officers decided to stop respondent and investigate further.

> The officers pulled their squad car into the alley and ordered respondent to stop and submit to a pat-down search. The search revealed no weapons, but the officer conducting the search did take an interest in a small lump in respondent's nylon jacket. The officer later testified: "As I pat-searched the front of his body, I felt a lump, a small lump, in the front pocket. I examined it with my fingers and it slid and it felt to be a lump of crack cocaine in cellophane." The officer then reached into repsondent's pocket and retrieved a small plastic bag containing one-fifth of one gram of crack cocaine. Respondent was arrested and charged in Hennepin County District Court with possession of a controlled substance.

These paragraphs work because they are well planned. These paragraphs are part of a United States Supreme Court opinion. The Court sets the scene for the reader.

11-4 SENTENCES

Sentences are groups of words expressing a complete thought. This grouping of words must have a noun and a verb. In legal writing, it is best to keep your sentences short and direct. A concise, well-thought-out sentence is easy to read and understand. Long convoluted sentences are hard to follow and may actually present unwanted ambiguities.

We can learn from case law and statutes, but using their organization and general format may not be the best approcah for the legal researcher who is writing to inform (predict) or convince (persuade).

A Point to Remember

Students are sometimes confused by what might be called the legal "Do as I say, not as I do" approach. The study of law involves reading law, often case law, rather than summaries, discussions, explanations, and factual characterizations written for the court or for clients by legal professionals. Courts structure case opinions to inform or instruct the legal community. Legislatures create statutes to inform all of us as to the status of the law. Statutes are often very long and written in a complex format. This is not a signal to you that you should write in this fashion. Similarly, case opinions may not always offer great examples of clear and concise legal writing.

Use Topic Sentences

The topic sentence is the writer's initial tool. Even thesis paragraphs need topic sentences. Some sentences serve as transitions from one topic to another or one paragraph to another.

Use Active Voice

Use **active voice** whenever possible. Sentences written in active voice usually follow this pattern of construction: subject–verb–object. In other words, open with the actor, move to the action, and then on to the object of the action. These active voice sentences are very easy to read because they open with a specific actor who then does something to someone.

active voice. Active voice is a tool used by writers to shorten sentences. A sentence written in active voice uses the simple subject–verb–object approach.

Examples:

Active voice: She soon regretted her actions.

Passive voice: It was not long before her actions made her sorry that she had done what she had.

Active voice: Victor kicked the ball.

Passive voice: The ball was kicked by Victor.

Active voice: Susan drove the vehicle.

Passive voice: The vehicle was driven by Susan.

Notice that the active voice sentences are shorter than the passive voice sentences. Check for passive voice while you edit your writing. If you think about it while you are drafting, it will slow you down and you may even lose your thoughts. Most word-processing grammar-check programs help with identifying and correcting passive voice. Notice that the passive voice sentences use too many words. When we edit for passive voice, we also edit out extra words.

Avoid Noise Words

Most sentences contain two types of words—words of "value" and "noise" words. Grammatically correct sentences contain both types of words. The key is to use very few noise words. The noise words help to hold the sentence together, but they add little to the meaning of the sentence. Editing for noise words is easy. First, count the number of words in the sentence. Second, count the number of noise words. Third, subtract the number of noise words from the total number of words. That provides you with the number of "value" words. These words are the factually and legally relevant words. Strive to create a much larger proportion of value, factually, and legally relevant words.

Examples:

Poor: A <u>motion</u> to <u>suppress</u> the <u>confession</u> was <u>brought</u> <u>by</u> the <u>defendant</u>.
[There are eleven words in this sentence. The value words are underlined. This sentence has six value words and five noise words.]

Better: The <u>defendant</u> <u>moved</u> to <u>suppress</u> the <u>confession</u>.
[There are seven words in this sentence. There are four value words, they are underlined. The noise words are reduced to three. The entire sentence is shortened by four words. This is a better sentence.]

Use Front-Loaded Sentences

A front-loaded sentence places the important information at the beginning of the sentence. The best practice is to (1) open a sentence with the actor of the sentence, (2) move to the action, and (3) then move to the object. The "better" sentence above is crafted in this fashion.

The defendant moved to suppress the confession.
↓   ↑   ↓
[actor]   [action]   [object]

Notice that the "poor" sentence above is out of order, it does not follow the logical actor first, action second, and object third approach. Good sentence structure is easy for a reader to follow.

11-5 KEEP LEGAL WRITING SIMPLE

Use Short Sentences

Keep sentences short. Use twenty-five words or less as the benchmark of an easily readable sentence. Long sentences become hard to read or even unreadable. As you review your written work, look for sentences that are longer than three lines. Edit these; in most cases they are too long for your reader to easily follow. Editing may involve cutting the sentence down in size or rewriting it as more than one sentence.

A Point to Remember

Your legal writing is not meant to entertain the reader, but rather to inform or convince. Many of the tools writers of fiction use to entertain—for example, varying sentence length, creative use of adjectives, and unnecessary words—must be avoided in legal writing. You are writing with a very specific purpose. Stay focused on the purpose of the document and the ultimate audience.

Avoid Unnecessary Words

Keep your legal writing simple. Get to the point, rather than introduce the point. Over the years, somewhere in an English course, we were told to introduce the topic.

So we learned to open our sentences with a phrase intended to tell the reader what we were about to do. Edit those phrases and words out of your legal writing. If an introductory phrase adds nothing to the meaning of the sentence, delete it.

Examples:

Poor: "Over the years many courts have held that the Fourth Amendment provides protection. . . ."

Better: "The Fourth Amendment provides protection. . . ."

The citations that follow this sentence will show the case precedent for this statement. Extra words are not helpful to open the sentence. In the "poor" sentence above, the reader must trudge through nine words before anything of value is presented. Get to your point, and do it quickly. Readers lose patience with writers who submerge good ideas inside long, poorly worded sentences.

Use Specific, Concrete Terms

The use of specific terminology is essential. Ambiguity arises when vague words invade legal writing. Be as specific as the facts of your situation allow. Use the most important facts to tell a clear story about people. For example, if it was "cold," tell the reader how cold. If the tree was "big," tell the reader it was 50 feet high. If the officer "demanded" something, do not say he "asked" for something. In the examples below, if the writer is describing an accident from the plaintiff's position, the first sentence is poor. However, if the accident is described from the defendant's point of view, the first sentence may be the better choice. Point of view makes a difference.

Examples:

Poor: The defendant's truck moved into the right lane hitting plaintiff's car.

Better: The defendant unexpectedly swerved his Chevrolet Tahoe into plaintiff's lane, seriously injuring the plaintiff and demolishing plaintiff's Ford Prius.

11-6 PREDICTIVE WRITING

"Predictive writing" is a fancy reference to writing that predicts a legal outcome. The drafter remains neutral; there is no attempt to "persuade" the reader. The strength or soundness of the rules of law and the application of those rules to a client's situation provides guidance for the reader. These documents are typically drafted in one of several formats, whichever format you choose, the general information is the same.

A simple predictive memorandum may contain the following **point headings:**

Facts: short statement of the most relevant facts

Issues: legal question arising from the facts

Brief Answer: simple, direct answer to the legal question (prediction)

Discussion: analysis of the relevant law to the facts

The IRAC method involves a document with four sections.

Issue: the legal question presented by the facts

Rule: the rules of law (constitution, statutes, rules/regulations, and case law)

Analysis: the explanation of the rules of law and the application of the rules to the client's facts

Conclusion: the logical outcome based upon the law used to analyze the facts (prediction)

point headings. Point headings provide the reader with a road map of the document. Use them to make a point you want to stress for the reader.

The CRAC method also involves a document with four sections.

Conclusion: this method opens with the legal conclusion (often stated in terms of the legal issue)

Rule: the rules of law (constitution, statutes, rules/regulations, and case law)

Analysis: the explanation of the rules of law and the application of the rules to the client's facts

Conclusion: the logical outcome based upon the law used to analyze the facts (prediction)

A predictive memorandum follows here:

Facts

Our client, the Town of Grand View, approved the Jones' application for site development and building permits. Throughout construction of the Jones' home, the Town's only building inspector, David Williams, inspected the Jones' property. Williams' duty was to ensure construction complied with building codes. Williams initialed the Jones' project inspection card, indicating the home's electrical wiring passed inspection. Construction was completed and Williams issued a certificate of occupancy.

The Jones' home caught on fire. The Central Fire District's investigation revealed that the fire started in the home's circuit box, and that the electrical wiring failed to meet building codes. The fire caused over $250,000 in property damage. The Jones' also suffered personal injuries, with medical treatment exceeding $350,000.

The Jones' believe that in response to two letters they sent to the Town manager, complaining about Williams, that Williams acted with corruption or malice in misrepresenting the electric wiring. The first letter complained that Williams failed to appear for four inspections. The second letter complained that Williams failed to appear on time for three more inspections, and that he acted rudely toward the Jones'. The Jones' seek compensation for property damages and personal injuries.

Questions Presented

Is the Town of Grand View immune from liability under Cal. Gov. Code Section 818.8 for misrepresentations made by a public employee?

Is the Town's building inspector, Williams, immune from liability for misrepresentation under Cal. Gov. Code Section 822.2 when Williams: (1) made several inspections of the Jones' property, (2) initialed the Jones' inspection card indicating the home's electrical wiring passed inspection, (3) issued a certificate of occupancy, (4) failed to appear on time for seven inspections, and (5) acted rudely toward the Jones'?

Brief Answer

The Town of Grand View is probably immune from liability. Generally, a public entity is not liable for injury resulting from misrepresentations by public employees.

In addition, Williams is probably immune from liability. A public employee is generally immune from liability for his own misrepresentation, unless he or she also acted with corruption, or actual malice. On Williams' facts, a court would almost certainly hold that he committed negligent misrepresentation when he misrepresented the condition of the electrical wiring. However, the court would probably hold that the evidence is insufficient to show Williams acted with corruption or actual malice. The evidence shows that subsequent to the Jones' first letter complaining about Williams, Williams acted rudely toward the Jones, failed to arrive on time to inspections, and misrepresented the safety of the electrical wiring. However, no evidence indicates Williams knew of the letters. Therefore, because evidence of malice is probably insufficient, Williams would probably be immune from liability for misrepresentation.

Discussion

Issue I: The court will almost certainly hold the Town of Grand View immune from liability for Williams' misrepresentation.

California Government Code Section 818.8 provides a governmental entity with immunity from liability for an injury resulting from misrepresentation by an employee. "A public entity is not liable for an injury caused by misrepresentation by an employee of the public entity, whether or not such misrepresentation be negligent or intentional." Cal. Gov. Code § 818.8 (West 20XX). Section 818.8 provides a public entity with immunity from liability for an employee's misrepresentations which result in an interference with a person's financial interests. *Tokeshi v. State*, 217 Cal. App. 3d 999 (1990). In *Tokeshi*, a state employee, instructed plaintiff, Tokeshi, to spray pesticide on his crop. Later, Tokeshi was prohibited from selling his crop due to excess pesticide. The court stated, "'misrepresentation,' . . . applies to interferences with financial . . . interests. The Legislature designed Section 818.8 to exempt the governmental entity from this type of liability." *Id.* at 1005 citing *Johnson v. State of California*, 69 Cal. 2d 782, 800 (1968). The court found "plaintiffs' alleged losses are commercial in scope, and therefore the defendants are shielded from liability under the immunity statutes." *Id.* at 801.

The Town of Grand View's case is similar to *Tokeshi* because courts have held that a home is a financial interest. *See Harshbarger v. City of Colton*, 197 Cal. App. 3d 1335 (1998). In *Harshbarger*, "homeowners sued . . . after they had to reconstruct their residence because city inspectors allegedly misrepresented and suppressed facts concerning the structure's compliance with the building code." *Tokeshi*, 217 Cal. App. 3d at 1007. The court determined that "misrepresentation immunity barred the action against the public entity because the injury resulted from an interference with the homeowners' financial concerns." *Harshbarger*, 197 Cal. App. 3d at 1342, *quoted in Tokeshi*, 217 Cal. App. 3d at 1007. Similarly, in the Town of Grand View's case, the injuries also resulted from a city inspector who misrepresented a home's compliance with building codes.

Therefore, since the Jones' personal and financial injuries resulted from the fire caused by Williams' misrepresentation about the Jones' home, a financial interest, the Town of Grand View will almost certainly be immune from liability.

Issue II: The court will probably hold that Williams is immune from liability for misrepresentation.

California Government Code Section 822.2 provides a public employee with limited immunity from liability for his own misrepresentation. "A public employee acting in the scope of his employment is not liable for an injury caused by his misrepresentation be negligent or intentional, unless he is guilty of actual fraud, corruption or actual malice." Cal. Gov. Code § 822.2 (West 20XX). Courts have interpreted Section 822.2 as having three requirements. First, "misrepresentation" was interpreted in the *Schonfeld* case to mean common law deceit. *Schonfeld v. City of Vallejo*, 50 Cal. App. 3d 401, 408 (1975). Second, *Schonfeld* held that where "a plaintiff saw . . . the property as to which the alleged misrepresentations were made . . . he must establish that he was justified in . . . relying on the other party. . . ." *Schonfeld*, 50 Cal. App. 3d at 412. Third, courts have interpreted "actual fraud" and "actual malice" as "a conscious intent to deceive, vex, annoy or harm the injured party in his business." *Id.* at 401. Therefore, a public employee is not immune from liability for misrepresentation if the following conditions are satisfied:

1. the employee is guilty of common law deceit; and
2. the plaintiff is justified in relying on the employee; and
3. the employee is motivated by corruption, or actual malice.

See id. at 410–412.

> **A. Williams probably committed common law deceit. When Williams initialed the inspection card he misrepresented the safety of the electrical wiring. Courts have held that negligent misrepresentation is a type of common law deceit.**

The court in *Schonfeld* lists four kinds of common law deceit, including negligent misrepresentation. *See id.* at 408. Negligent misrepresentation is, "[t]he assertion, as a fact, of that which is not true, by one who has no reasonable ground for believing it to be true." Ca. Civ. Code, § 1572, subd. 2.

In the Town of Grand View's case, no facts establish Williams knew the electric wiring was unsafe; however, the facts probably establish that Williams committed negligent misrepresentation. As the Town's sole building inspector, Williams had a duty to ensure that construction of the Jones' home complied with all building codes. Furthermore, Williams signed-off on the project's inspection card, indicating that the home's wiring complied with building codes. However, after the fire, the Central Fire District's investigation revealed that the fire started in the main circuit box, which failed to meet any known building codes. Therefore, the court will almost certainly hold that Williams had "no reasonable grounds for believing . . . [the electrical wiring was safe] to be true." Ca. Civ. Code, section 1572, subd. 2, *quoted in Schonfeld*, 50 Cal. App. 3d at 409. This fulfills the requirements for negligent misrepresentation.

> **B. The Jones' were almost certainly justified in relying on Williams' representations. Williams was the Town's sole building inspector and certified that the Jones' home complied with building codes. Courts have held that a person is justified in relying on the representations of a government employee who holds himself or herself out as an expert.**

The court in *Schonfeld* held that where "a plaintiff saw . . . the property as to which the . . . misrepresentations were made . . . he must establish that he . . . was justified in not making an inspection or in relying on the other party. . . ." *Id.* at 412.

In *Schonfeld*, plaintiff, Schonfeld, invested in a marina after the city manager made representations about the marina's quality. Specifically, one alleged misrepresentation was that the marina was "a first class harbor" and "the best berthing facility in Northern California." *Id.* at 413. The court stated, "[t]he city manager did not hold himself out as an expert on marinas but indicated that the marina was completed according to the city's plans. . . ." *Id.* The court found that the plaintiff was not justified in relying on the city manager's representations and that the city manager did not commit misrepresentation.

The Town of Grand View's case differs from *Schonfeld.* Williams, the Town's sole building inspector, was supposed to ensure that the Jones' home complied with building codes. In addition, he inspected the Jones' home, initialed the inspection card indicating the electric wiring passed inspection, and issued the certificate of occupancy. Unlike *Schonfeld,* the facts indicate that Williams appears to have held himself out to be an expert in building inspections. Therefore, the court will almost certainly hold that because Williams held himself out to be an expert in building inspections that the Jones' were justified in relying on his representations.

> **C. The evidence is probably insufficient to indicate Williams was motivated by corruption, or actual malice. Although the Jones' letters indicate that Williams acted rudely after the first letter, no evidence indicates Williams knew about the letters.**

In *Schonfeld* the court states, "section 822.2 applies unless, . . . a public employee is motivated by corruption or actual malice. . . ." *Id.* at 411. In *Schonfeld,* plaintiff, Schonfeld, alleged that the city manager misrepresented the city's title to the marina. The court held, "there was no evidence from which it could be inferred that the city manager made any representations with the actual malice as required by the statute." *Id.* at 416. This differs from the City of Grand View's case. The Jones' first letter did not complain that Williams acted rudely; however, the second letter did. This may indicate that Williams was angry about the first letter, and in response acted rudely toward the Jones'. From Williams' conduct, a court may infer that Williams' misrepresentation was in response to the Jones' letters.

On the other hand, no evidence indicates Williams knew about the letters. If Williams knew about the letters, it is important to find out whether he learned about them before misrepresenting the electric wiring. Additionally, knowing if Williams was rude before the first letter could establish that he was not acting rudely in response to the letters, and that the misrepresentation was not in response to the letters.

Therefore, the court will probably hold the evidence is insufficient to infer Williams acted with malicious intent or corruption. Since Section 822.2 provides immunity for misrepresentation without corruption or malicious intent, Williams will probably be immune from liability.

11-7 PERSUASIVE WRITING

Some documents must be persuasive. That is, the document is written so that the reader is persuaded to adopt the writer's point of view. Examples of such documents are trial briefs, points and authorities in support of motions, declarations, and demand letters. In persuasive writing, every word, phrase, and sentence must be carefully drafted. The writer must consider the impact the document will have on the reader. This goes beyond informative writing.

Set forth below are excerpts from briefs filed with the United States Supreme Court in the *Minnesota v. Dickerson* case.

This excerpt is from the opening argument section of the Brief for the United States as Amicus Curiae Supporting Petitioner.

ARGUMENT

I. OFFICER ROSE WAS CONDUCTING A LAWFUL PAT-DOWN SEARCH WHEN HE ACQUIRED PROBABLE CAUSE TO BELIEVE THAT RESPONDENT POSSESSED CONTRABAND.

The Minnesota Supreme Court not only declined as a general matter to recognize a "plain feel" corollary to the "plain view" doctrine; it also held that the crack seized from respondent's pocket would not be admissible under a "plain feel" analysis in any event. The latter holding was based on the court's view that, in the course of determining that the object in respondent's pocket was crack, Officer Rose exceeded the scope of the protective pat-down search authorized under *Terry v. Ohio*. To the contrary, we submit that Officer Rose was acting within the scope of *Terry* when he developed probable cause to believe that respondent was in possession of contraband.

At the outset, we agree with the premise underlying the state court's *Terry* holding: a "plain feel" corollary to the "plain view" doctrine would not authorize a police officer to seize evidence without a warrant if the police officer violated the Fourth Amendment in the course of developing probable cause to support the seizure. An "essential predicate" of a seizure based on "plain feel," like one based on "plain view," is that "the officer did not violate the Fourth Amendment in arriving at the place from which the evidence could be plainly [felt]." *Horton v. California* 469 U.S. 128, 136 (1990). Thus, if a police officer reaches into a suspect's pocket without reasonable suspicion or probable cause and feels an object that the officer knows to be contraband, the seizure of that object cannot be justified on the ground that the seizure was the product of a "plain feel" of the object. In *Sibron v. New York*, 392 U.S. 40, 65 (1968), this Court held that such an intrusion was unlawful, because the intrusion was not justified by reasonable suspicion or probable cause to believe that the suspect had contraband or a weapon in his pocket. The Court therefore ordered suppression of the contraband found in the course of that search.

Officer Rose's conduct, however, was a far cry from the sort of intrusion held to violate the Fourth Amendment in *Sibron*. This was not a case of retroactively justifying a search by what it turned up; rather, because the pat-down search was lawful, the fruits of that search could be considered in determining the lawfulness of Officer Rose's further investigative steps.

This next excerpt is from the opening argument section of the Brief filed for the American Civil Liberties Union and the Minnesota Civil Liberties Union as Amici Curiae in Support of Respondent.

ARGUMENT

I. THE WARRANTLESS SEARCH OF RESPONDENT'S POCKET CONTRAVENED THE FOURTH AMENDMENT BY EXCEEDING THE SCOPE OF *TERRY*.

A. A *Terry* frisk is limited solely to a narrowly-tailored search for weapons.

In *Terry v. Ohio*, this Court set forth the standard governing pat-downs of temporarily detained suspects: an officer can only conduct a limited protective search for weapons (a "frisk") when there is "reason to believe that he is dealing with an armed and dangerous individual . . ." 392 U.S. at 27. Although subsequent cases have extended *Terry's* reach to other contexts, this Court has never deviated from the fundamental rule that a frisk is singularly limited to weapon searches, and thus cannot be conducted simply to locate contraband or evidence of crime.

These principles were reaffirmed in *Ybarra v. Illinois:* "The *Terry* case created an exception to the requirement of probable cause," an exception whose 'narrow scope' this Court 'has been careful to maintain.' Under that doctrine a law enforcement officer, for his own protection and safety, may conduct a pat-down to find weapons that he reasonably believes or suspects are then in the possession of the person he has accosted. . . . Nothing in *Terry* can be understood to allow a generalized "cursory search for weapons" or, indeed, any search whatever for anything but weapons.

Both briefs go on for many pages. Both are convincing. Compare and contrast these two opening arguments.

11-8 OVERVIEW OF THE EDITING AND REVISION PROCESS

1. Print the document. If time permits, let it sit for a day before you look at it again. Reread your instructions. Have you adequately responded to the initial questions?
2. Look over the document; do not read it, just glance through it.
3. Is the organization of the document readily apparent, without actually reading it? If not, go back and work in appropriate point headings.
4. Check to see that each paragraph contains a topic sentence or a sentence that serves as a transition from the previous paragraph.
5. Does the discussion or argument section begin with a thesis paragraph? If not, insert a thesis paragraph now.
6. Make sure each paragraph contains facts or law to support your position.
7. Identify the verbs. Highlight the following: *was, were, is, are, has been, have been, had been, becomes, became, went, did,* and *came.* Where possible, replace these with active verbs. Active verbs create a mental picture of a specific sensation, activity, or sound in the reader's imagination.
8. Place transition words or phrases between sentences and paragraphs where appropriate.
9. Reread the opening of your document. Does it clearly and concisely introduce the topic of your writing? If not, revise or rewrite.
10. Reread the conclusion. Does it clearly and concisely conclude your document? If not, edit or rewrite. When you complete the conclusion ask yourself if you have created a tone of finality.

Online Legal Research

Go to www.supremecourtpreview.org. This Web site is supported by the American Bar Association. It provides a great deal of useful information.

Go to http://press-pubs.uchicago.edu/garner/. This Web site provides excellent legal writing practice and guidance.

CITATION MATTERS

USE OF THE ELLIPSIS

THE BLUEBOOK—RULE 5.3

Legal writers often find it useful to use quoted language, but may not need all of the sentence or paragraph. The omission of a word or many words is indicated by inserting an ellipsis in place of the omitted word or words. An ellipsis consists of three periods separated by spaces and set off by a space before the first period and after the last period.

For example:

The "core of the judicial system . . . relies on early disclosure of all the facts."

Omission of words at the end of a quoted sentence is shown by an ellipsis between the last word of the quote and the final punctuation of the quoted sentence.

For example:

The "core of the judicial system . . . relies on early disclosure. . . ."

Never use an ellipsis to begin a quotation. When language at the beginning of a sentence is deleted, capitalize the first letter of the first word used and place it in brackets (unless that word is already capitalized).

For example:

"[T]he statute imposes special prohibitions on those speakers who express views on the disfavored subject of race, color, creed, religion or gender."

This is a simple way to alert the reader that the word *The* was not the first word in the quoted sentence. The use of brackets indicates that the writer only changed the case of the letter. This same tool (the bracket) is used to change a capital letter to lowercase when the writer needs to incorporate a phrase from the beginning of a quoted sentence into one of the writer's own sentences.

For example:

It is true that "[t]he ordinance, even as narrowly construed by the State Supreme Court, is facially unconstitutional. . . ."

In this example, *The* was the first word in the quoted sentence. But the writer needed to incorporate the quoted sentence into a new sentence. By placing the lowercase *t* in brackets, the writer signals the reader that he or she changed the case of the letter.

CHAPTER SUMMARY

Keep your legal writing clear and concise. Strive to communicate in a straightforward manner. Before you begin to write, go back and check your instructions; have you followed them? Have you responded to all of the questions? Are your answers clear and concise? Is your research accurate, current, and validated? Have you been thorough? Be sure you understand the parameters of your project. Good legal writing opens with a thesis paragraph. Good paragraphs open with topic sentences. The body of a good legal discussion or argument follows a pattern of rule of law explanation paragraphs followed by application of the law to the facts paragraphs. Use active voice when possible. Keep your sentences short and avoid the use of unnecessary words. Be specific and always edit your work before passing it along to anyone to review.

TERMS TO REMEMBER

thesis paragraph   persuasive document   active voice
predictive office   topic sentence   point headings
 memorandum

QUESTIONS FOR REVIEW

1. Why should a writer use the Overview of a Legal Research and Writing Project form set forth in Section 11-2?
2. Discuss the purpose and importance of a thesis paragraph.
3. How should a thesis paragraph be arranged?
4. What is the role of the topic sentence?
5. Why should you use active voice whenever possible?

BUILDING YOUR WRITING AND ANALYSIS SKILLS: ASSIGNMENTS AND EXERCISE

1. Compare and contrast the arguments set forth in the briefs filed with the United States Supreme Court in the *Minnesota v. Dickerson* case located in Section 11-6.
2. Write a factual summary of the Meyers grand jury testimony located in Appendix A.

BUILDING YOUR ONLINE RESEARCH SKILLS: ASSIGNMENTS AND EXERCISES

1. Locate the briefs filed in the *Kyllo* case [533 U.S. 27 (2001)]. How many briefs were filed? List each document filed and the party (or interested party) who filed the brief.
2. Read the Brief for the Petitioner in the *Kyllo* case. Locate one paragraph of at least four sentences. First, type the paragraph as it is in the original. Second, redraft the paragraph using shorter sentences and the other suggestions provided in this chapter.
3. Go to www.supremecourtpreview.org. Open "Merit Briefs." Choose a current case and read the Petitioner's and Respondent's briefs. Write a short summary of the facts of the case and the issues before the United States Supreme Court. Clearly cite the case you chose for your instructor.

CASE PROJECT

Review the same case you researched in previous chapters. Answer the questions found in Sections 11-1 and 11-2 of this chapter to determine if you are prepared to write, and if so, how you should proceed.

chapter 122

PREDICTIVE LEGAL WRITING: THE MEMORANDUM OF LAW

S KILL OBJECTIVES FOR CHAPTER 12

When you complete this chapter you should be able to

- Explain the purpose of a legal memorandum.
- Describe the format for a memorandum of law.
- Explain the components of a memorandum of law.
- Write a predictive office memorandum.
- Explain the purpose of each component of a memorandum of law.

FROM THE DESK OF W. J. BRYAN, ESQ.

TO: Research Assistant

We are still working on pretrial motions in the Meyers case. Your previous memoranda were very helpful. Now I need you to check on a different issue. As you recall from the facts (review the Grand Jury transcript), our client made several statements in the police car while being transported to jail. Please research the law regarding the admissibility of these statements. If we move to suppress the statements, what are our chances of winning?

12-1 INTRODUCTION

As a legal researcher, you understand the importance of locating the cases or codes that answer your legal questions. However, your job as a researcher is not complete until you communicate your findings in an appropriate manner. In earlier chapters you learned that legal research is performed for different reasons and the results are conveyed to different types of audiences. The result of your research may be conveyed to a layperson or an attorney in an *objective* manner. An objective evaluation or analysis of the case often includes a *prediction* of how a court might rule on the issues of the case. In other cases, it may be conveyed to an attorney or judge, not in an objective manner, but in an *argumentative* or *persuasive* fashion.

A research assistant does research for a supervising attorney that, initially, is communicated in an objective manner. Ultimately, the research may be used to form the basis of advice given to a client or to form the basis of a formal legal document sent to another attorney and to the court.

Documents conveying the results of legal research are known by various names. A **memorandum of law** is a document written in an objective manner where the researcher explains the law governing a specific situation. An **opinion letter** is formal correspondence from an attorney to a client or other attorney explaining an attorney's interpretation of the law as applied to a factual situation. Usually, it contains an objective evaluation of the law and the facts. A **memorandum of points and authorities** is a more formal document, filed with the court, and advocating the client's position. In such a document, the author attempts to persuade the court to follow an interpretation of the law that favors the author's client. A memorandum of points and authorities is often used to support or oppose a motion made in court

memorandum of law. An objectively written document where the researcher informs the reader of the law governing a specific situation.

opinion letter. Formal correspondence from an attorney to a client or other attorney explaining an attorney's interpretation of the law as applied to a factual situation.

memorandum of points and authorities. A formal document, written in an argumentative or persuasive manner, filed with the court, and advocating a certain position.

trial brief. A document filed with the court at the beginning of the trial in which the author is trying to persuade the trial judge to interpret the law in a way that is favorable to the author's client.

appellate brief. A document filed in support of or in opposition to an appeal, containing arguments related to legal errors that may have occurred at trial.

in connection with a civil or criminal case. A **trial brief** is a formal document, filed with the court at the beginning of the trial, in which the author tries to persuade the trial judge to interpret the law in a way that is favorable to the author's client. An **appellate brief** is a document filed in a court of appeal in support of or in opposition to an appeal. It contains arguments related to legal errors that may have occurred at trial. This chapter deals with writing in a predictive objective manner for attorneys and clients. The following chapter addresses persuasive documents.

12-2 MEMORANDUM OF LAW

A researcher's initial findings and analysis are often written in a document called a memorandum of law. This document is included in the client file and is relied upon by the author or by other attorneys. It may form the basis for advice to the client or it may serve as the starting point for drafting persuasive documents to be filed with the court. It is important that a memorandum of law be complete and thorough. A memorandum of law is often written by a research assistant, such as a law clerk or paralegal. (The term *memorandum of law* is most commonly used to describe this type of document, but not always. Lawyers sometimes call this a *memo*, a *legal memorandum*, or even an *interoffice memo*.) It is intended to inform the reader, usually an attorney, of the state of the law concerning a certain issue. It contains a legal analysis of the facts and the law and should contain *all* relevant law, even law that does not support your client's position. The analysis in this type of document should include all reasonable arguments and inferences that can be drawn from the law, whether they support your client or not. The researcher, however, often gives an opinion, a prediction, as to what law and what arguments seem to be the strongest. The opinion must be supported by relevant legal authority. Such a memorandum is sometimes referred to as a *predictive* memorandum because it strives to predict how a court will rule on the issue.

Attorneys who rely on research assistants depend a great deal on a memorandum of law. A properly researched and written memorandum saves an attorney a great deal of time. Instead of spending hours researching, reading, and analyzing cases and statutes, the attorney can read a memorandum of law summarizing and synthesizing relevant law. Because an attorney may rely exclusively on such a memorandum, it is essential that this document be complete and accurate.

A Point to Remember

If you rely on a memorandum of law found in an office file, always check the date that the memo was written. Many cases take years before they are completed; a memo found in a file might have been researched years ago. Remember that laws change; if any significant amount of time passed since the memo was written, you must validate and update the research.

Although a memorandum of law is not filed with the court, it may later form the basis of an opinion letter to a client, or a more formal legal memorandum or brief used to convince another attorney or the court of your client's legal position. Read Appendix D. See how the memoranda of law on pages 437 and 438 (in Appendix D) were used to prepare the formal memorandum of points and authorities.

12-3 FORMAT FOR A MEMORANDUM OF LAW

There are no absolute formalities for a memorandum of law, although most do follow similar formats. Because this document is likely to be included in a client file, it should contain basic information found in all office memoranda. It should identify the author of the document, the person for whom it is prepared, the date, and the subject matter. The subject matter must always identify the office client so that if the document is separated from the file, it can be properly identified. The beginning of a memorandum should look as follows.

MEMORANDUM OF LAW

To:

From:

Date:

Subject:

The memorandum itself should contain the following components: a concise statement of relevant facts, a statement of the issue(s) or question(s) forming the basis of the research, a discussion of the law and the facts and a conclusion. Each component part should be clearly labeled with a heading. For example, a basic template for a memorandum looks like this.

Facts

[State the relevant and explanatory facts. Review Chapter 3 for identifying and writing a concise statement of facts. Remember, you identified these facts before you started your research.]

Issue(s)

[List the legal questions or issues. If you are writing an objective memorandum of law, these questions were probably given to you by the supervising attorney. Refer to Chapter 2 for a review of writing issue statements.]

Discussion

[This is the most important part of the memorandum. In this section, you discuss each of the issues, present the authorities you found in your research, and explain or discuss why and how these authorities apply to your factual situation. In discussing your research, you should use the IRAC method. Review Chapters 4 and 6 on using the IRAC method with cases and statutes. Also, do not forget the basic writing techniques discussed in Chapter 11.]

Conclusion

[Although you give a conclusion to each issue you discuss, you may provide a general conclusion summarizing all of your main points. Sometimes, in lieu of a conclusion or in addition to a conclusion, a memorandum contains a section titled "Brief Answer." This is usually placed at the beginning of the memo, immediately following the statement of issues.]

Some attorneys prefer a slightly different order; consider the following

- **Issue**
- **Brief Answer** (This is similar to the conclusion.)
- **Facts**
- **Discussion**

12-4 PREPARING TO WRITE THE MEMORANDUM OF LAW

Whether you realize it or not, you begin preparing to write a memorandum of law the moment you analyze the factual dispute and identify the legal issues. (Recall how and why you do this from Chapter 2.) In doing legal research, you look for relevant law. Your determination that law is relevant requires you to analyze the law you find and determine if and how it applies to your factual situation. You should recall from earlier chapters that this analysis is really a part of the research process. The memorandum of law *communicates* your analysis to the reader in an organized and logical manner.

Prior to writing the "Discussion," it is imperative that you organize your ideas and findings. Making an outline is a good way to do this. An outline for your discussion in a memorandum of law should contain the main points and the law that support each point in some logical order. Within the memorandum, the main points are usually stated in the topic sentences for each of your paragraphs.

In preparing an outline, remember that legal analysis usually follows the IRAC rule. Any legal analysis requires that you first identify the **I**ssue or question. That is followed by the rules of law that apply. These **R**ules of law are found in cases, codes, and constitutions. You then **A**pply the law to your facts. Finally, you reach a **C**onclusion. One of the most important results of making an outline before you begin to write is that you are forced to organize your ideas. Sticking to your outline while you write forces you to stay organized. There are, of course, different ways to organize the discussion in a memorandum. The following suggestions provide some assistance, but remember, they are not the only ways to organize your ideas.

An outline of the research in the Town of Grand View memorandum in Chapter 11 might look like this:

FACTS

    Parties

        Town of Grand View—Defendant

        Mr. and Mrs. Jones (fire damage to home)—Plaintiffs

        Inspector Williams—Defendant and employee of Town of Grand View

    Issues

        Is Town immune from liability?   Probably.

        Is Inspector immune from liability?   Probably.

(continued)

Discussion

I. The court will probably hold the Town immune from liability

Cal. Gov. Code Section 818.8—provides gov. immunity from liability for an injury resulting from misrepresentation by an employee

Case law: *Tokesi v. State; Johnson v. California; Harshbarger v. City of Colton*

II. The court will probably hold that Inspector is immune from liability for misrepresentation

Cal. Gov. Code Section 822.2—provides a public employee with limited immunity from liability for his misrepresentations

Case law: *Schonfeld v. City of Vallejo*

A. William probably commited common law deceit.

Schonfeld and Cal. Civ. Code Section 1572

B. The Jones' were justified in relying on the Inspector's representations

Schonfeld

C. The evidence is insufficient to indicate the Inspector was motivated by corruption or actual malice

Cal. Gov. Code Section 822.2

Schonfeld

Organizing a Memorandum

The organization of a memorandum of law often depends on the type of legal authorities controlling your case.

Situations Controlled by Statutory Law

Probably the easiest memorandum to write is one where you are asked to analyze a factual situation and determine whether a particular code section controls the facts. Suppose you are asked to write a memorandum addressing the following question: Is an off-duty police officer who uses excessive force in making a traffic stop criminally responsible for his acts under the Federal Civil Rights Act?

A written memorandum answering this question is easily organized around the relevant code section, which provides the following:

Whoever, under color of any law, statute, ordinance, regulation, or custom, willfully subjects any person in any State, Territory, Commonwealth, Possession, or District to the deprivation of any rights, privileges, or immunities secured or protected by the Constitution or laws of the United States, or to different punishments, pains, or penalties, on account of such person being an alien, or by reason of his color, or race, than are prescribed for the punishment of citizens, shall be fined under this title or imprisoned not more than one year, or both; and if bodily injury results from the acts committed in violation of this section or if such acts include the use, attempted use, or threatened use of a dangerous weapon, explosive, or fire, shall be fined under this title or imprisoned not more than ten years, or both; and if death results from the acts committed in violation of this section or if such acts include kidnapping or an attempt to kidnap, aggravated sexual abuse or an attempt to commit aggravated sexual abuse, or an attempt to kill, shall be fined under this title, or imprisoned for any term of years or for life, or both, or may be sentenced to death. 18 U.S.C. § 242

In this situation, break down the relevant code section into the various elements and then discuss each separately. (Keep in mind that you have already done this type of analysis. As part of the research process, you analyzed the statute to determine if it applied. At this point, you are communicating this analysis in written form. Refer to Chapter 6.)

In the discussion section, you may need to refer to case law interpreting some or all of the elements of the code. In discussing these elements, you can arrange them in the same order that they appear in the code. Alternatively, you can first discuss elements that are fairly obvious and then discuss those that present problems and require a more detailed analysis.

One question that arises occasionally with this type of memorandum is whether you need to discuss every element of the code section. If the code section applies to your facts, then you do need to discuss each element (assuming, of course, that this is what you were asked to research). If, on the other hand, it is clear to you that the statute does *not* apply, you may only need to discuss those elements that make the statute inapplicable. For example, suppose that a defendant is a private security guard rather than a police officer. The Federal Civil Rights Act requires that one be "acting under color of law." Because a private security guard does not act under color of authority, the section is clearly not applicable and it would not be necessary to discuss all the other elements of the code section.

An outline of a memo to be written in this case might look as follows.

Sample Outline

I. Introduction
   A. A violation of 18 U.S.C. § 242 requires that a person acting under color of law willfully deprive another of a constitutional right or subject another to different punishments or penalties because of color or race.
   B. Facts indicate defendant's actions meet each of the elements.

II. Were Defendant's Actions Under Color of Law? *(This is a statement of the issue.)*
   A. 18 U.S.C. § 242 requires that action be under color of law. *(This is the rule of law.)*
   B. Defendant was in police uniform.
   C. Defendant was performing a regular police function—a traffic stop.
      (B. and C. constitute the analysis. Here you apply the facts to the language of the code.)

III. Was Defendant's Conduct Willful?
   A. Code requires that conduct be willful.
   B. Defendant's actions were intentional.

IV. Did Defendant Deprive Another of Constitutional Rights?
   A. Code requires a deprivation of constitutional rights.
   B. A traffic stop is a seizure under the Fourth Amendment to the U.S. Constitution.
   C. Defendant's actions, in particular his use of excessive force, were not reasonable as required by the Constitution.

V. Did Defendant Inflict Different Punishment Due to Color or Race?
   A. As an alternative to a deprivation of constitutional rights, a violation of 18 U.S.C. § 242 can be based on infliction of different punishments due to color or race.
   B. Defendant inflicted extraordinary injury or punishment to victim.
   C. Defendant's statements indicate racial bias.

VI. Conclusion

A Point to Remember

During the research process, if you take notes on index cards, using a separate card for each authority, you can arrange these cards according to your outline. Writing your memorandum is much easier.

Situations Controlled by Case Law

A legal memorandum based on a situation controlled entirely by case law is often more difficult to organize. The organization depends on the research question. One common research task is to determine whether a party has a certain **cause of action,** entitling that party to some sort of relief (most often money). A cause of action is a set of facts that the law recognizes as entitling a person to relief from the courts. Whether a cause of action exists or not is dependent on the substantive law. Like many code sections, causes of action can be broken down into elements that are almost always listed in relevant case law. Organizing this type of memorandum is very similar to organizing a memorandum based on statutory law. You begin by setting out the elements of the cause of action as described in case law. You then discuss each of the elements, bringing in additional case law where needed. If there are affirmative defenses, they must also be discussed. For example, consider the case described below, Victoria V. v. U Shop Mall.

cause of action. The basis upon which a lawsuit may be brought to the court.

In this case, the relevant law is the law of negligence. Assume that this situation is controlled by the law of the state of California and your research uncovered the case of *Ann M. v. Pacific Plaza*, found on page 312. In this opinion, the court states what must be shown for a cause of negligence to exist. The court states: "An action in negligence requires a showing that the defendant owed the plaintiff a legal duty, that the defendant breached the duty, and that the breach was a proximate or legal cause of injuries suffered by the plaintiff."

In organizing your research for the memorandum of law regarding the Victoria V. case, you could take each of the factors mentioned by the court and discuss them separately, either in the order listed by the court or in any other logical order. Before going on, read the *Ann M.* case found later in this chapter.

Victoria V. v. U Shop Mall

Victoria V. was sexually assaulted in the parking lot of U Shop Mall one evening about 9 p.m. When she entered the shopping center at 6:30 p.m. it was still light outside but Victoria knew that she would shop for several hours and it would probably be dark when she left. Therefore, she parked under a light. Unknown to her, the light was not working.

The shopping center also employs a security guard to patrol its two parking areas, one in front and one in back. It takes the security guard about 30 minutes to patrol each of these. Incidentally, the security guard reported that the parking light was out about 24 hours prior to the assault on Victoria. However, the shopping center did not have any replacement bulbs on hand. Records also indicate that in the past month (before the assault) there were three reports of cars being broken into and items stolen. There was also one report of a mugging of an elderly gentleman that took place in the parking area. Finally, a report of a sexual assault that took place in a shopping center about two miles away was received by the U Shop Mall about two weeks prior to the assault on Victoria. No sexual assault had ever been reported in the U Shop Mall or its parking lot.

Your law firm represents Victoria and wants to file a civil lawsuit against U Shop Mall for its negligence. You are asked to research whether such a claim has any merit.

The first part of an outline for your memorandum might look something like this.

Sample Outline

I. Introduction
   A. Any action by Victoria must be based on the tort of negligence.
   B. An action for negligence requires the existence of a legal duty, breach of the duty, and the proximate or legal cause of injuries.

II. Does a landowner have a duty to protect others from criminal attack by third parties?

   *(This is a statement of the **issue**. Note that it corresponds to the first element of the cause of action described in B above, i.e., the existence of a legal duty.)*

   A. Before a landowner owes a duty to protect a person from criminal attack, the harm must be foreseeable. This requires other similar incidents.

   (State the rule of law or holding from the Ann M. *case and from any other authorities that might relate to this issue. At this point, you give the proper cite for your authorities.)*

   B. Comparison of facts of *Ann M.* with the facts of Victoria V.

   *(This is the **analysis**. Because your authorities for this issue consist of case law, your analysis requires that you compare facts of the case law to facts of Victoria. Your outline should list the facts of* Ann M. *that you want to discuss with the facts of the Victoria V. case.)*

   C. Conclusion.

   (Discuss your conclusion on this issue. An objective memorandum may not reach a definitive answer to the issue or question. You might be summarizing the various possibilities.)

III. *(Continue with each element of the cause of action and any defenses that may exist.)*

CASE 12-1

Ann M. v. Pacific Plaza Shopping Center
6 Cal. 4th 666, 863 P.2d 207, 25 Cal.Rptr. 2d 137 (1993)

OPINION:

We granted review in this case to determine whether the scope of the duty owed by the owner of a shopping center to maintain common areas within its possession and control in a reasonably safe condition includes providing security guards in those areas. We conclude that, under the facts of this case, the owner did not owe a duty to provide security guards.

I. BACKGROUND:

This case arises out of a civil complaint filed by Ann M. after she was raped at her place of employment. Unless otherwise indicated, the facts as stated herein are not in dispute.

On June 17, 1985, Ann M. was employed by the Original 60 Minute Photo Company, a photo processing service located in a secluded area of the Pacific Plaza Shopping Center (hereafter shopping center). The shopping center, owned and operated by defendants (hereafter sometimes collectively referred to as Pacific Plaza), is a strip mall located on Garnet Avenue in the Pacific Beach area of San Diego. Approximately 25 commercial tenants occupy the shopping center at any one time.

The lease between the photo store and the shopping center granted the owners of the shopping center the exclusive right to control the common areas. Although the lease gave Pacific Plaza the right to police the common areas, the lease did not purport to impose an obligation to police either common areas or those areas under the exclusive control and management of the tenants. In fact, Pacific Plaza hired no security guards.

At approximately 8 a.m. on June 17, Ann M. opened the photo store for business. She was the only employee on duty. The door was closed but unlocked. The store was equipped with a "drop gate" that was designed to prevent customer access behind the counter but it had been broken for some period of time. Shortly after Ann M. opened the store, a man she had never seen before walked in "just like a customer." Ann M. greeted the man, told him that she would assist him shortly, and turned her back to the counter. The man, who was armed with a knife, went behind the counter, raped Ann M., robbed the store, and fled. The rapist was not apprehended.

In 1984 and 1985 violent crimes occurred in the census tract in which the shopping center is located. While the record includes some evidence of criminal activity on the shopping center's premises prior to Ann M.'s rape—bank robberies, purse snatchings, and a man pulling down women's pants—there is no evidence that Pacific Plaza had knowledge of these alleged criminal acts. In fact, Pacific Plaza offers uncontroverted evidence that it "is the standard practice of [Pacific Plaza] to note or record instances of violent crime" and that Pacific Plaza's records contain no reference to violent criminal acts in the shopping center prior to Ann M.'s rape.

Ann M. presented evidence that the employees and tenants were concerned about their safety prior to her rape. These concerns centered around the presence of persons described as transients, who loitered in the common areas. One of the employees of the photo store called the police on two different occasions prior to the incident involved herein to complain that she felt threatened by persons loitering outside her employer's store. The photo store ultimately granted this employee permission to bring her dog to work for protection. This employee worked a late night shift, while Ann M. worked during the day. During periodic meetings of the merchants' association, an organization to which all tenants belonged, the tenants voiced complaints about a lack of security in the shopping center and the presence of transients. There is no evidence to indicate, however, that Ann M.'s rapist was one of the loitering transients or that the presence of the transients contributed in any way to Ann M.'s attack.

According to Ann M.'s deposition testimony, the merchants' association invited a security company to address the tenants' concerns at one of its meetings. During that meeting, the security company informed the tenants of different security options and recommended that regular walking patrols be instituted. Ann M. stated in her deposition that she was told that the merchants' association decided not to hire the security patrols, because the cost would be prohibitive. Ann M. further testified that she was told at these meetings that the merchants' association requested that the shopping center provide such patrols. No such patrols were provided. According to the lease, if the shopping center had provided the requested patrols, the tenants would have borne the cost in the form of additional rent. Ultimately, the merchants' association hired a security company to drive by the area three or four times a day instead of arranging for foot patrols. Ann M. was raped sometime thereafter.

After the rape, Ann M. filed a civil complaint for damages in the superior court, alleging causes of action for negligence against Amapho Corp. (the owner and operator of the photo store), Glen Hutchinson (the president of Amapho Corp.), the shopping center, and La Jolla Development Co. (the corporation employed to manage the shopping center at the time of the rape). Ann M. alleged that the defendants were negligent in failing to provide adequate security to protect her from an unreasonable risk of harm. This risk specifically was alleged to be the presence of transients and the potential for violent confrontation between transients and employees of the shopping center.

Pacific Plaza filed a motion for summary judgment or summary adjudication of issues, claiming that it owed no legal duty to Ann M., primarily because Ann M.'s attack was unforeseeable. Ann M. countered that a duty was owed: the attack was foreseeable because Pacific Plaza permitted transients to congregate in the common areas of the shopping center. Ann M. contended that "[s]ecurity patrols to roust the center's transient population would have provided the [necessary] 'first line of defense'" that Pacific Plaza allegedly had a duty to provide. The trial court granted the motion, finding that Pacific Plaza owed Ann M. no duty of care, and entered judgment in favor of Pacific Plaza.

Ann M. appealed. Following rehearing, the Court of Appeal affirmed the judgment of the trial court, but on different grounds. The Court of Appeal held that Pacific Plaza owed a duty to tenants and their employees to maintain the common areas and leased premises in a reasonably safe condition, including the duty to take reasonable precautions against foreseeable criminal activity by their persons; however, based on the evidence presented, the Court of Appeal held that no reasonable jury could have concluded that Pacific Plaza acted unreasonably in failing to provide the security patrols that Ann M. claims were necessary.

We granted Ann M.'s petition for review.

II. DISCUSSION

A. Standard of review

Although Ann M.'s complaint is phrased in broader terms, Ann M. concedes that the gravamen of her complaint is that Pacific Plaza's failure to provide security patrols in the common areas constituted negligence. We therefore confine our review to this issue (*Cf. Chern v. Bank of America* (1976) 15 Cal. 3d 866, 873 ["purpose of summary procedure is to penetrate through evasive language and adept pleading and ascertain the existence or absence of triable issues"]; *FPI Development, Inc. v. Nakashima* (1991) 231 Cal. App. 3d 367, 381–382 [pleadings serve as the outer measure of materiality in a summary judgment proceeding].)

An action in negligence requires a showing that the defendant owed the plaintiff a legal duty, that the defendant breached the duty, and that the breach was a proximate or legal cause of injuries suffered by the plaintiff. [emphasis added] (*United States Liab. Ins. Co. v. Haidinger-Hayes, Inc.* (1970) 1 Cal. 3d 586, 594; 6 Witkin, *Summary of Cal. Law* (9th ed. 1988) Torts, § 732, at 60.) On review of a summary judgment in favor of the defendant, we review the record de novo to determine whether the defendant has conclusively negated a necessary element of the plaintiff's case or demonstrated that under no hypothesis is there a material issue of fact that requires the process of trial. (*Molko v. Holy Spirit Assn.* (1988) 46 Cal. 3d 1092, 1107.)

For the reasons discussed below, we conclude that, under the facts of this case, the scope of any duty owed by Pacific Plaza to Ann M. did not include providing security guards in the common areas. Accordingly, we do not address whether Pacific Plaza's failure to provide security guards was a proximate cause of Ann M.'s injuries (*See Nola M. v. University of Southern California* (1993) 16 Cal. App. 4th 421 [hereafter *Nola M.*].)

B. DUTY

The existence of a duty is a question of law for the court. (*Isaacs v. Huntington Memorial Hospital* (1985) 38 Cal. 3d 112, 124 [hereafter *Isaacs*]; *Southland Corp. v. Superior Court* (1988) 203 Cal. App. 3d 656, 663.) Accordingly, we determine de novo the existence and scope of the duty owed by Pacific Plaza to Ann M.

It is now well established that California law requires landowners to maintain land in their possession and control in a reasonably safe condition. (Civ. Code, § 1714; *Rowland v. Christian* (1968) 69 Cal. 2d 108.) In the case of a landlord, this general duty of maintenance, which is owed to tenants and patrons, has been held to include the duty to take reasonable steps to secure common areas against foreseeable criminal acts of third parties that are likely to occur in the absence of such precautionary measures. (*Frances T. v. Village Green Owners Assn.* (1986) 42 Cal. 3d 490, 499–501 [hereafter *Frances T.*]; *O'Hara v. Western Seven Trees Corp.* (1977) 75 Cal. App. 3d 798, 802–803 [hereafter *O'Hara*]; *Isaacs, supra*, 38 Cal. 3d at pp. 123–124.)

Pacific Plaza argues that its relationship with Ann M. is insufficient to support the extension to Ann M. of the duty that it owes to its patrons and tenants to take reasonable steps to secure the common areas of its land. Ann M. counters that she is, in effect, Pacific Plaza's invitee and that this status creates a "special relationship" sufficient to support the imposition on Pacific Plaza of a duty to her.

In this state, duties are no longer imposed on an occupier of land solely on the basis of rigid classifications of trespasser, licensee, and invitee. (*Peterson v. San Francisco Community College Dist.* (1984) 36 Cal. 3d 799, 808, fn. 5; *Rowland v. Christian, supra*, 69 Cal. 2d at 119.) The purpose of plaintiff's presence on the land is not determinative. We have recognized, however, that this purpose may have some bearing upon the liability issue. (*Rowland v. Christian, supra*, 69 Cal. 2d at 119.) This purpose therefore must be considered along with other factors weighing for and against the imposition of a duty on the landowner.

We conclude that it is appropriate in this case to apply the rules specifying the duty of a landowner to its tenants and patrons. Ann M.'s reason for being upon Pacific Plaza's land at the time of her attack fully supports this conclusion. As stated above, it is established that a landlord owes a duty of care to its tenants to take reasonable steps to secure the common areas under its control. In this case, Ann M. admittedly was not Pacific Plaza's tenant; her employer was. Nevertheless, in "the commercial context where the tenant generally is not a natural person and must, therefore, act through its employees, it cannot be seriously asserted that a tort duty that a landlord owes to protect the personal safety of its tenant should not extend to its tenant's employees. (*Cf. DeGraf v. Anglo California Nat. Bank* (1939) 14 Cal. 2d 87, 93 ["plaintiff, as manager of the business of a tenant of the building, stood in a position equal to that of an actual tenant thereof"].) Therefore, the issue of the existence and scope of Pacific Plaza's duty to Ann M. is not resolved by the fact that Ann M.'s employer, rather than Ann M. herself, was Pacific Plaza's tenant.

Pacific Plaza next contends that it owed no duty to Ann M. in this case because the crime occurred on property not within its possession and control. While it is true that Ann M. was raped within the tenant's premises, Ann M. alleges that it was Pacific Plaza's failure to adequately maintain the common areas that caused her injury. As a result, she contends that the location of the crime does not necessarily determine the landowner's liability for injuries resulting from criminal acts. (*Frances T., supra*, 42 Cal. 3d at 503; *O'Hara, supra*, 75 Cal. App. 3d at 803.)

In *O'Hara, supra*, 75, Cal. App. 3d 798, a tenant sued her landlord, alleging that it was liable for injuries resulting from her rape inside her apartment. Knowing of several previous rapes of tenants and of conditions indicating a likelihood that the rapist would repeat his attacks, the landlord induced the plaintiff to rent an apartment in the complex without disclosing any of the above information, and by falsely assuring her that the premises were safe and patrolled at all times by professional guards. (at 802.) The landlord also failed to share with the plaintiff knowledge of the suspect's mode of operation and composite drawings of the suspect. (*Ibid.*) The Court of Appeal held that the landlord had a duty to take reasonable precautions to safeguard the common areas against the types of crimes of which it had notice and which were likely to recur if the common areas were not secure. (at 803–804.) Because the landlord's failure to take "reasonable precautions to safeguard the common areas under [its] control could have contributed substantially, as alleged, to [the tenant's] injuries" (at 803), the Court of Appeal reversed the judgment of the trial court with directions to overrule the general demurrer (at 806).

In *Frances T., supra*, 42 Cal. 3d 490, this court adopted the reasoning of the *O'Hara* court and extended it to the context of residential condominiums. We reasoned that a condominium association functions as a landlord in maintaining the common areas of a large condominium complex and, thus, has a duty to exercise care for the residents' safety in those areas under its control. (at 499.) In *Frances T.*, the trial court had sustained the condominium association's demurrer to a unit owner's allegations that it had negligently failed to install adequate lighting in the common areas and was therefore liable for injuries she sustained from a rape that occurred inside her unit. (at 495, 498.) We reversed. Although the rape occurred within the unit and not in a common area, we held that the association owed a duty to the plaintiff on the theory that an exterior condition over which the association had control contributed to the rape. (at 498–503.)

Since the existence of a duty on the part of Pacific Plaza to Ann M. is not precluded in this case either by the lack of a direct landlord-tenant relationship or by the lack of control over the premises where the crime occurred, we turn to the heart of the case: whether Pacific Plaza had reasonable cause to anticipate that criminal conduct such as rape would occur in the shopping center premises unless it provided security patrols in the common areas. For, as frequently recognized, a duty to take affirmative action to control the wrongful acts of a third party will be imposed only where such conduct can be reasonably anticipated. (*e.g., Frances T., supra,* 42 Cal. 3d at 501; *Isaacs, supra,* 38 Cal. 3d at 123–124; *Peterson v. San Francisco Community College Dist., supra,* 36 Cal. 3d at 807.)

In this, as in other areas of tort law, foreseeability is a crucial factor in determining the existence of duty. (*Isaacs, supra,* 38 Cal. 3d at 123; *Lopez v. McDonald's Corp.* (1987) 193 Cal. App. 3d 495, 506.) Our most comprehensive analysis to date of the foreseeability required to establish the existence of a business landowner's duty to take reasonable steps to protect its tenants and patrons from third party crime is found in *Isaacs, supra,* 38 Cal. 3d 112.

In *Isaacs,* a doctor affiliated with a private hospital was shot while in one of the hospital's parking lots. The doctor sued the hospital for failure to take reasonable security measures. Although the plaintiff presented evidence of several prior threatened assaults at the nearby hospital emergency room, he presented no evidence of prior assaults in the parking lot where he was shot. The trial court granted the defendant's motion for nonsuit because the plaintiff failed to show that prior similar incidents had occurred on the premises. We granted the petition for review to decide whether the plaintiff might "establish foreseeability other than by evidence of prior similar incidents on [the] premises." (*Isaacs, supra,* 38 Cal. 3d at 120.)

We held that foreseeability, for tort liability purposes, could be established despite the absence of prior similar incidents on the premises. We explained that "foreseeability is determined in light of all the circumstances and not by a rigid application of a mechanical 'prior similars' rule." (*Isaacs, supra,* 38 Cal. 3d at 126.) We also explained that prior similar incidents are "helpful to determine foreseeability but they are not necessary." (at 127.) We further explained that foreseeability should be assessed in light of the "totality of the circumstances," including such factors as the nature, condition and location of the premises. (at 127–129.) We concluded that the totality of the circumstances in *Isaacs* strongly suggested that the foreseeability of an assault in the parking lot should have been presented to the jury. (at 130.)

Since *Issacs* was decided, lower court opinions have questioned the wisdom of our apparent abandonment of the "prior similar incidents" rule. (*See Nola M., supra,* 16 Cal. App. 4th at 438–439.) ["If there is a flaw in our analysis finding the landowner not liable due to lack of causation between alleged security deficiencies and injury, we suggest it may be time for the Supreme Court to reexamine the concept of duty it articulated in [*Isaacs*] in the context of a society which appears unable to effectively stem the tide of violent crime."]; *Onciano v. Golden Palace Restaurant, Inc.* (1990) 219 Cal. App. 3d 385, 396 [conc. & dis. opn. of Woods (Fred), J., following *Isaacs,* but observing that its holding leads to inequity. In addition to judicial criticism, at least one commentator has noted that California is the only jurisdiction to adopt a "totality of the circumstances" rule in the business landowner context. Kaufman, *When Crime Pays: Business Landlords' Duty to Protect Customers from Criminal Acts Committed on the Premises* (1990) 31 S. Tex. L.Rev. 89, 97 [hereafter Kaufman, *When Crime Pays*].

Unfortunately, random, violent crime is endemic in today's society. It is difficult, if not impossible, to envision any locale open to the public where the occurrence of violent crime seems improbable. Upon further reflection and in light of the increase in violent crime, refinement of the rule enunciated in *Isaacs, supra,* 38 Cal. 3d 112, is required. We are not reluctant to revisit the rule announced in *Isaacs* because it was unnecessary for this court to consider the viability of the "prior similar incidents" rule in order to decide the *Isaacs* case: the record contained evidence of prior, violent, third party attacks on persons on the hospital's premises in close proximity to where the attack at issue in that case occurred. *Isaacs, supra,* 38 Cal. 3d at 121.

Moreover, broad language used in *Isaacs* has tended to confuse duty analysis generally in that the opinion can be read to hold that foreseeability in the context of determining duty is normally a question of fact reserved for the jury. *Isaacs, supra*, 38 Cal. 3d at 126, 127, 130. Any such reading of *Isaacs* is in error. Foreseeability, when analyzed to determine the existence or scope of a duty, is a question of law to be decided by the court. *Ballard v. Uribe* (1986) 41 Cal. 3d 564, 572–573, fn. 6; *Lopez v. McDonald's Corp., supra*, 193 Cal. App. 3d at 507, fn. 6.)

Turning to the question of the scope of a landlord's duty to provide protection from foreseeable third party crime, we observe that, before and after our decision in *Isaacs*, we have recognized that the scope of the duty is determined in part by balancing the foreseeability of the harm against the burden of the duty to be imposed. (*Isaacs, supra*, 38 Cal. 3d at 125.) "'[I]n cases where the burden of preventing future harm is great, a high degree of foreseeability may be required. [Citation.] On the other hand, in cases where there are strong policy reasons for preventing the harm, or the harm can be prevented by simple means, a lesser degree of foreseeability may be required.' [Citation.]" (*Ibid.*) Or, as one appellate court has accurately explained, duty in such circumstances is determined by a balancing of "foreseeability" of the criminal acts against the "burdensomeness, vagueness, and efficacy" of the proposed security measures. (*Gomez v. Ticor, supra*, 145 Cal. App. 3d at 631.)

While there may be circumstances where the hiring of security guards will be required to satisfy a landowner's duty of care, such action will rarely, if ever, be found to be a "minimal burden." The monetary costs of security guards is not insignificant. Moreover, the obligation to provide patrols adequate to deter criminal conduct is not well defined. "No one really knows why people commit crime, hence no one really knows what is 'adequate' deterrence in any given situation." *7735 Hollywood Blvd. Venture v. Superior Court* (1981) 116 Cal. App. 3d 901, 905. Finally, the social costs of imposing a duty on landowners to hire private police forces are also not insignificant. *See Nola M., supra*, 16 Cal. App. 4th at 437–438. For these reasons, we conclude that a high degree of foreseeability is required in order to find that the scope of a landlord's duty of care includes the hiring of security guards. We further conclude that the requisite degree of foreseeability rarely, if ever, can be proven in the absence of prior similar incidents of violent crime on the landowner's premises. To hold otherwise would be to impose an unfair burden upon landlords and, in effect, would force landlords to become the insurers of public safety, contrary to well-established policy in this state. *See Riley v. Marcus* (1981) 125 Cal. App. 3d 103, 109; *7735 Hollywood Blvd. Venture v. Superior Court, supra*, 116 Cal. App. 3d at 905.)

Turning to the facts of the case before us, we conclude that violent criminal assaults were not sufficiently foreseeable to impose a duty upon Pacific Plaza to provide security guards in the common areas. *Cf. Ballard v. Uribe, supra*, 41 Cal. 3d 564, 572–573, fn. 6. First, Pacific Plaza did not have notice of prior similar incidents occurring on the premises. Ann M. alleges that previous assaults and robberies had occurred in the shopping center, but she offers no evidence that Pacific Plaza had notice of these incidents. While a landowner's duty includes the duty to exercise reasonable care to discover that criminal acts are being or are likely to be committed on its land (*Peterson v. San Francisco Community College Dist., supra*, 36 Cal. 3d at 807), Pacific Plaza presented uncontroverted evidence that it had implemented "a standard practice . . . to note or record instances of violent crime" and that Pacific Plaza's records contain no reference to violent criminal acts prior to Ann M.'s rape. Moreover, even assuming that Pacific Plaza had notice of these incidents, Ann M. concedes that they were not similar in nature to the violent assault that she suffered. Similarly, none of the remaining evidence presented by Ann M. is sufficiently compelling to establish the high degree of foreseeability necessary to impose upon Pacific Plaza a duty to provide security guards in the common areas. Neither the evidence regarding the presence of transients nor the evidence of the statistical crime rate of the surrounding area is of a type sufficient to satisfy this burden.

We, therefore, conclude that Pacific Plaza was entitled to summary judgment on the ground that it owed no duty to Ann M. to provide security guards in the common areas.

III. DISPOSITION

The judgment of the Court of Appeal is affirmed.

Lucas, C. J., Kennard, J., Arabian, J., Baxter, J., and George, J., concurred.

12-5   WRITING THE MEMORANDUM OF LAW

Statement of Facts

The statement of facts should be a concise statement of all relevant and explanatory facts. The information for this statement comes from the client or from documents found in the client file. You identified key facts before you started the research. However, what is or is not a key fact is often affected by the results of your research. Therefore, the statement of facts for a memorandum should not be written until your research is complete.

Facts are generally presented in one of the following ways.

1. **Chronologically:**   A common and easy way of organizing facts in a memorandum of law is in the order in which they occurred chronologically.

2. **By Party:**   Another way of organizing the facts is by party. Where multiple parties exist, they may all have their own version of the facts. State each version separately.

3. **According to the Elements of a Cause of Action:**   When your memorandum concerns whether a cause of action exists, the facts can be presented in the same order in which you discuss the elements of the cause of action.

See Figure 12-1 for an example of a predictive memo. Read the Facts section.

Issue Statement

The issue statement is the question you research. Sometimes start with a very general research question and after doing your research you determine that other questions or issues must also be addressed. Many research problems have more than one issue. These questions should also be included in the issue statements of your memorandum. The issue part of a memorandum should be phrased as a question or questions. Review Chapter 2 for a more thorough discussion of identifying and stating the issues.

Read the Issues section of the predictive memo in Figure 12-1.

Discussion

The discussion section in a memorandum is where you explain the results of the research. In this section, you answer the question or questions stated in the issue section. You provide the reasons for your answers. This is called *legal analysis*.

Within the discussion, there will probably be several "issues"; these are often sub-issues raised by the general issue. For example, the main issue in the civil rights violation case described earlier in the chapter is whether the defendant faces criminal responsibility under 18 U.S.C. § 242. In researching this, you discover that you must also answer other questions, such as "Is an off-duty police officer acting under color of authority?" or "Were the victims deprived of any constititutional rights?" In writing the discussion or analysis, you should discuss each issue separately.

Within the memorandum you can also use point headings to separate the discussion of different issues. Point headings are required in more formal argumentative writing. They are similar to chapter titles or titles of various sections within a chapter. Headings not only help the reader stay focused on your ideas, but also help you, the writer, stay focused. See Figure 12-1 and note the use of headings in the discussion.

FACTS

Smith signed a job offer acceptance with West Coast Industries in June, 2XXX. The job offer letter contained a clause stating "[t]his position is terminable at the will of either party." Smith worked for the company for the next four and a half years until January 2XXX, when his employment was terminated.

Throughout Smith's employment, he received five performance evaluations. The evaluation system includes ratings of "fully effective" and "commendable." A "fully effective" review is defined as a "[g]ood, solid, consistent performance accomplished in a reliable and professional manner." A "commendable" rating is better than a "fully effective" rating. In Smith's first two annual evaluations, he received "commendable" reviews. In his last three evaluations, he received "fully effective" reviews with an improving trend in performance.

Smith also received three promotions during his employment. He was hired as a Tax Accountant II. Three months after beginning employment, he was promoted to Tax Accountant III. Less than five months later, he was promoted to Tax Supervisor, where he remained for one year and seven months. Finally, he was promoted to Tax Manager, where he remained until termination.

In the fall of 2XXX, Gomez, Smith's supervisor, began to examine Smith's punctuality. Smith spoke to the company vice president regarding the tardiness problem. Both men agreed on acceptable guidelines with regard to tardiness.

West Coast Industries has a guideline for the purpose of administering corrective action. The guideline contains suggested steps for corrective action, and the company reserves the right to alter or delete steps of the procedure.

ISSUES

I.   Whether a signed job offer constituted an integrated agreement which precludes a subsequent, implied-in-fact employment agreement, where the offer contains a clause stating, "[t]his position is terminable at the will of either party," and where no further at-will employment agreement was signed.

II.   Whether an implied-in-fact contract not to terminate Smith's employment but for good cause exists where Smith was employed for four and a half years, received "commendable" and "fully effective" reviews, met with the vice president to determine acceptable guidelines to solve tardiness problems, and where West Coast Industries maintained company guidelines for corrective actions.

DISCUSSION

I.   Is Smith precluded from asserting an implied-in-fact employment agreement since he signed a job offer stating his position was terminable at the will of either party?

In order to assert an implied-in-fact employment agreement, Smith must show that the job offer does not preclude subsequent, implied-in-fact agreements. He must show that the

FIGURE 12-1 Sample Predictive Memorandum of Law

clause in the job offer is merely a statement of California Labor Code section 2922. Generally, if the employment relationship is not reduced to an integrated, written agreement, then language that there is an at-will employment relationship does not establish the relationship as a matter of law. *Walker v. Blue Cross of California*, 4 Cal. App. 4th 985, 993, 6 Cal. Rptr. 2d 184, 189 (1992). Therefore, the clause in question may be a re-statement of section 2922, this creates a rebuttable presumption. *Wilkerson v. Wells Fargo Bank*, 212 Cal. App. 3d 1217, 1225, 261 Cal. Rptr. 185, 189 (1989). Smith can show the clause is a re-statement of section 2922, which creates a presumption that can be rebutted by an implied-in-fact contract. *Id.* Therefore, the clause does not preclude a subsequent implied-in-fact employment agreement.

      a.   California Labor Code section 2922 creates a rebuttable presumption of "at-will employment."

The rule of law governing employment termination is California Labor Code section 2922. This section states that "[a]n employment, having no specified term, may be terminated at the will of either party on notice to the other." Cal. Lab. Code § 2922 (West 2XXX). Consequently, an employer may terminate an employee without just cause. However, section 2922 "creates a presumption which may be superseded by a contract, express or implied, limiting the employer's right to discharge the employee." *Wilkerson*, 212 Cal. App. 3d at 1225, 261 Cal. Rptr. at 189. Therefore, the presumption of "at will employment" created by section 2922 may be overcome by an implied contract to the contrary.

      b.   The at-will employment clause of Smith's job offer merely restates the California Labor Code section 2922.

Walker helps distinguish which written agreements preclude the possibility of subsequent contracts. *Walker* states that "the employment relationship must be reduced to an integrated written agreement, signed by the employee." 4 Cal. App. 4th at 993, 6 Cal. Rptr. 2d at 189. "Language in the handbook that there is an at-will employment relationship does not establish the nature of the relationship as a matter of law." *Id.* This suggests that an integrated agreement signed by the employee must be present to create an at-will employment that cannot be overcome by a subsequent contract. An integrated agreement is defined as a "final expression of [the parties'] agreement." *Slivinsky v. Watkins,* 221 Cal. App. 3d 799, 804, 270 Cal. Rptr. 585, 588 (1990). In *Slivinsky*, the court held that a signed offer and employment agreement were enough to preclude the creation of a subsequent employment contract. *Id.* at 805, 270 Cal. Rptr. at 588. The signed offer stated that there "will be no agreement expressed or implied, between the Company and Slivinksy for any specific period of employment...." *Id.* The employment agreement used similar language, along with an explicit declaration that employment could be terminated with or without cause. *Id.*

Smith's employment situation can be distinguished from *Slivinsky* in several ways. The clause in the job offer Smith signed is less clear than the clause in Slivinky's offer. This language in *Slivinsky* is specific and manifests an agreement between the parties. Smith's

FIGURE 12-1
(continued)

offer states "[t]his position is terminable at the will of either party." Such a statement requires neither Smith's acceptance, nor agreement thereto. It is merely a statement of a presumed condition present in every employment situation, as set forth by section 2922. Additionally, Slivinsky signed an express employment agreement that there would be no other contract, express or implied, for continuing employment. *Slivinsky,* 221 Cal. App. 3d at 805, 270 Cal. Rptr. at 588. Smith never signed any such agreement. Smith's offer contained no language stating that his employment precluded the existence of an express or implied employment contract. In *Slivinsky,* the court ruled that the writing was intended by the parties as a final expression of their agreement. *Id.* In the case at hand, the offer probably cannot be construed as a final expression of the parties' agreement. The offer is too vague, and does not require explicit acceptance of the clause in question. It follows that the clause in the job offer Smith signed is not an agreement that employment will be exclusively at-will. Hence, the offer does not preclude a subsequent, implied in fact employment agreement.

     c.   The parol evidence rule probably will not prohibit the introduction of evidence that contradicts the written instrument of the job offer.

West Coast Industries will argue that the parol evidence rule "generally prohibits the introduction of any extrinsic evidence to vary or contradict the terms of an integrated, written instrument." *Wilkerson,* 212 Cal. App. 3d at 1227, 261 Cal. Rptr. at 190. In order to assert this claim, Pacific must show that the offer is an integrated, written instrument. It is undisputed that the offer is a written instrument. However, to be integrated, it must be a "final expression of [the parties'] agreement." *Slivinsky,* 221 Cal. App. 3d at 804, 270 Cal. Rptr. at 586. As formerly explained, it is unlikely that this offer can be construed as a final expression of an agreement. The terms are too vague and indefinite. Additionally, the language does not preclude subsequent employment. Therefore, the parol evidence rule is probably not an issue.

II.   Has an implied-in-fact contract not to terminate Smith but for good cause been created?

Smith must prove that the circumstances of his employment created an implied-in-fact agreement requiring Pacific to offer a good cause for his termination. Furthermore, he must show that such an agreement is sufficient to overcome the presumption of section 2922. Several factors may be considered to determine an employment agreement. Such factors include personnel policies, employee's longevity of service, communications by the employer, and practices of the industry. *Miller v. Pepsi-Cola Bottling Co.,* 210 Cal. App. 3d 1554, 1557, 259 Cal. Rptr. 56, 58 (1989). Smith can satisfy many of these factors. Taking into account all of the circumstances of Smith's employment, he might be able to establish an implied-in-fact contract strong enough to overcome the presumption of section 2922.

     a.   The circumstances of Smith's employment might have created an implied-in-fact agreement that termination requires good cause. This agreement might be sufficient to overcome the presumption of section 2922.

FIGURE 12-1
(continued)

The factors of an employment agreement are defined in *Miller* as "personnel policies…, the employee's longevity of service … communications by the employer reflecting
assurance of continued employment, and practices of the industry…." *Id.* In *Miller*, the appellant based his case on a single job assurance statement at the beginning of his employment,
commendations, promotions, and an employment term of 11 years. The court found that no
implied contract existed. *Id.* at 1559, 259 Cal. Rptr. at 59.

In *Walker*, the court found the circumstances of the appellant's employment created
a triable issue for the existence of an implied-in-fact contract for good cause termination. The
factors considered were over nineteen years of service, consistent promotions, satisfactory
evaluations, and personnel policies. *Smith,*4 Cal. App. 4th at 993, 6 Cal. Rptr. 2d at 189.
Many of the factors are present in the case at bar. Smith was employed for four and one-half
years. Smith also consistently received satisfactory or above satisfactory performance evaluations, and promotions. Finally, Pacific has personnel policies governing the administration of
corrective action. These factors are all similar to those in *Walker*. Furthermore, Smith spoke
to the vice president of Pacific. This communication set forth "acceptable guidelines" agreeable to both men on the issue of Smith's occasional tardiness. The communication supports
the reasonableness in a belief of a good cause termination policy. Since both men agreed on a
way to solve the problem, it shows that the company only wants to terminate an employee
for a good cause. All of these factors could lead a reasonable person in Smith's position
to believe he could only be terminated for a good cause, and would create an implied-
in-fact contract.

West Coast Industries will argue that Smith's employment was similar to that in
Miller. The defense will argue that promotions and salary increases alone "should not change
the status of an "at-will" employee to one dischargeable only for "just cause." *Miller,* 210
Cal. App. 3d at 1559, 259 Cal. Rptr. at 58. As stated above, Smith has more than promotions
and salary increases to support his position. He has good performance reviews, a company
policy that defines steps for corrective actions to be taken, and a communication with the
company vice president. The defense will argue that the company policies can be altered at
any time to undermine the reasonableness of Smith's belief. However, such an assertion is not
problematic for Smith's case. Pacific would not create policies it did not intend to use. The
very existence of such policies manifests an intention by the company to only terminate
an employee for good cause. The court might find the circumstances create an implied-
in-fact contract.

West Coast Industries will distinguish Smith's case from *Foley*. In *Foley* and
Walker, many of the same factors were presented to support an implied-in-fact contract.
However, other factors in *Foley* were "a mandatory seven-step pretermination procedure" and
"independent consideration for [Foley's] employment contract." *Miller,* 210 Cal. App. 3d at
1558, 259 Cal. Rptr. at 58. The *Foley* court found that all of these factors create a "reasonable expectation that [the employee] would not be terminated but for good cause." *Walker,* 4

FIGURE 12-1
(continued)

Cal. App. 4th at 993, 6 Cal. Rptr. 2d at 189. This result is distinguishable from the *Walker* case in which the court found that the factors would only create a triable issue of fact. The defense will therefore argue that since Smith's argument lacks consideration and a mandatory termination procedure, Smith could not reasonably expect to be terminated only for good cause. However, the court in *Foley* did not state that all of the factors were required. The court's conclusion in *Walker* set forth factors that were sufficient such that a jury could find an implied-in-fact contract. Hence, the court should rule in favor of Smith on this issue.

CONCLUSION

The language in Smith's job offer should not preclude him from asserting the existence of a subsequent, implied-in-fact contract requiring Pacific to terminate only for good cause. The clause in the offer is a statement of California Labor Code section 2922. It is not an integrated written agreement. The issue of an implied-in-fact contract for good cause termination is less clear than the first issue. Smith's case would be stronger if he had proof of further assurances by his superiors of his job security. However, he does satisfy the factors set forth in *Walker*. Therefore, Smith might be able to prove the existence of an implied-in-fact contract requiring termination to be for a good cause.

FIGURE 12-1
(continued)

In discussing or analyzing each of your issues, you should follow the IRAC approach discussed in earlier chapters. There are, however, a few additional pointers for using the IRAC approach within a memorandum.

Issue   State the issues in your case in the "Issue" section of the memorandum. It is not necessary to restate the question in your analysis. Where there is more than one issue, it is, however, necessary to let the reader know what issue you are discussing. This can be done with the use of a point heading or by the use of a **topic sentence** that lets the reader know the subject of the following paragraph.

topic sentence. A topic sentence introduces the issues or sub-issues and connects back to the thesis paragraph.

Stating the Rule of Law   The rule of law is taken from one or more of the primary sources of law (constitution, statutes, rules and regulations, or case law). In stating the rule of law, state the rule and then give the proper citation for the source. (For a review of citation format, see Appendix B.) At times, the rule of law may be a composite of law from several sources.

The following are examples of the different ways you can state a rule of law.

Case Law

- An off-duty police officer acts under color of authority when the air of official authority pervades the incident. *United States v. Tarpley*, 945 F.2d 806 (1991).
- In the case of *United States v. Tarpley*, 945 F.2d 806 (1991), the appellate court held that an off-duty police officer acts under color of authority when the air of official authority pervades the incident.

Statutory Law

- Federal law makes it a crime for anyone acting under color of authority to deprive any person of any constitutional right or to subject that person to different punishments, pains, or penalties, because of that person's race or color. 18 U.S.C. § 242.
- Title 18 section 242 of the United States Code makes it a crime for anyone acting under color of authority to deprive any person of any constitutional rights or to subject any person to different punishments, pains, or penalties, because of that person's race or color.

This is not an exhaustive list. You may also use direct quotations from the case or statute to confirm the statement of the rule of law. In most cases, state the rule of law in your own words and then use a quotation to verify your statement. You should avoid simply using a quotation without clarification or explanation.

Analysis

The analysis varies depending on whether the rule of law is based on statutory law or on case law. If it is statutory law, your analysis involves breaking the statute down into its elements and applying the language of the law to the facts of your case. If the rule of law comes from case law, analysis involves comparing the facts of the case law to your facts. It may also involve applying the reasoning of the case to your facts. In many situations, the analysis involves both statutory and case law.

An example of a Discussion section of a predictive memo follows on page 327.

Conclusion   The conclusion is usually the answer to the questions you raised in your statement of the issues. The conclusion should always be stated, even if you think it is obvious.

An example of a Conclusion section of a predictive memo follows on page 329.

Citing Authorities

Format   Citation of legal authorities in any type of legal writing should be in commonly accepted format. Often this means complying with the rules set out in a citation manual. Your state may have its own style manual. If so, you should follow those rules. An attorney may use your memorandum as the basis for the more formal memorandum of points and authorities or trial or appellate brief. If you follow the proper citation rules or your state's style manual, you may find that when you cite a case, it is only necessary to give the official cite. Parallel cites may not be needed.

A Point to Remember

If you have photocopied or downloaded important cases or statutes for your research, you might want to attach them to your memorandum. The attorney may want to read important legal authority. Attaching it to your memorandum saves time.

Using Id. and Supra   In writing any type of legal memorandum, you occasionally use a shorthand or abbreviated way of citing cases. Once a case is fully cited within the memorandum, it is not necessary to use a complete citation each time you refer to it. If the case was the immediately preceding citation, the term *Id.* is substituted for the case name and citation. Thus, the case *United States v. Tarpley*, 945 F.2d 806 (1991) becomes *Id.* If the citation is used to support a quotation, it then becomes, *Id.* at 807. *Id.* is only used when the citation is the immediately preceding citation. If citations to any legal authorities (not just cases) intervene, you cannot use *Id.* The following are accepted shorthand ways of abbreviating this case.

Tarpley, 945 F.2d 806

Tarpley, 945 F.2d at 807

945 F.2d at 807

     Normally when using a shorthand abbreviation you use the first name of the first party listed in the case name, rather than the second name. Thus, in abbreviating the case name *Smith v. Jones*, you would use *Smith*. However, where the first name is a common one, such as *People* or *U.S.*, you must use the second name to avoid confusion.

     Supra is used for authorities other than cases and statutes. (Although not approved by *The Bluebook* you see *supra* used with cases by attorneys and judges.) Review Figure 12-1 to see how these terms are used.

Using Quotations   Using quotations to emphasize your point can be an effective writing tool. Overuse, on the other hand, distracts the reader. You should keep quotations to a minimum. If your quotation is longer than three or four lines, read it to see if you really need all of it. Also, remember that quotations of less than three lines or less than 50 words are incorporated into the text with quotation marks. Longer quotations are indented on both right and left margins, are single spaced, and quotation marks are not used. This is called a "blocked quote." You saw this tool used in the Argument involving the drug detection dog in Chapter 11. All quotations must be followed by the citation, including the page—this cite to the actual page where the quote is found is called a "pin cite."

Conclusion

Every memorandum should have either a conclusion or a brief answer section. Some have both. This is a short summary of your findings. Often it contains a short and concise answer to the questions raised in your issue statement.

A Point to Remember

When you write a memorandum of law, follow the directions of the supervising attorney. If you are asked to research an issue, research that issue in a complete and objective manner. Do not research an issue that you think is more interesting or you think is more important. If you are not sure what your supervising attorney wants, be sure to ask before you spend hours researching and writing.

    Review Figure 12-2 for another sample of an interoffice memorandum.

To: Susan Springer, Assistant District Attorney

From: Research Assistant

Date: November 2, 2XXX

Re: Prosecution of Mr. David Johnston under California Penal Code

                Section 186.22(a)

STATEMENT OF ASSIGNMENT

You asked me to re-evaluate the case against David Johnston in order to establish that he meets the requisite elements for participation in a criminal street gang, under section 186.22(a) of the California Penal Code.

FACTS

The People of the State of California charged Mr. David Johnston with participation in a criminal street gang, under section 186.22(a) of the California Penal Code. Mr. Johnston's record shows that he has two prior arrests, one for vandalism in July 2002, and one for theft in September 2001. He was not convicted of either offense. Witness Wilson, a former member of the Rockets gang, will testify under subpoena for the People. His testimony will confirm Mr. Johnston's involvement in the gang.

The San Jose Police received an anonymous tip that two gangs were planning to assemble in San Jose on June 30, 2XXX. When Detective Castillo arrived at the scene, two groups of people were gathered around a fight between Peter Davis, the leader of the Rockets, and Andre Soprano, the leader of the Cobras. Both leaders had knives and Soprano was wounded. Castillo was informed by a witness that Davis cut Soprano with a knife. She recognized several people as members of the Rockets and Cobras. Castillo did not recognize the defendant, Johnston. He was not wearing a Rockets jacket, but he was standing in the group Castillo identified as the Rockets. Castillo called for backup and the officers stopped the fight. As the officers approached, Castillo heard the defendant shout, "Stop, Peter! Stop!" Many people ran, but the officers arrested the two fighters and charged them with assault with a deadly weapon. Johnston and several persons known to be gang members were also arrested.

Witness Wilson was a member of the Rockets from 2XXX to July 2XXX. He claims Johnston was a member when Wilson joined in 2000. Johnston left the gang in October of 2XXX, but continues to communicate with Wilson. Johnston is still friends with, and has been seen with, Davis. Wilson believes that Johnston was at the scene of his arrest on June 30, 2XXX, to assist Davis. Wilson claims that Davis wanted to affiliate the Rockets with the Cobras and wanted Johnston's help to keep things calm if arguments ensued. Johnston did not have anything to do with the fight, and Wilson heard him say, "Stop, Peter, stop Andre!"

ISSUE

Is David Johnston an active participant in the Rockets criminal street gang according to the California Penal Code, where he was once a member of the Rockets and continues to associate with the members, he has a prior arrest record, and he was recently arrested at the scene of a gang fight?

FIGURE 12-2
Sample Predictive
Memorandum of Law

DISCUSSION

1. Johnston was an active participant in the Rockets gang. The evidence establishes all of the elements for participation in a criminal street gang.

A person actively participates in a criminal street gang, regardless of actual membership, (1) by being more than passively involved, (2) having knowledge of the gang's pattern of criminal activity, and (3) aiding and abetting a felony committed by gang members. David Johnston actively participated in the Rockets gang through his previous membership, his continuous association with the members, his prior arrests on felony charges, and his recent arrest with other gang members at the scene of an alleged assault with a deadly weapon.

A. The California Penal Code provides the requirements for establishing participation in a criminal street gang.

The rule of law governing participation in a criminal street gang in California is found in section 186.22 of the California Penal Code. Under this code section, a person is guilty if he/she "actively participates in any criminal street gang, with knowledge that its members engage in or have engaged in a pattern of criminal gang activity, and who willfully promotes, furthers, or assists in any felonious criminal conduct by members of that gang. . . ." Cal. Penal Code § 186.22 (a) (West 2XXX). In order to establish active participation, "it is not necessary for the prosecution to prove that the person devotes all, or a substantial part of his or her time or efforts to the criminal street gang, nor is it necessary to prove that the person is a member of the criminal street gang." Cal. Penal Code § 186.22 (i).

Active participation in a criminal street gang means that a person has involvement with a gang that is "more than nominal or passive." *People v. Castenada*, 23 Cal. 4th 743, 747, 97 Cal. Rptr. 2d 906, 909, 3 P.3d 278, 281 (2000). The defendant does not need to hold a leadership position in the gang in order to actively participate in a gang. *Id.* at 745, 97 Cal. Rptr. 2d at 908, 3 P.3d at 280. *Scales v. United States* articulated the guilty knowledge and intent requirements, holding that "mere association with a group cannot be punished unless there is proof that the defendant knows of and intends to further its illegal aims." *Castenada*, 23 Cal. 4th at 747, 97 Cal. Rptr. 2d at 909, 3 P.3d at 281, citing *Scales v. United States*, 367 U.S. 203 (1961). *People v. Green* further acknowledged that someone who violates section 186.22(a) has also aided and abetted a criminal offense committed by gang members. *Castenada*, 23 Cal. 4th at 747, 97 Cal. Rptr. 2d at 909, 3 P.3d at 283, citing *People v. Green*, 227 Cal. App. 3d 692, 703-704, 278 Cal. Rptr. 140.

B. Johnston actively participated in the Rockets gang with the knowledge that its members engage in a pattern of criminal activity.

In *Castenada*, the defendant was convicted of robbery, attempted robbery, and active participation in Goldenwest, a criminal street gang. *Castenada*, 23 Cal. 4th at 745, 97 Cal. Rptr. 2d at 908, 3 P.3d at 280. The defendant and two others robbed and attempted to rob

FIGURE 12-2
(continued)

victims of their money, watch, and gold chain. *Id.* Police observed the defendant in the presence of gang members seven times. *Id.* at 756, 97 Cal. Rptr. 2d at 908, 3 P.3d at 280. The defendant claimed that he was never initiated into the gang, but just helped out the gang. *Id.* An officer testified that the defendant's numerous contacts and admitted association with the gang indicated his knowledge of the gang's activities. *Id.* Police even warned the defendant that Goldenwest was considered a criminal street gang, but the defendant continued to associate with them. *Id.* at 753, 97 Cal. Rptr. 2d at 914, 3 P.3d at 285. The joint robbery at issue in *Castenada* was sufficient evidence that the defendant promoted, furthered, and assisted felonious criminal conduct of the gang. *Id.* The court ruled that there was enough proof that the defendant actively participated in a criminal street gang within the meaning of section 186.22 (a) of the California Penal Code. *Id.*

In *In re Jose P.*, the defendant was arrested and convicted for robbery, burglary, false imprisonment, and participation in Norteno, a criminal street gang. *In re Jose P.*, 106 Cal. App. 4th 458, 130 Cal. Rptr. 2d 810 (2003). The defendant Jose P. and two other gang affiliates stole two safes from a home and pointed a gun at and put duct tape over the eyes and mouth of the seven-year-old who lived at the home. *Id.* at 462, 130 Cal. Rptr. 2d at 810. Jose P. was convicted of active participation in a criminal street gang. *Id.* at 467, 130 Cal. Rptr. 2d at 816. He admitted to the police that he associated with the Norteno gang, he was contacted in the presence of gang members, and was seen wearing red, the gang's color, at least twice. *Id.* at 468, 130 Cal. Rptr. 2d at 816. He further confessed that if his fellow gang members asked him to do something for them, he would. *Id.* In addition, he was involved in crimes of car theft, attempted robbery, and the robbery in question at trial. *Id.* The evidence was sufficient to prove that the defendant was an active participant in the Norteno gang. *Id.*

Similar to *Castenada* and *In re Jose*, Johnston was seen with the leader of the gang and remains friends with Wilson. He might not have been wearing a jacket on the day of the assault, but it is not necessary to prove that he is currently a member of Rockets, only that he participates more than nominally or passively. *Castenada,* 23 Cal. 4th at 747, 97 Cal. Rptr. 2d at 909, 3 P.3d at 281. Since Johnston was once a member of the Rockets, he has more than "mere association" with the gang. *Castenada,* 23 Cal. 4th at 747, 97 Cal. Rptr. 2d at 909, 3 P.3d at 281, citing *Scales v. United States*, 367 U.S. 203 (1961). His criminal record of multiple arrests shows that he is not someone who remains passively involved. Even if Johnston is no longer a member, he continues to remain friends with members and was arrested at the scene of a crime with gang members. From this evidence, it can be inferred that Johnston continues to have the requisite knowledge of the gang's pattern of criminal activity.

C. Johnston actively participated in the Rockets gang by promoting and assisting in felonious criminal conduct by gang members.

Just as in *Castenada* and *In re Jose*, Johnston was arrested at the scene of a crime with other gang members. Since Johnston was present during an assault with a deadly weapon in order to help out the Rockets gang leader, his involvement was more than nominal or passive. *Castenada,* 23 Cal. 4th at 747, 97 Cal. Rptr. 2d at 909, 3 P.3d at 281.

FIGURE 12-2
(continued)

Scales articulated that a defendant must know of, and intend to further, the gang's illegal aims. *Castenada*, 23 Cal. 4th at 747, 97 Cal. Rptr. 2d at 909, 3 P.3d at 281, citing *Scales*, 367 U.S. 203 (1961). In addition, *Green* further acknowledged that a defendant must have aided and abetted a criminal offense committed by gang members. *Castenada*, 23 Cal. 4th at 747, 97 Cal. Rptr. 2d at 909, 3 P.3d at 283, citing *Green,* 227 Cal. App. 3d 692, 703–704, 278 Cal. Rptr. 140. The California Jury Instruction on Culpability for Crime states that one aids and abets the commission of a crime when one: "(1) With knowledge of the unlawful purpose of the perpetrator, and (2) With the intent or purpose of committing or encouraging or facilitating the commission of the crime, and (3) By act or advice aids, promotes, encourages or instigates the commission of the crime…." Mere presence at the scene of a crime which does not itself assist the commission of the crime does not amount to aiding and abetting. The fact that Johnston was at the scene of a gang fight in order to assist the Rockets in becoming affiliated with the Cobras, with knowledge of what might ensue, establishes that he aided and abetted the assault. Since he was no longer a member of the gang, he could have chosen not to attend the event. There is no evidence that he was simply present for peacemaking because a fight broke out and no peacemaking occurred. After the police arrived, Johnston was heard shouting at the gang members to stop fighting. This can be interpreted as attempting to prevent the gang's arrest, not necessarily to stop the assault. Johnston aided the assault when he agreed to be present to help the Rockets gang leader and he did not stop the fight. In addition, his prior arrests might also show his affiliation and attempt to further the gang's illegal aims. *Castenada* , 23 Cal. 4th at 747, 97 Cal. Rptr. 2d at 909, 3 P.3d at 281.

The defense might argue that there is no evidence that his prior arrests were at all related to the gang. In addition, the defense might insist that he was at the scene of his arrest to prevent crime, not to assist in it. The evidence of Johnston's former membership and prior arrests shows his "guilty knowledge" of the gang's activities. *Id.* Furthermore, Johnston's voluntary attendance at the gang fight and his inaction to actually prevent the crime shows that he also has the requisite "guilty intent." *Id.* Johnston had more than passive or nominal knowledge of the gang's activities and he aided in the gang's felonious conduct. *Id.* There seems to be sufficient evidence to suggest that Johnston actively participated in a criminal street gang.

CONCLUSION

A criminal street gang is an ongoing organization of three or more persons, with a common name or symbol, that has as one of its primary activities the commission of enumerated crimes, and whose members engage in a pattern of criminal activity. A person actively participates in a criminal street gang by being more than passively involved, having knowledge of the gang's activities, and aiding in the felonious activity of other members. Johnston actively participated in a criminal street gang.

FIGURE 12-2
(continued)

Online Legal Research

For examples of outlining techniques, check the following sites:

http://owl.english.purdue.edu/handouts/general/gl_outlin.html

http://lib.jjay.cuny.edu/research/outlining.html

Legal memoranda are often posted on the Internet. To see available documents, do a Google search for "legal memorandum."

CITATION MATTERS

SHORT CITATION FORMAT

THE BLUEBOOK—RULE 4

Legal writing often contains a large number of citations. The "short citation formats" help the reader sort through the citations. The amount of repetition is cut down for both the writer and the reader.

Probably the most common short citation form is *Id.* Use *id.* when citing the immediately preceding legal authority. This tells the reader that the material originated in the same location as the material cited immediately preceding it.

For example:

The Ferber *case upheld a prohibition on the distribution and sale of child pornography, as well as its production, because these acts were "intrinsically related" to the sexual abuse of children in two ways.* New York v. Ferber, *458 U.S. 747, 759 (1982). First as a permanent record of a child's abuse, the continued circulation itself would harm the child who had participated.* See id. *Second, because the traffic in child pornography was an economic motive for its production, the State had an interest in closing the distribution network.*

Id. *at 760.*

In this example of a blocked quote, the reader is alerted that the material in the first sentence is found in the *Ferber* case. The entire citation is provided because this is the first time the case is used. The second sentence is followed by a short format citation. The "signal" *see* is followed by *id.*, meaning that the writer is asking the reader to look at page 759 in the case (page 759 is listed as the "pinpoint" page in the *Ferber* citation sentence). The *i* in *id.* is lowercase because *id.* is not the first word in the citation sentence. The third sentence is followed simply by "*Id.* at 760." This tells the reader that this information is found on page 760 of the *Ferber* case.

The Bluebook—The Bluepages—B5.2

Short Forms in Court Documents and Legal Memoranda

The Bluepages at B5.2 offers a good list of short forms for cases, constitutions, statutes and regulations, and books, pamphlets, and other non-periodic materials. For example, acceptable short form citations for *Ashcroft v. Free Speech Coalition*, 535 U.S. 234, 245 (2002) are the following:

Free Speech Coalition, 535 U.S. at 245.

535 U.S. at 245.

Id. at 245.

CHAPTER SUMMARY

The legal research process is usually not complete until the results are communicated to another person in either an objective or persuasive way, depending on the situation. Documents objectively conveying research findings are generally memoranda of law and opinion letters. Documents utilizing a persuasive approach include memoranda of points and authorities, trial briefs, and appellate briefs.

A memorandum of law, which is usually prepared for an attorney, contains an overview of all of the law related to the question that was researched. It must be accurate and complete. While there are no required formalities for such a document, a memorandum of law should identify the author, the recipient, the date, the subject matter, a statement of the facts, a statement of the issue or issues, a discussion of the relevant law, and a conclusion. Within the discussion, it is common to use the IRAC method of analysis. This includes stating the issue, stating the applicable rule of law (case law, statutory law, or consitutional law), applying the law to the facts, and reaching a conclusion.

TERMS TO REMEMBER

memorandum of law	trial brief	cause of action
opinion letter	appellate brief	topic sentence
memorandum of points and authorities		

QUESTIONS FOR REVIEW

1. Identify and describe the different types of documents used to convey the results of legal research.
2. List other names used to refer to a memorandum of law.
3. What is the purpose of a memorandum of law?
4. Why is it important that a memorandum of law include all law, even that which may be contrary to your client's position?
5. Describe the general format of a memorandum of law.

6. What steps should you follow in preparing to write a memorandum of law?

7. Describe one way of organizing a memorandum where the controlling law is found primarily in statutory law.

8. Describe one way of organizing a memorandum where the controlling law is found primarily in case law.

BUILDING YOUR WRITING AND ANALYSIS SKILLS: ASSIGNMENTS AND EXERCISES

1. Write a predictive memorandum of law based solely on the Victoria V. facts and the *Ann M.* case found in this chapter.

2. Review the hypothetical case of Speeker v. South Bay County School District found in (Appendix A, Problem 12). Read the authorities cited at the end of the factual background. Using these authorities write a memorandum of law, addressing the following issues:

   a. Did the school district have the right to suspend Susie for her action?

   b. Assuming that the school district was not justified in its actions, does Susie have a claim under 42 U.S.C. § 1983?

3. Review sections III, IV, and V of the memorandum in Figure 12-1. As indicated in the margin, these sections are incomplete and contain various rules of law that are not supported by legal authorities. Identify each statement that requires a citation to a legal authority and describe the type of authority you would expect to find.

BUILDING YOUR ONLINE RESEARCH SKILLS: ASSIGNMENTS AND EXERCISES

1. Locate: http://bartleby.com/141/

   This is the Web site where you may access William Strunk Jr.'s *The Elements of Style*. This is the classic reference book for English composition. Open Section: "V. Words and Expressions Commonly Misused." What does this resource say about each of the following:

   a. certainly

   b. very

   c. whom

2. Locate: www.wilbers.com

   This is Stephen Wilbers's *Writing for Business and Pleasure* site. Complete the two 30-second exercises. Be sure to show your instructor the actual exercise and your rewrite.

3. Locate: drgrammar.org

   This site was created by Dr. Grammar. Open "A Writer's Resources." Choose three of the links. Write a short summary of each resource.

CASE PROJECT

Write a predictive memorandum of law detailing the rights of the parties in the Appendix A hypothetical case you researched in the previous chapter.

PERSUASIVE WRITING: WRITING TO THE COURT

S **KILL OBJECTIVES FOR CHAPTER 13**

When you complete this chapter you should be able to

- Explain rules of court.
- List and describe common features found in legal memoranda and briefs.
- Describe the purpose of a memorandum of points and authorities.
- Explain how and why declarations are used.
- Describe the purpose of a trial brief.
- Describe the purpose of an appellate brief.
- Write a memorandum of points and Authorities.

FROM THE DESK OF W. J. BRYAN, ESQ.

TO: Research Associate

We were served with a memorandum of points and authorities in opposition to our motion to suppress in the Meyers case. Please read the document and the cases cited within it. Then prepare a draft of a reply memorandum of points and authorities. You need to check the rules of court to see how long we have before this needs to be filed. I know it is only a few days.

---

advocate. Arguing one side of an issue.

memorandum of points and authorities. Research document filed with the court containing legal analysis of disputed issues occuring in a case pending in court; often used to support or oppose motions.

trial brief. Research document filed with the court prior to trial addressing legal issues in the case.

appellate brief. Research document filed in an appeal addressing the legal issues forming the basis of the appeal.

motion. A request for a court order in connection with a case that is pending in court.

13-1 INTRODUCTION

In the previous chapter you saw how the results of legal research are objectively communicated in a memorandum of law. However, when research findings are communicated to a court, they are not presented in an objective manner but rather in a persuasive or argumentative way. The researcher **advocates** a position that is most favorable to his or her client. In advocating a position, the researcher tries to convince the court that the law supports the client's position.

When a researcher writes to the court, formal documents are used and technical rules must be followed. The documents used to present a legal argument to the court are **memoranda of points and authorities, trial briefs,** and **appellate briefs.** A memorandum of points and authorities is filed when a legal question arises in a case that is pending in court. Often it is used to support or oppose a **motion** in a case. A trial brief is a document filed at the beginning of a trial. In this document, the attorney presents legal authorities and arguments showing that his or her client should prevail at trial. Trial briefs might also contain legal arguments regarding evidentiary issues that are expected to arise at trial. Appellate briefs are prepared and filed after a case is decided in the trial court. These briefs contain arguments regarding the validity of the trial court judgment.

13-2 RULES OF COURT

Documents filed in a court must comply with rules regarding form and content. Most courts have these rules, which are part of their **rules of court,** sometimes called **local rules of court.** These rules usually cover such things as acceptable length, citation format, content requirements, and the number of copies that must be submitted. If the rules regarding form and content of a memorandum or brief are not followed, a court may refuse to consider the document.

Figure 13-1 contains a copy of one rule from the U.S. Supreme Court regarding briefs that are to be filed in that Court.

rules of court. Rules regulating law practice in a particular court or courts.

local rules of court. Procedural rules adopted by an individual court for practice in that specific court.

RULE OF COURT FOR SUPREME COURT

Rule 24. Briefs on the Merits: In General

1. A brief on the merits for a petitioner or an appellant shall comply in all respects with Rules 33.1 and 34 and shall contain in the order here indicated:

(a) The questions presented for review under Rule 14.1(a). The questions shall be set out on the first page following the cover, and no other information may appear on that page. The phrasing of the questions presented need not be identical with that in the petition for a writ of certiorari or the jurisdictional statement, but the brief may not raise additional questions or change the substance of the questions already presented in those documents. At its option, however, the Court may consider a plain error not among the questions presented but evident from the record and otherwise within its jurisdiction to decide.

(b) A list of all parties to the proceeding in the court whose judgment is under review (unless the caption of the case in this Court contains the names of all parties). Any amended list of parent companies and nonwholly owned subsidiaries as required by Rule 29.6 shall be placed here.

(c) If the brief exceeds five pages, a table of contents and a table of cited authorities is needed.

(d) Citations of the official and unofficial reports of the opinions and orders entered in the case by courts and administrative agencies.

(e) A concise statement of the basis for jurisdiction in this Court, including the statutory provisions and time factors on which jurisdiction rests.

(f) The constitutional provisions, treaties, statutes, ordinances, and regulations involved in the case, set out verbatim with appropriate citation. If the provisions involved are lengthy, their citation alone suffices at this point, and their pertinent text, if not already set out in the petition for a writ of certiorari, jurisdictional statement, or an appendix to either document, shall be set out in an appendix to the brief.

(g) A concise statement of the case, setting out the facts material to the consideration of the questions presented, with appropriate references to the joint appendix, e. g., App. 12, or to the record, e. g., Record 12.

(h) A summary of the argument, suitably paragraphed. The summary should be a clear and concise condensation of the argument made in the body of the brief; mere repetition of the headings under which the argument is arranged is not sufficient.

(i) The argument, exhibiting clearly the points of fact and of law presented and citing the authorities and statutes relied on.

(j) A conclusion specifying with particularity the relief the party seeks.

2. A brief on the merits for a respondent or an appellee shall conform to the foregoing requirements, except that items required by subparagraphs 1(a), (b), (d), (e), (f), and (g) of this Rule need not be included unless the respondent or appellee is dissatisfied with their presentation by the opposing party.

FIGURE 13-1

Supreme Court Rule of Court 24

FIGURE 13-1
(continued)

3. A brief on the merits may not exceed the page limitations specified in Rule 33.1(g). An appendix to a brief may include only relevant material, and counsel are cautioned not to include in an appendix arguments or citations that properly belong in the body of the brief.

4. A reply brief shall conform to those portions of this Rule applicable to the brief for a respondent or an appellee, but, if appropriately divided by topical headings, need not contain a summary of the argument.

5. A reference to the joint appendix or to the record set out in any brief shall indicate the appropriate page number. If the reference is to an exhibit, the page numbers at which the exhibit appears, at which it was offered in evidence, and at which it was ruled on by the judge shall be indicated, e. g., Pl. Exh.14, Record 199, 2134.

6. A brief shall be concise, logically arranged with proper headings, and free of irrelevant, immaterial, or scandalous matter. The Court may disregard or strike a brief that does not comply with this paragraph.

13-3 COMMON FEATURES

A memorandum of points and authorities (often referred to by lawyers as "P' and A's"), a trial brief, and an appellate brief, contain several common features: a case caption, table of contents, a table of authorities, a statement of facts, a statement of issues or questions presented, an argument, and a conclusion.

Case Caption

filed.   To become part of the court record.

caption.   A caption identifies the parties to the case, the court in which the case is pending, the docket number and the title of the document.

In all jurisdictions, any document **filed** in a court must contain a case **caption.** A caption identifies the parties to the case, the court in which the case is pending, the docket number, and the title of the document. Review Figure 13-5 and identify the caption.

Table of Contents

table of contents.   A list of the sections of a document with the page on which they appear within the document.

A **table of contents** is a list of the various sections found in the document with the corresponding page. The various sections include, but may not be limited to, the following:

- Table of Authorities
- Statement of Facts
- Issues
- Summary of the Argument
- Argument: Each point heading, and the page on which it appears, is restated under the argument in the table of contents.
- Conclusion
- Signature

A table of contents is generally required for trial briefs and appellate briefs. It is required in a memorandum of points and authorities only if the memorandum exceeds a certain page length. Local rules of court govern this. Some appellate documents may also contain a Statement of the Case (this is often a summary of the judicial history of the case), Jurisdiction Statement, Corporate Disclosure Statement, or a Statement of the Standard of Review.

See Figure 13-2 for an example of a table of contents from an appellate brief.

Table of Authorities

A **table of authorities** contains a list of all legal authorities, primary and secondary, that are cited within the document and the page or pages on which the citation appears. There are several acceptable formats for setting up the table of authorities; a common way follows.

table of authorities. A list of primary and secondary authorities cited within a memorandum or brief and the page numbers on which they appear.

TABLE OF CONTENTS

ii

FIGURE 13-2
Table of Contents for Appellate Brief

TABLE OF CONTENTS--Continued

FIGURE 13-2
(continued)   iii

TABLE OF CONTENTS--Continued

FIGURE 13-2
(continued)

Reprinted with permission of the author, Kenneth Rosenblatt, Esq.

Constitutional Provisions and Statutes

- Cite constitutional provisions in the order where they appear in the Constitution and give all pages on which they appear.
- Cite *United States Code* sections in numerical order and give all pages where they appear in the document.
- Cite state code sections (either alphabetically or numerically, depending on how the code is cited) and give all pages where they appear in the documents.
- Cite federal and state regulations.

Case Law

- Cite all cases, listing them alphabetically, and give *all* pages where they appear in the memorandum or brief. Another way to list the case law is to separate the federal and state case law into two lists. When this is done, it is common to follow this format:
- **Under the list of the federal cases,** first, list the United States Supreme Court cases in alphabetical order, second, follow with the federal circuit court cases in alphabetical order, third, list the miscellaneous reporters (Bankruptcy, Military, etc.) in alphabetical order, and fourth, list the district cases in alphabetical order.
- **Under the list of state cases,** list the state supreme court cases in alphabetical order and follow with the state appellate court cases in alphabetical order.

Miscellaneous Sources

- Cite secondary source material and any other source material used (usually alphabetically); include all pages where each source appears.

See Figure 13-3 for an example of a table of authorities. Note how all primary authority is listed first and how the primary authority is organized and labeled.

Like a table of contents, a table of authorities is usually required in trial briefs and appellate briefs. It is generally required in a memorandum of points and authorities only if it exceeds a certain page length. Local rules of court govern this.

Statement of Facts

A brief statement of the factual dispute before the court is usually presented in any argumentative document. The facts should be supported in the **court record** or in **declarations** or **affidavits** that are attached to the memorandum or brief. Although facts must always be accurate and truthful, the statement of facts is presented in a way most favorable to the party filing the memorandum or brief.

This section of the brief is usually presented after the table of contents and table of authorities. In this way, the reader has the opportunity to become acquainted with what actually happened before the legal issues or the argument is presented. (Sometimes the question presented may appear first. In fact, in a brief to the U.S. Supreme Court, the question presented is placed first, even before the table of contents and table of authorities.) Remember, all legal issues revolve around the facts. The facts contained in a brief are written so that your client is placed in the best light. Sometimes this is referred to as "slanting the facts to favor your client." *Caution:* Never change the facts, never add facts that do not exist, and never omit damaging facts. Write the facts for the court so that the client is placed in the best possible position.

court record. Documents and transcripts of proceedings in connection with a case.

declaration. A statement under penalty of perjury containing factual statements.

affidavit. A statement under penalty of perjury sworn to before a notary.

Vocabulary choices and descriptive terms can often produce different pictures of the same event. For example, consider the Rambeaux case (Appendix A, Problem 9). In describing the facts here, Rambeaux's attorney might state the facts as follows:

> Facing multiple suspects and fearing for his safety, Rambeaux used a reasonable amount of force in order to effect a legal arrest.

TABLE OF AUTHORITIES

Cases:

Arizona v. Manypenny, 451 U.S. 232 (1981) 13, 35, 36
Barr v. Matteo, 360 U.S. 564 (1959) 30
Bigelow v. Forrest, 76 U.S. 339 (1869) 16
Buck v. Colbath, 70 U.S. 334 (1865). 12, 16
City of Aurora v. Erwin, 706 F.2d 295
(10th Cir. 1983) 47-48
Cleveland C. & c. R.R. v. McClung,
119 U.S. 454 (1886) 21-22
Colorado v. Symes, 286 U.S. 510 (1932) . . . 17, 18, 20, 27, 34
Commonwealth of Pennsylvania v. Newcomer,
618 F.2d 246 (3d Cir. 1980) 33-35
Davis v. South Carolina, 107 U.S. 597 (1882) 14, 16, 25
Ellis v. Railway Clerks, 466 U.S. 435 (1984) 36
Erlenbaugh v. United States, 409 U.S. 239 (1972) 20
Fourco Glass Co. v. Transmirra Prod. Corp.,
353 U.S. 222 (1957) 18
Garcia v. United States, 469 U.S. 70 (1984) 6
Gay v. Ruff, 292 U.S. 25 (1934) 12, 15-17, 20
Georgia v. Grady, 10 Fed. Cas. 245 (1876) (No. 5,352) . . 13
Illinois v. Fletcher, 22 F. 776 (N.D. Ill. 1884) 25
In re Debs, 158 U.S. 564 (1895) 45
In re Neagle, 135 U.S. 1 (1890) 13, 14, 49
Jarecki v. Searle & Co., 367 U.S. 303 (1961) 6
Kelly v. Robinson, 479 U.S. __, 107 S.Ct. 353 (1986) 46
Little York Gold-Washing & Water Co. v. Keyes,
96 U.S. 199 (1887) 38
Martin v. Hunter's Lessee, 14 U.S. 304 (1816) 4, 8
Maryland v. Soper (No. 1),
270 U.S. 9 (1926) 2, 18, 20, 23-33, 35, 49

v

FIGURE 13-3
Table of Authorities for
Appellate Brief

TABLE OF AUTHORITIES--Continued

Maryland v. Soper (No. 2), 270 U.S. 36 (1926) 13, 49
McKee v. Rains, 77 U.S. 22 (1870) 11, 12, 16, 20
Morgan v. Willingham, 383 F.2d 139
(10th Cir. 1967), *reversed in*
Willingham v. Morgan, 395 U.S. 402 (1969) 31
Muniz v. Hoffman, 422 U.S. 454 (1975) 18
Northern Pipeline Construction. Co.
v. Marathon Pipeline Co. and United States,
458 U.S. 50 (1982) 42, 43
Oregon v. Wood, 268 F. 975 (D.Or. 1920) 25
Osborn v. Bank of the United States,
22 U.S. 738 (1824) . . . . 9 ,10, 36-39, 43
People of the State of California v. Mesa,
813 F.2d 960 (9th Cir. 1987) 2, 36, 40, 49
People of the State of California v. Morgan,
743 F.2d 728 (9th Cir. 1984) 49
Reiter v. Sonotone, 442 U.S. 330 (1979) 6
Salem & L.R. Co. v. Boston & L.R. Co.,
21 Fed. Cas. 229 (1857) (No. 12,249) 11
Screws v. United States, 325 U.S. 91 (1945) 20
Shoshone Mining Co. v. Rutter, 177 U.S. 505 (1900) 38
State of Alabama v. Peak, 252 F. 306 (D. Ala. 1918) 25
Tennessee v. Davis,
100 U.S. 257 (1880) 13, 16, 20, 24, 25, 34, 45
Texas & P.R. Co. v. Cody, 166 U.S. 606 (1897) 38
Textile Workers Union v. Lincoln Mills,
353 U.S. 448 (1956) 43-45
The Justices v. Murray, 76 U.S. 274 (1869) 11, 20
The Mayor v. Cooper, 73 U.S. 247 (1867) 11, 20
United States ex rel. Drury v. Lewis, 200 U.S. 1 (1906) . . 49
United States v. Kirby, 74 U.S. 482 (1868) 43
United States v. Mendoza, 464 U.S. 154 (1984) 43

vi

FIGURE 13-3
(continued)

TABLE OF AUTHORITIES--Continued

United States Constitution and statutes:

FIGURE 13-3
(continued)

TABLE OF AUTHORITIES--Continued

Miscellaneous authorities:

9 Congressional Debates, Part II, 22nd Cong.,
2d Sess., at 260, 419, and 461. 11

American State Papers, 1802-15, Finance, page 881 8

Amsterdam, *Criminal Prosecutions Affecting
Federally Guaranteed Civil Rights:
Federal Removal and Habeas Corpus
Jurisdiction to Abort State Court Trial,*
113 U.Pa.L.Rev. 793 (1965) 13, 34

Annals of Congress, 13th Cong., 3d Sess. at 757-61 . . . . 8, 9

Collins, Galie, Kincaid, *State High Courts,
State Constitutions, and Individual Rights
Litigation Since 1980: A Judicial Survey,*
13 Hastings Const. L.Q. 599 (1985-86) 48

Collins and Galie, State Constitutional Law
Insert to The National Law Journal,
September 29, 1986, S-8 48

Currie, *The Constitution in the Supreme Court;
The First Hundred Years, 1789-1888* (1985) 13

Katlein, *Administrative Claims and the
Substitution of the United States as
Defendants Under the Federal Drivers Act:
The Catch-22 of the Federal Tort Claims Act?,*
29 Emory L.J. 755 (1980) 19

Mishkin, *The Federal Question in the
District Courts,* 53 Colum. L. Rev. 157 (1953) 44, 45

Note, *The Theory of Protective Jurisdiction,*
57 N.Y.U.L. Rev. 933 (1982) 42

viii

FIGURE 13-3
(continued)

On the other hand, the attorney for the victims might characterize the events as follows:

> Rambeaux maliciously, violently, and unreasonably attacked and beat minority individuals, clearly using excessive force in light of the alleged minor infractions.

Damaging facts are downplayed or offset when possible. Writing an effective factual statement is mastered with practice.

Figure 13-4 contains the beginning sections of the Fact Statements presented to the United States Supreme Court in the *United States v. Virginia* (*VMI*) case. Notice the differences between the Petitioner's statement and the Respondent's statement. Citations to other documents and transcripts have been omitted. Also, as you read the Memorandum of Points and Authorities in Figure 13-5, note how factual statements are supported by references to other materials, such as depositions.

Statement of Issue(s) or Question(s) Presented

This section of a memorandum or brief states in simple terms the legal question or questions before the court. An issue statement sets forth the legal question *and* it provides the reader with the most significant facts. The issue is often stated as a question. Remember, it is the question presented to the court for resolution. Sometimes there is only one issue. Other times there are many. Each issue should generally be no more than one sentence. Proper identification and statement of the issues are critical to the success of the parties. Failure to raise all important issues or misstating the issue can result in the court's refusing to consider legal authorities or arguments that might favor your client. Proper identification of the issues obviously must be done before you finish your research and prior to writing a memorandum or brief. Review carefully the section in Chapter 2 dealing with issue statements. The following is the issue statement found in a brief to the Supreme Court in the case of *Paula Jones v. William Clinton:*

Question Presented

Whether a private civil action for damages against the President of the United States, based on events occuring before the President took office, should be permitted to go forward during the President's term of office.

The following are the questions presented in the *VMI* case, mentioned previously.

Petitioner's Question Presented

Whether the Equal Protection Clause permits a State, as one alternative in a primarily coeducational system of higher education, to afford its citizens the option of receiving the acknowledged benefits of single-sex education through methodologies designed by professional educators to accomplish optimal and substantively comparable pedagogical results for both women and men.

Respondent's Questions Presented

1. Whether a State that provides a rigorous military-style public education program for men can remedy the unconstitutional denial of the same opportunity to women by offering them a different type of single-sex educational program deemed more suited to the typical woman.

2. Whether coeducation is the required remedy in the context of this case.

After reading these questions, can you figure out which party is the petitioner and which is the respondent? What clues are provided in the questions?

PETITIONER S STATEMENT OF FACTS

1. The Virginia Military Institute. The Virginia Military Institute (VMI) is a state military college in Lexington, Virginia. Since its founding in 1839, VMI has maintained a policy of admitting only men to its four-year undergraduate degree program. The fourteen other public colleges in Virginia are all coeducational. Approximately 1300 male students are enrolled at VMI.

VMI's mission statement declares that VMI's goal is to produce "citizen-soldiers," described as "educated and honorable men who are suited for leadership in civilian life and who can provide military leadership when necessary." The VMI curriculum includes liberal arts, science and engineering courses, and VMI confers both Bachelor of Arts and Bachelor of Science degrees.

As the district court found, VMI has a strong reputation for producing leaders, and has an exceptionally loyal and powerful alumni network. That network is "enormously influential," especially in the male-dominated fields of engineering, the military, business, and public service in which VMI graduates tend to pursue careers, "VMI alumni overwhelmingly perceive that their VMI educational experience contributed to their obtaining personal goals." VMI enjoys the largest endowment on a per-student basis of any undergraduate institution in the United States.

VMI employs an "adversative" method of character development and leadership training not currently used by any other college-level institution. That method is based on techniques used in "English public schools" and "earlier military training," although it has long been abandoned at the United States military academies. The method "emphasizes physical rigor, mental stress, absolute equality of treatment, absence of privacy, minute regulation of behavior, and indoctrination of values." "As a consequence of completing the rigorous tasks, succeeding, and actually graduating from VMI, VMI cadets have a sense of having overcome almost impossible physical and psychological odds. They have been put through great physical pressures and hazards, and just to have made it yields a feeling of tremendous accomplishment."

VMI's adversative method is implemented through a pervasive military-style system. The system includes the "rat line," which is a seven-month regimen during which first-year cadets, or "rats," are "treated miserably," like "the lowest animal on earth." "Rats" are subjected to a strict system of punishments and rewards that creates "a sense of accomplishment and a bonding to their fellow sufferers and former tormentors." The "rat line" experience is accompanied by "rat training," "a tough physical training program" "designed to foster self-confidence and physical conditioning in fourth classmen [i.e., freshmen] by creating training situations which are stressful enough to show them that they are capable of doing tasks which surpass their previously self-imposed limits."

The "class system" assigns roles to each class of cadets within a hierarchy in order to "cultivate leadership." "After the rat line strips away cadets' old values and behaviors, the class system teaches and reinforces through peer pressure the values and behaviors that VMI exists to promote." VMI's program also includes the "dyke system," an arrangement by which each "rat" is assigned a senior as a mentor to give some "relief from the extreme stress of the rat line." VMI's honor code—providing that a cadet "does not lie, cheat, steal nor tolerate those who do"—provides "the single penalty of expulsion for its violation."

VMI requires cadets to "live within a military framework; they wear the cadet uniform at the Institute, eat most meals in the mess hall, live in a barracks, and regularly take part in parades and drills." "The most important aspects of the VMI educational experience occur in the barracks." There, cadets live at close quarters with one another,

FIGURE 13-4
Petitioner's and Respondent's Statement of Facts in the *Virginia Military Institute* Case

three to five together in stark and unattractive rooms, with poor ventilation, unappealing furniture, windowed doors with no locks and no window coverings. "[A] cadet is totally removed from his social background," and placed in an environment the principal object of which is "to induce stress."

Although VMI has always restricted admission to men, some women "would want to attend [VMI] if they had the opportunity." (Recruitment of women would likely yield a 10% female student body at VMI.) Between 1988 and 1990 VMI received 347 letters from women inquiring about admission, or indicating interest in attending VMI. It is not disputed that some women can succeed within the VMI-type methodology and are capable of doing all of the individual activities required of VMI cadets. The district court expressly found that the VMI methodology "could be used to educate women."

RESPONDENT'S STATEMENT OF FACTS

Petitioner's opening brief presents an incomplete picture of the VMI program and glosses over or contradicts crucial facts found by the courts below. This brief sets forth a more accurate and representative statement of the record and the remedial proceedings below.

A. Mary Baldwin College

Mary Baldwin College (MBC), an historically women's college, was founded in 1842. MBC has responded to the changing role of women in society by expanding its curriculum "to include the new options open to women in business and the professions." MBC has "developed an emphasis on career planning," has "computerized the campus," and has added "new state of the art equipment for its science labs." MBC "is committed to the education of women for a world of expanding opportunity."

MBC enrolls over 700 residential undergraduate students, has a Phi Beta Kappa chapter, is accredited by the Southern Association of Colleges and Schools, and is now ranked first among regional liberal arts colleges in the South. See *U.S. News & World Rep. 141* (Sept. 18, 1995. MBC's 55-acre campus in Staunton, Virginia, includes the facilities of the former Staunton Military Academy, residence halls, classroom buildings, computer and science laboratories, a 40,000-square-foot physical education facility, playing fields, tennis courts, and a swimming pool.

The student-faculty ratio in MBC's residential program is 11 to 1. MBC offers 28 undergraduate majors, including degrees in mathematics, the sciences, business, and the arts, and also offers pre-law and pre-med programs and a joint-degree engineering program with the University of Virginia. MBC is "geared in the direction of trying to encourage women to persist in math and physics."

MBC enjoys "a record of success in developing new programs and operating distinctive and unique programs within the larger traditional undergraduate residential community." For example, MBC has successfully established a unique residential baccalaureate program for academically gifted, high-school-age students tailored to "the academic, emotional and developmental needs of young women."

FIGURE 13-4
(continued)

Michael Thomas

State Bar Number 341

Thomas and Gomez

892 First Street

San Diego, California 92103

(619) 123-4567

thomas@gomez.com

Attorney for the Defendants

SUPERIOR COURT OF THE STATE OF CALIFORNIA

COUNTY OF SAN DIEGO

MISSION HILLS HOMEOWNERS)   NO. CIV-3654

ASSOCIATION,)

           Plaintiff,)   MEMORANDUM OF POINTS AND AU-

     vs.)   THORITIES IN SUPPORT OF DEFEN-

GLORIA JENNINGS,)   DANT'S MOTION FOR SUMMARY

           Defendant)   JUDGMENT, OR IN THE ALTERNATIVE,

)   SUMMARY ADJUDICATION.

)

)

)

FIGURE 13-5 Memorandum of Points and Authorities

Now into court, through undersigned counsel, comes Defendant Gloria Jennings, who moves for summary judgment, or in the alternative, summary adjudication, as follows, and asks this Court to grant this motion after due proceedings.

STATEMENT OF THE FACTS

In March of 2007, Defendant Gloria Jennings's nephew was killed in Iraq while honorably serving in the military. Distraught and heartbroken over her loss, Jennings decided to peacefully and respectfully express her opposition to the war. She erected a sixteen square foot sign that displays two sets of numbers. These numbers correspond to the number of military and civilian casualties incurred during the war in Iraq. No words are displayed on the sign and the Defendant took no measures to explain the sign's meaning to the public. Jennings placed the sign so that it was visible from her neighbor's property and from the community center. Jennings knew that the placement of the sign would gain added meaning because of the nearby military base and the American flag flying over the community center. The sign did not have any words because the sign represented all of those who have died and can no longer speak for themselves.

"The Mission Hills Restrictions" are recorded with the Recorder of San Diego County. Section 3.02(h) of this declaration states, in pertinent part: "No signs whatsoever, including but without limitation, commercial, political, and similar signs, visible from neighboring property, shall be erected or maintained upon any private area...." Jennings's sign caused a slight increase in traffic through the area as motorists slow down to view the sign. In May 2007, three notices were sent to Jennings informing her that the sign violated Section 3.02(h) and demanded that the sign be removed. Jennings has not removed the sign to date.

QUESTIONS PRESENTED

1. Is the Plaintiff's nuisance action barred under the Free Speech clause of the First Amendment because disallowing the sign serves no essential governmental interest as the sign is relatively small, only contains two sets of numbers and no words, and the presence of the sign merely created an increase in neighborhood traffic?

2. Is the restrictive covenant of the Mission Hills Subdivision unreasonable, and therefore unenforceable because the covenants only restrict certain types of signs, and are therefore arbitrary, and because the covenant restricting the use of signs abridges the vital public policy of permitting free speech?

FIGURE 13-5
(continued)

ARGUMENT

I. <u>THIS TORT ACTION IS BARRED BY THE FIRST AMEND-MENT'S FREE SPEECH CLAUSE BECAUSE THE DEFEN-DANT'S SIGN CONSTITUTES SYMBOLIC SPEECH AND THERE IS NO SIGNIFICANT STATE INTEREST TO JUSTIFY THIS INFRINGEMENT.</u>

Jennings's sign is symbolic speech that is entitled to First Amendment protection because Jennings intended the sign to express her opposition to the war, and this message was received and understood by others. By enforcing the restrictive covenant and forcing Jennings to remove the sign, California, through it's judiciary, would infringe Jennings's constitutional rights. There is no governmental interest that justifies abridging Jennings's right to free speech. The only negative impact is a slight increase in traffic through her neighborhood. The court should not allow mere inconvenience to trample the fundamental right of free speech.

    A. <u>Judicial action in this case constitutes state action for the purposes of the First and Fourteenth Amendments.</u>

The First Amendment protects an individual's freedom of speech from government intervention. U.S. Const. amend. I. It states that "Congress shall make no law. . . . abridging the freedom of speech. . . ." *Id*. This protection extends to the states through the Fourteenth Amendment: "no state shall make or enforce any law which shall abridge the privileges or immunities of citizens of the United States. . . ." U.S. Const.amend. XIV, § 1. Therefore, the First Amendment provides protection for freedom of speech and the Fourteenth Amendment prohibits states from making laws that curtail this individual "privilege." *Id*.

The Constitution protects individual liberties from governmental intrusion. In order to possess a constitutional claim, the government, not an individual, must take some action that infringes upon a personal freedom. This dichotomy was discussed by the Supreme Court in *Shelley v. Kraemer*. 334 U.S. 1 (1948). This case addressed a private restrictive covenant prohibiting property ownership by minorities. *Id*. at 5. The Court stated that the agreement could only be enforced through "judicial enforcement by state courts of the restrictive terms of the agreements." *Id*. at 13–14. Enforcement of the agreements necessarily entailed actions by the state through it's

FIGURE 13-5
(continued)

judiciary. Thus, the judicial enforcement of the restrictive covenant constituted state action that was entitled to constitutional protection.

Just as in *Shelley*, Jennings contends that the restrictive covenant abridges her constitutional rights. If the court hears this case, then it will be taking state action, because the court would be enforcing the restrictive covenant against Jennings. Therefore, constitutional analysis under the First Amendment is appropriate.

B. <u>The Defendant's sign is symbolic speech protected by the First Amendment because Defendant intends to communicate a specific message, and the message is receive d and understood by others.</u>

1. Symbolic Speech is protected under the First Amendment.

While most associate "speech" with the spoken word, the Court extends First Amendment protection to certain expressive acts. *Spence v. Washington*, 418 U.S. 405, 411 (1974). These expressive acts are called symbolic speech. However, the Court does not "accept the view that an apparently limitless variety of conduct can be labeled 'speech' whenever the person engaging in the conduct intends to . . . express a message." *United States v. O'Brien,* 391, U.S. 367, 376 (1968). The Court in *Spence v. Washington* set the standard for determining if expressive activity constitutes symbolic speech. *Spence,* 418 U.S. at 405. The Defendant was convicted under a washington statute prohibiting unlawful use of the American flag when he attached a peace symbol to a flag which hung outside his apartment. *Id.* The Court found that expressive activity is speech (1) when the act intends to express a particularized message, and (2) when the act is likely to be understood by others. *Id.* at 415. These factors were met in *Spence* and the Court reversed the conviction.

2. Jennings's sign is symbolic speech because it expresses a specific message and is understood by others.

In a case strikingly similar to Jennings's, the Supreme Court in *Ladue v. Gilleo* held that a city ordinance that restricted the placement of signs on private property violated the Defendant's free speech rights. 512 U.S. 43 (1994). The City of Ladue, in an attempt to "minimize visual clutter," prohibited all signs except those that fell within certain categories. *Id.* at 54. In analyzing the signs as a medium of

FIGURE 13-5
(continued)

expression, the court stated: "displaying a sign in one's own residence often carries a message quite distinct from placing the sign somewhere else . . . A sign advocating "Peace in the Gulf" in the front lawn of a retired general or decorated war veteran may provoke a different reaction than the same sign in a 10-year-old child's bedroom. . . ." *Id.* at 56. The Court indicates that the mere placement of a sign on one's property may express a particularized message. This message may gain added meaning through the context in which it is placed.

In *Texas v. Johnson*, the Court found that burning the American flag was expressive conduct protected by the First Amendment. 491 U.S. 397, 399 (1989). The Defendant burned the flag during a political demonstration protesting the Reagan administration. *Id.* The Court again relied on the context in which the act was executed to determine if the act was protected symbolic speech. "Johnson burned the American flag as part ... of a political demonstration that coincided with the convening of the Republican Party and its renomination of Ronald Reagan .... a more powerful statement of symbolic speech . . . couldn't have been made at that time." *Id.* at 406. The *Johnson* Court concluded that "Johnson's burning of the flag was conduct 'sufficiently imbued with elements of communication' to implicate the First Amendment." *Johnson,* 491 U.S. at 406, quoting *Spence v. Washington,* 418 U.S. 405, 409 (1974).

By applying these principles to Jennings's sign, it is evident that the *Spence* two part test is satisfied. First, Jennings intended "to convey a particularized message." *Spence,* 418 U.S. at 415. Jennings's nephew was killed while honorably serving in the military. Distraught over her loss, Jennings placed the sign on her property to respectfully display her opposition to the war. Jennings intentionally placed the sign such that it was visible from the neighbor's property and the community center. *See* Haley Deposition at 3. She also erected the sign knowing that it would be near an American flag and a military base. *See* Haley Deposition at 6. By placing the sign in proper context, as did the courts in *Ladue* and *Johnson,* the sign's communicative power is apparent. By placing the sign on her property, Jennings is intentionally conveying to the community that she is experiencing the tragedy of war, and that she is opposed to the government's involvement in Iraq. The sign is powerful expressive conduct designed to express Jennings's "particularized message." *Spence,* 418 U.S. at 415.

FIGURE 13-5
(continued)

Second, Jennings's message is understood by others. Ben's death was reported in the *Empire News Guardian*, a weekly newsletter distributed to all residents of Mission Hills. Hames Deposition at 3. Therefore, members of the community were aware of Jennings's loss. While Jennings's sign did not include words indicating what the numbers referred to, the casualty figures were readily available in the media. Also, Jennings had conversations with her neighbors regarding her opposition to the war. Hames Deposition at 3. Since her neighbors were aware of Jennings's views, they would assume the sign had something to do with the war. Therefore, the second part of the *Spence* test is satisfied and the sign constitutes symbolic speech.

      C. <u>State Action to disallow the sign is unconstitutional because it serves no significant state interest.</u>

While the sign is symbolic speech, the Supreme Court limits constitutional protection for some types of symbolic speech. *See United States v. O'Brien*, 391 U.S. 367 (1968). Generally, state action prohibiting expressive speech is permissible if there is a government interest that sufficiently justifies the regulation. In *O'Brien*, the Court held that Defendant's act of burning his selective service registration card was not afforded First Amendment protection. *Id.* at 370. There was a sufficient government interest in ensuring the preservation of the certificates.

Defendants were suspended from school for wearing black armbands to protest the Vietnam War in *United States v. Tinker*, 393 U.S. 503 (1968). The Court found that the armbands were symbolic speech and did not find any substantial governmental interest sufficient to waive First Amendment protection. It held that the school "must be able to show that its action was caused by something more than a mere desire to avoid the discomfort and unpleasantness that always accompany an unpopular viewpoint." *Id.* at 509.

In Jennings's case, no sufficient government interest is served by enforcing the restrictive covenant. The only negative impact on the community is the slight increase in traffic. As *Tinker* holds, the desire to avoid the display of an unpopular or uncomfortable viewpoint is not enough to deny extension First Amendment protection. *Id.*

FIGURE 13-5
(continued)

II. <u>THE RESTRICTIVE COVENANT IS UNREASONABLE, AND THERE-</u>
<u>FORE UNENFORCEABLE BECAUSE THE RESTRICTION IS</u>
<u>ARBITRARY, VIOLATES A FUNDAMENTAL PUBLIC POLICY, AND</u>
<u>IMPOSES A BURDEN ON THE USE OF THE LAND THAT OUTWEIGHS</u>
<u>ANY BENEFIT.</u>

Jennings merely wants to express her views in a peaceful and respectful manner. The sign is not obscene and is not excessively large. Jennings looked across the
street and saw the American flag flying above the community center, and thought that
it was reasonable that she be able to express her ideas too. However, the restrictive
covenant unjustly and unreasonably strips her of this right. The restriction is unreasonable, and conflicts with the inherent right of free expression.

California Civil Code Section 1354 deals with the enforceability of restrictive
covenants. It states that "the covenants and restrictions in the declaration shall be en-
forceable as equitable servitudes, unless unreasonable. . . ." Cal. Civ. Code § 1354
(West 2007). The rules governing equitable servitudes generally require a purchaser
of property to have actual notice of the restrictions. *Narstedt v. Lakeside Village Con-*
dominium Association, 8 Cal. 4th 361, 375, 33 Cal. Rptr. 2d 63, 71, 878 P.2d 1275,
1283 (1994). However, "the inclusion of covenants and restrictions in the declaration
recorded with the county recorder provides sufficient notice to permit the enforcement
of such recorded covenants and restrictions as equitable servitudes." *Id.* at 379, 33
Cal. Rptr. 2d at 73, 878 P.2d at 1285. The Mission Hills Restrictions were recorded
in June 1996, they meet the requirements of equitable servitudes and fall under the
control of Section 1354.

The California Supreme Court held that restrictive covenants that are
recorded with the county recorder are "presumed to be reasonable" and the burden
of proving otherwise is upon the challenging party. *Id.* at 379, 33 Cal. Rptr. 2d at 73,
878 P.2d at 1285. A party may show that the restriction is unreasonable by proving
the restriction is "arbitrary, imposes burdens on the use of lands it affects that substantially outweigh the restriction's benefits. . . . , or violates a fundamental public policy."
Id. at 382, 33 Cal. Rptr. 2d at 75, 878 P.2d at 1287. In analyzing the reasonableness
of a restriction, the evaluation must be made "not by reference to facts that are specific
to the objecting homeowner, but by reference to the common interest development as

FIGURE 13-5
(continued)

a whole."*Id.* at 386, 33 Cal. Rptr. 2d at 78, 878 P.2d at 1290. The enforcement of the restriction "must be fair and applied uniformly." *Id.* Therefore, a party may overcome a restriction's presumptive validity by establishing that the restriction is (1) arbitrary, (2) violates public policy, or (3) its burdens outweigh the benefits as applied to the community as a whole.

A. <u>The restrictive covenant is arbitrary, and therefore unreasonable, because it bears no rational relationship to the protection, preservation, operation, or purpose of the land and it is not evenly applied.</u>

In *Dolan King v. Rancho Santa Fe Association*, a community association sought to enforce its restrictive covenant to prevent a resident from making certain additions to her home. 81 Cal. App. 4th 965, 97 Cal. Rptr. 2d 280 (2000). The association sought to "preserv[e] the character" of the community by restricting the appearance of its resident's homes. *Id.* at 970, 97 Cal. Rptr. 2d 280, 283. Dolan King asserted that the restriction was arbitrary because of its subjective guidelines. The California Supreme Court stated that "a restriction is arbitrary when it bears no rational relationship to the protection, preservation, operation, or purpose of the affected land." *Narstedt,* 8 Cal.4th at 381, 33 Cal. Rptr. 2d at 75, 878 P.2d at 1287. Here, the court determined that maintaining a community that is artistically pleasing is not arbitrary because it bears a relationship to preserving the value of the homeowner's property.

In *Liebler v. Point Loma Tennis Club*, a condominium owner challenged a restriction that excluded nonresident owners from using the community's recreational facilities. 40 Cal. App. 4th 1600, 47 Cal. Rptr. 2d 783 (1995). Liebler, who owned property but did not reside in the development, used the development's tennis court in violation of the restriction. The California Supreme Court held that the restriction was not arbitrary because "there were valid reasons why members of a tennis-oriented residential condominium might choose to restrict access to their private tennis courts." *Id.* at 1611, 47 Cal. Rptr. 2d at 788-789. Hence, the restriction was related to the "operation" and "purpose" of the development.

The Mission Hills restrictive covenant limiting the use of certain signs is arbitrary because there is no rational reason to justify its enforcement. Section 3.02(H) strictly prohibits the use of certain kinds of signs, including "commercial, political,

FIGURE 13-5
(continued)

and similar signs." Mission Hills Restrictions, § 3.02H. There is no articulated reason why the community is attempting to restrict these types of signs. The restrictions have no relationship to the "protection, preservation, operation or purpose" of the land. *Narstedt,* 8 Cal. 4th at 381, 33 Cal. Rptr. 2d at 75, 878 P.2d at 1287. First, the restriction does not serve to increase security in the area. Second, there is no evidence indicating that a sign would cause any deterioration to the property or surrounding properties, and, thus, does not affect the "preservation" of the community. Third, a sign, at most, has a negligible effect on the operation of the land. Finally, the purpose of the land is to provide a means of shelter and enjoyment. The presence of a sign will in no way affect the "purpose" of the land.

The Mission Hills restrictions must be "fair and uniformly applied." *Narstedt,* 8 Cal. 4th at 386, 33 Cal. Rptr. 2d at 78, 878 P.2d at 1290. The Mission Hills community center bears an American flag the same size as Jennings's sign. It is wholly arbitrary to prohibit residents in the community from expressing their views through the use of a sign, while at the same time allowing the Homeowner's Association to express its views through the use of a flag. The restrictions, therefore, are not "uniformly applied." Thus, the restrictive covenant is arbitrary because there is no rational explanation for it, and it is not uniformly applied to the whole community.

> B. <u>The restrictive covenant violates the fundamental public policy of free</u>
>   <u>speech.</u>

As discussed in detail in Issue I above, the restrictive covenant violates Jennings's constitutionally protected right to freedom of expression. The Supreme Court addressed this issue in *Ladue v. Gilleo,* in which the City of Ladue enacted an ordinance prohibiting the display of any sign on residential property. 512 U.S. 43 (1994). The Court described that "a special respect for individual liberty in the home has been a part of our culture and our law; that principle has special resonance when the government seeks to constrain a person's ability to speak there." *Id.* at 58. The Mission Hills restrictive covenant attempts to constrain Jennings's ability to express her views through the use of her property. The covenant violates public policy because it violates the United States Constitution, and, therefore, is unreasonable.

FIGURE 13-5
(continued)

C. <u>The restrictive covenant is unreasonable because the harmful effects of enforcement outweigh any possible benefits.</u>

The benefits of enforcing this restriction are few, if any. The use of signs does not reduce the security of the area, nor does it inhibit those in the surrounding properties from using and enjoying their property. There is no evidence before the court that the use of signs will decrease property values. While the benefits are few, the burdens are great. Enforcing this restriction will infringe on one of the strongest and most important privileges in our society. The restriction serves to deny Jennings a fundamental medium to peacefully and respectfully express her views. By balancing these considerations, it is evident that the burden of infringing on the freedom of speech far outweighs the slight inconvenience of the sign.

CONCLUSION

Ms. Jennings respectfully submits that the Mission Hills restrictive covenant infringes on her First Amendment rights of free speech. The sign constitutes symbolic speech because she intends to convey a particularized message and this message is received by others. The restriction is also unreasonable because it is arbitrary, violates the fundamental public policy of free speech, and its burdens outweigh any benefits. Ms. Jennings simply wants to respectfully and peacefully express her views, and this right should not be discarded because of a few extra cars on a street.

Respectfully Submitted,

Dated:

_____
(signature line)

Attorney for Defendant

FIGURE 13-5
(continued)

Summary of Argument

In lengthy memoranda and in appellate briefs, the court requires the parties to include a brief summary of the argument before the argument itself. Figure 13-6 shows three short summaries of the argument in the *Illinois v. Caballes* case (printed in Chapter 3).

BRIEF FOR THE RESPONDENT (Caballes)

SUMMARY OF ARGUMENT

Respondent was stopped for speeding, for which the stopping officer decided to issue him a warning. A second officer, apparently in accordance with standard procedure, drove his drug detection dog to the scene and had it sniff the stopped car—even though the sniff could not have disclosed anything relevant to the traffic violation, and the police had no reasonable suspicion of a drug offense. The State argues that the Fourth Amendment did not require any justification for the drug sniff, beyond probable cause to believe that respondent had violated a traffic law.

1. This Court has viewed dog sniffs in particular contexts as imposing only modest burdens on Fourth Amendment interests. Nothing, however, in *United States v. Place, City of Indianapolis v. Edmond*, or any of the Court's other cases establishes the sweeping proposition the State advances here: That use of a trained dog to sniff a locked car trunk requires no individualized justification whatsoever, because it is a "Fourth Amendment non-event."

While dog sniffs are not physically invasive, they do intrude on reasonable privacy interests. Bringing a drug dog to the scene of a traffic stop for the specific purpose of sniffing a motorist's locked trunk is not at all analogous to observing some contraband item in "plain view" during the ordinary course of another investigation. Moreover, using a drug dog during an otherwise routine stop can be intimidating, accusatory and humiliating. Without any substantive limit on when a sniff is permissible, officers' decisions about when to use a dog are open to the reality or perception of discriminatory investigation. And while drug sniffs may in theory be designed to detect only the presence of contraband, in practice they are prone to errors—including, for example, the detection of non-contrab and currency—that will inevitably result in further unjustified invasions of motorists' privacy.

FIGURE 13-6
Summaries of the
Argument

Because investigatory sniffs by drug dogs during routine traffic stops implicate such Fourth Amendment interests, they should not be authorized in the absence of some reasonable, articulable, individualized suspicion of wrong-doing that could be either sharpened or dispelled by the sniff. Requiring that modest level of justification will not interfere with any legitimate investigative activity. It will, however, prevent police from using roving, suspicionless drug sniffs at the scene of routine traffic stops to replace the indiscriminate checkpoints, serving only a general interest in crime control, that this Court specifically disapproved in *Edmond*.

2. The fact that the police had probable cause to stop Caballes for speeding did not authorize them to undertake an investigatory dog sniff, designed solely to prospect for possible evidence of an unrelated offense. Standard Fourth Amendment principles, reflected in *Terry v. Ohio* and many other decisions, require particularized justification not only for the initiation of a non-consensual police encounter, but for its scope. Those principles apply even when an encounter is justified by probable cause (or, for that matter, even when the police are executing a warrant). They cannot be reconciled with the State's submission that officers who have probable cause to stop a driver for speeding need no further justification to conduct a dog sniff designed to detect illegal drugs. Adopting that standard would be an open invitation to abuse.

The Illinois Supreme Court held only that when officers stop a driver on the highway, they may not take the additional, targeted investigative step of having a dog sniff the car for drugs unless that measure is either reasonably related to the circumstances that justified the initial stop, or otherwise supported by some reasonable suspicion of drug-related wrongdoing. That standard appropriately balances the government's interest in law enforcement against the important personal interests protected by the Fourth Amendment.

BRIEF FOR THE PETITIONER (State of Illinois)
SUMMARY OF ARGUMENT

The Fourth Amendment does not require police to have reasonable suspicion that illegal drugs are present before using a drug-detection dog to sniff the exterior of a vehicle during a legitimate traffic stop. Because the sniff is not a Fourth Amendment

FIGURE 13-6
(continued)

search, it requires no independent justification when conducted on a vehicle that has already been detained following an observed traffic violation. That is, a traffic stop justified by probable cause does not lose its legitimacy when a canine sniff occurs during the stop.

In holding otherwise, the Illinois Supreme Court failed to acknowledge settled precedent establishing that canine sniffs are not Fourth Amendment searches. Instead, scrutinizing the sniff of respondent's car under the *Terry* doctrine, the majority invalidated the sniff upon concluding that the officers did not have reasonable suspicion that illegal drugs were present. The majority's analysis erred in two respects. First, the *Terry* doctrine does not govern traffic stops justified by probable cause or canine sniffs that occur during such stops. Second, even if the *Terry* doctrine applied, the sniff of respondent's car still was lawful under the Fourth Amendment because it did not entail any additional intrusion on respondent's legitimate privacy or possessory interests.

FOR THE RESPONDENT

SUMMARY OF THE ARGUMENT (Amicus brief)

The Supreme Court of Illinois correctly held that the Fourth Amendment requires that law enforcement officers have reasonable suspicion that a vehicle contains contraband before using a drug-detection dog to sniff the vehicle during a routine traffic stop. This is true for four reasons. First, suspicionless dog sniffs are not reasonably related in scope to the circumstances that justified the initial stop, when the right of motorists to remain free from arbitrary police interference is balanced against the public interests advanced by the seizure. Such suspicionless sniffs prolong the length and increase the intrusiveness of seizures, without contributing substantially to the interdiction of contraband. In addition, suspicionless sniffs allow unfettered police discretion and present the risk of involuntary consents. Second, requiring reasonable suspicion will reduce the incidence of false positives, a significant problem with drug-detection dogs that results in intrusions upon motorists' Fourth Amendment rights. Third, requiring reasonable suspicion is consistent with this Court's precedents. Fourth, petitioner and its amici are wrong in arguing that suspicionless dog sniffs are justified where police have probable cause to make the traffic stop.

FIGURE 13-6
(continued)

Argument

The **argument** is the main part of any memorandum of points and authorities or brief. This is where the law and facts are analyzed. In the argument section, each issue should be discussed separately, preferably in the order in which the issues are stated in the "Issue" section of the document. Major points are stated in point headings and then discussed in detail following the point heading. Legal authorities are cited and analyzed. (Hence, the phrase "Points and Authorities.") Just as with the "Discussion" section of a memorandum of law, the argument should be outlined and organized prior to the actual writing.

Proper phrasing of the point headings is an important part of the drafting of this section of the document. Remember you are making an argument, not just identifying the issue under discussion. Your position should thus be stated in positive and conclusionary terms. You tell the court how and why it should rule on the issues or questions presented. Refer back to Figure 13-2, the table of contents, and review the point headings found under "Argument." Note how the headings try to "persuade" the court to rule in a certain way. Also review the point headings found in the memorandum in Figure 13-5.

The IRAC method of analysis often forms the basis of the argument just as it does in a discussion. However, in more complex cases and in cases of **first impression,** the argument also includes more analysis of the reasoning behind the law. Most often, a reported case opinion includes a detailed analysis of why the court is ruling the way it is. In writing an argument, the researcher shows how and why this reasoning applies to his or her case. Short quotations from the reported case help to support this.

argument. The section of a memorandum or brief containing the legal analysis supporting that party's position on a legal issue.

first impression. A case where the legal issue is adjudicated for the first time.

Conclusion

Every memorandum and brief should contain a conclusion. Sometimes this is a brief summary of the main points. Other times, especially in appellate briefs where the argument contains summaries of the main points, attorneys conclude the legal arguments with this simple paragraph:

> For the foregoing reasons, the petitioner requests that the judgment of the lower court be affirmed.

Signature

Any document submitted to the court must contain the signature of the attorney submitting it. Because this is a legal document filed in court, an attorney—not a paralegal or law clerk—must sign it. However, a research associate can do much of the research for a memorandum or brief. Research associates may prepare drafts of the final document for review by the attorney.

A Point to Remember

A court is obligated to follow authorities that you cite only when those authorities are mandatory authority in your jurisdiction. If you are in a state court, mandatory authority is found in case law from your state courts and constitutional and statutory law of your state. Only if these do **not** exist should you use other authorities. If you are in federal court, and the issue is a constitutional or federal one, then cite cases from the U.S. Supreme Court and federal appellate courts from your circuit. Only if these do not exist should you cite cases from other jurisdictions. If you do not cite mandatory authority, the court can ignore your arguments. Review Chapter 3.

13-4 MEMORANDUM OF POINTS AND AUTHORITIES

As mentioned above, a memorandum of points and authorities is a document filed with a court where the author argues for or against a legal position on a matter. This type of document is often filed in support of or in opposition to a motion. A motion is a request for an order from the court in either criminal or civil cases. It is made when an attorney makes a request in connection with a pending case, such as a motion to dismiss a case, a motion for summary judgment, or a motion to suppress evidence that was illegally obtained. A memorandum of points and authorities contains an argument based on the law and the facts of the case.

Unlike a memorandum of law, the object of a memorandum of points and authorities is not to present an objective and thorough treatment of the law. In this document, attorneys advocate their client's position in a matter before the court. Although it is an ethical violation to misstate either the law or the facts, attorneys generally try to present the material in a way that is most favorable to their clients.

Even though the purpose is different, in many ways a memorandum of points and authorities resembles a memorandum of law. It generally contains a statement of facts, a statement of issues, legal analysis, and a conclusion. In lieu of a discussion, however, a memorandum of points and authorities contains an argument. Within this argument, the attorney sets forth the points he or she is making and then gives the legal authorities for these points. The IRAC method of analysis is used within the argument, just as it is in a discussion. The points are usually set out in point headings that precede each section of the argument.

Memoranda of points and authorities are used in adversary proceedings and, therefore, each side has the opportunity to submit a memorandum to the court. Memoranda are filed as follows.

moving party. The party making a motion.

Memorandum of Points and Authorities in Support of the Motion   This is the first memorandum filed by the **moving party,** the party making the motion. In this motion, the party, who may be the plaintiff or the defendant in the action, sets forth the legal argument for the court to grant the motion. This memorandum contains a caption, statement of facts, statement of issues, argument, conclusion, and attorney signature. It may also include a table of contents and a table of authorities if it is lengthy.

Memorandum of Points and Authorities in Opposition to the Motion   This motion is filed by the responding party within strict time limits set by law. In this memorandum, the responding party tries to accomplish two goals: (1) set forth the strongest argument in support of his or her position, and (2) refute arguments set forth by the moving party. This document may or may not include a statement of facts and a statement of issues. If the responding party is satisfied with the statements set forth in the opening memorandum, it is not necessary to repeat them.

Reply Memorandum   The moving party generally has the opportunity to file a reply memorandum, again within very strict time limits. This document replies to points raised in the responding memorandum.

In addition to rules regarding time limits for filing, many courts have rules regarding the maximum number of pages allowable in the memorandum of points and authorities. Review Figure 13-5 for an example of a memorandum of points and authorities filed in support of a motion for summary judgment. Because this is a relatively short memorandum, no table of contents or table of authorities was required. Review Appendix D, for examples of memoranda prepared by research associates and the memorandum of points and authorities drafted by the attorney and based in part on those memoranda.

13-5 DECLARATIONS

The statement of facts in a memorandum or brief must be supported by evidence in the court record. When parties file a memorandum of points and authorities, they often use declarations or affidavits, rather than live testimony, to present the facts to the court. A declaration is a statement made under penalty of perjury. An affidavit is also a statement made under penalty, but it is sworn to before a notary.

Facts contained in a declaration take on a tone quite different from those in a fact statement in a memorandum or brief. The declaration is made by the person having firsthand knowledge of the facts. It may be the client's words or it might be an attorney's statement. This is the declarant's story. A declaration often reads like a narrative of the *events from the client's point of view*. Even though it may be the client's story, and even though it may be signed by the client, it is still drafted by the attorney or the attorney's associate. A well-written declaration may be a powerful tool when combined with a motion. The following is an example of a declaration written in support of a request for a temporary restraining order in a family law matter:

Example

Declaration of Alma Steinman:

1. I am the plaintiff in the above-entitled action.
2. On July 3, 2007, my husband, the Defendant, Robert Steinman, arrived at my home about 11:45 p.m. drunk and angry. At that time, we had been separated and living apart for almost one year. That night he yelled horrible things at me. The children were in their rooms but they could hear him. He said things like, "You will pay for everything you have done," and "I will make sure you never leave me."
3. When I tried to close the door he pushed me to the floor and began slapping me and punching me. I was screaming and crying. Our oldest child, Marcy, called 911 for help. The police came and took my husband away.
4. Since that day he has called my office and home at least six times every day. He continues to threaten me. Some of his threats are really violent. He told me on August 19 that he would "kill me" if I see another man. I am very afraid of him.

I declare that the foregoing is true and correct under penalty of perjury.

You can see that this simple declaration in the client's own words is a powerful statement, much more so than the statement of facts in the memorandum itself. See Figure 13-7 for an example of a declaration by an attorney prepared in connection with a motion.

In some cases, facts presented in a memorandum of points and authorities are supported by deposition testimony, rather than by declarations or affidavits. A deposition is an out-of-court proceeding where a witness is questioned by attorneys. The witness is sworn to tell the truth under penalty of perjury and a written transcript of the questions and answers is prepared. Review Figure 13-5 to see how references to deposition testimony appear in the memorandum.

IN THE SUPERIOR COURT OF THE STATE OF CALIFORNIA

IN AND FOR THE COUNTY OF SANTA CLARA

THE PEOPLE OF THE STATE OF CALIFORNIA,	)	Case No. 196239
Plaintiff,	)	DECLARATION OF
	)	MARK B. HAMES
vs.	)	IN OPPOSITION TO
	)	MOTION TO DISMISS
RANDOLPH RAMBEAUX,	)	
	)	Date: November 20, 2007
Defendant.	)	Time: 9:00 a.m.
	)	Dept: 2

I, Mark Hames, do declare as follows:

1. I am a Supervising Deputy District Attorney as to the prosecution and preliminary examination of the above-entitled case;

2. On or about May 1, 2007, I received a call from the then attorney for the defendant, to resolve a Penal Code §1275 source of bail issue. As I was not available, I asked to take up the matter on May 2, 2005, as we would both be in Judge Phillips' department for preliminary examination;

3. On May 2, 2007 at 8:30 a.m. counsel and I appeared in Judge Phillips' department. We both advised the court in chambers that we were trying to resolve a Penal Code §1275 issue. These discussions lasted approximately 30 minutes at which time the court took the bench and the preliminary examination started;

4. During the course of the Penal Code §1275 discussions Judge Phillips stated that he had viewed the complaint and prior history and was "inclined" to raise the bail;

5. Thereafter, defendant's counsel made his CCP §170.6 for the first time, it was denied as being untimely;

6. Throughout the preliminary examination, neither counsel nor the defendant stated or implied that Judge Phillips had previously represented the defendant in 1990.

7. Throughout the preliminary examination, Judge Phillips did not state or imply that he had represented the defendant almost 16 years ago.

I declare, under penalty of perjury, that the above is true and correct, and that this declaration was executed in San Jose, California on November 12, 2007.

MARK B. HAMES
Supervising Deputy District Attorney

FIGURE 13-7
Declaration in
Opposition to Motion

13-6 TRIAL AND ARBITRATION BRIEFS

A trial brief is a document filed with the trial court, usually immediately prior to the start of the trial. The purpose of this document is to establish the legal support for the party's claims or defenses at trial. A second purpose is to present legal argument for evidentiary issues that a party anticipates will arise during trial. For example, in a medical malpractice case, the defendant, a doctor, might want to be assured that the plaintiff does not present any evidence relating to the doctor's insurance. In a trial brief filed before the case begins, the doctor's attorneys can present legal authorities supporting such a request. Trial briefs can also provide legal support for jury instructions.

In many jurisdictions, trial briefs are not required, but are filed only when attorneys anticipate that legal questions will arise during trial. If a trial brief is filed, it is for the benefit of the judge. If the case is being tried by a jury, the jurors never see the document. Furthermore, because there are no requirements that a party file a trial brief, the plaintiff is not necessarily the first one to file such a document. It is possible for both parties to file a trial brief simultaneously or for the defendant to file first. In any event, if one party has filed a brief, the other will often respond to the issues that are raised. The court might even ask the attorneys to do this.

Today, many cases go to **arbitration** rather than to trial. Arbitration is an out-of-court proceeding that takes place before a neutral party. This neutral party, an arbitrator, hears evidence from both parties and makes a decision. In an arbitration proceeding, parties may file **arbitration briefs,** which are similar to trial briefs and serve the same purposes.

arbitration. An out-of-court proceeding where parties submit a dispute to a neutral person for resolution.

arbitration brief. A document submitted in an arbitration proceeding addressing the legal issues in the arbitration.

13-7 APPELLATE BRIEFS

When a trial court decision is appealed, the parties are required to file briefs with the reviewing court. The initial brief, filed by the party who appeals, is called the *brief for the petitioner.* The brief filed by the other party is called the *brief for the respondent.* The petitioner, or appellant, also files a reply brief. In the opening, or petitioner's, brief, the appealing party describes legal errors that it contends occurred at trial. These form the basis for the legal issues in the brief that contains legal argument supporting these contentions. The respondent's brief answers these contentions, arguing that no legal errors occurred, or if they did, they were harmless and do not justify a reversal. In the reply brief, the petitioner answers points raised in the respondent's brief. Like a memorandum of points and authorities, an appellate brief is a persuasive document. Also, as with memoranda of points and authorities, strict time limits govern the filing dates for each brief.

A Point to Remember

Be careful not to confuse parties in an appellate brief. Often the appellant is called the *petitioner.* This is not the same as the plaintiff at the trial level. The petitioner, or appellant, may be either the plaintiff or the defendant.

Appellate briefs generally contain the following sections: Table of Contents, Table of Authorities, Statement of Facts, Statement of the Case, Issues or Questions Presented, Summary of Argument, Argument, and Conclusion. A statement of the case, which is usually not included in a memorandum of points and authorities or a trial brief, is a brief summary of the procedural history of the case. In substance, an appellate brief is very similar to a memorandum of points and authorities. The respondent's brief may or may not contain a statement of facts, a statement of the case, or an issue statement. If the respondent accepts the statements of the petitioners, there is no need to repeat it. Reply briefs generally do not contain any of the above.

Writing an appellate brief requires one step not usually required for a memorandum of points and authorities or for a trial brief. Because the appellate brief deals with what happened at trial, frequent mention is made of testimony or documents from the lower court. When this is done, reference or citation to the testimony or documents must be made in the brief. When a case is appealed, two types of records are prepared, a **clerk's transcript** and a **reporter's transcript.** The clerk's transcript consists of all the documents filed in the case or introduced at trial as exhibits. They are bound together and each page is numbered. The reporter's transcript contains a verbatim record of oral proceedings.

A reference to the clerk's transcript in a brief may look like this:

> On September 15, 1998, plaintiff filed a complaint accusing defendant of having violated the Civil Rights Act and asking for damages. (CT 7-12)

A reference to the reporter's transcript in a brief may look like this:

> During trial, the judge denied plaintiff's request to admit a videotape of the incident. (RT 125)

Another requirment that is unique to appellate briefs is a color-coded cover. Appellate court rules dictate the color of a cover for the particular brief.

clerk's transcript. Copies of all documents filed in a case and compiled by the clerk of the court at a party's request.

reporter's transcript. A verbatim record of oral proceedings in a case.

13-8 ROLE OF THE RESEARCH ASSOCIATE

Any legal memorandum or brief filed in court must bear the signature of an attorney rather than of a paralegal or law clerk. This does not mean, however, that research associates play no role in the preparation of a legal memorandum or brief; indeed the opposite is often true. Tasks performed by paralegals and law clerks include researching the legal issues, drafting memoranda of law explaining their research findings, reviewing and summarizing transcripts that are connected to the proceeding, and cite-checking and proofreading the final document. Occasionally, a research associate prepares a draft of a memorandum of points and authorities or brief for the attorney. Review Appendix D for an example of how two research associates helped in the preparation of a memorandum of points and authorities.

BOX 13-1   CLOSE-UP WITH GERALD UELMEN, ATTORNEY— CONSTITUTIONAL LAW SCHOLAR—PROFESSOR OF LAW

Professor Uelmen, who often uses research associates, provides the following insights and advice about legal research and writing.

The *key* to good research is thoroughness. All research must be updated and current. Researchers must use the most current sources available. The research project must be complete. A complete research project includes the "bad news" as well as the law that supports the client's interests. Counterarguments and weaknesses must be thoroughly researched.

BOX 13-1 (Continued)

He advises researchers to strive for clarity. Clarity is an essential element of good writing. Researchers must have a clear idea of where they are going *during* the research process. This initial focus enables the researcher to produce a writing that is clear and well reasoned. When doing his own research, much of his initial effort is through the LEXIS service. He often supplements his computer-assisted legal research with various printed materials.

At the time of this interview, Professor Uelmen was one of several defense attorneys working on the Marijuna Club cases in Federal Court in San Francisco, California. The attorneys divided up the issues, with Professor Uelmen focusing on four issues. Law student volunteers performed the initial research and provided memos to Professor Uelmen, which he then transformed into an argument, which, as a portion of the Memorandum of Points and Authorities, was filed with the Federal Court. In Appendix D, you will see some of this research and the Memorandum of Points and Authorities that was filed in this case.

Professor Uelmen is former dean of the School of Law at Santa Clara University. His publications include *Lessons from the Trial: The People v. O. J. Simpson; Disorderly Conduct: Verbatim Excerpts from Actual Cases; Supreme Folly;* and *Drug Abuse and Law: Cases, Text, Materials.* He has litigated many high-profile cases; his former clients include O. J. Simpson and Christian Brando.

Online Legal Research

For examples of briefs/arguments written for the court, there may be no better sources than LEXIS and Westlaw. Both databases offer the user the opportunity to view the briefs submitted to the United States Supreme Court over the past few decades. In addition, in newsworthy litigation the pleadings and briefs are often available through these resources. This may be the best way to fully understand the arguments made by both parties in a case before the United States Supreme Court.

Note: The transcripts of the oral arguments may be available.

Court TV provides the pleadings and briefs on some current cases. The archives include a wide variety of documents.

www.courttv.com

The 7th Circuit provides a great deal of very useful information. Check the Web site at: www.ca7.uscourts.gov/ (look under Rules and Guides).

CITATION MATTERS

USE OF PINPOINT CITATIONS

THE BLUEBOOK—RULE 3.2

Legal writers use pinpoint citations to direct the reader to the exact page where the information cited to is located. This allows a reader to go directly to the relevant portion of a case, book, article, or periodical. Pinpoint citations also direct readers to specific subdivisions of a document or a statute. These pinpoint citations are widely used by good legal writers.

For example:

Ashcroft v. Free Speech Coalition, 535 U.S. 234, 241 (2002).

This citation includes the pinpoint to page 241 of the *Ashcroft* decision. This citation follows material taken from page 241. All quotes must be followed by a citation that includes a pinpoint cite, unless the material quoted from is not paginated. This is probably the most widely used type of pinpoint citation. Rule 3.2 illustrates how to use pinpoint citations for books, law review articles, the *Congressional Record*, the *United States Code*, and more.

The use of *id.* is not limited to quotations. Any time material is borrowed, even general ideas, citations must be used. The audience of a legal document expects to see well-chosen and properly cited law.

CHAPTER SUMMARY

Research memoranda written for the courts are persuasive or argumentative documents where an attorney advocates a position favorable to the client. These documents, which include a memorandum of points and authorities, a trial brief, and an appellate brief, are formal documents that must adhere to technical rules of form and content. Rules govern such things as length, content, citation format, and filing deadlines. Rules regarding form and content are often found in rules of court.

Research documents filed in court have several common features. These include a case caption, a table of contents, a table of authorities, a statement of facts, a statement of issues or questions presented, an argument, a conclusion, and a signature. A table of contents and a table of authorities are often not required in short documents.

When legal issues arise in a pending case, those issues are addressed in a memorandum of points and authorities, prepared by the attorneys for the disputing parties. These are often used to support or oppose a motion. Trial briefs are used to analyze legal issues anticipated to arise at trial. These include substantive issues in the case as well as anticipated evidentiary problems. Appellate briefs analyze legal questions that form the basis of an appeal. All documents filed in court must bear the signature of an attorney rather than a paralegal or law clerk. However, research associates often help in the preparation of these documents by (1) researching the law, (2) preparing research memoranda, (3) drafting memoranda of points and authorities or briefs for attorney review, (4) summarizing and reviewing transcripts of hearings or trials that are relevant to the issues, (5) checking cites, and (6) proofreading the final document to be filed with the court.

TERMS TO REMEMBER

advocate	filed	first impression
memorandum of points and authorities	caption	moving party
	table of contents	arbitration
trial brief	table of authorities	arbitration brief
appellate brief	court record	clerk's transcript
motion	declaration	reporter's transcript
rules of court	affidavit	
local rules of court	argument	

QUESTIONS FOR REVIEW

1. Briefly describe the three types of research documents submitted to a court.
2. How do rules of court affect research documents?
3. What is the difference between a table of contents and a table of authorities?
4. What are point headings and how are they used in an argument?
5. What type of documents usually require a table of contents and a table of authorities?
6. What is the significance of the court record, declarations, or affidavits to research documents?
7. Why must an attorney and not a paralegal or a law clerk sign a memorandum or brief that is filed with the court?
8. Describe the three types of memoranda of points and authorities.
9. Compare and contrast a memorandum of law with a memorandum of points and authorities.
10. Compare and contrast a trial brief with an appellate brief.

BUILDING YOUR ANALYTICAL SKILLS: ASSIGNMENTS AND EXERCISES

1. After comparing and contrasting the summaries of the arguments in the *Illinois v. Caballes* case (Figure 13-6), explain the theory of the case for each party. (Think of the "theory of the case" as the foundation of the argument.)
2. Prepare a table of authorities for the memorandum in Figure 13-5.
3. Prepare a table of contents for the memorandum in Figure 13-5.

CASE PROJECT

Refer to the hypothetical case in Appendix A that you researched in previous chapters. Assume that the case is going to trial. Write a trial brief for either side addressing the legal issues in the case.

LEGAL CORRESPONDENCE

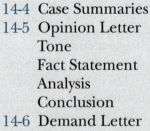

S KILL OBJECTIVES FOR CHAPTER 14

When you complete this chapter you should be able to

- Write a business letter using standard business letter format.
- Describe the different types of general correspondence that law firms use.
- List and describe the type of information contained in a case summary.
- Summarize a case file.
- Describe the content and tone of an opinion letter.
- Draft an opinion letter based on provided facts.
- Describe the content and tone of a demand letter.
- Draft a demand letter based on provided facts.

FROM THE DESK OF W. J. BRYAN, ESQ.

TO: Research Assistant

I recently received an offer from the prosecutor allowing Meyers to plead guilty to involuntary manslaughter rather than murder, providing that he does so before the motion to suppress is decided by a judge. I discussed this matter with our client and gave him my evaluation and opinion in the matter. I want to follow this up with a letter setting out the arguments for and against his accepting this offer and my recommendation. Please check my calendar and schedule a time when I can discuss this with you. You will write a draft of the letter. I will review and sign it.

14-1 INTRODUCTION

An important type of legal writing is the business letter. The efficient functioning of any law office depends on this communication method. Letters are used to communicate with other lawyers, clients, and with the courts. They serve many different purposes. In some instances business letters are used to communicate factual information. For example, if documents are sent to a court for filing, a letter provides the court with a description of the documents and instructions for filing. Such a letter is referred to as a **transmittal letter** or **cover letter** and is fairly simple. Simple business letters are also used to set up or confirm appointments or court dates, to request information from a client, or to confirm conversations. More complex correspondence involves the legal issues in a case. Sometimes correspondence includes a *summary* of a legal position, providing the reader with an objective explanation of the law. For example, an attorney might write a letter to a client (especially an insurance company) summarizing the legal position of an opposing party who made a motion in court. Other times, the correspondence includes not only an explanation of the law, but also a legal opinion regarding the client's rights or obligation. This type of letter is referred to as an **opinion letter** and is a type of predictive writing. Letters are also used to initiate settlement of a case. Such a letter utilizes

transmittal letter. A letter sent with documents or other items, explaining the nature of the documents or items as well as directions to the recipient for any actions to be taken with the documents or items; also referred to as a cover letter.

cover letter. A letter sent with documents or other items, explaining the nature of the documents or items as well as directions to the recipient for any actions to be taken with the documents or items; also referred to as a transmittal letter.

opinion letter. Formal correspondence from an attorney to a client or other attorney explaining an attorney's interpretation of the law as applied to a factual situation.

demand letter. Formal correspondence from an attorney to a party or other attorney demanding that action be taken or requesting a settlement of a claim or dispute.

persuasive techniques to encourage an opposing party to settle a case, either by paying a sum of money or by taking some other action. Such a letter is referred to as a **demand letter,** because it "demands" that some action be taken by the person to whom it is directed. All letters, regardless of how simple or how complex, must look professional, be grammatically correct, and be clear and understandable.

In addition to formal business letters, today's law office sees correspondence exchanged through e-mail and fax. Even though this results in instant communication and has some definite advantages, e-mail and fax present numerous potential problems.

This chapter discusses the different types of legal correspondence.

14-2 BUSINESS LETTER FORMAT

Legal correspondence follows the standard format for any type of business letter. It includes the following:

1. Name and address of the sender
2. The date
3. Special mailing or delivery methods
4. The inside address
5. A reference line
6. The salutation
7. The body
8. The closing
9. The signature block
10. Notations of enclosures, initials of preparer, and notation of copies sent

Letterhead and Date

The name and address of the sender is normally in a letterhead, preprinted on office stationery. In the case of a multi-attorney law firm, the letterhead usually includes the name of the firm as well as the name of all attorneys in the firm. A paralegal's name may or may not be included, depending on the law of the state and the policy of the office. Below the letterhead is the date.

Special Mailing or Delivery Methods

Below the date, a notation is made of special types of mailing or delivery methods. Legal correspondence is sometimes sent using certified mail or overnight delivery. These methods may have legal consequences. Today it is common to send correspondence first by fax, then followed by first-class mail. This is indicated in the letter.

Inside Address and Reference Line

The inside address contains the name, title, and address of the person to whom the correspondence is sent. Following the inside address is a reference line describing the subject matter of the legal correspondence. A reference line serves two purposes. It allows the recipient to know immediately what the letter concerns. If the recipient is another law office, an insurance company, or other business, this allows the person opening the mail to attach the letter to the office file before giving it to the named recipient. Also, should the letter ever be separated from your file (this happens in busy law offices, especially when attorneys remove documents from files), anyone finding it knows where it belongs. The information on the reference line varies. The most obvious is your client's name. However, that may not be very helpful to recipients of the letter, especially if they represent someone else. It is, therefore, preferable to include not only your client's name, but also the name of the client to whom the letter is sent. If legal correspondence is sent in response to other letters that contain client names or file numbers, these should be referenced in your letter. Such a reference line might read as follows:

Re: Victoria V. v. U Shop Mall
Your File No.: A12345

Salutation

The salutation in a letter from the law office should be kept formal. Unless some special relationship exists between you and the recipient, avoid the use of first names and use the terms "Mr." and "Ms." If the communication is sent to an unknown person, such as the clerk of the court, the person's title can be used—for example, "Dear Clerk."

Body

The body of the letter depends on the purpose of the letter. Some of the more common purposes are discussed in the following sections. However, regardless of the purpose, always keep the tone professional and businesslike. Avoid slang and never use contractions (such as didn't instead of did not). Be concise and to the point. Know what you want to say before you begin writing. Start with the end in mind.

Closing and Signature Block

The closing is very simple in a business letter. The phrases "Sincerely," "Sincerely yours," and "Very truly yours," are most commonly used. The signature block includes the name of the person sending the correspondence and his or her title. If you work as a paralegal, you might be allowed to sign letters on your own behalf. If so, always indicate your title following your name (such as "Paralegal" or "Legal Assistant"). In many cases, however, you draft letters on behalf of your supervising attorney. In such a case, the attorney's name and signature appear at the end of the letter.

Closing Notations

With any legal correspondence, the question of who receives copies is important. In addition to the named recipient, copies of legal correspondence are sometimes sent to the client. This lets the client know what is happening on the case. However, before sending copies to the client, always check with the attorney. If legal correspondence is sent in connection with a pending lawsuit and multiple attorneys are involved in the case, copies of correspondence between two of the attorneys are usually sent to all of the attorneys, especially if the matter relates to any time deadlines, court appearances, or other action pertaining to the case.

See Figure 14-1 on page 378 and note the various parts of a business letter.

14-3 GENERAL CORRESPONDENCE

Effectively operating a law office requires constant correspondence with clients, opposing attorneys, the courts, and miscellaneous parties. Four types of letters regularly found in a law office file include confirming letters, appointment letters, cover or transmittal letters, and information letters.

Confirming Letters

In order to avoid misunderstandings, confirming letters are sent to confirm an oral (usually telephone) conversation. Confirming letters are sent to confirm the following:

1. Substantive agreements relating to the case. (For example, in a family law matter parties may agree to a child visitation schedule.)
2. Agreements regarding the due date of any document, especially if an extension of time is granted.
3. Agreements setting or changing a court date, deposition, or other legal proceeding.
4. Any conversation that might need verification at a later date.

Confirming letters are sent for several reasons. Primarily, of course, the reason is to avoid misunderstandings that sometimes result from oral communications. They are also necessary because of the way that law firms operate. Often, files in offices are reassigned, or attorneys and paralegals may leave one firm and join another. The result is that the new attorney or paralegal has no way of knowing what agreements were reached by their predecessors unless some written memorandum or letter is contained in the file.

Appointment Letters

When a person is represented by an attorney, all notices from the courts or other attorneys in the case are sent to the attorney—not the client. This is true even when the notice requires that the client appear in court or at some other legal proceeding. The attorneys are obligated to notify their clients of the time, date, and place of any appearance or appointment. Although such notice can be given by telephone, an appointment letter should also be sent. The letter should clearly set forth the essential information, such as time, date, and place. The place should be completely described; if the client is to appear in court, the letter should give the address of the court, not just a reference to the "district court." Furthermore, always make certain that you have some way of confirming that the client received the letter and will appear as directed. This is done either by asking the client to call you to confirm his or her appearance or by your calling the client at some future date.

Cover or Transmittal Letters

A cover letter is used to explain documents that are sent. A cover letter should state exactly what documents are enclosed with the letter and what the recipient is to do with the documents, and any due dates for a response. In other words, is the recipient to review the documents, sign the documents, file the documents, or record the documents. The cover letter should also describe any expected response. Do you want the recipient to sign the documents and return them to you? If so, are the documents due by a certain date? Do you want the court to file the documents and return copies to you? If you want copies returned to you, enclose a self-addressed stamped envelope. Many courts will not return documents unless you do this.

Information Letters

A letter requesting or conveying information may be used to obtain information from a client, a witness, or some other third party. Sometimes the information sought is solely related to a specific case. For example, in an automobile accident case you might need a client to provide copies of all medical bills. Other times, the information is more general. For example, suppose you have a client who wants to obtain a zoning variance for a piece of real estate and you need to know whether the local regulating agency has any specific forms or guidelines to follow. The most difficult part about preparing a letter requesting information is identifying the party who has the information. This may take some preliminary work on your part.

In addition to requesting information, letters are sent conveying information. This might involve advising a client about the status of his or her case or responding to an inquiry from another attorney. In all cases, be sure that you understand the information to be conveyed before writing any letter. If you are in doubt, check your facts.

14-4 CASE SUMMARIES

Information letters are common in law firms that handle claims covered by insurance. In these instances, insurance companies not only are responsible for any ultimate judgment or settlement, they also bear the expense of litigation. These companies expect to receive periodic reports or summaries of the litigation. Case summaries must be prepared. In complex cases, case summaries are also routinely prepared to help the attorney handling the litigation. Case summaries are an important type of legal writing.

The purpose of a summary of any document or information is to inform the reader of the main ideas found in the summarized documents or data. The summary is read in lieu of the multiple pages found in the original data. Recall the case briefs discussed in Chapter 4. These briefs contain the main ideas found in the case opinion. By reading a case brief, the reader knows what is found in the case opinion without having read the entire case opinion. Also recall from Chapter 13 that when a memorandum of points and authorities exceeds a certain length many courts demand a summary of the argument be included in the memorandum.

A summary of any document requires that the writer extract the main points or ideas. A good way to begin this process is by looking for topic sentences in each paragraph of the document. Well-written topic sentences provide the main topic of the paragraph.

A case summary is usually completed by reviewing and summarizing the factual basis supporting the case as well as summarizing all of the documents found in a case file. One way of summarizing the factual basis of a case is to prepare a chronology of events. The chronology is often prepared in a column format with the following information:

Date   Event   Source of Information   Comments

Summarizing documents is similar. The main topics from documents include the date the document was prepared, the type of document (i.e., a complaint, a motion, a letter, etc.), the parties who wrote or received copies of the documents as well as any parties mentioned within the document, the main ideas or topics found within the document (e.g., if it is a memorandum of points and authorities, a summary should include a summary of the argument and all authorities cited within it), and finally any comments (e.g., a note that one document conflicts with another). Such a summary might be organized as follows:

Date   Type of Document   Parties   Content   Comments

Before preparing any case summary, you should always know any specific purpose for which the summary will be used. This affects both the information contained in the summary and the organization of the summary.

A Point to Remember

When preparing a case summary, do not just describe what the case is about. The summary must contain the main topics or ideas found in the case. The summary may be read in lieu of the entire case file.

14-5 OPINION LETTER

An opinion letter analyzes a particular factual situation in light of existing law and offers a legal opinion to the reader. For example, consider the Meyers case development as set forth in the note at the beginning of this chapter. The prosecutor offered a plea bargain if Meyers pleads guilty immediately. Rather than a murder charge that might involve a life sentence, the prosecutor agreed to accept a plea of involuntary manslaughter, a charge that carries much less jail time. However, Meyers must drop his motions to suppress evidence. Before deciding whether to accept this offer, Meyers would undoubtedly rely on the advice and opinion of his attorney. The attorney must evaluate the chances of the judge granting the motions as well as evaluating what might happen at a trial. This evaluation requires the attorney to analyze both the facts and the law. Based on those evaluations, the attorney makes recommendation or gives his opinion to Meyers. Even though such opinions are discussed with the client, an attorney might also want to include this information in a written *opinion* letter to the client.

Tone

Opinion letters are often written in response to an inquiry of a party who has a dispute with another party and is trying to determine what course of action to take. When an attorney recommends a specific course of action, he or she must first "predict" how a court would resolve the dispute. Only based on this prediction, can an attorney advise a client. Predictions, of course, are never 100% accurate and this must be conveyed to the recipient of an opinion letter. When writing the legal analysis in an opinion letter, you use the predictive writing techniques described in Chapter 12.

Fact Statement

An example of an opinion letter is found in Figure 14-1. In this letter, attorney Birk-Ramiriz is responding to a client, Frank Bennett, who has a dispute with a neighbor over the height of a fence. Like most opinion letters, the analysis and recommendations are based on facts related to the attorney by the client. Note that prior to analyzing the law and giving an opinion, the attorney is careful to relate the facts that were provided and to limit any opinion to those specific facts.

Analysis

Following the statement of the facts is an explanation and analysis of the law and a prediction of a probable outcome. An opinion letter requires that you do legal research and analysis, skills that were discussed in earlier chapters. However, remember that in writing such a letter, you are not writing it for an attorney or other legal professional. Try to avoid legal jargon. (Jargon should be avoided in any legal writing, but it is particularly important to do so here.) When writing an opinion letter, you often need to decide whether to include legal citations to cases or statutes. Practice differs on this point. Some attorneys believe that clients do not understand citations, so including them in a letter is unnecessary or possibly confusing. However, other attorneys are so used to citing law that they automatically include citations. There is an additional consideration. A copy of an opinion letter is included in the office client file. Should an attorney or other legal professional review the file and read the opinion letter, it is very helpful to have citations for authorities mentioned in the letter.

Conclusion

Finally, the letter provides the client with possible courses of actions or recommendations. Sometimes the letter expresses an opinion about the party's rights and obligations. Other times it recommends possible action that the party can take. Because an opinion letter gives legal advice, it must always be signed by an attorney. A paralegal cannot sign this type of letter.

See Figure 14-1 for an example of an opinion letter.

BOX 14-1   OPINION LETTER CHECKLIST

✓ State all facts upon which the opinion is based.

✓ Explain the relevant law.

✓ Explain how the law applies to the given facts.

✓ State opinion or conclusion.

JANET BIRK-RAMIRIZ
Attorney at Law
573 Second Ave. Suite 234
San Jose, CA 95110
Tel. (408) 555-1234   Fax. (408) 555-2345

jbr@online.com   www.jbrlaw.com

July 31, 2XXX

VIA FAX AND FIRST CLASS MAIL

Frank Bennett
3085 Monteverde Dr.
Cupertino, CA 94123

Re: Fence Dispute

Dear Mr. Bennett,

This letter is in response to your recent inquiry regarding a dispute you have with your neighbor over a fence. The facts you related to me are as follows. Your neighbor recently tore down a six-foot-high split rail fence located on the boundary between your two homes, and erected a brick fence measuring ten feet high in its place. This new fence blocks your view of neighboring hills. You also informed me that you have a history of problems with your neighbor, dating back over ten years. In the past, your neighbor has trampled on your flowers, thrown garbage in your yard and on several occasions shouted loud obscenities to you and your wife. Last summer, while you were on a two week vacation, evidently your neighbor called the police complaining that your car was parked on the street where it remained during your vacation. You now want to know if you can force your neighbor to tear down the brick fence and if you are entitled to any monetary damages because of your neighbor's conduct. Pursuant to your request I have researched the matter. My findings and opinions are dependent on the facts you presented being complete and accurate.

California law contains a specific provision regarding "spite fences." This provision, section 841.4 of the California Civil Code, provides as follows:

> Any fence or other structure in the nature of a fence unnecessarily exceeding 10 feet in height maliciously erected or maintained for the purpose of annoying the owner or occupant of adjoining property is a private nuisance. Any owner or occupant of adjoining property injured either in his comfort or the enjoyment of his estate by such nuisance may enforce the remedies against its continuance prescribed in Title 3, Part 3, Division 4 of this code.

Under this section you must show (1) that the fence exceeds 10 feet in height, (2) that the height is unnecessary, and (3) that it was maliciously erected. The facts related to me indicate that the fence is 10 feet high. The code section applies to fences that exceed 10 feet. You must obtain exact measurements of the height of the fence. Even if the fence does not exceed 10 feet, other legal theories may apply to your case. Before spending time researching this, however, I advise that you obtain exact measurements. Assuming that the fence exceeds 10 feet, even by a small amount, I believe you have strong evidence of a malicious motive on the part of your neighbor. Your neighbor's past conduct provides a history of ill will and bad feelings and is strong evidence of his intent in building this fence. In fact, there is a California case from the court of appeals, *Griffin v. Northridge* (1944) 67 Cal. App. 2d 69 that closely parallels your situation. The court held that conduct such as has occurred in your case, is strong evidence of malicious intent. For your information, I am including a copy of this case.

If your neighbor will not voluntarily remove the fence, you can file a lawsuit and ask the court to order the removal of the fence. Alternatively, you may ask for money damages. At this point, if you wish to proceed further, I suggest that you call me and set up an appointment to discuss the next action to take.

Sincerely,

Janet Birk-Ramiriz
Attorney at Law

JBK:hen

Enclosures (1)

FIGURE 14-1
Example of Opinion
Letter

14-6 DEMAND LETTER

A demand letter generally seeks resolution of a dispute or settlement of some matter, utilizing persuasive writing techniques. Sometimes it requests (or demands) that a party stop certain conduct (i.e., creating a nuisance or infringing on a patent) or comply with an existing obligation (i.e., payment of money owed.) Other times a demand letter is sent in the hopes of settling an existing or potential lawsuit (e.g., a claim resulting from an automobile accident). Regardless of the reason for the letter, most demand letters include (1) a statement of facts establishing that the client has a legitimate legal claim, (2) a discussion of the law showing the legal basis for a cause of action, (3) an itemization of damages that were incurred, and (4) a demand for a specific settlement.

Tone

The tone used in demand letters varies considerably. In some cases, the letter may be as harsh as the name suggests. For example, if your client in a divorce case advises you that the separated spouse (who is not represented by an attorney) is harassing your client at work, you might send a letter *demanding* that the behavior stop immediately. Likewise, if your client is owed money on an overdue promissory note, a demand letter might demand immediate payment. On the other hand, some demand letters are much more conciliatory in their tone, especially where the attorney is attempting to reach a monetary settlement in a case. (Demand letters are frequently sent to insurance companies for this purpose.) All demand letters are intended to be persuasive. The object of the letter is to convince the recipient of the letter to do something.

Fact Statement

The statement of facts in a demand letter is a critical part of the letter. If the reader does not accept your version of the facts, there may be little reason to settle a case. The persuasive nature of the demand letter begins here. If possible, facts stated in a demand letter should be supported by more than your own client's statement. Support for the facts giving rise to the claim is found in the following sources: witness statements, police reports, investigative reports, documents, photographs, and statements made by the opposing party. In writing the factual background in a demand letter, the source of all facts should be identified. In many instances, verifying documents or photographs may even be attached to the letter.

Analysis

The legal analysis is likewise written using persuasive techniques. These techniques are described in Chapter 13. Here controlling statutory and case law is discussed and applied to the stated facts.

Damages and Injuries

Like the statement of facts, the itemization of damages and description of injuries should be verified. Copies of medical bills or other out-of-pocket expenses should be included with the letter. Verification of any personal or property damage should also be included. Medical reports, photographs, and property appraisals are commonly included.

The Demand or Offer to Settle

A demand letter concludes with a clear statement of the action requested or offer of settlement. Generally, time limits for compliance or acceptance are also included. See Figure 14-2 for an example of a demand letter. The demand letter is based on the case Victoria V. v. U Shop Mall and the *Ann M.* case found in Chapter 12.

Roberta Jenkins
Attorney at Law
156 Oak St.
Central City, CA 91111
Tel. 510 555-1212   Fax. 510 555-2121

January 5, 20XX

Thomas Lord
Claims Adjuster
Goodhands Insurance Co.
78 Woodland Rd.
Central City, CA 96111

Re: Victoria V. v. U Shop Mall

Dear Mr. Lord:

I am writing on behalf of my client Victoria V., regarding her claim for personal injuries against your client U Shop Mall. The injuries were incurred when my client was assaulted on your client's premises on June 15, 20XX. I was advised by U Shop Mall that your company insures the mall and that all correspondence in this matter should be directed to you. After reviewing the statements of parties and witnesses and after examining various documents, I conclude that liability of your client is clear and that an early settlement in this matter is in everyone's best interests. The following information provides substantial justification for our offer of settlement.

Factual Basis
My client, Victoria V., was sexually assaulted in your client's parking lot at approximately 9 p.m. on June 15 of last year by an unknown assailant. The details of this event are found in a Central City Police Report dated June 16 of last year. The police report contains statements of Ms. V. as well as statements of two witnesses who observed an individual running from the scene and who assisted Ms. V. immediately after the assault. The report also contains a statement from a security guard employed by your client as well as the manager of the U Shop Mall. The statements from the witness substantiate the attack and resulting injuries. The statement from your employee, the security guard, confirms that the light in the parking lot was not operating. His statement also confirms that he reported this defective and dangerous condition several days prior to June 15. He also indicated that it takes him approximately 30 minutes to patrol the parking lot. The statement from your manager confirms that your client had prior notice of criminal acts on its premises and on nearby premises. He even admits, "I was afraid something like this would happen." A copy of the police report including all relevant statements is attached to this letter.

Legal Basis
The law in this jurisdiction is clear. Landowners owe a duty to maintain their premises in a reasonably safe condition. Cal. Civ. Code § 1714. This includes a duty to protect against criminal assaults by third parties when the landowner has knowledge that prior attacks have occurred. *Ann. M. v. Pacific Plaza Shopping Center*, 6 Cal. 4th 666 (1993). In this case, the facts prove that your client had such knowledge. Prior criminal acts occurred on the premises and on nearby premises. Your own client admits that he feared something like this would happen. Your client therefore had a duty to protect my client against attacks and breached that duty by failing to repair lights and by failing to provide adequate security guards.

Injuries and Damages
As a result of your client's negligence my client suffered severe physical and psychological injuries. She was treated at Central City Hospital where she was admitted. She also saw Dr. B. Feldon for her physical injuries and received therapy from Dr. K. Gordon, a psychiatrist. Copies of medical reports from Dr. Feldon and Dr. Gordon are attached to this letter. As the medical reports indicate, Ms. V. suffered numerous contusions and abrasions, as well as lumbar strain. She continues to have back pain. The emotional distress was severe and post traumatic stress syndrome may continue for the remainder of her life. To date Ms. V.'s medical expenses are as follows:

Central City Hospital	$10,569
Dr. Feldon	$ 1,250
Dr. Gordon	$ 2,400

It is anticipated that therapy will be needed for at least an additional six months, at a cost of $4,500. Copies of medical bills are enclosed.

In addition to medical expenses, Ms. V. was unable to work for 2 months. She has a management position at A & B Enterprises and her income is $120,000 per year. She lost approximately $40,000 in income.

FIGURE 14-2

Example of
Demand Letter

Settlement Offer
In view of the clear liability and the nature and extent of the injuries and damages, my client is agreeable to settling this matter for the sum of $250,000. I believe this to be fair and reasonable and hope to hear from you soon. The offer will remain open for 30 days.

Sincerely,

Roberta Jenkins
Attorney at Law

RJ:op

Enclosures (3)

cc: Victoria V.

FIGURE 14-2
(continued)

14-6 FAX AND E-MAIL

Most legal correspondence is still sent by mail. However, fax and e-mail correspondence offer speed in communicating and for that reason are sometimes favored by attorneys. There are, however, some concerns when using a fax machine or e-mail to transmit a letter. Confidentiality is a concern. Sending information via fax or e-mail does not assure any degree of confidentiality, because anyone can be on the receiving end. Many lawyers add a paragraph to any information they transmit by fax or e-mail asserting the confidentiality of the matter. Such a paragraph might read as follows:

Caution—Confidential
The document being transmitted to you may contain information protected by attorney-client privilege. It is intended only for the person to whom it is addressed. If you have received this facsimile in error, please notify us immediately and destroy the document.

However, this serves little purpose if the receiver is not an attorney or is not otherwise bound by an ethical standard of behavior. Faxing and e-mail are not safe with highly confidential or sensitive material.

E-mail presents additional problems. Because law offices need to keep copies of correspondence that is sent and received, e-mail cannot be used without making hard copies of messages sent and received. Because of the informal nature of e-mail, sometimes there is a tendency to forget that a communication from a law office is business correspondence. E-mails should always be carefully read and reviewed before sent.

Online Legal Research

Several government agencies are responsible for providing opinions on a variety of topics. Two such agencies are the U.S. Department of Labor and the Federal Trade Commission. Several of their opinion letters are found online at the following sites:

http://www.dol.gov/esa/whd/opinion/opinion.htm (Opinion letters issued by the Department of Labor)
http://www.ftc.gov/os/statutes/fcra/index.shtm (Opinion letters issued by the Federal Trade Commission)

CITATION MATTERS

THE USE OF BRACKETS

THE BLUEBOOK—**RULE 5.2**

Brackets are used when a letter needs to be changed from lower to uppercase, or vice versa.

1. Substituted letters (possibly to change tense)
2. Words (possibly to correct agreement or provide clarification)
3. Other inserted material

The Bluebook provides an excellent example:

> [P]ublic confidence in the [adversary] system depend[s upon] full disclosure of all the facts, within the framework of the rules of evidence.

In this example, a lowercase *p* was capitalized and *adversary* and *s upon* were added to make the sentence read well.

When there is a significant error in the original quote, place [*sic*] directly following the mistake.

> The Court noted that the judgment were [*sic*] not necessarily harsh, given the circumstances under which the crime was committed.

CHAPTER SUMMARY

Law offices routinely use business letters for numerous purposes. Regardless of the purpose, these letters follow standard business letter format and contain the name, address, and other contact information of the sender, the date, a notation of special delivery methods, an inside address, a reference line, a salutation, the body of the letter, a closing, a signature block, and notation of enclosures or copies. Letters are used for routine law office procedures such as confirming information, setting appointments, and conveying or requesting information. Cover or transmittal letters are used when documents are transmitted. In addition to routine office proceedings, attorneys use two special types of letters, opinion letters and demand letters. Opinion letters are written to clients to explain and analyze a legal problem and contain an opinion of the client's rights and obligations or a recommendation for a course of action. Demand letters are written to demand specific action from a party or to offer to settle a dispute.

TERMS TO REMEMBER

transmittal letter	opinion letter
cover letter	demand letter

QUESTIONS FOR REVIEW

1. What are the components of a standard business letter?
2. Can a paralegal's name be included in office letterhead?
3. What is a cover or transmittal letter?
4. Describe situations in which an information letter might be used.
5. What is the purpose of a case summary?
6. What is an opinion letter?
7. List the components of an opinion letter.
8. What is a demand letter?
9. List the component parts of a demand letter.
10. Describe some problems using fax and e-mail as methods of legal correspondence.

BUILDING YOUR WRITING AND ANALYSIS SKILLS: ASSIGNMENTS AND EXERCISES

1. Mr. and Mrs. Robert Smith contacted a lawyer with the following issue: Their son, Jeffrey turned 18 four months ago. He is a senior in high school, living at home, and will graduate in 5 months. He has a part-time job at a local fast-food restaurant and earns approximately $400 per month, most of which he spends on his car and entertainment. He is not married. Jeffrey has become a problem for Mr. and Mrs. Smith. He refuses to follow house rules, and stays out extremely late. He is causing a great deal of stress at home. The Smiths are demanding that Jeffrey find another place to live, but they want to know if they will be responsible for his support, and if so, how long this duty exists. Assume that the following Family Code section applies in your state:

   Subject to this division, the father and mother of a minor child have an equal responsibility to support their child in the manner suitable to the child's circumstances.

   The duty of support imposed herein continues as to an unmarried child who has attained the age of 18 years, is a full-time high school student, and who is not self-supporting, until the time the child completes the 12th grade or attains the age of 19 years, whichever occurs first. (Family Code §3.456)

   Based on this code section, write a draft of an opinion letter to the Smiths regarding their obligation to support Jeffrey.

2. Refer to Figure 14-1. Assume that your client, Frank Bennett, contacts your office and tells you that he hired a contractor to measure the fence in question. He presents you with a written report from the contractor, James Hammer, stating that precise measurements were taken and the fence measures 10 feet, 2 inches. James Hammer is a licensed general contractor. Write a demand letter to Mr. Bennett's neighbors, Paul and Marie Vista, demanding that he tear down the fence and pay Mr. Bennett the sum of $5000 to cover the cost of having the fence measured and for damages destroying your client's view. The Vistas live at 3087 Monteverde Dr.

3. Consider the following facts: Because of uninsured medical expenses, Dora Speckles incurred credit card charges of several thousand dollars. She was also unable to work for several months and was unable to pay the credit card

bill. Once her health was restored, Dora found employment in a small business office. However, she was still unable to make payments on the credit card account. The credit card company eventually turned the account over to Collect 'R Else collection agency. The Collection Agency learned of Dora's employment and telephoned her there to demand payment on the account. Dora advised the agency that she was not allowed to receive any nonemergency personal calls and requested that the collection agency not call her at work. Nevertheless, the collection agency continued to call her once a day. After two weeks, Dora was fired. Her employer told her she was terminated because of all the personal telephone calls. Dora worked as a receptionist for the Allied Title Company, earning $500 per week. After losing her job, Dora became very depressed, although she cannot afford to obtain medical treatment for this condition. After being unemployed for 2 months, Dora has finally found another job. Fearing that the collection agency will learn of this employment, Dora sought legal advice. Your law firm has agreed to represent Dora and advised her that she has remedies under the Fair Debt Collection Practices Act.

Draft a letter to the Collect 'R Else Collection Agency demanding that it have no further direct contact with Dora, either at home or any place of employment. Also demand damages for their past conduct in accordance with the Fair Debt Collection Practices Act. The relevant portions of the act are set forth below:

Fair Debt Collection Practices Act:

Communication in connection with debt collection [15 U.S.C. §1692c]

(a) COMMUNICATION WITH THE CONSUMER GENERALLY. Without the prior consent of the consumer given directly to the debt collector or the express permission of a court of competent jurisdiction, a debt collector may not communicate with a consumer in connection with the collection of any debt—

   (1) at any unusual time or place or a time or place known or which should be known to be inconvenient to the consumer. In the absence of knowledge of circumstances to the contrary, a debt collector shall assume that the convenient time for communicating with a consumer is after 8 o'clock antimeridian and before 9 o'clock postmeridian, local time at the consumer's location;

   (2) if the debt collector knows the consumer is represented by an attorney with respect to such debt and has knowledge of, or can readily ascertain, such attorney's name and address, unless the attorney fails to respond within a reasonable period of time to a communication from the debt collector or unless the attorney consents to direct communication with the consumer; or

   (3) at the consumer's place of employment if the debt collector knows or has reason to know that the consumer's employer prohibits the consumer from receiving such communication.

(b) COMMUNICATION WITH THIRD PARTIES. Except as provided in section 804, without the prior consent of the consumer given directly to the debt collector, or the express permission of a court of competent jurisdiction, or as reasonably necessary to effectuate a postjudgment judicial remedy, a debt collector may not communicate, in connection with the collection of any debt, with any person other than a consumer, his

attorney, a consumer reporting agency if otherwise permitted by law, the creditor, the attorney of the creditor, or the attorney of the debt collector.
Civil liability [15 U.S.C. §1692k]

(c) Except as otherwise provided by this section, any debt collector who fails to comply with any provision of this title with respect to any person is liable to such person in an amount equal to the sum of—

(1) any actual damage sustained by such person as a result of such failure;

(2) (A) in the case of any action by an individual, such additional damages as the court may allow, but not exceeding $1,000;

BUILDING YOUR ONLINE RESEARCH SKILLS: ASSIGNMENTS AND EXERCISES

1. Access the Web sites for the Department of Labor and the Federal Trade Commission found in the Online Legal Research feature. Select one opinion letter from each source and write a summary of the letters.

2. Using a general Internet search engine, find examples of different types of business letters.

Research and Writing Problems Based on Stated Fact Patterns and Case File Documents

Problem 1

People v. Baxter

In a busy shopping mall, Baxter grabs a bag of merchandise from Simpson. Simpson gives chase. In the course of the chase, Simpson has a heart attack and dies. With what crimes, if any, should Baxter be charged?

Problem 2

Flowers v. Mitchells

Peggy Mitchells is an aspiring fiction writer. She responds to a contest in a national magazine, *Sixteen*, and submits a short story. The short story is based on a teenage experience of Peggy revolving around a conflict with another girl, Tiffany Flowers, over a boy. In the short story, which is written in the first person, Peggy describes Tiffany as a "slut." Unfortunately, Peggy did not change Tiffany's name in the story. Tiffany has sued both Peggy and the magazine for libel.

Are Peggy and the magazine liable to Tiffany for damages?

Problem 3

Anystate v. Sutter

Sutter, a hospital, and Anystate, an insurance provider, signed a contract regarding health care services. The contract contained a provision requiring binding arbitration in the event of a dispute. Anystate claims that the contract was void and unenforceable and filed a lawsuit for declaratory relief and for rescission. Sutter filed an answer. Soon after the answer was filed, Anystate petitioned the court to require Sutter to submit to binding arbitration. Sutter claims that Anystate waived the arbitration provision by (1) claiming that the contract was void and unenforceable and by (2) filing a lawsuit in court.

Is Sutter correct?

1. Assume the contract is governed by state law.
2. Assume the contract is governed by federal law and the Federal Arbitration Act.

Problem 4

Drummond v. Jergins

Drummond, a customer in a bar, gets into a heated discussion with the bartender (Bob) over politics. Bob gets very angry and throws a glass of scotch at Drummond, splashing him in the face with the alcohol. The alcohol causes severe burning of Drummond's eyes. Bob then asks Bouncer Bill to eject Drummond from the bar. Bill grabs Drummond, dislocating Drummond's arm. Drummond sues Joe Jergins, the owner of the bar, for $100,000 for the damage to his eyes and his arm. Bob, the bartender, had worked for Jergins for only two weeks, during which time there were no complaints. Jergins did a background check of Bob before hiring him and found nothing to suggest he had violent tendencies. Is Jergins liable for the injuries claimed by Drummond?

Problem 5

Matter of Estate of Starr

Marjorie Starr had one natural child, a daughter, Evelyn Starr, and one foster child, Anthony Dilman. Anthony became her foster child when he was 16 years old. Marjorie's daughter Evelyn left home when she turned 18 and only contacted her mother when she needed money. Anthony, on the other hand, remained at home until he completed college. When Marjorie developed a terminal illness, Anthony moved back home and became her primary caregiver. Marjorie was dependent on Anthony for the last 2 years of her life. During this time, Evelyn rarely called and never visited.

When Anthony was 27, Marjorie died. She left no will, but surprisingly left an estate valued in excess of $2 million. Evelyn claims the entire estate as the sole child. Anthony has made a claim, contending that there was an equitable adoption. Pretrial discovery indicates the following facts: Marjorie and Anthony had a very close relationship from the time he first came to live with Marjorie. While in high school, Marjorie attended mother-son events with him and always referred to him as "my boy." She wore a "mother's ring" with the birthstones of both Evelyn and Anthony. However, Anthony was never formally adopted, nor were any attempts made to adopt. Anthony always kept his own name.

Does Anthony have a legitimate claim against the estate?

Problem 6

Owens v. Adams

Adams saw an advertisement on the Internet for the sale of a "wooded real estate lot." This was the only property advertised on this site. The lot was offered at $50,000, and interested parties were asked to e-mail the owner. Adams, who was familiar with the property in question, e-mailed the owner (Owens) as follows.

To: owens@aol.com

Re: Purchase of wooded real estate lot as seen on www.woodedlot.com

I am interested in your lot and hereby offer to purchase the property at $45,000, all cash, with the sale to close in 30 days.
M. Adams

Owens responded as follows:

To: madams@yahoo.com

Re: Offer to purchase lot

I will sell you the land at $47,500.
Owens

Adams replied immediately:

To: owens@aol.com

Re: Offer to purchase lot

Great! We have a deal
☺

Two weeks later, after doing considerable legal research on the Internet, Adams backed out of the deal, claiming that the transaction did not meet the requirements of the statute of frauds.

Is Adams correct?

Problem 7

People v. Barker

While on routine traffic patrol, police officer Matthew Dillon spotted Sonny Barker driving a late model white Mercedes automobile. Barker was well known to the police department and was suspected of being a drug dealer, although he had never been convicted of any drug offenses. Barker appeared to be obeying all traffic laws. Officer Dillon then noted that the vehicle did not have current registration tags and decided to stop the car, hoping that he might just see something related to the drug dealing. After stopping the vehicle, Dillon asked to see Barker's driver's license and the car registration. Barker could not produce either his license or the car's registration. Barker told Dillon that the car belonged to his mother. Dillon checked on Barker's driver's license and the car license. There were no warrants and the car had not been reported as stolen. He then asked Barker if he could search the car. Barker said yes. Dillon looked in the glove box and found the following: Barker's wallet, a little over one ounce of what looked like marijuana, and a piece of paper with the following writing—sbarker@digicom.com ("doobie"). Officer Dillon then reached under the front seat and found a large quantity of marijuana in a clear plastic bag. At this point he arrested Barker.

Later, Officer Dillon, who happens to be a computer fanatic and recognized the writing on the paper as being an Internet e-mail address, accessed the e-mail of S. Barker (*doobie* being the password). Dillon used his own computer to do this. Barker's e-mail contained the following message,

"Sold latest shipment of maryjane for a cool million; deposited your share in your mutual fund account at Citibank. Love, Ma."

Based on all of the above information, Sonny was charged with possession for sale.

The following issues have been raised in the criminal case.

1. Was the original stop good?
2. Was the search of the car good?
3. Was the officer's accessing Sonny's e-mail proper?

Problem 8

Su v. KILR

KILR, a local radio station, sponsored a "treasure chest" type contest. The station had buried a treasure ($5000) and periodically gave clues as to its location. The first one to find the treasure won the money. Steven Shriver heard a clue and was sure he knew the location of the money. However, several clues had been given over a period of time and Shriver was fairly certain that other people would also be able to figure out the clues. In order to get to the treasure first, Shriver therefore ignored the posted speed limits and was travelling 40 mph in a 25 mph zone (largely a residential neighborhood). When Shriver was about five blocks from the "treasure site," he noticed a police car behind him signaling him to pull over. Instead of pulling over, Shriver increased his speed to 50 mph. The police followed. Shriver kept increasing his speed, as did the police car following him. A high-speed chase ensued for about three

blocks, at which time Shriver ran a stop sign, colliding with another car and injuring the driver of that car. The injured party, Sally Su, has sued Shriver, KILR Radio Station, and Metro City Police Department for her injuries.

Su is a 35-year-old computer programmer. She is married and has two children. As a result of the accident, she suffered a cervical strain and was unable to work for three weeks following the accident. She did not have her seat belt on at the time of the accident.

Shriver is a 19-year-old college student. He was uninsured at the time of the accident.

Analyze the liability of the following parties:

a. KILR Radio Station
b. Metro City Police Department

Problem 9

The Rambeaux Matter

Randy Rambeaux, a San Diego city police officer, is facing both civil liability and criminal charges as a result of injuries he caused during a traffic stop. Although

he is accused of using excessive force, Rambeaux claims he acted in self-defense and always used an appropriate amount of force. The incident occurred as follows:

Rambeaux, who was not on duty at the time, observed a pickup truck with a defective tail light. He was, however, still in uniform since he had just completed his shift. After observing the truck, Rambeaux pulled up alongside the truck (Rambeaux was operating his own motorcycle), and motioned for the truck to pull over. The pickup pulled over to the side of the road and stopped. At this point there is some disagreement as to what happened. The accounts of the incident have been taken from a police report filed by Rambeaux, depositions of various parties, and statements from witnesses. However, uncontroverted is the fact that the driver of the truck suffered a severe blow to his head, resulting in a serious brain injury from which he has not recovered. One passenger in the truck has also been injured.

The following information was obtained from police reports and depositions of the parties:

Police Report

On March 21 of last year, San Diego Police Officer Randy Rambeaux stopped a 1989 Ford pickup truck with a camper shell, license, 123 ABC, because of defective brake lights. When he approached the vehicle Rambeaux saw numerous individuals crowded together in the camper shell. Rambeaux states that he ordered these individuals out of the vehicle. None of the individuals obeyed the officer's request. The request was repeated and still no one obeyed. Believing that the individuals might not understand English, Officer Rambeaux opened the driver's door, placed his hand on the arm of the driver (later identified as Jose Alcosta), and gestured for him to exit the vehicle. Alcosta resisted and more force was used to remove him from the vehicle. Fearing attack from the other passengers, Rambeaux removed his baton for self-protection. When Alcosta was pulled from the vehicle, he stumbled and fell, injuring himself. After Alcosta fell, suspect #2, Roberto Alcosta, jumped out of the vehicle. He slipped on the street, scraping his arms and legs. It was later determined that all passengers in the vehicle were in this country illegally. Both Alcostas were taken to San Diego County Hospital so that their injuries could be treated. The individuals in the camper shell, who were all under 18 years of age, were taken to county child protective services.

Deposition of Roberto Alcosta (taken through an interpreter)

Jose Alcosta is a citizen of Mexico who decided to come to the United States. Jose is 19 years old and has worked in construction in Mexico. Roberto is his 17-year-old brother. They lived a life of poverty in Mexico and hoped to find a better life in California. Friends told them that they could find work in California. Neither speaks English.

On the date of the incident, he recalls the following: The Alcosta family came across the border in a Ford pickup truck with a camper shell. At some point in time, police stopped their vehicle. The officer appeared to be saying something to them, but it was in English and they did not understand. Alcosta told the officer in Spanish that he did not understand him. The officer then grabbed Jose Alcosta and dragged him out of the vehicle. He then hit him repeatedly with a baton. Roberto Alcosta attempted to come to the aid of his brother and was grabbed and thrown to the ground by the officer. Jose suffered a severe blow to the head, a broken right arm, and internal injuries requiring the removal of his spleen. He has not recovered from the head injury. Roberto suffered numerous contusions and abrasions, but no broken bones.

Deposition of Rock MacMillan, Chief of Police

Chief MacMillan testified that it is highly unusual for off-duty police to make traffic stops and they are not encouraged to do so. Chief MacMillan also testified that the following is San Diego office policy regarding the use of force: Police officers are allowed to use reasonable force to effect an arrest or defend themselves. This includes the use of their baton or gun where appropriate. In the past year, the department has received twenty-six citizen complaints of excessive force. Fourteen of these complaints concerned arrests of illegal aliens. Of the twenty-six complaints made, the department determined that only two had any merit. In both cases the officers involved received reprimands.

The police department investigated the Rambeaux matter. Police talked to one witness who told them that Rambeaux ordered the driver and passengers out of the vehicle. Then, without giving them a chance to exit, he reached into the vehicle and pulled the driver out, throwing him on the ground. He drew his baton and struck the driver, saying, "Why don't you guys go back where you came from?"

Other evidence consists of a video showing Rambeaux pulling Jose Alcosta from the car and hitting him with a baton. The video also shows the officer pushing Roberto Alcosta to the ground. There is no sound on the video.

Deposition of Randy Rambeaux

Officer Rambeaux took the Fifth Amendment when deposed.

In addition to the depositions and police report, other discovery (mostly record production) revealed the following about the officer:

Randy Rambeaux is a ten-year veteran with the police department. He is married and has three children, ages 4, 7, and 13. He graduated from UCLA with a degree in criminal justice. He graduated cum laude. He had a minor in psychology. He has received two commendations for his work as a police officer. One of the commendations revolved around an incident where he went into a burning building and saved a young child. The child was Latino. On two prior occasions complaints have been made against Rambeaux for use of excessive force. One incident involved two African-American teenagers. The other involved Anglo teenagers. These two incidents were investigated by the department, which found that there was insufficient evidence against Rambeaux to take any action. Both incidents occurred five years ago.

1. Is Rambeaux criminally responsible for his actions under 18 U.S.C. § 242?
2. Is Rambeaux civilly liable under 42 U.S.C. § 1983?
3. Is the Rambeaux's employer, the city, liable under 42 U.S.C. § 1983?

Problem 10

People v. Meyers, Selected Documents from Case File

The following documents are excerpts from the case file, People v. Meyers. The search warrant and Grand Jury transcript selection contain facts relevant to the defendant's claim that physical evidence (drug paraphernalia) and statements should be suppressed.

**CIRCUIT COURT STATE OF NEW BRUNSWICK
COUNTY OF LOS DIABLOS**

In the Matter of the Search of:

The person of JUSTIN MEYERS, further described as a male caucasion, 5'10", 175 pounds, brown hair, brown eyes, D.O.B. 5/27/1980; and

The premises at 24870 Lake View Place, Apartment 17, Centerville, and further described as a two-bedroom apartment in a four story apartment complex bearing the name, "Lake View Apartments," including all containers, rooms and other parts therein; and also including a detached parking area and storage compartment designated as belonging to the resident of Apartment 17.

SEARCH WARRANT

TO: Any sheriff, policeman or peace officer in the county of Los Diablos:

Affidavit(s) having been made before me by Matthew A. Alonza who has reason to believe that on the person of JUSTIN MEYERS, or on the premises known as "Lake View Apartments," Apartment 17 located at 24870 Lake View Place, Centerville in the County of Los Diablos there is now concealed a certain person or property, namely:

> Cocaine, and cocaine paraphernalia including milk sugar, scales and other weighing devices, balloons, condoms, paper bundles, measuring devices, miniature spoons, short straws; articles tending to establish and document sales of cocaine including U.S. currency, buyer lists, seller lists, and recordations of sales including personal computers; articles of personal property tending to establish the identity of person in control of the premises, vehicles, storage areas and containers being searched including company receipts, rent receipts, address mail and keys.

I am satisfied that the affidavit(s) and any record testimony establish probable cause to believe that the person or property so described is now concealed on the person or premises above-described and establish grounds for the issuance of this warrant.

YOU ARE HEREBY COMMANDED to search on or before November 23, 20XX (not to exceed 10 days) the person or place named above for the person or property specified, serving this warrant and making the search ☒ in the daytime—6:00 AM to 10:00 P.M.
☐ at anytime in the day or night

as I find reasonable cause has been established and if the person or property be found there to seize same, leaving a copy of this warrant and receipt for the person or property taken, and prepare a written inventory of the person or property seized and promptly return this warrant to as required by law.

Dated:

_____   _____

Name and Title of Judge   Signature of Judge

PEOPLE OF THE STATE OF NEW BRUNSWICK, COUNTY OF LOS DIABLOS,
           Plaintiff,
 	
vs.
 	
JUSTIN MEYERS,
           Defendant
	Case No.: 07-7507
	
	TRANSCRIPT OF GRAND JURY PROCEEDING

Dated this 27th day of May, 20XX

_____

(continued)

Questioning by Deputy District Attorney Margaret Yow of witness Matthew A. Alonza:

Q. Please state your name and occupation.

A. Matthew Alan Alonza, Detective with the Los Diablos County Sheriff's Department.

Q. How long have you been so employed?

A. I have been employed by the Sheriff's Department for 15 years. I have been a detective for the last 7 years.

Q. Are you assigned to a specific unit within the Sheriff's Department?

A. Yes.

Q. What unit is that?

A. The narcotics investigation unit.

Q. How long have you been assigned to that unit?

A. For 3 years.

Q. And before that what was your assignment within the Department?

A. Well, I have had several different assignments. I started as a sheriff's deputy assigned to traffic patrol. As a sheriff's deputy I was also assigned to the jails and to court security. After about 4 years I became a sergeant and then in another two years I was promoted to detective. As a detective I am involved in investigating numerous types of crimes, including burglaries, assaults, including domestic violence, a variety of theft crimes, sex offenses and homicides.

Q. What is your educational background?

A. I have a Bachelor's Degree in Administration of Justice.

Q. Have you taken any police investigation courses?

A. Of course. Some courses were included in my undergraduate degree program, but since that time I have taken various courses at the state college as well as attending numerous seminars offered by various police agencies.

Q. And did any of these courses cover crime scene investigation?

A. Yes, several courses covered this.

Q. Now, as a member of the sheriff's department, I assume that you investigated numerous crime scenes.

A. That is correct.

Q. And have any of these investigations involved the execution of search warrants?

A. Yes.

Q. Can you estimate how many involved search warrants?

A. Many. I couldn't give you a specific number.

Q. Detective Alonza, I would like to direct your attention to a search warrant that you served on November 16 of last year. I have here a copy of a search warrant identified as people's exhibit A. I would ask you to examine this and state whether you have seen this search warrant prior to today.

A. Yes, I have seen this.

Q. Is this a copy of a search warrant that you served?

A. Yes it is.

Q. And this search warrant allows you to search the apartment occupied by the accused, Justin Meyers. Is that correct?

A. Yes it is.

Q. And did you participate in the execution or search pursuant to this warrant?

A. Yes I did.

Q. In general this warrant allows you to search the apartment of Mr. Meyers for cocaine or cocaine paraphernalia, along with any evidence showing that Mr. Meyers was engaged in the sale of cocaine. Is that correct?

(continued)   A. Yes it is.

Q. And this warrant also allows you to search and seize any evidence that tends to prove that Mr. Meyers was the occupant or resident of the premises identified in the search warrant?

A. Yes it does.

Q. Now on November 16, of last year you searched Mr. Meyers pursuant to this search warrant. Is that correct?

A. Yes.

Q. When you served that search warrant was Mr. Meyers present in the apartment?

A. Yes, he was.

Q. During your search, did you find evidence showing that Justin Meyers occupied the premises?

A. Yes we did.

Q. Please describe this.

A. Well, we found utility bills addressed to Mr. Meyers at the apartment address. We were also able to access a personal computer on the premises that clearly belonged to Mr. Meyers.

Q. During your search, did you find evidence of cocaine possession or sale?

A. Yes, we did. We found drugs and scales in the living and kitchen areas.

Q. Would you describe Mr. Meyers's apartment.

A. As you enter the apartment you walk into a living area with an attached kitchen toward the back. To the left was a short hallway leading to two bedrooms. Off one bedroom was a bathroom.

Q. Please describe how the bedrooms were furnished.

A. One room was furnished as a typical bedroom and the other was furnished as an office.

Q. Now, the bedroom furnished as an office—did it contain a bed?

A. No.

Q. Was Mr. Meyers's the sole occupant of this apartment?

A. Yes.

Q. And what led you to this conclusion?

A. A number of factors. There was only one bed. The clothing in the closet was all the same size. And when we checked with the manager of the apartment he told us that Mr. Meyers's was the only person on the rental agreement and he had never seen anyone else in the apartment on any regular basis.

Q. While serving the search warrant marked as exhibit A, did you search all the rooms in the apartment?

A. Of course.

Q. While searching the room used as a bedroom, did you find anything unusual?

A. Yes.

Q. Please describe.

A. The first thing I noticed was a photograph on the top of the accused's dresser. The photo showed 5 people all smiling and huddled together. One of the individuals in the photo was the accused, Justin Meyers. Another of the individuals appeared to be a young woman, Nadine Bostick, who was reported missing approximately 2 weeks earlier. Foul play was suspected in her disappearance and a small task force from our department was assigned to her case.

Q. Were you on the task force?

A. No.

Q. To your knowledge was the accused a suspect in her disappearance?

A. No, he was not.

Q. Would you have known if he was a suspect?

A. Probably. We are a relatively small department.

Q. After noticing the photograph, what did you do?

A. I continued searching the dresser and closet for drugs.

(continued)

Q. And did you find anything?

A. I didn't find drugs, but I did find a handkerchief with dried blood on it. The handkerchief was in the pocket of a jacket hanging in the closet.

Q. What did you do with this?

A. I placed it in a plastic container and seized it.

Q. Why did you take the handkerchief?

A. Well, there were a few reasons. I thought it might have traces of cocaine on it. I thought maybe that the accused might have used it to wipe off some of the paraphernalia we found. But I was also suspicious of the bloody rag. It just seemed strange. I guess in the back of my mind I was thinking about the young woman in the photograph. I was suspicious.

Q. What made you suspicious, then?

A. I don't know, but I have been a police officer for over 15 years and I do not believe in coincidences. We had a woman who had disappeared, a known drug dealer and a bloody handkerchief. I just thought there might be some connection.

Q. Did you ask the accused about the handkerchief?

A. Yes, as soon as I finished searching the bedroom I returned to the living room, where the accused was detained by another officer. He was handcuffed, sitting on the sofa and I showed him the handkerchief and asked him where the blood came from.

Q. What did he say?

A. He said he must have had a bloody nose. He didn't remember.

Q. Did you ask him anything else?

A. Yes, I asked him if he knew Nadine Bostick.

Q. And what did he say?

A. He said he had met her once—she was a friend of a friend.

Q. Did you ask him anything else?

A. Yes, I continued to ask him about Nadine. He looked very nervous to me, and I told him if he knew anything about her disappearance he should let us know. He told me that he didn't know anything.

Q. What did you do next?

A. We placed Mr. Meyers under arrest and put him in the patrol car to transport him to the jail.

Q. Did you read Mr. Meyers his *Miranda* rights?

A. Yes. We read his rights as soon as we placed him under arrest.

Q. And what did he say?

A. He said he wanted a lawyer.

Q. While you were transporting him to the jail, did you engage in any further conversations.

A. Yes. The defendant asked us if we had any leads in Nadine's disappearance. This made us all very cautious and I then asked the defendant why he wanted to know. He responded that he was just curious and hoped that she was o.k.

Q. Was anything else said?

A. Yes. I told the defendants that Nadine's parents were devastated at her disappearance and if he knew anything that could lead to finding her, he should let us know. He then said that with the time that has gone by, didn't we all think that she was probably dead. At this point I told him that we hoped she was not, but if she was, her parents deserved to know this so that they could give her a proper burial and find some peace in their lives. The defendant hesitated for a moment and then said that if he were investigating the case he would look in the Diablo Dam near the picnic area known as Cedar Point. I asked him why he would do this and he then said that he didn't want to talk about this anymore until he had a lawyer.

Q. What did you do in response to the statements of the defendant?

A. I immediately contacted the head of the task force. The next morning they had a team of divers at the location mentioned by the defendant. After a few hours they found her body.

(continued)

Q. What did you do with the bloody handkerchief?

A. I took it to our crime lab and asked them to run DNA tests to check the blood against Nadine's.

Q. And did they do this?

A. Yes.

Q. What did they report to you?

A. They reported that Nadine's DNA matched the DNA of the blood on the handkerchief.

Q. How long did it take for you to receive these test results?

A. I think it was a few weeks.

Q. And where was the accused during this time?

A. Well, he had been arrested for the sale of drugs and was in jail on that charge.

(continued)

Problem 11

Case v. Spend Less Foods, Selected Documents from Case File

Cort Case filed a complaint for wrongful termination against Spend Less Foods. Subsequently, Spend Less Foods made a motion to dismiss the case. The motion was denied. Following are excerpts from a deposition of Cort Case and from the declaration of Boss Hoggs, a Spend Less Foods employee, filed with the motion to dismiss. Assume that Cort Case claims that the drug tests violated his right to privacy under both a state and federal law. He specifically claims that he had the right to use marijuana for a physical condition.

Research Question:

Prepare a memorandum of law analyzing Case's position on both the state and federal claim of privacy.

(Excerpt from Deposition of Plaintiff, Cort Case)

Questioning by W. J. Bryan, Esq., attorney for Spend Less Food Stores:

Q. Please state your name and address for the record.

A. Cort Case; 784 Willow St., San Jose.

Q. How long have you lived at that address?

A. I think it's been about 4 years. I can't remember exactly.

Q. What was your previous address?

A. I can't remember. It was some place in Sunnyvale.

Q. What is your date of birth?

A. May 4, 1968.

Q. Are you currently employed?

A. No.

Q. Who was your last employer?

A. Spend Less Food Stores.

(continued)

Q. What was your position with Spend Less?

A. I worked in the warehouse, mostly loading and unloading heavy merchandise.

Q. Were you ever required to operate a forklift?

A. This was not my responsibility, but on one or two occasions I helped out and did this.

Q. Were you operating a forklift on January 29, 2006?

A. Yes, the regular operator was on a break and my supervisor asked me to load some items on a shelf in the store.

Q. And on January 29, 2006 did the fork lift strike a child while you were driving it?

A. No.

Q. No? You were not involved in an accident on January 29, 2006?

A. Yes, I was involved in an accident, but the child ran into me. I didn't run into her.

Q. Within 24 hours preceding this accident, had you consumed any alcohol?

A. No.

Q. Within 24 hours preceding this accident had you taken any medication?

A. Only what my physician has prescribed for me.

Q. And what was that?

A. Marijuana—I have frequent back aches from my job and the only thing that ever seemed to help was marijuana.

Q. And where did you acquire this marijuana?

Objection by Mr. Darrow: Objection, irrelevant. Do not answer the question.

Q. O.k. I'll withdraw the question. Mr. Case, did you submit to drug testing following this incident?

A. Yes.

Q. And you are aware that the results showed the presence of marijuana in your system.

A. Yes.

Q. Is there any reason to think that the test results were not accurate?

A. No.

Q. Did you tell the technician who conducted the test that you had a prescription for marijuana?

A. Yes.

Q. Did you have any verification of this?

A. Yes.

Q. What was that?

A. I keep a copy of the prescription.

Q. Did you show that to the lab tech?

A. Yes.

Q. You do realize, however, that possession of marijuana is illegal under federal law?
Mr. Darrow: Objection, argumentative and irrelevant. Mr. Case, don't answer the question.

Declaration of Boss Hoggs in Support of Motion to Dismiss

I, Boss Hoggs, declare as follows:

1. I am employed by defendant, Spend Less Food Stores, as a supervising manager, and have been so employed since March, 2002.
2. In my capacity as manager I have supervised Cort Case, plaintiff in the above entitled action, between September 25, 2003 and February 15, 2006.

(continued)

3. During that period of time, Cort Case worked in the warehouse of Spend Less Foods and was responsible for loading and unloading merchandise. As part of his responsibilities he was occasionally required to drive a small forklift through the store aisles.

4. At the time of his hiring, in September of 2003, Spend Less Foods did not have any drug testing policy in effect. A policy was implemented by the store, however in January of 2005. The drug policy provided that all employees engaged in dangerous activities could be tested for illegal drugs at any time, without notice. Any employee found to have illegal drugs was subject to immediate termination. However, if any employee could show a valid physician's prescription for any drug, the presence of that drug in his system would remain confidential with the testing laboratory and would not be grounds for any disciplinary proceedings at work.

5. On January 29, 2006, while operating a forklift within the Spend Less Foods Store, Cort Case hit a small child with the vehicle.

6. Immediately after the incident, I spoke to Cort Case who told me that he did not see the child. At the time I observed that plaintiff Case seemed to demonstrate some signs of intoxication. His speech was slightly slurred and he seemed somewhat incoherent. I reported this to my immediate supervisor and together we agreed that Smith should submit to chemical testing for alcohol and/or drugs.

7. A test was performed at Drug Testing Laboratories and they reported to us that marijuana was present in Mr. Case's system.

8. As a result, Cort Case was terminated on February 15, 2006.

I declare the foregoing to be true under penalty of perjury.
Executed on April 27, 2XXX

(continued)

Problem 12

Facts and Law Provided

Susie Speeker is a student at Oliver Wendell Holmes High School, located in South Bay County School District. South Bay County is a small community and has only one high school. Recently Susie Speeker was suspended from school by Principal Pat Strickland for her involvement with drugs. The factual background is as follows.

For several months the high school has had a special program directed at promoting the health of students. One of the topics stressed in this program is the harmful effects of drug use. In May of last year, the community of South Bay sponsored a community-wide health fair held in a city park. Various private and public community entities were invited to set up informational booths at the fair. There was no fee for participating, nor did any of the participants have any voice in the organization or operation of the fair. South Bay High School was invited to have a booth and they agreed to do so. At the booth, volunteers from the school (mostly teachers) agreed to disseminate material on a number of health issues, including the use of drugs.

The school administration and various teachers at Oliver Wendell Holmes High School encouraged students to attend the fair and promised "extra credit" if they attended the fair. Attendance would be verified by students signing an attendance sheet to be kept at the school-sponsored booth.

Susie Speeker attended the fair with her parents and older brother. The Speeker family believes that marijuana should be legalized for compassionate use by those who suffer from different illnesses. Susie's mother is a breast cancer survivor and her experiences led to this belief. At the fair, Susie held a sign which read, "Be compassionate, legalize marijuana for medical purposes." Susie was photographed carrying the sign by another Oliver Wendell Holmes student who worked on the school newspaper. The picture of Susie, with the sign, was published in the school paper. Principal Pat Strickland saw the picture and after a brief meeting with Susie and her parents, suspended Susie from school for 10 days pursuant to a school policy that allows suspension for students who "use, advocate or promote the use of any illegal drug at a school function." Susie and her parents appealed the suspension to the South Bay County School District, which upheld the suspension.

As a result of the suspension, Susie claims to have suffered ridicule and harassment from other students and faculty, causing great emotional damage. She also claims that as a result of her suspension, her grades have suffered and this may have a long-term effect of jeopardizing her college choices.

Susie has filed a lawsuit in federal district court claiming a violation of her civil rights under 42 U.S.C. § 1983.

Analyze the following questions:

1. Did the school district have the right to suspend Susie for her action?
2. Assuming that the school district was not justified in its actions, does Susie have a claim under 42 U.S.C. §1983?

In writing the memorandum use the following authorities:

Morse v. Frederick, 541 U.S. _____, 127 S.Ct. 2618, 168 L. Ed. 2d 290 (2007)
Tinker v. Des Moines Independent Community School Dist., 393 U.S. 503, 89 S.Ct. 733, 21 L. Ed. 2d 731 (1969)
U.S. Constitution Amend. 1
42 U.S.C. §1983

The majority opinions from the two cases are included in Appendix G.

Basic Citation Reference Guide

This citation information is taken from *The Bluebook: A Uniform System of Citation* (Harvard 18th ed. 2005).

Learning to cite correctly and consistently is essential. *The Bluebook* is a reference manual. It has more citation rules than you will ever need to learn. However, this tool is indispensable. The "rules" and conventions are all here. It takes patience to become familiar with *The Bluebook*. Take the time to look through this tool before you need to find answers quickly. The index to *The Bluebook* is excellent: Use it.

Note: Many states have their own legal style or citation manual. Check with your instructor for your state guidelines.

CASE LAW

The United States Supreme Court

Most case citations follow this basic format:

Name	Volume	Reporter	Page	Year
Miranda v. Arizona,	384	U.S.	436	(1966)

Miranda v. Arizona is the name of the case. Case names are underlined or italicized. This makes them easy to see on the page.

The *Miranda* case is located in volume 384 of the *United States Reports*. The *United States Reports* is the official reporter for United States Supreme Court cases. It is "official" because it is published by the United States Government. The proper abbreviation for this reporter is: U.S.

In volume 384, the *Miranda* case is located at page 436. The case was decided in 1966. The year is placed in parentheses.

This information allows anyone looking at the citation to locate the actual decision.

All United States Supreme Court cases are located in print form in three separate reporters, published by three different publishers. The full citation for the *Miranda* case is as follows:

Miranda v. Arizona, 384 U.S. 436, 86 S. Ct. 1602, 16 L. Ed. 2d 694 (1966).

86 S. Ct. 1602 and 16 L. Ed. 2d 694 are referred to as *parallel citations.*

A Point to Remember

When you refer to or "cite" a case be sure to provide your reader with a complete citation. Use the name, volume, reporter, page number, year, and if necessary, the parallel citations.

GO TO: *The Bluebook,* Table 1 (pages 200–201)

STATE CASE LAW

State cases are cited much the same as Supreme Court cases.

For example, in the state of California, either of the following citations is correct for a California case.

Long Beach v. Superior Court, 64 Cal. App. 3d 65, 134 Cal. Rptr. 468 (1976).

or

Long Beach v. Superior Court (1976) 64 Cal. App. 3d 65, 134 Cal. Rptr. 468.

In California and other states, there is an unofficial publisher of state case law. In the citation above, Cal. Rptr. is the abbreviation for the California Reporter, published by West Publishing. 134 Cal. Rptr. 468 is the parallel citation.

Sometimes you will see references to "regional reporters." The regional reporter abbreviations follow.

Atlantic Reporter	A.2d
North Eastern Reporter	N.E.2d
North Western Reporter	N.W.2d
Pacific Reporter	P.2d
Southern Reporter	So. 2d
South Eastern Reporter	S.E.2d
South Western Reporter	S.W.2d

The *2d* following the regional reporter abbreviation indicates that each of these reporters is in the second series.

A Point to Remember

Most legal sources follow the general format of

Title

Volume

Book or Reporter (abbreviated)

Page

Year

When you are looking at an unfamiliar citation, try to identify these elements. This will enable you to understand the various citations you come across in your legal studies.

GO TO: *The Bluebook*, Table 1 (pages 193–242)

UNITED STATES CONSTITUTION

The Fourteenth Amendment to the United States Constitution is written as follows:

U.S. Const. amend. XIV.

If you want to indicate a certain section of the Amendment you add: § 1
The full citation looks like this:

U.S. Const. amend. XIV, § 1.

GO TO: *The Bluebook*, Rule 11 (page 100)

THE UNITED STATES CODE (STATUTES)

The United States Code is cited in the following manner:

Number of Code Title	Code	Section Cited	Date
28	U.S.C.	§ 1291	(XXXX)

The proper cite is 28 U.S.C. § 1291 (XXXX).

GO TO: *The Bluebook*, Rule 12 (pages 101–113)

STATE CODES (STATUTES)

A statute citation must show

1. the numbers of the statutory topic,
2. the abbreviated name of the publication,

3. the specific statute or section of the statute, and

4. the year of the publication.

Examples

Ariz. Rev. Stat. Ann. § ## (XXXX)	Arizona Revised Statutes Annotated
Cal. Educ. Code § ## (XXXX)	California Education Code
Conn. Gen. Stat. § ## (XXXX)	Connecticut General Statutes
Ind. Code § ## (XXXX)	Indiana Code

GO TO: *The Bluebook*, Table 1 (pages 193–242)

The Bluebook Index (Eighteenth Edition)

When Citing	*Check Bluebook Page*	*Rule/Table*
A.L.R. Annotation	145	Rule 16.6.6
American Jurisprudence	135	Rule 15.8
Books	129–137	Rule 15
Brackets	69–70	Rule 5.2
Briefs	96–97	Rule 10.8.3
States and the District of Columbia	193–242	T.1
Capitalization	76–78	Rule 8
Case History	92–93	Rule 10.7
Case Names	81–86	Rule 10.2
Constitution, The	100	Rule 11
Corpus Juris Secundum (C.J.S.)	135	Rule 15.8
Dictionaries	135	Rule 15.8
Dissenting Opinions	91–92	Rule 10.6
Federal Cases	193–196	T.1
Federal Rules	110	Rule 12.8.3
Footnotes	59–61	Rule 3.2
Internet Sources	151–158	Rule 18
Introductory Signals	46–48	Rule 1.2
Law Review Articles	138–139	Rule 16
LEXIS	151–153	Rule 18
Looseleaf Services	162–163	Rule 19
Model Codes	111–112	Rule 12.8.5
Newspapers	141	Rule 16.5
Official Reporters	6–13, 86–88, 193–242	B5, Rule 10.3, T.1
Pages	59–61	Rule 3.2
Parenthetical Explanation of Authorities	91–92, 109	Rule 10.6, 12.7
Pending and Unreported Cases	95–96	Rule 10.8.1
Periodical Abbreviations (Law Reviews)	349–372	T.13
Periodicals	138–147	Rule 16
Pinpoint Citations	59–61	Rule 3.2

Quote Marks	68–71	Rule 5
Restatements	111–112	Rule 12.8.5
Short Citation Forms	64–67	Rule 4
State Cases	193–242	T.1
Statutes	101–113	Rule 12
Treatises	129–137	Rule 15
Uniform Acts	111	Rule 12.8.4
United States Supreme Court Cases	79, 193	Rule 10, T.1
Westlaw	151–153	Rule 18

QUOTATIONS

When you quote, you must alert the reader that you are using quoted language. Usually this means you must use quote marks. A citation must follow a quote. This citation lets the reader know where the borrowed material originated. Quotations of fifty words or more are blocked. A blocked quote is single spaced and indented on the left and right margins. No quote marks are used with a blocked quotation.

GO TO: *The Bluebook,* Rule 5 (page 68–71)

SIGNALS

Signals serve a variety of purposes. Signals indicate support, suggest comparisons, indicate contradictions, or indicate background material. When there is no signal, the cited authority is the source of the quoted material. A common introductory signal is *See.* When the signal *see* is placed in front of the cited authority, it means that the cited authority, clearly supports the proposition found in the quoted language.

GO TO: *The Bluebook,* Rule 1.2 (pages 46–48)

Information on the Order of Signals is found in *The Bluebook* at Rule 1.3 (page 48)

ELLIPSIS

When you omit a word or phrase from a quote, you must alert the reader that you have done so. The ellipsis is the tool we use for this purpose. For example: "The motion to suppress, after much heated debate and loud gavel banging, was denied." could become: "The motion to suppress . . . was denied." Do not use an ellipsis at the beginning of a quote. This tool is properly used in the middle of a quoted language or at the end of the quote. When used at the end of a quote you need to use four rather than three points. Never use more than three points internally in a quote. Never use more than four points at the end of a quote. The number of points does not indicate the amount of material omitted.

GO TO: *The Bluebook,* Rule 5.3 (pages 70–71)

Research Strategies:
An Overview

CREATE THE VOCABULARY LIST

Every fact pattern provides an initial vocabulary or terminology list. Sort the terms into two lists: one factual and the other legal.

As you review what you know, some terms are easily placed into your vocabulary list. At this point, do not worry too much about which list a certain fact actually belongs on; just pull out the key terminology. Some terms or concepts may seem to be both legal and factual. Do not let that confuse you. Your research will help you separate the legal from the factual.

From personal experience you may want to add terms or phrases. The important thing is that you have a list of words and phrases identified before you even consider going to the law library. If case law research becomes important, other facts will be important when you begin to compare and contrast the facts of your client's case and the facts of the reported decisions your research produces. You now have a list of terms to take to an index.

FORMULATE THE ISSUE

Attempt to articulate the legal issue. Remember, a well-written legal issue contains the cause of action (or legal problem) and the key facts. However, rather than attempting to write a formal issue statement at this early stage of the research, just ask a simple question.

Your initial research will clarify the cause of action. Once the elements of the cause of action are known, you will be better able to determine which of the facts are most important. This initial research also helps you to articulate the issue in a more formal format, that is, a format acceptable to send to the court. For now, keep it simple and remain focused on the research project.

USE THE LEGAL DICTIONARY AND THESAURUS

Once the initial vocabulary list is complete, take a few moments to consult a legal dictionary and a legal thesaurus. These resources expand your research list. That is, you will have a larger list of terms to take to the indexes of the legal research resources.

With this list of terms you are ready to begin work in the indexes. The questions become "Which set of books?" and "Which index?"

CREATE A RESEARCH PLAN BEFORE GOING TO THE LAW LIBRARY

Before going to the law library, sit down and consider where to begin the research. Make a list of books or sets of books you plan to review. Break that list into primary sources and secondary sources.

Most states have a state legal encyclopedia. This can be a good starting place when you know very little about the topic you are researching. Pleading and practice guides provide good examples. These secondary resources provide the researcher with a foundation to perform the research in primary sources. Once the vocabulary list and a list of library resources are prepared, you are ready to begin the initial research.

TAKE YOUR RESEARCH TERMS/VOCABULARY TO THE INDEXES

Step One

Determine which resource to attack first. Take a moment to look the set over. Notice how much information is on the spine of every volume. Notice that some of the volumes may say "Index" on them. This is a good sign. It means that in addition to a large comprehensive index at the end of the set, there is also a topical index for each topic.

Step Two

Locate the index for the set. The comprehensive index is usually at the end of the set of books. In most instances, the index is a large multivolume set. Sometimes these indexes are called "Descriptive Word Indexes" or "General Index." They are arranged alphabetically. Begin to methodically look up your vocabulary words and phrases. An early understanding of the cause of action provides an overall understanding of the materials you will locate.

EFFECTIVE USE OF THE INDEX VOLUMES

As you look at the index pages, you may locate terms that are not on your initial list, but look interesting. Add them to your list and pursue them.

Legal researchers must be armed with as many vocabulary terms as possible. With this expanded vocabulary list you are ready to begin the actual research in the sources you have chosen.

WHEN TO BEGIN THE RESEARCH IN PRIMARY SOURCES

Although your first inclination may be to begin all research in primary sources, this may not always be the best choice. Remember: Primary sources contain the law, not a discussion or explanation of the law. Primary sources are often annotated, but this information is usually a brief summary of case law, not an explanation or discussion written to educate or inform the reader.

Primary sources are a good place to begin research when you are familiar with the area of law to be researched and you are familiar with the vocabulary involved in the factual situation. In such cases, you may not need to perform foundation research.

Remember to begin with the terms directly produced by the initial fact pattern. However, you may need to expand the list of terms through a dictionary, thesaurus, and various indexes. As the list expands and becomes more complex, your understanding of the terminology may diminish. Good legal researchers work to expand their vocabulary. Take the time to understand all terminology before beginning the research.

With a good foundation of basic vocabulary and a clear legal issue, you are prepared to begin research in the statutes. You will have already used the index to look for terms; while searching for terms, you must begin to make a list of codes that may be applicable to your fact pattern. Methodically, list the code section names and numbers. When the initial list is complete, begin to locate and read the statutes you identified from the index.

In addition to a general index, usually a multivolume set located at the end of the set of books you are researching, there may be an index located at the end of the specific subject within the set of books. For example, if you know your topic is summary judgment motions, and you know that the general information on these motions is found in the civil procedure section of the state code, you could go to the last volume of the civil procedure sections of the state code to find the index to just the civil procedure statutes. This allows the researcher to limit or pinpoint the research. Think of this as a way to filter out other references that may be irrelevant.

WHEN TO BEGIN RESEARCH IN SECONDARY SOURCES

The set you choose to work in reflects how much prior knowledge you bring to the research situation. Legal encyclopedias, *American Law Reports*, and law review articles often provide a great deal of basic information. When a researcher knows very little about the topic, this is a good place to begin to build a research foundation.

Caution: When performing state-specific research, if possible, use your state's legal encyclopedia and try to find articles and *American Law Reports* annotations that include your state. If your issue is federal, you may want to look at the *American Law Reports Federal* edition and search out law review articles that focus on federal issues.

If your topic is somewhat narrow and you must search for case law, consider using the appropriate digest. The digest provides narrow topics listed in alphabetical order. Following each topic are references to specific cases. These references are often referred to as *annotations*.

The specialty sets and pleading and practice sets work well when the researcher is focused and understands the basic vocabulary associated with the topic to be researched.

Make a list of potential resources to be reviewed. Prioritize the list. Start with the set you feel will provide the most efficient path to your answers. Make sure you have thought about what you already know and what you need to know. Remember: Your goal is to locate relevant primary law.

Another approach to locating background information is to locate and read an *American Law Reports* annotation (article). There may even be a specialty set appropriate to your research situation.

As you can see, there are several places to begin your research. With practice, you will develop preferences for certain resources over other, less user-friendly resources. Do not lose sight of the research plan. Create a plan and follow it until you have good reason to believe that the initial plan is not producing reliable results.

TAKE NOTES WHEN WORKING WITH PRINTED MATERIALS

Finding the law is a good starting point. Try not to go too far into the research without slowing down and checking the validity of your research results. In addition, make sure you have the most current information available.

Use *Shepard's* to update and validate your research. *Shepard's* is available in print and on LEXIS. Shepardize any case or statute you feel you may rely on. Do not forget that you may Shepardize law review articles and *A.L.R.* annotations.

In addition to *Shepard's* you should consider using some of the features available through *LEXIS* and *Westlaw*. In LEXIS you may use the Auto-Cite feature, discussed in Chapter 9. Westlaw offers a similar service called KeyCite; this is also introduced in Chapter 9. These services are designed to be used in addition to *Shepard's*.

TAKE NOTES WHEN WORKING WITH PRINTED MATERIALS

ORGANIZATION AND ATTENTION TO DETAIL	
Get ready to take notes.	You need pencils, pens, underliners, self-adhesive notes, paperclips.
Be prepared to take notes.	Get your materials out and ready; be organized at each step of the research process.
Think about the paper you will use.	Loose leaf paper? Bound tablet? Large index cards? Adhesive notes?

Loose leaf paper is easy to shuffle and organize later. It is also easy to misplace. These pages may look a lot like the other notes in your notebooks.

A bound tablet will keep everything in one place, but does not provide much flexibility when shuffling becomes necessary. At some point it becomes necessary to organize the notes in a logical order. Remember: Your research results may not proceed in the same order you will eventually write up your memorandum or brief.

Large index cards, sometimes color-coded, prove useful because of their versatility. Many researchers color-code their issues. All research on a specific issue is placed, for example, on blue 5×7 cards. On the back of each card, the researcher notes the date the research is performed, the source of the data, and any personal notes. It is easy later to shuffle and organize by color. Sometimes a researcher places each case reviewed on a separate card. The notes on each statute are also noted on separate cards. This makes later organization much easier.

Self-adhesive notes are small, come unstuck, and are easily misplaced. Consider using them only in addition to other resources.

Work toward establishing a personal preference. Consider the nature of your research. If you plan to take a good number of written notes, maybe index cards or loose leaf paper will provide you with the ability to easily organize and rearrange your results. Try several approaches and work toward finding a note-taking process that is comfortable and reliable.

TAKE NOTES AND RECORD RESULTS WHEN WORKING WITH ONLINE OR CD-ROM MATERIALS

Instead of making handwritten notes from the screen during online research, consider printing or downloading the relevant information. Some handwritten notes may be necessary, however: keep in mind that the database in which you are researching may be quite expensive and note taking is time consuming.

When working with CD-ROM products, the time element is not critical. Still, you may want to take minimal notes while you print and download the most useful data. Be sure that you note why you printed the material and how you plan to use it.

ORGANIZATION OF PHOTOCOPIED OR DOWNLOADED MATERIALS

Organization of Materials

In the process of legal research, you will photocopy and download many documents, probably too many. It is critical that you organize these documents *as you acquire them.* Staple pages that belong together; do not paperclip them. On the reverse side of every document copied or printed, note the date you acquired the material, the reason you copied it, the source and the issue(s) it pertains to. Over days or weeks of research, you *will* forget why you copied materials and where they originated. You may also find that some of the documents you copy in the early stages of research may not be as relevant as they seemed at the time you copied them. The date notation may help you place perspective on the data.

Create folders or files. Organize the materials issue by issue or separate the documents into groups of case law and statutes. If you organize from the very beginning, the process of creating the written document is made much easier.

Defendants' Joint Memorandum of Points and Authorities in Opposition to Plaintiff's Motions for Preliminary Injunction: Initial Research Memoranda

This appendix is a complex Memorandum of Points and Authorities dealing with a law that purportedly legalized the use of marijuana for medicinal purposes. In part, this Memorandum is based on work done by research associates. Their research memoranda follow the Memorandum of Points and Authorities. Sections II.C, II.D, and II.E.5 of Defendants' Joint Memorandum of Points and Authorities in Opposition to Plaintiff's Motions for Preliminary Injunction incorporate the work of the research associates. Their work is found beginning on page 437.

IN THE UNITED STATES DISTRICT COURT
FOR THE NORTHERN DISTRICT OF CALIFORNIA

UNITED STATES OF AMERICA,	) Nos.	C 98-00085 CRB
	)	C 98-00086 CRB
Plaintiff,	)	C 98-00087 CRB
	)	C 98-00088 CRB
v.	)	C 98-00089 CRB
	)	C 98-20013 CRB
CANNABIS CULTIVATORS' CLUB;	)	
and DENNIS PERON,	)	
	)	DEFENDANTS' JOINT MEMORANDUM
Defendants.	)	OF POINTS AND AUTHORITIES IN
	)	OPPOSITION TO PLAINTIFF'S
	)	MOTIONS FOR PRELIMINARY
AND RELATED ACTIONS.	)	INJUNCTION
	)	

Date: March 24, XXXX
Time: 2:30 p.m.
Courtroom: 8

TABLE OF CONTENTS

<u>TABLE OF AUTHORITIES</u>

TO THE HONORABLE CHARLES R. BREYER, UNITED STATES DISTRICT JUDGE,
AND TO ALL PARTIES TO THE ABOVE-CAPTIONED ACTION:

Defendants herein, by and through their respective counsel, specially appearing, submit the following Opposition to Plaintiff United States' Motion For Preliminary Injunction And Permanent Injunction And For Summary Judgment:

I. INTRODUCTION

On January 9th 1998, the Government filed the instant suit against six medical cannabis dispensaries pursuant to 21 USC § 882. On January 30, 1998, over the government's objections, this Honorable Court granted defendants' Motion for Continuance and directed defendants to file Memoranda addressing the effect of federal law on defendants' activities protected by Proposition 215, codified as California Health & Safety Code § 11362.5. Defendants submit their Opposition herein.

A. History of Medical Marijuana

The medicinal use of cannabis can hardly be characterized as a "recent" phenomenon. The first recorded use of marijuana medicinally was over five thousand years ago. During the reign of the Chinese Emperor, Chen Nung, it was written that cannabis provided relief for malaria, constipation, rheumatic pains, and other conditions.

In the *Anatomy of Melancholy*, published in 1621, the English clergyman Robert Burton suggested the use of cannabis in the treatment of depression. The New English Dispensary of 1764 recommended applying a cannabis compress to the skin to relieve inflammation.

Between 1840 and 1900, more than 100 papers were published in Western medical literature concerning the medicinal benefits of cannabis. In 1839, Dr. W. B. O'Shaughnessy, a professor at the medical college of Calcutta wrote that a tincture made of hemp proved to be an effective analgesic.

Cannabis was first listed in the United States Dispensatory in 1854. It was common during that era for commercial cannabis preparations to be available in drugstores. In 1860, Dr. R. R. M'Meens reported numerous medical uses for cannabis to the Ohio State Medical Society. In 1887, H. A. Hare wrote of the benefits of cannabis in the treatment of terminal patients. In 1891, Dr. J. B. Mattison urged physicians to use hemp as an analgesic and to treat such conditions as chronic rheumatism and migraine. In 1937, the United States passed the Marihuana Tax Act at the urging of Harry Anslinger, a government agent who had essentially been put out of business with the repeal of prohibition. Mr. Anslinger was instrumental in convincing the public of the dangers of marijuana through such means as the film "reefer madness."

In 1938, Mayor Fiorello LaGuardia appointed a committee of scientists to study the medical, sociological, and psychological effects of marijuana use in New York. The study was published in 1944, finding no proof that major crime was associated with marijuana, or that it caused any aggressive or antisocial behavior. Harry Anslinger denounced this report and it was essentially ignored by the government.

In 1970, Congress passed the Controlled Substances Act, at which time President Nixon appointed the Presidential Commission on Marihuana and Drug Abuse, aka the Shafer Commission, to study marijuana and report back to Congress. The purpose was to assist Congress in determining the appropriate scheduling of marijuana. When the Commission found that there was no basis for placing marijuana in Schedule I, Congress and the President virtually ignored its scientific judgment.

On September 6, 1988, after a Court order forced the DEA to hold two years of hearings before its own administrative law judge, the Honorable Francis L. Young ruled that approval by a significant minority of physicians was enough to meet the standard of "currently accepted medical use in treatment in the United States" established by the Controlled Substances Act for a Schedule II drug. Judge Young wrote that "marihuana, in its natural form, is one of the safest therapeutically active substances known to man. . . . One must reasonably conclude that there is accepted safety for use of marihuana under medical supervision. To conclude otherwise, on the record, would be unreasonable, arbitrary, and capricious." Judge Young's findings were, not surprisingly, ignored by the government.

B.   History of Dispensaries

Proposition 215 was not the first effort in California to allow for the use of medicinal marijuana. In two consecutive years, the California legislature passed medical marijuana bills, only to see them vetoed by Gov. Pete Wilson. Finally, in 1996, the voters of the state placed an initiative on the ballot. It passed on November 5, 1996, receiving 56% of the vote. In response to the voters' demand that "seriously ill Californians have the right to obtain and use marijuana for medical purposes where the medical use is deemed appropriate by a physician," numerous medical cannabis dispensaries, including the defendants herein, sprang up to meet the needs of patients. These dispensaries provided safe and affordable medicine that patients had previously only found available on the black market, and then only at exorbitant prices and of questionable quality.

II.   ARGUMENT

Defendants herein contend that the government's pending motion should be denied. Defendants' argument can be summarized as follows:

A.   Substantive Due Process Bars The Government From Enforcing The Sections Of The Controlled Substances Act It Seeks To Apply To Defendants.

B.   The Controlled Substances Act Does Not Reach The Defendants' Activities Which Are Wholly Intrastate In Nature.

C.   Defendants' Activities Are Exempt From Application Of The Controlled Substances Act.

D.   Defendants' Activities Are Justified By The Defense Of Necessity.

E.   The Government Cannot Meet The Standards For The Injunctive Relief It Seeks.

A.   SUBSTANTIVE DUE PROCESS BARS THE GOVERNMENT FROM ENFORCING THE SECTIONS OF THE CONTROLLED SUBSTANCES ACT IT SEEKS TO APPLY TO DEFENDANTS.

1.   Substantive Due Process Protects Individuals from Government Actions That Violate Protected Personal Liberty Interests.

The United States Supreme Court has established that individuals are protected under the Due Process clauses of the Fourteenth and Fifth Amendments from State or Federal intrusions into their "fundamental liberty interests." Substantive Due Process has come to stand for protection of numerous un-enumerated liberties. As Justice Rehnquist recently described in *Washington v. Glucksberg*, U.S._____, 117 S.Ct. 2258 (1997).

> The Due Process Clause guarantees more than fair process, and the "liberty" it protects includes more than the absence of physical restraint. . . . The Clause also provides heightened

protection against government interference with certain fundamental rights and liberty interests. In a long line of cases, we have held that, in addition to the specific freedoms protected by the Bill of Rights, the "liberty" specially protected by the Due Process Clause includes the rights to marry; to have children; to direct the education and upbringing of one's children; to marital privacy; to use contraception; to bodily integrity; and to abortion. We have also assumed, and strongly suggested, that the Due Process Clause protects the traditional right to refuse unwanted lifesaving medical treatment.

Glucksberg, at 2267, (citations omitted).

In applying Substantive Due Process analysis, the Chief Justice in *Glucksberg* explained that government action must be "narrowly tailored to serve a compelling [government] interest" where a "fundamental liberty interest" is involved. Such interests arise where the interest protected is firmly rooted in history and tradition and is carefully described:

Our established method of substantive due process analysis has two primary features: First, we have regularly observed that the Due Process Clause specially protects those fundamental rights and liberties which are, objectively, "deeply rooted in this Nation's history and tradition," ("so rooted in the traditions and conscience of our people as to be ranked as fundamental"), and "implicit in the concept of ordered liberty," such that "neither liberty nor justice would exist if they were sacrificed". . . . Second, we have required in substantive due process cases a "careful description" of the asserted fundamental liberty interest. Our Nation's history, legal traditions, and practices thus provide the crucial "guideposts for responsible decision-making," that direct and restrain our exposition of the Due Process Clause. As we stated recently . . ., the Fourteenth Amendment "forbids the government to infringe . . . 'fundamental' liberty interests at all, no matter what process is provided, unless the infringement is narrowly tailored to serve a compelling state interest."

Glucksberg, at 2268 (citations omitted).

Justice Souter in his concurrence to *Glucksberg* argues the application of Substantive Due Process based on a "concept of 'ordered liberty' . . . comprising a continuum of rights to be free from 'arbitrary impositions and purposeless restraints.'" *Glucksberg,* at 2281–2 (Souter, J., concurring). Justice Souter described his standard for a substantive due process right as follows:

This approach calls for the court to assess the relative "weights" or dignities of the contending interests. . . . [This] method is subject to two important constraints. . . . First, such a court is bound to confine the values that it recognizes to those truly deserving constitutional stature, either to those expressed in constitutional text, or those exemplified by "the traditions from which [the nation] developed" or revealed by contrast with "the traditions from which it broke."

The second constraint, again, simply reflects the fact that constitutional review, not judicial lawmaking, is a court's business here. . . . It is only when the legislation's justifying principle, critically valued, is so far from being commensurate with the individual interest as to be arbitrarily or pointlessly applied that the statute must give way.

Glucksberg, at 2283 (Souter, J., concurring) (citations omitted).

Under either the Rehnquist or Souter standard, the High Court would resolve Defendants' Substantive Due Process claims similarly.

2.   The Due Process Clause Protects Clearly Established Fundamental Liberty Interests.

Defendants' liberty interests meet the first prong of the Rehnquist analysis of Substantive Due Process: The right of patients to obtain physician-recommended treatment that would alleviate pain and preserve life is strongly reflected in our nation's traditions and the Supreme Court's historic Substantive Due Process analysis. The Court has found Due Process interests in preserving life and caring for oneself. *Id.* Moreover, Substantive Due Process analysis indicates that the Fourteenth and Fifth Amendments protect a fundamental interest *to receive palliative treatment for a painful medical condition. Id.*

"Many of the rights and liberties protected by the Due Process Clause sound in personal autonomy." *Glucksberg*, at 2271. There is no liberty more firmly established than the fundamental interest to be free from physical pain imposed by the government for arbitrary and capricious reasons. The highest Court in the land has continuously and persistently measured and evaluated Substantive Due Process claims in terms of the physical pain imposed upon the individual by government restraints. *Furman v. Georgia*, 408 U.S. 238 (1972). (Substantive Due Process implicated where death penalty imposed under a method inflicting "unnecessary pain"); *Doe v. Bolton*, 410 U.S. 179 (1973), (considerations of an individual's Substantive Due Process right to abortion include the fact that pregnancy requires one "to incur pain" and a "higher mortality rate"); *Ingraham v. Wright*, 430 U.S. 651 (1977) (school children's Substantive Due Process violated by corporal punishment, discussed *infra*); *Los Angeles v. Lyons*, 461 U.S. 95 (1983) (arrestee's Substantive Due Process violated by police utilizing unnecessarily painful chokeholds); *Cruzan v. Director, MDH*, 497 U.S. 261 (1990), (pain suffered by patient in persistent vegetative state relevant to inquiry of fundamental interest to deprive oneself of nutrition and hydration, discussed *infra*); *Planned Parenthood v. Casey*, 505 U.S. 833 (1992) ("anxieties," "physical constraints," and "pain" of women carrying child to term basis of Substantive Due Process right for a woman to elect an abortion); *Rochin v. California*, 342 U.S. 165 (1952) (violation of Substantive Due Process to pump arrestee's stomach to preserve evidence); and *Washington v. Glucksberg*, ____ U.S. ____ (1997) (terminally ill patient rights to palliative treatment implicate to Substantive Due Process, discussed *infra*).

In *Ingraham v. Wright, supra*, the Supreme Court cited the long history and tradition of constitutional rights respecting individual integrity:

> The Due Process Clause of the Fifth Amendment, later incorporated into the Fourteenth, was intended to give Americans at least the protection against governmental power that they had enjoyed as Englishmen against the power of the Crown. The liberty preserved from deprivation without due process included the right "generally to enjoy those privileges long recognized at common law as essential to the orderly pursuit of happiness by free men." Among the historic liberties so protected was a *right to be free from, and to obtain judicial relief for, unjustified intrusions on personal security.*

> While the contours of this historic liberty interest in the context of our federal system of government have not been defined precisely, they always have been thought to encompass freedom from bodily restraint and punishment. It is fundamental that the state cannot hold and physically punish an individual except in accordance with due process of law.

> This constitutionally protected liberty interest is at stake in this case. . . . where school authorities, acting under color of state law, inflict *appreciable physical pain*, we hold that [Due Process] liberty interests are implicated.

Ingraham, at 672–3 (footnotes and citations omitted) (*emphasis added*).

Not only is the prevention of unnecessary pain established under the Due Process Clause, but is also clearly established as a basic *enumerated* fundamental right in regard to punishment under the

Eighth Amendment barring cruel and unusual punishment. As was true in *Ingraham*, the High Court has drawn from the history of the Eighth Amendment in defining the parameters of Substantive Due Process. Where the issue of unnecessary pain is involved, Substantive Due Process is often analyzed as a parallel to the Eighth Amendment. Thus, in *Furman v. Georgia*, 408 U.S. (1972), the Court surmised a confluence between the two approaches. "[C]ruel and unusual punishment and substantive due process become so close as to merge." *Furman*, at 359.

The relevance of infliction of pain by the state as the basis for Substantive Due Process claims is not limited to those areas involving discipline or criminal punishment. Pain analysis was also highly relevant to Substantive Due Process analysis in *Cruzan, supra.* There, the Court considered whether the state of Missouri could require "clear and convincing" evidence that a patient wished to terminate artificial nutrition treatment after an automobile accident left her in a persistent vegetative state.

Most recently, the Supreme Court considered whether an individual had a Substantive Due Process right to have the assistance of a physician in committing suicide. *Washington v. Glucksberg, supra.* In that case, four terminally ill patients and their doctors petitioned the court for the permission to proceed with doctor-assisted suicides. As in the previous instances, the notion that the state would subject an individual to unnecessary pain weighed heavy in the minds of the Justices.

Although the Court's opinion in *Glucksberg* was unanimous in result, it was not so in its reasoning. Justice O'Connor and four other Justices filed separate concurrences, each of which supports the position maintained by Defendants herein that Substantive Due Process protects an individual's right to obtain medical treatment that alleviates unnecessary pain. Her opinion makes clear that suffering patients are presumed to have access to any palliative medication that would alleviate pain even where such medication might hasten death. "[A] patient who is suffering from a terminal illness and who is experiencing great pain has *no legal barriers* to obtaining medication, from qualified physicians." *Glucksberg*, at 2303 (*emphasis added*).

Similarly, Justice Breyer's concurrence turned on issues of a consideration of the pain suffered by patients. Breyer's opinion suggested that a "right to die with dignity" may in fact be protected under the Constitution. He argued that such a right would include a right to "professional medical assistance" and "the avoidance of unnecessary and severe physical suffering." *Glucksberg*, at 2311 (J. Breyer, concurring). Justice Breyer made clear that the presence of pain was a determinative factor in his mind: "[I]n my view, the avoidance of severe physical pain (connected with death) would have to comprise an essential part of any successful claim". *Id.*

Justice Souter's concurrence similarly stresses an individual's right to make decisions with one's own doctor along with considering the pain and incumbent indignity suffered by an individual. Justice Souter writes, "[The] liberty interest in bodily integrity was phrased . . . by [Justice] Cardozo when he said, '[e]very human being of adult years and sound mind has a right to determine what shall be done with his own body' in relation to his medical needs." *Glucksberg* at 2288 (Souter, J., concurring). He explained further,

> [T]he Court [has] recognized that the good physician is not just a mechanic of the human body whose services have no bearing on a person's moral choices, but one who does more than treat symptoms, one who ministers to the patient. . . . This idea of the physician as serving the whole person is a source of the high value traditionally placed on the medical relationship.

Glucksberg, at 2288–89, (citation omitted).

Finally, Justice Stevens asserts with regard to the protected "sphere of substantive liberty":

> Whatever the outer limits of the concept may be, it definitely includes protection for matters "central to personal dignity and autonomy." It includes, "the individual's right to make certain unusually important decisions that will affect his own, or his family's, destiny. The Court has referred to such decisions as implicating 'basic values,' as being 'fundamental,' and as being dignified by history and tradition.

Glucksberg, at 2307 (Stevens, J., concurring) (citation omitted).

Defendants herein assert that they maintain a fundamental liberty interest in physician recommended treatment to alleviate physical pain in the face of governmental restraint. The Defendant dispensaries are cooperatives composed of members who are patients whose doctors have recommended cannabis for medical purposes. Many of the members are terminally ill cancer or AIDS patients. As a result of their conditions, they experience intense pain and nausea. Others are glaucoma patients, threatened with permanent blindness. Defendants can prove that cannabis is unique in its ability to relieve these symptoms. The government now seeks an injunction that would prevent these Defendants from obtaining this necessary treatment.

In a similar vein, Defendants' interests are bolstered by a second established fundamental interest in the *right to provide care for oneself.* Although this right is usually implicated where an individual is incarcerated and does not have access to necessary medical treatment, the argument is equally applicable to a situation where the government denies medical treatment by enacting laws proscribing such:

> [W]hen the State by the affirmative exercise of its power so restrains an individual's liberty that it renders him unable to care for himself, and at the same time fails to provide for his basic human needs—e.g., food, clothing, shelter, *medical care,* and reasonable safety—it transgresses the substantive limits on state action set by the Eighth Amendment and the Due Process Clause. In the substantive due process analysis, it is the State's affirmative act of restraining the individual's freedom to act on his own behalf—through incarceration, institutionalization, or other *similar restraint of personal liberty*—which is the "deprivation of liberty" triggering the protections of the Due Process Clause.

Deshaney v. Winnebago Cty. Soc. Servs. Dept., 489 U.S. 189, 200 (1989) (citation omitted).

The government's restraint on the distribution of cannabis prevents the defendant patients from obtaining medical care for themselves, as protected by *Deshaney.* This is particularly egregious where the treatment sought is that to alleviate pain as discussed above.

The interest of some of these member/patients in preventing unnecessary pain, in treating themselves, and in preserving eyesight, is surpassed only by a third firmly rooted liberty interest, that of preserving life. It is without question that an individual has a liberty interest in preserving his or her life. As the Supreme Court explained in *Cruzan, supra,* "[i]t cannot be disputed that the Due Process Clause protects an interest in life." *Cruzan,* at 281. Many of the cooperative members would needlessly place their lives in jeopardy were they denied the right to the medical use of cannabis. Many chemotherapy patients and AIDS patients are so plagued with nausea and discomfort that they are unable to eat. Without basic nourishment, their conditions are aggravated and they are essentially at risk of starving to death.

Defendants herein present compelling circumstances. The history and traditions of Substantive Due Process make clear that bodily integrity is an area of fundamental importance. The interests protected, relief from pain, self care, and preservation of life, are so ingrained in our nation's traditions and are so firmly rooted in our concepts of ordered liberty that they are fundamental. The right to live, painfree under the care of one's physician without arbitrary interference from the government, is at stake.

3.   The Substantive Due Process Interest At Issue Is Narrowly Defined.

The Defendant patients assert Constitutional protection from the federal government's interference with their right legally to obtain cannabis, with a doctor's recommendation, for treatment of painful and life-threatening medical conditions. Unlike the plaintiff doctors in *Glucksberg* various Defendants in the instant action assert personal interests as the Controlled Substances Act applies specifically to them. Each of the Defendant cooperative's members has a medical condition for which a physician has recommended treatment with cannabis. Without the treatment some will suffer pain, some will risk blindness, and others will die of malnutrition. The only barrier to this treatment is the broad federal proscription against the distribution of marijuana. The interest asserted by Defendants is sufficiently defined to pass the "narrowly described" standard of the Rehnquist analysis.

4. The Government Cannot Establish That The Broad Federal Proscription Against Distribution And Use of Marijuana Is Narrowly Tailored To Meet a Compelling State Interest.

As the Court laid out in *Glucksberg*, where fundamental liberty interests that are narrowly described are demonstrated, any restraint on those interests must be narrowly tailored to serve a compelling state interest. Defendants contend that the federal proscription against the possession and distribution of marijuana is unnecessarily overbroad and arbitrary where it restrains the terminally ill and others in chronic pain from obtaining an essential medication to alleviate their pain and in some cases contribute to the preservation of life.[1]

Congress has recognized and declared that "[m]any . . . drugs . . . have a useful and legitimate medical purpose and are necessary to maintain the health and general welfare of the American people." 21 USC § 801 (1). Congress has also declared that "[t]he illegal importation, manufacture, distribution, and possession and improper use of controlled substances have a substantial and detrimental effect on the health and general welfare of the American people." 21 USC § 801 (2). Thus the government has a legitimate interest both in assuring that appropriate medicines are made available, and in stemming the abuse of controlled substances.

In the case of numerous other substances, the government has acted to provide for medical use while limiting abuse. In the case of marijuana, however, the means employed by the government abysmally fail to accomplish the purpose stated in 21 USC § 801 (1) and are therefore an affront to the concept of Substantive Due Process.

B. The Controlled Substances Act Is
Not Applicable to Defendants' Activities

1. Congress May Only Regulate Those Purely Intrastate Activities Which Have A Substantial Effect On Interstate Commerce.

In determining whether Congress may properly regulate an activity pursuant to its power derived under the Commerce Clause, Courts have recognized that the activity to be regulated must fall into one of three categories.

> "First, Congress may regulate the use of the channels of interstate commerce. Second, Congress is empowered to regulate and protect the instrumentalities of interstate commerce, or persons or things in interstate commerce, even though the threat may come only from intrastate activities. Finally, Congress's commerce authority includes the power to regulate those activities having a substantial relation to interstate commerce, i.e., those activities that substantially affect interstate commerce." *Lopez*, _____ U.S. at _____,
> 115 S.Ct. at 1629–30 (citations omitted); see also *Perez*, 402 U.S. at 150, 91 S.Ct. at 1359 (same).

U.S. v. Pappadopoulos, 64 F.3d 522, 525–526 (9th Cir. 1995).

In the *Lopez* case, the Supreme Court declared the Gun-Free School Zones Act unconstitutional on the basis that the act purported to reach purely intrastate conduct that had no substantial effect on interstate commerce. *United States v. Lopez*, 514 U.S. 549 (1995). Relying on this holding, this Circuit found that a particular activity may be regulated by the Controlled Substances Act, (21 USC § 801, et seq.), only if it can be found to fall into one of the three categories identified in *Lopez*. *U.S. v. Tisor*, 96 F.3d 370, 374 (9th Cir. 1996).

---

1. Although Defendants do not present evidence in support of this claim in the present briefing, they certainly will be prepared to do so at an evidentiary hearing. Such evidence would include not only medical evidence verified by volumes of scientific research, but also thousands of testimonials from patients who have obtained relief from pain and other conditions and who have gained a life-saving appetite from the medical use of cannabis.

It cannot be argued that defendants' activities constitute either 1) channels or 2) instrumentalities of interstate commerce. Defendants will be able to prove that their activities are purely intrastate in nature. Thus, in order for Congress to lawfully regulate defendants' activities through the promulgation, and enforcement of the sections of the Controlled Substances Act now advanced by the Government, (21 USC §§ 841, 846, and 856), the Government must establish that defendants' intrastate activities are substantially related to or affect interstate commerce. *Tisor*, at 375.

This Circuit previously considered and rejected Commerce Clause challenges to prosecutions under the Controlled Substances Act, both before and after *Lopez*. However, a review of these cases, when juxtaposed against defendants' activities, establishes that they are materially distinguishable from the matter now before the Court.

        a)   Pre-*Lopez* Cases

Prior to the Supreme Court's recent decision in *Lopez*, this Circuit considered four cases in which defendants, charged with one or more of the sections of the Controlled Substances Act now relied upon by the Government, challenged the applicability of the Act to their allegedly intrastate activities: *U.S. v. Rodriquez-Camacho*, 468 F.2d 1220, (9th Cir. 1972), (possession of 99 pounds of marijuana with intent to distribute, in violation of 21 U.S.C. § 841); *U.S. v. Montes-Zarate*, 522 F.2d 1330 (9th Cir. 1977), (possession of marijuana with intent to distribute, in violation of 21 U.S.C. § 841); *U.S. v. Thornton*, 901 F.2d 738 (9th Cir. 1990), (sale of PCP within 1000 feet of a school, in violation of 21 USC § 845a, (currently § 860), which provided for an enhancement to the penalty for violation of § 841); and *U.S. v. Visman*, 919 F.2d 1390 (9th Cir. 1990), (cultivation of marijuana, in violation of §§ 841, 846, and 856).

In these cases this Circuit recognized that Congress could regulate wholly intrastate activity only if it had an effect on interstate commerce. *Rodriquez-Camacho*, at 1221; see also *Visman*, at 1392.

In finding such a relationship in each case, the court relied on Congressional findings, as set forth in 21 USC § 801, that the intrastate activities in controlled substances affects interstate commerce. *Rodriquez-Camacho*, at 1221; *Montes-Zarate*, at 1331; *Thornton*, at 741; *Visman*, at 1392.

This Circuit recognized, however, that the Congressional findings in 21 USC § 801 were not inherently dispositive, but created, in effect, a rebuttable presumption. "This court will certainly not substitute its judgment for that of Congress in such a matter unless the relation of the subject to interstate commerce and its effect upon it are clearly nonexistent. [Citation Omitted]." *Rodriquez-Camacho*, at 1222; *Visman*, at 1393.

        b)   Post-*Lopez* Cases

Following the *Lopez* decision, this Circuit revisited the question of regulation of intrastate activity under the Controlled Substances Act, considering four new challenges: *U.S. v. Staples*, 85 F.3d 461 (9th Cir. 1996), (use of firearm while distributing cocaine, in violation of 18 U.S.C. § 924(c)(1), the underlying offense being a violation of § 841); *U.S. v. Kim*, 94 F.3d 1247, 1248 (9th Cir. 1996), (possession of methamphetamine with the intent to distribute, in violation of 21 USC § 841); *U.S. v. Tisor*, 96 F.3d 370 (9th Cir. 1996), (conspiracy to distribute and distribution of methamphetamine, in violation of §§ 841 and 846); and *U.S. v. Henson* 123 F.3d 1226 (9th Cir. 1997), (distribution of PCP in violation of §§ 841 and 846).

In these cases considered in the aftermath of *Lopez*, this Circuit noted that Congress could properly regulate intrastate activity that "*substantially* affected interstate commerce." [Emphasis added]. *Staples*, at 463; see also *Tisor*, at 375; *Henson*, at 1233. Once again, the decisions in these cases rested upon Congressional findings that intrastate drug trafficking has a substantial effect on interstate commerce. *Kim*, at 1250;

As the *Tisor* Court explained:

The challenged laws are part of a wider regulatory scheme criminalizing interstate and intrastate commerce in drugs. In adopting the Controlled Substances Act, Congress expressly found that intrastate drug trafficking had a "substantial affect" on interstate commerce. Accordingly, we hold that the Controlled Substances Act does not exceed Congressional authority under the Commerce Clause.

Tisor, at 375.

Each of these cases, both pre- and post-*Lopez*, is materially distinguishable from the matter now before the Court on two distinct grounds: 1) each of the above cases involved intrastate activities that inarguably constituted violations of state law, as opposed to the case at bar where the defendants' activities are sanctioned by California Health & Safety Code § 11362.5; and 2) each of these cases involved intrastate illicit drug trafficking activities in the same "class of activities" as those interstate activities prohibited by the Controlled Substances Act, while the defendants now before the Court, as will be established below, are involved in conduct that is not in the "class of activities" prohibited by the sections of the Controlled Substances Act relied upon by the government.

2.   Congress Did Not Intend The Controlled Substances Act To Reach
       Defendants' Activities.

As noted above, Courts have consistently found that Congress may lawfully regulate those purely intrastate activities which substantially affect interstate commerce. In applying this principle to prosecutions under the Controlled Substances Act, Courts have deferred to Congressional findings that intrastate drug trafficking has just such a substantial effect on interstate drug trafficking. Just as consistently, though, it has been recognized that a Court will not defer to this Congressional finding where "the relation of the subject to interstate commerce and its effect upon it are clearly nonexistent." *Stafford v. Wallace*, 258 U.S. 495, 521, (1922); *U.S. v. Rodriquez-Camacho*, 468 F.2d 1220, 1222 (9th Cir. 1972); *U.S. v. Visman*, 919 F.2d 1390, 1392 (9th Cir. 1990).

A review of the Congressional findings to which the Courts refer in the above-referenced decisions, in the context of defendants' conduct herein, is illustrative of the inapplicability of §§ 841, 846, and 856 of the Controlled Substances Act to these defendants.

The first Congressional finding, 21 USC § 801(1), states:

(1) Many of the drugs included within this subchapter have a useful and legitimate medical purpose and are necessary to maintain the health and general welfare of the American people.

Thus it is clear that Congress has recognized that a drug may serve a legitimate, beneficial medical purpose.[2] In subsection (2), Congress recognized the converse:

(2) The illegal importation, manufacture, distribution, and possession and improper use of controlled substances have a substantial and detrimental effect on the health and general welfare of the American people.

Here Congress focused specifically on "illegal" and "improper" use which has a "detrimental" effect on health. The conduct of the defendants (providing cannabis for the relief of seriously ill patients who have obtained a recommendation and/or approval of a physician for the medical use of cannabis, all under color of state law) can only rationally be viewed as falling within the activities envisioned by Congress in subsection (1) as opposed to subsection (2).

---

2.   It is interesting to note that the government, in quoting 21 USC § 801 in its Memorandum, left this particular subsection out of its argument. (See e.g. Government Memorandum in Oakland Case, 3:15).

In subsection (3) Congress declared:

(3) A major portion of the traffic in controlled substances flows through interstate and foreign commerce. Incidents of the traffic which are not an integral part of the interstate or foreign flow, such as manufacture, local distribution, and possession, nonetheless have a substantial and direct effect upon interstate commerce because—

(a) after manufacture, many controlled substances are transported in interstate commerce,

(b) controlled substances distributed locally usually have been transported in interstate commerce immediately before their distribution, and

(c) controlled substances possessed commonly flow through interstate commerce immediately prior to such possession.

Here Congress identified three distinct grounds for its conclusion that intrastate trafficking in controlled substances substantially effects interstate commerce.

Congress first noted that controlled substances are often transported across state lines after manufacture. Such a concern is not applicable to defendants' activities. Defendants will be able to prove that they distribute individually small amounts of cannabis to a discrete class of persons for relatively immediate medicinal use in California, all in accordance with the state law that specifically prohibits diversion for nonmedical purposes. (See H&S § 11362.5(b)(2)).

Congress next recognized that controlled substances are often transported over state lines immediately prior to their distribution. Again this concern is not applicable to defendants' activities. Defendants will be able to prove that the medicinal cannabis they distribute is cultivated under controlled conditions in California.

Finally Congress found that controlled substances are often transported over state lines immediately prior to their possession. As established above, this concern is equally inapplicable to defendants' activities as defendants will be able to prove that the medicinal cannabis they distribute is grown, distributed, and consumed wholly within the borders of California.

Congress next found, in subsection (4), that:

(4) local distribution and possession of controlled substances contribute to swelling the interstate traffic in such substances.

In considering this finding it is easy to see how defendants' activities, which are condoned by state law, have no relation to the illicit interstate trafficking Congress sought to proscribe. Unlike the intrastate trafficking considered by this Circuit in previous cases, defendants' activities in providing a medicine to a discreet class of persons do not have any effect on interstate illicit drug trafficking. Judge Fern Smith of this Honorable Court recognized such when she ruled that "the government's fears in this case are exaggerated and without evidentiary support. It is unreasonable to believe that use of medical marijuana by this discrete population for this limited purpose will create a significant drug problem." *Conant v. McCaffrey*, 172 F.R.D. 681, 694 n5 (N.D.Cal. 1997).

Congress next found that:

(5) Controlled substances manufactured and distributed intrastate cannot be differentiated from controlled substances manufactured and distributed interstate. Thus, it is not feasible to distinguish, in terms of controls, between controlled substances manufactured and distributed interstate and controlled substances manufactured and distributed intrastate.

If considering intrastate illicit drug trafficking versus interstate illicit drug trafficking, Congress' findings here are clearly applicable. However, the concerns evidenced by Congress in this subsection are once again allayed when viewed in the context of defendants' conduct. Defendants will be able to prove that the medicinal cannabis they distribute is clearly and unambiguously labeled as such. No reasonable person could confuse the labeled medicinal cannabis distributed by the defendants herein with illicit black market marijuana, or vice versa.

In subsection (6) Congress noted that:

(6) Federal control of the intrastate incidents of the traffic in controlled substances is essential to the effective control of the interstate incidents of such traffic.

Again, it is clear that Congress is concerned with intrastate trafficking effecting interstate trafficking. As noted above and recognized by Judge Smith, the suppression of defendants' activities, clearly separate from and unrelated to black market drug trafficking, be it intrastate or interstate, is not essential to the control of illegal interstate commerce in drugs. In fact, the converse is true: Barring these defendants from providing a safe affordable source of medicinal cannabis will only serve to drive seriously ill patients into the waiting and willing arms of the black marketeers, thus swelling the interstate illicit drug trade. This certainly was not the intention of Congress in promulgating the Controlled Substances Act.

Finally, Congress recognized the international attempt to curb the illicit traffic in drugs, finding that:

(7) The United States is a party to the single convention on narcotic drugs, 1961, and other international conventions designed to establish effective control over international and domestic traffic in controlled substances.

Here again, the emphasis is on "drug trafficking," a class of activity in which the defendants herein are not involved.

Thus it is readily apparent that the Congressional findings stated in 21 USC § 801 are not applicable to the defendants' conduct herein. When defendants' activities are observed under the illumination of these findings, it is clear that defendants' activities are not within the "class of activities" that adversely effect interstate commerce. (See *U.S. v. Kim*, 94 F.3d 1247, 1249 (9th Cir. 1996); *U.S. v. Visman*, 919 F.2d 1390, 1392–93 (9th Cir. 1990). The Government cannot show that defendants' purely intrastate activities have any substantial effect on interstate commerce. Under these circumstances, the Controlled Substances Act is unconstitutional as applied to these defendants.

C.   Defendants' Activities Are Exempt From Application Of The Controlled Substances Act

1.   Joint Acquisition and Use of Cannabis for Medical Purposes Is Not "Distribution" or "Possession for Distribution" under the Federal Controlled Substances Act.

In *United States v. Swiderski*, 548 F.2d. 445 (2nd Cir. 1977), two individuals purchased cocaine together, then shared it. After they were convicted of the federal crime of distribution, the Second Circuit Court of Appeal held that "where two or more individuals simultaneously and jointly acquire possession of a drug for their own use, intending only to share together, the only crime is personal drug abuse—simple joint possession, without any intent to distribute the drug further." *Id.* at 450. The court reasoned that Congress, in making the penalties much harsher for distributing drugs than for possessing them, was concerned that distribution has the dangerous, unwanted effect of drawing additional participants into the web of drug abuse. *Id.* Because the concerns are not present in a situation of joint purchasers, it was error not to instruct the jury that it could find possession without any distribution. *Id.* at 452

At a trial on the merits, Defendants herein would be able to demonstrate that under *Swiderski*, they are not guilty of the federal crimes of distribution, or possession for distribution, because their alleged control of medical cannabis is established through a cooperative enterprise, shared equally among all of the members thereto, for the exclusive medicinal use of each of them, individually. Defendants will be able to demonstrate that there are no third parties involved, nor is anyone else being brought into a "web" of drug use.

Further, Defendants will be able to establish that this is an enterprise that is legal under the laws of the State of California. Cooperatives are a commonly authorized legal entity. The activity allegedly being conducted is lawful and authorized under the Compassionate Use Act of 1996 (H&S § 11362.5).

In the context of illicit drug transactions, the Ninth Circuit limited *Swiderski* to its facts in *United States v. Wright*, 593 F.2d 105 (1979), In *Wright*, a person asked the defendant to purchase heroin, and gave him money for that purpose. The defendant went out on his own, procured the heroin, brought it back and then participated in its consumption. The court held that it was not error to deny a jury instruction based on the doctrine of joint possession, because the defendant "facilitated the transfer of the narcotic; he did not simply simultaneously and jointly acquire possession of a drug for their (his and another's) own use. *Id.*

At a trial of this matter on the merits, Defendants in this case will be able to demonstrate that, unlike the situation in *Wright*, defendants do not give money to others for the purposes of procuring drugs for recreational use. Rather, Defendants in this case act in concert as cooperatives to ensure the safe and affordable access to cannabis for medicinal purposes for each of the members. In *Wright*, the Court was concerned with defendants using the *Swiderski* defense in a "typical" drug deal. Here, any cannabis possessed is exclusively for medicinal purposes. The activity is not illicit, because it is medicinal in nature and authorized by California Law.

In *United States v. Rush*, 738 F.2d 497 (1st Cir. 1984), the Court upheld a *Swiderski* instruction in a case involving "tons" of marijuana. The Court concluded, "[T]he *Swiderski* defendants were entitled to pursue whatever factual defense they could support, however implausible it might seem to a finder of fact in this case they may have had a colorable alternative." *Id.* at 514. As the Court noted in *United States v. Escobar De Bright*:

> [T]he general principle is well established that a criminal defendant is entitled to have a jury instruction on any defense which provides a legal defense to the charge against him and which has some foundation in the evidence, even though the evidence be weak, insufficient, inconsistent and doubtful of credibility.

Id., 742 F.2d 1196, 1198 (9th Cir. 1984).

Here, the evidence is strong, sufficient, consistent, and credible and would almost certainly result in an acquittal of the Defendants by a jury.

2.   Defendants Are Not in Violation of the Controlled Substances Act, Because They Are "Ultimate Users".

Section 802(27) of the Controlled Substances Act defines an "ultimate user" as "a person who has lawfully obtained, and who possesses a controlled substance for his own use or for the use of a member of his household. . . . "Under the Act, an ultimate user is permitted to possess a Schedule I controlled substance, including marijuana, without being in violation of the Act and without being required to register with the Attorney General.

At a trial on the merits, Defendants would be able to demonstrate that they fit squarely into the "ultimate user" exemption of the Controlled Substances Act. Defendants could show that California Health & Safety Code § 11362.5 authorizes their possession of cannabis. Further, under *Swiderski, supra*, any medical cannabis possessed by any of the Defendants as members of their respective cooperatives would be for the exclusive medicinal purposes of each of them under the doctrine of joint possession. See also, *United States v. Bartee*, 479 F.2d 1390 (10th Cir. 1973) (ultimate user "obtain[s] the drug for his own use").

D. Defendants' Activities Are Justified by the Defense of Necessity.

1.   The Defense Of Medical Necessity Provides Complete Justification For The Defendants' Acts.

The common law defense of necessity is well-established as a defense to federal criminal prosecutions not involving homicides. *United States v. Holmes*, 26 Fed. Cas.No. 15, 383, p. 360 (C.C.E.D. Pa. 1842); *United States v. Ashton*, 24 Fed.Cas.No. 14,470 p. 873 (C.C.D. Mass. 1834). In *United States v. Bailey*, 444 U.S. 394, 414 (1980), the Supreme Court held that criminal defendants may assert the defense of necessity when charged with prison escape, provided they proffer the necessary; evidence to support the claim. The defense of medical necessity is simply a specialized application of the common law defense of necessity available in all federal criminal prosecutions. 1 LaFave & Scott, *Substantive Criminal Law*, § 5.4(c)(7), pp. 631–33 (1986). Although neither the Supreme Court nor this Circuit have ruled directly on the issue in the context of marijuana use, ample authority exists to recognize the viability of the defense of medical necessity in prosecutions for possession, distribution, and cultivation of marijuana.

In *United States v. Randall*, 104 Daily Wash.L.Rptr. 2249, 2252 (D.C. Super. 1976), a defendant successfully asserted medical necessity as a defense to a charge of marijuana possession in the Washington D.C. Superior Court. He grew marijuana plants and used them to treat his own condition of glaucoma after conventional medications were ineffective. The court concluded that the defendant's right to preserve his sight outweighed the government's interest in outlawing the drug.

In *United States v. Burton*, 894 F.2d 188 (6th Cir. 1990), the defendant, who also suffered from glaucoma, asserted a defense of medical necessity when charged with three counts of possession of marijuana with intent to distribute. The jury convicted him of the lesser offense of simple possession, however, and on appeal the Court declined to hold that the medical necessity defense was available to the possession charge, while noting, "Medical necessity has been recognized by some courts and by some authority." *Id.* at 191. The reason the court found the defense unavailable was that, subsequent to the *Randall* case, a government program was established to study the effects of marijuana on glaucoma sufferers, and the defendant failed to utilize this "reasonable legal alternative." Since the *Burton* decision, however, that experimental governmental program has been closed to additional applicants. Thus, the "reasonable legal alternative" is no longer available, and the *Burton* court's grudging acceptance of the medical necessity defense remains good law.

The medical necessity defense has received a warmer reception in the Appellate Courts of many states in this Circuit. In *State v. Hasting*, 801 P.2d 563 (Idaho 1990), the Supreme court of Idaho held that a defendant who claimed her use of marijuana was necessary to control the pain and muscle spasms associated with rheumatoid arthritis presented a legitimate defense of necessity, and it was "for the trier of fact to determine whether or not she has met the elements of that defense." *Id.* at 565. In *State v. Diana*, 604 P.2d 1312 (Wash.App. 1979), the Washington Court of Appeals, citing *United States v. Randall*, held that medical necessity was encompassed in the common law defense of necessity:

> The wisdom of the Randall decision was recognized by the legislature in our State when it enacted the Controlled Substances Therapeutic Research Act, Laws of Washington 1979, Reg.Sess. Ch. 136, eff. March 27, 1979. That legislation recognizes marijuana as a medicinal drug and makes it available under controlled circumstances to alleviate the effects of glaucoma and cancer chemotherapy. The patient must be certified to the State Board of Pharmacy by a licensed physician. In addition, under the Act other disease groups may be included if pertinent medical data is presented to the Board. We believe that the defendant here should be given the opportunity to demonstrate the alleged beneficial effect, if any, of marijuana on the symptoms of multiple sclerosis. Accordingly, we remand his case to the trial court, here the trier of fact, for determination of whether medical necessity exists.

604 P.2d at 1316–17.

In *State v. Bachman*, 595 P.2d 287 (Hawaii 1979), the Hawaii Supreme court concluded "it is entirely possible that medical necessity could be asserted as a defense to a marijuana charge in a proper case." However, the Court held the defense was properly rejected in that case because the defense failed to proffer competent medical testimony "of the beneficial effects upon the defendant's condition of marijuana use, as well as the absence or ineffectiveness of conventional medical alternatives." *Id.* at 288.

Most recently, the California Court of Appeal, assuming that a medical necessity defense is valid in California, and that it is composed of the same elements as the general necessity defense, concluded that the defendant's offer of proof was insufficient to meet those elements because she failed to establish she had no adequate alternative but to possess and transport the marijuana as charged. Nonetheless, based on the subsequent enactment of H&S § 11362.5 and its retroactive application, the court remanded the case for a limited retrial to determine whether H&S § 1362.5 provided a partial defense to the charges. *People v. Trippet*, 56 Cal.App.4th 1532, (1997).

Thus, clear authority exists for the availability of a medical necessity defense in a federal criminal prosecution for marijuana distribution or possession with intent to distribute. The medical necessity defense is simply a corollary of the fully accepted common law defense of necessity, and presents a factual question for the jury to determine in a particular case.

The Ninth Circuit has established a four part test regarding the availability of the necessity defense. To invoke the necessity defense Defendants must offer proof that: "(1) they were faced with a choice of evils and chose the lesser evil; (2) they acted to prevent imminent harm; (3) they reasonably anticipated a direct causal relationship between their conduct and the harm to be averted; and (4) they had no legal alternatives to violating the law." *United States v. Aguilar*, 883 F.2d 662, 693 (9th Cir.1989), *cert. denied*, 498 U.S. 1046, (1991).

Defendants are able to prove each element of the necessity defense. Defendants faced a choice of evils. Thousands of people within the Defendants' geographic range suffer from debilitating and often deadly diseases, including cancer, AIDS, and glaucoma.

A common cause of death for AIDS patients is wasting syndrome. Those afflicted lose all appetite and literally waste away from starvation. Similarly, chemotherapy often causes intense nausea and loss of appetite. Patients face the choice of quitting chemotherapy or enduring it and risking starvation and malnutrition. For many people afflicted with these two diseases, cannabis provides relief as a pain reliever and, more importantly, as an appetite stimulant. In short, cannabis saves these people's lives. Similarly, many glaucoma patients find that cannabis is the only medication that effectively relieves the intraocular pressure in their eyes, a condition that threatens permanent blindness.

But cannabis is, for many, difficult or impossible to obtain. The Defendants solve this problem by providing cannabis to their members. By doing so they run the risk of potentially running afoul of federal drug laws. Such is the choice of evils, and Defendants have clearly chosen the lesser one.

The Defendants also meet the second and third prongs of the necessity test: The harm sought to be averted was (and continues to be) imminent and life threatening and the act of supplying cannabis is a necessary component to averting that harm.

The fourth prong of the necessity defense is the one the government will most likely insist the Defendants have not met. The Defendants are prepared to show that there are no legal alternatives to the distribution of medical cannabis via the cannabis cooperative. The Defendants will present evidence from doctors and patients showing that for many people Marinol or other "legal" drugs simply do not work in treating their symptoms. Cannabis, however, does work. Defendants will also show that their members have no legal or safe alternative to acquire marijuana from other sources, including the government. Additionally, Defendants will show that they have attempted (and continue to attempt) to change marijuana laws at the local, state, and federal level. Such legal alternatives have, for purposes of a necessity defense, been exhausted. Moreover, even if such legal alternatives as rescheduling were an option, such "alternatives" are not adequate to render the necessity defense unavailable to patients who will likely die, waste away, or go blind long before any rescheduling actually is accomplished.

Defendants' actions fall squarely within those contemplated by the necessity defense as articulated by the Ninth Circuit. As such, Defendants possess a valid defense to the charges underlying the government's motions for an injunction.

2.   The Defense of Entrapment Is Available to the Extent That a Defense of Medical Necessity Would Be Precluded for Distribution to DEA Agents.

The entrapment defense was first recognized by the United States Supreme Court in *Sorrels v. United States*, 287 U.S. 435 (1932). The Court held that the defense should be available when the government instigates criminal activity by an otherwise innocent defendant. This subjective test, focused on the predisposition of the defendant, was reaffirmed in *United States v. Russell*, 411 U.S. 423 (1972).

When examining a defendant's predisposition, the court looks to persistent and extended efforts by government agents to target the defendant. Illustrative is *Sherman v. United States*, 356 U.S. 369 (1958), where the government agent met the defendant while both were undergoing treatment for drug abuse. The government agent claimed he was suffering from withdrawal and repeatedly implored the defendant to provide a source for illicit drugs. The Court found the government conduct so extreme that it ruled Sherman was entrapped as a matter of law. In determining the defendant was not "predisposed," the Court distinguished the "unwary innocent" from the "unwary criminal," and examined both the personal characteristics of the defendant and the persistent and extended government behavior.

Clearly, the defendants in this case were not predisposed to commit any crime. The cannabis dispensaries were established for the sole purpose of providing marijuana to patients with doctors' recommendations, to alleviate the nausea associated with cancer chemotherapy, AIDS treatment, and the symptoms of other debilitating diseases. The DEA initiated an extensive undercover sting operation lasting over seven months, to infiltrate the clubs under the guise of needing medical marijuana. The DEA created phony physician's orders, with an agent posing as a doctor to verify the orders. Similar to the egregious behavior in *Sherman*, the undercover DEA agents falsely simulated illness to gain the sympathy of the defendants, resulting in the entrapment of "unwary innocents."

The defendants' reasonable belief that the marijuana they were providing to the DEA agents would be used for medicinal purposes confirms their lack of predisposition. The Cannabis Buyers' Co-operatives can be analogized to the drug treatment center in *Sherman*. Government infiltration of a humanitarian venture to alleviate pain should be viewed with great skepticism. Certainly a jury would be justified in questioning the vast investment of governmental investigative resources demonstrated here in order to seduce "unwary innocents" whose primary motivation is providing comfort and relief for those who are seriously ill. In part, the entrapment defense is an effective way of controlling the behavior of overzealous police who themselves create the "crime" they are responsible for suppressing.

In *Matthews v. United States*, 485 U.S. 58 (1988), the defendant denied having committed the crime and simultaneously requested an instruction on entrapment. The lower court denied his request to present the entrapment defense to the jury, requiring that he admit the crime before he could assert the defense of entrapment. The Supreme Court reversed, holding that he was entitled to an entrapment instruction as long as a reasonable juror could find that entrapment existed. The Court restated the well-established rule applicable to all defenses:

> As a general proposition a defendant is entitled to an instruction as to any recognized defense for which there exists evidence sufficient for a reasonable jury to find in his favor.

Id. at 63.

Once the defendant presents some evidence of entrapment, the prosecution bears the burden of proving beyond a reasonable doubt that the defendant was predisposed to commit the crime of which he is charged before he was approached by the government. *Notaro v. United States*, 363 F.2d 169 (9th Cir. 1966); *United States v. Jacobson*, 112 S.Ct. 1535, 1540–41 (1992). Here, the only "predisposition" on the part of the defendants was a humane willingness to respond to the legitimate medical needs of the sick, in the context of a cooperative venture approved by state law. The government inducements to persuade them to provide marijuana to DEA agents who had no legitimate medical need would be entrapment as a matter of law.

E.   The Government Cannot Meet the Standards for The Injunctive Relief it Seeks.

1.   Traditional Equitable Principles Apply To An Injunction Sought under Section 882.

Section 882 grants federal courts jurisdiction to enjoin violations of the Controlled Substances Act.

The district courts of the United States and all courts exercising general jurisdiction in the territories and possessions of the United States shall have jurisdiction in proceedings in accordance with the Federal Rules of Civil Procedure to enjoin violations of this subchapter.

21 USC § 882(a).

Although Congress has the power to limit a court's equitable jurisdiction, it has not done so here. The statute contains no language that suggests any limitation on a court's equitable powers. On the contrary, by explicitly stating that injunction proceedings must follow the Federal Rules of Civil Procedure, Congress intended courts to conduct § 882 actions in the same manner as any other civil proceeding in equity.

The Supreme Court squarely addressed the issue of the application of equitable principles to statutory enforcement actions in *Weinberger v. Romero-Barcelo*, 456 U.S. 305 (1982). In *Romero*, the Court explained, "unless a statute in so many words, or by a necessary and inescapable inference, restricts the court's jurisdiction in equity, the full scope of that jurisdiction is to be recognized and applied." *Id.* at 313. As the Court further explained:

[A] major departure from the long tradition of equity practice should not be lightly implied . . . we construe the statute at issue in favor of that interpretation which affords a full opportunity for equity courts to treat enforcement proceedings . . . in accordance with their traditional practices, as conditioned by the necessities of the public interest which Congress has sought to protect.

Id. at 320.

Section 882 does not restrict the court's jurisdiction in equity, and consequently the full scope of that jurisdiction applies.

2.   The Government Has Failed To Meet The Equitable Criteria For A Preliminary Injunction.

The Ninth Circuit has established a four pronged analysis to use in determining whether to grant a preliminary injunction. A court should consider:

(1) [T]he likelihood of the moving party's success on the merits; (2) the possibility of irreparable injury to the moving party if relief is not granted; (3) the extent to which the balance of hardships favors the respective parties; and (4) in certain cases, whether the public interest will be advanced by granting the preliminary relief.

Miller v. California Pacific Medical Center, 19 F.3d 449, 456 (9th Cir. 1994) (en banc).

The moving party must show:

> [E]ither (1) a combination of probable success on the merits and the possibility of irreparable harm, or (2) the existence of serious questions going to the merits, the balance of hardships tipping sharply in its favor, and at least a fair chance of success on the merits. These two formulations represent two points on a sliding scale in which the required degree of irreparable harm increases as the probability of success decreases."

Id. at 456.

The government has failed to make the requisite showing under either test to warrant granting it a preliminary injunction.

a).   The Government Has Failed To Show Probability Of Success On The Merits.

The government has not shown probability of success on the merits. To succeed on the merits the government must prove that Defendants violated §§ 841(a)(1), 856(a)(1), and 846 of the Controlled Substances Act. The government in its moving papers has not done so. Even if the facts were, as the government claims, uncontroverted, the government has not shown violations of the Controlled Substances Act. As explained in detail above, the Controlled Substances Act *cannot* constitutionally reach the Defendants' behavior. Even if it could reach the Defendants' behavior, the Controlled Substances Act *does not* reach their behavior in this circumstance. Finally, even if the federal statutes were applied to the Defendants' acts, the Defendants possess valid defenses that would preclude a finding of probability of success on the merits for the government.

b).   The Government Has Not Established Irreparable Injury.

The government claims that it need not prove irreparable injury. It cites *United States v. Odessa Union Warehouse Co-op*, (833 F.2d 172 (9th Cir. 1987)), for the proposition that in statutory enforcement actions irreparable injury is presumed. Such a presumption is limited, however, to situations in which the statutory violation underlying the injunctive action is conceded. The Ninth Circuit sitting en banc clarified the limits of *Odessa Union*.

> There, the traditional requirement of irreparable injury was inapplicable because the parties *conceded* that the federal statute involved was violated. However, when the violation is *disputed* (as it is here), *Odessa Union* does not relieve the governmental agency of its burden of showing that the statutory conditions are met. See *Id.* Rather, as we recently indicated in *United States v. Nutri-Cology, Inc.*, 982 F.2d 394 (9th Cir. 1992), the strength of the government's showing on the likelihood of prevailing on the merits will affect the degree to which it must prove inseparable injury.

Miller, 19.F.3d at 459 (emphasis added).

In *Nutri-Cology*, because the statutory violation was disputed and the government did not establish likelihood of success on the merits, the court held, "the government is not entitled to a presumption, rebuttable or otherwise, of irreparable injury." *Nutri-Cology*, at 398.

In the instant case Defendants do not concede that any federal statute is being violated. Whether or not such statutes are being violated is the central factual and legal issue in this action. Because the government has not shown probability of success on the merits, it is certainly not entitled to a presumption of irreparable injury.

Other than relying on a presumption of irreparable injury, to which it is not entitled, the government has proffered no evidence to show an injury to the public caused by Defendants' acts.

The government has made no such showing because it *cannot* make such a showing. As noted above, in a case arising out of another recent attempt by the federal government to interfere with patients' access to medical marijuana, Judge Smith of this Honorable Court found the government's claims of injury and hardship unsubstantiated.

> Moreover, the government's fears in this case are exaggerated and without evidentiary support. It is unreasonable to believe that use of medical marijuana by this discrete population for this limited purpose will create a significant drug problem.

Conant v. McCaffrey, 172 F.R.D. 681, 694–5 (N.D. Cal. 1997).

If the government truly possessed a good faith belief that the activities of the Defendants was causing irreparable injury, it would not have waited over two years from the opening of the first cooperative to its bringing this suit in equity. Likewise, the government could have brought criminal charges against members of cooperatives and shut them down long ago, rather than waiting to bring this politically opportune case.

The use of medical cannabis by the members of the cooperatives that are defendants in this action cannot rationally be characterized as an irreparable injury to the United States.

c). Balance of Hardships

The government has made no showing that the balance of hardships tips sharply in its favor. Just as with irreparable injury, the government has relied on an inapplicable presumption that the purported statutory violations it wishes to enjoin are *per se* hardships on the public. It has offered no evidence of any actual hardships suffered by the public as a result of the Defendants' operations. Even if the government were entitled to some presumption of hardship in this case, it has not shown that the balance tips sharply in its favor. As in *Conant,* the "government's fears are exaggerated and without evidentiary support." *Id.*

Moreover, the government still possesses an adequate remedy at law. It will suffer no hardship by being denied the extraordinary remedy of an injunction. As with irreparable injury, if the government were truly burdened by the cooperatives' existence it could move to shut them down in criminal proceedings. That it has not attempted to do so makes the government's claims of hardship ring hollow.

Defendants, in contrast, are prepared to show substantial hardships to be suffered by their members and by the general public if this Court were to enjoin the Defendants. Collectively, the six cooperatives the government seeks to shut down serve the medical needs of several thousand patients. Numerous members are afflicted with AIDS, cancer, glaucoma, and other serious illnesses for which, for many, cannabis is the only effective treatment for intractable pain and conditions that could otherwise lead to death, blindness or other permanent debilitation. For the government to assert that such hardships can be alleviated by petitioning the DEA to reschedule marijuana, *Plaintiff's Motion* at p. 18, (a process in which Defendants have attempted in the past and continue to pursue), shows a lack of compassion and a distorted view of reality that is truly frightening. The patients who Defendants serve suffer hardships that are immediate and life threatening. These cannot be alleviated by an administrative process that all parties agree could take years to effectuate, even if the government abandoned its arbitrary and capricious practices and dealt with this issue in good faith.

d). Public Interest Favors Denial Of The Government's Motion.

Just as it does with irreparable injury and the balancing of hardships, the government relies on unsubstantiated presumptions it claims weigh in its favor. As with those other factors the government is only entitled to such a presumption when it has clearly shown a statutory violation. This Honorable Court must weigh such presumptions against the effect issuance of an injunction would have on the public interest. Inflicting substantial and life-threatening medical and legal hardships on patients who are reliant upon the Defendants surely offends the public interest. Moreover, issuance of an injunction that frustrates the declared intent of the majority of voters in California, that seriously ill people have access to medical marijuana, would clearly run contrary to the public interest.

3.   No Injunction Should Issue.

As demonstrated above, the government has met none of the equitable criteria for the issuance of an injunction against defendants. Even if the government were able to establish that Defendants' actions were violative of the federal law, the facts and circumstances of this case do not, as the government contends, require that an injunction automatically issue. The Supreme Court made this clear in *Romero*. "The grant of jurisdiction to ensure compliance with a statute hardly suggests an absolute duty to do so under any and all circumstances, and a federal judge sitting as chancellor is not mechanically obligated to grant an injunction for every violation of law." *Romero*, at 313. The public interest and the balance of hardships dictate that no injunction should issue here.

4.   Equitable Defenses Preclude Injunctive Relief.

The government's attempt to invoke equitable relief against defendants is barred by the doctrine of unclean hands.

a).   Unclean Hands

The government cannot prevail in its attempt to prohibit the distribution of medical marijuana since it comes to the Court with unclean hands. The applicability of the doctrine to government action was explained by the Ninth Circuit in *Equal Employment Opportunity Commission v. Recruit U.S.A.*, 939 F.2d 746 (1991).

> They [defendants] rely on the "clean hands" doctrine, which insists that one who seeks equity must come to the court without blemish. See, e.g., *Johnson v. Yellow Cab Transit Co.*, 321 U.S. 383, 387, 64 S.Ct. 622, 624, 88 L.Ed. 814 (1944). This maxim "is a self-imposed ordinance that closes the doors of a court of equity to one tainted with an inequitableness or bad faith relative to the matter in which he seeks relief, however improper may have been the behavior of the defendant. "*Precision Instrument Mfg. Co. v. Automotive Maintenance Mach. Co.*, 324 U.S. 806, 814, 65 S.Ct. 993, 997, 89 L.Ed. 1381 (1945). This rule applies to the government as well as to private litigants. See *United States v. Desert Gold Mining Co.*, 448 F.2d 1230, 1231 (9th Cir. 1971).

Id. at 752.

The government's record regarding marijuana in general and medical marijuana specifically demonstrates a pattern of bad faith that should preclude it from attaining equitable relief. The government has at least a twenty-five year history of bad faith and unclean hands in its dealings with medical marijuana. Such behavior is violative of the legislative intent of the Controlled Substances Act and of the United States' obligations under the Single Convention Treaty. It also flies in the face of virtually every comprehensive study commissioned by the government during the twentieth century. Defendants are prepared to show that 1) numerous and uncontroverted scientific studies exist firmly establishing the medical efficacy of marijuana and 2) the government has obstructed, suppressed or ignored all attempts by citizens to reschedule or otherwise make marijuana legally available for medical purposes. Having in bad faith resisted all attempts by Defendants and others to explicitly legalize medical marijuana under federal law, the government cannot now invoke equity in its attempts to squelch Defendants' good faith efforts to legally provide medical marijuana through the cooperatives. One who comes to equity must do so with clean hands. The government, in this instance, does not.

Perhaps the most glaring example of the government's unclean hands is that of the Investigative New Drug (IND) program. Under the IND program the federal government provides marijuana to eight individuals suffering from a variety of ailments including cancer and glaucoma. The government claims in prosecuting this action that there are no medically accepted uses for marijuana, while, simultaneously, the DEA distributes marijuana for those very same medical purposes that the cooperatives serve. The government's own actions demonstrate the falsity of its arguments. Not only does the very existence of the IND program counter the government argument of no legitimate medical use for marijuana, but the government's administration of the program exhibits a complete lack of good faith. Only eight people currently receive marijuana under the program. No new enrollments are accepted. These eight people do not differ from the several thousand members of the cannabis club in any medical sense. Their illnesses are no more or less severe than those of the club members not part of the IND program. The only distinction is political. The IND patients were all enrolled prior to the War on Drugs of the 1980's. They also predate the AIDS epidemic. The government admits that it stopped approving applications under the program because it feared an upswing in applications by AIDS patients would "send the wrong message." The decision had nothing to do with the efficacy of marijuana as medicine. The history of the IND program demonstrates that the federal government has not dealt with medical marijuana in a rational, scientific good faith manner. For the government to seek injunctive relief here, when it has itself failed to treat its ailing citizens in an equitable fashion, runs afoul of all principles upon which equitable jurisdiction is based.

5.   The Government Is Not Entitled To Summary Judgment And A Permanent Injunction.

      a)   Because Genuine Issues of Fact Exist That Are Material to the Defenses
              Raised By Defendants, Summary Judgment and Permanent Injunctive
              Relief Are Inappropriate.

If the Court does grant the government's request for a preliminary injunction it must not simultaneously grant its request for summary judgment and a permanent injunction. Even without considering issues of facts, it is apparent that plaintiffs have violated the procedural rules governing summary judgment, and as such, should be precluded from a final judgment. According to the summary judgment rules applicable to claimants, "[a] party seeking to recover upon a claim, . . . may, at any time after the expiration of 20 days from the commencement of the action . . ., move with or without supporting affidavits for a summary judgment in the party's favor upon all or any part thereof." Fed.R.Civ.P.56(a). Defendants were served with plaintiff's *Motion for Preliminary and Permanent Injunction, and for Summary Judgment* on January 8, 1998, thereby commencing this action. As demonstrated by the motion's title, plaintiffs included with their request for a preliminary injunction a request for summary judgment. Such a procedure of including at the commencement of the action a motion for summary judgment, is barred by the federal rules. To be in compliance, plaintiff was required to wait until 20 days after the filing of the complaint to move for summary judgment. Since the government failed to do so, the motion should be denied.

Aside from plaintiff's procedural error, the existence of issues of material fact also warrants denial of plaintiff's motion. The threshold inquiry in summary judgment motions is "determining whether there is the need for a trial—whether, in other words, there are any factual issues that can be properly resolved only by a finder of fact because they may reasonably be resolved in favor of either party." *Anderson v. Liberty Lobby, Inc.*, 477 US 242, 250, 106 S.Ct. 2505, 91 L.Ed.2d 202 (1986). A factual dispute is genuine if the nonmovant's evidence is substantial enough to require trial. *Id.* at 249–250. All reasonable inferences to be drawn from the facts "must be viewed in the light most favorable to the party opposing the motion." *Matsushita Elec. Indus. Co. v. Zenith Radio Corp.*, 475 U.S. 574, 587 (1986).

Defendants have sustained their burden of identifying for the Court a multitude of facts that illustrate the presence of genuine issues requiring a hearing. In outlining their defenses above, Defendants have made fact specific offers of proof regarding constitutional, legal, and equitable defenses to the government's charges.

Since no legally adequate notice has been provided to Defendants, summary judgment at this juncture would be premature. Moreover, as previously discussed, genuine issues of fact exist which mandate a hearing. By granting summary judgment on the basis of the current record, Defendants would be effectively deprived of their day in court. Thus, the government's motion for summary judgment and permanent injunctive relief should be denied.

F.   The Court Should Fashion Protective Measures to Ensure That Defendants' Procedural Due Process Rights Are Not Violated.

The Government has brought the within action under 21 USC § 882, a novel use of a statute for which there is a dearth of precedence. In so doing, the government has placed the defendants at a critical disadvantage. If the government had sought to prosecute Defendants criminally, Defendants would have been afforded the Constitutional protections of the Fourth, Fifth, and Sixth Amendments. By seeking to enjoin Defendant's lawyers the government is interfering with the right to counsel to such a degree that in a criminal context would surely be a Sixth Amendment violation. Perhaps most importantly, by first bringing a civil proceeding against Defendants, the government has placed them in an unavoidable Fifth Amendment conundrum. Defendants cannot adequately defend the civil proceedings without effectively waiving Constitutional rights against self-incrimination in any future criminal proceedings. At a minimum, before the government can seek equitable relief against defendants it must guarantee them immunity from any possible criminal prosecutions for the acts which it seeks to enjoin. The government cannot fairly contend that legal remedies are unavailable and at the same time waive the hammer of those very same legal remedies over the heads of Defendants.

III.   CONCLUSION

It is unfortunate that the federal government is undertaking this effort to prohibit access to the only supply of affordable, safe medical cannabis on which numerous seriously ill and suffering patients depend for relief. The federal government is acting in direct defiance to the will of the voters of California who clearly and unambiguously mandated that patients who can attain relief through the use of medical marijuana should be allowed to do so under a physician's care. The citizens of California have called on the federal government to make medical cannabis available. Instead the federal government has responded by initially threatening California physicians. When Judge Smith of this Honorable Court barred the government from making good on its threats, the government aimed its crosshairs at the sick and dying. Accordingly, defendants request that this Honorable Court deny the government's request for a preliminary injunction, permanent injunction and summary judgment.

Dated: February 27, 1998   Respectfully submitted,

Review section II.D.1 of Defendants' Joint Memorandum to see how this work was incorporated into the final product.

MEMORANDUM OF LAW

I. The Defense of Medical Necessity Provides Complete Justification for the Defendant's Acts

It is well established that the common law defense of necessity is recognized in federal criminal prosecutions that do not involve homicides. In *US v. Bailey*, 444 U.S. 394, 414 (1980), the United States Supreme Court held that criminal defendants may assert the defense of necessity when charged with prison escape provided they proffer the necessary evidence to support the claim. Moreover, in *US v. Lemon*, 824 F.2d 763, 765 (9th Cir. 1987), the Ninth Circuit recognized the common law defense in the context of a charge of unlawful possession of a handgun. Therefore, it is clear that the courts recognize the common law defense in federal criminal prosecutions. The defense of medical necessity is simply a specialized application of the common law defense of necessity available in all federal criminal prosecutions. 1 LaFave & Scott, *Substantive Criminal Law* § 5.4(c)7, 631–633 (1986). Although neither the United States Supreme Court nor the Ninth Circuit have ruled directly with the issue in the context of marijuana use, authority exists that does recognize the viability of the defense of medical necessity in prosecutions for possession and cultivation of marijuana.

In *US v. Randall*, 104 Wash.D.C.Rep. 2249, 2252, 104 Daily Wash.L.Rptr. 2249 (D.C. Super. 1976), a Washington D.C. Superior Court allowed the defendant to assert medical necessity as a defense for possession of marijuana. There, the defendant grew marijuana plants and used them to treat his own glaucoma because conventional medications were ineffective. The court concluded that the defendant's right to preserve his sight outweighed the government's interest in outlawing the drug. *Id.* at 2252. In *Hawaii v. Bachman*, 61 Haw. 71, 72 (1976), the Hawaii Supreme Court stated that "it is entirely possible that medical necessity could be asserted as a defense to a marijuana possession charge in a proper case." However, in that case, the court rejected the defense because the defendant failed to show by competent medical testimony the beneficial effects upon the his condition of marijuana use. *Id.* at 73.

Moreover, in *Washington v. Diana*, 24 Wash. App. 908, 916 (1979), the court stated that medical necessity was a viable defense in a prosecution for possession of marijuana. There, the defendant used marijuana as treatment for his multiple sclerosis, but was not allowed to present the medical necessity defense at trial. The appellate court remanded the case holding that the defendant should have been permitted to present the defense of medical necessity. *Id.*, at 915–916. Finally, in *Jenks v. Florida*, 582 So. 2d 676, 677 (CA 1991), the defendant, who suffered from AIDS and used marijuana to combat the side effects of AZT treatment, was convicted of cultivation of marijuana. A Florida Court of Appeals reversed the conviction and entered a judgment of acquittal holding that state legislation which forbids all use of marijuana does not automatically preclude the defense of medical necessity to a charge of possession. *Id.* at 679. Therefore, ample persuasive authority exists which recognizes the viability of the defense in state criminal prosecutions.

However, case law does exist where courts have refused to extend the doctrine of medical necessity to federal prosecutions for possession of marijuana. In *U.S. v. Belknap*, 1993 U.S. App. LEXIS 2183 (4th Cir. 1993), the court refused to allow an instruction on medical necessity. There, the defendant was using marijuana to alleviate pain and overcome previous drug addiction. However, the defendant did not offer evidence to support an instruction on medical necessity because he failed to show that his alternatives were limited and testified that he never tried to treat his suffering through legal means. Additionally, in *U.S. v. Burton*, 894 F.2d 188, 191 (6th Cir. 1990), the court refused to hold that defense of medical necessity was available to a charge of possession with intent to distribute. The court refused to extend the medical necessity defense because the defendant failed to utilize an existing government program under which he could treat his glaucoma with marijuana under the government's supervision. The defendant was aware of this alternative, thus he failed to meet the elements of medical necessity. However, in *Burton*, the Sixth Circuit expressly recognized that authority did exist for allowing the medical necessity defense in federal prosecutions. *Id.* at 191. Thus, although two federal cases have refused to extend the defense, the facts of those cases are insufficient to assert the defense on a basic level.

Notwithstanding *Burton* and *Belknap*, medical necessity is a common law defense which should be available in federal criminal prosecutions. Clear authority exists establishing that the common law defense of necessity is recognized in federal criminal prosecutions. Medical necessity is merely a particular application of common law necessity. A myriad of persuasive authority exists where courts have extended the defense of medical necessity in state criminal prosecutions. Therefore, the defense should be available in federal criminal prosecutions.

Review sections II.C and II.E.5 of the Defendants' Joint Memorandum to see how this work was incorporated into the final product.

MEMORANDUM OF LAW ARGUMENT FOR CANNABIS CLUB DEFENSE: "JOINT-PURCHASERS"

I. The Motion for a Summary Judgment and Request for Injunction should not be Granted Because it Unduly Deprives the Defendants of the Opportunity to Present a Legally Viable Defense to a Jury of their Peers

A. INTRODUCTION

The United States is charging the defendants with the crime of distributing marijuana in violation of 21 U.S.C. section 882(a), referred to as the Controlled Substances Act. Instead of charging the defendants criminally, which would afford them the right to present legally viable defenses to a jury of their peers, the United States is attempting to obtain a preliminary and permanent injunction against the Defendants, ultimately depriving them of the right to present their defenses to the alleged criminal violations.

The United States Constitution guarantees the right to trial by jury in order to prevent oppression by the government. U.S.C.A. Const. Amends 6, 14; *Duncan v. State of La.*, 391 U.S. 145, 194 (1968). As such, a right to a jury trial is inherent in our governmental system which purports to guarantee fairness, and the United States is attempting to deprive the defendants of this right by the institution of this motion for a preliminary and permanent injunction. There is a well-established principle that in proceedings for criminal contempt, a defendant has no right to a jury trial for petty crimes such as ones that result in imprisonment of less than six months. *Bloom v. State of Ill.*, 391 U.S. 194 (1968). It seems apparent that the United States is purposely attempting to avoid a traditional criminal prosecution so that they can pursue criminal contempt proceedings against the Defendants for any violations of the requested injunction, ultimately avoiding a jury trial and depriving the Defendants of their right to present any viable defenses.

The case at hand presents an issue never presented to a court before. The case involves Cannabis Clubs who provide marijuana to their members for medicinal purposes which is legal under California law. (Prop. 15) The United States is requesting an injunction to halt this alleged illegal conduct. However, the Defendants have a viable defense to the allegations that they are engaged in the illicit distribution of marijuana. Under *U.S. v. Swiderski*, 548 F.2d 445 (2nd Cir. 1977), it was held that a statutory "transfer" could not occur between two individuals in joint possession of a controlled substance simultaneously acquired for their own use. It is the Defendant's contention that under *Swiderski*, they and their members should be considered "joint purchasers" thus relieving them of any liability for distributing an illicit substance.

At this juncture, the issue is not whether this defense will ultimately persuade a jury, rather the issue is whether the defendants have a guaranteed right to present such a defense to a jury. The Defendants will argue that they should be accorded such a right and by issuing an injunction at this stage, they will be denied any possibility of defending their alleged conduct.

B. THE DEFENDANTS RIGHT TO PRESENT A LEGALLY VIABLE DEFENSE TO A JURY OF THEIR PEERS WOULD BE UNDULY DENIED WITH THE ISSUANCE OF AN INJUNCTION

As stated above, the U.S. Constitution affords individuals the right to a jury trial when dealing with legal issues. It is true that a jury trial is not guaranteed to those seeking relief in equity. *Kalish v. Franklin Advisers, Inc.*, 928 F.2d 590 (1991). However, when a case involves both legal and equitable claims, right to trial by jury must be preserved. *Glezos v. Amalfi Ristorante Italiano, Inc.*, 651 F.Supp. 1271 (1987).

In the case at hand, the United States is seeking equitable relief in the form of a preliminary and permanent injunction against the defendants. If the United States were to charge the defendants criminally based on the same alleged conduct, there would be no question to the defendant's right to a jury trial in a criminal action. So, although equitable relief is being sought by the United States, the issues are legal in nature thus supporting the defendant's right to a jury trial.

In fact, "the general principle is well-established that a criminal defendant is entitled to have a jury instruction on any defense which provides a legal defense to the charge against him and which has some foundation in the evidence, even though the evidence may be weak, insufficient, inconsistent, or of doubtful credibility." *U.S. v. Escobar De Bright*, 742 F.2d 1196, 1198 (9th Cir. 1984). So, no matter how insufficient the United States will claim the Defendant's defenses are, if prosecuted a jury would have to be instructed on any viable defenses. It seems obvious that the prosecution is attempting to avoid this by the institution of these proceedings requesting an injunction, so they can ultimately charge the Defendants with criminal contempt without a jury.

C. THE DEFENDANTS SHOULD BE CONSIDERED "JOINT PURCHASERS" THUS MAKING IT IMPOSSIBLE FOR THEM TO BE CHARGED WITH DISTRIBUTION OF AN ILLICIT SUBSTANCE

In *U.S. v. Swiderski*, 548 F.2d 445 (2d Cir. 1977), two individuals purchased cocaine and then snorted it. After they were charged with distribution, the court held that "where two or more individuals simultaneously and jointly acquire possession of a drug for their own use, intending only to share it together, the only crime is personal drug abuse-simple joint possession, without any intent to distribute the drug further." *Id.* at 450. The court reasoned that Congress, in making the penalties much harsher for distributing narcotics than for just possessing them, was concerned that such conduct tends to have the dangerous, unwanted effect of drawing additional participants into the web of drug abuse. *Id.* Because these concerns were not present in a situation of joint purchasers, it was error for the jury not to be instructed that they could find mere possession without any distribution. *Id.* at 452.

This case presents a factual scenario whereby the Defendants are involved in a cooperative enterprise with the members of their clubs. "Members" of the Defendant's

Cannabis clubs jointly obtain marijuana for medicinal purposes. All members are screened and only those with diagnosed medical problems and a doctor's prescription may obtain the marijuana. This is an enterprise that is legal under California law, thus leaving the Defendants without any intent to violate the law. Basically, they jointly acquire the marijuana and jointly use it to treat their medical conditions. The Defendants act as caregivers, making the marijuana available as a remedy for their member's ailments. Alternatively, the members are using the marijuana to alleviate their ailments as a patient would use the medicine his doctor gave him to alleviate his pain. There are no third parties involved. It is simply a joint enterprise that is absolutely legal under California law.

Congress' concerns over drawing additional participants into the web of drug abuse are not jeopardized. As in *Swiderski*, nobody other than the co-purchasers are involved in the marijuana use. The members are not drawn into drug use through the Defendants, rather they seek the drug to alleviate their ailments. These individuals are not using marijuana for recreational purposes. They are merely attempting to alleviate their painful ailments through the use of physician prescribed medicinal marijuana. Basically, there is no distribution taking place, for the clubs and their members jointly acquire the marijuana for medicinal purposes to be shared among them and nobody else. The arrangement actually furthers the federal goal of eliminating illicit drug trafficking, by providing a safe environment for those who frequently suffer from debilitating ailments to conveniently gain access to necessary medication. If these cooperative enterprises are shut down, patients will be left to seek individual transactions with illicit dealers.

In the context of illicit drug transactions, The Ninth Circuit has limited *Swiderski* to its facts. In *U.S. v. Wright*, 593 F.2d 105 (1979), the defendant was asked to purchase heroin and was given money by another. The defendant went out on his own, procured the heroin, brought it to the individual who requested it where they snorted the heroin together. The court held that it was not an error to deny a jury instruction based on the joint purchaser defense presented in *Swiderski, Id.* at 108. The court reasoned that the defendant "facilitated the transfer of the narcotic; he did not simply simultaneously and jointly acquire possession of a drug for their (his and another's) own use." *Id.*

This case presents a factual scenario unlike *Wright*. As opposed to *Wright*, the members of the club do not give money to the Defendants and have them go procure drugs for their recreational use. Rather, the marijuana is originally acquired for the club and its members from the outset. In *Wright*, the court was concerned with defendants using the *Swiderski* defense in a "typical" drug deal. Here, the drugs are not being used for illicit purposes. In fact, the club and its members are engaged in legal activity under state law and the use of the drugs is not for recreational purposes but instead for purely medicinal purposes.

The present case is one of first impression and the Defendants would have the opportunity to present the joint purchaser defense to a jury. *Wright* would not automatically preclude such a defense because the facts of this case are in such discord with the facts of *Wright*. In *U.S. v. Rush*, 738 F.2d 497 (1st Cir. 1984), a group of defendants were in possession of tons of marijuana and argued the *Swiderski* defense. Despite the large amount of marijuana that was retrieved, which usually leads to an inference that they intended to distribute it, the court stated "[T]he *Swiderski* defendants were entitled to pursue whatever factual defense they could support, however implausible it might seem to a finder of fact; in this case they may have had no colorable alternative." *Id.* at 514. Thus, despite *Wright*, the Defendants would still be afforded the opportunity to present the defense to a jury if they were prosecuted criminally. Based on the novel facts of this case as well as the legality of the operation under state law, it cannot be denied that the *Swiderski* defense has direct applicability to these Defendants.

D. CONCLUSION

Although many courts have decided to limit or even not recognize the defense presented in *Swiderski*, it is still a viable defense. As stated above, a defendant has the right to present any defenses that can be supported by the evidence, no matter how improbable or insufficient it might seem. The reason we have a jury system is to allow a group of our peers to be the ultimate decision-maker. We must trust a jury to ultimately determine if the joint purchaser defense can be applied to the Defendants in this case.

There is no doubt that if the prosecution decided to prosecute the Defendants criminally in this matter, the defense would have the right to present any defense that is allowed under the law or any reasonable extension thereof. In the present case, the situation involving a marijuana club that is involved in a cooperative enterprise with its members to help them get the medicine that their doctors are prescribing is unlike any factual scenario this court has seen before.

As described above, the current situation can be analogized to *Swiderski*, and the cases that have limited the holding have involved situations where individuals were engaged in the illicit use of drugs in direct contravention to Congress' concerns in passing the Controlled Substances Act. Here, those concerns are not raised because the Defendants are operating under a legal scheme under state law. Additionally, marijuana is not being made available to the general public nor those that want marijuana for commercial or recreational purposes. Only those members involved in the cooperative enterprise with the Defendants who have medical prescriptions for marijuana are the ones using the marijuana. This is not a typical drug deal and it would unduly deny the Defendants their rights if they were not allowed to present this defense to a jury of their peers.

Appellate Brief

**IN THE SUPREME COURT
OF THE UNITED STATES**

OCTOBER TERM, 1988

———

No. 87-1206

KATHRYN ISABELLA MESA, PETITIONER

v.

PEOPLE OF THE STATE OF CALIFORNIA

———

SHABBIR A. EBRAHIM, PETITIONER

v.

PEOPLE OF THE STATE OF CALIFORNIA

———

*ON WRIT OF CERTIORARI TO THE UNITED STATES
COURT OF APPEALS FOR THE NINTH CIRCUIT*

———

BRIEF FOR THE RESPONDENT

———

QUESTION PRESENTED

Whether 28 U.S.C. §1442(a)(1) allows a federal employee charged with committing a traffic offense while on duty to remove the ensuing prosecution to federal court where the employee does not allege a defense to the charges based upon any right, duty, privilege, or immunity provided under federal law?

<u>TABLE OF CONTENTS</u>

<u>TABLE OF AUTHORITIES</u>

Cases:

<u>TABLE OF AUTHORITIES</u>—Continued

United States Constitution and Statutes:

<u>TABLE OF AUTHORITIES</u>—Continued

Miscellaneous Authorities:

STATEMENT

This Court is presented with two otherwise ordinary traffic cases. Petitioner Shabbir A. Ebrahim was given a traffic ticket for speeding and failing to yield after he struck a police car with the mail truck he was driving. Petitioner Kathryn Isabella Mesa was charged with misdemeanor vehicular manslaughter after she struck and killed a bicyclist with the mail truck she was driving.

Each mail carrier filed a petition for removal based solely upon their having been federal employees on duty when the incidents occurred. Neither petitioner alleged that his/her actions were justified by federal law. There has been no suggestion that these prosecutions were motivated by animus toward federal officials or federal law.

The United States District Court for the Northern District of California simultaneously granted the petitions and denied the State of California's motions for remand. California sought review by the Ninth Circuit Court of Appeals by direct appeal and mandamus.

The Ninth Circuit held that mandamus was available to challenge the District Court's decision, and petitioners do not challenge that ruling. The Ninth Circuit found that removal was prohibited by this Court's decision in *Maryland v. Soper* (*No. 1*), 270 U.S. 9, 33–35 (1926), which required that the employee have alleged in his petition a defense to the state charges based upon federal law. *People of the State of California v. Mesa*, 813 F.2d 960 (9th Cir. 1987). This Court granted certiorari.

SUMMARY OF ARGUMENT

Petitioners seek to expand federal jurisdiction radically at the expense of State sovereignty and common sense. Petitioners' theory would allow federal employees to force local prosecutors to travel hundreds of miles from county seats to federal courthouses to contest traffic tickets and other criminal offenses completely unconnected with federal law or authority. The tactical advantage of such a procedure will ensure its use, and create a separate criminal court for federal employees. District courts will be burdened with new cases presenting purely state law issues. Those cases will generate a disproportionate number of appeals because there is uncertainty concerning the proper incorporation of state procedural and substantive law into federal criminal procedure.

Such an expansion of federal jurisdiction would breach this Court's fundamental policy against federal interference with state criminal prosecutions, and is both unnecessary and contrary to the intent of Congress in enacting section 1442(a)(1). Petitioners rely upon their construction of other statutes dissimilar in language and heritage to section 1442(a)(1). because the structure and history of section 1442 (a)(1) demonstrates that Congress has always required a federal defense for removal. This is not a case where this Court must choose between two plausible statutory constructions based upon the desirability of the result, although the difficulties posed by creating a separate criminal court for federal officials would tip the balance in favor of California. Rather, petitioners' construction of section 1442 (a)(1) renders both section 1442 (a)(3) and the Federal Drivers Act (28 U.S.C. 2679(b)) superfluous. It also ignores the distinction made by Congress between "under color of office" and "in performance of duties". A chronological view of the legislative history illuminates that distinction and demonstrates that Congress has always intended to require a federal defense under section 1442(a)(1).

When it enacted the first federal official removal statute, Congress only intended to protect federal law against defiance or misinterpretation by State courts. Congress did not provide for removal of all torts and petty crimes committed while on duty, as those cases did not present a challenge to federal law. Moreover, that first statute was enacted before it was clear that Article III, section 2, permitted federal jurisdiction over state court judgments presenting *federal* questions. *See Martin v. Hunter's Lessee*, 14 U.S. 304 (1816). Congress would not have provided for removal of cases presenting purely state law issues under those circumstances. Indeed, removal of these cases would still violate Article III because these traffic offenses do not present federal questions.

Petitioners concede that Congress retained its original intent when it enacted subsequent removal statutes. The history of those enactments confirms that Congress intended to protect federal law by requiring a federal defense for removal.

The lack of cases allowing removal confirms that conclusion. There are no reported cases decided before 1980 (when the Third Circuit "reinvented" Congressional intent), allowing removal where the federal employee did not rely upon his enforcement or compliance with federal law as a defense. Certainly officials sued for miscellaneous torts or prosecuted for petty crimes in "hostile" states would have produced hundreds of reported decisions over 165 years had there been no federal defense requirement. The absence of a case explicity allowing removal without a federal defense, combined with the absence of such reported decisions, is only consistent with the federal defense requirement.

Finally, the decision of this Court in both civil and criminal cases uniformly mandate the federal defense requirement once the term "federal defense" is understood as including all cases where the official's defense raises issues of federal law. Petitioners ignore the official's claim of federal immunity in many of those decisions, and are unable to explain this Court's denial of removal to on-duty officials in the remainder.

ARGUMENT

1.   Congress Always Intended to Require a Federal Defense for Removal

A.   READING SECTION 1442(a) AS A WHOLE ESTABLISHES THAT CONGRESS REQUIRED A FEDERAL DEFENSE FOR REMOVAL

Section 1442(a)(1) allows removal for suits and prosecutions for acts "under color of office". That phrase is inherently ambiguous.[1] Petitioners claim it mandates removal of suits and prosecutions for any acts committed by officials in performance of their duties. But reading section 1442(a) as a whole prohibits that construction. Section 1442(a)(3) allows removal to "[a]ny officer of the courts of the United States, for any Act under color of office *or* in the performance of his duties" (emphasis added). Terms connected in the disjunctive are to be given separate meanings. *See Garcia v. United States*, 469 U.S. 70, 73 (1984), *Reiter v. Sonotone*, 442 U.S. 330, 339 (1979). Thus, "under color of office" must restrict removal to something less than all acts committed while on duty. The only logical reading of section 1442(a)(1) is that "under color of office" refers to acts which the official seeks to justify or immunize by the laws creating and protecting his exercise of federal authority (i.e. his "office").

In addition, petitioners' reading of the phrase "under color of office" in section 1442(a)(1) must be rejected because it would allow court officers to remove cases based upon any act committed while in performance of their duties under section 1442(a)(1), rendering all of section 1442(a)(3) superfluous. *See Jarecki v. Searle & Co.*, 367 U.S. 303 (1961) (this Court reads statutes as a whole and seeks to give effect to each section).

B.   THE LEGISLATIVE HISTORY OF SECTION 1442(a)(1) DEMONSTRATES THAT CONGRESS ALWAYS REQUIRED A FEDERAL DEFENSE FOR REMOVAL

The history of the removal statutes set forth below demonstrates that Congress employed removal sparingly, as befits a threat to State sovereignty. From the outset, Congress crafted the removal statutes to protect only certain federal laws from State misinterpretation or defiance. Congress periodically reenacted removal statutes protecting different classes of federal officials only when the laws which those officials enforced were the subject of State hostility. Protecting federal officials who enforced federal law was the only mechanism available to protect the law itself. Congress provided for removal to protect enforcement of federal law, not to allow federal officials to remove all torts or crimes committed while on duty.

1.   Congress enacted the first federal official removal statute solely to provide an efficient mechanism to transfer suits challenging federal authority to federal court before trial.

Section 25 of the Judiciary Act of 1789 (1 Stat. 85) provided for removal after trial of state court judgments purporting to invalidate federal law or authority exercised under federal law. There was no

---

1.   Petitioners do not address the "plain meaning" of "under color of office". Rather, they attempt to construe section 1442(a)(1) *in pari materia* with other statutes purportedly united by a common purpose and legacy. AB 9–12, 27. The failure of that attempt is discussed below after examination of the legislative history of section 1442(a)(1).

provision for removal of cases lacking federal questions. Indeed, when the first federal official removal statute was enacted in 1815, this Court had yet to rule that federal courts could review any state court judgments, even those presenting federal questions. Compare Act of February 4, 1815, 3 Stat. 198 ("1815 Act") with Martin v. Hunter's Lessee, 14 U.S. 304 (1816) (decided after Congress enacted the 1815 Act). Congress would not have attempted to expand federal jurisdiction to include cases presenting no federal questions under such circumstances. Rather, the legislative history of the 1815 Act demonstrates that it was only a modest and temporary extension of the Judiciary Act.

The 1815 Act was proposed to protect federal customs agents in their enforcement of federal law against States sympathetic to smugglers during the 1812 War. The only available legislative history for that Act consists of a letter from its proponent, the Secretary of the Treasury. *See* Annals of Congress, 13th Cong., 3d Sess. at 757–61 (also appearing in the American State Papers, 1802–15, Finance, at 881). The Secretary related that the Vermont courts were frustrating the enforcement of federal law by routinely granting civil judgments against customs officials for seizures authorized under federal law. Under the Judiciary Act, decisions in such civil cases could only be removed to federal courts *after* the judgement was affirmed by the highest court in the State. That delay would allow Vermont to forestall review until after the war ended.

The Secretary wanted to allow removal of civil cases before adjudication by any State court. *Id.*, at 760. The Secretary only intended to adjust the Judiciary Act for the duration of the war to allow immediate transfer to federal court of State challenges to federal law authorizing searches and seizures by customs inspectors. He quoted section 25 of the Judiciary Act as allowing removal of cases "where is drawn in question the validity of an authority, exercised under the United States (as in the case of an official of the customs,) and the decision is against the validity." *Id.*, at 760 (quoting the Judiciary Act). His proposal mirrors the Judiciary Act, except that he suggested that removal occur before trial.

"A more effectual provision should be made for transferring, from the State courts to the Federal courts, suits brought against persons *exercising* an authority under the United States, so that such suits may be transferred, as soon as conveniently may be, after they are commenced."

Id., at 761 (emphasis added). Congress passed the 1815 Act, which allowed certain officials and those assisting them to remove civil and criminal cases where the charged acts were "agreeable to the provisions of this act, or under colour thereof" until the war ended. 1815 Act, secs. 8, 13. Thus, Congress allowed removal of suits only where the validity of the authority "exercised" by the official was relied upon as a defense. Congress was only worried about preserving federal law. Protecting officials relying upon that law was necessary to ensure its enforcement.[2]

2.   Subsequent reenactments of the federal official removal statute maintained the federal defense requirement

The provisions of the 1815 Act were revived during the next State-Federal conflict, when South Carolina purported to nullify the federal tariff by passing the Nullification Act in 1832. See Act of March 2, 1833,

---

2. Although there is no case law construing the 1815 Act, one of the briefs filed in *Osborn v. Bank of the United States*, 22 U.S. 738 (1824), suggests that contemporaries understood that Act to allow removal only when the revenue officer alleged a defense based upon federal law. "A revenue officer may commit a trespass while executing his official duties, and *if he justifies under the statutes of the United States, a question will arise under them*, in which an appellate jurisdiction is given to this court, to correct the errors of the state courts. But could Congress give additional jurisdiction to the federal courts, in all suits brought by or against revenue officers?" *Id.*, at 814 (emphasis added).

The absence of case law is also evidence that Congress maintained a "federal question" requirement. A sudden expansion of jurisdiction to encompass all torts committed by federal employees would have sparked litigation well before the brief was filed in *Osborn* in 1824.

4 Stat. 632, sec. 3 ("1833 Act"). The Senate debate indicates that Congress did not intend to expand federal jurisdiction.3 The 1833 Act tracked the language of the 1815 Act. Most important, courts understood that a federal defense was required for removal. See Salem & L.R. Co. v. Boston & L.R. Co., 21 Fed. Cas. 229 (1857)(No. 12, 249)(official must allege facts in petition demonstrating excuse or justification under the revenue laws).

The next federal official removal statute was enacted during the Civil War. The Act of March 3, 1863, sec. 5, 12 Stat. 756, ("1863 Act") provided for removal where the official acted "by virtue or under color of any authority derived from or exercised by or under the President of the United States, or any Act of Congress." *Id.* This statute by its plain terms required a federal defense.

This Court confirmed that requirement in three cases. In *The Mayor v. Cooper*, 73 U.S. 247 (1867), the Court upheld the constitutionality of the 1863 Act4 based upon the power of federal courts to hear *federal* questions. *Id., see also The Justices v. Murray*, 76 U.S. 274 (1869)(noting that the 1863 Act only allowed removal of federal questions). In *McKee v. Rains*, 77 U.S. 22 (1870), a United States Marshal was sued for trespass after entering a dwelling and seizing property pursuant to a writ of execution. This Court rejected his petition for removal under the 1863 Act because "[n]o Act of Congress has been cited from which authority can be derived to the Marshal of any court of the United States to seize the goods of one person for the satisfaction of the debts of another." *Id.*, at 25. Although the Marshal was in performance of his duties when executing a court order, he was denied removal because he could not base his defense upon federal law.5 Petitioners cannot reconcile *McKee* or the 1863 Act with their theory that Congress always intended to allow removal for acts "in performance of duties."

The next removal statutes were part of internal revenue laws.6 The Act of July 13, 1866 was the first statute to use the phrase "under color of office" in providing for removal. Congress did not discuss this new language, and this Court's view of the federal defense requirement did not change. "That the act of Congress does provide for the removal of criminal offenses against the State laws; *when there arises in them the claim of the Federal right or authority, is too plain to admit of denial." Tennesse v. Davis*, 100 U.S. 257, 261 (1880)(emphasis added). Again, this Court required a federal defense.7

---

3.   Petitioners rely upon Senator Webster's concern that federal officials would not receive a fair trial from jurors who had sworn allegiance to the Nullification Act. AB 13–14. But the Senator did not suggest that federal officials could not receive a fair trial because of universal hostility to federal officials. Rather, he argued that allowing trial in South Carolina's courts would be futile because jurors were sworn to support the Nullification Act in defiance of the federal *law* upon which the official would rest his defense. Thus, removal was needed to "give a chance to the officer to defend himself *where the authority of the law was recognized* (sic)." 9 Congressional Debates, Part II, 22nd Cong., 2d Sess., at 461 (same remarks of Sen. Daniel Webster)(emphasis added), 419 (statute would frustrate attempts by States to preclude an official from "appealing to the constitution and laws under which he acted")(Sen. Dallas), 260 (Sen. Wilkins).

4.   The Court construed the 1863 Act as amended by the Act of May 11, 1866, 14 Stat 46. The changes to the Act were not significant for the issue presented here.

5.   Although the Marshal was also clearly enforcing federal law by enforcing a court order, the 1863 Act required that the official act under authority "derived from the President of the United States, or from an Act of Congress." Court orders were held not to be covered by the Act. *See Buck v. Colbath*, 70 U.S. 334 (1865). As discussed *infra*, at page 14, this problem prompted Congress in 1916 to add section 1442(a)(3) protecting court officers.

6.   The 1833 Act applied only to collection of duties on imports. The Internal Revenue Act of June 30, 1864, ch. 173, section 50, 13 Stat. 241 ("1864 Act"), provided that the 1833 Act was to be "taken and deemed as extended to and embracing all cases arising under the laws for the collection fo [revenue]." That provision was repealed and replaced in 1866 with a different removal statute. *See* Act of July 13, 1866, ch. 184, section 67, 14 Stat. 98, 171 ("1866 Act"), *Gay v. Ruff*, 292 U.S. 25 n.8 (1934). That Act was codified in 1874 as section 643 of the Revised Statutes, and recodified as Section 33 of the Judicial Code of 1911, 36 Stat. 1097.

7.   This Court upheld the constitutionality under Article III of section 643 of the 1874 Revised Statutes (*see supra* note 6) based upon the assumption that a federal defense was required for removal. Petitioners' theory that *Davis* did not require a defense based upon federal authority is refuted by virtually every sentence of that case. *Id.*, at 271, 272 (allowing removal of prosecutions where "there arises a federal question" or in which "there arises a defense under United States law"). Petitioners argue that *Davis* did not require a federal defense because "self-defense" is a "state-law" defense. AB 19–20, n.7. But petitioner concedes that this Court stated in *Maryland v. Soper (No. 2)*, 270 U.S. 36 (1926), that acts of self-defense are "part of the exercise of official authority." *Id.*,

3.   The addition of section 1442(a)(3) in 1916 is compelling evidence that Congress maintained the federal defense requirement

Congress added section 1442(a)(3) in 1916. As discussed above, that amendment allows a court officer to remove civil and criminal actions "for or on account of any act done under color of his office *or in the performance of his duties as such officer." Id.* (emphasis added). Petitioners' reading of "under color of office" as referring to all acts in performance of duties not only renders section 1442(a)(3) superfluous as read today, but makes no sense historically.

Petitioners claim that Congress read both phrases as "coterminous." AB 26. But this does not explain why Congress added "in performance of duties" to section (a)(3) if "under color of office" achieved the same result. Nor does it explain why Congress added section (a)(3) at all, instead of simply amending section (a)(1) to include court officers.

This Court's decision in *Gay v. Ruff,* 292 U.S. 25 (1934), indicates that Congress intended both phrases to encompass only those acts justifiable by federal law or authority. Defendant in *Ruff* was a receiver appointed by federal court order to run a railroad. Plaintiff sued the receiver for the death of his son allegedly caused by the negligent operation of a train by railroad employees. The receiver sought removal under section 1442(a)(3) based on his having been a court officer when the incident occurred.

This Court held that the receiver was a court officer for purposes of section 1442(a)(3). *Id.,* at 39. But this Court also noted that the case was *dissimilar* to cases removable under section 1442(a)(3) *because no federal questions were presented. Id.,* at 34. (Petitioners' construction would require removal in the absence of a federal question.) This Court denied removal, holding that Congress only intended "in performance of duties" to protect court officers relying upon the federal authority embodied in the court order. *Id.,* at 35, 38–39. Thus, even that broader phrase requires reliance upon federal authority.

This Court also rejected petitioners' construction of the phrase "under color of office", which appears in sections 1442(a)(1) and (a)(3). Petitioners read "under color of office" as allowing removal for all acts committed while on duty. Under that construction, the receiver in *Ruff* should have been allowed removal because he was accused of negligence in performing his duties. But *Ruff* held that the receiver could not have been acting "under color of office" under section 1442(a)(3) because he had no federal defense. *Id.,* at 39 ("nor is there reason to assume that he will in this case rest his defense on his duty to cause the train to be operated").[8]

---

at 42. The official in *Davis* relied upon the federal immunity defense, very much a "common law of 'justification' applicable to crimes committed by federal employees in the performance of their duties." AB n.7, *see Arizona v. Manypenny,* 451 U.S. 232, 236–237 (1981), *In re Neagle,* 135 U.S. 1 (1890), Amsterdam, *Criminal Prosecutions Affecting Federally Guaranteed Civil Rights: Federal Removal and Habeas Corpus Jurisdiction to Abort State Court Trial,* 113 U.Pa.L.Rev. 793, 874 n.328 (1965) (*Davis* demonstrates the rule under section 1442(a)(1) that the official must show colorable protection under federal law), Currie, *The Constitution in the Supreme Court, The First Hundred Years, 1789–1889* (1985), 393–94 n.172 (recognizing that *Davis* was a federal immunity case). Although the district court in *Georgia v. Grady,* 10 Fed. Cas. 245 (1876) (No. 5, 352) (AB 20–21) chose to couch the necessary and proper test later set forth in *In re Neagle,* in terms of state law with which the jury might be more familiar, the gravamen of the defense still remains reliance upon federal authority.

The officer in *Davis v. South Carolina,* 107 U.S. 597 (1882), also alleged a federal immunity defense. This Court noted that the official relied upon federal law as justifying his presence at the scene. *Id.,* at 600. The official's petition averred that the shooting occurred only after the fugitive attempted to evade arrest, and that the fugitive's sudden appearance had frightened his horse and caused his firearm to discharge. *Id.,* at 598. Thus, the official alleged that his acts while on duty were necessary and proper because the firearm discharged as a result of his attempt to enforce federal law (i.e. guarding the house when the fugitive emerged). Although this immunity defense might not prevail at trial, it was certainly "colorably" alleged for purposes of removal. *See In re Neagle, Willingham v. Morgan,* 395 U.S. 402 (1969) (discussed in a later section in this brief).

8.   That the two phrases are not "coterminous" is demonstrated by the motive of Congress in adding section 1442(a)(3). Court officers serving arrest warrants for violations of revenue laws could remove to federal court under section 1442(a)(1) by raising a federal immunity defense based upon their duty to enforce those laws. *See Tennessee v. Davis, supra, Davis v. South Carolina, supra.* However, section 1442(a)(1) referred only to revenue laws. Court officers executing court orders where the underlying authority for the order was *not* a revenue law were held to be unprotected by section 1442(a)(1). *See Gay v. Ruff,* 292 U.S. 25, 37–38

Only two years before *Ruff*, this Court had construed *section 1442(a)(1)* as prohibiting removal where the federal official failed to present a federal defense. *See Colorado v. Symes*, 286 U.S. 510 (1932). Petitioners suggest that this Court denied removal because the official did not provide enough information to allow the Court to determine if he acted in "proper discharge of his duty." AB 23–24. But the official's detailed narrative established at the very least that he acted in performance of his duties. *Id.*, at 516–17. This Court denied removal because the official failed to establish a federal immunity defense.[9] Petitioners' construction of "under color office" has been refuted repeatedly by this Court.

4.   Congress did not eliminate the federal defense requirements when it enacted the present statute

Congress amended section 1442(a)(1) to include "[a]ny officer of the United States or any agency thereof" as part of the Revision of the Judicial Code in 1948. The Reviser's Note to that section states only that the Revision extended the right to remove to all federal employees. Petitioners concede that the extension of protection to all federal employees did not change the character of that protection. AB 16. This Court has repeatedly held that changes in language made during the 1948 Revision are presumed not to have changed the scope and meaning of the statute unless Congress clearly expressed such an intent in the Reviser's Notes. *See Fourco Glass Co. v. Transmirra Prod. Corp.*, 353 U.S. 222, 226 (1957), *see also Walters v. National Assn. of Radiation Survivors*, 473 U.S. 305, 318 (1985), *Muniz v. Hoffman*, 422 U.S. 454, 467–74 (1975) (collected authority).

5.   The Federal Drivers Act is further evidence that Congress still requires a federal defense for removal

Congress in 1961 refuted petitioners' vision of federal official removal when it added the Federal Drivers Act (28 U.S.C. 2679 (b)), allowing federal officials to remove *civil* suits arising out of the performance of their duties. The Act provides for removal of civil suits against federal drivers upon certification by the Attorney General that the incident occurred while the official was performing his duties. It does not encompass criminal cases. This section would be superfluous under petitioners' construction of section

---

(1934). This Court has held that federal law did not protect those court officers when sued in state court for a variety of torts even though those suits were based upon the officer's execution of a court order. *See McKee v. Rains, supra, Bigelow v. Forrest,* 76 U.S. 339, 348 (1869), *Buck v. Colbath,* 70 U.S. 334, 342–44 (1865). The defense of federal immunity per the revenue laws, and thus removal, was unavailable to those officers.

Congress sought to provide court officers with the same protection afforded to revenue officers *and* to members of Congress. *Ruff,* at 38–39 (quoting House Judiciary Committee report). Since revenue officers were allowed to remove acts committed "under color of office", that phrase was also included within section 1442 (a)(3). But additional protection was needed because of this Court's decisions holding that federal law did not provide a defense to suits challenging the marshal's execution of court orders. Section 1442(a)(4), added in 1875, allows members of Congress to remove any suit on account of "any act in the discharge of his official duty *under an order of such House." Id.* (emphasis added). Congress incorporated this protection of all acts committed pursuant to federal authority into section 1442(a)(3) by adding the phrase "in performance of duties." *Ruff,* at 39.

Had Congress read "under color of office" as protecting all acts committed while on duty (*see* AB 26), then it would not have added another section to subsection 1442(a). Congress simply would have amended section 1442(a)(1) to include court officers. But Congress needed to add protection that petitioners claim was already present. California's reading of the two phrases is the only reading consistent with *Ruff* and the history and intent of the 1916 Act. Petitioners' reading defies common sense by making "under color of office" broader than "in performance of duties."

9.   "The statements of the petition are so vague, indefinite and uncertain as not to commit petitioner in respect of essential details of the *defense* he claims. They are not sufficient to enable the court to determine whether his *claim of immunity* rests on any substantial basis or is made in good faith." *Id.*, at 521 (emphasis added). As discussed in a later section, this Court in *Maryland v. Soper (No. 1), supra,* required officials seeking to allege an immunity defense to make a complete account of the incident prompting prosecution to ensure that all acts which could form the basis of that prosecution were protected by federal law. In *Symes,* this Court held that the official had failed to give a sufficiently complete account. *Id.*, at 519–20 (citing *Soper (No. 1)*).

1442(a)(1). The Federal Drivers Act was necessary because section 1442(a)(1) does not allow removal in the absence of a federal defense.[10]

     6.   This Court has held that section 1442(a)(1) is not *in pari materia* with civil rights laws

Statutes may be considered in *pari materia* only if they share the same object. *Erlenbaugh v. United States*, 409 U.S. 239, 243–45 (1972). This Court held in *Screws v. United States*, 325 U.S. 91, 111 (1945), that the language "under color of law" in the civil rights statutes cannot be construed *in pari materia* with the phrase "under color of office" in section 1442(a)(1) precisely because the statues were enacted for different purposes. *Id.,* at 111–12. The civil rights laws were enacted to punish state or federal officials who deprived others of their constitutional rights under the assumption of authority. Insistence that the official had acted within his federal authority would have vitiated the statutory purpose of punishing abuse of power. *Id.* Section 1442(a)(1), in contrast, was enacted to protect federal law by protecting officials relying upon that law in state courts. Restricting removal to cases featuring federal defenses makes sense.

    That the dissent would have construed civil rights laws in accordance with section 1442(a)(1) does not help petitioners, since the dissent, *along with the majority,* construed "under color of office" as requiring the official to justify his conduct under federal law. *Id.,* at 111–112, 145–46. Petitioners cannot reconcile *Screws* with their construction of section 1442(a)(1). *See also Gay v. Ruff, supra, Colorado v. Symes, supra, Maryland v. Soper (No. 1), supra, Tennessee v. Davis, The Mayor v. Cooper, The Justices v. Murray, McKee v. Rains, supra.*

II.   This Court has never Abolished the Federal Defense Requirement

    A.   THIS COURT'S DECISION IN *CLEVELAND V. MCCLUNG* IS CONSISTENT
           WITH THE FEDERAL DEFENSE REQUIREMENT

When a railroad company holding a lien on certain freight informed customs collectors of that lien, federal law required the collectors to notify that railroad before releasing the freight to a consignee or owner. The collectors were not allowed to release the freight until the owner discharged the lien. *Cleveland C. & C. R. R. v. McClung,* 119 U.S. 454, at 454–55. Plaintiff in *McClung* was a railroad holding a lien on particular goods. Defendant was the customs collector bearing responsibility for notifiying plaintiff and holding those goods once they arrived at the station. Plaintiff alleged that defendant had allowed his deputy on prior occasions to release goods to the consignees after collecting the amounts due on the liens. The deputy would then deliver the money to the railroad. Plaintiff complained that the deputy on one occasion had failed to turn over the money, and sought to hold the defendant responsible for the deputy's omission. *Id.,* at 454–55, 461, 462.

    Plaintiffs alleged that defendant had failed to adhere to federal law by allowing his deputy to release the goods without notification. *Id.,* at 456. Defendant's petition stated that he had at all times acted "under color of office". After removal, defendant claimed that it was not his duty under federal law to collect money for the lienholders, and that he was therefore not responsible for his deputy's alleged failure to pay that money to the railroad. *Id.,* at 461. He also claimed that since the money had already been paid and the lien discharged, he had no duty under federal law to notify the railroad or retain the goods. *Id.,* at 458.

---

    10.   Although the Federal Tort Claims Act (28 U.S.C. 1346) provides for removal of tort suits against the United States pursuant to that Act, plaintiffs could still sue employees individually in state courts until 1961. Congress enacted the Federal Drivers Act to protect those employees against suits alleging negligent driving, which did not give rise to a federal defense. *See* Comment, *Katlein, Administrative Claims and the Substitution of the United States as Defendants Under the Federal Drivers Act: The Catch-22 of the Federal Tort Claims Act?,* 29 Emory L. J. 755, 761–63 (1980).

This case is confusing because, unlike the instant cases, defendant was accused of violating *federal* law. That allegation necessarily put the interpretation of federal law into issue as a defense. Moreover, while defendant's petition by today's standards was overly cryptic, he alleged a federal defense by stating in effect that he defended the charges based upon his duties (or lack thereof) under federal law. *Id.*, at 456. Thus, the Court proceeded to evaluate the case against the collector in those terms.

> The real question here is, therefore, whether the collection of the carrier's charges was a part of the official duty of the collector. If it was, the collection by the deputy was an official act, and the principal officer is liable accordingly.

Id., at 462. The Court found that the collector's federal defense was valid, and affirmed the lower court's instruction to the jury on that defense. *Id.*, at 463. The Court also stated that the defendant's denial of the allegation did not vitiate his right to removal. That ruling was correct because removal depends upon the allegations in the petition; officials may rely upon any defense at trial. The instant cases present no federal issues because petitioners do not defend their allegedly negligent driving by recourse to federal law.

B.   THE "CAUSAL CONNECTION" TEST EMPLOYED IN *WILLINGHAM* WAS
      DEVELOPED TO PROVIDE A REMEDY FOR HARASSMENT AND
      ASSUMES THE FEDERAL DEFENSE REQUIREMENT

Petitioners' interpretation of this Court's recent authority is easily stated. Petitioners observe that *Willingham v. Morgan*, 395 U.S. 402 (1969), granted removal in a civil case where the official had alleged only that he was on duty. They quote the language in *Willingham* stating that the official was entitled to removal because he had established a "causal connection" between the charged act and his official authority. AB 17. And they note that section 1442(a)(1) does not distinguish between civil and criminal cases on its face. Petitioners conclude that this "causal connection" test allows them removal in these criminal cases because they too alleged only that they were on duty.

California *agrees* that the test for removal is identical for civil and criminal cases, but suggests that petitioners misunderstand the "causal connection" test. As discussed herein, this Court has always held that a federal defense is required for all cases. Petitioners' argument collapses because they assume that the "causal connection" test outlined in *Willingham* is the exclusive test for removal. But that test already assumes that the federal official attempts to justify his conduct by relying upon federal law. The "casual connection" test only defines what facts must be alleged to put that federal defense into issue. This distinction is critical and is illustrated by *Maryland v. Soper*, 270 U.S. 9 (1926) ("*Soper (No. 1)*").

The "causal connection" test arose out of the problem posed by petitioners: the official who is harassed by State authorities attempting to frustrate Federal policy. *See* AB 7, 8, 27, 29–30. Petitioners' suggestion that officials may remove prosecutions without admitting having committed the charged act and alleging that the act was justified under federal law is not new. *Cf.* AB 6, 8, 22–23, 31. But the suggestion arose in a different context.

It was assumed that the official had to allege a defense to the charges based upon federal law. *See Tennessee v. Davis, supra.* However, occasionally an official would be disabled from pleading a federal defense to the prosecution by the usual method, which was to admit having committed the charged act and to justify those acts under federal law. This occurred when the official had no knowledge of the incident prompting the prosecution.

In *Maryland v. Soper (No. 1)*, 270 U.S. 9 (1926), prohibition agents discovered a homicide victim while raiding an illegal still. They reported their discovery to local authorities and were promptly arrested for murder. The agents had a choice. They had no knowledge of the homicide. If they admitted killing the decedent, they falsely incriminated themselves. Moreover, since they had no knowledge of the incident, they were not in a position to assert that the killing was required by their duties. Their other alternative was to deny the killing and claim that they did nothing but their federal duty. But asserting that they did nothing but their duty did not necessarily put a federal defense into issue. One court refused to grant removal to an official who denied having committed the charged act, reasoning that the official, by denying having committed the charged act, had failed to allege a defense relevant to the prosecution. *Compare Illinois v. Fletcher*, 22 F. 776 (N.D. Ill. 1884) with *Oregon v. Wood*, 268 F. 975 (D.Or. 1920), and *State of Alabama v. Peak*, 252 F. 306 (D. Ala. 1918).

Although that ruling may appear unfair, allowing removal based only upon a denial of the charges would have eliminated the federal defense requirement. In most cases, the ruling did not affect officials because they had knowledge of the incident and alleged a federal immunity defense justifying the charged act. *See Tennessee v. Davis, supra, South Carolina v. Davis, supra.* This Court in *Soper (No. 1)* created a means by which officials lacking knowledge of the incident could obtain removal while ensuring that prosecutions based upon acts *unjustifiable* under federal law remained in state courts.

To allow removal by an official lacking knowledge about the incident (the agents), there had to be a means of determining whether the prosecution, either deliberately or mistakenly, had been based solely upon the official's performance of federal duties. Even if the prosecutor's motive was innocently based upon the official's presence at the wrong place at the wrong time (i.e. the agent finding the decedent), such a prosecution would in effect penalize compliance with federal law and violate the Supremacy Clause. The Supremacy Clause would then supply the federal defense justifying removal. Otherwise, States could prosecute federal officials for offenses which they had not committed, knowing that the official would be unaware of the incident and thus be unable to formulate a federal defense sufficient for removal. The problem was how to put this Supremacy Clause defense in issue in the appropriate case.

It was clear that an official claiming no knowledge of the incident should have the burden of producing evidence that his presence and activities as a federal official prompted the prosecution. But too strict a test would require the official to prove his defense in order to proceed to trial in federal court, and would defeat the purpose of removal. And too lax a "causal connection" test would allow any official to obtain removal merely by denying having committed the act and claiming ignorance of the incident prompting prosecution.

The agents in *Soper (No. 1)* denied knowledge of the murder, but argued that they were entitled to removal because they had found the slain man while on duty. This Court fashioned a very strict test allowing the official lacking knowledge about the incident to allege a connection between his federal activities and the prosecution sufficient for removal. The official had to demonstrate the "causal connection" by: 1) detailing all of his actions and showing that each act was in enforcement of federal law; and (2) negating the possibility that he was prosecuted for an act unprotected by federal law.

> There must be a "causal connection" between what the officer has done under asserted official authority and the state prosecution. It must appear that the prosecution of him for whatever offense has arisen out of the acts done by him under color of Federal authority *and in enforcement of Federal law*, and he must by direct averment *exclude the possibility* that it was based on acts or conduct of his, *not justified* by his Federal duty. But the statute does not require that the prosecution must be for the very acts which the officer admits to have been done by him under Federal authority. It is enough that his acts or his presence at the place in performance of his official duty constitute the basis, *though mistaken or false*, of the state prosecution.

* * * *

> The defense he is to make is that of his immunity from punishment by the State, *because what he did was justified by his duty under the Federal law*, and because *he did nothing else* on which the prosecution could be based.

Id., at 33, 34 (emphasis added).[11] By showing that each of his acts was indisputably in enforcement of federal law, the official declared that the only basis of the prosecution was either: 1) an act protected by a federal defense;[12] or 2) his mere presence at the scene while enforcing federal law. *Id.* (language quoted above). As noted above, a prosecution based upon his mere presence would provide a Supremacy Clause defense. The phrase "it is enough that his acts or his presence at the place in performance of his official duty constitute the basis, though mistaken or false, of the state prosecution" (*id.*) was intended to govern *only* those cases where the official alleged a lack of knowledge of the events underlying the prosecution.

That "presence" language required more than simply being on duty. Thus, this Court in *Soper (No. 1)* denied the removal petition because "[t]hese averments amount to hardly more than to say that the homicide on account of which they are charged with murder was at a time when they were engaged in performing their official duties." *Id.*, at 33. *Petitioners not only misread Soper (No. 1), but rely upon the same allegation that was rejected in that case.*

The language in *Soper (No. 1)* suggests that in order to obtain removal based solely upon the official's presence at the scene, the official must demonstrate that: 1) he committed no acts other than those required by his duties; 2) there was a discernible reason for his prosecution, even though based upon mistake (or animus toward federal authority); and 3) the reason was connected with his having been present carrying out his duties at the time the charged act was allegedly committed.[13] Petitioners fail to meet this test, and instead rely upon the language used by this Court in *Willingham* to justify removal.

Plaintiff inmate in *Willingham* sued his prison warden and doctor for maltreatment. *Willingham* is confusing because this Court had to reconcile its decision in *Soper (No. 1)* with the relatively new federal defense of official immunity. That doctrine had always shielded legislative and judicial officials for acts performed as part of their judicial functions. But after deciding *Soper (No. 1)*, this Court had expanded that doctrine *for civil suits* to shield all federal officials who could show that the charged acts were committed as part of their official duties. *See Barr v. Matteo*, 360 U.S. 564 (1959).

The official immunity defense is a federal defense because it immunizes federal officials in civil cases; the scope of that immunity is a federal question.[14] However, this federal defense differed fundamentally

---

11.   This Court required officials to waive their Fifth Amendment rights and give a complete account of their role in the incident. *Id.*, at 34, 35. Such a waiver would have been unnecessary if an official could obtain removal by alleging only that he was on duty, as such a statement could not be inculpatory.

12.   The "causal connection" test also applied where the official acknowledged having committed the charged act but alleged a federal defense. The Court, in the language quoted above, held that in order to put a federal immunity defense into issue, the official had to negate any inference that the prosecution could properly be based upon an act unprotected by federal law. This explains this Court's denial of removal in *Colorado v. Symes, supra. See supra* note 9. This Court later relaxed this part of the "causal connection" test for the official immunity defense in civil cases in *Willingham, supra*, at n.4. *See infra* note 16. Petitioners do not allege any federal defense.

13.   Thus, this Court posed the hypothetical of a prosecution commenced "merely on account of the presence of the officer in discharge of his duties in enforcing the law, at or near the place of the killing, under circumstances casting suspicion of guilt on him. He may not even know who did the killing, and yet his being there and his official activities may have led to the indictment." *Id.*, at 33. This Court stated that removal was proper if the prosecution arose out of the officer's acts committed "under authority of Federal law in the discharge of his duty *and only by reason thereof.*" *Id.*, at 33 (emphasis added).

It is not enough to show that the prosecution would not have occurred *but for* the official's physical presence at the scene, because such a test would be tautological. Had our petitioners not been at the scene of accidents by virtue of their driving, these prosecutions would not have occurred. The official must demonstrate that his mere presence enforcing or executing federal law was the proximate cause of the prosecution.

The official in *Soper (No. 1)* alleged that his identity and activity as a federal agent (and not just his presence at the scene as the reporter of the crime), was the proximate cause of his prosecution. This Court stated that such a showing might have been sufficient. However, this Court denied removal because the official had failed to provide enough information to negate an inference that he might have committed an act apart from his duties (i.e. by having shot the slain man). *Id.*, at 35–36.

14.   This explains the distinction between the instant cases and the hypothetical federal officials posed in petitioners' brief. *See* AB 11–12. The FBI agents, the federal engineer, and the EPA inspector would rely upon official immunity as a defense to a civil suit, and upon federal immunity in a criminal action.

from other defenses because the official could put it into issue by alleging only that he was performing his duties when he committed the act.[15] This difference posed a problem for lower courts because *Soper (No. 1)* in a criminal case had rejected the idea that an official could obtain removal by alleging only that he was on duty when the charged act was committed. *Soper (No. 1)* required defendant to provide a complete account of the incident and negate any inference that he committed an act unprotected by federal law. That an official was on duty was not enough for removal under *Soper (No. 1)*. And there was no reason to believe that *Soper (No. 1)* did not apply to both civil and criminal cases. Thus, even though Congress intended to allow removal of all federal defenses per section 1442(a)(1), the court below in *Willingham* denied removal because it did not recognize official immunity as such a federal defense in light of *Soper (No. 1)*. *See Morgan v. Willingham*, 383 F.2d 139, 141 (10th Cir. 1967) (distinguishing between the breadth of the immunity defense and the scope of removal jurisdiction) (citing *Soper (No. 1)*), *reversed* in *Willingham v. Morgan*, 395 U.S. 402 (1969).

This Court in *Willingham* recognized this new defense of official immunity as a federal defense for purposes of section 1442(a)(1). *Id.*, at 406, 407. But, as in *Soper (No. 1)*, this Court had to determine what facts were sufficient to put that federal defense in issue. *See id.*, 407–09. This Court was seeking to define what "causal connection" between the official's acts and the civil suit had to be shown in order to demonstrate that the official had a "colorable" official immunity defense. In *Soper (No. 1)*, this Court had required the officials to meticulously detail all of their actions with regard to the victim to negate the inference that an act unprotected by a federal defense was the basis of the prosecution. But such a strict test imposed a burdensome standard in *Willingham* because the defendant prison officials might have had dozens of contacts with plaintiff. *Id.*, at 408–09.

The solution was simple. The official immunity defense covered acts committed in the performance of duties. Thus, that federal defense could be put into issue by alleging that all contacts between the officials and plaintiffs occurred while the officials were on duty. The Court merely eliminated, *for civil cases only*, the requirement that the official alleging a federal defense negate any inference that he had committed an act unprotected by federal law.[16] But petitioners' confusion arises from the Court's implementation of that decision. This Court elected to employ the "presence" language of the *Soper (No. 1)* decision in allowing removal.[17]

In hindsight, that decision was the source of later confusion. Averring that the official was on duty was sufficient to allege the official immunity defense. It was not sufficient to allege other federal defenses (e.g. federal immunity). But this Court in *Willingham* used some of the same language to define the "causal connection" test for the official immunity defense as it had used earlier in *Soper (No. 1)*

---

15.   This Court only recently resolved a split among the Circuits by holding that the official must allege that his act was discretionary in addition to having been committed while on duty. *See Westfall v. Erwin*, 484 U.S._____, 108 S.Ct. 580, 98 L.Ed. 2d 619, n.4 (1988). It was assumed in *Willingham* that the warden and doctor had the discretion to impose medical treatment. This Court ultimately allowed removal without requiring the official to allege that the charged act was discretionary. Whether *Westfall* affects the showing required to put the official immunity defense in issue is not relevant here.

16.   In *Soper (No. 1)*, even those officials who admitted the charged act and asserted federal immunity defenses had to negate any inference that they were prosecuted for acts unprotected by federal law. *See supra* note 12. This Court relaxed that requirement for civil cases, but stated in footnote 4 that it had not decided whether to relax that requirement for criminal cases. That issues is not presented here because petitioners do not present a federal defense.

17.   "Past cases have interpreted the 'color of office' test to require a showing of a 'causal connection' between the charged conduct and asserted official authority. *Maryland v. Soper (No. 1), supra*, at 33. 'It is enough that [petitioners'] acts or [their] presence at the place in performance of [their] official duty constitute the basis, though mistaken or false, of the state prosecution.' *In this case*, once petitioners had shown that their only contact with respondent occurred inside the penitentiary, while they were performing their duties, we believe that they had demonstrated the required 'causal connection'. The connection consists, simply enough, of the undisputed fact that petitioners were on duty, at their place of federal employment, at all the relevant times." *Id.*, at 490 (brackets in original, emphasis added).

Note, however, that this Court also made clear that the causal connection test was intended only to define the allegations necessary to put *federal defenses* in issue. "Petitioners sufficiently put in issue the questions of official justification and immunity; the validity of their defenses should be determined in the federal courts." *Id.* This Court did not abolish the federal defense requirement.

to define the "causal connection" test for a defense based upon enforcement of federal law. *See supra* note 17. Lower courts considering cases where the official immunity defense was not available (i.e. criminal cases) could fail to understand that *Willingham* only defined the showing required to put the official immunity defense in issue. They could infer that *Willingham* mandated removal in *all* cases where federal employees merely alleged that they "were on duty, at their place of federal employment, at all the relevant times." *Willingham*, at 409.

However, this Court did limit its ruling to civil suits. *Willingham*, at n.4. *See supra* note 16. And there was no reason to believe that this Court had elected to overrule 100 years of precedent and radically expand federal jurisdiction when its purpose was to create a means of removing a new federal defense. Nonetheless, the Third Circuit read *Willingham* as having eliminated the federal defense requirement. *See Commonwealth of Pennsylvania v. Newcomer*, 618 F.2d 246 (3d Cir. 1980) (*Newcomer*).

C.   THE THIRD CIRCUIT'S DECISION ABOLISHING THE FEDERAL DEFENSE REQUIREMENT IGNORED CONGRESSIONAL INTENT AND MISINTERPRETED *WILLINGHAM*

The Third Circuit relied upon two arguments in dismantling the federal defense requirement in *Newcomer*. The Circuit stated that the original removal statutes "were enacted not so much to provide federal forums for federal defenses, as to protect federal officers from interference with the operations of federal government by the state." *Id.*, at 250. But this Court in *Willingham* did not suggest that view of legislative intent, and the Third Circuit presented no legislative history supporting it.[18]

The Circuit's second argument contradicted its first. Instead of relying upon its view of Congressional intent, the Circuit stated that "the liberal construction to be afforded the statute, *see Willingham*, at 406; *Colorado v. Symes*, 286 U.S. at 517, 52 S.Ct. at 637, and the interpretation of 'color of office' supplied by *Willingham compel* our result in this case." *Id.*, at 250 (emphasis added). Specifically, the Circuit relied upon the holdings in *Willingham* and *Soper (No. 1)* that the official need not admit that he committed the charged act in order to obtain removal. The Circuit reasoned that "in such a case, of course, the denial does not involve a federal defense." *Newcomer*, at 250. But *Soper (No. 1)* requires that such a denial must be accompanied by facts establishing a "causal connection" between the prosecution and the official's enforcement of federal law sufficient to implicate the Supremacy Clause. The denial *is* the allegation of a federal defense.

D.   THIS COURT'S *DICTA* IN *ARIZONA V. MANYPENNY* SUPPORTS THE FEDERAL DEFENSE REQUIREMENT

Petitioners' attempt to deny the importance of federal immunity in *Arizona v. Manypenny*, 451 U.S. 232 (1981), is unconvincing. Although an immunity defense had not been alleged at trial, this Court assumed that the removal petition had made out a claim of federal immunity *and* that such a defense was necessary for removal.

> Federal involvement is necessary in order to insure a federal forum, but it is *limited* to assuring that an impartial setting is provided in which the federal defense of immunity can be considered during prosecution under state law. Thus, while giving full effect to the purpose or

---

18.   The Third Circuit relied instead upon *Tennessee v. Davis, supra*, and Amsterdam, *Criminal Prosecutions Affecting Federally Guaranteed Civil Rights: Federal Removal and Habeas Corpus Jurisdiction to Abort State Court Trial*, 113 U.Pa.L.Rev. 793 (1965). As discussed above, the legislative history indicates that Congress was concerned with protecting federal law against State interference. Moreover, Professor Amsterdam cited *Davis* as an example of the rule under section 1442(a)(1) that the official must show colorable protection under federal law. *See supra* note 7. And the Third Circuit conceded that the official in *Davis* had alleged a federal defense. *Newcomer*, at 250.

removal, this Court retains the highest regard for a State's right to make and enforce its own criminal laws.

Id., at 242–43 (emphasis added).[19]

III.   Article III Prohibits Removal of Cases Lacking a Federal Defense

Article III, section 2, extends federal jurisdiction only to those cases "arising under" the laws or Constitution of the United States. *Id.* Article III on its face does not allow removal of these traffic cases because petitioners fail to raise federal defenses. California has argued that a reasonable construction of section 1442(a)(1) avoids the obvious constitutional difficulty posed by the absence of federal issues in these cases. *See Ellis v. Railway Clerks*, 466 U.S. 435, 444 (1984) (this Court will first determine whether a reasonable construction of the statute supporting the constitutionality of the statute exists). Should this Court disagree, California reluctantly requests this Court to declare section 1442(a)(1) unconstitutional insofar as it purports to confer federal jurisdiction in this case.

The dissent below suggests that the cases "arise under" Article III because the officials were employed to perform duties that were authorized by federal law. *See Mesa*, at 968 (Noonan, J., dissenting) (citing *Osborn v. Bank of the United States*, 22 U.S. 738, 823 (1824) ("*Osborn*")). *Osborn* does not support jurisdiction here. The only other basis for jurisdiction beyond *Osborn* is the controversial and dubious theory of "protective jurisdiction".

A.   EVEN THE BROAD READING OF "ARISING UNDER" JURISDICTION PROPOUNDED IN *OSBORN V. BANK OF UNITED STATES* DOES NOT CONFER JURISDICTION IN THIS CASE

Osborn has been described as reflecting a "broad conception" of Article III jurisdiction. *See Verlinden B. V. v. Central Bank of Nigeria*, 461 U.S. 480, 492 (1983). However, this Court has refused to hold that *Osborn* allows Article III jurisdiction over cases presenting only "potential" federal issues. *Verlinden*, at 492–93 (declining to decide whether "a mere speculative possibility that a federal question may arise at some point in the proceeding" is sufficient under Article III). The holding and reasoning of *Osborn* demonstrates that only those "potential" issues which are necessarily implied by plaintiff's complaint "arise" under Article III.

There are two types of cases which must be kept separate. First, there are cases where the character of the action always presents federal issues. These issues are "potential" because they may or may not be asserted, or "raised", by one or both of the parties in the action. Such issues may be so well-settled that it is highly unlikely that they will be "raised" by the parties (e.g. the right of the Bank of the United States to sue or contract). However, these issues are present at the outset of the case because it is apparent from the facts presented in the complaint (i.e. the status of the Bank as a federal instrumentality) that the rights of the parties are dependent upon the resolution of those issues. The "original ingredient" test established by *Osborn* confers jurisdiction in such cases.[20]

The second class of cases encompasses suits where the facts of the case stated in the complaint do not automatically raise federal issues. Such cases can "arise under" Article III only if a party "raises" a

---

19. By "state-law questions", the Court referred to remaining defenses available to defendant under state law in addition to the federal immunity defense (e.g. lack of criminal intent, identity, etc.). *Id.*, at 241–42.

20. This was the point of contention between the majority and dissent in *Osborn*. Justice Johnson, dissenting, stated that a federal issue did not "arise" for purposes of Article III until a party "raised" the issue *Id.*, at 888–889. Justice Marshall decided that issues necessarily implied by the complaint, though well-settled and not raised by either party, presented federal issues sufficient for jurisdiction. *Id.*, at 824–25. But neither Justice Marshall nor Justice Johnson suggested that issues which were not necessarily implied by plaintiff's complaining, but could conceivably appear later in the action depending upon facts later presented, could serve as the foundation for Article III jurisdiction. *Id.*, at 825. *See Shoshone Mining co. v. Rutter*, 177 U.S. 505, 509–10 (1900) (interpreting *Osborn*).

federal issue that is dispositive of that lawsuit.[21] In the absence of an "original ingredient", *Osborn* does not allow a party to create jurisdiction merely by stating a set of facts from which a federal issue might, or might not, arise upon the development of other facts. *See Little York Gold-Washing & Water Co. v. Keyes*, 96 U.S. 199, 203 (1887) (construing Justice Marchall's language in *Osborn* as preventing removal under the admittedly narrower general federal question removal statute where a federal question only *might* be presented at a later point in the litigation).

Turning to the issue presented here, petitioners' status is not an "original ingredient" in these prosecutions. California is not required to allege that defendants are federal officials. California may prevail without first proving that petitioners did not act in enforcement of federal law, just as a plaintiff in an ordinary contract action need not show that his contract is unaffected by federal law. Furthermore, while the Bank's status created an actual federal issue is *Osborn*, petitioners' status as federal employees does not do so here. Federal employees are not "creatures of federal law" (*Osborn*, at 823), and the fact that they are employed by the United States when they commit the charged act does not create a federal issue. Justice Marshall recognized that the mere status of the Bank as an entity created by the United States could not by itself create federal jurisdiction.

> It is said that a clear distinction exists between the party and the cause; that the party may originate under a law with which the cause has no connection; and that Congress may, with the same propriety, give a naturalized citizen, who is the mere creature of a law, a right to sue in the courts of the United States, as give that right to the bank. *This distinction is not denied.*

Id., at 826–27 (emphasis added). The same must be true for persons employed by an entity created by federal law, or else Article III jurisdiction would extend to all suits by federal employees arising out of off-duty activities. Indeed, Justice Marshall's concession was prompted by the dissent's argument that focusing upon the identity of the party instead of the issues raised by the case would create jurisdiction for any case involving federal officials. *Id.*, at 901–02. Justice Marshall did not rely upon the status of the Bank to create jurisdiction directly, but upon the fact that the Bank's status created federal questions concerning all of its acts, including its right to sue. *Id.*, at 827. Thus, petitioners' employment, without more, cannot serve as the basis for Article III jurisdication.

The petitions also failed to raise a federal issue. Since petitioners did not assert that their charged acts (negligent driving) were justified under the laws authorizing their duties, the issue of whether they acted in their official capacity cannot be in dispute. A case cannot "arise under" a law that is irrelevant to the disposition of the action. To argue that Article III jurisdiction encompasses such acts because they were committed "within the scope of his employment" begs the question. *See e.g. Messa*, at 968 (Noonan, J., dissenting). Assume that a mail carrier drives his truck down the sidewalk, running over pedestrians. The mail carrier's actions other than the charged act may have been committed within the scope of his employment. But the issue of whether his hitting pedestrians was within the scope of employment for purposes of a criminal action is an issue to be raised via federal defense (i.e. justification under federal law), and only then decided.

In our cases, simply stating that hitting a bicyclist (or a police car) was an act committed within the "scope of employment" does not put the laws authorizing those duties into issue. Petitioners certainly do not contend that those laws authorized the negligent driving charged herein. (If they do, then the District Court erred by allowing removal based upon such a frivolous defense contrary to 28 U.S.C. 1446(a)(4) and (5)). Rather, petitioner Mesa alleges that the accident occurred "*while* defendant was on duty and acting in the course and scope of her employment." (J.A. 5) (emphasis added). Mr. Ebrahim's petition merely states that he was on duty. (J.A. 10). Stating that the alleged criminal act

---

21. Although *Osborn* was read in later cases as having provided federal jurisdiction for suits against instrumentalities, that jurisdiction was based upon the requirement that plaintiff allege defendant's corporate and federal status in the complaint. *See Texas & P.R. Co. v. Cody*, 166 U.S. 606, 609–10 (1897).

occurred while they were discharging their duties does not present a federal issue because it says nothing about why the particular charged act was committed; petitioners only tell us that they were doing other proper things when the incident occurred. "Scope of employment" in practice means nothing more than that the official was on duty.

The phrase "scope of employment" appears to have been borrowed from official immunity cases, where the official may assert a federal defense in a *civil* suit by showing that he had the discretion to commit the act by virtue of his federal authority. *See Westfall v. Erwin*, 484 U.S.____, 108 S.Ct. 580, 98 L.Ed. 2d 619 (1988). But facts which raise federal issues in such cases do not necessarily raise them in criminal actions. A simple statement that the official was on duty in a typical case may well raise a federal issue sufficient for removal because it actually alleges a federal defense. *See Willingham v. Morgan*, 395 U.S. 402, 409 (1969). But the same statement in these criminal cases does not raise a federal defense. Thus, federal jurisdiction is lacking.

B.   THIS COURT SHOULD DECLINE PETITIONERS' INVITATION TO ADOPT PROTECTIVE JURISDICTION AS A BASIS FOR FEDERAL JURISDICTION OVER TRAFFIC TICKETS

This Court has not found it necessary to embrace protective jurisdiction in the more than 200 years since Article III was written. *See e.g. Verlinden v. Central Bank of Nigeria*, 461 U.S. 480, 491–93 (1983), *Northern Pipeline Construction. Co. v. Marathon Pipeline Co. and United States*, 458 U.S. 50, 72–74 (1982) (rejecting federal jurisdiction based upon Article I). Petitioners invite this Court to abandon a reasonable construction of section 1442(a)(1) to create a special district court for federal employees. To accept this invitation would be unsound because the theory is suspect and the consequences unpredictable.

There appear to be two theories of protective jurisdiction. First, that Congress may provide jurisdiction over any case where it has the power under Article I to enact laws governing the outcome of that case. *See* Wechsler, *Federal Jurisdiction and the Revision of the Judicial Code*, 13 Law and Contemporary Problems, 216, 224–25 (1948). Second, that Congress has the power to create a federal forum to protect federal "interests". *See* Note, *The Theory of Protective Jurisdiction*, 57 N.Y.U.L. Rev. 933 (1982).

Justice Frankfurter discussed the limits of Professor Wechsler's theory.

> But, under the theory of 'protective jurisdiction', the 'arising under' jurisdiction of the federal courts would be vastly extended. For example, every contact or tort arising out of a contract affecting commerce might be a potential cause of action in the federal courts, even though only state law was involved in the decision of the case.

Textile Workers Union v. Lincoln Mills, 353 U.S. 448, 481–82 (1956) (Frankfurter, J., dissenting).[22] Moreover, even such an all-inclusive theory does not include our cases because Congress lacks the power under Article I to enact federal criminal laws preempting those state laws which govern prosecution of ordinary traffic offenses.[23] Finally, adherents of this theory indicate that Congress provides jurisdiction

---

22.   *See Northern Pipeline*, at 72–74. The majority in *Lincoln Mills* did not reach our Article III issue because it held that the challenged statute directed federal courts to fashion federal common law in that area. *Id.* Congress did not intend section 1442(a)(1) to create federal law governing suits and/or prosecutions of federal officials.

23.   The Commerce power is unaffected by the choice of forum for prosecution of federal officials for acts unrelated to federal authority. Extending jurisdiction on the basis that a guilty verdict might sideline a federal employee would extend jurisdiction to all cases involving employees arrested while off-duty. This was the result Justice Marshall chose to avoid in *Osborn*. The postal power (Art. 1, sec. 8) is also unaffected by the choice of forum for trial of mail carriers. Indeed, this Court has questioned the constitutionality of federal statutes preventing execution of state felony warrants against carriers actually *delivering* mail. *See United States v. Kirby*, 74 U.S. 482 (1868). The United States fisc cannot be affected by a guilty verdict because the United States cannot be the subject of non-mutual offensive collateral estoppel. *See United States v. Mendoza*, 464 U.S. 154 (1984).

by moving to protect its regulation of an area. *See* Mishkin, *The Federal Question in the District Courts*, 53 Colum. L. Rev. 157, at 184–96. Congress has heretofore not invaded State sovereignty over State criminal law, and has no policy concerning federal officials charged with acts unrelated to their federal authority.

The theory that Congress may provide jurisdiction based upon its "interest" in providing a federal forum for federal officials has been rejected by this Court. In *Verlinden B. V. v. State Bank of Nigeria, supra*, this Court noted that a jurisdictional statute could not serve as the federal statute under which the case arises under Article III. *Id.*, at 496. Since this species of protective jurisdiction is based upon a "federal interest", and not an actual federal statute, the only federal law available for the case to "arise under" would be the jurisdictional statute.

In addition, protective jurisdiction stretches the "arising under" language of Article III past the breaking point because cases would not arise under "the law and Constitution", but under "federal interests". "The law and Constitution" is definable; "federal interests" mean whatever Congress or the courts say they mean at a particular time. Moreover, the rationale behind this "forum-based" jurisdiction does not extend to the instant cases because the United States has no legitimate interest in conferring jurisdiction over federal officials acting outside of their official capacity.[24] The United States has no interest in providing federal jurisdiction for those who do not contend that their prosecution seeks to penalize compliance with federal law or obstruct the operations of the United States.

IV.   This Court Should Refuse to Create a Special Federal Court for
Federal Employees at the Expense of State Sovereignty

This case turns on the proper construction of a statute. Petitioners' reliance on policy considerations is misplaced because the intent of Congress is clear. However, since petitioners invoke federal interests in support of removal, California urges that allowing removal would burden the federal courts at the expense of State sovereignty.

> The right to formulate and enforce penal sanctions is an important aspect of the sovereignty retained by the States. This Court has emphasized repeatedly "the fundamental policy against federal interference with state criminal prosecutions."

Kelly v. Robinson, 479 U.S._____ , 107 S.Ct. 353, 360 (1986) (quoting *Younger v. Harris.* 401 U.S. 37, 46 (1971)). This Court should not abrogate that policy by insulating federal employees from State judicial process where there is no challenge to federal authority.

---

24. *But see Textile Workers Union v. Lincoln Mills*, 353 U.S. 448, 475 (Frankfurter, J., dissenting). Justice Frankfurter argued that the limits of federal distrust of state courts had to be the Constitution as expressed by Article III (i.e. diversity jurisdiction). As part of that argument, he discussed section 1442(a)(1). He first properly distinguished the removal statute by finding that the statute had been interpreted as requiring a federal defense. *Id.*, at 475 n. 5 ("that put federal law in the forefront as a defense") (interpreting *Tennessee v. Davis, supra*). Thus, petitioners receive no comfort from Justice Frankfurter.

However, Justice Frankfurter also attempted to provide an alternate, and incorrect, rationale accounting for section 1442(a)(1). "In any event, the fact that officers of the Federal Government were parties *may* be considered sufficient to afford access to the federal forum. *See In re Debs*, 158 U.S.564, 584–86 (1895); Mishkin, 53 Col. L. Rev., at 193: 'Without doubt, a federal forum should be available for all suits involving the Government, its agents and instrumentalities, regardless of the source of the substantive rule.'" *Lincoln Mills*, at 482 n. 5. (emphasis added).

Justice Frankfurter's use of the word "may" indicates some uncertainty about this pronouncement. In addition, he appears to have misinterpreted the quotation from Professor Mishkin's article as referring to federal officials instead of government agencies. *See Mishkin, supra*, at 193. Or Justice Frankfurter may have assumed that federal officials would be acting in their official capacities when suing or being sued. *Id.* He appears not to have considered the possibility that the official might have been on duty but acting outside of his official capacity (i.e. without a federal defense). Thus, Justice Frankfurter's only support for the statement (aside from Mishkin) was *In re Debs, supra*, which held that Congress could apply to the courts for an injunction against activities interfering with its Article I powers over interstate commerce. *Id.*

The instant cases are excellent examples of why this Court should not construe section 1442(a)(1) to allow removal to all on-duty employees. Both are traffic cases; one is a simple traffic ticket. These cases were removed even though petitioners do not allege local or State hostility to mail carriers or federal law. Many federal officials will seek to remove such cases, not because of concerns over harassment, but to gain a tactical advantage.

For example, in California and other large states, the distance between a particular county and the nearest federal court may be measured in hundreds of miles.[25] Very few county prosecutors can afford to spend the time and money necessary to contest minor infractions in federal court. Fewer witnesses will be willing or able to travel long distances. Many offenses may be dismissed or compromised because prosecutions have been removed.

Removal in inappropriate cases injures Federal and State governments. Federal courts will be burdened with hundreds or thousands of new cases each year presenting no issues of federal law, including traffic tickets. *Pro se* litigants with distinctive and uninformed views about our Constitution and legal system can be expected to make a federal case out of a traffic ticket.

The spectacle and expense of a separate criminal court for federal employees are themselves good reasons for restricting removal. But such cases will also generate numerous appeals because there is little guidance available concerning the trial of removed cases in federal courts. It appears that district courts are forced to provide most protections available under State law to criminal defendants even where those protections conflict with federal criminal procedure. *See City of Aurora v. Erwin*, 706 F.2d 295 (10th Cir. 1983) (reversing conviction because defendant was not afforded a jury trial guaranteed under Colorado law.) Conflicts between federal and state criminal procedure will raise issues of first impression and create errors requiring reversal or retrial. Differences between federal procedure and procedure mandated by each of the fifty States' constitutions concerning, *inter alia*, discovery, voir dire, and jury instructions will spawn confusion and appeals.[26]

Finally, petitioners urge that section 1442(a)(1) and the federal defense requirement will disrupt "federal government functions" and leave officals vulnerable to harassment by States hostile to federal authority. But federal officials alleging harassment have effective remedies. This Court allows federal officials to obtain removal by pleading the facts suggesting harassment. As discussed above, the official need only show that his actions were in enforcement of, or compliance with, federal law and negate the possibility that he was prosecuted for an act unprotected by federal law. *See Soper (No. 1), supra*, at 33–34. Congress can amend section 1442(a)(1) if this standard is considered too burdensome. *See e.g. Maryland v. Soper (No. 2)*, 270 U.S. 36, 43–44 (1926). Finally, the Ninth Circuit below specifically stated that it might have allowed removal had petitioners alleged harassment. *Mesa, supra*, at 967.

Moreover, the writ of *habeas corpus* is an equally potent weapon against harassment. *See* 28 U.S.C. 2241 (c)(2) and (c)(3). *See In re Neagle*, 135 U.S. 1 (1890). Federal officials may apply for the writ before trial. *United States ex rel. Drury v. Lewis*, 200 U.S. 1 (1906). Instead of having to prevail at an evidentiary hearing and again at trial (*see* 28 U.S.C. 1446(a)), the successful official is released immediately after the hearing on the writ. *Id.* The official need only show that the prosecution was motivated by animus toward

---

25.   In California, the county seat of Del Norte County is Crescent City. Crescent City is in the Northern District of California. The nearest federal court within that district is over 350 miles away in San Francisco. Many other county seats are located over 100 miles away from their respective federal district courts.

26.   Any State retaining independent and adequate state grounds based upon its constitution may present conflicts with federal criminal procedure. State Supreme Courts have handed down at least 450 decisions based upon State constitutions which conflict with federal law, and the majority of those decisions involve criminal cases. Collins, Galie, Kincaid, *State High Courts, State Constitutions, and Individual Rights Litigation Since 1980: A Judicial Survey*, 13 Hastings Const. I.Q. 599, 613 (1985–86), Wermiel, *State Supreme Courts Are Feeling Their Oats*, Wall St. Journal, June 15, 1988, at 1, col. 1, (updating the Hastings article), Collins and Galie, State Constitutional Law Insert to The National Law Journal, September 29, 1986, S-8 (listing some of those cases sorted by category). Moreover, the definition of state "substantive law" may encompass state statutes, as well as State constitutional provisions. *See Virginia v. Felts*, 133 F. 85 (C.C. Va. 1904) (suggesting that State rules of evidence, voir dire, and sentencing must prevail over federal law).

the performance of federal duties. *See e.g. People of the State of California v. Morgan*, 743 F.2d 728, 731 (9th Cir. 1984). Thus, this Court's decision reaffirming the federal defense requirement will not affect the remedies available to federal officials claiming harassment.

In sum, requiring a federal defense for removal preserves Congressional intent and over 100 years of this Court's precedent. Affirming the judgment below will protect the legitimate interest of the United States in ensuring enforcement of federal law without invading State sovereignty.

CONCLUSION

For the foregoing reasons, the judgment of the court of appeals should be affirmed.

Respectfully submitted.

LEO HIMMELSBACH
District Attorney for the
County of Santa Clara,
State of California

KENNETH ROSENBLATT
Deputy District Attorney

AUGUST 1988

To read the Court's decision in this case, go to *Mesa v. California*, 489 U.S. 121 (1989).

Case Briefing Practice

Brendlin v. California

The following case briefs have one or more sections incomplete. Read the cases and complete the briefs. The majority opinions for the cases are found in Appendix G.

Brendlin v. California, 551 U.S. _____ (2006)

Judicial History

After petitioner was charged with possession and manufacture of methamphetamine in state court, he made a motion to suppress evidence obtained from a search of his person and a search of the vehicle in which he was a passenger. The motion was denied by the trial court. Petitioner then pled guilty and appealed the ruling on the motion. The California Court of Appeals reversed the denial of the motion. The California Supreme Court reversed the Court of Appeals decision and reinstated the conviction. The U.S. Supreme Court granted certiorari.

Facts

[To be completed]

Issue

When a police officer makes a traffic stop is a passenger seized within the meaning of the Fourth Amendment?

Rules

Delaware v. Prouse, 440 U.S. 648 (1979) and *Whren v. United States,* 517 U.S. 806 (1996) A traffic stop entails a Fourth Amendment seizure of the driver "even though the purpose of the stop is limited and the resulting detention quite brief."

United States v. Mendenhall, 446 U.S. 544 (1980) Where the actions of police or a suspect are ambiguous, a seizure of the suspect occurs if "in view of all the circumstances surrounding the incident, a reasonable person would have believed he was not free to leave."

Florida v. Bostick, 501 U.S. 429 (1991) and *California v. Hodari D.,* 499 U.S. 621 (1991) When a person voluntarily submits to police, whether a seizure occurs is measured by asking whether a reasonable person would feel free to decline the officers request or otherwise terminate the encounter.

Analysis

Although the issue here is one of first impression, dicta in *Prouse* and *Whren* suggest that the Court has long believed that passengers and drivers should be treated the same in determining whether a traffic stop

467

results in a seizure. In these cases the Court clearly ruled that even a brief traffic stop results in a Fourth Amendment seizure of the driver. In reaching this conclusion, the Court described the petitioner driver as an occupant rather than as a driver, suggesting that the ruling should apply to all occupants of the vehicle, not just the driver.

The Court further resolved the issue here by applying the tests stated in *Mendenhall*, *Bostick* and *Hodari* and asking whether a reasonable person in petitioner Brendlin's position when the car stopped would have believed himself free to terminate the encounter between the police and himself. The Court believed that no reasonable person would believe this. It is not reasonable for passengers to believe that once a car is stopped passengers would be allowed to move about freely.

Conclusion

[To be completed]

Elk Grove Unified School District v. Newdow,
542 U.S. _____ (2004)

Judicial History

Respondent filed a complaint against petitioner in the federal district court on his own behalf and on behalf of his minor daughter, alleging that school recitation of the Pledge of Allegiance violates the First Amendment. The District Court ruled that the Pledge of Allegiance is constitutional and dismissed the complaint. Respondent appealed and the federal appellate court reversed holding that as a parent, respondent had standing to sue and that the school district's policy violated the First Amendment. After the appellate court ruling, the mother of the child filed a petition to intervene or dismiss the complaint. The school district filed a petition for writ of certiorari in the Supreme Court and the Court granted a hearing.

Facts

Students of Petitioner school district, including Respondent's daughter, recite the Pledge of Allegiance each day in class. Respondent, who is an atheist, objects to this practice because of the words "under God." Respondent is divorced from his daughter's mother. The parents share physical custody of their daughter, however, the mother has sole legal custody.

Issues

1. Does a parent who has joint physical custody but no legal custody have standing to sue a school district on behalf of his daughter, or on his own behalf, where the school district's policy requires the recitation of the Pledge of Allegiance?

2. Does a school district's policy requiring recitation of the Pledge of Allegiance violate the First Amendment?

Rules

[To be completed]

Analysis

[To be completed]

Conclusion

The Supreme Court reversed the Court of Appeals decision because it found that under California state law a father who has no legal custody does not have standing to sue on behalf of his daughter. The Court also found that Respondent had no standing to sue on his own behalf because the school district's policy did not affect his rights. Because the Court found no standing, it did not address the second issue, the constitutionality of the school district's policy regarding the Pledge of Allegiance.

Marshall v. Marshall,
547 U.S. _____ (2006)

Judicial History

[To be completed]

Facts

Petitioner, Vicki Marshall, aka Anna Nicole Smith, was the surviving spouse of Howard Marshall. Respondent E. Pierce Marshall was the son of decedent J. Howard Marshall. J. Howard Marshall's will left no provision for his surviving spouse, although she claimed that he told her he would provide for her in a "catch all" trust. Petitioner and Respondent were parties to a Texas state court action regarding the validity of the will when petitioner filed an action for bankruptcy in California. Respondent filed a claim for a debt in the bankruptcy court alleging that petitioner had defamed him by saying that he engaged in forgery, fraud and overreaching to gain control of his father's assets. Petitioner counterclaimed that respondent had tortiously interfered with the execution of the will, causing decedent to omit petitioner from the will.

Issue

Does a tort action involving the enforceability of a will which is the subject of a state probate action, fall within the "probate exception" to federal court jurisdiction?

Rules

Ankenbrandt v. Richards, 504 U. S. 689 (1992) The "domestic relations" exception to federal jurisdiction is limited in scope and does not apply to a tort action between parent and child where the court would have jurisdiction based on diversity.

28 U.S.C. §1334 Federal district courts have jurisdiction in bankruptcy cases and related proceedings.

Markham v. Allen, 326 U.S. 490 (1946) Federal courts have jurisdiction to hear lawsuits to determine the rights of creditors, legatees, heirs and other claimants, so long as the federal court does not interfere with the probate proceedings.

Analysis

Among longstanding limitations on federal jurisdiction which would otherwise be proper are the "domestic relations" and "probate" exceptions. These exceptions are not found expressly stated in federal law, but are derived from historical jurisdiction of the English courts. Nothing in Article III of the U.S. Constitution prohibits jurisdiction in such matters. The Court in this case acknowledged that while such exceptions are recognized, the exceptions are limited by case law, in particular, *Ankenbrandt v. Richards*, a 1992 case dealing with the domestic relations exception. In *Ankenbrandt* a lawsuit was filed on behalf of children against their father for damages for sexual abuse. The action was filed in federal court based on diversity. The Supreme Court found that this was an exception to the domestic relations exception which applied only to divorce and support proceedings. The Court analogized the *Marshall* situation to that in *Ankenbrandt* and found that there

was no reason to treat the probate exception any differently than the domestic relations one. If a tort action was proper in the domestic relations case, it should also be proper in the probate action.

The Court also reasoned that this result is supported by both 28 U.S.C. § 1334, which gives the federal district courts jurisdiction in bankruptcy cases and related proceedings and the earlier case of *Markham v. Allen*, 326 U.S. 490 (1946). In *Markham*, the Court stated that the probate exception applied only where the claim in bankruptcy does not interfere with the probate proceedings or assume general jurisdiction of the probate or control of the property in the custody of the state court. Although, the Court in *Marshall* found this language somewhat confusing, it did find that in *Marshall*, the actions of the bankruptcy court did not interfere with the probate proceedings and that therefore federal jurisdiction was proper.

Conclusion

The Court held that the bankruptcy court did have jurisdiction and reversed and remanded the case to the Ninth Circuit Court of Appeals so that it could review the case on its merits.

San Diego v. Roe 543 U.S._____ (2004)

Judicial History

Roe brought suit in District Court claiming the termination violated his First Amendment right to free speech. District court granted summary judgment in favor of the City of San Diego. The Court of Appeals reversed. The Supreme Court granted a writ of certiorari.

Facts

Respondent, John Roe, a San Diego police officer made a sexually explicit video and sold it on the adults-only section of eBay. He also sold an official SDPD police uniform and various other material. Roe's activity was discovered by his supervisor, a police sergeant, who reported it to police authorities. An investigation by SDPD's internal affairs department concluded with a report that Roe's conduct violated department policies including conduct unbecoming an officer, outside employment and immoral conduct. Roe was ordered to stop the sales. Roe failed to follow this order and Roe was dismissed from the police force.

Issue

[To be completed]

Rules

Connick v. Myers, 461 U.S. 138 (1983) Public employees have a First Amendment right to speak on matters of public concern.

United States v. Treasury Employees, 513 U.S. 454 (1995) (NTEU) Government employees have a First Amendment right to speak or write on their own time on topics unrelated to their employment, absent some governmental justification "far stronger than mere speculation."

Pickering v. Board of Ed. of Township High School Dist. 205, Will Cty., 391 U.S. 563 (1968) The court shall balance an employee's right to engage in speech with the government employer's right to protect its own legitimate interests in performing its mission.

Analysis

The Court noted that the proper test to be applied in this action is based on the *Connick* and *Pickering* cases. *Pickering* adopted a balancing test, requiring the court to evaluate restraints on a public employee's speech with the interests of an employee as a citizen, in commenting upon matters of public concern. But *Pickering* did not hold that any and all statements by a public employee were entitled to balancing. A threshold inquiry is whether the speech touches on a matter of public concern.

Although the boundaries of public concern are not well drawn, cases make it clear that public concern is something that is a subject of legitimate news interest, or touch on matters of public concern such as comments about the President. The Court stated that the court of appeals erred when it concluded that Respondent's actions were a matter of public concern. Historically, First Amendment protections have been applied to off-duty employees whose writings or speech contributed substantially to literature or art. Respondent's activities here did not do this. (*NTEU*) On the contrary, his use of a uniform and law enforcement references were injurious to his employer. The Court concluded that Roe's expression does not qualify as a matter of public concern under any view of the public concern test. His speech was detrimental to the mission and functions of the employer and of no benefit to the community. As a result he failed the threshold test and the *Pickering* balancing test did not come into play.

Conclusion

[To be completed]

Supplemental Cases

Ohio v. Robinette, 519 U.S. 33 (1996)

Cancellier v. Federated Department Stores, 672 F.2d 1312 (9th Cir. 1981)

Richards v. Wisconsin, 520 U.S. 385 (1997)

Marshall v. Marshall, 547 U.S. _____ (2006)

City of San Diego v. Roe, 543 U.S. _____ (2006)

Elk Grove School District v. Newdow, 542 U.S. _____ (2006)

Brendlin v. California, 551 U.S. _____ (2007)

Tinker v. Des Moines School Dist., 393 U.S. 503 (1969)

Morse v. Frederick, 551 U.S. _____ (2007)

Ohio v. Robinette,
519 U.S. 33 (1996)

OPINION: CHIEF JUSTICE REHNQUIST delivered the opinion of the Court.

We are here presented with the question whether the Fourth Amendment requires that a lawfully seized defendant must be advised that he is "free to go" before his consent to search will be recognized as voluntary. We hold that it does not.

This case arose on a stretch of Interstate 70 north of Dayton, Ohio, where the posted speed limit was 45 miles per hour because of construction. Respondent Robert D. Robinette was clocked at 69 miles per hour as he drove his car along this stretch of road, and was stopped by Deputy Roger Newsome of the Montgomery County Sheriff's office. Newsome asked for and was handed Robinette's driver's license, and he ran a computer check which indicated that Robinette had no previous violations. Newsome then asked Robinette to step out of his car, turned on his mounted video camera, issued a verbal warning to Robinette, and returned his license.

At this point, Newsome asked, "One question before you get gone: Are you carrying any illegal contraband in your car? Any weapon of any kind, drugs, anything like that?" App. To Brief for Respondent 2 [internal quotation marks omitted]. Robinette answered "no" to these questions, after which Deputy Newsome asked if he could search the car. Robinette consented. In the car, Deputy Newsome discovered a small amount of marijuana and, in a film container, a pill which was later determined to be methylenedioxymethamphetamine (MDMA). Robinette was then arrested and charged with knowing possession of a controlled substance, MDMA, in violation of Ohio Rev. Code Ann. § 2925.11(A) (1993).

Before trial, Robinette unsuccessfully sought to suppress this evidence. He then pleaded "no contest," and was found guilty. On appeal, the Ohio court of appeals reversed, ruling that the search resulted from an unlawful detention. The Supreme Court of Ohio, by a divided vote, affirmed. 73 Ohio St. 3d 65, 653 N.E.2d 695 (1995). In its opinion, that court established a bright-line prerequisite for consensual interrogation under these circumstances:

"The right, guaranteed by the federal and Ohio Constitutions, to be secure in one's person and property requires that citizens stopped for traffic offenses be clearly informed by the detaining officer when they are free to go after a valid detention, before an officer attempts to engage in a consensual interrogation. Any attempt at consensual interrogation must be preceded by the phrase 'At this time you legally are free to go' or by words of similar import." *Id.*, at 650–651, 653 N.E. 2d at 696.

We granted certiorari, 516 U.S. _____ (1996), to review this *per se* rule, and we now reverse.

We must first consider whether we have jurisdiction to review the Ohio Supreme Court's decision. Respondent contends that we lack such jurisdiction because the Ohio decision rested upon the Ohio Constitution, in addition to the Federal Constitution. Under *Michigan v. Long*, 463 U.S. 1032 (1983), when "a state court decision fairly appears to rest primarily on federal law, or to be interwoven with the federal law, and when the adequacy and independence of any possible state law ground is not clear from the face of the opinion, we will accept as the most reasonable explanation that the state court decided the case the way it did because it believed that federal law required it to do so." *Id.*, at 1040–1041. Although the opinion below mentions Article I, Section 14 of the Ohio Constitution in passing (a section which reads identically to the Fourth Amendment), the opinion clearly relies on federal law nevertheless. Indeed, the only cases it discusses or even cites are federal cases, except for one state case which itself applies the federal constitution.

Our jurisdiction is not defeated by the fact that these citations appear in the body of the opinion, while, under Ohio law, "the Supreme Court speaks as a court only through the syllabi of its cases." *See Ohio v. Gallagher*, 425 U.S. 257, 259 (1976). When the syllabus, as here, speaks only in general terms of "the federal and Ohio Constitutions," it is permissible for us to turn to the body of the opinion to discern the grounds for decision. *Zacchini v. Scripps-Howard Broadcasting Co.*, 433 U.S. 562, 566 (1977).

Respondent Robinette also contends that we may not reach the question presented in the petition because the Supreme Court of Ohio also held, as set out in the syllabus (1): "When the motivation behind a police officer's continued detention of a person stopped for a traffic violation is not related to the purpose of the original, constitutional stop, and when that continued detention is not based on articulable facts giving rise to a suspicion of some separate illegal activity justifying an extension of the detention, the continued detention constitutes an illegal seizure," 73 Ohio St. 3d at 650, 653 N.E.2d at 696.

In reliance on this ground, the Supreme Court of Ohio held that when Newsome returned to Robinette's car and asked him to get out of the car, after he had determined in his own mind not to give Robinette a ticket, the detention then became unlawful.

Respondent failed to make any such argument in his brief in opposition to certiorari. *See* this Court's Rule 15.2. We believe the issue as to the continuing legality of the detention is a "predicate to an intelligent resolution" of the question presented, and therefore "fairly included therein." This Court's rule 14.1 (a); *Vance v. Terrazas*, 444 U.S. 252, 258–259, n. 5 (1960). The parties have briefed this issue, and we proceed to decide it.

We think that under our recent decision in *Whren v. United States*, 517 U.S. _____ (1996) (decided after the Supreme Court of Ohio decided the present case), the subjective intentions of the officer did not make the continued detention of respondent illegal under the Fourth Amendment. As we made clear in *Whren*, "'the fact that [an] officer does not have the state of mind which is hypothecated by the reasons which provide the legal justification for the officer's action does not invalidate the action taken as long as the circumstances, viewed objectively, justify that action' . . . Subjective intentions play no role in ordinary, probable-cause Fourth Amendment analysis." *Id.*, at (slip op. at 6–7) (quoting *Scott v. United States*, 436 U.S. 128, 138 (1978)). And there is no question that, in light of the admitted probable cause to stop Robinette for speeding, Deputy Newsome was objectively justified in asking Robinette to get out of the car, subjective thoughts notwithstanding. *See Pennsylvania v. Mimms*, 434 U.S. 106, 111, n. 6 (1977) ("We hold . . . that once a motor vehicle has been lawfully detained for traffic violation, the police officers may order the driver to get out of the vehicle without violating the Fourth Amendment's proscription of unreasonable searches and seizures.")

We now turn to the merits of the question presented. We have long held that the "touchstone of the Fourth Amendment is reasonableness." *Florida v. Jimeno*, 500 U.S. 248, 250 (1991). Reasonableness, in turn is measured in objective terms by examining the totality of the circumstances.

In applying this test we have consistently eschewed bright-line rules, instead emphasizing the fact-specific nature of the reasonableness inquiry. Thus, in *Florida v. Royer*, 460 U.S. 491 (1983), we expressly disavowed any "litmus-paper test" or single "sentence or . . . paragraph . . . rule," in recognition of the "endless variations in the facts and circumstances" implicating the Fourth Amendment. *Id.*, at 506. Then in *Michigan v. Chesternut*, 486 U.S. 567 (1988), when both parties urged "bright-line rules applicable to all investigatory pursuits," we rejected both proposed rules as contrary to our "traditional contextual approach." *Id.*, at 572–573. And again, in *Florida v. Bostick*, 501 U.S. 429 (1991), when the Florida Supreme Court adopted a per se rule that questioning aboard a bus always constitutes a seizure, we reversed, reiterating that the proper inquiry necessitates a consideration of "all the circumstances surrounding the encounter." *Id.*, at 439.

We have previously rejected a per se rule very similar to that adopted by the Supreme Court of Ohio in determining the validity of a consent to search. In *Schneckloth v. Bustamonte*, 412 U.S. 218 (1973), it was argued that such a consent could not be valid unless the defendant knew that he had a right to refuse the request. We rejected this argument: "While knowledge of the right to refuse consent is one factor to be taken into account, the government need not establish such knowledge as the *sine qua non* of an effective consent." *Id.*, at 227. And just as it "would be thoroughly impractical to impose on the normal consent search the detailed requirements of an effective warning," *Id.*, at 231, so too would it be unrealistic to require police officers to always inform detainees that they are free to go before a consent to search may be deemed voluntary.

The Fourth Amendment test for a valid consent to a search is that the consent be voluntary, and "voluntariness is a question of fact to be determined from all the circumstances," *Id.*, at 248–249. The Supreme Court of Ohio having held otherwise, its judgment is reversed, and the case is remanded for further proceedings not inconsistent with this opinion.

It is so ordered.

CONCUR: JUSTICE GINSBURG, concurring in the judgment.

Robert Robinette's traffic stop for a speeding violation on an interstate highway in Ohio served as a prelude to a search of his automobile for illegal drugs. Robinette's experience was not uncommon in Ohio. As the Ohio Supreme Court related, the sheriff's deputy who detained Robinette for speeding and then asked Robinette for permission to search his vehicle "was on drug interdiction patrol at the time." 73 Ohio St. 3d 650, 651, 653 N.E. 2d 695, 696 (1995). The deputy testified in Robinette's case that he routinely requested permission to search automobiles he stopped for traffic violations. *Ibid.* According to the deputy's testimony in another prosecution, he requested consent to search in 786 traffic stops in 1992, the year of Robinette's arrest. *State v. Retherford*, 93 Ohio App. 3d 586, 594, n. 3, 639 N.E. 2d 498, 503 n. 3, *dism'd*, 69 Ohio St. 3d 1488, 635 N.E. 2d 43 (1994).

From their unique vantage point, Ohio's courts observed that traffic stops in the State were regularly giving way to contraband searches, characterized as consensual, even when officers had no reason to suspect illegal activity. One Ohio appellate court noted: "Hundreds, and perhaps thousands of Ohio citizens are being routinely delayed in their travels and asked to relinquish to uniformed police officers their right to privacy in their automobiles and luggage, sometimes for no better reason than to provide an officer the opportunity to "practice" his drug interdiction technique." 932 Ohio App. 3d at 594, 639 N.E. 2d, at 503 (footnote omitted).

Against this background, the Ohio Supreme Court determined, and announced in Robinette's case, that the federal and state constitutional rights of Ohio citizens to be secure in their persons and property called for the protection of a clear-cut instruction to the State's police officers: An officer wishing to engage in consensual interrogation of a motorist at the conclusion of a traffic stop must first tell the motorist that he or she is free to go. The Ohio Supreme Court described the need for its first—tell-then-ask rule this way:

"The transition between detention and a consensual exchange can be so seamless that the untrained eye may not notice that it has occurred. . . .

"Most people believe that they are validly in a police officer's custody as long as the officer continues to interrogate them. The police officer retains the upper hand and the accouterments of authority. That the officer lacks legal license to continue to detain them is unknown to most citizens, and a reasonable person would not feel free to walk away as the officer continues to address him.

"While the legality of consensual encounters between police and citizens should be preserved, we do not believe that this legality should be used by police officers to turn a routine traffic stop into a fishing expedition for unrelated criminal activity. The Fourth Amendment to the federal Constitution and Section 14, Article I of the Ohio Constitution exist to protect citizens against such an unreasonable interference with their liberty." 73 Ohio St. 3d at 654–655, 653 N.E. 2d at 698–699.

Today's opinion reversing the decision of the Ohio Supreme Court does not pass judgment on the wisdom of the first-tell-then-ask rule. This Court's opinion simply clarifies that the Ohio Supreme Court's instruction to police officers in Ohio is not, under this Court's controlling jurisprudent the command of the Federal Constitution. *See ante*, at 5–6. The Ohio Supreme Court invoked both the Federal Constitution and the Ohio Constitution without clearly indicating whether state law, standing alone, independently justified the court's rule. The ambiguity in the Ohio Supreme Court's decision renders this Court's exercise of jurisdiction proper under *Michigan v. Long*, 463 U.S. 1032, 1040–1042 (1983), and this Court's decision on the merits is consistent with the Court's "totality of the circumstances" Fourth Amendment precents, *see ante*, at 5. I therefore concur in the Court's judgment.

I write separately, however, because it seems to me improbable that the Ohio Supreme Court understood its first-tell-then-ask rule to be the Federal Constitution's mandate for the Nation as a whole. "[A] State is free as a matter of its own law to impose greater restrictions on police activity than those this Court holds to be necessary upon federal constitutional standards." *Oregon v. Haas*, 420 U.S. 714, 719. But ordinarily, when a state high court grounds a rule of criminal procedure in the Federal Constitution, the court thereby signals its view that the Nation's Constitution would require the rule in all 50 States. Given this Court's decisions in consent-to-search cases such as *Schneckloth v. Bustamonte*, 412 U.S. 218 (1973), and *Florida v. Bostick*, 501 U.S. 429 (1991), however, I suspect that the Ohio Supreme Court may not have homed in on the implication ordinarily to be drawn from a state court's reliance on the Federal constitution. In other words, I question whether the Ohio court thought of the strict rule it announced as a rule for the governance of police conduct not only in Miami County, Ohio, but also in Miami, Florida.

The first-tell-then-ask rule seems to be a prophylactic measure not so much extracted from the text of any constitutional provision as crafted by the Ohio Supreme Court to reduce the number of violations of textually guaranteed rights. In *Miranda v. Arizona*, 384 U.S. 436 (1966), this Court announced a similarly motivated rule as a minimal national requirement without suggesting that the text of the Federal Constitution required the precise measures the Court's opinion set forth. *See id.*, at 467 ("The *Miranda* exclusionary rule . . . sweeps more broadly than the Fifth Amendment itself".) Although all parts of the United States fall within this Court's domain, the Ohio Supreme Court is not similarly situated. That court can declare prophylactic rules governing the conduct of officials in Ohio, but it cannot command the police forces of sister States. The very ease with which the Court today disposes of the federal leg of the Ohio Supreme Court's decision strengthens my impression that the Ohio Supreme Court saw its rule as a measure made for Ohio, designed to reinforce in that State the right of the people to be secure against unreasonable searches and seizures.

The Ohio Supreme Court's syllabus and opinion, however, were ambiguous. Under *Long*, the existence of ambiguity regarding the federal- or state-law basis of a state court decision will trigger this Court's jurisdiction. *Long* governs even when, all things considered, the more plausible reading of the state court's decision may be that the state court did not regard the Federal Constitution alone as a sufficient basis for its ruling. Compare *Arizona v. Evens*, 514 U.S. _____ (1995) (slip op., at 4–7), with *id.*, at _____ (slip op., at 10–11) (GINSBURG, J., dissenting).

It is incumbent on a state court, therefore, when it determines that its State's laws call for protection more complete than the Federal constitution demands, to be clear about its ultimate reliance on state law. Similarly, a state court announcing a new legal rule arguably derived from both federal and state law can definitively render state law an adequate and independent ground for its decision by a simple declaration to that effect. A recent Montana Supreme Court opinion on the scope of an individual's privilege against self-incrimination includes such a declaration:

"While we have devoted considerable time to a lengthy discussion of the application of the Fifth Amendment to the United States constitution, it is to be noted that this holding is also based separately and independently on [the defendant's] right to remain silent pursuant to Article II, Section 25 of the Montana Constitution." *State v. Fuller*, _____ Mont. _____ 915 P.2d 809, 816, *cert. denied*, 519 U.S. _____ (1996).

An explanation of this order meets the Court's instruction in *Long* that "if the state court decision indicates clearly and expressly that it is alternatively based on bona fide separate, adequate, and independent grounds, [this Court] will not undertake to review the decision." *Long*, 463 U.S. at 1041.

On remand, the Ohio Supreme Court may choose to clarify that its instructions to law-enforcement officers in Ohio find adequate and independent support in state law, and that in issuing these instructions, the court endeavored to state dispositively only the law applicable in Ohio. *See Evans*, 514 U.S. at _____ (slip op., at 8–12) (GINSBURG, J., dissenting). To avoid misunderstanding, the Ohio Supreme Court must itself speak with the clarity it sought to require of its State's police officers. The efficacy of its endeavor to safeguard the liberties of Ohioans without disarming the State's police can then be tested in the precise way Our Federalism was designed to work. *See e.g., Kaye, State Courts at the Dawn of a New Century: Common Law Courts Reading Statutes and Constitutions*, 70 N.Y.U.L. Rev. 1, 11–18 (1995); Linda, *First Things First: Rediscovering the States' Bills of Rights*, 9 U. Ballet. L. Rev. 379, 392–396 (1980).

Cancellier v. Federated Department Stores,
672 F.2d 1312 (9th Cir. 1981)

Prior History:

Appeal from the United States District Court for the Northern District of California.

Opinion:

The plaintiffs below and appellants here, Philip D. Cancellier, John W. Costello, and Zelma Smith Ritter, are former employees of I. Magnin, the defendant below and cross-appellant here. They won a jury verdict in the district court totaling $1.9 million, plus court-awarded attorneys' fees of $400,000, on their claims under the Age Discrimination in Employment Act (ADEA), 29 U.S.C. §§ 621–634 (1976 & Supp. II 1978) and pendent state claims. They appeal denial of their motions for reinstatement and for an injunction against I. Magnin. I. Magnin cross-appeals the judgment primarily on grounds of improper ADEA instructions, use of a general verdict, and an erroneous award of compensatory and punitive damages for breach of the implied covenant. We affirm.

Facts:

Plaintiffs-appellants are former executives of I. Magnin. Cancellier was vice president for stores and operations. Costello was divisional merchandise manager for accessories. Ritter was a buyer of sportswear. In early 1978 they were terminated after having been employed at I. Magnin for twenty-five, seventeen, and eighteen years, respectively. In July 1979 they brought this action in the United States District Court for the Northern District of California alleging that their terminations violated the ADEA. They sought back pay, liquidated damages, reinstatement to their former positions, and an injunction against further age discrimination at I. Magnin. Appellants also raised claims under California law for breach of employment contract and breach of the implied covenant of good faith and fair dealing. Costello sought additional relief claiming fraud in connection with a promise of future employment at I. Magnin.

After a six-week trial the jury returned general verdicts in favor of Cancellier in the amount of $800,000, Costello in the amount of $600,000, and Ritter in the amount of $500,000. The jury also returned verdicts in favor of I. Magnin on Costello's fraud claims. Both sides appeal. For convenience, I. Magnin's cross-appeal is discussed first.

II.

I. Magnin's Cross-Appeal

A. ADEA "Determining Factor" Standard

The ADEA makes it unlawful for an employer to discharge any individual because of such individual's age. 29 U.S.C. § 623(a) (1976). In *Kelly v. American Standard, Inc.*, 640 F.2d 974, 984–85 (9th Cir. 1981), this court set out the requirements for a proper jury instruction on age discrimination. We adopted the "determining factor" test established in *Laugesen v. Anaconda*, 510 F.2d 307, 317 (6th Cir. 1975), and restated as a "but for" test in *Loeb v. Textron*, 600 F.2d 1003, 1019 (1st Cir. 1979). We rejected the argument that plaintiff must prove age was the sole factor in his discharge, and upheld a jury instruction stating that plaintiff has the burden of proving that one of the reasons he was terminated was because of his age, and that he should prevail if this factor "made a difference" in determining whether the plaintiff was retained or discharged.

The essence of a proper jury instruction under *Kelly* is that it requires the jury to focus on the marginal effect of the age factor. Age need not be the sole factor in a discharge or other discriminatory practice. Conversely, it is not enough that age discrimination be present or even that it figure in the decision to fire; age must "make a difference" between termination and retention of the employee in the sense that, but for the presence of age discrimination, the employee would not have been discharged.

Here the district judge instructed the jury that "age must be a determining factor in an employer's personnel policies or practices before violation of the Act occurs." The district judge completely failed to give any guidance as to the meaning of "determining factor" in lawsuits under the ADEA, or to refer to the *Laugesen* and *Loeb* test we adopted in *Kelly v. American Standard, Inc.* This was error. The words "determining factor" are not self-explanatory. In general, fair application of the Act requires the trial judge to formulate precisely what employer conduct the ADEA redresses and what employer conduct it leaves undisturbed. Because the attribute with which the statute is concerned comes to each of us in time, it will inevitably be present in a multitude of employee discharges. It will be a factor in many and a determining factor in some. It is only this last group that can obtain relief under the ADEA, even though, in the broad sense, it aims to benefit the entire aged employment force.

However, a careful reading of the transcript and record convinces us that in this case the instruction does not require reversal. Giving it was harmless error. There is little or no indication in the proceedings that the outcome would have changed if the *Kelly* jury instruction had been given. This case was not decided by a hairsbreadth. There was ample evidence that consideration of age "made a difference" in the termination of Cancellier, Costello, and Ritter. Moreover, it was conceded at oral argument that the challenged instruction was fashioned by the judge from language submitted by I. Magnin. While we are extremely reluctant to affirm verdicts based on jury instructions different from those approved in *Kelly* or their equivalent, we find that on the facts of this case refusing a new trial is consistent with substantial justice. Fed.R.Civ.P. 61; *Ginsburg v. Ginsburg,* 276 F.2d 94, 96 n.2 (9th Cir. 1960); 7 J. Moore & J. Lucas, Moore's Federal Practice P 61.11 & n.1a (2d ed. 1979). The instruction approved in *Kelly* adequately protects against mistaken inferences either that age must be the sole factor in the discharge, or that age may be less than a "but for" cause of the discharge. It is strongly preferred. Here, however, we find the error harmless.

Use of General Verdict

I. Magnin contends that the district court committed reversible error by using simple general verdict forms without requiring special interrogatories or any breakdown of the verdict by source of damages. Thus, I. Magnin contends, the possibility of punitive damages not recoverable under the ADEA in this lawsuit or of duplicative damages in the pendent state claims requires a new trial.

Submission of special interrogatories is a matter committed to the discretion of the district judge. Fed.R.Civ.P. 49(b); *Monsma v. Central Mutual Insurance Co.,* 392 F.2d 49 (9th Cir. 1968); 5A J. Moore & J. Lucas, Moore's Federal Practice P 49.04 & n.3 (2d ed. 1981). A jury generally is not required to itemize the components that enter into an award of damages. *Neal v. Saga Shipping Co.,* 407 F.2d 481, 489 (5th Cir.), *cert. denied,* 395 U.S. 986, 89 S. Ct. 2143, 23 L. Ed. 2d 775 (1969), cited in *Frito-Lay, Inc. v. Local 137, International Brotherhood of Teamsters,* 623 F.2d 1354, 1365 (9th Cir. 1980), *cert. denied,* 449 U.S. 1013, 101 S. Ct. 571, 66 L. Ed. 2d 472 (1981), and *cert. denied,* 449 U.S. 1112, 101 S. Ct. 922, 66 L. Ed. 2d 841 (1981) (district court sitting as trier of fact not required to itemize damage award).

When state claims for breach of the implied covenant of good faith and fair dealing are joined to claims of age discrimination under the ADEA, however, review of jury verdicts presents special difficulty to appellate courts. A general verdict may conceal punitive damages which may not be allowed under the ADEA. If the state claims are flawed, the entire verdict may have to be reversed. For these reasons, a separate verdict for each claim and a separate verdict on punitive damages is strongly preferred.

Nevertheless, failure to submit special interrogatories was not an abuse of discretion. The amounts awarded here are consistent with a reasonable award on the ADEA and pendent state claims. We find no reversible error. I. Magnin's claim that it is impossible to tell which plaintiffs prevailed on which of their claims is unpersuasive. The court submitted general verdict forms in favor of the defendant on each claim. The jury returned general verdict forms in favor of I. Magnin on Costello's fraud claim and Costello's negligent misrepresentation claim; clearly, all other claims were resolved in favor of the plaintiffs. The verdict is clear as to which plaintiffs prevailed on which claims.

C. Tort Damages for Breach of the Implied Covenant

Breach of the Implied Covenant

I. Magnin contends that a claim for breach of the implied covenant under the circumstances here is contrary to California law. The contention is without merit.

California law recognizes an implied covenant of good faith and fair dealing in certain contracts that neither party will do anything to deprive the other of the benefit of the contract. *See, e.g., Gruenberg v. Aetna Insurance Co.,* 9 Cal.3d 566, 578, 108 Cal.Rptr. 480, 510 P.2d 1032 (1973) (*en banc*); *Comunale v. Traders & General Insurance Co.,* 50 Cal.2d 654, 658, 328 P.2d 198 (1958). California courts have recently applied the duty created by the implied covenant to the situation where the employee alleges no more than long service and the existence of personnel policies or oral representations showing an implied promise by the employer not to act arbitrarily in dealing with its employees. Such claims sound in both contract and tort and may give rise to emotional distress damages and punitive damages. *Pugh v. See's Candies, Inc.*, 116 Cal.App.3d 311, 171 Cal.Rptr. 917 (1981); *Cleary v. American Air Lines*, 111 Cal.App.3d 443, 168 Cal.Rptr. 722 (1980) (alternative holding). *See Tameny v. Atlantic Richfield Co.*, 27 Cal.3d 167, 179 n.12, 164 Cal.Rptr. 839, 610 P.2d 1330 (1980) (dicta). Cf. Note, Defining Public Policy Torts in At-Will Dismissals, 34 Stan.L.Rev. 153 (1981) (arguing against application of implied covenant to employment context).

Preemption

The ADEA does not preempt the award of tort damages on pendent state claims. *Kelly v. American Standard, Inc.*, 640 F.2d 974, 983 (9th Cir. 1981) (upholding emotional distress damages under state age discrimination statute). The award of tort damages on state claims here did not duplicate ADEA relief. Plaintiffs' ADEA claims were based on age discrimination in firing. Plaintiffs' contract and covenant claims were based on I. Magnin's obligation not to deal arbitrarily or unfairly in terminating plaintiff's employment, an obligation created by I. Magnin's personnel policies and the fact of long service by the employee. Punitive and emotional distress damages for this violation, unavailable under the ADEA, do not duplicate the ADEA award for back pay, lost benefits, and liquidated damages. While the wisdom of allowing open-ended state claims for breach of the implied covenant to coexist with ADEA claims whose financial redress Congress has carefully limited to specific damage elements, *see* 29 U.S.C. § 626(b) (1976); *Kelly v. American Standard, Inc.*, 640 F.2d at 983, is arguable, it is for Congress, not us, to decide whether state common law remedies trench too closely on the federal scheme. Pendent jurisdication, of course, is a doctrine of discretion. We recognize that in appropriate circumstances dismissal of the state claims without prejudice is proper. *United Mineworkers v. Gibbs*, 383 U.S. 715, 726–27, 86 S. Ct. 1130, 1139, 16 L. Ed. 2d 218 (1966). Such circumstances may exist, for example, where the trial judge finds that the state issues predominate in terms of the comprehensiveness of the remedy sought, or that there is a sufficient likelihood of jury confusion in treating divergent legal theories of relief to justify separating state and federal claims. *Id.*

Punitive Damages

A jury may award punitive damages if it finds by a preponderance of the evidence that defendant was guilty of malice, oppression, or fraud. Cal.Civ.Code § 3294 (West 1981); *Egan v. Mutual of Omaha Insurance Co.*, 24 Cal.3d 809, 819, 169 Cal.Rptr. 691, 620 P.2d 141 (1979). It is a question for the jury whether defendant's conduct was fraudulent, malicious, or oppressive. *Id.* at 821, 169 Cal.Rptr. 691, 620 P.2d 141. The evidence before the jury adequately supported a finding against I. Magnin on the issue of punitive damages.

D. Other Alleged Errors

I. Magnin's additional claims of error are without merit. A thorough review of the record below establishes that the trial was fairly and properly conducted.

III.

Appeal of Cancellier, Costello, and Ritter

A. Reinstatement and Injunction

The ADEA provides that "in any action brought to enforce (the Act) the court shall have jurisdication to grant such legal or equitable relief as may be appropriate . . . including without limitation judgments compelling employment, reinstatement or promotion. . . ." 29 U.S.C. § 626(b) (1976). Reinstatement is not a mandatory remedy; it lies within the discretion of the trial court after careful consideration of the particular facts of the case. *Combes v. Griffin Television, Inc.*, 421 F. Supp. 841, 846 (W.D.Okl.1976). Ordinarily a verdict for plaintiff on the age discrimination claim is res judicata on plaintiff's equitable reinstatement claim. *Cleverly v. Western Electric Co.*, 450 F. Supp. 507, 511 (W.D.Mo.1978), aff'd, 594 F.2d 638 (8th Cir. 1979).

However, courts have refused to grant reinstatement where the employer continued a reduction in force for permissible business reasons, *id.*, or where discord and antagonism between the parties made it preferable to fashion relief from other available remedies, *Combes v. Griffin Television, Inc., supra*, at 846–47.

Damages in lieu of reinstatement may be awarded in addition to liquidated damages. However, the value of reinstatement is often speculative. Thus, availability of a substantial liquidated damages award may be a proper consideration in denying additional damages in lieu of reinstatement. *Loeb v. Textron, Inc.*, 600 F.2d 1003, 1021–23 (1st Cir. 1979).

The trial judge in this case denied reinstatement because he found evidence of acrimony in the record and because he was "fully satisfied that (the verdict) has made the plaintiffs whole." Clerk's Record 124. The court noted the testimony of an I. Magnin officer who referred to plaintiff Ritter as a "cancer." I. Magnin's numerous attacks during the trial on plaintiffs' abilities support the trial judge's conclusion that plaintiffs and I. Magnin could no longer "co-exist in a business relationship that would be productive to the consumer, community or to the business itself." Clerk's Record 125. By virtue of his position in conducting the trial, the judge was peculiarly well-situated to observe the demeanor of plaintiffs and defendants in making this determination. Moreover, in view of the substantial verdict the judge did not abuse his discretion in finding that it had made the plaintiffs whole.

Like the reinstatement remedy, injunctive relief is available under the ADEA when appropriate. The trial judge found that the $2.3 million judgment against I. Magnin, including attorneys' fees, was sufficient to discourage I. Magnin from practicing age discrimination in the future. This finding was not an abuse of discretion.

B. Attorneys' Fees on Appeal

A grant of fees on appeal is within the discretion of the appellate court. *Kelly v. American Standard, Inc.*, 640 F.2d 974, 986 (9th Cir. 1981). Although plaintiffs did not prevail on their reinstatement and injunction claims, an award of fees on appeal in some amount is appropriate to reflect successful defense of the verdict below. *See id.; Cleverly v. Western Electric Co.*, 594 F.2d 638, 642 (8th Cir. 1979) (fees awarded to plaintiff denied reinstatement). We remand to the district court for a determination of the proper amount.

IV.

Conclusion

While the instructions approved in *Kelly v. American Standard, Inc., supra*, and separate verdict forms for each claim, as well as a separate verdict form for punitive damages, are preferred, the trial judge did not commit reversible error in instructing the jury on "determining factor" under the ADEA, in using a general verdict, or in allowing tort damages on pendent state claims. Nor was denial of plaintiffs' motions for reinstatement and for injunctive relief against continuing age discrimination at I. Magnin an abuse of discretion. Plaintiffs are entitled to reasonable attorneys' fees in light of the outcome on appeal. The judgment of the district court is affirmed.

AFFIRMED.

Richards v. Wisconsin,
520 U.S. 385 (1997)

STEVENS, J., delivered the opinion for a unanimous Court.

In *Wilson v. Arkansas*, 514 U.S. 927, 131 L. Ed. 2d 976, 115 S. Ct. 1914 (1995), we held that the Fourth Amendment incorporates the common law requirement that police officers entering a dwelling must knock on the door and announce their identity and purpose before attempting forcible entry. At the same time, we recognized that the "flexible requirement of reasonableness should not be read to mandate a rigid rule of announcement that ignores countervailing law enforcement interests," *id.* at 934, and left "to the lower courts the task of determining the circumstances under which an unannounced entry is reasonable under the Fourth Amendment." *Id.* 936.

In this case, the Wisconsin Supreme Court concluded that police officers are never required to knock and announce their presence when executing a search warrant in a felony drug investigation. In so doing, it reaffirmed a pre-*Wilson* holding and concluded that *Wilson* did not preclude this *per se* rule. We disagree with the court's conclusion that the Fourth Amendment permits a blanket exception to the knock-and-announce requirement for this entire category of criminal activity. But because the evidence presented to support the officers' actions in this case establishes that the decision not to knock and announce was a reasonable one under the circumstances, we affirm the judgment of the Wisconsin court.

I.

On December 31, 1991, police officers in Madison, Wisconsin obtained a warrant to search Steiney Richards' hotel room for drugs and related paraphernalia. The search warrant was the culmination of an investigation that had uncovered substantial evidence that Richards was one of several individuals dealing drugs out of hotel rooms in Madison. The police requested a warrant that would have given advance authorization for a "no-knock" entry into the hotel room, but the magistrate explicitly deleted those portions of the warrant.

The officers arrived at the hotel room at 3:40 A.M. Officer Pharo, dressed as a maintenance man, led the team. With him were several plainclothes officers and at least one man in uniform. Officer Pharo knocked on Richards' door and, responding to the query from inside the room, stated that he was a maintenance man. With the chain still on the door, Richards cracked it open. Although there is some dispute as to what occurred next, Richards acknowledges that when he opened the door he saw the man in uniform standing behind Officer Pharo. He quickly slammed the door closed and, after waiting two or three seconds, the officers began kicking and ramming the door to gain entry to the locked room. At trial, the officers testified that they identified themselves as police while they were kicking the door in. When they finally did break into the room, the officers caught Richards trying to escape through the window. They also found cash and cocaine hidden in plastic bags above the bathroom ceiling tiles.

Richards sought to have the evidence from his hotel room suppressed on the ground that the officers had failed to knock and announce their presence prior to forcing entry into the room. The trial court denied the motion, concluding that the officers could gather from Richards' strange behavior when they first sought entry that he knew they were police officers and that he might try to destroy evidence or to escape. *Id.* at 54. The judge emphasized that the easily disposable nature of the drugs the police were searching for further justified their decision to identify themselves as they crossed the threshold instead of announcing their presence before seeking entry. *Id.* at 55. Richards appealed the decision to the Wisconsin Supreme Court and that court affirmed. 201 Wis. 2d 845, 549 N.W.2d 218 (1996).

The Wisconsin Supreme Court did not delve into the events underlying Richards' arrest in any detail, but accepted the following facts: "On December 31, 1991, police executed a search warrant for the motel room of the defendant seeking evidence of the felonious crime of Possession with Intent to Deliver a Controlled Substance in violation of Wis. Stat. Section 161.41 (lm) (1991–92). They did not knock and announce prior to their entry. Drugs were seized." *Id.* at 849, 549 N.W.2d at 220.

Assuming these facts, the court proceeded to consider whether our decision in *Wilson* required the court to abandon its decision in *State v. Stevens*, 181 Wis. 2d 410, 511 N.W.2d 591 (1994), *cert. denied*, 515 U.S. 1102 (1995), which held that "when the police have a search warrant, supported by probable cause, to search a residence for evidence of delivery of drugs or evidence of possession with intent to deliver drugs, they necessarily have reasonable cause to believe exigent circumstances exist" to justify a no-knock entry. 201 Wis. 2d at 852, 549 N.W.2d at 221. The court concluded that nothing in *Wilson's* acknowledgment that the knock-and-announce rule was an element of the Fourth Amendment "reasonableness" requirement would prohibit application of a *per se* exception to that rule in a category of cases. 201 Wis. 2d at 854–855, 549 N.W.2d at 220. In reaching this conclusion, the Wisconsin court found it reasonable—after considering criminal conduct surveys, newspaper articles, and other judicial opinions—to assume that all felony drug crimes will involve "an extremely high risk of serious if not deadly injury to the police as well as the potential for the disposal of drugs by the occupants prior to entry by the police." *Id.* at 847–848, 549 N.W.2d at 219. Notwithstanding its acknowledgment that in "some cases, police officers will undoubtedly decide that their safety, the safety of others, and the effective execution of the warrant dictate that they knock and announce," *id.* at 863, 549 N.W.2d at 225, the court concluded that exigent circumstances justifying a no-knock entry are always present in felony drug cases. Further, the court reasoned that the violation of privacy that occurs when officers who have a search warrant forcibly enter a residence without first announcing their presence is minimal, given that the residents would ultimately be without authority to refuse the police entry. The principal intrusion on individual privacy interests in such a situation, the court concluded, comes from the issuance of the search warrant, not the manner in which it is executed. *Id.* at 864–865, 549 N.W.2d at 226. Accordingly, the court determined that police in Wisconsin do not need specific information about dangerousness, or the possible destruction of drugs in a particular case, in order to dispense with the knock-and-announce requirement in felony drug cases.

Justice Abrahamson concurred in the judgment because, in her view, the facts found by the trial judge justified a no-knock entry. *Id.,* at 866–868, 549 N.W.2d at 227. Specifically, she noted that Richards' actions in slamming the door when he saw the uniformed man standing behind Officer Pharo indicated that he already knew that the people knocking on his door were police officers. Under these circumstances, any further announcement of their presence would have been a useless gesture. *Id.* at 868–869, n3, 549 N.W.2d at 228. While agreeing with the outcome, Justice Abrahamson took issue with her colleagues' affirmation of the blanket exception to the knock-and-announce requirement in drug felony cases. She observed that the constitutional reasonableness of a search has generally been a matter left to the court, rather than to the officers who conducted the search, and she objected to the creation of a blanket rule that insulated searches in a particular category of crime from the neutral oversight of a reviewing judge. *Id.* at 868–875, 549 N.W.2d at 228–230.

II.

We recognized in *Wilson* that the knock-and-announce requirement could give way "under circumstances presenting a threat of physical violence," or "where police officers have reason to believe that evidence would likely be destroyed if advance notice were given." 514 U.S. at 936. It is indisputable that felony drug investigations may frequently involve both of these circumstances. The question we must resolve is whether this fact justifies dispensing with case-by-case evaluation of the manner in which a search was executed.

The Wisconsin court explained its blanket exception as necessitated by the special circumstances of today's drug culture, 201 Wis. 2d at 863–866, 549 N.W.2d at 226–227, and the State asserted at oral argument that the blanket exception was reasonable in "felony drug cases because of the convergence in a violent and dangerous form of commerce of weapons and the destruction of drugs." Tr. of Oral Arg. 26. But creating exceptions to the knock-and-announce rule based on the "culture" surrounding a general category of criminal behavior presents at least two serious concerns.

First, the exception contains considerable over-generalization. For example, while drug investigation frequently does pose special risks to officer safety and the preservation of evidence, not every drug investigation will pose these risks to a substantial degree. For example, a search could be conducted at a time when the only individuals present in a residence have no connection with the drug activity and thus will be unlikely to threaten officers or destroy evidence. Or the police could know that the drugs being searched for were of a type or in a location that made them impossible to destroy quickly. In those situations, the asserted governmental interests in preserving evidence and maintaining safety may not outweigh the individual privacy interests intruded upon by a no-knock entry. Wisconsin's blanket rule impermissibly insulates these cases from judicial review.

A second difficulty with permitting a criminal-category exception to the knock-and-announce requirement is that the reasons for creating an exception in one category can, relatively easily, be applied to others. Armed bank robbers, for example, are, by definition, likely to have weapons, and the fruits of their crime may be destroyed without too much difficulty.

If a *per se* exception were allowed for each category of criminal investigation that included a considerable—albeit hypothetical—risk of danger to officers or destruction of evidence, the knock-and-announce element of the Fourth Amendment's reasonableness requirement would be meaningless.

Thus, the fact that felony drug investigations may frequently present circumstances warranting a no-knock entry cannot remove from the neutral scrutiny of a reviewing court the reasonableness of the police decision not to knock and announce in a particular case. Instead, in each case, it is the duty of a court confronted with the question to determine whether the facts and circumstances of the particular entry justified dispensing with the knock-and-announce requirement.

In order to justify a "no-knock" entry, the police must have a reasonable suspicion that knocking and announcing their presence, under the particular circumstances, would be dangerous or futile, or that it would inhibit the effective investigation of the crime by, for example, allowing the destruction of evidence. This standard—as opposed to a probable cause requirement—strikes the appropriate balance between the legitimate law enforcement concerns at issue in the execution of search warrants and the individual privacy interests affected by no-knock entries. *Cf. Maryland v. Buie*, 494 U.S. 325, 337, 108 L. Ed. 2d 276, 110 S. Ct. 1093 (1990) (allowing a protective sweep of a house during an arrest where the officers have "a reasonable belief based on specific and articulable facts that the area to be swept harbors an individual posing a danger to those on the arrest scene"); *Terry v. Ohio*, 392 U.S. 1, 30, 20 L. Ed. 2d 889, 88 S. Ct. 1868 (1968) (requiring a reasonable and articulable suspicion of danger to justify a pat-down search). This showing is not high, but the police should be required to make it whenever the reasonabless of a no-knock entry is challenged.

III.

Although we reject the Wisconsin court's blanket exception to the knock-and-announce requirement, we conclude that the officers' no-knock entry into Richards' hotel room did not violate the Fourth Amendment. We agree with the trial court, and with Justice Abrahamson, that the circumstances in this case show that the officers had a reasonable suspicion that Richards might destroy evidence if given further opportunity to do so. The judge who heard testimony at Richards' suppression hearing concluded that it was reasonable for the officers executing the warrant to believe that Richards knew, after opening the door to his hotel room the first time, that the men seeking entry to his room were the police. Once the officers reasonably believed that Richards knew who they were, the court concluded, it was reasonable for them to force entry immediately given the disposable nature of the drugs. *Id.* at 55.

In arguing that the officers' entry was unreasonable, Richards places great emphasis on the fact that the magistrate who signed the search warrant for his hotel room deleted the portions of the proposed warrant that would have given the officers permission to execute a no-knock entry. But this fact does not alter the reasonableness of the officers' decision, which must be evaluated as of the time they entered the hotel room. At the time the officers obtained the warrant, they did not have evidence sufficient, in the judgment of the magistrate, to justify a no-knock warrant. Of course, the magistrate could not have anticipated in every particular the circumstances that would confront the officers when they arrived at Richards' hotel room. These actual circumstances—petitioner's apparent recognition of the officers combined with the easily disposable nature of the drugs—justified the officers' ultimate decision to enter without first announcing their presence and authority.

Accordingly, although we reject the blanket exception to the knock-and-announce requirement for felony drug investigations, the judgment of the Wisconsin Supreme Court is affirmed.

It is so ordered.

NOTICE: This opinion is subject to formal revision before publication in the preliminary print of the United States Reports. Readers are requested to notify the Reporter of Decisions, Supreme Court of the United States, Washington, D. C. 20543, of any typographical or other formal errors, in order that corrections may be made before the preliminary print goes to press.

SUPREME COURT OF THE UNITED STATES

No. 04-1544

VICKIE LYNN MARSHALL, PETITIONER v. E. PIERCE MARSHALL

ON WRIT OF CERTIORARI TO THE UNITED STATES COURT OF
APPEALS FOR THE NINTH CIRCUIT

[May 1, 2006]

Justice Ginsburg delivered the opinion of the Court.

In *Cohens v. Virginia*, Chief Justice Marshall famously cautioned: "It is most true that this Court will not take jurisdiction if it should not: but it is equally true, that it must take jurisdiction, if it should. . . . We have no more right to decline the exercise of jurisdiction which is given, than to usurp that which is not given." 6 Wheat. 264, 404 (1821). Among longstanding limitations on federal jurisdiction otherwise properly exercised are the so-called "domestic relations" and "probate" exceptions. Neither is compelled by the text of the Constitution or federal statute. Both are judicially created doctrines stemming in large measure from misty understandings of English legal history. *See, e.g.*, Atwood, Domestic Relations Cases in Federal Court: Toward a Principled Exercise of Jurisdiction, 35 Hastings L. J. 571, 584–588 (1984); *Spindel v. Spindel*, 283 F. Supp. 797, 802 (EDNY 1968) (collecting cases and commentary revealing vulnerability of historical explanation for domestic relations exception); Winkler, The Probate Jurisdiction of the Federal Courts, 14 Probate L. J. 77, 125–126, and n. 256 (1997) (describing historical explanation for probate exception as "an exercise in mythography"). In the years following Marshall's 1821 pronouncement, courts have sometimes lost sight of his admonition and have rendered decisions expansively interpreting the two exceptions. In *Ankenbrandt v. Richards*, 504 U. S. 689 (1992), this Court reined in the "domestic relations exception. " Earlier, in *Markham v. Allen*, 326 U. S. 490 (1946), the Court endeavored similarly to curtail the "probate exception."

Nevertheless, the Ninth Circuit in the instant case read the probate exception broadly to exclude from the federal courts' adjudicatory authority "not only direct challenges to a will or trust, but also questions which would ordinarily be decided by a probate court in determining the validity of the decedent's estate planning instrument." 392 F. 3d 1118, 1133 (2004). The Court of Appeals further held that a State's vesting of exclusive jurisdiction over probate matters in a special court strips federal courts of jurisdiction to entertain any "probate related matter, " including claims respecting "tax liability, debt, gift, [or] tort." *Id.*, at 1136. We hold that the Ninth Circuit had no warrant from Congress, or from decisions of this Court, for its sweeping extension of the probate exception.

I

Petitioner, Vickie Lynn Marshall (Vickie), also known as Anna Nicole Smith, is the surviving widow of J. Howard Marshall II (J. Howard). Vickie and J. Howard met in October 1991. After a courtship lasting more than two years, they were married on June 27, 1994. J. Howard died on August 4, 1995. Although he lavished gifts and significant sums of money on Vickie during their courtship and marriage, J. Howard did not include anything for Vickie in his will. According to Vickie, J. Howard intended to provide for her financial security through a gift in the form of a "catch-all" trust.

Respondent, E. Pierce Marshall (Pierce), one of J. Howard's sons, was the ultimate beneficiary of J. Howard's estate plan, which consisted of a living trust and a "pourover" will. Under the terms of the will, all of J. Howard's assets not already included in the trust were to be transferred to the trust upon his death.

Competing claims regarding J. Howard's fortune ignited proceedings in both state and federal courts. In January 1996, while J. Howard's estate was subject to ongoing proceedings in Probate Court in Harris County, Texas, Vickie filed for bankruptcy under

Chapter 11 of the Bankruptcy Code, 11 U. S. C. §1101 *et seq.*, in the United States Bankruptcy Court for the Central District of California. *See* 275 B. R. 5, 8 (CD Cal. 2002). In June 1996, Pierce filed a proof of claim in the federal bankruptcy proceeding, *id.*, at 9; see 11 U. S. C. §501, alleging that Vickie had defamed him when, shortly after J. Howard's death, lawyers representing Vickie told members of the press that Pierce had engaged in forgery, fraud, and overreaching to gain control of his father's assets. 275 B. R., at 9. Pierce sought a declaration that the debt he asserted in that claim was not dischargeable in bankruptcy. *Ibid.*[1] Vickie answered, asserting truth as a defense. She also filed counterclaims, among them a claim that Pierce had tortiously interfered with a gift she expected. *Ibid.;* see App. 23–25. Vickie alleged that Pierce prevented the transfer of his father's intended gift to her by, among other things: effectively imprisoning J. Howard against his wishes; surrounding him with hired guards for the purpose of preventing personal contact between him and Vickie; making misrepresentations to J. Howard; and transferring property against J. Howard's expressed wishes. *Id.*, at 24.

Vickie's tortious interference counterclaim turned her objection to Pierce's claim into an adversary proceeding. *Id.*, at 39; see Fed. Rule Bkrtcy. Proc. 3007. In that proceeding, the Bankruptcy Court granted summary judgment in favor of Vickie on Pierce's claim and, after a trial on the merits, entered judgment for Vickie on her tortious interference counterclaim. *See* 253 B. R. 550, 558–559 (2000). The Bankruptcy Court also held that both Vickie's objection to Pierce's claim and Vickie's counterclaim qualified as "core proceedings" under 28 U. S. C. §157, which meant that the court had authority to enter a final judgment disposing of those claims. See 257 B. R. 35, 39–40 (2000). The court awarded Vickie compensatory damages of more than $449 million—less whatever she recovered in the ongoing probate action in Texas—as well as $25 million in punitive damages. *Id.*, at 40.

Pierce filed a post-trial motion to dismiss for lack of subject-matter jurisdiction, asserting that Vickie's tortious interference claim could be tried only in the Texas probate proceedings. *Id.*, at 36. The Bankruptcy Court held that "the 'probate exception' argument was waived" because it was not timely raised. *Id.*, at 39. Relying on this Court's decision in *Markham*, the court observed that a federal court has jurisdiction to "adjudicate rights in probate property, so long as its final judgment does not undertake to interfere with the state court's possession of the property. " 257 B. R., at 38 (citing *Markham*, 326 U. S., at 494).

Meanwhile, in the Texas Probate Court, Pierce sought a declaration that the living trust and his father's will were valid. 392 F. 3d, at 1124–1125. Vickie, in turn, challenged the validity of the will and filed a tortious interference claim against Pierce, *ibid.*, but voluntarily dismissed both claims once the Bankruptcy Court entered its judgment, *id.*, at 1128. Following a jury trial, the Probate Court declared the living trust and J. Howard's will valid. *Id.*, at 1129.

Back in the federal forum, Pierce sought district-court review of the Bankruptcy Court's judgment. While rejecting the Bankruptcy Court's determination that Pierce had forfeited any argument based on the probate exception, the District Court held that the exception did not reach Vickie's claim. 264 B. R. 609, 619–625 (CD Cal. 2001). The Bankruptcy Court "did not assert jurisdiction generally over the probate proceedings. . . or take control over [the] estate's assets, " the District Court observed, *id.*, at 621, "[t]hus, the probate exception would bar federal jurisdiction over Vickie's counterclaim only if such jurisdiction would 'interfere' with the probate proceedings," *ibid.* (quoting *Markham*, 326 U. S., at 494). Federal jurisdiction would not "interfere" with the probate proceedings, the District Court concluded, because: (1) success on Vickie's counterclaim did not necessitate any declaration that J. Howard's will was invalid, 264 B. R., at 621; and (2) under Texas law, probate courts do not have exclusive jurisdiction to entertain claims of the kind asserted in Vickie's counterclaim, *id.*, at 622–625.

---

1. Among debts not dischargeable in bankruptcy, see 11 U. S. C. §523(a), are those arising from "willful and malicious injury by the debtor," §523(a)(6).

The District Court also held that Vickie's claim did not qualify as a "core proceedin[g] arising under title 11, or arising in a case under title 11." 28 U. S. C. §157(b)(1); see 264 B. R., at 625–632. A bankruptcy court may exercise plenary power only over "core proceedings. " *See* §157(b)–(c).[2] In non-core matters, a bankruptcy court may not enter final judgment; it has authority to issue only proposed findings of fact and conclusions of law, which are reviewed *de novo* by the district court. *See* §157(c)(1). Accordingly, the District Court treated the Bankruptcy Court's judgment as "proposed[,] rather than final, " and undertook a "comprehensive, complete, and independent review of" the Bankruptcy Court's determinations. 264 B. R., at 633.

Adopting and supplementing the Bankruptcy Court's findings, the District Court determined that Pierce had tortiously interfered with Vickie's expectancy. Specifically, the District Court found that J. Howard directed his lawyers to prepare an *inter vivos* trust for Vickie consisting of half the appreciation of his assets from the date of their marriage. *See* 275 B. R., at 25–30, 51–53. It further found that Pierce conspired to suppress or destroy the trust instrument and to strip J. Howard of his assets by backdating, altering, and otherwise falsifying documents, arranging for surveillance of J. Howard and Vickie, and presenting documents to J. Howard under false pretenses. See *id.*, at 36–50, 57–58; see also 253 B. R., at 554–556, 559–560. Based on these findings, the District Court awarded Vickie some $44. 3 million in compensatory damages. 275 B. R., at 53–57. In addition, finding "overwhelming" evidence of Pierce's "willfulness, maliciousness, and fraud," the District Court awarded an equal amount in punitive damages. *Id.*, at 57–58.

The Court of Appeals for the Ninth Circuit reversed. The appeals court recognized that Vickie's claim "does not involve the administration of an estate, the probate of a will, or any other purely probate matter." 392 F. 3d, at 1133. Nevertheless, the court held that the probate exception bars federal jurisdiction in this case. In the Ninth Circuit's view, a claim falls within the probate exception if it raises "questions which would ordinarily be decided by a probate court in determining the validity of the decedent's estate planning instrument," whether those questions involve "fraud, undue influence[, or] tortious interference with the testator's intent." *Ibid.*

The Ninth Circuit was also of the view that state-court delineation of a probate court's exclusive adjudicatory authority could control federal subject-matter jurisdiction. In this regard, the Court of Appeals stated: "Where a state has relegated jurisdiction over probate

---

2. "Core proceedings include, but are not limited to—

"(A) matters concerning the administration of the estate;

"(B) allowance or disallowance of claims against the estate or exemptions from property of the estate, and estimation of claims or interests for the purposes of confirming a plan under chapter 11, 12, or 13 of title 11 but not the liquidation or estimation of contingent or unliquidated personal injury tort or wrongful death claims against the estate for purposes of distribution in a case under title 11;

"(C) counterclaims by the estate against persons filing claims against the estate;

"(D) orders in respect to obtaining credit;

"(E) orders to turn over property of the estate;

"(F) proceedings to determine, avoid, or recover preferences;

"(G) motions to terminate, annul, or modify the automatic stay;

"(H) proceedings to determine, avoid, or recover fraudulent conveyances;

"(I) determinations as to the discharge ability of particular debts;

"(J) objections to discharges;

"(K) determinations of the validity, extent, or priority of liens;

"(L) confirmations of plans;

"(M) orders approving the use or lease of property, including the use of cash collateral;

"(N) orders approving the sale of property other than property resulting from claims brought by the estate against persons who have not filed claims against the estate;

"(O) other proceedings affecting the liquidation of the assets of the estate or the adjustment of the debtor-creditor or the equity security holder relationship, except personal injury tort or wrongful death claims; and

"(P) recognition of foreign proceedings and other matters under chapter 15 of title 11." 28 U. S. C. A. §157(b)(2) (1993 ed. and July 2005 Supp.).

matters to a special court and [the] state's trial courts of general jurisdiction do not have jurisdiction to hear probate matters, then federal courts also lack jurisdiction over probate matters." *Id.*, at 1136. Noting that "[t]he [P]robate [C]ourt ruled it had exclusive jurisdiction over all of Vickie['s] claims, " the Ninth Circuit held that "ruling . . . binding on the United States [D]istrict [C]ourt. " *Ibid.* (citing *Durfee v. Duke*, 375 U. S. 106, 115–116 (1963)).

We granted certiorari, 545 U. S. _____ (2005), to resolve the apparent confusion among federal courts concerning the scope of the probate exception. Satisfied that the instant case does not fall within the ambit of the narrow exception recognized by our decisions, we reverse the Ninth Circuit's judgment.

II

In *Ankenbrandt v. Richards*, 504 U. S. 689 (1992), we addressed both the derivation and the limits of the "domestic relations exception" to the exercise of federal jurisdiction. Carol Ankenbrandt, a citizen of Missouri, brought suit in Federal District Court on behalf of her daughters, naming as defendants their father (Ankenbrandt's former husband) and his female companion, both citizens of Louisiana. *Id.*, at 691. Ankenbrandt's complaint sought damages for the defendants' alleged sexual and physical abuse of the children. *Ibid.* Federal jurisdiction was predicated on diversity of citizenship. *Ibid.* (citing 28 U. S. C. §1332). The District Court dismissed the case for lack of subject-matter jurisdiction, holding that Ankenbrandt's suit fell within "the 'domestic relations' exception to diversity jurisdiction." 504 U. S., at 692. The Court of Appeals agreed and affirmed. *Ibid.* We reversed the Court of Appeals' judgment. *Id.*, at 706–707.

Holding that the District Court improperly refrained from exercising jurisdiction over Ankenbrandt's tort claim, *id.*, at 704, we traced explanation of the current domestic relations exception to *Barber v. Barber*, 21 How. 582 (1859). *See Ankenbrandt*, 504 U. S., at 693–695. In *Barber*, the Court upheld federal-court authority, in a diversity case, to enforce an alimony award decreed by a state court. In dicta, however, the *Barber* Court announced—without citation or discussion—that federal courts lack jurisdiction over suits for divorce or the allowance of alimony. 21 How., at 584–589; see *Ankenbrandt*, 504 U. S., at 693–695.

Finding no Article III impediment to federal-court jurisdiction in domestic relations cases, *id.*, at 695–697, the Court in *Ankenbrandt* anchored the exception in Congress' original provision for diversity jurisdiction, *id.*, at 698–701. Beginning at the beginning, the Court recalled:

> "The Judiciary Act of 1789 provided that 'the circuit courts shall have original cognizance, concurrent with the courts of the several States, of *all suits of a civil nature at common law or in equity, where the matter in dispute exceeds*, exclusive of costs, the sum or value of *five hundred dollars*, and . . . an alien is a party, or the suit is *between a citizen of the State where the suit is brought, and a citizen of another State.*'" *Id.*, at 698 (quoting Act of Sept. 24, 1789, §11, 1 Stat. 78; emphasis added in *Ankenbrandt*).

The defining phrase, "all suits of a civil nature at common law or in equity," the Court stressed, remained in successive statutory provisions for diversity jurisdiction until 1948, when Congress adopted the more economical phrase, "all civil actions." 504 U. S., at 698; 1948 Judicial Code and Judiciary Act, 62 Stat. 930, 28 U. S. C. §1332.

The *Barber* majority, we acknowledged in *Ankenbrandt*, did not expressly tie its announcement of a domestic relations exception to the text of the diversity statute. 504 U. S., at 698. But the dissenters in that case made the connection. They stated that English courts of chancery lacked authority to issue divorce and alimony decrees. Because "the jurisdiction of the courts of the United States in chancery is bounded by that of the chancery in England," *Barber*, 21 How., at 605 (opinion of Daniel, J.), the dissenters reasoned, our federal courts similarly lack authority to decree divorces or award alimony, *ibid.* Such relief, in other words, would not fall within the diversity statute's original grant of jurisdiction over "all suits of a civil nature at common law or in equity." We concluded in *Ankenbrandt* that "it may be inferred fairly that the jurisdictional limitation recognized by the *[Barber]* Court rested on th[e] statutory basis" indicated by the dissenters in that case. 504 U. S., at 699.

We were "content" in *Ankenbrandt* "to rest our conclusion that a domestic relations exception exists as a matter of statutory construction not on the accuracy of the historical justifications on which [the exception] was seemingly based." *Id.*, at 700. "[R]ather," we relied on "Congress' apparent acceptance of this construction of the diversity jurisdiction provisions in the years prior to 1948, when the statute limited jurisdiction to 'suits of a civil nature at common law or in equity.'" *Ibid.* (quoting 1 Stat. 78). We further determined that Congress did not intend to terminate the exception in 1948 when it "replace[d] the law/equity distinction with the phrase 'all civil actions.'" 504 U. S., at 700. Absent contrary indications, we presumed that Congress meant to leave undisturbed "the Court's nearly century-long interpretation" of the diversity statute "to contain an exception for certain domestic relations matters." *Ibid.*

We nevertheless emphasized in *Ankenbrandt* that the exception covers only "a narrow range of domestic relations issues." *Id.*, at 701. The *Barber* Court itself, we reminded, "sanctioned the exercise of federal jurisdiction over the enforcement of an alimony decree that had been properly obtained in a state court of competent jurisdiction." 504 U. S., at 702. Noting that some lower federal courts had applied the domestic relations exception "well beyond the circumscribed situations posed by *Barber* and its progeny," *id.*, at 701, we clarified that only "divorce, alimony, and child custody decrees" remain outside federal jurisdictional bounds, *id.*, at 703, 704. While recognizing the "special proficiency developed by state tribunals . . . in handling issues that arise in the granting of [divorce, alimony, and child custody] decrees," *id.*, at 704, we viewed federal courts as equally equipped to deal with complaints alleging the commission of torts, *ibid.*

III

Federal jurisdiction in this case is premised on 28 U. S. C. §1334, the statute vesting in federal district courts jurisdiction in bankruptcy cases and related proceedings. Decisions of this Court have recognized a "probate exception," kin to the domestic relations exception, to otherwise proper federal jurisdiction. *See Markham v. Allen*, 326 U. S., at 494; see also *Sutton v. English*, 246 U. S. 199 (1918); *Waterman v. Canal-Louisiana Bank & Trust Co.*, 215 U. S. 33 (1909). Like the domestic relations exception, the probate exception has been linked to language contained in the Judiciary Act of 1789.

Markham, the Court's most recent and pathmarking pronouncement on the probate exception, stated that "the equity jurisdiction conferred by the Judiciary Act of 1789. . . , which is that of the English Court of Chancery in1789, did not extend to probate matters." 326 U. S., at 494. See generally Nicolas, Fighting the Probate Mafia: A Dissection of the Probate Exception to Federal Jurisdiction, 74 S. Cal. L. Rev. 1479 (2001). As in *Ankenbrandt*, so in this case, "[w]e have no occasion . . . to join the historical debate" over the scope of English chancery jurisdiction in 1789, 504 U. S., at 699, for Vickie Marshall's claim falls far outside the bounds of the probate exception described in *Markham*. We therefore need not consider in this case whether there exists any uncodified probate exception to federal bankruptcy jurisdiction under §1334.[3]

---

3. We note that the broad grant of jurisdiction conferred by §1334(b) is subject to a mandatory abstention provision applicable to certain state law claims. Section 1334(c)(2) provides:

"Upon timely motion of a party in a proceeding based upon a State law claim or State law cause of action, related to a case under title 11 but not arising under title 11 or arising in a case under title 11, with respect to which an action could not have been commenced in a court of the United States absent jurisdiction under this section, the district court shall abstain from hearing such proceeding if an action is commenced, and can be timely adjudicated, in a State forum of appropriate jurisdiction."

That provision is, in turn, qualified: "Non-core proceedings under section 157(b)(2)(B) of title 28, United States Code, shall not be subject to the mandatory abstention provisions of section 1334(c)(2)." §157(b)(4). Because the Bankruptcy Court rejected Pierce's motion for mandatory abstention as untimely, 257 B. R. 35, 39 (CD Cal. 2000), we need not consider whether these provisions might have required abstention upon a timely motion.

In *Markham*, the plaintiff Alien Property Custodian[4] commenced suit in Federal District Court against an executor and resident heirs to determine the Custodian's asserted rights regarding a decedent's estate. 326 U. S., at 491–492. Jurisdiction was predicated on §24(1) of the Judicial Code, now 28 U. S. C. §1345, which provides for federal jurisdiction over suits brought by an officer of the United States. At the time the federal suit commenced, the estate was undergoing probate administration in a state court. The Custodian had issued an order vesting in himself all right, title, and interest of German legatees. He sought and gained in the District Court a judgment determining that the resident heirs had no interest in the estate, and that the Custodian, substituting himself for the German legatees, was entitled to the entire net estate, including specified real estate passing under the will.

Reversing the Ninth Circuit, which had ordered the case dismissed for want of federal subject-matter jurisdiction, this Court held that federal jurisdiction was properly invoked. The Court first stated:

> "It is true that a federal court has no jurisdiction to probate a will or administer an estate. . . . But it has been established by a long series of decisions of this Court that federal courts of equity have jurisdiction to entertain suits 'in favor of creditors, legatees and heirs' and other claimants against a decedent's estate 'to establish their claims' so long as the federal court does not interfere with the probate proceedings or assume general jurisdiction of the probate or control of the property in the custody of the state court." 326 U. S., at 494 (quoting *Waterman*, 215 U. S., at 43).

Next, the Court described a probate exception of distinctly limited scope:

> "[W]hile a federal court may not exercise its jurisdiction to disturb or affect the possession of property in the custody of a state court, . . . it may exercise its jurisdiction to adjudicate rights in such property where the final judgment does not undertake to interfere with the state court's possession save to the extent that the state court is bound by the judgment to recognize the right adjudicated by the federal court." 326 U. S., at 494.

The first of the above-quoted passages from *Markham* is not a model of clear statement. The Court observed that federal courts have jurisdiction to entertain suits to determine the rights of creditors, legatees, heirs, and other claimants against a decedent's estate, "so long as the federal court does not *interfere with the probate proceedings.*" *Ibid.* (emphasis added). Lower federal courts have puzzled over the meaning of the words "interfere with the probate proceedings," and some have read those words to block federal jurisdiction over a range of matters well beyond probate of a will or administration of a decedent's estate. *See, e.g., Mangieri v. Mangieri,* 226 F. 3d 1, 2–3 (CA1 2000) (breach of fiduciary duty by executor); *Golden ex rel. Golden v. Golden,* 382 F. 3d 348, 360–362 (CA3 2004) (same); *Lepard v. NBD Bank,* 384 F. 3d 232–237 (CA6 2004) (breach of fiduciary duty by trustee); *Storm v. Storm,* 328 F. 3d 941, 943–945 (CA7 2003) (probate exception bars claim that plaintiff's father tortiously interfered with plaintiff's inheritance by persuading trust grantor to amend irrevocable *inter vivos* trust); *Rienhardt v. Kelly,* 164 F. 3d 1296, 1300–1301 (CA10 1999) (probate exception bars claim that defendants exerted undue influence on testator and thereby tortiously interfered with plaintiff's expected inheritance).

We read *Markham*'s enigmatic words, in sync with the second above-quoted passage, to proscribe "disturb[ing] or affect[ing] the possession of property in the custody of a state court." 326 U. S., at 494. True, that reading renders the first-quoted passage in part redundant,

---

4. Section 6 of the Trading with the Enemy Act, 40 Stat. 415, 50 U. S. C. App., authorizes the President to appoint an official known as the "alien property custodian," who is responsible for "receiv[ing,] . . . hold[ing], administer[ing], and account[ing] for" "all money and property in the United States due or belonging to an enemy, or ally of enemy. . . ." The Act was originally enacted during World War I "to permit, under careful safeguards and restrictions, certain kinds of business to be carried on" among warring nations, and to "provid[e] for the care and administration of the property and property rights of enemies and their allies in this country pending the war." *Markham v. Cabell,* 326 U. S. 404, 414, n. 1 (1945) (Burton, J., concurring) (quoting S. Rep. No. 113, 65th Cong., 1st Sess., p. 1 (1917)).

but redundancy in this context, we do not doubt, is preferable to incoherence. In short, we comprehend the "interference" language in *Markham* as essentially a reiteration of the general principle that, when one court is exercising *in rem* jurisdiction over a *res*, a second court will not assume *in rem* jurisdiction over the same *res*. *See, e. g., Penn General Casualty Co. v. Pennsylvania ex rel. Schnader*, 294 U. S. 189, 195–196 (1935); *Waterman*, 215 U. S., at 45–46. Thus, the probate exception reserves to state probate courts the probate or annulment of a will and the administration of a decedent's estate; it also precludes federal courts from endeavoring to dispose of property that is in the custody of a state probate court. But it does not bar federal courts from adjudicating matters outside those confines and otherwise within federal jurisdiction.

A

As the Court of Appeals correctly observed, Vickie's claim does not "involve the administration of an estate, the probate of a will, or any other purely probate matter." 392 F. 3d, at 1133. Provoked by Pierce's claim in the bankruptcy proceedings, Vickie's claim, like Carol Ankenbrandt's, alleges a widely recognized tort. *See King v. Acker*, 725 S. W. 2d 750, 754 (Tex. App. 1987); Restatement (Second) of Torts §774B (1977) ("One who by fraud, duress or other tortious means intentionally prevents another from receiving from a third person an inheritance or gift that [s]he would otherwise have received is subject to liability to the other for loss of the inheritance or gift."). Vickie seeks an *in personam* judgment against Pierce, not the probate or annulment of a will. *Cf. Sutton*, 246 U. S., at 208 (suit to annul a will found "supplemental to the proceedings for probate of the will" and therefore not cognizable in federal court). Nor does she seek to reach a *res* in the custody of a state court. *See Markham*, 326 U. S., at 494.

Furthermore, no "sound policy considerations" militate in favor of extending the probate exception to cover the case at hand. *Cf. Ankenbrandt*, 504 U. S., at 703. Trial courts, both federal and state, often address conduct of the kind Vickie alleges. State probate courts possess no "special proficiency . . . in handling [such] issues." *Cf. id.*, at 704.

B

The Court of Appeals advanced an alternate basis for its conclusion that the federal courts lack jurisdiction over Vickie's claim. Noting that the Texas Probate Court "ruled it had exclusive jurisdiction over all of Vickie Lynn Marshall's claims against E. Pierce Marshall," the Ninth Circuit held that "ruling . . . binding on the United States [D]istrict [C]ourt." 392 F. 3d, at 1136. We reject that determination.

Texas courts have recognized a state-law tort action for interference with an expected inheritance or gift, modeled on the Restatement formulation. *See King*, 725 S. W. 2d, at 754; *Brandes v. Rice Trust, Inc.*, 966 S. W. 2d 144, 146–147 (Tex. App. 1998).[5] It is clear, under *Erie R. Co. v. Tompkins*, 304 U. S. 64 (1938), that Texas law governs the substantive elements of Vickie's tortious interference claim. It is also clear, however, that Texas may not reserve to its

---

5.   Texas appellate courts have on occasion held claims of tortious interference with an expected inheritance "barred" by a prior probate court judgment, apparently applying ordinary principles of preclusion. *See, e. g., Thompson v. Deloitte & Touche*, 902 S. W. 2d 13, 16 (Tex. App. 1995) (final probate court judgment bars claim of tortious interference with inheritance expectancy because probate court "necessarily found that [the decedent] signed the will with testamentary capacity, and that it reflected his intent, was not the result of coercion or undue influence, and was valid"); *Neill v. Yett*, 746 S. W. 2d 32, 35–36 (Tex. App. 1988) (complaint alleging fraud and tortious interference with inheritance expectancy, filed more than two years after will was admitted to probate, was barred by both the statute of limitations and the final probate judgment, and failed to state the elements of the claim). Neither *Thompson* nor *Neill* questions the Texas trial courts' subject-matter jurisdiction over the claims in question.

Pierce maintains that *Thompson, Neill*, and other Texas decisions support his contention that preclusion principles bar Vickie's claim. See Brief for Respondent 36–38. Vickie argues to the contrary. See Brief for Petitioner 42 n. 30 (urging that preclusion does not apply because (1) Vickie's claim was not litigated to final judgment in the Texas probate proceedings; (2) having presented her claim in the Bankruptcy Court years before she joined the Texas will contest, Vickie was not obliged to present her claim in the Texas proceedings; (3) the Bankruptcy Court's judgment preceded the Probate Court judgment; and (4) the Texas Probate Court did not have before it important evidence). See also Tex. Rule Civ. Proc. 97; *Ingersoll-Rand Co. v. Valero Energy Corp.*, 997 S. W. 2d 203, 206–207 (Tex. 1999). The matter of preclusion remains open for consideration on remand. See *infra*, at 18.

probate courts the exclusive right to adjudicate a transitory tort. We have long recognized that "a State cannot create a transitory cause of action and at the same time destroy the right to sue on that transitory cause of action in any court having jurisdiction." *Tennessee Coal, Iron & R. Co. v. George*, 233 U. S. 354, 360 (1914). Jurisdiction is determined "by the law of the court's creation and cannot be defeated by the extraterritorial operation of a [state] statute . . . , even though it created the right of action." *Ibid.* Directly on point, we have held that the jurisdiction of the federal courts, "having existed from the beginning of the Federal government, [can] not be impaired by subsequent state legislation creating courts of probate." *McClellan v. Carland*, 217 U. S. 268, 281 (1910) (upholding federal jurisdiction over action by heirs of decedent, who died intestate, to determine their rights in the estate (citing *Waterman*, 215 U. S. 33)).

Our decision in *Durfee v. Duke*, 375 U. S. 106 (1963), relied upon by the Ninth Circuit, 392 F. 3d, at 1136, is not to the contrary. *Durfee* stands only for the proposition that a state court's final judgment determining *its own* jurisdiction ordinarily qualifies for full faith and credit, so long as the jurisdictional issue was fully and fairly litigated in the court that rendered the judgment. See 375 U. S., at 111, 115. At issue here, however, is not the Texas Probate Court's jurisdiction, but the federal courts' jurisdiction to entertain Vickie's tortious interference claim. Under our federal system, Texas cannot render its probate courts exclusively competent to entertain a claim of that genre. We therefore hold that the District Court properly asserted jurisdiction over Vickie's counterclaim against Pierce.

IV

After determining that Vickie's claim was not a "core proceeding," the District Court reviewed the case *de novo* and entered its final judgment on March 7, 2002. 275 B. R., at 5–8. The Texas Probate Court's judgment became final on February 11, 2002, nearly one month earlier. App. to Pet. for Cert. 41. The Court of Appeals considered only the issue of federal subject-matter jurisdiction. It did not address the question whether Vickie's claim was "core"; nor did it address Pierce's arguments concerning claim and issue preclusion. 392 F. 3d, at 1137. These issues remain open for consideration on remand.

*　　　*　　　*

For the reasons stated, the judgment of the Court of Appeals for the Ninth Circuit is reversed, and the case is remanded for further proceedings consistent with this opinion.

It is so ordered.

SUPREME COURT OF THE UNITED STATES

City of San Diego, California et al. v. John Roe

ON PETITION FOR WRIT OF CERTIORARI TO THE UNITED STATES
COURT OF APPEALS FOR THE NINTH CIRCUIT

No. 03-1669. Decided December 6, 2004

PER CURIAM. The city of San Diego (City), a petitioner here, terminated a police officer, respondent, for selling videotapes he made and for related activity. The tapes showed the respondent engaging in sexually explicit acts. Respondent brought suit alleging, among other things, that the termination violated his First and Fourteenth Amendment rights to freedom of speech. The United States District Court for the Southern District of California granted summary judgment to the City. The Court of Appeals for the Ninth Circuit reversed.

The petition for a writ of certiorari is granted, and the judgment of the Court of Appeals is reversed.

I

Respondent John Roe, a San Diego police officer, made a video showing himself stripping off a police uniform and masturbating. He sold the video on the adults-only section of eBay, the popular online auction site. His user name was "Codestud3@aol. com," a word play on a high priority police radio call. 356 F. 3d 1108, 1110 (CA9 2004). The uniform apparently was not the specific uniform worn by the San Diego police, but it was clearly identifiable as a police uniform. Roe also sold custom videos, as well as police equipment, including official uniforms of the San Diego Police Department (SDPD), and various other items such as men's underwear. Roe's eBay user profile identified him as employed in the field of law enforcement.

Roe's supervisor, a police sergeant, discovered Roe's activities when, while on eBay, he came across an official SDPD police uniform for sale offered by an individual with the user-name "Codestud3@aol. com." He searched for other items Codestud3 offered and discovered listings for Roe's videos depicting the objectionable material. Recognizing Roe's picture, the sergeant printed images of certain of Roe's offerings and shared them with others in Roe's chain of command, including a police captain. The captain notified the SDPD's internal affairs department, which began an investigation. In response to a request by an undercover officer, Roe produced a custom video. It showed Roe, again in police uniform, issuing a traffic citation but revoking it after undoing the uniform and masturbating.

The investigation revealed that Roe's conduct violated specific SDPD policies, including conduct unbecoming of an officer, outside employment, and immoral conduct. When confronted, Roe admitted to selling the videos and police paraphernalia. The SDPD ordered Roe to "cease displaying, manufacturing, distributing or selling any sexually explicit materials or engaging in any similar behaviors, via the internct, U. S. Mail, commercial vendors or distributors, or any other medium available to the public." 356 F. 3d, at 1111 (internal quotation marks omitted). Although Roe removed some of the items he had offered for sale, he did not change his seller's profile, which described the first two videos he had produced and listed their prices as well as the prices for custom videos. After discovering Roe's failure to follow its orders, the SDPD—citing Roe for the added violation of disobedience of lawful orders— began termination proceedings. The proceedings resulted in Roe's dismissal from the police force.

Roe brought suit in the District Court pursuant to Rev. Stat. §1979, 42 U. S. C. §1983, alleging that the employment termination violated his First Amendment right to free speech. In granting summary judgment to the City, the District Court decided that Roe had not demonstrated that selling official police uniforms and producing, marketing, and selling sexually explicit videos for profit qualified as expression relating to a matter of "public concern" under this Court's decision in *Connick v. Myers*, 461 U. S. 138 (1983).

In reversing, the Court of Appeals held Roe's conduct fell within the protected category of citizen commentary on matters of public concern. Central to the Court of Appeals' conclusion was that Roe's expression was not an internal workplace grievance, took place while he was off-duty and away from his employer's premises, and was unrelated to his employment. 356 F. 3d, at 1110, 1113–1114.

II

A government employee does not relinquish all First Amendment rights otherwise enjoyed by citizens just by reason of his or her employment. *See, e. g., Keyishian v. Board of Regents of Univ. of State of N. Y.*, 385 U. S. 589, 605–606 (1967). On the other hand, a governmental employer may impose certain restraints on the speech of its employees, restraints that would be unconstitutional if applied to the general public. The Court has recognized the right of employees to speak on matters of public concern, typically matters concerning government policies that are of interest to the public at large, a subject on which public employees are uniquely qualified to comment. *See Connick, supra; Pickering v. Board of Ed. of Township High School Dist. 205, Will Cty.*, 391 U. S. 563 (1968). Outside of this category, the Court has held that when government employees speak or write on their own time on topics unrelated to their employment, the speech can have First Amendment protection, absent some governmental justification "far stronger than mere speculation" in regulating it. *United States v. Treasury Employees*, 513 U. S. 454, 465, 475 (1995) *(NTEU)*. We have little difficulty in concluding that the City was not barred from terminating Roe under either line of cases.

A

In concluding that Roe's activities qualified as a matter of public concern, the Court of Appeals relied heavily on the Court's decision in *NTEU*. 356 F. 3d, at 1117. In *NTEU* it was established that the speech was unrelated to the employment and had no effect on the mission and purpose of the employer. The question was whether the Federal Government could impose certain monetary limitations on outside earnings from speaking or writing on a class of federal employees. The Court held that, within the particular classification of employment, the Government had shown no justification for the outside salary limitations. The First Amendment right of the employees sufficed to invalidate the restrictions on the outside earnings for such activities. The Court noted that throughout history public employees who undertook to write or to speak in their spare time had made substantial contributions to literature and art, *NTEU, supra*, at 465, and observed that none of the speech at issue "even arguably [had] any adverse impact" on the employer. *Ibid.*

The Court of Appeals' reliance on *NTEU* was seriously misplaced. Although Roe's activities took place outside the workplace and purported to be about subjects not related to his employment, the SDPD demonstrated legitimate and substantial interests of its own that were compromised by his speech. Far from confining his activities to speech unrelated to his employment, Roe took deliberate steps to link his videos and other wares to his police work, all in a way injurious to his employer. The use of the uniform, the law enforcement reference in the Web site, the listing of the speaker as "in the field of law enforcement," and the debased parody of an officer performing indecent acts while in the course of official duties brought the mission of the employer and the professionalism of its officers into serious disrepute. 356 F. 3d, at 1111 (internal quotation marks omitted).

The Court of Appeals noted the City conceded Roe's activities were "unrelated" to his employment. *Id.*, at 1112, n. 4. In the context of the pleadings and arguments, the proper interpretation of the City's statement is simply to underscore the obvious proposition that Roe's speech was not a comment on the workings or functioning of the SDPD. It is quite a different question whether the speech was detrimental to the SDPD. On that score the City's consistent position has been that the speech is contrary to its regulations and harmful to the proper functioning of the police force. The present case falls outside the protection afforded in *NTEU*. The authorities that instead control, and which are considered below, are this Court's decisions in *Pickering, supra, Connick, supra*, and the decisions which follow them.

B

To reconcile the employee's right to engage in speech and the government employer's right to protect its own legitimate interests in performing its mission, the *Pickering* Court adopted a balancing test. It requires a court evaluating restraints on a public employee's speech to balance "the interests of the [employee], as a citizen, in commenting upon matters of public concern and the interest of the State, as an employer, in promoting the efficiency of the public services it performs through its employees." 391 U. S., at 568; *see also Connick, supra*, at 142.

Underlying the decision in *Pickering* is the recognition that public employees are often the members of the community who are likely to have informed opinions as to the operations of their public employers, operations which are of substantial concern to the public. Were they not able to speak on these matters, the community would be deprived of informed opinions on important public issues. See 391 U. S., at 572. The interest at stake is as much the public's interest in receiving informed opinion as it is the employee's own right to disseminate it.

Pickering did not hold that any and all statements by a public employee are entitled to balancing. To require *Pickering* balancing in every case where speech by a public employee is at issue, no matter the content of the speech, could compromise the proper functioning of government offices. *See Connick*, 461 U.S., at 143. This concern prompted the Court in *Connick* to explain a threshold inquiry (implicit in *Pickering* itself) that in order to merit *Pickering* balancing, a public employee's speech must touch on a matter of "public concern." 461 U. S., at 143 (internal quotation marks omitted).

In *Connick*, an assistant district attorney, unhappy with her supervisor's decision to transfer her to another division, circulated an intra office questionnaire. The document solicited her co-workers' views on, *inter alia*, office transfer policy, office morale, the need for grievance committees, the level of confidence in supervisors, and whether employees felt pressured to work in political campaigns. *See id.*, at 141.

Finding that—with the exception of the final question—the questionnaire touched not on matters of public concern but on internal workplace grievances, the Court held no *Pickering* balancing was required. 461 U. S., at 141. To conclude otherwise would ignore the "common-sense realization that government offices could not function if every employment decision became a constitutional matter." *Id.*, at 143. *Connick* held that a public employee's speech is entitled to *Pickering* balancing only when the employee speaks "as a citizen upon matters of public concern" rather than "as an employee upon matters only of personal interest." 461 U. S., at 147.

Although the boundaries of the public concern test are not well-defined, *Connick* provides some guidance. It directs courts to examine the "content, form, and context of a given statement, as revealed by the whole record" in assessing whether an employee's speech addresses a matter of public concern. *Id.*, at 146–147. In addition, it notes that the standard for determining whether expression is of public concern is the same standard used to determine whether a common-law action for invasion of privacy is present. *Id.*, at 143, n. 5. That standard is established by our decisions in *Cox Broadcasting Corp. v. Cohn*, 420 U. S. 469 (1975), and *Time, Inc. v. Hill*, 385 U. S. 374, 387–388 (1967). These cases make clear that public concern is something that is a subject of legitimate news interest; that is, a subject of general interest and of value and concern to the public at the time of publication. The Court has also recognized that certain private remarks, such as negative comments about the President of the United States, touch on matters of public concern and should thus be subject to *Pickering* balancing. *See Rankin v. McPherson*, 483 U. S. 378 (1987).

Applying these principles to the instant case, there is no difficulty in concluding that Roe's expression does not qualify as a matter of public concern under any view of the public concern test. He fails the threshold test and *Pickering* balancing does not come into play.

Connick is controlling precedent, but to show why this is not a close case it is instructive to note that even under the view expressed by the dissent in *Connick* from four Members of the Court, the speech here would not come within the definition of a matter of public concern. The dissent in *Connick* would have held that the entirety of the questionnaire circulated by the employee "discussed subjects that could reasonably be expected to be of interest to persons seeking to develop informed opinions about the manner in which . . . an elected official charged with managing a vital governmental agency, discharges his responsibilities." 461 U. S., at 163 (opinion of Brennan, J.). No similar purpose could be attributed to the employee's speech in the present case. Roe's activities did nothing to inform the public about any aspect of the SDPD's functioning or operation. Nor were Roe's activities anything like the private remarks at issue in *Rankin*, where one coworker commented to another co-worker on an item of political news. Roe's expression was widely broadcast, linked to his official status as a police officer, and designed to exploit his employer's image.

The speech in question was detrimental to the mission and functions of the employer. There is no basis for finding that it was of concern to the community as the Court's cases have understood that term in the context of restrictions by governmental entities on the speech of their employees.

The judgment of the Court of Appeals is *Reversed*.

Notice: This opinion is subject to formal revision before publication in the preliminary print of the United States Reports. Readers are requested to notify the Reporter of Decisions, Supreme Court of the United States, Washington, D. C. 20543, of any typographical or other formal errors, in order that corrections may be made before the preliminary print goes to press.

SUPREME COURT OF THE UNITED STATES

No. 02–1624

*Elk Grove Unified School District and David W. Gordon, Superintendent,
Petitioners v. Michael A. Newdow et al.*

ON WRIT OF CERTIORARI TO THE UNITED STATES COURT OF
APPEALS FOR THE NINTH CIRCUIT

[June 14, 2004]

JUSTICE STEVENS delivered the opinion of the Court.

Each day elementary school teachers in the Elk Grove Unified School District (School District) lead their classes in a group recitation of the Pledge of Allegiance. Respondent, Michael A. Newdow, is an atheist whose daughter participates in that daily exercise. Because the Pledge contains the words "under God," he views the School District's policy as a religious indoctrination of his child that violates the First Amendment. A divided panel of the Court of Appeals for the Ninth Circuit agreed with Newdow. In light of the obvious importance of that decision, we granted certiorari to review the First Amendment issue and, preliminarily, the question whether Newdow has standing to invoke the jurisdiction of the federal courts. We conclude that Newdow lacks standing and therefore reverse the Court of Appeals' decision.

I

"The very purpose of a national flag is to serve as a symbol of our country," *Texas* v. *Johnson*, 491 U. S. 397, 405 (1989), and of its proud traditions "of freedom, of equal opportunity, of religious tolerance, and of good will for other peoples who share our aspirations," *id.*, at 437 (STEVENS, J., dissenting). As its history illustrates, the Pledge of Allegiance evolved as a common public acknowledgement of the ideals that our flag symbolizes. Its recitation is a patriotic exercise designed to foster national unity and pride in those principles.

The Pledge of Allegiance was initially conceived more than a century ago. As part of the nationwide interest in commemorating the 400th anniversary of Christopher Columbus' discovery of America, a widely circulated national magazine for youth proposed in 1892 that pupils recite the following affirmation: "I pledge allegiance to my Flag and the Republic for which it stands: one Nation indivisible, with Liberty and Justice for all."[1] In the 1920's, the National Flag Conferences replaced the phrase "my Flag" with "the flag of the United States of America."

In 1942, in the midst of World War II, Congress adopted, and the President signed, a Joint Resolution codifying a detailed set of "rules and customs pertaining to the display and use of the flag of the United States of America." Chapter 435, 56 Stat. 377. Section 7 of this codification provided in full:

> "That the pledge of allegiance to the flag, 'I pledge allegiance to the flag of the United States of America and to the Republic for which it stands, one Nation indivisible, with liberty and justice for all', be rendered by standing with the right hand over the heart; extending the right hand, palm upward, toward the flag at the words 'to the flag' and holding this position until the end, when the hand drops to the side. However, civilians will always show full respect to the flag when the pledge is given by merely standing at attention, men removing the headdress. Persons in uniform shall render the military salute." *Id.*, at 380.

---

1.   J. Baer, The Pledge of Allegiance: A Centennial History, 1892–1992, p. 3 (1992) (internal quotation marks omitted). At the time, the phrase "one Nation indivisible" had special meaning because the question whether a State could secede from the Union had been intensely debated and was unresolved prior to the Civil War. See J. Randall, Constitutional Problems Under Lincoln 12–24 (1964). See also W. Rehnquist, Centennial Crisis: The Disputed Election of 1876, p. 182 (2004).

This resolution, which marked the first appearance of the Pledge of Allegiance in positive law, confirmed the importance of the flag as a symbol of our Nation's indivisibility and commitment to the concept of liberty.

Congress revisited the Pledge of Allegiance 12 years later when it amended the text to add the words "under God." Act of June 14, 1954, ch. 297, 68 Stat. 249. The House Report that accompanied the legislation observed that, "[f]rom the time of our earliest history our peoples and our institutions have reflected the traditional concept that our Nation was founded on a fundamental belief in God." H. R. Rep. No. 1693, 83d Cong., 2d Sess., p. 2 (1954). The resulting text is the Pledge as we know it today: "I pledge allegiance to the Flag of the United States of America, and to the Republic for which it stands, one Nation under God, indivisible, with liberty and justice for all." 4 U. S. C. §4.

II

Under California law, "every public elementary school" must begin each day with "appropriate patriotic exercises." Cal. Educ. Code Ann. §52720 (West 1989). The statute provides that "[t]he giving of the Pledge of Allegiance to the Flag of the United States of America shall satisfy" this requirement. *Ibid.* The Elk Grove Unified School District has implemented the state law by requiring that "[e]ach elementary school class recite the pledge of allegiance to the flag once each day."[2] Consistent with our case law, the School District permits students who object on religious grounds to abstain from the recitation. See *West Virginia Bd. of Ed. v. Barnette*, 319 U. S. 624 (1943).

In March 2000, Newdow filed suit in the United States District Court for the Eastern District of California against the United States Congress, the President of the United States, the State of California, and the Elk Grove Unified School District and its superintendent.[3] App. 24. At the time of filing, Newdow's daughter was enrolled in kindergarten in the Elk Grove Unified School District and participated in the daily recitation of the Pledge. Styled as a mandamus action, the complaint explains that Newdow is an atheist who was ordained more than 20 years ago in a ministry that "espouses the religious philosophy that the true and eternal bonds of righteousness and virtue stem from reason rather than mythology." *Id.*, at 42, ¶ 53. The complaint seeks a declaration that the 1954 Act's addition of the words "under God" violated the Establishment and Free Exercise Clauses of the United States Constitution,[4] as well as an injunction against the School District's policy requiring daily recitation of the Pledge. *Id.*, at 42. It alleges that Newdow has standing to sue on his own behalf and on behalf of his daughter as "next friend." *Id.*, at 26, 56.

The case was referred to a Magistrate Judge, whose brief findings and recommendation concluded, "the Pledge does not violate the Establishment Clause." *Id.*, at 79. The District Court adopted that recommendation and dismissed the complaint on July 21, 2000. App. to Pet. for Cert. 97. The Court of Appeals reversed and issued three separate decisions discussing the merits and Newdow's standing.

In its first opinion the appeals court unanimously held that Newdow has standing "as a parent to challenge a practice that interferes with his right to direct the religious education of his daughter." *Newdow v. U. S. Congress*, 292 F. 3d 597, 602 (CA9 2002) (*Newdow I*). That holding sustained Newdow's standing to challenge not only the policy of the School District, where his daughter still is enrolled, but also the 1954 Act of Congress that had amended the

---

2. Elk Grove Unified School District's Policy AR 6115, App. to Brief for United States as Respondent Supporting Petitioners 2a.

3. Newdow also named as defendants the Sacramento Unified School District and its superintendent on the chance that his daughter might one day attend school in that district. App. 48. The Court of Appeals held that Newdow lacks standing to challenge that district's policy because his daughter is not currently a student there. *Newdow v. U. S. Congress*, 328 F. 3d 466, 485 (CA9 2003) (*Newdow III*). Newdow has not challenged that ruling.

4. The First Amendment provides in relevant part that "Congress shall make no law respecting an establishment of religion, or prohibiting the free exercise thereof." U. S. Const., Amdt. 1. The Religion Clauses apply to the States by incorporation into the Fourteenth Amendment.

See *Cantwell v. Connecticut*, 310 U. S. 296, 303 (1940).

Pledge, because his "'injury in fact'" was " 'fairly traceable'" to its enactment. *Id.*, at 603–605. On the merits, over the dissent of one judge, the court held that both the 1954 Act and the School District's policy violate the Establishment Clause of the First Amendment. *Id.*, at 612.

After the Court of Appeals' initial opinion was announced, Sandra Banning, the mother of Newdow's daughter, filed a motion for leave to intervene, or alternatively to dismiss the complaint. App. 82. She declared that although she and Newdow shared "physical custody" of their daughter, a state-court order granted her "exclusive legal custody" of the child, "including the sole right to represent [the daughter's] legal interests and make all decision[s] about her education" and welfare. *Id.*, at 82, ¶¶ 2–3. Banning further stated that her daughter is a Christian who believes in God and has no objection either to reciting or hearing others recite the Pledge of Allegiance, or to its reference to God. *Id.*, at 83, ¶ 4. Banning expressed the belief that her daughter would be harmed if the litigation were permitted to proceed, because others might incorrectly perceive the child as sharing her father's atheist views. *Id.*, at 85, ¶ 10. Banning accordingly concluded, as her daughter's sole legal custodian, that it was not in the child's interest to be a party to Newdow's lawsuit. *Id.*, at 86. On September 25, 2002, the California Superior Court entered an order enjoining Newdow from including his daughter as an unnamed party or suing as her "next friend." That order did not purport to answer the question of Newdow's Article III standing. *See Newdow v. U. S. Congress*, 313 F. 3d 500, 502 (CA9 2002) (*Newdow II*).

In a second published opinion, the Court of Appeals reconsidered Newdow's standing in light of Banning's motion. The court noted that Newdow no longer claimed to represent his daughter, but unanimously concluded that "the grant of sole legal custody to Banning" did not deprive Newdow, "as a noncustodial parent, of Article III standing to object to unconstitutional government action affecting his child." *Id.*, at 502–503. The court held that under California law Newdow retains the right to expose his child to his particular religious views even if those views contradict the mother's, and that Banning's objections as sole legal custodian do not defeat Newdow's right to seek redress for an alleged injury to his own parental interests. *Id.*, at 504–505.

On February 28, 2003, the Court of Appeals issued an order amending its first opinion and denying rehearing en banc. *Newdow v. U. S. Congress*, 328 F. 3d 466, 468 (CA9 2003) (*Newdow III*). The amended opinion omitted the initial opinion's discussion of Newdow's standing to challenge the 1954 Act and declined to determine whether Newdow was entitled to declaratory relief regarding the constitutionality of that Act. *Id.*, at 490. Nine judges dissented from the denial of en banc review. *Id.*, at 471, 482. We granted the School District's petition for a writ of certiorari to consider two questions: (1) whether Newdow has standing as a noncustodial parent to challenge the School District's policy, and (2) if so, whether the policy offends the First Amendment. 540 U. S. 945 (2003).

III

In every federal case, the party bringing the suit must establish standing to prosecute the action. "In essence the question of standing is whether the litigant is entitled to have the court decide the merits of the dispute or of particular issues." *Warth v. Seldin*, 422 U. S. 490, 498 (1975). The standing requirement is born partly of "'an idea, which is more than an intuition but less than a rigorous and explicit theory, about the constitutional and prudential limits to the powers of an unelected, unrepresentative judiciary in our kind of government.'" *Allen v. Wright*, 468 U. S. 737, 750 (1984) (quoting *Vander Jagt v. O'Neill*, 699 F. 2d 1166, 1178–1179 (CADC 1983) (Bork, J., concurring)).

The command to guard jealously and exercise rarely our power to make constitutional pronouncements requires strictest adherence when matters of great national significance are at stake. Even in cases concededly within our jurisdiction under Article III, we abide by "a series of rules under which [we have] avoided passing upon a large part of all the constitutional questions pressed upon [us] for decision." *Ashwander v. TVA*, 297 U. S. 288, 346 (1936) (Brandeis, J., concurring). Always we must balance "the heavy obligation to exercise jurisdiction," *Colorado River Water Conservation Dist. v. United States*, 424 U. S. 800, 820 (1976), against the "deeply rooted" commitment "not to pass on questions of constitutionality" unless adjudication of the constitutional issue is necessary, *Spector Motor Service, Inc. v. McLaughlin*, 323 U. S. 101, 105 (1944). *See also Rescue Army v. Municipal Court of Los Angeles*, 331 U. S. 549, 568–575 (1947).

Consistent with these principles, our standing jurisprudence contains two strands: Article III standing, which enforces the Constitution's case or controversy requirement, *see Lujan v. Defenders of Wildlife*, 504 U. S. 555, 559–562 (1992); and prudential standing, which embodies "judicially self-imposed limits on the exercise of federal jurisdiction," *Allen*, 468 U. S., at 751. The Article III limitations are familiar: The plaintiff must show that the conduct of which he complains has caused him to suffer an "injury in fact" that a favorable judgment will redress. *See Lujan*, 504 U. S., at 560–561. Although we have not exhaustively defined the prudential dimensions of the standing doctrine, we have explained that prudential standing encompasses "the general prohibition on a litigant's raising another person's legal rights, the rule barring adjudication of generalized grievances more appropriately addressed in the representative branches, and the requirement that a plaintiff's complaint fall within the zone of interests protected by the law invoked." *Allen*, 468 U. S., at 751. *See also Secretary of State of Md. v. Joseph H. Munson Co.*, 467 U. S. 947, 955–956 (1984). "Without such limitations—closely related to Art. III concerns but essentially matters of judicial self-governance—the courts would be called upon to decide abstract questions of wide public significance even though other governmental institutions may be more competent to address the questions and even though judicial intervention may be unnecessary to protect individual rights." *Warth*, 422 U. S., at 500.

One of the principal areas in which this Court has customarily declined to intervene is the realm of domestic relations. Long ago we observed that "[t]he whole subject of the domestic relations of husband and wife, parent and child, belongs to the laws of the States and not to the laws of the United States." *In re Burrus*, 136 U. S. 586, 593–594 (1890). *See also Mansell v. Mansell*, 490 U. S. 581, 587 (1989) ("[D]omestic relations are preeminently matters of state law"); *Moore v. Sims*, 442 U. S. 415, 435 (1979) ("Family relations are a traditional area of state concern"). So strong is our deference to state law in this area that we have recognized a "domestic relations exception" that "divests the federal courts of power to issue divorce, alimony, and child custody decrees." *Ankenbrandt v. Richards*, 504 U. S. 689, 703 (1992). We have also acknowledged that it might be appropriate for the federal courts to decline to hear a case involving "elements of the domestic relationship," *id.*, at 705, even when divorce, alimony, or child custody is not strictly at issue:

> "This would be so when a case presents 'difficult questions of state law bearing on policy problems of substantial public import whose importance transcends the result in the case then at bar.' Such might well be the case if a federal suit were filed prior to effectuation of a divorce, alimony, or child custody decree, and the suit depended on a determination of the status of the parties." *Id.*, at 705–706 (quoting *Colorado River*, 424 U. S., at 814).

Thus, while rare instances arise in which it is necessary to answer a substantial federal question that transcends or exists apart from the family law issue, *see, e. g., Palmore v. Sidoti*, 466 U. S. 429, 432–434 (1984), in general it is appropriate for the federal courts to leave delicate issues of domestic relations to the state courts.[5]

As explained briefly above, the extent of the standing problem raised by the domestic relations issues in this case was not apparent until August 5, 2002, when Banning filed her motion for leave to intervene or dismiss the complaint following the Court of Appeals' initial decision. At that time, the child's custody was governed by a February 6, 2002, order of the California Superior Court. That order provided that Banning had "'*sole* legal custody as to the rights and responsibilities to make decisions relating to the health, education and welfare of'" her daughter. *Newdow II*, 313 F. 3d, at 502. The order stated that the two parents should

---

5. Our holding does not rest, as THE CHIEF JUSTICE suggests, *see post*, at 2–5, on either the domestic relations exception or the abstention doctrine. Rather, our prudential standing analysis is informed by the variety of contexts in which federal courts decline to intervene because, as *Ankenbrandt v. Richards*, 504 U. S. 689 (1992), contemplated, the suit "depend[s] on a determination of the status of the parties," *id.*, at 706. We deemed it appropriate to review the dispute in *Palmore* because it "raise[d] important federal concerns arising from the Constitution's commitment to eradicating discrimination based on race." 466 U. S., at 432. In this case, by contrast, the disputed family law rights are entwined inextricably with the threshold standing inquiry. THE CHIEF JUSTICE in this respect, see *post*, at 3, misses our point: The *merits* question undoubtedly transcends the domestic relations issue, but the *standing* question surely does not.

"'consult with one another on substantial decisions relating to'" the child's "'psychological and educational needs,'" but it authorized Banning to "'exercise legal control'" if the parents could not reach "'mutual agreement.'" *Ibid.*

That family court order was the controlling document at the time of the Court of Appeals' standing decision. After the Court of Appeals ruled, however, the Superior Court held another conference regarding the child's custody. At a hearing on September 11, 2003, the Superior Court announced that the parents have "joint legal custody," but that Banning "makes the final decisions if the two . . . disagree." App. 127–128.[6]

Newdow contends that despite Banning's final authority, he retains "an unrestricted right to inculcate in his daughter—free from governmental interference—the atheistic beliefs he finds persuasive." *Id.*, at 48, ¶ 78. The difficulty with that argument is that Newdow's rights, as in many cases touching upon family relations, cannot be viewed in isolation. This case concerns not merely Newdow's interest in inculcating his child with his views on religion, but also the rights of the child's mother as a parent generally and under the Superior Court orders specifically. And most important, it implicates the interests of a young child who finds herself at the center of a highly public debate over her custody, the propriety of a widespread national ritual, and the meaning of our Constitution.

The interests of the affected persons in this case are in many respects antagonistic. Of course, legal disharmony in family relations is not uncommon, and in many instances that disharmony poses no bar to federal-court adjudication of proper federal questions. What makes this case different is that Newdow's standing derives entirely from his relationship with his daughter, but he lacks the right to litigate as her next friend. In marked contrast to our case law on *jus tertii, see, e. g., Singleton v. Wulff*, 428 U. S. 106, 113–118 (1976) (plurality opinion), the interests of this parent and this child are not parallel and, indeed, are potentially in conflict.[7]

Newdow's parental status is defined by California's domestic relations law. Our custom on questions of state law ordinarily is to defer to the interpretation of the Court of Appeals for the Circuit in which the State is located. *See Bishop v. Wood*, 426 U. S. 341, 346–347 (1976). In this case, the Court of Appeals, which possesses greater familiarity with California law, concluded that state law vests in Newdow a cognizable right to influence his daughter's religious upbringing. *Newdow II*, 313 F. 3d, at 504–505. The court based its ruling on two intermediate state appellate cases holding that "while the custodial parent undoubtedly has the right to make ultimate decisions concerning the child's religious upbringing, a court will not enjoin the noncustodial parent from discussing religion with the child or involving the child in his or her religious activities in the absence of a showing that the child will be thereby harmed."

---

6. The court confirmed that position in a written order issued January 9, 2004:

"The parties will have joint legal custody defined as follows: Ms. Banning will continue to make the final decisions as to the minor's health, education, and welfare if the two parties cannot mutually agree. The parties are required to consult with each other on substantial decisions relating to the health, education and welfare of the minor child, including . . . psychological and educational needs of the minor. If mutual agreement is not reached in these areas, then Ms. Banning may exercise legal control of the minor that is not specifically prohibited or is inconsistent with the physical custody." App. to Reply Brief for United States as Respondent Supporting Petitioners 12a.

Despite the use of the term "joint legal custody"—which is defined by California statute, *see* Cal. Fam. Code Ann. §3003 (West 1994)—we see no meaningful distinction for present purposes between the custody order issued February 6, 2002, and the one issued January 9, 2004. Under either order, Newdow has the right to consult on issues relating to the child's education, but Banning possesses what we understand amounts to a tie breaking vote.

7. "There are good and sufficient reasons for th[e] prudential limitation on standing when rights of third parties are implicated—the avoidance of the adjudication of rights which those not before the Court may not wish to assert, and the assurance that the most effective advocate of the rights at issue is present to champion them." *Duke Power Co. v. Carolina Environmental Study Group, Inc.*, 438 U. S. 59, 80 (1978). Banning tells us that her daughter has no objection to the Pledge, and we are mindful in cases such as this that "children themselves have constitutionally protectible interests." *Wisconsin v. Yoder*, 406 U. S. 205, 243 (1972) (Douglas, J., dissenting). In a fundamental respect, "[i]t is the future of the student, not the future of the parents," that is at stake. *Id.*, at 245.

In re Marriage of Murga, 103 Cal. App. 3d 498, 505, 163 Cal. Rptr. 79, 82 (1980). *See also In re Marriage of Mentry*, 142 Cal. App. 3d 260, 268–270, 190 Cal. Rptr. 843, 849–850 (1983) (relying on *Murga* to invalidate portion of restraining order barring noncustodial father from engaging children in religious activity or discussion without custodial parent's consent). Animated by a conception of "family privacy" that includes "not simply a policy of minimum state intervention but also a presumption of parental autonomy," 142 Cal. App. 3d, at 267–268, 190 Cal. Rptr., at 848, the state cases create a zone of private authority within which each parent, whether custodial or noncustodial, remains free to impart to the child his or her religious perspective.

Nothing that either Banning or the School Board has done, however, impairs Newdow's right to instruct his daughter in his religious views. Instead, Newdow requests relief that is more ambitious than that sought in *Mentry* and *Murga.* He wishes to forestall his daughter's exposure to religious ideas that her mother, who wields a form of veto power, endorses, and to use his parental status to challenge the influences to which his daughter may be exposed in school when he and Banning disagree. The California cases simply do not stand for the proposition that Newdow has a right to dictate to others what they may and may not say to his child respecting religion. *Mentry* and *Murga* are concerned with protecting "'the fragile, complex interpersonal bonds between child and parent,'" 142 Cal. App. 3d, at 267, 190 Cal. Rptr., at 848, and with permitting divorced parents to expose their children to the "'diversity of religious experiences [that] is itself a sound stimulant for a child,'" *id.*, at 265, 190 Cal. Rptr., at 847 (citation omitted). The cases speak not at all to the problem of a parent seeking to reach outside the private parent-child sphere to restrain the acts of a third party. A next friend surely could exercise such a right, but the Superior Court's order has deprived Newdow of that status.

In our view, it is improper for the federal courts to entertain a claim by a plaintiff whose standing to sue is founded on family law rights that are in dispute when prosecution of the lawsuit may have an adverse effect on the person who is the source of the plaintiff's claimed standing. When hard questions of domestic relations are sure to affect the outcome, the prudent course is for the federal court to stay its hand rather than reach out to resolve a weighty question of federal constitutional law. There is a vast difference between Newdow's right to communicate with his child—which both California law and the First Amendment recognize—and his claimed right to shield his daughter from influences to which she is exposed in school despite the terms of the custody order. We conclude that, having been deprived under California law of the right to sue as next friend, Newdow lacks prudential standing to bring this suit in federal court.[8]

The judgment of the Court of Appeals is reversed.

It is so ordered.

JUSTICE SCALIA took no part in the consideration or decision of this case.

NOTICE: This opinion is subject to formal revision before publication in the preliminary print of the United States Reports. Readers are requested to notify the Reporter of Decisions, Supreme Court of the United States, Washington, D. C. 20543, of any typographical or other formal errors, in order that corrections may be made before the preliminary print goes to press.

---

8. Newdow's complaint and brief cite several additional bases for standing: that Newdow "at times has himself attended—and will in the future attend—class with his daughter," App. 49, ¶ 80; that he "has considered teaching elementary school students in [the School District]," *id.*, at 65, ¶ 120; that he "has attended and will continue to attend" school board meetings at which the Pledge is "routinely recited," *id.*, at 52, ¶ 85; and that the School District uses his tax dollars to implement its Pledge policy, *id.*, at 62–65. Even if these arguments suffice to establish Article III standing, they do not respond to our prudential concerns. As for taxpayer standing, Newdow does not reside in or pay taxes to the School District; he alleges that he pays taxes to the District only "indirectly" through his child support payments to Banning. Brief for Respondent Newdow 49, n. 70. That allegation does not amount to the "direct dollars-and-cents injury" that our strict taxpayer-standing doctrine requires. *Doremus v. Board of Ed. of Hawthorne*, 342 U. S. 429, 434 (1952).

SUPREME COURT OF THE UNITED STATES

No. 06–8120

Bruce Edward Brendlin, Petitioner v. California

ON WRIT OF CERTIORARI TO THE SUPREME COURT OF CALIFORNIA

[June 18, 2007]

JUSTICE SOUTER delivered the opinion of the Court.

When a police officer makes a traffic stop, the driver of the car is seized within the meaning of the Fourth Amendment. The question in this case is whether the same is true of a passenger. We hold that a passenger is seized as well and so may challenge the constitutionality of the stop.

I

Early in the morning of November 27, 2001, Deputy Sheriff Robert Brokenbrough and his partner saw a parked Buick with expired registration tags. In his ensuing conversation with the police dispatcher, Brokenbrough learned that an application for renewal of registration was being processed. The officers saw the car again on the road, and this time Brokenbrough noticed its display of a temporary operating permit with the number "11," indicating it was legal to drive the car through November. App. 115. The officers decided to pull the Buick over to verify that the permit matched the vehicle, even though, as Brokenbrough admitted later, there was nothing unusual about the permit or the way it was affixed. Brokenbrough asked the driver, Karen Simeroth, for her license and saw a passenger in the front seat, petitioner Bruce Brendlin, whom he recognized as "one of the Brendlin brothers." *Id.*, at 65. He recalled that either Scott or Bruce Brendlin had dropped out of parole supervision and asked Brendlin to identify himself.[1] Brokenbrough returned to his cruiser, called for backup, and verified that Brendlin was a parole violator with an outstanding no-bail warrant for his arrest. While he was in the patrol car, Brokenbrough saw Brendlin briefly open and then close the passenger door of the Buick. Once reinforcements arrived, Brokenbrough went to the passenger side of the Buick, ordered him out of the car at gunpoint, and declared him under arrest. When the police searched Brendlin incident to arrest, they found an orange syringe cap on his person. A pat down search of Simeroth revealed syringes and a plastic bag of a green leafy substance, and she was also formally arrested. Officers then searched the car and found tubing, a scale, and other things used to produce methamphetamine.

Brendlin was charged with possession and manufacture of methamphetamine, and he moved to suppress the evidence obtained in the searches of his person and the car as fruits of an unconstitutional seizure, arguing that the officers lacked probable cause or reasonable suspicion to make the traffic stop. He did not assert that his Fourth Amendment rights were violated by the search of Simeroth's vehicle, *cf. Rakas v. Illinois*, 439 U. S. 128 (1978), but claimed only that the traffic stop was an unlawful seizure of his person. The trial court denied the suppression motion after finding that the stop was lawful and Brendlin was not seized until Brokenbrough ordered him out of the car and formally arrested him. Brendlin pleaded guilty, subject to appeal on the suppression issue, and was sentenced to four years in prison.

The California Court of Appeal reversed the denial of the suppression motion, holding that Brendlin was seized by the traffic stop, which they held unlawful. 8 Cal. Rptr. 3d 882 (2004) (officially depublished). By a narrow majority, the Supreme Court of California reversed. The State Supreme Court noted California's concession that the officers had no reasonable basis to suspect unlawful operation of the car, 38 Cal. 4th 1107, 1114, 136 P. 3d 845,

---

1. The parties dispute the accuracy of the transcript of the suppression hearing and disagree as to whether Brendlin gave his name or the false name "Bruce Brown." App. 115.

848 (2006),[2] but still held suppression unwarranted because a passenger "is not seized as a constitutional matter in the absence of additional circumstances that would indicate to a reasonable person that he or she was the subject of the peace officer's investigation or show of authority," *id.*, at 1111, 136 P. 3d, at 846. The court reasoned that Brendlin was not seized by the traffic stop because Simeroth was its exclusive target, *id.*, at 1118, 136 P. 3d, at 851, that a passenger cannot submit to an officer's show of authority while the driver controls the car, *id.*, at 1118–1119, 135 P. 3d, at 851–852, and that once a car has been pulled off the road, a passenger "would feel free to depart or otherwise to conduct his or her affairs as though the police were not present," *id.*, at 1119, 136 P. 3d, at 852. In dissent, Justice Corrigan said that a traffic stop entails the seizure of a passenger even when the driver is the sole target of police investigation because a passenger is detained for the purpose of ensuring an officer's safety and would not feel free to leave the car without the officer's permission. *Id.*, at 1125, 136 P. 3d, at 856.

We granted certiorari to decide whether a traffic stop subjects a passenger, as well as the driver, to Fourth Amendment seizure, 549 U. S. _____ (2007). We now vacate.

II

A

A person is seized by the police and thus entitled to challenge the government's action under the Fourth Amendment when the officer, "'by means of physical force or show of authority,'" terminates or restrains his freedom of movement, *Florida v. Bostick*, 501 U. S. 429, 434 (1991) (quoting *Terry v. Ohio*, 392 U. S. 1, 19, n. 16 (1968)), "*through means intentionally applied*," *Brower v. County of Inyo*, 489 U. S. 593, 597 (1989) (emphasis in original). Thus, an "unintended person . . . [may be] the object of the detention," so long as the detention is "willful" and not merely the consequence of "an unknowing act." *Id.*, at 596; *cf. County of Sacramento v. Lewis*, 523 U. S. 833, 844 (1998) (no seizure where a police officer accidentally struck and killed a motorcycle passenger during a high-speed pursuit). A police officer may make a seizure by a show of authority and without the use of physical force, but there is no seizure without actual submission; otherwise, there is at most an attempted seizure, so far as the Fourth Amendment is concerned. *See California v. Hodari D.*, 499 U. S. 621, 626, n. 2 (1991); *Lewis, supra*, at 844, 845, n. 7.

When the actions of the police do not show an unambiguous intent to restrain or when an individual's submission to a show of governmental authority takes the form of passive acquiescence, there needs to be some test for telling when a seizure occurs in response to authority, and when it does not. The test was devised by Justice Stewart in *United States v. Mendenhall*, 446 U. S. 544 (1980), who wrote that a seizure occurs if "in view of all of the circumstances surrounding the incident, a reasonable person would have believed that he was not free to leave," *id.*, 554 (principal opinion). Later on, the Court adopted Justice Stewart's touchstone, *see, e. g., Hodari D., supra*, at 627; *Michigan v. Chesternut*, 486 U. S. 567, 573 (1988); *INS v. Delgado*, 466 U. S. 210, 215 (1984), but added that when a person "has no desire to leave" for reasons unrelated to the police presence, the "coercive effect of the encounter" can be measured better by asking whether "a reasonable person would feel free to decline the officers' requests or otherwise terminate the encounter," *Bostick, supra*, at 435–436; *see also United States v. Drayton*, 536 U. S. 194, 202 (2002).

The law is settled that in Fourth Amendment terms a traffic stop entails a seizure of the driver "even though the purpose of the stop is limited and the resulting detention quite brief." *Delaware v. Prouse*, 440 U. S. 648, 653 (1979); *see also Whren v. United States*, 517 U. S. 806, 809–810 (1996). And although we have not, until today, squarely answered the question whether a passenger is also seized, we have said over and over in dicta that during a traffic stop an officer seizes everyone in the vehicle, not just the driver. *See, e. g., Prouse, supra*, at 653 ("[S]topping an automobile and detaining its occupants constitute a 'seizure' within the

---

2. California conceded that the police officers lacked reasonable suspicion to justify the traffic stop because a "'vehicle with an application for renewal of expired registration would be expected to have a temporary operating permit.'" 38 Cal. 4th, at 1114, 136 P. 3d, at 848 (quoting Brief for Respondent California in No. S123133 (Sup. Ct. Cal.), p. 24).

meaning of [the Fourth and Fourteenth] Amendments"); *Colorado v. Bannister*, 449 U. S. 1, 4, n. 3 (1980) (*per curiam*) ("There can be no question that the stopping of a vehicle and the detention of its occupants constitute a 'seizure' within the meaning of the Fourth Amendment"); *Berkemer v. McCarty*, 468 U. S. 420, 436–437 (1984) ("[W]e have long acknowledged that stopping an automobile and detaining its occupants constitute a seizure" (internal quotation marks omitted)); *United States v. Hensley*, 469 U. S. 221, 226 (1985) ("[S]topping a car and detaining its occupants constitute a seizure"); *Whren, supra*, at 809–810 ("Temporary detention of individuals during the stop of an automobile by the police, even if only for a brief period and for a limited purpose, constitutes a 'seizure' of 'persons' within the meaning of [the Fourth Amendment]").

We have come closest to the question here in two cases dealing with unlawful seizure of a passenger, and neither time did we indicate any distinction between driver and passenger that would affect the Fourth Amendment analysis. *Delaware v. Prouse* considered grounds for stopping a car on the road and held that Prouse's suppression motion was properly granted. We spoke of the arresting officer's testimony that Prouse was in the back seat when the car was pulled over, see 440 U. S., at 650, n. 1, described Prouse as an occupant, not as the driver, and referred to the car's "occupants" as being seized, *id.*, at 653. Justification for stopping a car was the issue again in *Whren v. United States*, where we passed upon a Fourth Amendment challenge by two petitioners who moved to suppress drug evidence found during the course of a traffic stop. See 517 U. S., at 809. Both driver and passenger claimed to have been seized illegally when the police stopped the car; we agreed and held suppression unwarranted only because the stop rested on probable cause. *Id.*, at 809–810, 819.

B

The State concedes that the police had no adequate justification to pull the car over, see n. 2, *supra*, but argues that the passenger was not seized and thus cannot claim that the evidence was tainted by an unconstitutional stop. We resolve this question by asking whether a reasonable person in Brendlin's position when the car stopped would have believed himself free to "terminate the encounter" between the police and himself. *Bostick, supra*, at 436. We think that in these circumstances any reasonable passenger would have understood the police officers to be exercising control to the point that no one in the car was free to depart without police permission.

A traffic stop necessarily curtails the travel a passenger has chosen just as much as it halts the driver, diverting both from the stream of traffic to the side of the road, and the police activity that normally amounts to intrusion on "privacy and personal security" does not normally (and did not here) distinguish between passenger and driver. *United States v. Martinez-Fuerte*, 428 U. S. 543, 554 (1976). An officer who orders one particular car to pullover acts with an implicit claim of right based on fault of some sort, and a sensible person would not expect a police officer to allow people to come and go freely from the physical focal point of an investigation into faulty behavior or wrongdoing. If the likely wrongdoing is not the driving, the passenger will reasonably feel subject to suspicion owing to close association; but even when the wrong doing is only bad driving, the passenger will expect to be subject to some scrutiny, and his attempt to leave the scene would be so obviously likely to prompt an objection from the officer that no passenger would feel free to leave in the first place. *Cf. Drayton, supra*, at 197–199, 203–204 (finding no seizure when police officers boarded a stationary bus and asked passengers for permission to search for drugs).[3]

It is also reasonable for passengers to expect that a police officer at the scene of a crime, arrest, or investigation will not let people move around in ways that could jeopardize his safety. In *Maryland v. Wilson*, 519 U. S. 408 (1997), we held that during a lawful traffic stop an officer may order a passenger out of the car as a precautionary measure, without reasonable

---

3. Of course, police may also stop a car solely to investigate a passenger's conduct. *See, e. g., United States v. Rodriguez-Diaz*, 161 F. Supp. 2d 627, 629, n. 1 (Md. 2001) (passenger's violation of local seatbelt law); *People v. Roth*, 85 P. 3d 571, 573 (Colo. App. 2003) (passenger's violation of littering ordinance). Accordingly, a passenger cannot assume, merely from the fact of a traffic stop, that the driver's conduct is the cause of the stop.

suspicion that the passenger poses a safety risk. *Id.*, at 414–415; *cf. Pennsylvania v. Mimms*, 434 U. S. 106 (1977) (*per curiam*) (driver may be ordered out of the car as a matter of course). In fashioning this rule, we invoked our earlier statement that "'[t]he risk of harm to both the police and the occupants is minimized if the officers routinely exercise unquestioned command of the situation.'" *Wilson, supra,* at 414 (quoting *Michigan v. Summers*, 452 U. S. 692, 702–703 (1981)). What we have said in these opinions probably reflects a societal expectation of "'unquestioned [police] command'" at odds with any notion that a passenger would feel free to leave, or to terminate the personal encounter any other way, without advance permission. *Wilson, supra,* at 414.[4]

Our conclusion comports with the views of all nine Federal Courts of Appeals, and nearly every state court, to have ruled on the question. *See United States v. Kimball*, 25 F. 3d 1, 5 (CA1 1994); *United States v. Mosley*, 454 F. 3d 249, 253 (CA3 2006); *United States v. Rusher*, 966 F. 2d 868, 874, n. 4 (CA4 1992); *United States v. Grant*, 349 F. 3d 192, 196 (CA5 2003); *United States v. Perez*, 440 F. 3d 363, 369 (CA6 2006); *United States v. Powell*, 929 F. 2d 1190, 1195 (CA7 1991); *United States v. Ameling*, 328 F. 3d 443, 446–447, n. 3 (CA8 2003); *United States v. Twilley*, 222 F. 3d 1092, 1095 (CA9 2000); *United States v. Eylicio-Montoya*, 70 F. 3d 1158, 1163–1164 (CA10 1995); *State v. Bowers*, 334 Ark. 447, 451–452, 976 S. W. 2d 379, 381–382 (1998); *State v. Haworth*, 106 Idaho 405, 405– 406, 679 P. 2d 1123, 1123–1124 (1984); *People v. Bunch*, 207 Ill. 2d 7, 13, 796 N. E. 2d 1024, 1029 (2003); *State v. Eis*, 348 N. W. 2d 224, 226 (Iowa 1984); *State v. Hodges*, 252 Kan. 989, 1002–1005, 851 P. 2d 352, 361–362 (1993); *State v. Carter*, 69 Ohio St. 3d 57, 63, 630 N. E. 2d 355, 360 (1994) *(per curiam); State v. Harris*, 206 Wis. 2d 243, 253–258, 557 N. W. 2d 245, 249–251 (1996). And the treatise writers share this prevailing judicial view that a passenger may bring a Fourth Amendment challenge to the legality of a traffic stop. *See, e. g.*, 6 W. LaFave, Search and Seizure §11. 3(e), pp. 194, 195, and n. 277 (4th ed. 2004 and Supp. 2007) ("If either the stopping of the car, the length of the passenger's detention thereafter, or the passenger's removal from it are unreasonable in a Fourth Amendment sense, then surely the passenger has standing to object to those constitutional violations and to have suppressed any evidence found in the car which is their fruit" (footnote omitted)); 1 W. Ringel, Searches & Seizures, Arrests and Confessions §11:20, p. 11–98 (2d ed. 2007) ("[A] law enforcement officer's stop of an automobile results in a seizure of both the driver and the passenger").[5]

C

The contrary conclusion drawn by the Supreme Court of California, that seizure came only with formal arrest, reflects three premises as to which we respectfully disagree. First, the State Supreme Court reasoned that Brendlin was not seized by the stop because Deputy Sheriff Brokenbrough only intended to investigate Simeroth and did not direct a show of authority toward Brendlin. The court saw Brokenbrough's "flashing lights [as] directed at the driver," and pointed to the lack of record evidence that Brokenbrough "was even aware [Brendlin] was in the car prior to the vehicle stop." 38 Cal. 4th, at 1118, 136 P. 3d, at 851. But that view of the facts ignores the objective *Mendenhall* test of what a reasonable passenger would understand. To the extent that there is anything ambiguous in the show of force (was it fairly seen as directed only at the driver or at the car and its occupants?), the test resolves the ambiguity, and here it leads to the intuitive conclusion that all the occupants were subject to like control by the successful display of authority. The State Supreme Court's approach, on the contrary, shifts the issue from the intent of the police as objectively manifested to the motive of the police for taking the intentional action to stop the car, and we have repeatedly rejected attempts to introduce this kind of subjectivity into Fourth Amendment analysis. *See, e. g., Whren*, 517 U. S., at 813 ("Subjective intentions play no role in ordinary, probable-cause Fourth Amendment

---

4. Although the State Supreme Court inferred from Brendlin's decision to open and close the passenger door during the traffic stop that he was "awar[e] of the available options," 38 Cal. 4th 1107, 1120, 136 P. 3d845, 852 (2006), this conduct could equally be taken to indicate that Brendlin felt compelled to remain inside the car. In any event, the test is not what Brendlin felt but what a reasonable passenger would have understood.

5. Only two State Supreme Courts, other than California's, have stood against this tide of authority. *See People v. Jackson*, 39 P. 3d 1174, 1184–1186 (Colo. 2002) (en banc); *State v. Mendez*, 137 Wash. 2d 208, 222–223, 970 P. 2d 722, 729 (1999) (en banc).

analysis"); *Chesternut*, 486 U. S., at 575, n. 7 ("[T]he subjective intent of the officers is relevant to an assessment of the Fourth Amendment implications of police conduct only to the extent that that intent has been conveyed to the person confronted"); *Mendenhall*, 446 U. S., at 554, n. 6 (principal opinion) (disregarding a Government agent's subjective intent to detain Mendenhall); cf. *Rakas*, 439 U. S., at 132–135 (rejecting the "target theory" of Fourth Amendment standing, which would have allowed "any criminal defendant at whom a search was directed" to challenge the legality of the search (internal quotation marks omitted)).

California defends the State Supreme Court's ruling on this point by citing our cases holding that seizure requires a purposeful, deliberate act of detention. See Brief for Respondent 9–14. But *Chesternut, supra*, answers that argument. The intent that counts under the Fourth Amendment is the "intent [that] has been conveyed to the person confronted," *id.*, at 575, n. 7, and the criterion of willful restriction on freedom of movement is no invitation to look to subjective intent when determining who is seized. Our most recent cases are in accord on this point. In *Lewis*, 523 U. S. 833, we considered whether a seizure occurred when an officer accidentally ran over a passenger who had fallen off a motorcycle during a high-speed chase, and in holding that no seizure took place, we stressed that the officer stopped Lewis's movement by accidentally crashing into him, not "through means intentionally applied." *Id.*, at 844 (emphasis deleted). We did not even consider, let alone emphasize, the possibility that the officer had meant to detain the driver only and not the passenger. Nor is *Brower*, 489 U. S. 593, to the contrary, where it was dispositive that "Brower was meant to be stopped by the physical obstacle of the roadblock—and that he was so stopped." *Id.*, at 599. California reads this language to suggest that for a specific occupant of the car to be seized he must be the motivating target of an officer's show of authority, see Brief for Respondent 12, as if the thrust of our observation were that Brower, and not someone else, was "meant to be stopped." But our point was not that Brower alone was the target but that officers detained him "through means intentionally applied"; if the car had had another occupant, it would have made sense to hold that he too had been seized when the car collided with the roadblock. Neither case, then, is at odds with our holding that the issue is whether a reasonable passenger would have perceived that the show of authority was at least partly directed at him, and that he was thus not free to ignore the police presence and go about his business.

Second, the Supreme Court of California assumed that Brendlin, "as the passenger, had no ability to submit to the deputy's show of authority" because only the driver was in control of the moving vehicle. 38 Cal. 4th, at 1118, 1119, 136 P. 3d, at 852. But what may amount to submission depends on what a person was doing before the show of authority: a fleeing man is not seized until he is physically overpowered, but one sitting in a chair may submit to authority by not getting up to run away. Here, Brendlin had no effective way to signal submission while the car was still moving on the roadway, but once it came to a stop he could, and apparently did, submit by staying inside.

Third, the State Supreme Court shied away from the rule we apply today for fear that it "would encompass even those motorists following the vehicle subject to the traffic stop who, by virtue of the original detention, are forced to slow down and perhaps even come to a halt in order to accommodate that vehicle's submission to police authority." *Id.*, at 1120, 136 P. 3d, at 853. But an occupant of a car who knows that he is stuck in traffic because another car has been pulled over (like the motorist who can't even make out why the road is suddenly clogged) would not perceive a show of authority as directed at him or his car. Such incidental restrictions on freedom of movement would not tend to affect an individual's "sense of security and privacy in traveling in an automobile." *Prouse*, 440 U. S., at 662. Nor would the consequential blockage call for a precautionary rule to avoid the kind of "arbitrary and oppressive interference by [law] enforcement officials with the privacy and personal security of individuals" that the Fourth Amendment was intended to limit. *Martinez-Fuerte*, 428 U. S., at 554.[6]

---

6. California claims that, under today's rule, "all taxi cab and bus passengers would be 'seized' under the Fourth Amendment when the cab or bus driver is pulled over by the police for running a red light." Brief for Respondent 23. But the relationship between driver and passenger is not the same in a common carrier as it is in a private vehicle, and the expectations of police officers and passengers differ accordingly. In those cases, as here, the crucial question would be whether a reasonable person in the passenger's position would feel free to take steps to terminate the encounter.

Indeed, the consequence to worry about would not flow from our conclusion, but from the rule that almost all courts have rejected. Holding that the passenger in a private car is not (without more) seized in a traffic stop would invite police officers to stop cars with passengers regardless of probable cause or reasonable suspicion of anything illegal.[7] The fact that evidence uncovered as a result of an arbitrary traffic stop would still be admissible against any passengers would be a powerful incentive to run the kind of "roving patrols" that would still violate the driver's Fourth Amendment right. *See, e. g., Almeida-Sanchez v. United States*, 413 U. S. 266, 273 (1973) (stop and search by Border Patrol agents without a warrant or probable cause violated the Fourth Amendment); *Prouse, supra*, at 663 (police spot check of driver's license and registration without reasonable suspicion violated the Fourth Amendment).

*   *   *

Brendlin was seized from the moment Simeroth's car came to a halt on the side of the road, and it was error to deny his suppression motion on the ground that seizure occurred only at the formal arrest. It will be for the state courts to consider in the first instance whether suppression turns on any other issue. The judgment of the Supreme Court of California is vacated, and the case is remanded for further proceedings not inconsistent with this opinion.

It is so ordered.

Tinker v. Des Moines School Dist.,
393 U.S. 503 (1969)

MR. JUSTICE FORTAS delivered the opinion of the Court.

Petitioner John F. Tinker, 15 years old, and petitioner Christopher Eckhardt, 16 years old, attended high schools in Des Moines, Iowa. Petitioner Mary Beth Tinker, John's sister, was a 13-year-old student in junior high school.

In December 1965, a group of adults and students in Des Moines held a meeting at the Eckhardt home. The group determined to publicize their objections to the hostilities in Vietnam and their support for a truce by wearing black armbands during the holiday season and by fasting on December 16 and New Year's Eve. Petitioners and their parents had previously engaged in similar activities, and they decided to participate in the program.

The principals of the Des Moines schools became aware of the plan to wear armbands. On December 14, 1965, they met and adopted a policy that any student wearing an armband to school would be asked to remove it, and if he refused he would be suspended until he returned without the armband. Petitioners were aware of the regulation that the school authorities adopted.

On December 16, Mary Beth and Christopher wore black armbands to their schools. John Tinker wore his armband the next day. They were all sent home and suspended from school until they would come back without their armbands. They did not return to school until after the planned period for wearing armbands had expired—that is, until after New Year's Day.

This complaint was filed in the United States District Court by petitioners, through their fathers, under 1983 of Title 42 of the United States Code. It prayed for an injunction restraining the respondent school officials and the respondent members of the board of directors of the school district from disciplining the petitioners, and it sought nominal damages. After an evidentiary hearing the District Court dismissed the complaint. It upheld the constitutionality of the school authorities' action on the ground that it was reasonable in

---

7. Compare *Delaware v. Prouse*, 440 U. S. 648, 663 (1979) (requiring "at least articulable and reasonable suspicion" to support random, investigative traffic stops), and *United States v. Brignoni-Ponce*, 422 U. S. 873, 880–884 (1975) (same), with *Whren v. United States*, 517 U. S. 806, 810 (1996) ("[T]he decision to stop an automobile is reasonable where the police have probable cause to believe that a traffic violation has occurred"), and *Atwater v. Lago Vista*, 532 U. S. 318, 354 (2001) ("If an officer has probable cause to believe that an individual has committed even a very minor criminal offense in his presence, he may, without violating the Fourth Amendment, arrest the offender").

order to prevent disturbance of school discipline. 258 F. Supp. 971 (1966). The court referred to but expressly declined to follow the Fifth Circuit's holding in a similar case that the wearing of symbols like the armbands cannot be prohibited unless it "materially and substantially interfere[s] with the requirements of appropriate discipline in the operation of the school." *Burnside v. Byars*, 363 F.2d 744, 749 (1966).

On appeal, the Court of Appeals for the Eighth Circuit considered the case en banc. The court was equally divided, and the District Court's decision was accordingly affirmed, without opinion. 383 F.2d 988 (1967). We granted *certiorari*. 390 U.S. 942 (1968).

I.

The District Court recognized that the wearing of an armband for the purpose of expressing certain views is the type of symbolic act that is within the Free Speech Clause of the First Amendment. *See West Virginia v. Barnette*, 319 U.S. 624 (1943); *Stromberg v. California*, 283 U.S. 359 (1931). *Cf. Thornhill v. Alabama*, 310 U.S. 88 (1940); *Edwards v. South Carolina*, 372 U.S. 229 (1963); *Brown v. Louisiana*, 383 U.S. 131 (1966). As we shall discuss, the wearing of armbands in the circumstances of this case was entirely divorced from actually or potentially disruptive conduct by those participating in it. It was closely akin to "pure speech" which, we have repeatedly held, is entitled to comprehensive protection under the First Amendment. *Cf. Cox v. Louisiana*, 379 U.S. 536, 555 (1965); *Adderley v. Florida*, 385 U.S. 39 (1966).

First Amendment rights, applied in light of the special characteristics of the school environment, are available to teachers and students. It can hardly be argued that either students or teachers shed their constitutional rights to freedom of speech or expression at the schoolhouse gate. This has been the unmistakable holding of this Court for almost 50 years. In *Meyer v. Nebraska*, 262 U.S. 390 (1923), and *Bartels v. Iowa*, 262 U.S. 404 (1923), this Court, in opinions by Mr. Justice McReynolds, held that the Due Process Clause of the Fourteenth Amendment prevents States from forbidding the teaching of a foreign language to young students. Statutes to this effect, the Court held, unconstitutionally interfere with the liberty of teacher, student, and parent. *See also Pierce v. Society of Sisters*, 268 U.S. 510 (1925); *West Virginia v. Barnette*, 319 U.S. 624 (1943); *McCollum v. Board of Education*, 333 U.S. 203 (1948); *Wieman v. Updegraff*, 344 U.S. 183, 195 (1952) (concurring opinion); *Sweezy v. New Hampshire*, 354 U.S. 234 (1957); *Shelton v. Tucker*, 364 U.S. 479, 487 (1960); *Engel v. Vitale*, 370 U.S. 421 (1962); *Keyishian v. Board of Regents*, 385 U.S. 589, 603 (1967); *Epperson v. Arkansas*, ante, p. 97 (1968). In *West Virginia v. Barnette, supra*, this Court held that under the First Amendment, the student in public school may not be compelled to salute the flag. Speaking through Mr. Justice Jackson, the Court said:

> "The Fourteenth Amendment, as now applied to the States, protects the citizen against the State itself and all of its creatures—Boards of Education not excepted. These have, of course, important, delicate, and highly discretionary functions, but none that they may not perform within the limits of the Bill of Rights. That they are educating the young for citizenship is reason for scrupulous protection of Constitutional freedoms of the individual, if we are not to strangle the free mind at its source and teach youth to discount important principles of our government as mere platitudes." 319 U.S., at 637.

On the other hand, the Court has repeatedly emphasized the need for affirming the comprehensive authority of the States and of school officials, consistent with fundamental constitutional safeguards, to prescribe and control conduct in the schools. *See Epperson v. Arkansas, supra*, at 104; *Meyer v. Nebraska, supra*, at 402. Our problem lies in the area where students in the exercise of First Amendment rights collide with the rules of the school authorities.

II.

The problem posed by the present case does not relate to regulation of the length of skirts or the type of clothing, to hair style, or deportment. *Cf. Ferrell v. Dallas Independent School District*, 392 F.2d 697 (1968); *Pugsley v. Sellmeyer*, 158 Ark. 247, 250 S. W. 538 (1923). It does not concern aggressive, disruptive action or even group demonstrations. Our problem involves direct, primary First Amendment rights akin to "pure speech."

The school officials banned and sought to punish petitioners for a silent, passive expression of opinion, unaccompanied by any disorder or disturbance on the part of petitioners. There is here no evidence whatever of petitioners' interference, actual or nascent, with the schools' work or of collision with the rights of other students to be secure and to be let alone. Accordingly, this case does not concern speech or action that intrudes upon the work of the schools or the rights of other students.

Only a few of the 18,000 students in the school system wore the black armbands. Only five students were suspended for wearing them. There is no indication that the work of the schools or any class was disrupted. Outside the classrooms, a few students made hostile remarks to the children wearing armbands, but there were no threats or acts of violence on school premises.

The District Court concluded that the action of the school authorities was reasonable because it was based upon their fear of a disturbance from the wearing of the armbands. But, in our system, undifferentiated fear or apprehension of disturbance is not enough to overcome the right to freedom of expression. Any departure from absolute regimentation may cause trouble. Any variation from the majority's opinion may inspire fear. Any word spoken, in class, in the lunchroom, or on the campus, that deviates from the views of another person may start an argument or cause a disturbance. But our Constitution says we must take this risk, *Terminiello v. Chicago,* 337 U.S. 1 (1949); and our history says that it is this sort of hazardous freedom—this kind of openness—that is the basis of our national strength and of the independence and vigor of Americans who grow up and live in this relatively permissive, often disputatious, society.

In order for the State in the person of school officials to justify prohibition of a particular expression of opinion, it must be able to show that its action was caused by something more than a mere desire to avoid the discomfort and unpleasantness that always accompany an unpopular viewpoint. Certainly where there is no finding and no showing that engaging in the forbidden conduct would "materially and substantially interfere with the requirements of appropriate discipline in the operation of the school," the prohibition cannot be sustained. *Burnside v. Byars, supra,* at 749.

In the present case, the District Court made no such finding, and our independent examination of the record fails to yield evidence that the school authorities had reason to anticipate that the wearing of the armbands would substantially interfere with the work of the school or impinge upon the rights of other students. Even an official memorandum prepared after the suspension that listed the reasons for the ban on wearing the armbands made no reference to the anticipation of such disruption. On the contrary, the action of the school authorities appears to have been based upon an urgent wish to avoid the controversy which might result from the expression, even by the silent symbol of armbands, of opposition to this Nation's part in the conflagration in Vietnam. It is revealing, in this respect, that the meeting at which the school principals decided to issue the contested regulation was called in response to a student's statement to the journalism teacher in one of the schools that he wanted to write an article on Vietnam and have it published in the school paper. (The student was dissuaded.)

It is also relevant that the school authorities did not purport to prohibit the wearing of all symbols of political or controversial significance. The record shows that students in some of the schools wore buttons relating to national political campaigns, and some even wore the Iron Cross, traditionally a symbol of Nazism. The order prohibiting the wearing of armbands did not extend to these. Instead, a particular symbol—black armbands worn to exhibit opposition to this Nation's involvement in Vietnam—was singled out for prohibition. Clearly, the prohibition of expression of one particular opinion, at least without evidence that it is necessary to avoid material and substantial interference with schoolwork or discipline, is not constitutionally permissible.

In our system, state-operated schools may not be enclaves of totalitarianism. School officials do not possess absolute authority over their students. Students in school as well as out of school are "persons" under our Constitution. They are possessed of fundamental rights which the State must respect, just as they themselves must respect their obligations to the State. In our system, students may not be regarded as closed-circuit recipients of only that which the State chooses to communicate. They may not be confined to the expression of those sentiments that are officially approved. In the absence of a specific showing of constitutionally valid reasons to regulate their speech, students are entitled to freedom of expression of their views. As Judge Gewin, speaking for the Fifth Circuit, said, school officials cannot suppress "expressions of feelings with which they do not wish to contend." *Burnside v. Byars, supra,* at 749.

In *Meyer v. Nebraska, supra,* at 402, Mr. Justice McReynolds expressed this Nation's repudiation of the principle that a State might so conduct its schools as to "foster a homogeneous people." He said:

> "In order to submerge the individual and develop ideal citizens, Sparta assembled the males at seven into barracks and intrusted their subsequent education and training to official guardians. Although such measures have been deliberately approved by men of great genius, their ideas touching the relation between individual and State were wholly different from those upon which our institutions rest; and it hardly will be affirmed that any legislature could impose such restrictions upon the people of a State without doing violence to both letter and spirit of the Constitution."

This principle has been repeated by this Court on numerous occasions during the intervening years. In *Keyishian v. Board of Regents,* 385 U.S. 589, 603, MR. JUSTICE BRENNAN, speaking for the Court, said:

> "'The vigilant protection of constitutional freedoms is nowhere more vital than in the community of American schools.' *Shelton v. Tucker,* [364 U.S. 479,] at 487. The classroom is peculiarly the 'marketplace of ideas.' The Nation's future depends upon leaders trained through wide exposure to that robust exchange of ideas which discovers truth 'out of a multitude of tongues, [rather] than through any kind of authoritative selection.'"

The principle of these cases is not confined to the supervised and ordained discussion which takes place in the classroom. The principal use to which the schools are dedicated is to accommodate students during prescribed hours for the purpose of certain types of activities. Among those activities is personal intercommunication among the students. This is not only an inevitable part of the process of attending school; it is also an important part of the educational process. A student's rights, therefore, do not embrace merely the classroom hours. When he is in the cafeteria, or on the playing field, or on the campus during the authorized hours, he may express his opinions, even on controversial subjects like the conflict in Vietnam, if he does so without "materially and substantially interfer[ing] with the requirements of appropriate discipline in the operation of the school" and without colliding with the rights of others. *Burnside v. Byars, supra,* at 749. But conduct by the student, in class or out of it, which for any reason—whether it stems from time, place, or type of behavior—materially disrupts classwork or involves substantial disorder or invasion of the rights of others is, of course, not immunized by the constitutional guarantee of freedom of speech. *Cf. Blackwell v. Issaquena County Board of Education,* 363 F.2d 749 (C. A. 5th Cir. 1966).

Under our Constitution, free speech is not a right that is given only to be so circumscribed that it exists in principle but not in fact. Freedom of expression would not truly exist if the right could be exercised only in an area that a benevolent government has provided as a safe haven for crackpots. The Constitution says that Congress (and the States) may not abridge the right to free speech. This provision means what it says. We properly read it to permit reasonable regulation of speech-connected activities in carefully restricted circumstances. But we do not confine the permissible exercise of First Amendment rights to a telephone booth or the four corners of a pamphlet, or to supervised and ordained discussion in a school classroom.

If a regulation were adopted by school officials forbidding discussion of the Vietnam conflict, or the expression by any student of opposition to it anywhere on school property except as part of a prescribed classroom exercise, it would be obvious that the regulation would violate the constitutional rights of students, at least if it could not be justified by a showing that the students' activities would materially and substantially disrupt the work and discipline of the school. *Cf. Hammond v. South Carolina State College,* 272 F. Supp. 947 (D.C. S. C. 1967) (orderly protest meeting on state college campus); *Dickey v. Alabama State Board of Education,* 273 F. Supp. 613 (D.C. M. D. Ala. 1967) (expulsion of student editor of college newspaper). In the circumstances of the present case, the prohibition of the silent, passive "witness of the armbands," as one of the children called it, is no less offensive to the Constitution's guarantees.

As we have discussed, the record does not demonstrate any facts which might reasonably have led school authorities to forecast substantial disruption of or material interference with school activities, and no disturbances or disorders on the school premises in fact occurred. These petitioners merely went about their ordained rounds in school. Their deviation consisted only in wearing on their sleeve a band of black cloth, not more than two inches wide. They wore it to exhibit their disapproval of the Vietnam hostilities and their advocacy of a truce, to make their views known, and, by their example, to influence others to adopt them. They neither interrupted school activities nor sought to intrude in the school affairs or the lives of others. They caused discussion outside of the classrooms, but no interference with work and no disorder. In the circumstances, our Constitution does not permit officials of the State to deny their form of expression.

We express no opinion as to the form of relief which should be granted, this being a matter for the lower courts to determine. We reverse and remand for further proceedings consistent with this opinion.

Reversed and remanded.

NOTICE: This opinion is subject to formal revision before publication in the preliminary print of the United States Reports. Readers are requested to notify the Reporter of Decisions, Supreme Court of the United States, Washington, D. C. 20543, of any typographical or other formal errors, in order that corrections may be made before the preliminary print goes to press.

SUPREME COURT OF THE UNITED STATES

No. 06-278

Deborah Morse, ET AL., Petitioners v. Joseph Frederick

ON WRIT OF CERTIORARI TO THE UNITED STATES COURT
OF APPEALS FOR THE NINTH CIRCUIT

[June 25, 2007]

CHIEF JUSTICE ROBERTS delivered the opinion of the Court.

At a school-sanctioned and school-supervised event, a high school principal saw some of her students unfurl a large banner conveying a message she reasonably regarded as promoting illegal drug use. Consistent with established school policy prohibiting such messages at school events, the principal directed the students to take down the banner. One student—among those who had brought the banner to the event—refused to do so. The principal confiscated the banner and later suspended the student. The Ninth Circuit held that the principal's actions violated the First Amendment, and that the student could sue the principal for damages.

Our cases make clear that students do not "shed their constitutional rights to freedom of speech or expression at the schoolhouse gate." *Tinker v. Des Moines Independent Community School Dist.*, 393 U. S. 503, 506 (1969). At the same time, we have held that "the constitutional rights of students in public school are not automatically coextensive with the rights of adults in other settings," *Bethel School Dist. No. 403 v. Fraser*, 478 U. S. 675, 682 (1986), and that the rights of students "must be 'applied in light of the special characteristics of the school environment.'" *Hazelwood School Dist. v. Kuhlmeier*, 484 U. S. 260, 266 (1988) (quoting *Tinker, supra*, at 506). Consistent with these principles, we hold that schools may take steps to safeguard those entrusted to their care from speech that can reasonably be regarded as encouraging illegal drug use. We conclude that the school officials in this case did not violate the First Amendment by confiscating the prodrug banner and suspending the student responsible for it.

I

On January 24, 2002, the Olympic Torch Relay passed through Juneau, Alaska, on its way to the winter games in Salt Lake City, Utah. The torchbearers were to proceed along a street in front of Juneau-Douglas High School (JDHS) while school was in session. Petitioner Deborah Morse, the school principal, decided to permit staff and students to participate in the Torch Relay as an approved social event or class trip. App. 22–23. Students were allowed to leave class to observe the relay from either side of the street. Teachers and administrative officials monitored the students' actions.

Respondent Joseph Frederick, a JDHS senior, was late to school that day. When he arrived, he joined his friends (all but one of whom were JDHS students) across the street from the school to watch the event. Not all the students waited patiently. Some became rambunctious, throwing plastic cola bottles and snowballs and scuffling with their classmates. As the torchbearers and camera crews passed by, Frederick and his friends unfurled a 14-foot banner bearing the phrase: "BONG HiTS 4 JESUS." App. to Pet. for Cert. 70a. The large banner was easily readable by the students on the other side of the street.

Principal Morse immediately crossed the street and demanded that the banner be taken down. Everyone but Frederick complied. Morse confiscated the banner and told Frederick to report to her office, where she suspended him for 10 days. Morse later explained that she told Frederick to take the banner down because she thought it encouraged illegal drug use, in violation of established school policy. Juneau School Board Policy No. 5520 states: "The Board specifically prohibits any assembly or public expression that . . . advocates the use of substances that are illegal to minors. . . ." *Id.*, at 53a. In addition, Juneau School Board Policy No. 5850 subjects "[p]upils who participate in approved social events and class trips" to the same student conduct rules that apply during the regular school program. *Id.*, at 58a.

Frederick administratively appealed his suspension, but the Juneau School District Superintendent upheld it, limiting it to time served (8 days). In a memorandum setting forth his reasons, the superintendent determined that Frederick had displayed his banner "in the midst of his fellow students, during school hours, at a school-sanctioned activity." *Id.*, at 63a. He further explained that Frederick "was not disciplined because the principal of the school 'disagreed' with his message, but because his speech appeared to advocate the use of illegal drugs." *Id.*, at 61a.

The superintendent continued:

"The common-sense understanding of the phrase 'bong hits' is that it is a reference to a means of smoking marijuana. Given [Frederick's] inability or unwillingness to express any other credible meaning for the phrase, I can only agree with the principal and countless others who saw the banner as advocating the use of illegal drugs. [Frederick's] speech was not political. He was not advocating the legalization of marijuana or promoting a religious belief. He was displaying a fairly silly message promoting illegal drug usage in the midst of a school activity, for the benefit of television cameras covering the Torch Relay. [Frederick's] speech was potentially disruptive to the event and clearly disruptive of and inconsistent with the school's educational mission to educate students about the dangers of illegal drugs and to discourage their use." *Id.*, at 61a–62a.

Relying on our decision in *Fraser, supra,* the superintendent concluded that the principal's actions were permissible because Frederick's banner was "speech or action that intrudes upon the work of the schools." App. to Pet. for Cert. 62a (internal quotation marks omitted). The Juneau School District Board of Education upheld the suspension.

Frederick then filed suit under 42 U. S. C. §1983, alleging that the school board and Morse had violated his First Amendment rights. He sought declaratory and injunctive relief, unspecified compensatory damages, punitive damages, and attorney's fees. The District Court granted summary judgment for the school board and Morse, ruling that they were entitled to qualified immunity and that they had not infringed Frederick's First Amendment rights. The court found that Morse reasonably interpreted the banner as promoting illegal drug use—a message that "directly contravened the Board's policies relating to drug abuse prevention." App. to Pet. for Cert. 36a–38a. Under the circumstances, the court held that

"Morse had the authority, if not the obligation, to stop such messages at a school-sanctioned activity." *Id.*, at 37a.

The Ninth Circuit reversed. Deciding that Frederick acted during a "school-authorized activit[y]," and "proceed[ing] on the basis that the banner expressed a positive sentiment about marijuana use," the court nonetheless found a violation of Frederick's First Amendment rights because the school punished Frederick without demonstrating that his speech gave rise to a "risk of substantial disruption." 439 F. 3d 1114, 1118, 1121–1123 (2006). The court further concluded that Frederick's right to display his banner was so "clearly established" that a reasonable principal in Morse's position would have understood that her actions were unconstitutional, and that Morse was therefore not entitled to qualified immunity. *Id.*, at 1123– 1125.

We granted certiorari on two questions: whether Frederick had a First Amendment right to wield his banner, and, if so, whether that right was so clearly established that the principal may be held liable for damages. 549 U. S. _____ (2006). We resolve the first question against Frederick, and therefore have no occasion to reach the second.[1]

II

At the outset, we reject Frederick's argument that this is not a school speech case—as has every other authority to address the question. See App. 22–23 (Principal Morse); App. to Pet. for Cert. 63a (superintendent); *id.*, at 69a (school board); *id.*, at 34a–35a (District Court); 439 F. 3d, at 1117 (Ninth Circuit). The event occurred during normal school hours. It was sanctioned by Principal Morse "as an approved social event or class trip," App. 22–23, and the school district's rules expressly provide that pupils in "approved social events and class trips are subject to district rules for student conduct." App. to Pet. for Cert. 58a. Teachers and administrators were interspersed among the students and charged with supervising them. The high school band and cheerleaders performed. Frederick, standing among other JDHS students across the street from the school, directed his banner toward the school, making it plainly visible to most students. Under these circumstances, we agree with the superintendent that Frederick cannot "stand in the midst of his fellow students, during school hours, at a school-sanctioned activity and claim he is not at school." *Id.*, at 63a. There is some uncertainty at the outer boundaries as to when courts should apply school-speech precedents, *see Porter v. Ascension Parish School Bd.*, 393 F. 3d 608, 615, n. 22 (CA5 2004), but not on these facts.

III

The message on Frederick's banner is cryptic. It is no doubt offensive to some, perhaps amusing to others. To still others, it probably means nothing at all. Frederick himself claimed "that the words were just nonsense meant to attract television cameras." 439 F. 3d, at 1117–1118. But Principal Morse thought the banner would be interpreted by those viewing it as promoting illegal drug use, and that interpretation is plainly a reasonable one.

As Morse later explained in a declaration, when she saw the sign, she thought that "the reference to a 'bong hit' would be widely understood by high school students and others as referring to smoking marijuana." App. 24. She further believed that "display of the banner would be construed by students, District personnel, parents and others witnessing the display of the banner, as advocating or promoting illegal drug use"—in violation of school policy. *Id.*, at 25; see *ibid.* ("I told Frederick and the other members of his group to put the banner down

---

1. JUSTICE BREYER would rest decision on qualified immunity without reaching the underlying First Amendment question. The problem with this approach is the rather significant one that it is inadequate to decide the case before us. Qualified immunity shields public officials from money damages only. *See Wood v. Strickland*, 420 U. S. 308, 314, n. 6 (1975). In this case, Frederick asked not just for damages, but also for declaratory and injunctive relief. App. 13. JUSTICE BREYER's proposed decision on qualified immunity grounds would dispose of the damages claims, but Frederick's other claims would remain unaddressed. To get around that problem, JUSTICE BREYER hypothesizes that Frederick's suspension—the target of his request for injunctive relief—"may well be justified on non-speech-related grounds." *See post*, at 9. That hypothesis was never considered by the courts below, never raised by any of the parties, and is belied by the record, which nowhere suggests that the suspension would have been justified solely on non-speech-related grounds.

because I felt that it violated the [school] policy against displaying . . . material that advertises or promotes use of illegal drugs").

We agree with Morse. At least two interpretations of the words on the banner demonstrate that the sign advocated the use of illegal drugs. First, the phrase could be interpreted as an imperative: "[Take] bong hits . . ."—a message equivalent, as Morse explained in her declaration, to "smoke marijuana" or "use an illegal drug." Alternatively, the phrase could be viewed as celebrating drug use—"bong hits [are a good thing]," or "[we take] bong hits"—and we discern no meaningful distinction between celebrating illegal drug use in the midst of fellow students and outright advocacy or promotion. *See Guiles v. Marineau*, 461 F. 3d 320, 328 (CA2 2006) (discussing the present case and describing the sign as "a clearly pro-drug banner").

The pro-drug interpretation of the banner gains further plausibility given the paucity of alternative meanings the banner might bear. The best Frederick can come up with is that the banner is "meaningless and funny." 439 F. 3d, at 1116. The dissent similarly refers to the sign's message as "curious," *post*, at 1, "ambiguous," *ibid.*, "nonsense," *post*, at 2, "ridiculous," *post*, at 6, "obscure," *post*, at 7, "silly," *post*, at 12, "quixotic," *post*, at 13, and "stupid," *ibid.* Gibberish is surely a possible interpretation of the words on the banner, but it is not the only one, and dismissing the banner as meaningless ignores its undeniable reference to illegal drugs.

The dissent mentions Frederick's "credible and uncontradicted explanation for the message—he just wanted to get on television." *Post*, at 12. But that is a description of Frederick's *motive* for displaying the banner; it is not an interpretation of what the banner says. The *way* Frederick was going to fulfill his ambition of appearing on television was by unfurling a pro-drug banner at a school event, in the presence of teachers and fellow students.

Elsewhere in its opinion, the dissent emphasizes the importance of political speech and the need to foster "national debate about a serious issue," *post*, at 16, as if to suggest that the banner is political speech. But not even Frederick argues that the banner conveys any sort of political or religious message. Contrary to the dissent's suggestion, see *post*, at 14–16, this is plainly not a case about political debate over the criminalization of drug use or possession.

IV

The question thus becomes whether a principal may, consistent with the First Amendment, restrict student speech at a school event, when that speech is reasonably viewed as promoting illegal drug use. We hold that she may.

In *Tinker*, this Court made clear that "First Amendment rights, applied in light of the special characteristics of the school environment, are available to teachers and students." 393 U. S., at 506. *Tinker* involved a group of high school students who decided to wear black armbands to protest the Vietnam War. School officials learned of the plan and then adopted a policy prohibiting students from wearing armbands. When several students nonetheless wore armbands to school, they were suspended. *Id.*, at 504. The students sued, claiming that their First Amendment rights had been violated, and this Court agreed.

Tinker held that student expression may not be suppressed unless school officials reasonably conclude that it will "materially and substantially disrupt the work and discipline of the school." *Id.*, at 513. The essential facts of *Tinker* are quite stark, implicating concerns at the heart of the First Amendment. The students sought to engage in political speech, using the armbands to express their "disapproval of the Vietnam hostilities and their advocacy of a truce, to make their views known, and, by their example, to influence others to adopt them." *Id.*, at 514. Political speech, of course, is "at the core of what the First Amendment is designed to protect." *Virginia v. Black*, 538 U. S. 343, 365 (2003). The only interest the Court discerned underlying the school's actions was the "mere desire to avoid the discomfort and unpleasantness that always accompany an unpopular viewpoint," or "an urgent wish to avoid the controversy which might result from the expression." *Tinker*, 393 U. S., at 509, 510. That interest was not enough to justify banning "a silent, passive expression of opinion, unaccompanied by any disorder or disturbance." *Id.*, at 508.

This Court's next student speech case was *Fraser*, 478 U. S. 675. Matthew Fraser was suspended for delivering a speech before a high school assembly in which he employed what this

Court called "an elaborate, graphic, and explicit sexual metaphor." *Id.*, at 678. Analyzing the case under *Tinker*, the District Court and Court of Appeals found no disruption, and therefore no basis for disciplining Fraser. 478 U. S., at 679–680. This Court reversed, holding that the "School District acted entirely within its permissible authority in imposing sanctions upon Fraser in response to his offensively lewd and indecent speech." *Id.*, at 685.

The mode of analysis employed in *Fraser* is not entirely clear. The Court was plainly attuned to the content of Fraser's speech, citing the "marked distinction between the political 'message' of the armbands in *Tinker* and the sexual content of [Fraser's] speech." *Id.*, at 680. But the Court also reasoned that school boards have the authority to determine "what manner of speech in the classroom or in school assembly is inappropriate." *Id.*, at 683. *Cf. id.*, at 689 (Brennan, J., concurring in judgment) ("In the present case, school officials sought only to ensure that a high school assembly proceed in an orderly manner. There is no suggestion that school officials attempted to regulate [Fraser's] speech because they disagreed with the views he sought to express").

We need not resolve this debate to decide this case. For present purposes, it is enough to distill from *Fraser* two basic principles. First, *Fraser*'s holding demonstrates that "the constitutional rights of students in public school are not automatically coextensive with the rights of adults in other settings." *Id.*, at 682. Had Fraser delivered the same speech in a public forum outside the school context, it would have been protected. *See Cohen v. California*, 403 U. S. 15 (1971); *Fraser, supra*, at 682–683. In school, however, Fraser's First Amendment rights were circumscribed "in light of the special characteristics of the school environment." *Tinker, supra*, at 506. Second, *Fraser* established that the mode of analysis set forth in *Tinker* is not absolute. Whatever approach *Fraser* employed, it certainly did not conduct the "substantial disruption" analysis prescribed by *Tinker, supra*, at 514. *See Kuhlmeier*, 484 U. S., at 271, n. 4 (disagreeing with the proposition that there is "no difference between the First Amendment analysis applied in *Tinker* and that applied in *Fraser*," and noting that the holding in *Fraser* was not based on any showing of substantial disruption).

Our most recent student speech case, *Kuhlmeier*, concerned "expressive activities that students, parents, and members of the public might reasonably perceive to bear the imprimatur of the school." 484 U. S., at 271. Staff members of a high school newspaper sued their school when it chose not to publish two of their articles. The Court of Appeals analyzed the case under *Tinker*, ruling in favor of the students because it found no evidence of material disruption to classwork or school discipline. 795 F. 2d 1368, 1375 (CA8 1986). This Court reversed, holding that "educators do not offend the First Amendment by exercising editorial control over the style and content of student speech in school-sponsored expressive activities so long as their actions are reasonably related to legitimate pedagogical concerns." *Kuhlmeier, supra*, at 273.

Kuhlmeier does not control this case because no one would reasonably believe that Frederick's banner bore the school's imprimatur. The case is nevertheless instructive because it confirms both principles cited above. *Kuhlmeier* acknowledged that schools may regulate some speech "even though the government could not censor similar speech outside the school." *Id.*, at 266. And, like *Fraser*, it confirms that the rule of *Tinker* is not the only basis for restricting student speech.[2]

Drawing on the principles applied in our student speech cases, we have held in the Fourth Amendment context that "while children assuredly do not 'shed their constitutional rights . . . at the schoolhouse gate,' . . . the nature of those rights is what is appropriate for children in school." *Vernonia School Dist. 47J v. Acton*, 515 U. S. 646, 655–656 (1995) (quoting *Tinker, supra*, at 506). In particular, "the school setting requires some easing of the restrictions to which searches by public authorities are ordinarily subject." *New Jersey v. T. L. O.*, 469 U. S. 325,

---

2. The dissent's effort to find inconsistency between our approach here and the opinion in *Federal Election Commission v. Wisconsin Right to Life, Inc.*, 551 U. S. _____ (2007), *see post*, at 12 (opinion of STEVENS, J.), overlooks what was made clear in *Tinker, Fraser*, and *Kuhlmeier*: student First Amendment rights are "applied in light of the special characteristics of the school environment." *Tinker*, 393 U. S., at 506. *See Fraser*, 478 U. S., at 682; *Kuhlmeier*, 484 U. S., at 266. And, as discussed above, *supra*, at 8, there is no serious argument that Frederick's banner is political speech of the sort at issue in *Wisconsin Right to Life*.

340 (1985). *See Vernonia, supra*, at 656 ("Fourth Amendment rights, no less than First and Fourteenth Amendment rights, are different in public schools than elsewhere . . ."); *Board of Ed. of Independent School Dist. No. 92 of Pottawatomie Cty. v. Earls*, 536 U. S. 822, 829-830 (2002) ("'special needs' inhere in the public school context"; "[w]hile schoolchildren do not shed their constitutional rights when they enter the schoolhouse, Fourth Amendment rights . . . are different in public schools than elsewhere; the 'reasonableness' inquiry cannot disregard the schools' custodial and tutelary responsibility for children" (quoting *Vernonia*, 515 U. S., at 656; citation and some internal quotation marks omitted).

Even more to the point, these cases also recognize that deterring drug use by schoolchildren is an "important—indeed, perhaps compelling" interest. *Id.*, at 661. Drug abuse can cause severe and permanent damage to the health and well-being of young people:

> School years are the time when the physical, psychological, and addictive effects of drugs are most severe. Maturing nervous systems are more critically impaired by intoxicants than mature ones are; childhood losses in learning are lifelong and profound; children grow chemically dependent more quickly than adults, and their record of recovery is depressingly poor. And of course the effects of a drug-infested school are visited not just upon the users, but upon the entire student body and faculty, as the educational process is disrupted." *Id.*, at 661–662 (citations and internal quotation marks omitted).

Just five years ago, we wrote: "The drug abuse problem among our Nation's youth has hardly abated since *Vernonia* was decided in 1995. In fact, evidence suggests that it has only grown worse." *Earls, supra*, at 834, and n. 5.

The problem remains serious today. See generally 1 National Institute on Drug Abuse, National Institutes of Health, Monitoring the Future: National Survey Results on Drug Use, 1975–2005, Secondary School Students (2006). About half of American 12th graders have used an illicit drug, as have more than a third of 10th graders and about one-fifth of 8th graders. *Id.*, at 99. Nearly one in four 12th graders has used an illicit drug in the past month. *Id.*, at 101. Some 25% of high schoolers say that they have been offered, sold, or given an illegal drug on school property within the past year. Dept. of Health and Human Services, Centers for Disease Control and Prevention, Youth Risk Behavior Surveillance—United States, 2005, 55 Morbidity and Mortality Weekly Report, Surveillance Summaries, No. SS–5, p. 19 (June 9, 2006).

Congress has declared that part of a school's job is educating students about the dangers of illegal drug use. It has provided billions of dollars to support state and local drug-prevention programs, Brief for United States as *Amicus Curiae* 1, and required that schools receiving federal funds under the Safe and Drug-Free Schools and Communities Act of 1994 certify that their drug prevention programs "convey a clear and consistent message that . . . the illegal use of drugs [is] wrong and harmful." 20 U. S. C. §7114(d)(6) (2000 ed., Supp. IV).

Thousands of school boards throughout the country—including JDHS—have adopted policies aimed at effectuating this message. See Pet. for Cert. 17–21. Those school boards know that peer pressure is perhaps "the single most important factor leading schoolchildren to take drugs," and that students are more likely to use drugs when the norms in school appear to tolerate such behavior. *Earls, supra*, at 840 (BREYER, J., concurring). Student speech celebrating illegal drug use at a school event, in the presence of school administrators and teachers, thus poses a particular challenge for school officials working to protect those entrusted to their care from the dangers of drug abuse.

The "special characteristics of the school environment," *Tinker*, 393 U. S., at 506, and the governmental interest in stopping student drug abuse—reflected in the policies of Congress and myriad school boards, including JDHS—allow schools to restrict student expression that they reasonably regard as promoting illegal drug use. *Tinker* warned that schools may not prohibit student speech because of "undifferentiated fear or apprehension of disturbance" or "a mere desire to avoid the discomfort and unpleasantness that always accompany an unpopular viewpoint." *Id.*, at 508, 509. The danger here is far more serious and palpable. The particular concern to prevent student drug abuse at issue here, embodied in established school policy, App. 92–95; App. to Pet. for Cert. 53a, extends well beyond an abstract desire to avoid controversy.

Petitioners urge us to adopt the broader rule that Frederick's speech is proscribable because it is plainly "offensive" as that term is used in *Fraser*. See Reply Brief for Petitioners 14–15. We think this stretches *Fraser* too far; that case should not be read to encompass any speech that could fit under some definition of "offensive." After all, much political and religious speech might be perceived as offensive to some. The concern here is not that Frederick's speech was offensive, but that it was reasonably viewed as promoting illegal drug use.

Although accusing this decision of doing "serious violence to the First Amendment" by authorizing "viewpoint discrimination," *post*, at 2, 5 (opinion of STEVENS, J.), the dissent concludes that "it might well be appropriate to tolerate some targeted viewpoint discrimination in this unique setting," *post*, at 6–7. Nor do we understand the dissent to take the position that schools are required to tolerate student advocacy of illegal drug use at school events, even if that advocacy falls short of inviting "imminent" lawless action. *See post*, at 7 ("[I]t is possible that our rigid imminence requirement ought to be relaxed at schools"). And even the dissent recognizes that the issues here are close enough that the principal should not be held liable in damages, but should instead enjoy qualified immunity for her actions. *See post*, at 1. Stripped of rhetorical flourishes, then, the debate between the dissent and this opinion is less about constitutional first principles than about whether Frederick's banner constitutes promotion of illegal drug use. We have explained our view that it does. The dissent's contrary view on that relatively narrow question hardly justifies sounding the First Amendment bugle.

*   *   *

School principals have a difficult job, and a vitally important one. When Frederick suddenly and unexpectedly unfurled his banner, Morse had to decide to act—or not act—on the spot. It was reasonable for her to conclude that the banner promoted illegal drug use—in violation of established school policy—and that failing to act would send a powerful message to the students in her charge, including Frederick, about how serious the school was about the dangers of illegal drug use. The First Amendment does not require schools to tolerate at school events student expression that contributes to those dangers.

The judgment of the United States Court of Appeals for the Ninth Circuit is reversed, and the case is remanded for further proceedings consistent with this opinion.

It is so ordered.

GLOSSARY

Active Voice   Active voice is a tool used by writers to shorten sentences; a sentence written in active voice uses the simple subject-verb-object approach

Administrative Procedures   Procedures used by agencies and boards

Advocate   Arguing one side of an issue

Affidavit   A statement under penalty of perjury sworn to before a notary

Affirm   To uphold; in connection with an appeal to uphold the lower court's decision

Affirmative Defenses   Defenses raised by the defendant in the answer; reasons why the plaintiff should not recover even if all of the allegations of the complaint are true

Amend   To change

Annotated   A brief summary of a statute or a case added to explain or clarify

Appeal   Review of a lower court decision

Appellant   One who appeals

Appellate Brief   A document filed in support of or in opposition to an appeal, containing arguments related to legal errors that may have occurred at trial

Appellee   Party in an appeal who did not file the appeal

Arbitration   An out-of-court proceeding where parties submit a dispute to a neutral person for resolution

Arbitration Brief   A document filed in an arbitration proceeding addressing the legal issues in the arbitration

Argument   The section of a memorandum or brief containing legal analysis supporting that party's position on a legal issue

Bill   Proposed legislation

Bill of Rights   First ten amendments to United States Constitution

Binding Authority   Another term for mandatory authority

Boolean   A special logic used in computerized legal research; utilizes the use of connective words

Brief   A written document that might contain a summary of the facts, issues, rules, and analysis used by a court and a comparison with a client's facts; a case brief is a short summary of a published case

Caption   A caption identifies the parties to the case, the court in which the case is pending, the docket number, and the title of the document

Case Brief   A short summary of a reported case

Case Law   A collection of reported cases

Case Law Reporters   Sets of published volumes of cases decided by various courts

Case Reporters   Books that contain case decisions from the courts

Causes of Action   The basis upon which a lawsuit may be brought to the court

CD-ROM Libraries   Legal materials, either primary or secondary sources, stored on a CD-ROM

Century Digest   Part of the American Digest System; containing case annotations for the years 1688 to 1896

Citators   Research materials used to update or "validate" legal authorities

Cited Authority   The authority you are Shepardizing (updating and validating)

Citing Authority   Authorities you are referred to when you Shepardize

Civil Law   The area of law dealing with private disputes between parties

Clerk's Transcript   Copies of all documents filed in a case and compiled by the clerk of the court at a party's request

Code   A topical organization of statutes

Code Books   Books that contain codes or statutes

Common Law   Body of law developed through the courts

Computer-Assisted Legal Research (CALR)   Legal research done with the use of a computer; includes the use of CD-ROM, online services such as LEXIS, Westlaw, Internet, and intranets

Concurrent Jurisdiction   Jurisdiction or power exercised by two different entities

Connectors   Words such as *and* or *or* used in a search query to show the relationship between key words or terms

Court Record   Documents and transcripts of proceedings in connection with a case

Cover Letter   A letter sent with documents or other items, explaining the nature of the documents or items as well as directions to the recipient for any actions to be taken with the documents or items; also referred to as a transmittal letter

Criminal Law   The area of law dealing with prosecution and defense of crimes

Database   Compilation of electronically stored information

Decennial Digest   Updates to the *Century Digest,* published every five years

Decision   The formal written resolution of a case; it explains the legal and factual issues, the resolution of the case, and the law used by the court in reaching its resolution

Declaration   A statement under penalty of perjury containing factual statements

Demand Letter   Formal correspondence from an attorney to a party or other attorney demanding that action be taken or requesting a settlement of a claim or dispute

De-publish   In rare instances, a court will decide a case and write and release a decision; however, before it is published in the official reporter, the court decides not to publish some or all of the case decision; a de-published case cannot be used as precedent

Descriptive Word Index   An alphabetical listing of words describing the topics contained in a book or a set of books; refers the researcher to the volume and page where the topic is discussed

Digest   An index to reported cases, arranged by subject; a short summary of cases is provided

Digest Topics   Topics included in an index (digest) to reported case law, arranged by subject

Document   An identifiable item located in a database; can refer to a case or a single code section

Double Jeopardy   Clause in the United States Constitution that generally prevents the government from trying a person more than once for the same offense

Editorial Enhancements   Helpful information included in many unofficial publications; the enhancements assist the researcher to understand the material. Most official publications have little or no editorial enhancements.

Electronic Search Query   Words that constitute a search request when using electronically stored data, that is, information on the Internet or on a CD-ROM

Elements   The components of a cause of action or of a statute

Express Powers   Powers given to the federal government that are expressly stated in the Constitution

Federal Reporter   The set containing all of the federal appellate decisions

Federal Rules Decisions   The set containing federal opinions, decisions, and rulings involving the Federal Rules of Civil Procedure and the Federal Rules of Criminal Procedure

Federal Supplement   The set containing the cases argued and determined in the United States District Courts, the United States Court of International Trade, and the rulings of the Judicial Panel on Multidistrict Litigation

Federalism   A system of government in which the people are regulated by both federal and state governments

Filed   To become part of the court record

First Impression   A case where the legal issue has not previously been decided

Forms of Pleading and Practice   Form books containing forms for use in connection with litigation

Full-text Search   Legal research method utilized in computer-assisted legal research, in which all documents in a database are searched for certain words

General Digest   Updates to the *Decennial Digest*

Good Law   Law that is still in effect or valid and can be cited as authority

Headnote   Editorial enhancement added to the front material of a case; useful summary of most of the legal topics addressed in the case

Holding   The legal principle to be taken from the court's decision

Hornbook   Name given to books published by West that are a type of treatise; commonly used by law students

Implied Powers   Power to make all laws that are necessary and proper for carrying into execution any of the stated or express powers of the government

Index   A list of words and phrases that reflect the topics covered in the book

Intranet   A secure database set up and accessible by a specific group, such as a law firm

Judicial History   The legal (courtroom) history of a case

Jurisdiction   The power or authority to act in a certain situation; the power of a court to hear cases and render judgments

Jury Instructions   Statements of the law read to the jury at the end of trial

Key Numbers   A research aid unique to the Thomson/West materials; these numbers allow a researcher to quickly access specific material in a digest

Key Word   Words that describe important aspects of a research question

Law Library   A library dedicated to legal resource material

Law Review   A type of legal periodical published by law schools containing articles on different legal topics

Lawyers' Edition   Lexis Law Publishing publishes this unofficial (nongovernment) printing of all United States Supreme Court case law

Legal Analysis   The process of analyzing facts and legal issues in light of existing constitutional, statutory, or case law

Legal Citations   Special abbreviations used to describe resource material

Legal Dictionary   A dictionary defining and explaining legal terms

Legal Encyclopedia   A collection of legal information arranged alphabetically by topic; a secondary source of the law

Legal Error   Application of law to a case in a mistaken way

Legal Issue   A question that must be decided by a court

Legal Thesaurus   A book providing synonyms for legal words

Legislative History   The proceedings that relate to a bill before it becomes law

Legislative Intent   The purpose of the legislature in passing a law

LEXIS   A computer-assisted legal research service

Local Rules of Court   Procedural rules adopted by an individual court for practice in that specific court

Looseleaf Service   Legal material published in a binder format, regularly supplemented with replacement pages

Mandatory Authority   Case law that must be followed by a court

Memorandum of Law   An objectively written document in which the researcher informs another of the law governing a specific situation

Memorandum of Points and Authorities   A formal document, written in an argumentative or persuasive manner, filed with the court, and advocating a certain position

Model Codes   A collection of sample laws, created for the states to adopt in whole or in part; helped to create uniformity in law

Motion   A request for an order from the court

Motion for Summary Judgment   A request that the trial court decide the case without a trial

Moving Party   The party making a motion

Nutshell Series   Condensed versions of hornbooks

Official Citation   This is the citation to the official publication of case law for a particular jurisdiction (this is usually a government publication); the official citation includes the name of the case, volume number in which the case is located, the first page of the case, and the year of the decision

Official Reporters   Sets of case law published by the government or the designee of the government

Opinion   A decision is sometimes referred to as an opinion

Opinion Letter   Formal correspondence from an attorney to a client or other attorney explaining an attorney's interpretation of the law as applied to a factual situation

Parallel Citations   Many case citations include references to unofficial publications as well as the official citation. These additional references are parallel citations; simply stated, you may find the exact case in more than one publication

Periodical   Legal material, published at regular intervals, consisting of magazines, journals, and law reviews

Persuasive Authority   Nonbinding case law that is nevertheless considered by a court

Persuasive Document   A persuasive document is drafted to persuade the reader to adopt the writer's legal analysis of a specific legal problem. The audience for most persuasive documents is a court (judge)

Petition for Writ of Certiorari   A request for a hearing in the Supreme Court

Petitioner   The person who files a petition with the court

Pleading and Practice Guides   Secondary sources providing sample pleadings and general practice advice; available in most states and for some federal practice areas

Pleadings   The formal written allegations filed with the court by both sides to a lawsuit; claims and defenses are clearly set out so that both parties are placed on notice of the position of the opposing party

Pocket Part   A removable supplement; includes all changes or additions to the material contained in the hardbound volume

Point Headings   Point headings provide the reader with a road map of the document. Use them to make a point you want to stress for the reader

Positive Law   Codes that were enacted into law by Congress

Practice Books   Books for use in federal and state legal practice; these often contain discussions of an area of law and provide forms needed for practice in that legal area

Precedent   The example set by the decision of an earlier court for similar cases or similar legal questions that arise in later cases

Predictive Office Memorandum   A predictive memorandum predicts the outcome of a legal issue, based upon legal research and analysis. This document does not "take sides" or try to convince the reader to adopt a position

Preempt   To assume sole responsibility to regulate

Prefatory Material   Material found in the front of a book or set of books, describing such matters as the purpose of the book and instructions for using the book

Prima Facie **Case**   On first view or on its face; for example, the plaintiff presented a strong *prima facie* case for establishing the negligence of the defendant

Primary Authority   The resources that provide the actual law; laws are found in constitutions, statutes, case law, and some administrative materials

Primary Source   A work that contains the law itself

Private Laws   Laws enacted by Congress that affect only selected individuals

Public Law   Laws enacted by Congress that affect the public in general

Query   Words that constitute a search request when using CD-ROM or online materials

Questions Presented   A statement of the legal issue presented to the court for resolution

Rationale   The reasoning or explanation for the court's ultimate resolution of a case

Real Party in Interest   A party who has a true interest in the action

Regional Reporters   A set of published volumes of cases by courts in specific regions of the United States; for example, the *Pacific Reporter* or the *North Eastern Reporter*

Remand   To send back

Repeal   To undo; to declare a law no longer in effect

Reported Case   A judicial decision that is published

Reporter's Transcript   A verbatim record of the oral proceedings in court prepared by the court reporter

Respondent   The party who answers the Petitioner's petition

Reverse   To change

Rules of Court   Procedural rules adopted by all courts regulating practice in the court

Secondary Source   A tool used to understand the law; one such tool is a legal encyclopedia that explains the law

Session Laws   Laws from state legislatures, published in chronological order

Shepardize   To check the validity of a citation in one of the *Shepard's* citations

Shepard's   System used to update, validate, and expand research results

Slip Law   First publication of a law; usually in pamphlet form

Specialized Reporters   Collections of cases grouped by specific topics rather than by level of court or jurisdiction

Stare Decisis   "It stands decided"; another term for *precedent*

Statutory Law   Law enacted through the legislative process

Statutory Requirements   Various requirements or elements of a statute that must be met before the statute will apply to a situation

Strategy   A well-thought-out plan or approach to a project

Style Manual   A manual illustrating the proper citation format for a particular state

Superseded   Replaced

Supplemented   Kept up-to-date

Supremacy Clause   Clause in the U.S. Constitution providing that the U.S. Constitution is the supreme law of the land

Supreme Court Reporter   Printed by Thomson/West, this is an unofficial publication of all U.S. Supreme Court case law

Table of Abbreviations   A common feature of legal publications containing an explanation of all abbreviations found in the book

Table of Authorities   A list of primary and secondary authorities cited with a memorandum or brief and the page numbers on which they appear

Table of Cases   A common feature of legal publications containing the names of all cases cited in the book or document

Table of Contents   A list of the sections of a document with the page on which they appear within the document

Table of Statutes   A common feature of legal publications containing a list of all statutes or codes that are referenced in the book or document

Thesis Paragraph   The thesis paragraph lays a solid foundation for the reader. This paragraph sets forth the client's problem, states the legal issue, briefly explains the legal rules governing the issues, and states the legal conclusion

Topic and Key Number   System used by the Thomson/West to integrate its various primary and secondary resource materials

Topic Sentence   A topic sentence introduces the issues or subissues and connects back to the thesis paragraph

Topical Index   An index arranged by subject-matter topics

Transaction Forms   Books that contain forms for use in connection with business and personal transactions

Transmittal Letter   A letter sent with documents or other items, explaining the nature of the documents or items as well as directions to the recipient for any actions to be taken with the documents or items; also referred to as a cover letter

Treatise   Either one book or a multivolume series of books dealing with one legal topic

Trial   A court proceeding before a judge or jury wherein each side presents evidence of the facts that form the basis for the lawsuit or the defense to the lawsuit

Trial Brief   A document submitted to the court; the trial brief contains a statement of facts, the issues, and the party's legal argument and the holding

Trial Court   Where cases originate and where the factual dispute is resolved at trial

Uniform Laws   Similar laws that are adopted by the legislatures of different states (i.e., Uniform Commercial Code); intended to create uniformity in the law

Uniform System of Citation   A reference manual; contains the rules for proper citation format; often called *The Bluebook*

United States Reports   Official publication of all U.S. Supreme Court case law; published by the federal government

Unofficial Publication   Material not published by a government entity or a government designee

Unofficial Reporters   Collections of printed decisions that are not government publications or sanctioned by government

Validate   To verify that an authority is still good law

Westlaw   A computer-assisted legal research service

Writ of Habeas Corpus   An order directing the release of one who is in custody

Writ of Mandate   Order from higher court to lower court to take some action

INDEX